SPIRIT HERMENEUTICS

Spirit Hermeneutics

Reading Scripture
in Light of Pentecost

what are the benefits?

Craig S. Keener

William B. Eerdmans Publishing Company
Grand Rapids, Michigan

Wm. B. Eerdmans Publishing Co.

2140 Oak Industrial Drive N.E., Grand Rapids, Michigan 49505

www.eerdmans.com

22 21 20 19 18 17 16   1 2 3 4 5 6 7

Library of Congress Cataloging-in-Publication Data

Names: Keener, Craig S., 1960- author.

Title: Spirit hermeneutics: reading scripture in light of Pentecost / Craig S. Keener.

Description: Grand Rapids: Eerdmans Publishing Company, 2016. |
Includes bibliographical references and index.

Identifiers: LCCN 2016013066 | ISBN 9780802874399 (cloth: alk. paper)

Subjects: LCSH: Bible—Hermeneutics. | Bible—Criticism, interpretation, etc. |
Holy Spirit. | Pentecostalism.

Classification: LCC BS476 .K45 2016 | DDC 220.601—dc23

LC record available at https://lccn.loc.gov/2016013066

Translations of Scripture are the author's own unless otherwise specified.

Baker has granted permission for use of material from Craig S. Keener, *Acts: An Exegetical Commentary*, volume 1, copyright © 2012, and volume 2, copyright © 2013; and for Craig S. Keener, *Miracles: The Credibility of the New Testament Accounts*, copyright © 2011. Used with permission from Baker Academic, a division of Baker Publishing Group.

Robert Danielson has granted permission for use of material from Craig S. Keener, "Scripture and Context: An Evangelical Exploration," *Asbury Journal* 70 (1, 2015): 17–62.

Regnum has granted permission for use of material from Craig S. Keener, "Biblical Fidelity as an Evangelical Commitment," 29–41 in *Following Jesus: Journeys in Radical Discipleship; Essays in Honor of Ronald J. Sider,* edited by Paul Alexander and Al Tizon. Regnum Studies in Global Christianity. Oxford: Regnum, 2013.

To my fellow scholars who value the works of the Spirit,
including all my colleagues at Asbury,
and particularly to Ben Witherington,
who years ago took a young new
scholar under his wings

movement?

Contents

Contents

Contents

Foreword

As coeditors of the Pentecostal Manifestos series published by William B. Eerdmans, James K. A. Smith and I have from the beginning been in conversation with Craig Keener and anticipating that someday he would make a contribution in the area of scriptural and biblical-theological hermeneutics. The series description suggests that volumes in the series "would include two different kinds of books: (a) shorter, crisply argued volumes of 128–200 pages that articulate a bold vision within a field; and (b) longer scholarly monographs . . . (250–300 pages)" that would be "bold statements of a distinctly Pentecostal interjection into contemporary discussions and debates, undergirded by rigorous scholarship." No doubt Keener is the right person to write a Pentecostal manifesto on hermeneutic "undergirded by rigorous scholarship," although even putting it that way is an understatement for those who know of his work; yet, we somehow underestimated that a Keener manifesto would be anything less than a multivolume undertaking—or did not anticipate that his habit of generating multivolume or dual-column-per-page commentaries would carry over into his other writing projects—and incredulously presumed that he would send us a book within the lengthier parameters outlined in (b) above. Well, duh! To put it mildly, once Keener finally produced the manuscript, it was twice the size of anything else in the Manifestos series, and Eerdmans has decided that it would be better to publish it as a stand-alone volume.

As I have already implicated myself in precipitating this project, let me now present nine reasons why readers who have gotten this far ought to press through the rest of these pages. I organize my rationale under three general headings: about how *Spirit Hermeneutics* makes a contribution to the ongoing discussion in biblical-theological hermeneutics; about its capacity to impact wider hermeneutical conversations; and about why this book holds the key to understanding Keener the biblical scholar and Christian, and to the Keenerian corpus as a whole (of which we have only a fragment so far, compared to the legacy that will eventually be left behind, God willing).

First, while this is not the first book on pentecostal hermeneutics (as the footnotes to this work will show), it is by far the most comprehensively articulated and registers authoritatively why it is essential to attend to pentecostal perspectives in the wider arena of biblical and theological hermeneutics. If world Christianity is exploding at least in part because of the growth of pentecostal and charismatic churches in the majority world, then pentecostal readings of scripture in particular and pentecostal hermeneutical orientations and approaches in general cannot be neglected in biblical interpretation and in the wider field of theological scholarship. In contrast to prior contributions to pentecostal hermeneutics, Keener's is the most global, more attentive to global cultures and transcultural dynamics than the others. For those concerned with the theological dimensions of the shift of the center of gravity of Christianity to the global South, this book provides as good a springboard as any for tracing the hermeneutical implications both for scriptural interpretation and for its theological consequences.

Second, *Spirit Hermeneutics* boosts pentecostal voices into the center of the present ferment in *theological interpretation of scripture* (TIS). Scholars—biblical theologians and systematicians—engaged in this discussion are presently contending about the role confessional traditions play in TIS. Pentecostalism is not quite a "confessional" form of Christianity so much as it is a spirituality, ethos, and set of sensibilities, but this combination could be potent in sparking conversation, even intensifying the contentiousness that has already germinated in TIS circles. The point is that pentecostal hermeneutics is no less theological in reading scripture with the expectation that the Holy Spirit works through the text, but such reading has the potential to scramble the established categories of disputation in TIS precisely because what is foregrounded is not just received theological (or creedal) traditions but existential experiences under the dynamic impact of the Spirit's ongoing work in the world.

Third, pentecostal Christianity emerged at least in part as did Reformation traditions in general and Lutheranism more specifically: as Luther never intended to found a new church (or denomination), so also pentecostal believers always only believed that they were retrieving and reappropriating the apostolic message in a more vital and comprehensive manner than they had heretofore experienced, so that such restorationism was understood from the beginning as living more fully into the apostolic path and tradition. In that sense, pentecostal spirituality or pentecostal Christianity is not another kind or way of Christ-following, but simply living fully into Christ's gift of the Spirit from the right hand of the Father (Acts 2:33). In that sense, then, pentecostal hermeneutics is nothing less than Christian hermeneutics, devoted to understanding and then living out life in Christ *through the Spirit.* Craig Keener is here a gentle and effective teacher: alert to the triumphalism that all too often pervades (and plagues) pentecostal spheres but yet inviting of all who trust in Jesus—those who go by the label of *pentecostal* and otherwise—to live more fully into the Holy Spirit's ongoing work in the world. In short, *Spirit Hermeneutics* is about biblical fidelity, not just for those who find themselves in pentecostal communities of faith, but for all who wish to follow Jesus as the man who was himself anointed by the Spirit and who is now the resurrected Christ precisely through the power of the Spirit.

If the above three reasons undergird more specifically how Keener's book impacts the field of biblical interpretation, the next three focus on how it makes a difference for those thinking about hermeneutics in general and hermeneutical philosophy in a broader sense. If hermeneutics after Friedrich Schleiermacher, the putative "father" of modern theology, continues to seek to understand (to "divine," as he put it) the mind of the author, and if hermeneutics after Karl Barth and Hans Frei intends to enter more fully into the so-called "strange new world of the Bible," then (fourth) Keener shows us how Christian hermeneutics is even more radical than the former's liberalism and the latter's postliberalism by explicating hermeneutical sensibilities that are attentive both to the otherness of ancient text and to such texts' affective dimensions. Yet the radicality of Keener's proposals consists precisely in opening up that the *how* of such attentiveness involves, not precludes, the affectivity and the horizons of contemporary readers and their reading communities. The latter does not eliminate the text's otherness but enables more effective engagement with these aspects of such distant horizons.

Further, and fifth, Keener shows that the understanding of ancient texts has contemporary implications. Christians call this discipleship, and Keener's biblical-theological commitments lead him to frame such in terms of the Bible's eschatological horizons. But from the standpoint of general hermeneutics, this forward-looking and anticipating momentum involves what is identified in such domains as the pragmatic or even teleological dimension of reading: How does our understanding and reception of the past lead to liberative activity in the present toward ends that anticipate a better future? If Marxist hermeneutics prioritizes the latter trajectory, *Spirit Hermeneutics* insists that such liberative dynamics are unleashed through the pentecostal realities of the

Spirit's work in the world as scripted—which is distinct from being *predetermined*—and even funded by the ancient text of Scripture.

Sixth, then, if Keener shows us how to live squarely into the Gadamerian hermeneutical dialectic that does not minimize the horizon of the Spirit-inspired text or subjugate such under the horizon of the reader, he then also enables Christian engagement with the Habermasian emancipatory hermeneutics in ways that highlight how communicative rationality can be deeply religious on the one hand and yet also truly public on the other. Keener is more alert than most Christian hermeneutical theorists to the character of world Christianity, particularly as manifest in its pentecostal and charismatic forms, and is therefore able to indicate how such global horizons can shape public discourse, both in terms of interfacing with such and in terms of effecting certain forms of liberative praxis. Christian thinkers seeking to make contributions into general hermeneutical theory cannot do much better than to pay attention to how Keener navigates a via media between the ancient text and the contemporary global and public contexts.

Many readers of this book, however, will be drawn to it because of the established and renowned stature of Keener as a biblical exegete and commentarian. For those in this group, these final three reasons will be anti-climatic since they will already be primed to enjoy long books in their exquisite details. However, let me venture these recommendations anyway, lifting up the obvious fact (seventh) that this book lays bare Keener's hermeneutical instincts and commitments that are only implicit in much of his earlier work. There is a sense in which any exegete's hermeneutical presuppositions can only be teased out from their body of writings (even as a systematician's theological method can only be traced out from their *oeuvre*), and that surely applies here also. But the beauty of this book is that Keener himself has now articulated clearly—and extensively—what his readership might otherwise have to guess at while working endlessly on his voluminous publications (no reader can ever catch up with what Keener writes!), but he does it in his own characteristic way that engages, rather than simply talks about, scripture. This means we have here insight into Keener the scholar and the person, and also into scripture.

Further (eighth), *Spirit Hermeneutics* gives us a window into how a pentecostal Christian—which can be left just at *Christian,* without the qualifier, given my earlier remarks—exemplifies the convergence of the life of the mind and life in the Spirit. Many Christians err on one or the other side, embracing one while rejecting the other, or thinking that one is incompatible with the other. In Craig Keener we finally have an exemplar that unveils how rigorous use of the intellect and prodigiousness in scholarly output are spiritual activities, compelled by life in the Spirit of Jesus, in anticipation of the coming reign of God. More pointedly, it may even be said that in a certain sense there is no life of the mind in his case without a spiritual life that sustains and impels intellectual pursuits.

Last (ninth) but not least, *Spirit Hermeneutics* does not simply model a Spirit-filled academic life but charts a way beyond the polarities that have hampered theological education even in the present generation. Intellectual versus pietistic; academic versus spiritual; cognitive versus affective; self-formational versus world-changing; rationalistic versus charismatic; speculative/theoretical versus pragmatic/practical; sectarian/parochial versus ecumenical/catholic; ecclesial versus public, etc.—in each case, Keener points to a way beyond the binaries and dualisms that some would prefer to exaggerate. How this plays out in this book means not that we have overcome the two sides, but that they are retained in ways that make us capable of a more robust spectrum of reading and living than if the edges were lost. Seminarians, not to mention those who teach in their schools, are urged to pay attention not just to the details of Keener's hermeneutical arguments but to the way in which he models discursive engagement with hugely contested issues, and how he attempts to carry the conversation forward by bringing disputants with him rather than leaving them behind.

No doubt readers will not agree with Keener in every case or on every point he makes. Yet such differences can be discerned and clarified only through engagement with this work of a master teacher. I am thankful that Keener took seriously the original invitation to write a Pentecostal Manifesto, and somehow, I think that its appearance outside that series not only facilitated the much larger book but will engage an even wider readership. May the breath of the Spirit be palpably felt and even transformative for those who find their attention focused on the following pages.

Amos Yong
Professor of Theology and Mission
Fuller Theological Seminary
Pasadena, California

Acknowledgments

I am grateful to my editors at Eerdmans for welcoming and editing this book: Michael Thomson, James Ernest, and Jenny Hoffman. I also wish to thank Amos Yong and James K. A. Smith for originally inviting the book, and, with Lalsangkima Pachuau, for prompting me to engage conceptually and cross-culturally.

Abbreviations

AAAM	American Anthropological Association Monographs
AARAS	American Academy of Religion Academy Series
AARTRSS	American Academy of Religion Teaching Religious Studies Series
AB	Anchor Bible
ABD	*Anchor Bible Dictionary*
ABIG	Arbeiten zur Bibel und ihrer Geschichte
ACCS	Ancient Christian Commentary on Scripture
AfSt	African Studies
AfThJ	*Africa Theological Journal*
AJPS	*Asian Journal of Pentecostal Studies*
AJPSS	Asian Journal of Pentecostal Studies Series
AmAnth	*American Anthropologist*
AmJEpid	*American Journal of Epidemiology*
AmSocMissMonS	American Society of Missiology Monograph Series
AmSocMissS	American Society of Missiology Series
AnnBehMed	*Annals of Behavioral Medicine*
ANTC	Abingdon New Testament Commentaries
AnthCons	*Anthropology of Consciousness*
AnthHum	*Anthropology and Humanism*
AnthrQ	*Anthropological Quarterly*
ARAnth	*Annual Review of Anthropology*
ATJ	*Asbury Theological Journal*
AUSS	*Andrews University Seminary Studies*
AUSt	American University Studies
BangTF	*Bangalore Theological Forum*
BAR	*Biblical Archaeology Review*
BASOR	*Bulletin of the American Schools of Oriental Research*

BBR	*Bulletin of Biblical Research*
BDAG	Danker, Frederick W., Walter Bauer, William F. Arndt, and D. Wilbur Gingrich. *Greek-English Lexicon of the New Testament and Other Early Christian Literature.* 3rd ed. Chicago: University of Chicago Press, 2000.
BDB	Brown, Francis, S. R. Driver, and Charles A. Briggs. *A Hebrew and English Lexicon of the Old Testament.*
BETL	Bibliotheca Ephemeridum Theologicarum Lovaniensium
BiBh	*Bible Bhashyam (Biblebhashyam)*
BibT	*The Bible Today*
Bijdr	*Bijdragen*
BIS	Biblical Interpretation Series
BMedJ	*British Medical Journal*
BrCanRes	*Breast Cancer Research*
BrillPauly	*Brill's New Pauly, Encyclopaedia of the Ancient World: Antiquity.* Ed. Hubert Cancik, Helmuth Schneider, and Christine F. Salazar. Leiden and Boston: Brill, 2002–.
BSac	*Bibliotheca Sacra*
BTCB	Brazos Theological Commentary on the Bible
BullHistMed	*Bulletin of the History of Medicine*
BurH	*Buried History*
CBC	Cambridge Bible Commentary
CBET	Contributions to Biblical Exegesis and Theology
CBull	*Classical Bulletin*
CCRMS	Cross-Cultural Research and Methodology Series
ChicSt	*Chicago Studies*
CJ	*Classical Journal*
CNT	Commentaire du Nouveau Testament
ConBOT	Coniectanea biblica: Old Testament Series
CrQ	*Crozer Quarterly*
CSPhilRel	Cornell Studies in the Study of Religion
CSR	*Christian Scholar's Review*
CT	*Christianity Today*
CurTM	*Currents in Theology and Mission*
DNTB	*Dictionary of New Testament Background.* Ed. Craig A. Evans and Stanley E. Porter. Downers Grove, IL: InterVarsity, 2000.
DPCM	*Dictionary of Pentecostal and Charismatic Movements.* Ed. Stanley M. Burgess, Gary B. McGee, and Patrick H. Alexander. Grand Rapids: Zondervan, 1988.
DPL	*Dictionary of Paul and His Letters.* Ed. Gerald F. Hawthorne,

	Ralph P. Martin, and Daniel G. Reid. Downers Grove, IL: InterVarsity, 1993.
Enr	*Enrichment*
ETR	*Études Théologiques et Religieuses*
EvQ	*Evangelical Quarterly*
ExpT	*Expository Times*
F&M	*Faith & Mission*
FidHist	*Fides et Historia*
FoiVie	*Foi et Vie*
FourR	*The Fourth R*
FPhil	*Faith and Philosophy*
HBT	*Horizons in Biblical Theology*
HealthPsy	*Health Psychology*
HistTh	*History and Theory*
HTIOPS	Hispanic Theological Initiative Occasional Paper Series
HTS/TS	*HTS Teologiese Studies/Theological Studies*
HUCA	*Hebrew Union College Annual*
HumSt	*Hume Studies*
HvTSt	Hervormde Teologiese Studies
IBC	Interpretation: A Bible Commentary for Teaching and Preaching
IBMR	*International Bulletin of Missionary Research*
ICC	International Critical Commentaries
IEJ	*Israel Exploration Journal*
IJPhilRel	*International Journal for Philosophy of Religion*
IntArHistI	International Archives of the History of Ideas
IntJEpid	*International Journal of Epidemiology*
IntJPsyMed	*International Journal of Psychiatry in Medicine*
IntRevMiss	*International Review of Missions*
ITQ	*Irish Theological Quarterly*
JAAR	*Journal of the American Academy of Religion*
JABFM	*Journal of the American Board of Family Medicine*
JAM	*Journal of Asian Mission*
JAnthRes	*Journal of Anthropological Research*
JASA	*Journal of the American Scientific Affiliation*
JBL	*Journal of Biblical Literature*
JChrDis	*Journal of Chronic Diseases*
JClinEpid	*Journal of Clinical Epidemiology*
Jeev	*Jeevadhara*
JETS	*Journal of the Evangelical Theological Society*
JGBSMS	*Journal of Gerontology Series A: Biological Sciences and Medical Sciences*

JGPSSS	*Journal of Gerontology Series B: Psychological Sciences and Social Sciences*
JGRCJ	*Journal of Greco-Roman Christianity and Judaism*
JHSocBeh	*Journal of Health and Social Behavior*
JITC	*Journal of the Interdenominational Theological Center*
JJS	*Journal of Jewish Studies*
JPFC	*The Jewish People in the First Century: Historial Geography, Political History, Social, Cultural and Religious Life and Institutions.* 2 vols. Ed. S. Safrai and M. Stern with D. Flusser and W. C. van Unnik. Section 1 of Compendia Rerum Iudaicarum ad Novum Testamentum. Vol. 1: Assen: Van Gorcum & Comp., B.V., 1974; Vol. 2: Philadelphia: Fortress, 1976.
JPHWMSM	J. Philip Hogan World Missions Series Monograph
JPT	*Journal of Pentecostal Theology*
JPTSup	Journal of Pentecostal Theology Supplement Series
JR	*Journal of Religion*
JRelAf	*Journal of Religion in Africa*
JSHJ	*Journal for the Study of the Historical Jesus*
JSJ	*Journal for the Study of Judaism in the Persian, Hellenistic, and Roman Periods*
JSNT	*Journal for the Study of the New Testament*
JSNTSup	Journal for the Study of the New Testament Supplements
JSOTSup	Journal for the Study of the Old Testament Supplements
JSQ	*Jewish Studies Quarterly*
JSS	*Journal of Semitic Studies*
JTS	*Journal of Theological Studies*
JTSA	*Journal of Theology for Southern Africa*
JValInq	*Journal of Value Inquiry*
LCL	Loeb Classical Library
LD	Lectio Divina
LEC	Library of Early Christianity
LNTS	Library of New Testament Studies
LumVie	*Lumière et Vie*
MaisD	*Maison Dieu*
MHR	*Mediterranean Historical Review*
MissSt	*Mission Studies*
NAC	New American Commentary
NatInt	*The National Interest*
NBf	*New Blackfriars*
NCamBC	New Cambridge Bible Commentary
NCCS	New Covenant Commentary Series

NIB	*The New Interpreter's Bible.* Ed. Leander E. Keck. 12 vols. Nashville: Abingdon, 1994–2004.
NICNT	New International Commentary on the New Testament
NICOT	New International Commentary on the Old Testament
NIGTC	New International Greek Testament Commentary
NIVAC	NIV Application Commentary
NovTSup	Supplements to Novum Testamentum
NRTh	*Nouvelle Revue Théologique*
NSPR	New Studies in the Philosophy of Religion
NTMon	New Testament Monographs
NTS	*New Testament Studies*
NTTS	New Testament Tools and Studies
OCD³	*The Oxford Classical Dictionary: The Ultimate Reference Work on the Classical World.* 3rd rev. ed. Ed. Simon Hornblower and Antony Spawforth. Oxford: Oxford University Press, 2003.
OHCC	Oxford History of the Christian Church
OrOnc	*Oral Oncology*
PAST	Pauline Studies
PHC	Penguin History of the Church
PhilChr	*Philosophia Christi*
PhilFor	*Philosophical Forum*
PhilSt	*Philosophical Studies*
PhilTheol	*Philosophy and Theology*
PNTC	Pillar New Testament Commentary
PRSt	*Perspectives in Religious Studies*
PrTMS	Princeton Theological Monograph Series
PScChrF	*Perspectives on Science and Christian Faith*
PsycTRPT	*Psychotherapy: Theory, Research, Practice, Training*
QC	*Qumran Chronicle*
RelS	*Religious Studies*
ResAg	*Research on Aging*
ResQ	*Restoration Quarterly*
RevExp	*Review and Expositor*
RevQ	*Revue de Qumran*
RNT	Regensburger Neues Testament
RStMiss	Regnum Studies in Mission
SBL	Society of Biblical Literature
SBLMS	Society of Biblical Literature Monograph Series
SBLSymS	Society of Biblical Literature Symposium Series
SBT	Studies in Biblical Theology
ScChrB	*Science and Christian Belief*

SCEthn	Series in Contemporary Ethnography
SCR	Studies in Comparative Religion
SEAJT	*South East Asia Journal of Theology*
SHBC	Smyth & Helwys Bible Commentary
SHCM	Studies in the History of Christian Mission
SHE	*Studia Historiae Ecclesiaticae*
SICHC	Studies in the Intercultural History of Christianity
SJRS	*Scottish Journal of Religious Studies*
SJT	*Scottish Journal of Theology*
SMedJ	*Southern Medical Journal*
SNTSMS	Society for New Testament Studies Monograph Series
SocG	*Sociologische Gids*
SP	Sacra Pagina
SPCI	Studies in Pentecostal and Charismatic Issues
SSMed	*Social Science & Medicine*
StMkRev	*St Mark's Review*
SWJT	*Southwestern Journal of Theology*
TJ	*Trinity Journal*
TJT	*Toronto Journal of Theology*
TQ	*Theologische Quartalschrift*
TSHP	Texts and Studies in the History of Philosophy
TynBul	*Tyndale Bulletin*
UCPLA	Unidade Cientifico-Pedagógica de Letras e Artes
UJT	Understanding Jesus Today
WBC	Word Biblical Commentary
WMQ	*William and Mary Quarterly*
WUNT	Wissenschaftliche Untersuchungen zum Neuen Testament
ZAW	*Zeitschrift für die Alttestamentliche Wissenschaft*
Zyg	*Zygon: Journal of Religion and Science*

Introduction

Purpose

Spirit Hermeneutics is primarily designed to function as biblical theological reflection supporting a dynamic, experiential reading of Scripture. At the same time, a genuine sensitivity to the Spirit's voice in Scripture should welcome deeper understanding of the historical and cultural milieu in which the Spirit shaped Scripture's form as we have it, a sensitivity against which some proponents of experiential and theological reading have sometimes overreacted.

Although concerned with Christian readings generally, this work engages in conversation particularly frequently with Pentecostal and charismatic traditions because of their special interest in the Spirit and my familiarity with historical examples and discussions in these circles. I am a charismatic biblical scholar at home, albeit sometimes in different ways, both in global pentecostalism[1] and in academic discussions of Scripture.

Because I am a biblical scholar, I can make the strongest distinctive contribution not by analyzing the current state of hermeneutical discussion (a work undertaken by many others) but by focusing on the biblical evidence itself.[2] Such evidence is relevant for all Christian interpretive traditions and is also where my own journey with Scripture, nurtured particularly by Pentecostals, began. Scripture itself provides many precedents for hearing earlier parts of Scripture as applicable to the hearers' time. Scripture itself thus models an experiential appropriation of its message.

I begin by showing the importance of (and time-honored appreciation for) this experiential emphasis, the value of hearing the text from multiple locations (global Christianity), and the potential consistency of these approaches with a grounding in the original, experiential message in its first context. I then show how these approaches reflect an epistemology grounded in the gospel of Christ and surfacing in multiple early Christian streams (including Pauline, Johannine, and Lukan approaches). I then work to show inductively how Scripture itself invites us to hear it in these ways, especially in terms of how

1

4 parts?

Jesus and Paul read the Scriptures. Finally, I briefly consider what implications these and some other factors might have for what is often called "pentecostal" or "charismatic" hermeneutics.

What This Book Is Not

When in the past I taught hermeneutics to master's-level pastoral ministry students, much of the course addressed basic exegetical method and models (plus some introductory-level theory). I generally offered an explicit integrative transition to other theological disciplines, especially preaching, yet only relatively briefly at the end of the course.

Yet I myself was regularly preaching, applying texts to my audience's settings, and even more regularly listened spiritually to what I could learn from the biblical text. I modeled this approach when I taught various Bible courses (including the aforementioned hermeneutics course), but I rarely reflected on or sought to explain it in a deliberate manner. In this book, I want to somewhat redress that theoretical deficiency by comments on why a spiritually sensitive, specifically Christian approach to the biblical text is for Christians a valuable companion to (yet not a replacement for) exegesis.

In this book I presuppose that most readers already understand the value of attention to literary and historical context, which I have addressed frequently elsewhere. This book is thus neither a manual addressing basic principles for basic Bible interpretation, which I have provided at no cost on a popular level elsewhere,[3] nor an advanced philosophic discussion of hermeneutics, which many other scholars (perhaps most notably and famously Anthony Thiselton) have provided better than I could.[4]

assumption

Thus this book mostly assumes readers' existing competence in basic literary hermeneutics (including the importance of literary and historical context and genre); that is what I usually teach, and that is more foundational for most ordinary readers of Scripture. This work is meant to complement and supplement these basic approaches, not to supplant them. As will become clear later in the book, I have little patience for approaches that claim to be "of the

intresting

Spirit" yet ignore the concreteness of the settings in which the Spirit inspired the biblical writings, settings that help explain the particularities in the shape of such writings.

This work thus addresses not everything one needs for understanding Scripture but focuses on a particular question or element of hermeneutics: How do we hear the Spirit's voice in Scripture? Other techniques, common to other sorts of literature, necessarily remain relevant to various genres of Scripture. After all, biblical texts are *texts,* communicated in real language, history, culture, and genres that at least resemble identifiable genres from their historical context. The shape of these texts invite interpretive approaches appropriate to their shape.

What is distinctive to Spirit hermeneutics, however, is *believers* reading the texts as *Scripture.*[5] During or once we have done responsible exegesis, how may we expect the Spirit to apply the text to our lives and communities? Those of us already trained in exegesis are often the ones who most need to be reminded of this latter concern, which we often do not cover when teaching traditional exegetical methodologies.

[margin note: interesting]

What Is Spirit Hermeneutics?

The title *Spirit Hermeneutics* suggests several theological lenses through which I believe Scripture invites us to read Scripture.[6] The genesis of this book further helps explain its trajectory and choice of analogies. Amos Yong and James K. A. Smith graciously invited me to contribute a volume on Pentecostal hermeneutics to their series on Pentecostal theology. Amos's suggestions also pushed me to consider how I personally read Scripture as Scripture—beyond the more restricted methods on which I have formally lectured in my interpretation courses. Because of the book's size, Michael Thomson, the series editors, and I agreed to publish this book outside the series, but its genesis explains its orientation.

[margin note: motivation to write!]

From the project's beginning, however, I insisted that the narrower title "Pentecostal Hermeneutics," accurate as it would be, could mislead potential readers, since I ultimately conclude that the elements that characterize a good "Pentecostal" hermeneutic are elements that should characterize *any* truly Christian and Spirit-led hermeneutic. That is, it is "Pentecostal" in the sense that all of us as Christians should read from the vantage of Pentecost and the experience of the Spirit. Although a significant proportion of my direct conversation partners in this book's notes come from Pentecostal, charismatic and other renewal traditions, the hermeneutical observations are hardly relevant for Pentecostals alone.

[margin note: Thesis?]

A title such as "Pentecostal hermeneutics" could further mislead readers because the book's objective is not a description of how various members of Pentecostal denominations interpret Scripture.[7] Indeed, the expression "global pentecostalism" (with a small "p") in current usage generally encompasses all those who claim a dynamic experience of the Spirit and his gifts, in no way limited to Pentecostal denominations or independent charismatic churches. Moreover, consensus definitions of "Pentecostal," and thus of Pentecostal hermeneutics, are elusive.[8] Even classical Pentecostal interpretive practices are as diverse as the historical roots and settings of these churches and the academic settings of their interpreters; most of their approaches are not in fact distinctive of Pentecostal experience per se.[9] Some Pentecostals in fact describe other Pentecostals' hermeneutical practices as problematic,[10] so mere description, helpful as it would be for sociological analysis, cannot in any case function prescriptively without considerable qualification.[11]

Rather, my objective here is to help to articulate how the experience of the Spirit that empowered the church on the day of Pentecost can and should dynamically shape our reading of Scripture. It is less about reading the Bible within a particular denominational or movement's interpretive community than about ways of reading the Bible that are faithful both to the Spirit-inspired biblical text and the experience of the Spirit within a believer or among believers as an interpretive community. That approach is relevant for denominational Pentecostals, but also for all who share their commitment to reading the Bible experientially, hearing in Scripture God's inspired voice for us, his people, in all ages.

Insights from Global Pentecostal Emphases on the Spirit

As already suggested, this approach is consistent with some key emphases of the early Pentecostal revival, but is relevant to the wider church as well. What early Pentecostals introduced (or often developed from the contemporary holiness revivals) was something that distinguished them and many of their peers from the widespread and fairly rigid cessationism of their day. But their original vision was ecumenical—the renewal of the entire end time church—and not the creation of simply one competing movement cut off from others.

Although denominational Pentecostals today comprise a significant proportion of the global church,[12] the contribution of what scholars today often call "global pentecostalism" has become far wider than their immediate circle.[13] Partly because of early Pentecostals' historic contribution, much of the church today recognizes the importance of depending on the Spirit and the value of the entire range of spiritual gifts. The hermeneutic addressed here must belong to that wider circle—to all who are people of the Spirit.[14]

Thus my focus here will be on some hermeneutical principles modeled by intrabiblical, hence Spirit-inspired, readings. In keeping with both my own interests and the editors' invitation to the series, I will engage Pentecostal scholarship and draw on what I believe are important insights from early Pentecostalism.[15] More broadly, however, the hermeneutic today is no longer merely a classical Pentecostal one but has become to some extent more generally a Christian one. All Christians should read Scripture as people who are living in the biblical experience—not in terms of ancient *culture,* but as people living by the same Spirit who guided God's people in Scripture.

This is, however, a distinctly noncessationist (i.e., it is a continuationist) approach to Scripture. As followers of the risen Messiah, we are people of the era of the Messiah and the Spirit, inaugurated at Pentecost, a prophetic, eschatological people. Referring to events that began at Pentecost, Acts announces the era of the Spirit that God had earlier promised: "In the last days . . . I will pour out my Spirit on all flesh, and your sons and daughters will prophesy." A "Spirit hermeneutic" seems an apt title for that interpretive location. Moreover, it is one shared by the first Pentecostals and most global Pentecostals and charismatics, including myself.

This means that we are interested in biblical texts not simply for what they teach us about ancient history or ideas (intriguing as that is to me), but because we expect to share the kind of spiritual experience and relationship with God that we discover in Scripture.[16] Jesus's resurrection is not a mere historical datum; it declares that the Jesus we learn about in the Gospels is now the exalted Lord, who has sent his Spirit so that we may continue to experience his presence.

Throughout Scripture we read about people hearing from God, prophesying, and experiencing miracles. Though we may not all experience all these activities of the Spirit daily, biblical patterns lead us to expect that the God who empowered these activities throughout Scripture is the God who still empowers them. Many traditional approaches fail to do justice to Scripture's own witness—for example, they read Scripture as if it were merely designed to satisfy our historical interest about past salvation history (the approach of some conservative interpreters) or past ideas (the approach of some liberal ones), or just teaches us doctrine about God without inviting a relationship with him, or exemplifies moral virtues without attesting the Spirit's power to implement them.

While careful study of Scripture helps counter the unbridled subjectivism of popular charismatic excesses, study that does not lead to living out biblical experience in the era of the Spirit misses the point of the biblical texts.[17]

5

of the · t
Spirit

All Christian experience in this era must be properly "Pentecostal"—that is, shaped by the experience of Pentecost, the outpouring of the Spirit on the church.

Pentecostal Hermeneutics and Spirit Hermeneutics

Because this book's genesis was an invitation to contribute a volume on hermeneutics to a series of studies on Pentecostal theology, the rest of my introduction addresses the relevance of more self-consciously Pentecostal hermeneutics to this book, and of this book to that kind of Pentecostal hermeneutics. Various Pentecostals have different views on how to do hermeneutics, and whether and in what ways Pentecostal hermeneutics are distinctive from others' hermeneutics.

One could approach a book on Pentecostal hermeneutics from various angles; as noted below, one valuable approach sociologically would be descriptive, but there are others far more qualified to survey descriptively all the various methods.[18] Instead, I am constructing an approach that I believe is biblical, and thus faithful to the original, biblically directed Pentecostal (and restorationist) ethos,[19] one that many other Pentecostal and other pastorally concerned biblical scholars will share.

Nevertheless, I believe that global Pentecostalism can help offer one valuable "inside" perspective on some of the sorts of Spirit-experiences emphasized in the NT.[20] Early Pentecostals believed that they lived within the larger narrative world of Scripture, a world where the supernatural and eschatology were real.[21] Because charismatic experience is an important part of New Testament experience, it provides a much more adequate starting point or preunderstanding for engaging the text than does the lack of such experience.[22] To suggest that pentecostals can offer this perspective is not by any means to limit it to Pentecostals (even in the broadest sense). It is simply to suggest that this is a distinctively Pentecostal emphasis, and one that is therefore a gift that Pentecostals have historically been bringing to much of the rest of the church.[23]

Key Pentecostal emphases draw on genuine biblical emphases, just as Anabaptist emphases on caring for the poor, evangelical emphases on understanding Scripture, and other parts of the church each contribute some genuine biblical insights to the rest of the church. Impoverished believers, Messianic Jewish believers, members of house churches, members of religious and often ethnic minorities, those who have experienced power encounters

6

or persecution, and others who have distinctive aspects of their identity in common with that of many or most members of the churches that appear in the New Testament can all offer somewhat "inside" perspectives on early Christian experience by offering sympathetic analogies. Their respective settings allow them to highlight aspects of experience that we might otherwise overlook.[24]

This book, then, is not meant to describe or prescribe an entire hermeneutic used by Pentecostal or charismatic exegetes; it is rather meant to highlight emphases that Pentecostals, charismatics and other people of the Spirit may add to hermeneutical wisdom already in place.[25]

Moreover, my interest in this book is not simply a hermeneutical approach, but a more fundamental epistemological approach on which it rests, an epistemology both suggested by and pointing toward the voice of Scripture. When I write for the secular academy, I work from the significantly more limited epistemological, hence hermeneutical, approaches shared as an accepted common ground by scholars from a diverse range of persuasions. But outside the academic sphere, barely anyone lives fully with the heavy agnosticism of such approaches; even if one starts with such agnosticism, sooner or later one will learn something and cease to be agnostic on that point. Those of us who embrace the Christian message as true share with one another a broader common ground than do academicians merely laboring for theological neutrality or agnosticism beyond a shared, limited methodology.[26] To adequately address any self-consciously Christian hermeneutic, I must explore elements of a specifically Christian epistemology. I believe that what some today call a Pentecostal hermeneutic is simply an emphatic expression of what should be a wider Christian hermeneutic.

The "Pentecostal" in "Pentecostal Hermeneutics"

The now-burgeoning scholarship on Pentecostalism in many major universities worldwide often speaks of Pentecostal in two ways: Pentecostal denominations (often with a capital "P") and those who share a basic pentecostal experience or ethos (often with a small "p"), including charismatics, members of Third Wave churches, and others who emphasize similar spiritual experience.[27] This book, like the series, presupposes the broader label, although many of the specific examples I engage derive from the earlier twentieth-century global revival movements that provide important antecedents for our more widespread current practice.

When I speak here of Pentecostal experience, I refer to an experience with God modeled in Acts 2, not a denomination or title that must contain it. Many of the earliest Pentecostals, in fact, disliked human organization; some left the Azusa Street Mission once it put up a title![28] Happily, Pentecostal denominations have since provided invaluable organization for missions, training, and other benefits. Nevertheless, from the beginning the vision for the Pentecostal revival was the renewal of Christianity as a whole.[29] Today, global Pentecostalism crosses many boundaries; for example, one of the largest single groups within the amorphous movement many sociologists classify as global pentecostalism is the Catholic charismatic movement.[30]

Similarly, people employ the term "charismatic" in a wide range of ways. I am using the term with reference to the affirmation of the *charismata* mentioned by Paul. Some churches today that fit this definition avoid the term because of its connotations in particular circles (which associate the term with, for example, prosperity teaching). Nevertheless, "charismatic" seems the more widely encompassing term (and more widely used than "pentecostal" with a small "p"), so I retain it with the definition offered here.

Although the term "charismatic" has taken on a range of meanings in various circles, the modern classification originates in Paul's depiction of *charismata,* or spiritual gifts (Rom 12:6–8; 1 Cor 12:4–11). Such gifts belong to the entire body of Christ; by definition, each member of the body has at least one gift to contribute to the larger body (Rom 12:4–6; 1 Cor 12:12–30). That is, all Christians should be considered charismatic by definition. I will use the title somewhat more narrowly later in the book (chapter 18; esp. Appendix C) only as a concession to popular usage and for lack of another term to describe practicing noncessationists.

Some Protestant thinkers traditionally argued for the specific cessation only of "supernatural" gifts. This dichotomy, however, has more to do with early Protestant reaction against Catholic tradition (similar to early Protestant rejection of missions because Catholics engaged in it) and accommodation to Enlightenment skepticism than it does with Scripture. For Paul, *all* gifts are empowered by the Spirit. A body that excludes particular kinds of gifts that Paul affirmed would, from a Pauline perspective, thus be a disabled or malformed body, lacking some of the member gifts needed to bring the body as whole to maturity. That some Christian bodies have traditionally amputated valuable members as purely vestigial cannot justify trying to build a new body out of all the amputated members.

In theory, most Christians today believe that the range of biblical gifts continue today, but in practice most churches have only some of the gifts represented. In fact, many churches that in principle allow that the gifts are for today are, with respect to public worship, practical cessationists on any biblical gifts that do not fit their traditional order of service. This is true even of many Pentecostal and charismatic churches, sometimes even with regard to gifts traditionally associated with those churches. It is admittedly true even of most churches where I have ministered (though not so much where I pastored). While I am happy to minister and worship there, I do believe that, biblically, we are missing something important. (Sometimes the size of the congregation prohibits exercise of many members' gifts, but these can often be accommodated through small groups.)

Descriptive or Prescriptive?

As noted above, a work addressing "Pentecostal hermeneutics" could be descriptive, showing how a range of Pentecostal interpreters read biblical texts. One common and valuable descriptive reader-response approach involves readings from different social locations, an approach that, like reception history, can broaden our interpretive horizons by placing a wider range of readings on the table.[31]

Pentecostal readings, however, can be quite diverse. They may include prosperity teaching as well as asceticism, local syncretism as well as mainstream church tradition, strict traditions against drinking any alcohol as well as eager contextualization. There is no Pentecostal magisterium to decide which views are "the Pentecostal view"—unless various scholars or groups who claim to speak for Pentecostal hermeneutics implicitly intend to set themselves up as one.[32] We cannot assume that by describing even much of Pentecostal hermeneutics that we have prescribed what such a hermeneutic *should* be;[33] it may be that what empowered Pentecostalism was not especially its hermeneutic,[34] and that Pentecostals can learn from other parts of Christ's body in this way.

After all, the early Pentecostal figure Smith Wigglesworth prophesied a future revival that would bring together Word and Spirit;[35] perhaps that means that, instead of early populist Pentecostalism supplying both elements, Pentecostal emphasis on the Spirit could combine with evangelical emphasis on the Word. With enough humility, Pentecostals and other evangelicals may and sometimes do learn much from one another.[36] Sometimes evangelicals fear charismatic excesses, and charismatics are impatient with evangelicals' reticence to engage some genuinely biblical experiences. In our pride and

interesting

fear, we fail to see how much we need each other as fellow gifts in Christ's body, and that both are considering genuine elements of the biblical message. Instead of reacting against each other, or posturing about which gifts are most important, let us embrace biblically affirmed experience in biblical ways. The Bible offers repeated models of spiritual experience; it also offers guidance and a framework within which we can keep our experience on track.[37]

Pentecostal hermeneutical approaches are as varied as the Pentecostal interpreters who use them; we often tend to favor those hermeneutical approaches in which we have been schooled (e.g., grammatical-historical, historical-critical, or postmodern). What is more helpful in descriptively identifying a common core for Pentecostal hermeneutics is looking at historic distinctives in Pentecostal approaches, especially where these remain useful for a wider readership.

Nevertheless, today the sort of hermeneutic historically characteristic of Pentecostals is not distinctive to them, but is widely shared among other Christians. A "Pentecostal" hermeneutic therefore need not be like some special-interest hermeneutical approaches that are designed simply to produce desired theological, ethical, or political outcomes, nor is any distinctive approach to Scripture needed to produce an outcome that emphasizes the Spirit. If read on its own terms (or even with a brief Pauline concordance search), the Bible does invite us to affirm the life, gifts, fruit and power of the Spirit. The New Testament pervasively emphasizes the new era of the Spirit in Christ, an emphasis missed not by concordance searches or exegesis but only by worldviews that cannot contend with it. This emphasis, then, is the result of a *biblical* hermeneutic simply attentive to the text; it is relevant for the entire church, and not just the massive segment that is called Pentecostal. If we define pentecostal in this wider sense, ideally all of the church should be pentecostal, reading from the vantage point of Pentecost.

A More Prescriptive Approach

As a biblical scholar rather than a church historian or sociologist, years of grappling with biblical texts has better qualified me to suggest ways to engage Scripture than to survey how some parts of the church do so. Nevertheless, just as readings from various locations may broaden our interpretive horizons and help us catch our blind spots, listening to Pentecostal/charismatic insights may bring to our attention—and *has* often brought to the church's attention—points that the wider church has missed.

Through charismatic movements, freer worship, and the like, positive Pentecostal values have affected the larger church. One of the strongest attractions of cessationism today (felt even by many charismatics such as myself) is the extreme subjectivism of some charismatics; evangelical emphasis on careful biblical teaching is crucial here. Yet life is full of subjective experiences, and those who genuinely heed Scripture cannot neglect spiritual experience. The Bible itself is full of dynamic experiences with God, and the broader church regularly needs to be reminded of these.

Whether we call those experiences "pentecostal" or not is a matter of semantics (in my wife's country, for example, most Christians can experience prophecy and healing, both true and false, outside of denominationally Pentecostal and neopentecostal circles). But if we are to be faithful to Scripture *qua* Scripture, we must not only explain what it meant to first-century hearers but also learn from its models. Most biblical scholars today recognize that cessationism lacks a strong biblical foundation, but biblical interpretation requires more than that recognition. Too often Western Christians are inconsistent: we are not cessationist in name, but we are in practice. Unfortunately, this has become true of some denominational Pentecostals as well.

We need to read the Bible dynamically as something that speaks to us about how God acts in our world—in our time and not just in the past. That is a contribution that much of the broader church still needs to grasp from global pentecostalism, even as the broader church offers its own contributions to global pentecostalism. Ideally, the entire church must be experiential if it wishes to be biblical.

Ultimately, a "pentecostal" approach is an apology for reading Christian texts in a specifically Christian way, rather than the way we sometimes read those texts in the academy. This is not to devalue the contribution of the historical-critical academic reading.[38] Historical information enriches and is often necessary for our full understanding of the text; the point is simply that analysis of historical questions by itself is not equivalent to understanding, welcoming, or embracing a text's message.

For now, suffice it to say that understanding a text's grammar or even recognizing its instructions differs from embracing its message with faith. Most scholars, whether or not they personally embrace the text in faith, recognize that merely knowing information about a text is not the same thing as embracing the text's message in faithful obedience.[39] Moreover, an approach sterilized from any direct faith in the supernatural differs significantly from how the biblical writers intended their works to be read. For some of the philosophic discussion of this distinction, see Appendix A.

The Wider Christian Hermeneutic of the Spirit

Although most Christian scholars, whatever their tradition, would be impatient with any approach that plays down disciplined study, most also value the Spirit's work in helping believers to understand and obey Scripture.

How Does Illumination Function?

Divine illumination does not mean pretending away the textual nature of the biblical text; insofar as it is textual, Scripture by virtue of its textual form must be approached in the sorts of ways in which we must approach texts. Some thus suggest that, ultimately, illumination's object may be less about enabling grammatical exegesis of the sort we are already capable of doing on our own, and instead about enabling us to recognize the text's demands for us and to embrace the text's message in faith.[40]

Other evangelical scholars further emphasize that the Spirit's role of illumining the reader is not meant to "redo," and certainly not to "undo," the Spirit's work in inspiration. The Spirit already generated meaning through the inspired human agents writing in their own language and setting. The Spirit's role of illumination thus focuses on the texts' perlocution, i.e., "the successful conclusion of the speech act": normally understanding and response. "Perlocution is what identifies the expected response to a speech act. If the illocution is a command, the perlocution would be obedience. . . . The Holy Spirit is largely involved at the perlocutionary level as we are enabled to understand the truthfulness of the text, recognize what it requires from us and then actually take the appropriate steps to actualize the intentions that the Holy Spirit initially delivered to the human instrument."[41]

Still, the Spirit can be active even on the level of exegesis, most often through the clear functioning of our cognitive faculties in exploring and embracing the text.[42] As one Pentecostal scholar suggests, "Illumination occurs in conjunction with, not in isolation from, normal application of hermeneutical principles."[43] We should expect such help in light of the Spirit's role as teacher and as one who reminds us of Jesus's teaching (John 14:26).[44]

In a seminal modern essay on illumination, Pentecostal exegete French L. Arrington notes the importance of the Spirit's activity in interpretation, in "(1) submission of the mind to God so that the critical and analytical abilities are exercised under the guidance of the Holy Spirit; (2) a genuine openness to the witness of the Spirit as the text is examined; (3) the personal experience of faith as part of the entire interpretive process; and, (4) response to the transforming call of God's Word."[45] The first of these points helpfully recognizes that the Spirit can work through as well as beyond our cognitive faculties.[46]

The Wider Christian Tradition Affirms Illumination

Seeking to hear the Spirit's voice in the biblical text has a long history.[47] It characterizes the meditative approach *lectio divina*, developed among Benedictines in the fifth century.[48] (Many elements of both *lectio divina* and Eastern Orthodox *hesychasm* can be meaningful for and adapted in ways relevant to believers in a range of cultures.)[49] Indeed, earlier Christian interpreters such as Origen, John Chrysostom, and Augustine insisted on the need for the Spirit's help in understanding Scripture, in addition to the reader's own diligence in study.[50]

Luther emphasized the need for interpreters to experience faith and the Spirit's illumination, in addition to grammatical and historical exegesis;[51] "Experience is necessary for the understanding of the Word," which must "be believed and felt."[52] Reading the Bible properly included prayer and meditation.[53] Calvin likewise insisted that people could understand God's Word only through the Spirit's enlightenment.[54] Both Puritans and Pietists insisted that only God's Spirit provides true understanding of Scripture's message.[55] Early founders of Princeton Seminary also emphasized illumination,[56] though in the nineteenth century a conservative scholasticism developed there that played down the Spirit's role in interpretation.[57] Francis Wayland of Brown University, the best-known Baptist scholar of the 1830s and 1840s, emphasized the need for the Holy Spirit's illumination of the Bible.[58]

Likewise, J. B. Lightfoot, an exegete sensitive to ancient culture and perhaps the leading British biblical scholar of the nineteenth century, articulates well our need to engage the Spirit when hearing Scripture. One of his remarks is so balanced that I must quote it here at length:

> Last of all, these remarks would be most defective, if I failed to remind you, as I need to be reminded myself, that above all things prayer is necessary for the right understanding of the Holy Scripture. As speaking to Christians, I might appeal at once to the authority of Scripture itself, an authority which you all recognize. But if it can be said that as a matter of argument, I am arguing in a circle, because the recognition of the duty of prayer presupposes a belief in the truth of Holy Scripture, I could put the matter in this light. If you are studying an ancient writer, a historian for instance such as

Thucydides or Tacitus, you would not expect to understand him unless you endeavored to transport yourself into the time at which he wrote, to think and feel with him, and to realize all the circumstances which influenced the life and actions of men of that day. Otherwise, your study would be barren of any results. So it is with the study of Holy Scripture. These documents come before you as spiritual writings, and to appreciate them you must put yourself in communication with the Spirit. Prayer is the medium of communication. And therefore it is necessary for the right understanding of the Bible.[59]

Major early-twentieth-century popular Christian interpreters also often emphasized this approach, sometimes even in ways that might invite some subsequent evangelicals' concern. While affirming written Scripture as God's Word, Oswald Chambers also "believed that the words of Scripture, though they are the Word of God, 'do not give us life unless Jesus speaks them to us.'"[60] One may compare also the Christian and Missionary Alliance devotional theologian A. W. Tozer: "It is the present Voice which makes the written Word all-powerful."[61]

Interdenominational Consensus

Pentecostal, Wesleyan, and earlier exegetes are not the only ones who value this level of engagement.[62] In terms of valuing application, classical scholars and philosophers often look to ancient texts for valuable wisdom.[63] How much more can we expect such interests among those who value biblical texts as canonical? Brethren scholar F. F. Bruce, for example, insisted that readers who engage Scripture as God's book must not stop with the grammatical and historical foundation, but also hear the text theologically.[64] Likewise, Bernard Ramm emphasized the necessity of devotional reading in the Pietist tradition, provided that it was not disconnected from sound contextual interpretation.[65] "The Holy Spirit alone," Grant Osborne urges, "can empower the preacher so that his message exemplified not 'persuasive words of [human] wisdom' but rather demonstrates 'the Spirit and the power' of God (1 Cor 2:4–5)."[66]

Advocates of inductive Bible study also recognize that spiritual experience of God helps readers appropriate biblical texts in the sorts of ways they were meant to be appropriated.[67] Simply objectifying and evaluating texts as if we may control them leaves little room for us to hear God there.[68] Catholic scholar Daniel J. Harrington notes that after examining the original meaning most interpreters also desire to hear the text's significance for us today.[69] The goal of hermeneutical theorists such as Fuchs and Ebeling is to hear Scripture speaking anew in new settings.[70] This interest certainly pervaded earlier Christian readings of Scripture, including among Reformers[71] and many modern interpreters.[72]

Most modern theologians also value the Spirit's role in interpretation. For example, Karl Barth welcomed historical criticism as a first step in engaging Scripture, but insisted that only the Spirit could provide full understanding beyond grammar and history.[73] Carl F. H. Henry considers this the orthodox Protestant position.[74] Donald Bloesch, Thomas F. Torrance, J. I. Packer and others likewise emphasize the Spirit's role in interpretation.[75] Some have described the traditional division of labor as biblical scholars (historical critics) studying what the text meant a long time ago and theologians figuring out God's message for today, without interfering much in the other's discipline.[76] Today, however, many biblical scholars and theologians have sought rapprochement through theological interpretation of the Bible.[77]

My Own Background

Many other parts of the body of Christ appreciate and share the pentecostal or charismatic ethos. Representatives of this ethos and experience now may be found among nearly all global communions today. For example, I am ordained as a Baptist minister and teach in a predominantly Wesleyan and Methodist environment. But I pray in tongues (probably often an hour a day), love deep worship in the Spirit, and attended a Pentecostal seminary, and the Baptist minister who offered the charge at my ordination both prayed in tongues over me and prophesied to me. My Baptist ordination did not have to do with complaints about Pentecostal practice but with my commitment to ethnic reconciliation and the local church and community where I was ordained.[78] I have also written works about the Spirit and spiritual experience that explicitly identify me as charismatic.[79] Indeed, presumably because Scripture allowed me no concessions to cessationism at all, a local newspaper review of one of my books by one conservative Presbyterian minister identified me as "wildly charismatic"![80]

My Own Development in Thinking

Nevertheless, this is not a book that I could have written several years ago, for two reasons. First, I was at the apex of my historical-critical work on the Gospels when I wrote *Historical Jesus of the Gospels* (2009).[81] I bent over backward to limit my arguments to consensus arguments and data for which I could offer sufficient support. I believed that my conclusions were from a neutral historiographic standpoint far more plausible and better informed historically than those of skeptics. To my disappointment, several skeptics simply dismissed my work by stereotyping it as evangelical "apologetic," as if only arguments favoring a more conventional position may be deemed a "defense" of something.[82]

Their reaction reinforced for me how deep biases can run, even among some scholars who claim to be unbiased, critical and open-minded. Unfortunately, fitting what is often of greatest popular interest in a media-saturated age, some scholarship is geared more toward novelty than accuracy. I often warn my doctoral students that while creativity is ideal, accuracy is more vital. After hearing and reading the most critical responses from scholars in a fairly skeptical tradition, I had to resist the temptation to give up even engaging this circle of scholars. My subsequent work on miracles then forced me to think outside the historical-critical box. Metahistorical questions need not devalue the use historical-critical methods in the historical-critical sphere; still, that sphere need not be viewed as the only one worthy of epistemological consideration.

Second, over the years I had taught biblical interpretation to perhaps a thousand students in person, plus written a short, practical book on the subject that has been circulated among tens of thousands of readers in Africa.[83] My emphasis in such courses was largely a correction of popular interpretation: I was leading my students in taking into account especially context, background, and genre. These are crucial emphases that popular readers often miss.

Yet while I modeled going from text to sermon and from text to living, I left mostly to homiletics and spiritual formation colleagues (if to anyone) the task of explaining the connections. Popular interpreters so often move from text to application that I did not believe that the process needed justification except at a more esoteric academic level, a justification already provided adequately by other scholars.

When Amos Yong invited me to write on Pentecostal hermeneutics, my academic reflex was still primarily corrective. Beyond literary context, my own primary academic contribution has been providing ancient material that helps readers reconstruct the setting, since that is what is most difficult for modern readers to acquire on their own. But Amos pressed me to consider the valuable contribution of a pentecostal hermeneutic, and the more that I wrestled with this question the more intrigued I became.

The result is this book. It is not written, to be sure, the way a theologian, philosopher, or historian of interpretation would have written it. I write as a biblical scholar and have touched more lightly on areas that others can address with much greater competence. Without trying to replace other important work on interpretation, I hope to stimulate some further discussion and contribute to this intriguing area at the interface of various disciplines and the Christian life. My interest is partly in showing that it is *biblical* for believers to read the text from a location within the biblical theological world.[84]

In contrast to my exegetical commentaries, my approach to the biblical witnesses here is deliberately integrative, moving back and forth among different biblical writers in an effort to show that the emphases in question are rarely limited to a single biblical writer. Many of these emphases, in fact, are pervasive. If we find parallels with other early Jewish ideas, we should hardly be surprised to find common streams of thought in early Christianity.

A Legacy from Pentecostal Scholars   influence on the author

Early Pentecostals emerged especially from the radical wing of late-nineteenth-century evangelicals ("evangelical" being the dominant North American religious expression in that century), a wing that emphasized holiness, missions, social justice and reform, and divine healing. Because lines eventually hardened, early-twentieth-century fundamentalists mostly excluded and sometimes demonized Pentecostals. At that time, Pentecostals would have been unwelcome in most fundamentalist educational institutions. Although Pentecostals still often drew on fundamentalist arguments, their primary agendas differed.[85] Partly because of earlier fundamentalist rejection, today many Pentecostal and charismatic scholars train in nonevangelical institutions.

I studied under a number of Pentecostal scholars, including Stanley Horton, Ben Aker, and Gary McGee. With Stanley's blessing before he passed, I was the first Horton lecturer after he passed. This was at the Assemblies of God Theological Seminary, one of the institutions where I studied with him. Stanley did some of his work at Harvard (about the same time as George Ladd), and Ben and Gary did doctoral studies at St. Louis University, a Catholic institution. At the time I went to study at Duke, I understood that as a Pentecostal I belonged to the broader evangelical tradition, but our Pentecostal perception was that we offered a special contribution that cessationists (in name or in practice) did not.

In one class debate at Duke a student kept hammering at me that my approach differed from that of Martin Luther (on some point that I no longer recall); I could not understand why he was arguing on that basis. Finally an Episcopalian colleague interceded for me: "Craig does not feel a commitment to that tradition." I shared Luther's valuing of Scripture, but not necessarily all of his interpretations. As an exegete, Luther was willing to challenge traditions of his day, and I was more eager to follow his example in valuing Scripture above tradition than to echo all his interpretations as my own tradition. Supporting any given historical interpretation was not a battle that I felt a stake in.[86]

Similarly, although I knew that many evangelicals opposed women in at least particular forms of ministry, I was bewildered by the harsh response that I received from many evangelicals when I argued in support of women in ministry. From the standpoint of some other evangelical traditions, I was now "liberal"—even though on that point I was faithful to my own, Pentecostal evangelical tradition[87] (and by this time the local circle of African-American Baptist churches where I ministered). My mentoring by and friendships with other evangelical scholars largely arose after my doctoral work. Many old barriers of misunderstanding have broken down, and I believe that this is therefore an ideal time for all of us to learn from many other movements in Christ's body.

The heart of my own calling, like that of many other biblical scholars (as well as the Reformers and many earlier and subsequent renewal movements), is to call the church back to the Scriptures. I recognize that there are other valid callings and that these supplement one another, but features of my calling, as it has worked out so far, seem to include teaching God's people to read biblical books the way God gave them to us (with concrete literary and cultural contexts), as well as correcting some popular interpretive errors.

At the same time, when we correctly understand the Scriptures, we find there also repeated testimony to divine encounters and a living relationship with Christ. Recognizing in Scripture the prevalence and promise of divine activity, and expecting the Spirit's presence and pedagogy as we read Scripture, is a Spirit hermeneutic.

PART I

A Theological Reading
toward Praxis and Mission

Scripture itself invites us to read it theologically with interest in praxis and mission.[1] That is, most biblical writers wanted their audience to implement the lessons they communicated, and their teaching frequently highlights God, Christ, and the church's mission. Although sometimes disparaged by modernist academic readers, reading Scripture for theological interests characterized premodern interpreters and finds itself back on the table of postmodern interpreters.[2] The church never abandoned this interest, and early Pentecostal emphases offer one example of this focus.

Scholars today often describe understanding texts in terms of two horizons, the original text's or author's horizon and the reader's horizon. Nearly all of my academic work in biblical studies has been dedicated to the ancient horizon, but because this book focuses on a *distinctive* element of Spirit hermeneutics I focus here more fully on reading that moves beyond that horizon. Nevertheless, if we truly respect the biblical text as authoritative, that horizon is a necessary foundation for interpretation, and I therefore return to it especially in chapters 8 and 9.

By contrast, recent discussions of Spirit hermeneutics have so focused on the reader that they have sometimes reacted against earlier interpretive emphases on the first horizon. The purposes for which a text was apparently designed, however, suggest its most obvious uses, and a genuinely Spirit-illumined interpretation should be consistent with the originally Spirit-inspired design. Our readings of Scripture as communication are best anchored, insofar as possible, in the contexts of the biblical texts.

But the recent discussions raise a crucial question: how do those texts go on to speak to us in different settings? Here informed analogies are helpful, a matter to which I turn later (especially in chapter 16). First, however, I want to show the value of experiential and eschatological readings of texts, provided that they correlate with the range of meaning implied in the original inspired communication.

CHAPTER 1

Reading Experientially

Read from a Christian standpoint, the biblical story moves toward our savior's coming and the ultimate consummation. The current period between Jesus's comings is an eschatological time in which we should expect the Spirit to act decisively in the church. Although the first Pentecostals typically read Scripture through the narrative grid of a "Latter Rain" rather than the more biblically accurate already/not yet kingdom eschatology, their reading was unquestionably eschatological.[3] They and other revival movements of the period can thus provide one helpful model of reading Scripture experientially and eschatologically, recognizing the significance of present experience. This way of reading is invited by our location in biblical history.

Early Pentecostalism's Missiological Reading of Acts 2

Late-nineteenth-century radical evangelicals emphasized the importance of the Great Commission, the mission of reaching all peoples with the gospel of Christ. Eschatologically, their frequent postmillenialism played a role in this expectation, but it was one that proponents of other eschatological schemes also shared. Many radical evangelicals, especially in circles emphasizing holiness, were praying for a special experience of empowerment.

Those in Keswick and some other circles rightly gathered that the focus of the Spirit's activity recounted in Acts is divine empowerment for mission (see esp. Acts 1:8), and they were praying accordingly. Some, believing that the global task was too great without miraculous help, believed that it could be accomplished only if missionaries could evangelize directly without having to learn all languages first (many languages had never yet even been mapped).

Tongues us empowerment to do missions (handwritten marginal note)

They were praying for missionary tongues — that is, that God would supernaturally empower them to speak languages without the need to learn them first.

When some Christians in holiness circles began speaking in tongues as part of their dramatic experience of the Spirit, they first believed that they were experiencing missionary tongues.[4] Although in most cases they subsequently discovered otherwise,[5] their interest in power for mission remained, and in its first modern century pentecostal forms of Christianity have expanded far faster than any other Christian movement, much of it globally by conversion growth.[6] The connection between tongues and missions, however, was often forgotten.[7]

Although Pentecostals did not always recognize the connection, Luke's narrative use of tongues was also mission-connected. Because Luke focuses on the Spirit's power for mission (Acts 1:8), he naturally emphasized the most conspicuous intersection between the prophetic dimension of the Spirit's activity and the cross-cultural element. What greater sign of cross-cultural prophetic empowerment could Luke emphasize than God's agents, inspired by the Spirit, worshiping him in other peoples' languages?[8]

Looking to Biblical Narratives for Models

When early Pentecostals read Acts looking for clues to the narratives' signs of Spirit baptism, some critics retorted that one cannot get theology from narrative. Of course, today scholars recognize that narratives do indeed often communicate perspectives, which can be theological, political, moral, or a combination of various emphases.[9] Against the dichotomy between history and theology that sometimes prevailed in mid-twentieth century biblical criticism, ancient historians often explicitly noted this purpose in their writing.[10] Biblical writers themselves affirmed this practice (e.g., Rom 15:4; 1 Cor 10:11; 2 Tim 3:16–17).

Scholars may debate whether early Pentecostals always noted the correct patterns in Acts (many argue, for example, that signs of Spirit baptism there may be more diverse than they anticipated). Their narrative hermeneutic, however, was more sensitive to the text than that of most of their critics. Biblical scholars in general grew more sensitive to the theological value of narratives after the rise of redaction criticism and especially narrative criticism and narrative theology.[11] Today many mainstream evangelical scholars, for example, recognize that consistent patterns in Acts are instructive, including Luke's connection between the Spirit and power for ministry.[12]

Critics also often responded to Pentecostal readings of Acts by citing clear statements from Pauline theology, which Pentecostals rightly often regarded as beside the point. James D. G. Dunn was one of the first scholars to take Pentecostalism seriously enough to write a major scholarly critique of its usual understanding of baptism in the Spirit.[13] (It should be noted that Dunn himself, while engaging in rigorous dialogue on exegetical points, has always been conciliatory and friendly toward Pentecostals and their practices. Indeed, although not charismatic by some popular definitions, he is a "Pauline charismatic"—affirming the continuance of all the charismata and excelling especially in his charism of teaching.)[14] Many Pentecostal exegetes responded that Dunn was reading Luke in light of Paul, instead of allowing their voices to be distinct but complementary. They also argued that this approach was ironic in view of Dunn's own emphasis on the diversity as well as unity of theology in the NT.[15]

Various renewal movements have looked to the early church in Acts as a model and sought to live out Acts in various ways.[16] Late-nineteenth-century missions movements and early Pentecostals rightly drew from Acts a model for mission. More importantly, Acts teaches us patterns of God's activity—even if part of the pattern is that God often pours out his Spirit in ways unexpected by his people.

Interestingly, although many of the debates about outpourings of the Spirit in Acts understandably focus on individual Christian experience, Luke's narratives focus on corporate outpourings—perhaps something like what American church historians call revivals. Elements of the "revivals" in Acts sometimes varied in particular characteristics, such as economic sacrifice (Acts 2:44–45; 4:32–35) or joy (13:52). Given Luke's focus, it is not surprising that he especially emphasizes the element of prophetic empowerment (2:17–18; Luke 1:67), including bold inspired speech for God (Acts 4:8, 31; 19:6), proclamation of a vision (7:55), and worship in tongues (2:4; 10:46; 19:6). But we also should not be surprised if various outpourings of the Spirit include various specific characteristics, whether sorrow for sin, joy in Christ (as in Acts 13:52), or the like.[17] (Ideally all believers should always express all the fruit of the Spirit, but in practice particular expressions sometimes come to the fore when God draws our attention to them in special ways.)

Some critics today believe that biblical narratives teach us only about God's actions but do not provide models for our responses to God. They argue that these texts teach us salvation history but not examples for our faith. But that is not how Paul reads Scripture. He sees Abram's faith (Gen 15:6) as a model for all believers (Rom 4); in a different way, so does James (Jas 2:21–23).

[handwritten margin note: Acts as model. Spirit often comes in unexpected ways]

That is not to say that every aspect of Abram's behavior is a positive model, but Abram's behavior that God reckoned as righteousness certainly was. Likewise, James uses the experiences of the prophets and Job as models for endurance (5:10–11). He not only recognizes Elijah's common humanity with us but for this very reason also treats his faith for divine action as a model for us (Jas 5:17–18).

I return to the application of narrative models more fully later in chapters 10 and 15. My point here is simply that this way of reading has characterized Pentecostal interpretation from the beginning.

The Value in Reading Devotionally

Critiques of charismatic hermeneutics, like critiques of revivals, often come from academicians or seminary-trained ministers criticizing popular charismatic interpretation. Some of these critiques may be as much a critique of popular approaches as of charismatic theology in particular. One wonders whether popular noncharismatic interpretations would fare significantly better if critiqued by charismatic academicians. Popular interpreters often take Scripture out of context, and as our culture moves increasingly further toward communicating in sound bites and concise tweets the ability to follow an entire argument, relevant to some genres in Scripture, will become increasingly scarce.

Having said that, popular, devotional interpretation does contribute an insight that many of us academicians, for all our methodological precision, have missed. That is, we need to hear Scripture with faith, embracing it in our personal lives. A reader may embrace a false idea when taking Scripture out of context, but a reader who understands it in context yet does not embrace its demands on one's trust also misses its function as Scripture. Hermeneutical distance has advantages at one level of interpretation,[18] but places the interpreter at a severe disadvantage when it comes to living the text's message.

This approach to hermeneutical proximity is not limited to Pentecostals,[19] but Pentecostals are among those who conventionally read this way.[20] As Christians, we read the Bible with personal *faith*—not only to understand it but to embrace its message and theological worldview as true for the world in which we live. One can still do scholarship for the academy that follows its rules, but such readings, while legitimate for their purposes, differ from the deliberately Christian reading emphasized here, which is also legitimate for its purpose.[21]

Wesley urged readers who found some biblical passages hard to understand to seek God in prayer.[22] Praying for understanding is certainly a biblical concept (e.g., 1 Kgs 3:9–10; Ps 25:4–5; Dan 2:18–19; Eph 1:17–18; Phil 1:9–10; Col 1:9–10; Phlm 6; Jas 1:5), and this principle certainly applies to understanding Scripture (Dan 9:2–3, 23); prayer for understanding of the law is a frequent refrain in Psalm 119 (119:27, 34, 73, 125, 144, 169). We do not need to wait until there is a passage that we do not understand cognitively, however. When reading Scripture devotionally, we can pray while reading, taking time to praise God for, and prayerfully ponder, what we find there. This approach need not require lingering over every point, but we can pray about the points that offer challenges or special insights to us. The prayer might be a brief whisper before moving on, or wrestling deeply with a matter particularly challenging to us.

Reading Biblically Is Reading Experientially

Purely subjective "experiential" readings are common on a popular level—seeking a particular "feeling" about a text or some "deep" meaning unrelated to the less "spiritual" surface meaning. Unfortunately, such subjective readings and purely "rational" readings often react against, and thus feed off of, one another. A purely rational way of reading is one that analyzes grammar and contextual sense, yet never engages with the text in terms of considering the demands or invitations or encouragements of its message. Such a rational reading can often address one side of the text, but it does not approach the message as God's word.[23] A persistent refusal to embrace the message in faith, conditioning one's habitual way of reading the text, can ultimately produce a hardness against it.

Experiential reading in a responsible way does not endorse pure subjectivity in interpretation. Nor do I refer to looking for a personal application or "takeaway" for each verse or even paragraph, although (as argued later in the book) application by responsible analogy helps us to hear and engage the text more sympathetically and concretely. Rather, by experiential reading I mean believing to the depths of our being what we find in the text. For example, it is one thing to affirm academically that God loves us. It is another to welcome that truth into our hearts that have felt wounded and untrusting. I myself have experienced both merely rational affirmation and subsequently the warm embrace of the Father's love. Although feelings are part of human experience and therefore an element in our spiritual life, the sort of experience I address here has more to do with faith and the action that it demands than with feeling.

Pentecostal spirituality has always read Scripture experientially.[24] By this I do not mean that pentecostal Christians simply read Scripture in light of their experience, although that has sometimes been the case (and not only for Pentecostals). Rather, I mean that we especially read and develop our experience in light of Scripture.[25]

Of course, experience, like our culture and tradition, also shapes how we read Scripture, for good or for ill. No one comes to texts without presuppositions, usually shaped by past experiences or instruction.[26] We may do our best to suspend judgment, and honestly engaging texts may adjust our presuppositions.[27] But we should not pretend that we do not have any presuppositions.[28] Even basic reflection requires "mental categories" and some frameworks for interpreting reality.[29] As Anthony Thiselton points out, "historical conditioning is two-sided: *the modern interpreter, no less than the text, stands in a given historical context and tradition.*"[30]

Contemporary experiences, however, can help us hear the biblical text in ways that resonate with its values. Just as dialogue with other cultures and vantage points or learning new information enables us to adjust our starting assumptions, so does engagement with the voice of Scripture. Thus Thiselton also notes that "the biblical text comes alive as a 'speech-act' . . . when some kind of correspondence or inter-relation occurs between the situation addressed by the biblical writer and the situation of the modern reader or hearer."[31] Scripture already holds authority and is true, but it is *experienced* as authoritative, for example on matters of forgiveness, when one personally embraces its truth.[32]

Experiences similar to those in Scripture often make Scripture more believable or close to us than it feels to those who do not have such experiences. I noted earlier that Messianic Jews or members of house congregations may hear emphases or resonate with experiences or emphases in Scripture that some others miss; likewise, those who have experienced miracles often find them more plausible than those who have not.[33] Further, an experience of spiritual power can also embolden us to stand for our convictions about truth in the face of a different prevailing consensus, an experience that can also have hermeneutical implications for both scholars and other readers.

The most distinctive contribution of classical Pentecostalism to the global church has been the restoration of the full slate of spiritual gifts as an experiential preunderstanding from which we read Scripture. This is no small contribution, but a full-fledged Spirit hermeneutic should emphasize not only elements that are distinctive to the early Pentecostal movement, but also those biblical experiences that have long been shared by the church movements from which it was birthed.

Valuable as some experiential preunderstanding is, however, my primary focus here is on how we read our experiences in light of analogous experiences in Scripture. To some degree, experiential reading of Scripture is inevitable. Yet it is not only inevitable; it is desirable and biblical, provided such devotional reading is also shaped by the careful discipline of how Scripture itself invites us to read it. Jesus, his followers, and earlier prophets all illustrate ways of reading Scripture experientially.

A Pentecostal Approach

Experience has long influenced interpretation. For example, Whitefield's and Wesley's experience of preaching in the fields gave them a fuller appreciation for Jesus's open-air preaching of which they already were aware from the Gospels. Wesley's experience of lay ministers and women accurately communicating Scripture opened him up to genuine dimensions of Scripture that he had initially resisted.[34] (Since for this book I have a friendly audience I would love to repeat my biblical case supporting women in ministry here, but given the other topics that I need to cover here, I simply refer readers to my earlier work on the subject, and that of others.)[35]

Late-nineteenth-century radical evangelicals, like many other readers of Scripture throughout history, wanted to live according to Scripture and expected God to meet them as they studied it. Their piety formed the intuitive backdrop of early Pentecostal practices, practices also attested widely today among global charismatics and other Christians. Early Pentecostal emphasis on the Spirit and experience actually does reflect a pervasive theme of Scripture and particularly the life of early Christianity exemplified in Acts and Paul's letters. Some Protestant interpreters had played down these biblical emphases, presumably because they seemed foreign to their own experience.

Pentecostalism was, like many of its precursors and (to a lesser extent) the Reformation and some Catholic monastic movements, a restorationist movement.[36] They wanted to go back behind inadequate church traditions to Scripture. Restorationism itself, of course, became a tradition, and like many traditions various forms of restorationism sometimes ossified into legalistic codes or a means of exalting one's group above others. Its original, fundamental interest, however, was valuable. The impetus of many medieval reformers and monastic movements was protest against corruption in the church; the Renaissance emphasis on recovering the early sources also helped fuel the Reformation.[37]

Although the fundamentalist-modernist controversy eventually forced more of a focus on doctrinal propositions, many restorationists (including again everything from monastic movements to the radical evangelicals) emphasized a return to the highest ideal lifestyle or spiritual experience depicted in the New Testament. This approach may idealize the earliest church, but it rightly calls us back to what Jesus, and virtually all Christian tradition, affirms is God's Word, and to what we therefore ought to value more than any other source of teaching in our tradition.[38]

In the global Pentecostal approach to Scripture, the supernatural God of the Bible is the God of the present, real world. The line between salvation history in the biblical narrative and continuing salvation history today is thin, so that readers approach the text as a model for life and ideally expect God to continue to act as he acted in Scripture. Like experiencing God's presence, experiencing his apparent absence is biblical, as some of the psalms show us. Thus the psalmist pleads to God, "Don't be far from me!" (Pss 22:11; 35:22; 38:21; 71:12), or questions, "How long won't you hear, Lord?" (e.g., Pss 13:1; 79:5; 89:46; also Hab 1:2). Far from being used exclusively for the psalmist's benefit, the biblical psalms spoke also to situations of those who joined in corporate worship in the temple (1 Chr 16:42; 2 Chr 20:21; Ezra 3:11; Neh 12:8, 27, 46) and after the temple's destruction (e.g., Ps 89:38); the Chronicler explicitly notes that earlier songs were reused for praise (2 Chr 29:30).[39]

Yet far from making excuses for a God who sometimes in fact seems absent, spirituality characterized by the experience of Pentecost typically starts with the premise that God is present and active. Even when he seems far off, that we have experienced the Spirit reminds us that God is with us, among us, and within us. Admittedly, the emphasis can err if not balanced with other biblical expectations; biblically, God's presence often brings suffering as well as restoration to wholeness. Sometimes starting with the expectation that God is active has led Pentecostals to a sort of reductionism that mirrors naturalistic reductionism. Pure naturalism allows no miracles; some supernaturalists have reduced God to a formula that treats miracles as automatic if given conditions are met. Conversely, one may view the world as an enchanted place, but this becomes a childish fantasy if not submitted to the biblical God's will; indeed, Jesus regards desiring only what mortals desire, while eschewing suffering for Christ, as Satanic (Mark 8:33–35). Provided that we recognize biblical themes of facing opposition and endurance, however, it is biblical to see the entire world as reflecting God's activity, and to recognize and expect God's activity in the course of fulfilling his will.

Some of those who are now reported as seeing significant miracles started by recognizing God at work even in smaller details of their daily lives—an attitude of *trust*.[40] Such people may sometimes assume more knowledge of God's working than they have and may wrongly construe the details of how God is working. Nevertheless, as Christians, we should never fault them for trusting God to be at work—often more than we do. That is a Pentecostal way of approaching reality, but it is not limited to Pentecostal tradition (Calvinists, for example, typically and rightly recognize God at work in everything in their lives).

This is not the approach to reality that we professors generally learn in our rigorous academic training, which focuses on predictable natural explanations and challenges all premises critically.[41] Some sources are more reliable than others, however, and the habit of critical evaluation applied to claims in texts is not always profitable when applied to relationships with persons deserving our trust. At the height of my historical Jesus research, for example, when my wife would inform me of something, for instance remind me about what she wrote her dissertation on, I would respond out of habit, "Can you provide me evidence for that assertion?" I did learn quickly that such an approach has its limitations and dangers, and that there is a place for healthy trust. This should be true most of all in our relationship with God.

At its best, Pentecostal spirituality is about living out a dynamic *relationship* with God. Such a spirituality reads Scripture dynamically, as stories of how the God with whom one has a relationship has worked with his people throughout history.[42] One who reads Scripture this way will naturally receive the narrative differently than someone for whom it is simply information or stories or myths. In some cases, our exegesis might be the same, but the ways we appropriate the narrative in our lives is completely different. Those who read with faith read with hope, and read according to the purpose some early Christians found in Scripture: "The matters written before (in Scripture) were written to teach us, so that through endurance and through the encouragement offered by the Scriptures we might have hope" (Rom 15:4).

Some consider such readings as naïve, setting one up for disappointment; but early Christians were confident that those who put their trust in God would not be disappointed or made ashamed of their hope (Isa 28:16, cited in Rom 9:33; 10:11; 1 Pet 2:6; cf. Ps 22:5; Rom 5:5). In practice, one might suffer yet not be abandoned; even in despair, God's presence provides help (2 Cor 4:8–9; 6:4–10). Indeed, medical studies suggest that not only does faith of some sort correlate with reduced mortality,[43] but it also apparently can give greater strength to face mortality (cf. Prov 17:22).[44]

Scientism?

Experiential Reading in Other Charismatic Hermeneutics

Various scholars have independently suggested many of the same distinctive characteristics of Pentecostal or charismatic exegesis that I identify and develop in this book. For example, one Anglican charismatic writer identifies as distinctive elements of a charismatic hermeneutic many of the same features I emphasize here as part of a Spirit hermeneutic, although I address these features at various points in this book rather than all in one place.[45] He finds and illustrates these features in Peter's Pentecost sermon.[46] I draw on some complementary aspects of the Pentecost experience later in this book.

1. An experiential reading[47]
2. An analogical reading[48]
3. A communal reading[49]
4. A christocentric reading[50]
5. An eschatological reading[51]
6. An emotional reading[52]
7. A practical reading[53]

Virtually all of these elements are biblical features of a Spirit-led hermeneutic, although interpreters do differ, sometimes substantially, in precisely how they implement them. My immediate focus in this section is experiential reading.

Experiential Reading Is Inevitable

People read texts with interests and agendas. Historians, for example, may have personal interests, specializing in church history, women's history, military history, and so forth, without thereby being any less historians.[54] It is likewise natural to read the Bible with pastoral and theological questions in mind, and also with the personal issues on each of our hearts. Many biblical principles will speak legitimately to those issues. Ancient Christians often heard Scripture as relevant to their communities; some, like Anthony or Augustine, also heard it personally and therefore abandoned wealth or sexual immorality.

Personal experience inevitably shapes how texts or communications affect us. The same report of a sports event will affect differently those who were rooting for different teams. A report about the rise in racism may feel more personally threatening to some people (including myself, since my family is interracial) than to others. Reports about violence in many parts of the world affect me, but when I learn of them in places where I have lived and have close friends, such as in northern Nigeria, they affect me most deeply. I am neither able nor willing to forego my experiential encounter with such texts or oral reports. This does not mean that I am privy to secret meanings of words used in such sources; it does mean that I cannot but read them in sometimes larger and sometimes more personal contexts.

This is what some scholars mean when they speak of texts' "fuller meaning," though others prefer the language of "application."[55] I personally prefer (and usually here use) the latter designation, not least for logistical reasons, since it is helpful to somehow distinguish present reception of the text's message from the likely experiences of its ideal receptors. But even those evangelical homiletical approaches *most* insistent on employing the label "application" would exclude this activity no more than would those who include it under the rubric of "meaning." Although many contemporary debates over meaning are more substantive, some of our differences might be better resolved by defining how we are using our key terms.

Studying Scripture inductively, like trying to hear other reports honestly, remains the ideal; by learning what biblical texts say in their own setting, we are most likely to catch accurately the principles that they are genuinely addressing. In science, applied research is likelier to find a particular, targeted cure faster than basic research would, but basic research (such as investigation of the human genome) cumulatively yields more cures in the long run. Preparing for sermons on Saturday night or speaking in the inspiration of a moment cannot substitute for extensive and diligent labor in the Scriptures. Inductive study of the Bible on its own terms thus uncovers more information in the long run than coming to the Bible with our questions (especially if a pastor is starting to prepare a sermon the night before he or she will be preaching it!).[56] It is by such faithful working through biblical books in disciplined ways that we open ourselves up to the Spirit's teaching on a wider range of topics than those we already were interested in.

Nevertheless, we *do* need to learn what the Bible says to our present situations. The only alternative to bringing our questions and struggles is to leave such issues untouched by Scripture. We must be open to biblical principles speaking to our situations. In fact, while anyone with a sound exegetical approach may discover exegetical insights for biblical (or other) texts, it is *disciples* who will hear the text's demands on their lives.

Ideally, a Christian reader should have both sound understanding of the original message and consequent insight into how it speaks to our settings. This is ideal because it is when we hear the original message of the text most carefully that we can be assured that our experience of the text is something relevant beyond us. The Spirit can spark our conscience through anything that reminds of us a biblical (or other) principle, even if that reminder does not arise from sound exegesis of the text. But the reason God gives us Scripture as well as the Spirit is to provide a more objective guide and framework for our personal experience of God; it defeats the purpose of having a Bible if it simply becomes a mine for what we hope to find there anyway, whether theologically or experientially.

I return to this discussion of a more objective resource in Part III of the book. But for now, I should note that listening to the Bible personally and experientially is not only inevitable; it is not in necessary conflict with reading Scripture in a way that respects the original message. Reading personally and experientially is desirable, provided it is shaped and instructed by the discipline of careful and consistent reading such as this book will discuss later.

Experiential Reading Is Desirable

Many parts of Scripture overtly invite experiential reading. For example, the psalms are meant to be prayed and sung more than exegeted in light of their specific settings (which are often unknown to us).[57] Psalms evoke feeling, employing a range of rhetorical devices, including some complex forms of parallelism (such as an aesthetically pleasing acrostic in Ps 119) or building to a crescendo (as in Ps 150).[58] We can try to reconstruct their historical situation (fairly difficult for many of the psalms), or compare them with liturgical forms from surrounding cultures (such as Canaanite psalms or Egyptian hymns to their deities). But once we have done all possible research, psalms by their very genre invite us to do more than study them: they invite us to pray them, sing them, or use them as models to jumpstart our own prayers. They provide us a historic vocabulary of prayer.

Certainly one way to "experience" Scripture is to use it, once it is rightly understood, in dynamic worship and prayer; these are traditionally characteristic expressions of a pneumatic approach.[59] These elements bring to the fore Scripture's affective impact as well as its cognitive challenges.[60] One of my predecessors in biblical interpretation at Asbury Seminary, Bob Mulholland, urged readers to consider how God's Spirit speaks to us when we engage the reasons for our emotive responses to the biblical text.[61]

Most readers would agree that psalms are meant to be prayed, as the Puritans prayed them. But does historical narrative invite experiential reading?

What about biography? Even here, however, narratives are meant to draw us into their world, to facilitate reader identification,[62] to invite us to imbibe something of their worldview. We may take for an example John's Gospel. When we read that Jesus taught his disciples to love one another, do we genuinely fulfill the intention of either the Fourth Gospel's author or the Jesus who spoke in the narrative to merely study the Greek terms used? Do we fulfill it by merely comparing ancient opinions about love and showing how the opinion expressed here is different? Such studies have supportive value, but presumably John wants us to respond to the text faithfully by actually loving one another.

Even those who read biblical narratives as matters of almost solely historical interest, without personal application, might make exceptions for teaching contained in those narratives. Nevertheless, someone could argue that these sayings address only Jesus's first disciples. Such an approach, however, is unsatisfactory. Within the narrative, Jesus addresses disciples present on that occasion, but why does John report these words? Presumably John also has his own audience in mind, probably including a potential audience larger than his immediate circle; soon after this Jesus himself applies his message not only to his immediate hearers but to all his followers (John 17:20).

Presumably we should approach in the same manner Jesus's sayings about the coming of the Spirit, sent to continue to reveal Jesus to us (14:16–17, 26; 15:26; 16:7–15). Some apply these promises specifically to the disciples who were with Jesus on that occasion, as authors of the New Testament message. Although such an application is appropriate, it does not exhaust all legitimate applications of these words; John himself was apparently not interested in that application exclusively. Granted, the Spirit comes specifically to the first disciples in John 20:22, but we also know that *all* who believe in Jesus would receive the Spirit (7:39). The indwelling of the Spirit and the greater works that Jesus promised (e.g., 14:12–13, 17, 23) thus as surely apply to all believers as the possibility of coming to Jesus through the Father because Jesus is the way (14:6).[63]

That this is the correct way to understand John's Gospel is clear from 1 John, which probably addresses the same circles as the Fourth Gospel and draws on its portrait of Jesus. Plainly the "new commandment" addresses not only Jesus's first disciples, as in John 13:34–35, but all of John's audience (1 John 2:7–10; 2 John 5). To "love one another" is what Jesus commanded "us" (1 John 3:23), in an immediate context in which "us" would seem to refer to all believers in Jesus Christ (3:14, 16, 18–24). In the same way, true believers have the Spirit living in them (3:24; 4:13), and just as Jesus said the Spirit would teach his followers all things (John 14:26), here the anointing teaches them concerning all things (1 John 2:20, 27).[64] John's Gospel is meant to be more than exegeted intellectually; it summons those who attend to it to feed on Jesus, the bread of life, to crave him as our very source of life.[65]

Someone may again object that such features are well and good for Jesus's teachings, but they do not apply to the narratives about Jesus. John's Gospel, however, uses Jesus's relationship with the Father as a model for believers' relationship with God (John 10:14–15). Although referring less explicitly to the Gospel, 1 John also invites its audience to use Jesus's behavior as a model: if we claim to abide in him, we should walk just as he walked (1 John 2:6).

Such observations cannot be limited to the Fourth Gospel. Most Lukan scholars believe that Luke, the one evangelist who includes a full sequel to his Gospel by a story about early Christian mission, deliberately parallels members of the church in the second volume, Acts, with Jesus in the first; the parallels appear quite extensive.[66] Moreover, the second volume's opening description of the first volume as narrating "all that Jesus *began* to do and teach" may indicate his continued working among his followers in the second volume.[67] The Spirit given to empower the first witnesses (Acts 1:8) is given to all believers (2:38–39), for the assigned work is not finished. The second volume's mission is open-ended, so that the mission to the nations continues.[68] Luke presents Jesus as a model (Luke 22:27); Acts also presents Paul as one (Acts 20:35). As noted above, ancient audiences expected to learn from narratives. Scholars may read biblical texts purely for information, but Christians (whether they are scholars or not) also read them for edification. Again, as Paul said, the Scriptures were "written for our instruction, that through endurance and through the encouragement given by the Scriptures we might have hope" (Rom 15:4).

Association plays a major role in human memory. While undisciplined free association often makes inappropriate links, association is inevitable and sometimes helpful. When we have encountered God in various ways through studying different texts, those associations will be triggered when we think of such texts. That is, a disciplined life of spiritual formation in connection with Scripture can yield cumulative insights by evoking a range of past spiritual experiences as we travel through Scripture again. (Bible training often separates us from those earlier experiences when those experiences built on misunderstanding of biblical texts, so it is ideal to learn to read texts in a way faithful to their message early in our spiritual development.) In this way, Scripture becomes a contact point for our relationship with God and useful for spiritual formation. Trusting God's sovereignty and/or the Spirit's leading can also invite us to particularly profitable associations, including analogies for our lives and ministries.

Experiential Reading Is Biblical

Those of us who seek to hear and translate the biblical message for the church recognize both its historical character and how we can learn from it by appropriate analogy.

Today we look back and understand, even with some OT support, that Jesus was a peaceful Messiah at his first coming. Sometimes we even criticize his contemporaries for not recognizing it in the OT (Isa 11:6–10 [but cf. 11:4]; Zech 9:9–10 [but cf. 9:1–8]). Yet there were a range of prophecies about the Messianic age and the work of the Messiah, and there was little way to discern securely what was literal from what was figurative, what pertained to a first coming as opposed to a second coming, and so forth. A reader before the first coming would not readily discern even that there *would be* two comings.

Early Christians learned the right texts from Jesus (see Luke 24:25–27, 44–45), and from what they found fulfilled in Jesus. In other words, they read the text in light of their experience of Jesus, which fit too well and was too divine to be an accident or a fabrication. Their experience helped them sort through a range of prophecies to understand how they fit together. Subsequent discussion in this book will turn to this issue in greater detail (see Part V, especially chapter 16).

When those schooled in Scripture criticized the faith of a man who based his faith on his experience, he could respond only, "Once I was blind, but now I see," and deconstruct the inconsistency of their arguments (John 9:25, 31–33). Such responses did not move the arrogant, but the man's experience with Jesus was undeniably genuine. Granted, others will sometimes challenge our experience by citing counterexperience (e.g., Exod 7:11–12; 2 Kgs 18:33–35). Providing answers to strengthen faith and refute objections is a valid ministry (Luke 21:15; Acts 18:28; Titus 1:9). Nevertheless, God does reveal truth to people in encounters such as happened repeatedly in Jesus's ministry; to fail to heed such experiences, which do fit a larger biblical context, is to miss God visiting his people.

Those concerned about the dangers of leaving such an experiential approach unfettered are of course right to be concerned.[69] But when experience is incontrovertibly divine and remains consistent with Scripture and with the character of experience in Scripture, it equips the experiencer with fresh, legitimate questions with which to search the Scriptures. As is often pointed out, Peter's vision in Acts 10 overturns centuries of practice already based on Scripture.[70] This experience did have external evidence that guaranteed that it transcended more than personal belief: it was confirmed through Cornelius's independent vision and through God sovereignly imparting his Spirit to these Gentiles. That is, Peter's revelation cannot readily be explained as purely subjective. Of course, other factors also supported this change in the church's theology and practice, but most of these had to do with the new experience of Jesus. Between the first and second comings, we are not having the same kind of new experience of Jesus (the incarnation is once for all), but we do continue to have experiences that help us understand our life with Christ.

Moreover, not only our subjective but also our objective resources are limited. There are many problems we cannot resolve exegetically, as any honest exegete will tell you. We often can discern enough to refute some subjective claims to revelatory interpretations of texts. Scripture is already revelation and offers us an objective grid through which we can evaluate other interpretive claims. Personal experiences of texts, where the Spirit may apply the wording or message in some ways, may be unique to the individual and do not determine or necessarily reveal the canonical meaning of the text. Nevertheless, there is clearly much meaning that has been lost to exegesis because we no longer understand particular aspects of the language, culture, or experience of the biblical writers. If we are to live in Christ as they were, we need what we can understand from Scripture, but we also need to be willing to live in and depend on Christ as they did.

The fruit of the Spirit, expected for all believers, is experiential, emotive and behavioral: love, joy, peace, longsuffering, and the rest. As already noted, one cannot read the psalms the way they were meant to be heard without embracing the emotion in them. Emotion, then, is not foreign to Scripture (which attributes emotions in some sense even to God), even if it is so to what some of us would consider the ideal, detached researcher. In contrast to some reading strategies considered more sophisticated and respectable, early Pentecostals, many of whom were not from the same social classes as respected academicians of the era, were not ashamed to embrace emotion.[71] They could enter texts with feeling, not just by cerebral dissection of grammar. (My binary contrast here is meant to underline the point graphically, though it may overstate the actual dichotomy, especially on the academic side.)

One-time Events

Of course, we are not meant to replicate today every kind of experience in Scripture. Clearly some events were once-for-all: obviously the angelic promise that Mary will conceive a child by the Holy Spirit (Luke 1:31–35) cannot double as a promise to any reader that they will also have a virgin birth. Nevertheless, we can learn from Mary's example; she receives God's message and submits to the Spirit and God's call as a "female servant" (δούλη) of the Lord (1:38; cf. 1:48). The next time we hear this same Greek term—its only other use in the NT—is toward the beginning of Luke's second volume, where all God's people are male and female servants empowered by the Spirit (Acts 2:18). Mary's submission to the Spirit offers a model of discipleship for all of us as we also submit to the reign of God's Spirit in our lives.

Likewise, some scholars emphasize that the lengthy narratives about David appear in the Bible only because he would become king over Israel, and eventually, in God's larger purpose, progenitor of our eternal king, the Messiah Jesus. These scholars are surely correct; we do not get such detailed accounts concerning most prophets in Scripture, even if some may have walked closer to God than David did. David served a special role that commanded ancient Israelites' special interest. His past kingdom and God's promises to him offered a hope for the future kingdom.

But this approach does not exclude us from discovering personal lessons from David's life. Of course, we must do this in a disciplined way; someone who tries to be a hero like David without David's call may face surprising defeat. His nephew Asahel tried to be a hero, perhaps like his uncle David or his brother Joab. In so doing, however, he simply brought about his own death, despite his athletic prowess (2 Sam 2:18–23). We must remember that when David confronted Goliath, he did so trusting that God would defend his honor (1 Sam 17:26), and also because David had just received a specific promise from God about his destiny (16:1, 13). David would face his own testing soon enough, learning, as did Sarah, and Joseph, and others, that God fulfills his promises, but not always as quickly as we might expect. The lessons we learn about God's faithfulness, however, apply to any calling; so also the lessons that God's calling is often costly, that his blessing matters more than what others count as strength (17:33), and so forth.

Yet we also learn even from David's actions as a character. Obviously David is not always a positive example (cf. 2 Sam 11:1–27), but his positive acts of faith are. They fit a pattern of positive examples in biblical narratives, and are explicitly hailed by the ancient collector of the material in Samuel-Kings (all a single, though multivolume, work) as a positive role model for his successors (e.g., 1 Kgs 11:33, 38; 15:3, 5, 11; 2 Kgs 14:3; 16:2; 18:3; 22:2). Other writers agreed (2 Chr 28:1; 29:2; 34:2). Likewise, the writer of Hebrews explicitly cites David as an example of faith from whom we can (selectively) learn (Heb 11:32; cf. Mark 2:25; Rom 4:7–8).

Conclusion

Early Pentecostals, like many readers in times of spiritual renewal, understood themselves as part of the continuing biblical narrative. They looked to biblical narratives not simply for information about the past, interesting as that may have been, but for truths about how God continues to work with human agents. They read devotionally, seeking to experience God in the text.

Reading our experiences in light of the Bible, and taking them into account when we read the Bible, is not a practice limited to early Pentecostals. Provided that our reading flows from the authentic message given in Scripture (see Part III), experiential reading is inevitable, desirable, and biblical.

CHAPTER 2

Reading from the Vantage of Pentecost

Although building on what came before, Pentecost ushered in something new. The experience of Pentecost in Acts 2 echoes many earlier biblical themes and particularly echoes Jesus's experience of the Spirit in Luke's Gospel.[1] Nevertheless, it simultaneously signifies something new: the last-days outpouring of God's Spirit prophetically empowering all God's people for ministry. No longer was prophetic empowerment restricted to only some prophets in Israel; now it was for all God's people, and for a mission to all peoples. The Spirit would be poured out on all flesh, so that all Jesus's followers, Jew and Gentile, would be empowered to share in that mission (1:8; 2:17–18, 38–39).[2]

How does the experience of Pentecost affect our reading of Scripture? The Spirit's coming necessarily adds an experiential dimension to our reading.[3] In this case, the central thrust of the Pentecost narrative is empowerment for mission, so reading from this standpoint invites us to read Scripture missionally: sensitive to the work that God has for us to do, not just work that believers might want God to do for them. Reading from the vantage point of Pentecost is also reading with the humble who depend on God's Spirit. Finally, a reading from the perspective of Pentecost is both an eschatological reading and a continuationist (noncessationist) reading, because Pentecost offers a "last days" vantage point on Scripture.

Knowing God's Heart

Inspired by the Spirit (Acts 2:4), Peter speaks God's message to his hearers, including from Scripture (2:17–21, 25–28, 34–35). In his Spirit-led explanation of these passages, Peter appeals to his hearers' knowledge of Jesus's signs (2:22), the apostles' experience with the risen Lord (2:32) and his hearers' experience of witnessing the effects of the Spirit's current activity (2:15–16, 33). Application of Scripture remains prominent in succeeding Spirit-led preaching in Acts, especially to those familiar with Scripture (3:22; 4:11, 24–26; 7:2–53; 13:15–41, 47; 15:16–18; 20:26; 23:5; 26:17–18, 22–23, 26–27; 28:26–27) but implicitly even among those who could not recognize it (10:24, 43; 14:15; 17:24–26; 24:14–15).

More generally, the Spirit's coming adds an experiential dimension to our reading. This dimension need not supplant all insights of earlier scribal approaches (cf. Matt 13:52) but instead supplements them with the transformed heart needed to live by biblical principles (Ezek 36:27). Preunderstanding shapes how we come to texts,[4] so the transformed heart should also transform how we approach Scripture (with eagerness, faith and obedience) and what we hear there.

Disciplined critical methods give us a framework for interpreting Scripture in many respects, but the most important element of hearing Scripture can elude even the best of critical scholarship. Obviously I believe that cultural background is essential; I have devoted most of my academic career to making more of that available. But an even deeper background comes in understanding the personality of the leading characters and the voice of the authors. If I personally know an author or lead character, I can hear them speaking in much the way in which they would have said it. I can usually grasp their basic intention even if some cultural or linguistic allusions elude me. This experience may not always affect our critical conclusions, but it will surely affect our reception of the text.

If we really hear God's heart in Scripture, we will read Scripture differently.[5] A rascal will read Paul's claims to be the least, because of Paul's past persecution of Christians, as clever, mock humility (1 Cor 15:9; Eph 3:8; 1 Tim 1:15); conversely, someone who has deeply experienced grace will identify with the gratitude such a claim expresses (cf. 2 Sam 16:10–12; Luke 7:44–47; 18:10–14). Those of us who experienced anger from authority figures early in our lives may recoil at expressions of God's anger in Scripture; but the larger narratives that encase these expressions usually make clear how slow to anger God is, despite how people provoked him and resisted faith.

For example, in the Gospels, Jesus heals the suffering and welcomes the marginalized. He models the perfect relationship with the Father, and laments over those who cannot understand the Father's heart. Religious people might judge others from a situation of superiority, and Jesus's denunciations of them were because these religious people were alienating from God's way those who esteemed themselves more lightly (cf. Matt 23:4, 13). Jesus came to lay down his life to save people, and loving service is the way of those who truly understand the Father's heart. Jesus explained that he was not seeking his own honor, but

40

just seeking to honor his Father (though his Father also loved him and sought his honor). "You've never come to know him," he lamented, "but I *do* know him. If I were to say that I don't know him, I would be lying just as you are. But I know him, and do what he says" (John 8:55).

One could hear Jesus as obliquely boasting (the appropriate way to boast in ancient urban contexts). But because I have experienced deep intimacy with the Father, I can hear Jesus here boasting not in himself but in the magnificence of a relationship with the Father that honors the Father's kindness. I can imagine how someone who has not experienced this joy could misconstrue my own words here. There are, however, some attitudes that we will never understand or identify with unless we have experienced them or known and trusted those who have.

Getting to know God's heart in Scripture where it is clearest helps us hear his voice elsewhere as well. We can recognize, for instance, that some words of judgment are spoken with pain (for a clear example, see Hos 11:5–8; cf. Judg 10:16), though of course even in such texts God communicates this pain in cultural and linguistic forms intelligible to his audience (cf. Hos 2:2–3).[6] Jesus said that his own know him, *just as* he knows the Father and the Father knows him (John 10:14–15). Perhaps this claim of us intimately knowing him describes the ideal or a divinely initiated potential, but the point is that believers must have a relationship with the Father.

The Johannine Christians' most elite critics were probably more academically skilled than they, and probably boasted a superior knowledge of the Torah;[7] but John assures his audience that they know the Torah even more fully than their critics, for John's audience knows the Word made flesh (1:1–18). They experience God through the Spirit that their critics did not even claim to possess.[8] The Spirit would continue to reveal Jesus to the world through them (16:7–11), and would continue to reveal even the secret matters of Jesus to all who love and follow Jesus (16:12–15; cf. the parallel with 15:15).[9] Believers have an experience of God, and this shapes the way we read Scripture. For us, no less than for Moses, the veil has been removed (2 Cor 3:14–18).[10] Critical knowledge, which has its place, may come from critical study, but this intimate knowledge of God comes through the activity of God's Spirit in us, transforming us into Christ's image (2 Cor 3:17–18).[11]

Thus one biblical scholar who after his training dramatically experienced the Spirit laments feeling torn: "The academic task requires that one stand, as it were, off-stage, like a critic or reviewer, so that one can observe the drama with the more objective eye of scholarship, whereas the Holy Spirit draws one on stage with the actors."[12] While acknowledging his great debt to academic study, he describes the tension as reflecting the difference between being "witnesses" and "analysts."[13] The tension is less for those of us who studied under professors who embodied both values, but I concede that it is one with which I myself struggled for a number of years.

I am not by any means claiming that a critical reading cannot aid our understanding. A narrative critic may analyze God as a character in the text, and if the critic is not suspending belief but embraces God's voice in the text, the critic experiences some of what the Spirit says in the text. But there is an added dimension when the critic (or non-critic) reads the text and embraces it in faith, or when one who already knows God hears directly in the text the voice of the God with whom one is already in intimate relationship. Sometimes, of course, this embrace leads to dissonance, as when one who knows God in Christ reads the conquest narratives in Joshua. How can a follower of the Prince of Peace stomach such violence? Such dissonance also benefits us, however, in forcing us to place the God of the book of Joshua in a wider theological context (including that of the law of Moses presupposed there) and to also be sensitive to clues within the book of Joshua[14] that point to that fuller picture of God. We wrestle with a text in light of what we know of God's heart until we understand better its point.

For another example, Jesus did not oppose divorce arbitrarily, to impose unnecessary hardship, but because the divorcing husband's action was "against" his wife (Mark 10:11). Betrayal is wrong, and Jesus refused to accommodate men's hardness of heart at their wives' expense (10:5; or vice versa, cf. 10:12).[15] Yet if we so understand Jesus's heart, we will also find tragic the common practice of later Christians to require celibacy of the innocent party. It further harms the partner that Jesus compassionately sought to protect.

Reading in light of God's heart may begin with the sense of God's personal involvement in one's life and reading. Eventually, as we grow in God's heart and caring about what he cares about, we will also grow to care for other people and especially his people. Because we are finite in our knowledge, no less than were biblical prophets (e.g., Matt 11:3//Luke 7:20; 1 Cor 13:9), we may not always make the best applications. But ideally the omniscient Spirit can guide us in showing us at least what we need to see for what he is calling us to do.

Reading Missionally

Jesus's promise of the Spirit for Pentecost was a promise of empowerment for mission (Luke 24:48–49; Acts 1:8). Jesus ascends and bestows the Spirit in a manner that evokes the model of Elijah and his successor who received a double portion of his spirit, namely, Elisha (Acts 1:8–11). If the Spirit empowers us especially for mission, it should not surprise us if a Spirit-led reading of Scripture should highlight the theme of mission.[16] Following Jesus's lead, then, Peter's biblical explanation of the outpoured Spirit is prophetic empowerment (2:17–18).

Luke reveals how pivotal this empowerment is by underlining its necessity in both his Gospel's conclusion and his sequel's introduction.[17] This is how the servant aspect of Jesus's ministry becomes that of his followers. Luke's primary emphasis regarding the Spirit involves mission, and most scholars acknowledge empowerment for mission as the Spirit's most prominent activity in Acts.[18]

Biblical narratives offered widely available models for Luke's connection between the gift of the Spirit and Jesus's ascension. Although Moses also imparted the Spirit to Joshua, so that he was filled with the Spirit of wisdom (Deut 34:9; cf. Acts 2:4; 6:3, 10), the transfer of Elijah's spiritual power and ministry to Elisha is even more relevant (2 Kgs 2:9, 15; cf. Sir 48:12).[19] This is because it also belongs to the Old Testament's only explicit ascension scene (explicitly connected to the transfer; 2 Kgs 2:10, 13; cf. Sir 48:9, 12). Such biblical models indicate that Jesus is delegating his prophetic empowerment to his followers.[20]

The opening of Peter's Pentecostal sermon highlights this feature. Indeed, what all Luke's programmatic texts (Luke 4:18–19; 24:45–49; Acts 1:8; 2:16–17; cf. Luke 3:4–6) share in common is God's Spirit empowering God's agents for their mission. The empowerment of the Spirit leads to mission and, to the extent that the seminal preaching about the experience offers a model for us, a missional reading of that empowerment.[21]

Reading from within Spirit-filled Experience

Peter explained the Pentecost experience in light of Scripture and Scripture in light of the Pentecost experience. "[I]s it not vain to speak of love to one who has not known love," one scholar inquires, "or of the joys of learning to those who reject it?"[22] Shared experience allows for a deeper understanding of the experience being communicated. Among other contexts to be considered in interpretation, such as historical and literary contexts, spiritual context also matters: authors of Scripture addressed audiences in particular historical situations, but sometimes also living communities of faith that shared the spiritual realities presupposed by the authors.[23]

Charismatic and prophetic experiences within the Bible take a variety of forms, so mere experience of prophecy or miracles does not mean that one's experience is ontologically identical to any given biblical experience. It does, however, provide a sympathy for the experience and a window into such experiences generally in a way with which those without such experiences will not so readily identify.[24] That is, if we have experienced the Spirit in any way at all, we will be more apt to give at least a knowing nod to such experiences in Scripture than would someone for whom all such descriptions are puzzling enigmas of a past era or some sort of literary fiction.

Sharing biblical experiences, such as particular spiritual gifts (or for that matter spiritual fruit), affects how we conceptualize those experiences in Scripture. Note, for example, the way that some movies based on Acts depict speaking in tongues; someone who has experienced the gift might depict it differently. Certainly someone who knows the kind Lord Jesus personally would not recognize much of him in the unblinking, morose Jesus of Nazareth film, despite the film's positive features.

Similarly, a long-term charismatic may identify with the ambiguities of prophetic experience depicted in 2 Kgs 2:3–5, 16–17 and Acts 21:4, 11–14, even though such ambiguities puzzle many other readers.[25] Likewise, interest in matters of the Spirit may help us to ask questions about and identify with experiences attested in Scripture but often ignored by interpreters. When Samuel was a boy visions were rare (1 Sam 3:1), but after his leadership prophets proliferated in Israel, even with multiple persons prophesying together, sometimes on the ground (10:5, 10; 19:20, 24). We may not all be groundbreaking prophetic leaders like Samuel but we can all learn from the spiritual experience depicted here and can pray for renewal.[26] The details of the experience are not filled in; the narrator probably assumes that his audience is familiar with the behavior of Israelite prophets. If we lack that familiarity, we may nevertheless understand better the prophets' dynamic experience of sometimes overwhelming inspiration through our own experience of the Spirit.

I resort to my own example here because some writers on the subject today suppose that by citing Pentecostal tradition they have resolved what a Pentecostal hermeneutic should look like. Because I have ministered regularly in the gift of prophecy in certain periods of my life, I have not only an empathy for biblical prophets but also a sense of what prophetic inspiration sometimes feels like (although I can readily assure concerned cessationists that I have never written anything canonical). I also find such an experience in Scripture impossible to dismiss and easy to resonate with.[27] From one period in my life, I can identify with the intense alienation of Jeremiah from a society that rejected his message; from another, I can weep with God's broken heart in the book of Hosea.

Whereas Dilthey found in common humanity a general means to connect author and reader, and those with traditional Middle Eastern or Mediterranean backgrounds[28] might find more specific common cultural connections with biblical texts, common spiritual experience also provides a valuable connection on a special level.[29] A more liberal or radical scholar who then experiences the activity of the Spirit will find it more difficult to dismiss reports in Scripture of supernatural activity;[30] someone from an anticharismatic background will after an experience of the Spirit find more sympathy for charismatic experience. Likewise, someone who experiences prophetic inspiration will find less plausible the archaic view of inspiration by mechanical dictation.[31]

As someone who has moved in the gift of prophecy, I recognize that prophecy must be evaluated. I also recognize that a prophecy that I give to someone can mean something more precise and profound in their context than I could have imagined.[32] At the same time, my personal context normally imposes some limitations on the range of possible meanings—prophecies normally come in the speaker's language and potential range of vocabulary, for example.

If someone prophesies, "The Lord says, 'I will raise up a sword against the nations,'" a hearer might be right to infer from this a further warning against living for the values of this world. By contrast, someone who used this prophecy to assure themselves of imminent financial wealth by linking this with some other proof-texts, such as the wealth of the sinner being laid up for the righteous (Prov 13:22), would most likely be departing from the spirit of the message. If even prophecies do not mean just anything, I am not inclined to think that ancient inspired texts in more determinate genres mean just anything either, especially those in which the authors' own use of sources and reasoning processes (as in, e.g., history or Paul's biblical argumentation, respectively) were more fully engaged.

Reading with the Humble

When Peter, filled with the Spirit (Acts 4:8), confronts Jerusalem's elite in Acts 4:8–12, the latter observe that Peter and John lack elite education (4:13). They recognize that these fishermen speak boldly because they have been with Jesus (4:13). Yet Peter and John return and pray for continued boldness for believers (4:24, 29), which God granted by filling them all with the Spirit (4:31). Jesus calls (Luke 5:2, 10; 6:13) and empowers (Acts 2:4) not the proud but the lowly who depend on him. That was at least part of why the Spirit was given not to the elite but to the humble who obeyed God (5:32).

Scripture often indicates that God is near the broken but far from the proud (Ps 138:6; Prov 3:34; Matt 23:12; Luke 14:11; 18:14; Jas 4:6; 1 Pet 5:5). We should expect this claim to have hermeneutical implications.[33] Why should God reveal himself differently among those who read (or hear) the Bible than when he reveals himself more generally? Exegetes are sometimes proud of our knowledge; knowledge does, as Paul noted, tend to lead us to overestimate our status (1 Cor 8:1). Many of the early Pentecostals came from circles that were poor and socially marginalized;[34] many of us today would consider the dictates of some of these marginal holiness-oriented believers (even as early as Wesley and certainly William Law and most Puritans) too radical at times,[35] yet they were determined to obey what they believed God was teaching, no matter what the social cost. Granted, those who excel in what such circles value can develop a pride of their own, but in general, these were much humbler circles than those that dominated the most prestigious theological institutions at the time.

Most of the places experiencing the most profound spiritual revival today are also circles among the poor and the marginalized.[36] Whitefield's and the Wesleys' revivals began in the fields; compare also nineteenth-century American frontier revivals such as at Cane Ridge, Kentucky,[37] or upstate New York.[38] Various revivals toward the beginning of the twentieth century fit this pattern; for example, the Welsh revival of 1904–1905 flourished initially among mine workers and other marginal elements of Welsh society;[39] revival came to Pandita Ramabai's orphanage in India in 1905;[40] a humble, one-eyed African-American Holiness preacher from the Jim Crow South led the Azusa Street Revival that began in 1906; "the Great Revival" of 1907 in Korea came at a time of national hardship and disappointment.[41] God has also poured out his Spirit among rural farmers in China in the 1980s, orphans in contemporary Mozambique, and others.[42]

Even some of the more notable exceptions are not foreign to the general pattern. Thus the noonday prayer revival that often featured businessmen in 1857–58 followed a market crash in 1857.[43] The revival among Nigerian students in Scripture Union starting in 1967 followed in the wake of a tragic civil war that particularly devastated the largely Christian Southeast.[44] The Jesus Revival in the United States flourished among disaffected youth, and many student revivals, such as those at Asbury College, came among students dissatisfied with their current state and hungry for more of God. "How wonderful it will be for those who are hungry and thirsty for righteousness, for they'll be fed" (Matt 5:6).

This is what liberation theology should lead us to expect,[45] and it is certainly what biblical theology leads us to expect. "How wonderful for the poor" (so Luke) and/or "How wonderful for the poor in spirit" (so Matthew), "for it's to them that heaven's kingdom belongs" (Matt 5:3; cf. Luke 6:20). "How wonderful for the humble," that is, for those who aren't puffed up with their own importance but are sensitive to others, "for they are the ones who will inherit the world to come" (Matt 5:5). Likewise, it is wonderful for the broken who will be comforted (5:4) and for those persecuted on account of righteousness and Jesus's name (5:10–12).

Jesus did not come into this world in a palace in Jerusalem, though that is presumably where Magi first looked for him (Matt 2:1–2). Luke, in fact, probably contrasts Jesus at his birth with the respected emperor Augustus, whose inconvenient decree establishes part of the geographic premise of Luke's birth narrative (Luke 2:1). Augustus claimed a universal empire, held together by force and propaganda; by contrast, Jesus was the true and benevolent ruler of humanity.[46]

Augustus, emperor of the Mediterranean world	Jesus, the true, Davidic king destined to rule creation
Augustus was in a palace	Jesus was in an animal feeding trough (2:7)
Earthly choirs praised Augustus	Heavenly choirs praise Jesus at his birth (2:13)
Augustus boasted that he had established the Pax Romana	Jesus is associated with "peace on earth" (2:14)
Augustus was hailed as a "savior" and "lord"	"Today . . . there has been born for you a savior, Christ the Lord" (2:11)
Augustus was attended by the powerful	Jesus's birth was attended by shepherds, a socially marginal group, and the hosts of heaven (2:8, 13)
Augustus held the highest status in the Mediterranean world	Jesus was born to a young Galilean couple in what could appear a scandalous situation (2:5)

Two chapters later, Luke summarizes Jesus's mission in part as good news to the poor (Luke 4:18). When Jesus summarizes his signs that indicate the messianic era, Jesus lists various miracles and then concludes—or perhaps even climaxes—with preaching good news to the poor (Matt 11:5//Luke 7:22). The poor are objects of Jesus's first beatitude (Luke 6:20; cf. Matt 5:3). Although Luke apparently dedicates his volume to a person of status (Luke 1:3), among the few wealthy people who make it through the eye of a needle (cf. 6:24; 8:14;

12:21; 16:22–23; esp. 18:25) in his Gospel are those who sacrifice for the poor (19:8; cf. 14:12–14) or who risk their very lives to honor Jesus (23:52).[47]

Likewise, Jesus chose fishermen (Luke 5:10) and a tax collector (5:27) as his disciples. That these are the only professions specifically named among Jesus's disciples may suggest that the other disciples had even less prestigious occupations; the vast majority of Galileans were probably peasants, so fishermen and tax collectors made a better living than most. By contrast, apparently none of Jesus's chief disciples were scribes; none belonged to the more prestigious sect of the Pharisees, and certainly none belonged to the Sadducean chief priestly elite in Jerusalem.[48] With few and private exceptions, it was not the intellectual elite of Jesus's day, but the lowly, who followed him. "I praise you, Father," Jesus prayed, "for you hid these matters from the wise and intellectual and revealed them to little children" (Matt 11:25//Luke 10:21). Only those who welcome the kingdom like a child will enter it (Mark 10:15).

On a spiritual level and beyond the methodological level, Augustine and Anselm speak of faith seeking understanding;[49] likewise Luther and Calvin elevated faith above reason.[50] For Luther, one not immersed in Scripture and engaged in the service of the church could understand it no more than one could understand Virgil's *Bucolics* or *Georgics* without being a herder or farmer.[51] Barth deemed faith necessary for true understanding.[52] Our information and intellects are finite, so the greater wisdom is to trust first the omniscient one. Intellectuals may not like it, since this is not the epistemic approach that we have cultivated and for which we have diligently labored, but Jesus declared that is the way God arranged matters. We are justified by trust, not by merit or personal advantage, including intellect.

Far be it from me to suggest that knowledge hinders our study of Scripture; Proverbs urges us to seek knowledge diligently (Prov 8:17; 15:14; 18:15). (I revisit this subject later when briefly responding to those who suppose otherwise.)[53] But Proverbs also warns us against considering ourselves wise (3:7; 12:15; 26:5, 12, 16), and that true wisdom and knowledge begin with fearing God (Prov 1:7; 9:10; 15:33; cf. Ps 111:10). It is a fool who counts his way right in his own eyes and is therefore unwilling to learn from others (Prov 12:15; cf. 26:12, 16). Isaiah, too, condemns those who are wise in their own eyes (Isa 5:21).

The humble read Scripture not simply to reinforce their knowledge, but with desperation and/or faith to hear God there. They read with dependence on God, trusting the Holy Spirit to lead them. Methods and information help us, but there is no mechanical substitute for expecting to meet God in the study of Scripture.[54] That was a way of reading among early Pentecostals and

48

remains prevalent in the Pentecostalism of the Majority World today (see further discussion in Part II). Early Pentecostals insisted on "a proper attitude of reception" toward the text; this would yield more fresh insights, they believed, than simply organizing biblical information systematically, which anyone without spiritual insight could also do.[55] The expectation of meeting God in the text, of course, was never limited to Pentecostals.[56] Wesley, for example, urged continual meditation on Scripture in order to "attain the best knowledge," namely, knowing God.[57]

Scholarship has gifts to bring to traditional Pentecostal spirituality; yet traditional Pentecostal spirituality also has gifts to bring to scholars as readers who are also human beings. These observations remain relevant even for some emerging scholarship in the Majority World, since the published, educated minority within the Majority World who often have Western-related education and a hearing in the West may differ from grassroots Christian voices.[58] That is, you do not need to abandon your precious experience of God simply in order to satisfy Western elites often insulated from wider realities. These observations serve as an even greater warning to us tenured Western professors who may teach and write in insulated cultural bubbles. "Whoever does not receive God's reign like a child will surely not enter it" (Mark 10:15).

An Eschatological Reading

Peter recognizes that Jesus's followers now live in a special, biblically promised time, the "last days" when God will pour out his Spirit and save those who call on Jesus Christ (Acts 2:17–21). Peter's understanding remains incomplete at this point (10:28–29), but already God is teaching a new messianic, and therefore eschatological, framework for conceptualizing Scripture (cf. Luke 24:27, 44–49; Acts 3:18, 24; 10:43).

On the Border of a New World

Early Pentecostals believed that they were in the last days. Reading the context of Joel's promised last-days outpouring in Joel 2:28–29, often they envisioned their own time as a "latter rain" corresponding to the "former rain" (2:23) on the day of Pentecost.[59] Unfortunately, this allegorical reading of Israel's climate conditions likely misses Joel's point. The heart of early Pentecostals' intuition about the last days, though, was surely right. They were biblically right to see themselves as part of an end-time church.[60] This eschatological perspective has often characterized the church in times of renewal.[61]

God did not pour out the Spirit on Pentecost, pour the Spirit back for most of history and then pour the Spirit out again in their own day. Nor did God start the last days, allow some days after those last days that were not really last days, and now will conclude with some more last days. Surely the Spirit did not cease his activity after the book of Acts concluded. The early Pentecostal restorationist approach simply adopted contemporary cessationism and modified it by making the cessation temporary. Whatever history looked like from early Pentecostals' vantage point or that of Reformers or restorationists before them, Scripture does not prescribe an intervening period of spiritual inactivity, even if spiritual activity is certainly necessary to achieve some events predicted before the end (Matt 24:14; Rom 11:12, 25–26).[62] Throughout Scripture, there was an ebb and flow of spiritual activity, of apostasy and what we call revival, of periods of abandonment and repentance.

The biblical approach was neither (with many cessationists) to envision a present interim era unlike the biblical period, nor (with many early Pentecostals) to envision a new revival that ended such an interim. Rather, the last-days Spirit poured out at Pentecost was God's empowerment for the church's mission in the world, hence should have been appropriated at all times. That much of history looked different speaks to the church's failures (today often included), not to any deficiency of the Spirit's availability. On the experiential level, however, this amounts to what Pentecostalism claimed to experience: God's Spirit-empowered people are eschatological.

From the standpoint of the New Testament, Jesus's people should always recognize ourselves as living in what scholars have dubbed the "already/not yet." Jesus not only announced the coming kingdom; his signs were a foretaste of the fulness of that kingdom (Matt 12:28//Luke 11:20). When John the Baptist heard that Jesus was healing the sick but not baptizing in fire, he questioned Jesus's identity (Matt 11:3//Luke 7:19). But Jesus responded by framing the healings in language that evoked the promised restoration (Matt 11:5//Luke 7:22; Isa 35:5; 61:1); his signs were a foretaste of the promised new world, when healing and deliverance would be complete. The majestic kingdom was already present like an obscure mustard seed, recognizable only to those who had the eyes of faith (Mark 4:31–32).

Similarly, Paul declares that Christ has delivered us from this present evil age (Gal 1:4), to which he urges us not to be conformed (Rom 12:2). Instead of being conformed to this age, we should think with minds made new—that is, conformed to the standards of the promised coming age.[63] This approach reveals Paul's understanding about the eschatological era impinging on the present, and naturally demands that we read Scripture from this eschatological perspective as well (cf. Paul's pneumatic qualification of biblical denials that mortals can understand God, in 1 Cor 2:9–10 and 2:16).[64] Paul read Scripture as relevant for God's people living at the ends of the ages (1 Cor 10:11). The Spirit is the first fruits of the promised future harvest (Rom 8:23), the down payment on our future inheritance in the world to come (2 Cor 1:22; 5:5; Eph 1:13–14). Thus the incomparable riches of the promised future, currently depicted in words only through the imagery of apocalyptic similitudes, is already experienced as a foretaste through the Spirit (1 Cor 2:9–10). As another early Christian put it, we have "tasted the powers of the coming world" (Heb 6:5).

If, as most commentators believe, the child snatched up to rule the nations in Rev 12:5 is Jesus, the believers suffering for his name in the rest of that chapter are living in an eschatological time. At least in passages like this one, the eschatological tribulation expected by many Jewish people probably represents instead the entire present era, a period of birth pangs preceding the new world (cf. also Rom 8:22).[65]

The Last Days of Acts 2:17[66]

In explaining the outpouring of the Spirit on the day of Pentecost, Peter depicts his own era as experiencing the "last days." Peter's "last days" alters the text of Joel, substituting "In the last days" for Joel's "afterward," but this change simply highlights the implications of the context that he does not go on to cite.[67] "In the last days" (and related expressions such as "last times") was a biblical phrase that applied especially to the period of Israel's promised restoration, which Jewish hopes now fixed in the eschatological time (Isa 2:2; Hos 3:5; Mic 4:1; Dan 2:28).[68]

This title for the eschatological period of restoration also applied to a period of great suffering just before that restoration (Jer 23:20; 30:24; Ezek 38:16; Dan 10:14),[69] a period that Jewish tradition expected to produce apostasy among the insincere.[70] Christian texts likewise mention an eschatological period of suffering and apostasy (cf. Mark 13:9–13; Rom 8:22; 1 John 2:18), often designating it as the present, final period before the end (1 Tim 4:1;[71] 2 Tim 3:1; 2 Pet 3:3). As a time of final suffering, the last days prefigured the final "day of the Lord" (Acts 2:20); as a time of Israel's restoration, they were identical with it or followed it. Thus the phrase roughly means "the eschatological time."

Early Christians consistently viewed this eschatological time as the period in which they were living (1 Tim 4:1; 2 Tim 3:1; Heb 1:2; Jas 5:3; 1 Pet 1:20; 2 Pet 3:3; Ign. *Eph.* 11.1).[72] There is no reason to suppose that Luke intends the phrase (Acts 2:17) any differently, especially since the title would be meaningless if it were to be followed by other periods not characterized as "last," "final" or "eschatological."

Luke thus surely means his programmatic use of Joel as theologically prescriptive and not merely historically descriptive; that is, he believes that the church of his day continues, or should continue, to experience the outpouring of the Spirit and concomitant prophesying. "In the last days . . . I will pour out my Spirit on all flesh, and your sons and daughters will prophesy; and your young people will see visions; and your elders will dream dreams. Indeed, I will pour out my Spirit on my male and female servants alike, and they will prophesy" (Acts 2:17–18). Lest anyone miss the point, Peter adds to the text of Joel a further, clarifying line, "and they will prophesy." Prophetic empowerment of God's people characterizes the eschatological era in which Jesus's followers live.

Luke must view the promise as valid for all believers in his day, given his appeal to a text referring to "all flesh" (i.e., all kinds of people, Acts 2:17) and his emphasis that the gift was for their descendants, even those far away (2:39). The idea that such empowerment or its prophetic expressions had ceased in his day, or was scheduled to cease before the Lord's return, is one that, given Luke's language, surely could not have occurred to Luke. For Luke, such activity characterizes the eschatological era in which the church lives; Luke would hardly emphasize that this era was inaugurated on Pentecost and then expect us to infer, without clear evidence, that the era would be phased out before its consummation at Christ's return.[73] God would hardly pour out his Spirit, then pour it back again![74] Indeed, such a contradiction would have played into the hands of those who questioned whether the eschatological Messiah had genuinely come, and would undermine Luke's apologetic and theology of fulfillment.

Further, Luke presents the interim messianic era of Christ's reign at the Father's right hand (2:34–35) as in continuity with God's activity in Scripture. If this eschatological era continues "biblical" experience, then it is relevant that, despite ebbs and flows, Luke believes that prophetism was always active in biblical history (Acts 3:18, 21, 24). Those who received the message would, indeed, be "children of the prophets" as well as of Abraham (cf. 3:25).[75] Not surprisingly, Christian prophecy did continue in later centuries,[76] and later opponents of Christianity continued to attack it.[77]

Pentecost and Its Subsequent Revivals

If God poured out the Spirit on the day of Pentecost, then much of what we envision as "revival" is simply part of the normal Christian life. It is not the sole possession of one part of the body of Christ, as if other parts may dismiss it as a sectarian or divisive issue; it is part of God's gift, and it is unholy and a sin against God to despise it (cf. 1 Thess 5:20). At the same time, it is not something that belongs to a label, as if calling ourselves "Pentecostal" or "charismatic" means that we have it, reducing it to a merely sectarian possession. It does not come with labels or with a theology that merely affirms it. It comes from obedient faith in God's gift to his church.

The early Christians saw themselves as living both in the last days and in the continuation of the biblical era, expecting God to act in their own day. As one Dominican observer noted, what was particularly distinctive about the early-twentieth-century Pentecostal movement was not so much tongues as that they belonged to "the life of the church of the apostles, the 'church of Pentecost'"; they understood the renewal of prophecy, healing and the like "as signs that they were bringing in the 'last times.'"[78] That is, their continuity with the apostolic church was also a foretaste and herald of the coming kingdom.

Although early Pentecostals, like other restorationist movements of their era, did overemphasize much of their own distinctive role in the history of the church, they rightly understood the biblical perspective that our experience of the Spirit is eschatological. Whether restorationists rightly understood the larger scheme of history, they were often right that they were restoring emphases or experiences that their contemporaries had forgotten. And, theological restorationism aside, early Pentecostals did ultimately play a historic role in restoring to the wider church the recognition that spiritual gifts should continue (although in so doing they were part of a wider movement of radical evangelical predecessors, such as A. B. Simpson's Missionary Alliance).

As various scholars have shown, early Pentecostals saw the restoration of the gifts as a sign of Christ's imminent return, and this eschatological hope helped drive the growth of Pentecostalism.[79] Although many early Pentecostals accepted the classical dispensationalist eschatology popular at the time, their perspective also continued the expectant eschatology of the holiness movement, which viewed the present era of the church as the era of the Spirit.[80] Moreover, in contrast to the classical dispensationalist relegation of certain events to the past and/or future, these believers appropriated more of the principles of Scripture for the present.[81] Classical dispensationalism's increasing dominance in the fundamentalist environment surrounding early Pentecostals to a great extent overwhelmed the more distinctive and relevant elements in early Pentecostal eschatology,[82] but biblical scholarship (not least George Eldon Ladd's emphasis on the already/not yet of the kingdom) has led to a widespread resurgence in what was much closer to the original spiritual impetus of the Pentecostal revival.

God sometimes acts in different ways in different times; Christians today often speak of those special periods as periods of revival or awakening. In some settings and times, miracles seem to happen regularly, and in other times more rarely; we need to recognize the element of God's sovereignty. At the same time, he welcomes us to pray for his activity (cf. Acts 4:29–30) and promises to hear us (Luke 11:13). Living in the reality of God's word and the presence of his Spirit is something that can characterize our lives all the time, and make us increasingly ready for whatever other ways God may pour out the Spirit in our time and place. Faith may be expressed in expectancy, and this faith may itself express the sense that God is moving, a sense based on God's own activity in our hearts. As noted further below (pp. 174–76), biblical faith is not "make-believe," or wishing hard;[83] it is a spiritual sense that has eyes to see and ears to hear, recognizing that God is trustworthy and, in light of some biblical passages, recognizing that God is acting or recognizing what God is doing. *Faith is the sound and appropriate response to God's reliability.*

Noncessationist, or Continuationist, Reading

When we apply texts, we look for continuity between the message of the text and circumstances today. This process is not limited to, but is much simpler for, those whose theology allows a greater degree of continuity. Without biblical support, hard cessationists (the sort of cessationists primarily criticized in this book) posit radical discontinuity at some significant points.[84]

When I was a young Christian I attended some Bible studies taught by a strong traditional dispensationalist (not the current, "progressive dispensationalist" kind). Some of these extreme dispensationalists did not believe that even baptism or the Lord's Supper was for this dispensation, accepting only what was taught in Paul's prison epistles. I found that approach extreme and disagreed with them regarding spiritual gifts. Nevertheless, I appreciated their love for the parts of the Bible that they did apply, and for several months I accepted the basic premise of radical discontinuity between the testaments until my continued study of Scripture made it unworkable.

Reading Paul, I soon realized that he grounds his arguments for salvation by faith in Christ in the Old Testament, himself accepting its relevance. If he was wrong, the most I could salvage of my young faith was Jesus plus the Old Testament, and I would need to practice the law. As I worked through Deuteronomy, however, I discovered that it was full of grace. God had *always* saved people by grace through faith; the change or discontinuity had to do not with grace but with newer revelations and revelatory events in salvation history, the ultimate one, of course, being God becoming flesh and dying and rising for us. But reading the Bible for continuity wherever possible helped me to welcome its message for my own life today.[85]

Some hard cessationists have argued that although no clear text announces that the gifts would pass away after the close of the canon, neither do any texts argue the opposite. This is truly a curious way of arguing, since one would expect such a dramatic shift away from both Old and New Testament prophetic models to be announced explicitly in Scripture. Instead Paul seems to assume that prophecy and tongues remain until we see Jesus face to face, partial knowledge being valuable until it is supplanted by perfect knowledge as we are known (1 Cor 13:8–12).

This cessationist argument also appears a curious tactic when we consider the selective nature of the reasoning. Would someone argue that the unity of Christ's multigifted body would pass away with the completion of the canon unless there is explicit evidence to the contrary (cf. Eph 4:11–13)? Or more analogously, would someone argue that once the canon is complete we no longer need the gift of teaching? Why some gifts and not others? (Teaching seems to run more risk of competing with the canon than tongues would.) Some people argue that we should not use instrumental music if it is not mentioned in the New Testament; others might respond that they might well then exclude cars and electric lights.[86]

But the hard cessationist makes a still stranger claim: he or she excludes something that *is* in the Bible (such as prophecy throughout biblical history and the biblical command to pursue it in 1 Cor 14:1, 39), without any evidence that it was supposed to stop. The basis for this is not Scripture but a theological inference about Scripture. Ironically, this is a postbiblical doctrine—the very thing that hard cessationists claim most to fear from allowing postbiblical prophecies!

In contrast to such an approach, it seems more biblically faithful to read the biblical narrative as a model for understanding how God works in our world, and to live in the light of that narrative. Such a reading takes faith, inviting an entirely new worldview or approach to reality around us. It introduces the expectation of a God who works actively in the world around us.

We thus both trust his providence in our lives, and expect his Spirit to guide us and to perform unusual works where he finds them appropriate to further his purposes.

Such a reading invites us to experience God's activity in the way that early Christians did, provided we are willing to engage in the same wholehearted commitment mission that they did. This was true in the radical evangelism of early US Methodism. From Francis Asbury's arrival in the US until his death, Methodists grew a thousand times over.[87] Near the end of his life, Asbury warned that the Reformation removed only some of the corruption that had quenched the spirit of the first-century church. The 1784 church conference in which he became the church's leader formed "an apostolic form of Church government."[88] Some, he warned, questioned whether the church of today could, "as in former apostolical days, have such doctrines, such discipline, such convictions, such conversions, such witnesses of sanctification, and such holy men. But I say that we can; I say we must; yea, I say we have . . ."[89]

Absorbing biblical perspectives is necessary for a healthy Christian life. Immersing ourselves only in world news can breed despair; some eschatological approaches breed fear. Immersion in Scripture, however, allows us to identify with God's people before us (e.g., 1 Cor 10:1–12); we have been through such crises before. Even biblical predictions of final suffering usually give way to final biblical hope beyond it. Immersing ourselves in Scripture reinforces our confidence that the ultimate future lies in the hands of the sovereign Lord, who is worthy of our trust.

Conclusion

As cultural background once shared by biblical authors and their first audiences may help readers to fill gaps in the text, so too shared spiritual experience may help us relate to experiences in the text, e.g., understanding what it feels like (at least in some cases) to experience the Spirit's guidance, visions, or prophecy. At times an inner restlessness guards me against approaching a passage as I intended, forcing me to prayerfully and exegetically wrestle with the text until both my intellect and my spirit are satisfied. Living by faith in God's present activity affects our reception of Scripture.

Reading from the vantage point of Pentecost includes knowing God's heart, reading missionally, reading from within Spirit-filled experience, reading with the humble, reading eschatologically, and reading with ourselves as part of the theological world that Scripture narrates.

Global Readings

Communities of interpretation have become prominent in hermeneutical and theological discussion, and many scholars who speak of Spirit hermeneutics emphasize the role of the community. Yet for Christians in general and especially various (and overlapping) Christians movements such as pentecostals, Catholics, and Anglicans, we belong to larger communities of interpretation today that are global. In Part II I will suggest that we may hear the Spirit's voice more clearly when we critically listen to one another.

Chapter 3 suggests that the Pentecost narrative in Acts, which is paradigmatic for most Christian movements emphasizing the Spirit, also invites global readings. Chapter 4 argues that contextualization is biblical, is modeled for us in Scripture, and must begin with the biblical message. Indeed, because ancient texts reflect cultures different from our own, exegeting them properly requires cross-cultural sensitivity (including to their original cultures), and applying their message in our setting requires recontextualization. Chapter 5 emphasizes the value of insights from a range of global cultures for understanding the biblical text. Chapter 6, concluding this section, highlights two specific case studies of areas where the Western church, long afflicted by its syncretism with radical Enlightenment philosophy, can learn from Majority World believers, namely, regarding spirits and miracles.

CHAPTER 3

Global Reading: The Biblical Model of Pentecost

Reading from the vantage point of Pentecost also means a cross-cultural, globally sensitive reading. Before examining the value of global readings today I must briefly draw attention to the connection in Acts 2 between the Pentecost experience of the Spirit in Acts 2 and the embracing of the contributions of fellow believers from all cultural settings.

The connection seems clear from the apparent reversal of (or, on some views, parallel with) Babel in Acts 2:5–13, a narrative that also highlights the cross-cultural element in Luke's pneumatology (1:8) and specifically his mention of prayer in tongues (2:4). Although Peter presumably does not recognize the significance of his words within the narrative world, in the larger context of Acts his "all flesh" (2:17) and "all who are far away" (2:39) presumably include Gentiles. Pentecost is for all peoples; its repetition among Samaritans (8:14–17) and Gentiles (10:44–48) emphasizes that believers from among new groups of people also receive empowerment for mission and become earlier believers' partners in mission.

Reversal of Babel[1]

Many scholars understand Acts 2 as a reversal of the Babel story and believe that Luke patterned his narrative after it;[2] some ancient commentators made the same connection.[3] Such an approach would certainly fit Luke's theme of mission transcending cultural and linguistic barriers.[4] Some object that although the connection may be a legitimate theological inference to draw for Luke's sources or others,[5] the text gives no indication that Luke made the connection.[6]

I contend, however, that the accumulation of various specific allusions seems compelling reason to affirm a deliberate connection,[7] and Luke offers subtle allusions even in the narrative's structure. If we surmise that the table of nations in Genesis 10 informs Luke's list of nations in Acts 2:9–11 (as Gen 10 informed most Jewish lists of nations), an allusion to Babel in Gen 11:1–9 in the same context seems likely.[8] This suggestion becomes even more likely when we consider that Babel represents the only scattering of languages in the OT and hence the only *potential* background for Luke's story shared by all his ideal audience. This is Scripture's seminal "language miracle." (Certainly, the Babel story, as part of the very popular book of Genesis, was widely told and retold[9] and was reapplied for new settings.)[10]

When the author of the Qumran *War Scroll* refers to a "confusion of tongues,"[11] we know that he refers to Babel because this mention follows the creation of Adam and his seed and it parallels scattering. Luke's use of a table of nations and his mention of scattered languages seem similarly transparent. Whatever the date of the triennial Jewish lectionary readings,[12] at least some of them reflect earlier traditions, and so it would probably not be a coincidence if we concluded on other grounds, with some, that the cycle's first year used Genesis 11 as a reading for Pentecost.[13] Even if the lectionary connection is pure coincidence, however, the Babel allusion in this narrative is clear enough. For what it is worth, at least some Jewish people also envisioned an eschatological reversal of Babel (cf. *Test. Jud.* 25:3).[14]

Differences between the narratives are clear, of course. God scattered nations at Babel for trying to deify themselves (Gen 11:4), paralleling Adam's revolt and his expulsion from the garden (3:5, 22–23). By contrast, the disciples at Pentecost are waiting in obedience to a divine command (Acts 1:4–5); instead of trying to reach heaven, they are waiting for their Lord, who *has* ascended to heaven (1:9–11), to send them the Spirit. In Gen 11:7, God descended to confound the transgressors (the wording reflects their rebellion in 11:3–4), but at Pentecost God descends, in one sense, in a different way (Acts 2:33). In Genesis, God descended and scattered tongues to prevent unity; in Acts, the Spirit descends and scatters tongues to create multicultural unity (1:14; 2:1, 42, 44–46).

Narrative Function of Tongues in Acts[15]

My interest here is not a full theology of tongues, but how they function in this context. Paul emphasizes a different aspect of tongues, but Luke uses the experience to emphasize that the Spirit empowered witnesses, and hence ultimately the church, to cross cultural barriers with their prophetically inspired message. What better symbol of this cross-cultural empowerment for mission could have been available than the phenomenon of tongues, which Luke understands as inspired speech in languages the speakers had not learned?[16]

That Luke emphasizes tongues is no surprise; as Barrett notes, "Speech is in Acts the characteristic mark of the Spirit's presence, sometimes in glossolalia (2.4; 10.46; 19.6), sometimes in prophecy (2.17, 18; 11.27; 13.1–3; 21.(4), (9), 10, 11), sometimes in proclamation (e.g., 4.31)."[17] As the Spirit's activity often produced prophetic speech in ancient Israel, Bruce observes, so now it produced "prophetic speech," but "of a peculiar kind."[18] Luke explicitly uses tongues to identify the activity of the Spirit of prophecy (2:17–18), yet by focusing particularly on crossing cultural boundaries.

Presumably, the prophetic aspect of the Spirit's empowerment that he articulates in general includes and could be evidenced by any speech inspired by the Spirit or perhaps by prophet-like miracles as well, provided they testified about Jesus. But in view of his likely thesis statement at 1:8, Luke's primary concern is not simply prophetic speech in general but especially prophetic speech that extended to other peoples (promoting what scholars typically identify as Luke's emphasis on the "Gentile mission").

Thus tongues function here as a sign of prophetic empowerment for the continuing cross-cultural mission. In contrast to this portrayal of the apostles early in Acts, Luke, toward the beginning of his first volume, reports a priest who initially disbelieved the divine message and was struck mute (Luke 1:20). When he was later filled with the Spirit, however, even he prophesied the divine message (1:67).[19] More in parallel with the scene here, Jesus, filled with the Spirit, foreshadows the Gentile mission (4:1, 14, 24–27). Tongues thus offer one kind of prophetic speech (Acts 2:16–18), one particularly relevant for Luke's emphasis on cross-cultural mission.

Association with Baptism in the Spirit in Classical Pentecostal Interpretation

Different revivals of the Spirit in subsequent history have had varying emphases;[20] although tongues occurred sporadically before,[21] the contribution of widespread personal worship in tongues has been one valuable emphasis of the twentieth-century Pentecostal revival. Even in the early Pentecostal revival, however, views varied regarding its necessity. Many influential early

Pentecostal proponents of tongues (e.g., Agnes Ozman, F. F. Bosworth, Minnie Abrams, and, according to many, even Azusa Street leader William Seymour) apparently denied or came to deny that tongues speaking was a necessary evidence of the seminal experience of the Spirit described in Acts.[22] This perspective was probably even more prevalent outside the United States.[23] Some other early Pentecostal leaders wished to place the focus of the movement elsewhere than on tongues.[24] This consideration will be important when we consider, later in the book, whether there is a single Pentecostal hermeneutic; even the most distinctive doctrine of early Pentecostalism was not a unanimous conclusion.

Despite dissent from some of Pentecostalism's early leading figures,[25] however, tongues as the "initial evidence" of baptism in the Spirit became the dominant view among classical Pentecostals.[26] This might be a minority view today among global charismatics and certainly among charismatics in most traditional denominations.[27] Without a legacy of the initial evidence doctrine behind them, perhaps even some traditional Pentecostal denominations, were they formulating their doctrines in today's climate, would have welcomed greater diversity of views.[28] Indeed, even the primary formulator of the largest Pentecostal denomination's doctrine of initial evidence apparently held that tongues sometimes culminated a *process* rather than always accompanying an initial Spirit baptism experience.[29]

Although interpreters even in Pentecostal and charismatic traditions differ as to whether tongues marks every individual who is baptized in the Spirit, a more general connection between tongues and baptism in the Spirit is grounded in a genuine observation about the text and Luke's overall narrative pattern, one that some earlier interpreters may have overlooked precisely because it was so foreign to their own experience. (This despite the fact that some of the earliest Christian interpreters apparently did recognize the connection.)[30] Both the early classical Pentecostals and their modern scholars who associate tongues with Spirit baptism observed a genuine feature of Luke's story.[31]

Nor are Pentecostals the only readers to notice this connection. James D. G. Dunn, who is known for challenging classical Pentecostalism by identifying Spirit baptism with conversion-initiation rather than with a subsequent experience, has noted, "It is undoubtedly true that Luke regarded the glossolalia of Pentecost as an external sign of the Spirit's outpouring." Luke used tongues the same way in 10:45–46 and 19:6, and Dunn thinks that tongues probably occurred in 8:17, though it is not mentioned.[32] Since these passages exhaust the "initial" fillings that are *described* in Acts (9:17 predicts but does not describe Paul's), Dunn recognizes that the case "that Luke *intended* to por-

interesting tray 'speaking in tongues' as 'the initial physical evidence' of the outpouring of the Spirit" makes far more sense than most scholars have noticed.[33]

Yet Dunn nevertheless demurs from the dominant traditional Pentecostal conclusion: Luke's intention is to demonstrate the Spirit's presence through tongues, not to "teach" that tongues will always accompany the Spirit (Luke does, after all, omit its mention in 8:17).[34] The majority of interpreters here agree with Dunn's conclusion, based on the very limited evidence we have in Acts: he concludes that Luke regarded tongues as one verbally inspired manifestation of the prophetic Spirit among several, along with praise (2:11; 10:46), prophecy (19:6; cf. 2:17–18), and boldness (4:8, 31).[35] Such expressions underline the prophetic character of the empowerment. Likewise, as noted further below, tongues speech evidences the experience of baptism in the Spirit (i.e., reveals its purpose and function), not the individual recipients of this baptism; it thus would not need to occur on every occasion to maintain its symbolic function.[36] Nevertheless, Luke's highlight of tongues is not arbitrary, but reflects a connection with cross-cultural mission.

Tongues and Cross-cultural Mission

Debates on this matter continue, but Luke's own emphasis may lie especially with what tongues signify theologically. The most conspicuous manifestations of the Spirit reported by Luke, especially in key, paradigmatic texts, are vocal (1:8; 2:4, 17–18). Luke does not focus on every aspect of the Spirit's activity mentioned by other early Christian writers; he focuses on inspired speech flowing from the prophetic Spirit (2:17–18). At the same time, Luke has a reason for emphasizing a particular form of inspired speech, namely, tongues, where he can (which is why I am more skeptical than Dunn, though not dogmatically so, that Luke found it in, or felt free to infer it for, his source for Acts 8): this particular form of prophetic speech provides the most obvious symbol of people empowered to cross cultural and linguistic barriers with the gospel, which fits Luke's emphasis (1:8).

Tongues speaking itself is not simply one sign among many, only arbitrarily connected with Spirit baptism. Rather, it is intrinsically connected with Luke's emphasis on the Spirit's empowerment to proclaim Christ cross-culturally (1:8).[37] This experience may not be necessary to evidence the cross-cultural facility of every individual recipient, but in Luke's narrative it does evidence the character of Spirit baptism itself, explicating for Luke the *nature* of that empowerment.

Some historians have noted that some nineteenth-century Holiness advocates initially sought the "gift of tongues" because they believed it relevant to missionary endeavor.[38] Following this expectation, many of Pentecostalism's early exponents understood tongues as a form of missionary xenoglossy,[39] a view attested also among some church fathers.[40] Although some cases of xenoglossy have appeared, most tongues experiences have not functioned this way (either in the New Testament or today).[41] Although most early Pentecostals fairly quickly abandoned the "missionary tongues" view after it generally failed the empirical test,[42] the early Pentecostal teacher Charles Parham insisted on it to the end, criticizing others for abandoning it.[43] Early Pentecostals continued to embrace both power for mission and tongues speaking, but with the latter as a more symbolic sign of the former.

Yet whereas most traditional Pentecostals no longer claimed a direct "missionary" function for tongues, and xenolalia is not the usual function of the gift, the doctrine's first advocates had noticed a genuine connection that most subsequent interpreters (including most Pentecostals) have missed: the connection in Luke's theology between tongues speech and the empowerment for global mission.[44]

The aspect of Spirit baptism on which Luke focuses is empowerment for cross-cultural mission; although tongues speaking provides a key illustration of this empowerment in Acts when Luke has it available, Luke's real pneumatic focus is prophetic inspiration to communicate Christ's message cross-culturally.[45] Recognition of this association is not limited to modern interpreters. As John Chrysostom noted, the Corinthians exalted tongues because it was the first spiritual gift on Pentecost; but it was first "because it was a sign that they were to go everywhere, preaching the gospel."[46] Similarly, the Venerable Bede believed that Acts 2:3–4 "indicated that the holy church, when it had spread to the ends of the earth, was to speak in the languages of all nations."[47]

For Luke, tongues is not an arbitrary evidence of baptism in the Holy Spirit but is highlighted because it is intrinsically related to the point of what Luke means by this experience.[48] From a narrative perspective, it seems evident that tongues is a sign that attests or explains the *nature* of the experience, even if Pentecostal scholars debate whether it is a mandatory sign of every *individual's* reception of that experience.

It should therefore come as no surprise that many interpreters today view the globalization of Christianity, the church's global multiculturalism, or the Christian mission's sensitivity to indigenous languages and cultures as a theological extension of Pentecost.[49]

The Bicultural Hellenists (Acts 6)

Despite the birthing of Pentecost in a multicultural way in Acts 2, cultural and social divisions have strained the Jerusalem church by the time that the reader reaches Acts 6. (Similarly, the fruits of the interracial, multicultural Azusa Street Revival were eventually forcibly split by Jim Crow and other worldly social factors.)[50] Widows from the Hellenist faction complain against the dominant "Hebrew" faction of the Jerusalem church. "Hellenists" probably refers to those who spoke Greek exclusively and were more prone to Greek customs—in many cases, probably immigrant Diaspora Jews from elsewhere in the Mediterranean world.[51] Diaspora Jews already appear in 2:7–12 and 4:36 and are plainly in view here (see 6:9).

The Twelve respond to the widows' complaints in a manner rare if not almost unprecedented in antiquity: they hand the food distribution over to mutually acceptable members of the offended minority, provided they are full of the Spirit and wisdom (6:3). Their Greek names suggest that these seven all belonged to the Hellenist minority. Granted, some Judeans had Greek names,[52] but some of those Judeans so named clearly *were* Hellenists. Overall, it was more likely for Diaspora Jews to bear biblical names than for even rich Judeans to bear Greek ones.[53] In Rome, where three-quarters of all Jewish inscriptions are in Greek and only 1 percent are Semitic, 15.2 percent of the Jewish names included some Semitic elements.[54] The linguistic mixture of names of the putative LXX translators in Pseudo-Aristeas is also informative.[55] Even centuries later, Palestinian rabbis recognized that Gentile names were particularly common in the Diaspora but much rarer in the Holy Land.[56]

That all seven here, by contrast, have Greek names is hardly a coincidence, was surely deliberate,[57] and would be recognized by Luke's ancient audience in regions where such Greek names were common; Luke's informed hearers are suddenly on ground familiar from their own environment. Most scholars concur that the Seven are members of the Hellenist faction.[58] As the "Twelve" (Acts 6:2; Luke 8:1; 9:1, 12; 18:31; 22:3, 47; cf. Mark 3:16; 1 Cor 15:5) led most of the church, the "Seven" (Acts 21:8) would provide recognized and universally accepted leadership for the minority subculture in the Jerusalem church.[59]

These new leaders, one of them even a proselyte (6:5), foreshadow leaders who would arise in the Diaspora (13:1) and for the Gentile mission. Their bicultural competence made the Hellenist Jewish Christians a natural bridge to reaching non-Jewish Hellenists (11:20).[60] Thus the bilingual milieu of the Jerusalem church already in this period provided a groundwork for the transition that would come.[61] Commissioned by the apostles (6:6), these Hellenists now expand the apostles' sphere of ministry theologically (Acts 7) and geographically and culturally (Acts 8). In so doing, they are led by the Spirit to push forward toward the work's goal specified by Jesus in 1:8.

As noted earlier, the repetition of the Spirit's outpouring among Samaritans (8:14–17) and Gentiles (10:44–48) emphasizes that believers from among new groups of people also are empowered for mission and become earlier believers' partners in mission. Although Luke's focus is empowerment to spread the good news, this mission must also include understanding and applying the Scriptures to their own new contexts.

Conclusion

Sometimes alternative frameworks prove more accurate than those we started with, a situation that also appears among the apostles in Acts. Why is it that bicultural Hellenist believers such as Stephen (theologically) and Philip (practically; Acts 6–8) were able to begin bridging cultural gaps before the Jerusalem apostles did? The apostles were the ones whom Jesus directly instructed to bring the good news to "the ends of the earth" (1:8), but initially they may have expected it to spread indirectly or by a sovereign miracle while they continued to work in Jerusalem. Yet once Peter and John witnessed and supported Philip's success in Samaria, they also began preaching in Samaritan villages (8:25). Is it possible that cultural lenses influenced who first understood Jesus's instructions most clearly?

If we read from the vantage point of Pentecost, we recognize that God speaks all languages and reaches out to all cultures. Different cultures may hear different aspects of the Spirit's voice more readily. A reading from the vantage point of Pentecost, then, invites us to trust the Spirit's work in the global church enough that we dialogue with one another, listen to one another, and share with one another.

The Spirit speaks through different gifts in the local church, and we all provide a safety net of discernment for one another's blind spots (1 Cor 14:29).[62] The same will be true with the global church; sometimes what others hear from the Spirit in the global church will challenge us, and sometimes what we hear will challenge others. Yet we are together one body in Christ, needing one another. The one Spirit is heard best through the one body into which the Spirit has baptized us (1 Cor 12:13; Eph 4:4–6).

This chapter has suggested that a reading from the standpoint of Pentecost must be a reading ready to engage multiple cultures. The next three chapters offer suggestions concerning how best to implement this vision exegetically.

CHAPTER 4

Global Reading: Contextualization and Scripture

If reading from the standpoint of Pentecost includes sensitivity to a range of cultures, as argued in the previous chapters, what implications should that recognition have for our Spirit-led exegesis?[1] One may compare how James, learning from the conversion of non-Jews, applies Scripture accordingly and this application is attributed to the Holy Spirit (Acts 15:14–18, 28). Paul's own new understanding of what Scripture said about Gentiles was in fact at the heart of his global mission, a fresh apostolic revelation (Rom 16:25–26; cf. Eph 3:5–6). The Spirit continues to move Christ's followers across cultural barriers as in the book of Acts (e.g., Acts 8:29; 10:19, 44; 11:12, 15; 13:2, 4; 15:8, 28), applying Scripture to new cultural situations.[2] Although others have explored this challenge more fully elsewhere, I survey some of the practical issues here.[3]

I begin by addressing contextualization and Scripture, suggesting the value of hearing texts from multiple cultural settings. Later I will suggest two concrete examples of matters conventionally associated with "pentecostal issues" where many Majority World readings could help Western readers to hear biblical texts more sympathetically and in ways closer to what the first audiences would have heard.

Introduction: Scripture and Context

Charismatic Anglican scholar N. T. Wright, one of the most creative and prolific NT theologians of our generation, has argued that Mark 13 "is advice 'more useful to a *refugee* from military invasion than to a man caught unawares by the last trumpet.'"[4] While this verdict is certainly true of part of the passage, I asked my wife, who was a refugee for eighteen months, about Mark 13:24–27. She replied that it sounded to her instead like "the end of the world," and noted that that was how people in Congo-Brazzaville read the passage whether they are refugees or not.[5] In this case, interpretive traditions may play as much of a role as social location. Nevertheless, social location inevitably influences how we hear texts.

Humans have long recognized that culture makes a difference in communication.[6] In addition to the ordinary complications of intercultural communication, however, hearing the messages of Scripture involves an additional cultural complication: what relevance theory (noted below) calls "secondary communication."[7] When my Congolese wife and I communicate, we can clarify our meaning through discussion—this is sometimes called negotiating meaning. If we are simply reading a report from another culture with which we are unfamiliar, however, the words are translated, but the idioms, the literary forms, and so forth are not, and direct conversation is not always possible.

Scripture as a Cross-cultural Canon

In secondary communication, the cultures of the receiver and the current communicator remain important. If we genuinely care to understand what the original communication was meant to communicate (which one might hope we would care about for an inspired communication), however, we also need some understanding of the cultural context of the original communication.[8] If the Scriptures are not just a decoration and prop for what we want to say, but themselves hold special authority for us, we want to hear what God inspired their authors to say. (Charismatics, of all people,[9] should recognize that God can inspire people to speak his message. Certainly we may infer this point from Acts 1:8, 2:4, and 2:17.) Yet these authors communicated their message in particular languages, cultures, and circumstances.

Cultural sensitivity in reading Scripture offers a foundation for believers across cultures, offering a common functional basis or canon for intercultural dialogue; it is a natural component of the same approach that invites us to listen to one another interculturally. As Christians, we share a common basis for conversation in the received canonical text.[10] That text did not originate in a cultural vacuum, but in a concrete linguistic, cultural and historical setting that may be explored.[11] The Hebrew, Aramaic, and Greek words and even letters are unintelligible markings when extracted from the particular linguistic settings in which they originated.[12]

"Neo-Aristotelian" "Chicago School" critics, like Booth, differ from the earlier New Critics in emphasizing the communication between writer and reader.[13] Authorial activity functions differently in different sorts of texts; it is more prominent in "transmissive" communication (such as letters) than in more "expressive" communication (such as poetry), with narratives (like Acts), which evoke a narrative world, standing between these poles.[14]

Today relevance theory, an approach concretely grounded in cognitive linguistics, approaches texts in terms of communications, taking into account the cultural assumptions that inform them.[15] To take a common example, cultural context fills in the missing semantic content of "Coffee, please." The query, "Where were you on 9/11?" makes sense in an early-twenty-first-century North American context but would have been meaningless or conveyed a different meaning to any reader in 1997—and still more in October of 1911.[16] To offer a less familiar example, if someone says to us, "It was good to see you briefly," shall we infer that she is saying to us, "It was good to see you, *albeit* briefly," or, "It was good to *have to* see you *only* briefly"?[17]

Literary or cultural allusions can prove even more elusive. Because my wife grew up in Congo, I cannot trade childhood Star Trek or Batman allusions with her; at least we both read Tarzan. But both we and our son can quote back and forth lines from biblical epics we watched together over the years. In 2015, a friend and I were lamenting fraudulent fundraising techniques and he offered, "I will gladly pay you Tuesday for a hamburger today." I responded, "Forget the hamburger—I need the spinach." Those who were North American children when we were would catch the allusions to Wimpy and Popeye, but the point of our banter (aside from perhaps its playfulness) would be virtually unintelligible without such knowledge.

Some contemporary approaches might conclude, "I don't care what the speaker/author intended." If we *do* care, however, as in the case of normal human communication, or in the case of any text where we respect what an author may have designed to communicate, only context (such as the relationship between speaker and intended hearer) will help us resolve the meaning. Part of our transcultural goal should be listening honestly to the texts. The more effectively that we hear texts in their first contexts, the greater the confidence with which we may recontextualize the principles for other settings, and the greater our *shared* basis for dialoguing about what the texts say to us today.[18]

Insights on Scripture from Diverse Cultures

Yet we also will hear the text more clearly when we listen to one another, because Christians in some cultures will intuitively hear customs and concepts in particular passages in ways closer to the original context. Even widespread customs such as brideprice or dowry, levirate marriage and so forth differ from one culture to another. Although a Ghanaian Christian may intuitively understand such customs better than a Westerner, she may still envision them somewhat differently than the way the biblical writers anticipated that their first audiences would understand them.

We intuitively interpret people's actions or sayings in light of our broader knowledge or cultural assumptions; interpreters from other cultures provide alternative possibilities for understanding. Sometimes one culture's or interpreter's reading explains the text more satisfactorily than another's; sometimes the diverse interpretive options drive us to explore more deeply the original cultural context, or simply serve to make us more cautious about our a prioris, especially when we lack means to reconstruct some details beyond the text.

Teachings about justice and sacrificial care for the poor constitute such a significant proportion of the Bible that they may be deemed among the Bible's most common themes.[19] Liberation theologians picked up on such important themes that traditional Western systematic theology, for all its value, had typically neglected as a topic of disciplined study.[20] If we make hamartiology a theological rubric, concerns about whether gluttony is a venial sin or whether street children in Brazil are abused represent different yet genuine contexts. I confess that being very *hungry* as an unpaid young pastor did affect my hermeneutical grid, but I think that experience highlighted for me a biblical emphasis (one that I already recognized in principle) rather than creating a bias analogous to that of those who have never experienced hunger.

Cross-cultural Communication within Scripture: A Case Study

Even within the Bible itself, cross-cultural communication could prove complicated. Thus when Jesus talks with the Samaritan woman in John 4, their conversation presupposes an undercurrent of hostility between Jews and Samaritans that John's audience probably took for granted. Jesus crosses three social barriers to communicate with this woman.[21] First, in Jesus's culture, conservative opinion frowned on men talking alone with women who were not relatives.[22] If anyone is tempted to doubt that this custom affected someone in the narrative, one need only recall the report of 4:27: Jesus's own disciples were amazed that he was "conversing with a woman." Of course, Jesus also transforms this situation, since in 4:29 she ends up inviting all her people to Jesus with virtually the same words ("Come and see") through which Philip earlier invited Nathanael in 1:46. That is, she becomes a witness for Jesus at an even more dramatic level—this in spite of the fact that women's testimony was usually demeaned in the wider culture.[23]

Second, both Jews and Samaritans agreed that upright people should avoid unnecessary contact with those known to be immoral. Jesus reaches across those barriers in the other Gospels, and, although the matter has generated more debate in this case, he probably does so here as well. Granted, this woman could have been widowed five times and living with her brother (4:18),[24] but this would not explain why she comes to the well alone, a conspicuous action since village women normally came to wells together.[25] Moreover, she specifically comes at the sixth hour (4:6)—noon—when, throughout ancient Mediterranean literature, people stopped work and rested in the shade, often even taking siestas.[26] She comes at the very time when no one else would come, probably because she was not welcome among the other women. That this woman must come alone to the well at the hottest hour of the day (4:6), instead of coming with the other village women, probably suggests that she was unwelcome among the other women.

In cross-cultural settings, actions intended one way can easily be misconstrued. When Jesus tells the woman to "call" her husband (a term earlier used, again, for Philip "calling" Nathanael, 1:48), she replies, "I don't have a husband" (4:16–17). Today we could read this response in various ways, but the reply may have struck John's first audience less subtly. In Jesus's milieu, people sometimes sought marital or sexual partners at wells;[27] the biblically informed would think of encounters with Rebekah, Rachel, and Zipporah (Gen 24:13–15; 29:10; Exod 2:15–21).[28] But if the woman suspects that Jesus's intentions are sexual or conjugal, his elaboration of her own domestic situation (John 4:18) clarifies the nature of his interest, and she recognizes that he is God's prophet (4:19).

The third barrier is the explicitly ethnic one. As John 4:9 puts it simply, "Jews do not associate with Samaritans." Jewish teachers considered Jewish women unclean one week per month—but Samaritan women unclean every week of every month since infancy.[29] It is therefore no wonder she is surprised by his request for a drink from her vessel; it violates Jewish tradition.

And yet the woman herself also now ventures beyond Samaritan tradition here. At least if our later sources are accurate, Samaritans did not believe in prophets between Moses and the future restorer who would be like Moses.[30] That is why, once she acknowledges Jesus as a prophet in 4:19, she immediately shifts into what might seem to us a different subject. "Our ancestors worshiped here, on Mount Gerizim—but you Jews say that Jerusalem is the only right place of worship" (4:20). If he is a prophet, Jews are right and Samaritans are wrong. Yet ever since Samaritans desecrated the Jerusalem temple, they were unwelcome there; there was therefore no hope for her or her people. Her use of past tense for their ancestral place of worship is also deliberate, evoking the history of division between them: Jews had destroyed the Samaritan temple on Mount Gerizim more than a century earlier.[31] Jesus goes on to transcend this ethnic division by speaking of a greater place for worship than Jerusalem or Mount Gerizim: in Spirit and in truth (4:22–24).

Culture as well as language is encoded in this text, and if we have only a translation without the cultural context, we will miss some of the meaning.[32] Cues in the narrative signalled this meaning for its first audience, but some of the meaning could be left implicit because certain information could be simply assumed as shared between the author and the audience.[33] (Returning again to relevance theory: communication often takes the simplest forms by leaving unsaid elements that those involved in the communication can take for granted.)[34]

This happens elsewhere in Scripture as well. Mark, for example, explains a Jewish custom in Mark 7:3–4. When Matthew retells the same story in Matt 15:1–2, he omits the explanation because Matthew's Jewish Christian audience would not need it. How often does the Bible leave cultural matters unexplained because its first audiences did not need these explanations—yet today we do?

Some protest that God has spoken to people adequately using verses out of their literary and historical context. Because God is sovereign, we may grant this concession; nevertheless, their experience does not supply the text's universal message, and we might expect them to hear God even more clearly through understanding better the texts the way that God inspired them.

Moreover, I might compare this protest about using background with someone in the sixteenth century protesting the value of vernacular Bible translations on the grounds that such works would imply that the Western church was not already doing fine with the Vulgate. Today we do have translations available, and we have a considerable amount of background available on a popular level as well.[35] The question today is whether we will use what others' sacrifices have given us.

If we dismiss the relevance of such background in Scripture, would we do the same for modern cross-cultural conversation? When my wife and I first married, I often affirmed, "I love you," to which she responded, "Thank you." I became despondent, because in my culture the anticipated response to "I love you" is "I love you, too," and I feared that she did not love me. Eventually we discovered that the expected response to this affirmation differs between our cultures; it was not a matter of love but a matter of cross-cultural communication. Is Scripture written in some magical code that, despite all appearances, suspends its cultures' normal rules of genre and communication? A truly sensitive and respectful reading of Scripture, a reading also consistent with the global nature of today's church, should take into account what we can know of the original cultural situation.

Contextualization within the Bible

I asked my dear friend, neighbor, and missiology colleague at my former seminary, Samuel Escobar, where biblical studies could be helpful for missiology. He suggested that biblical scholars could help missiologists to define the boundaries between contextualization and syncretism.[36] Because the entire Bible has a cultural context, the entire Bible offers us models for non-syncretistic contextualization.

Those of us who embrace Scripture as divine revelation must recognize that God communicated cross-culturally. All communication has a cultural context; no one communicates or hears in a cultural vacuum. Insofar as we wish to hear the Bible as communication, then, we need to take into account its cultural context.[37]

The Bible provides countless examples of God identifying with cultures—sometimes down to the terms used for various kinds of sacrifices; literary forms used for oracles; or Proverbs, Jesus, and Paul using rhetorical forms of contemporary sages. Yet it also provides countless examples of God challenging culture, for instance in warnings against deity statues. Genuine contextualization does not simply adopt all values of the host culture (an adoption that would include syncretism); rather, it communicates God's prior message in the language and idiom of local culture, making both its affirmations and its demands more intelligible.

God went further in relating to local cultures than many of us today are willing to do. In many cases God used forms that resembled forms used in the religious practices of Israel's neighbors, while infusing those forms with new meanings.

Although some of the Bible's examples represent limited cultural accommodation short of God's ideal (cf. Mark 10:5: "because of the hardness of your hearts"), others represent translation into the language and images intelligible in the host culture. For example, the Tabernacle[38] adapts the tripartite design standard in Egyptian and some Canaanite temples.[39] Similarly, like most ancient Near Eastern temples the Tabernacle has a sacred object in the innermost shrine.[40] Tent shrines were also part of their milieu.[41] The use of the most expensive dyes and metals nearest the ark may reflect a wider understanding of gradation of holiness, emphasizing the deity's majesty and the awe with which s/he should be approached.[42] Such features would help Israelites—whom the Egyptians may have employed in temple construction—better relate to the Tabernacle as a temple (see Exod 25–27).

Nevertheless, these cultural analogies heighten the significance of the explicit contrasts with other ancient Near Eastern sanctuaries: for example, the Tabernacle has no bed for the deity,[43] because YHWH neither slumbers nor sleeps (Ps 121:4). Indeed, most strikingly, the climax of other ancient temples was the image of the deity, but no image is enthroned above the ark's cherubim.[44] The Lord reminds his people that they must have no images and other gods in his sight (Exod 20:3–5). Elements of culture can be helpful or harmful; good contextualization avoids syncretism.

Priests in the ancient Near East often treated earthly temples as portals that mimicked the image of heavenly temples.[45] The idea of a heavenly temple becomes more common in apocalyptic sources. When Hebrews or Revelation speaks of a heavenly temple, they lack the Platonizing, allegorical details found in the Alexandrian Jewish philosopher Philo.[46] Nevertheless, they employ images that contemporary hearers would have understood.

The cross-cultural strategies of God's servants in Scripture can provide even more direct models for Spirit-led contextualization. In seeking to win as many people as possible, Paul says that he became all things to all people (1 Cor 9:19–23).[47] Paul preaches from Scripture in a synagogue (Acts 13:16–41), from nature in a farming community (14:15–17), and from Greek poets and philosophic themes that intersected biblical theology in Athens (17:22–31).[48] In his Gentile mission, Paul befriended Asiarchs, many of whom would have participated in some aspects of public pagan religion (Acts 19:31).[49] Likewise, reaffirming his solidarity with Israel's heritage (but not their ethnocentrism) he offered sacrifice in the Jerusalem temple (Acts 21:24–26).[50]

Paul's letters abound with sensitivity to local or cultural situations. For example, he affirms hair coverings, which to at least lower-class persons in the Eastern Mediterranean represented sexual modesty.[51] Although many of us today would recognize that Paul contextualized the principle helpfully for his setting, most of us would also feel comfortable expressing sexual modesty in different ways for very different cultures.

But contextualization requires interpretation, and some nuances and connections with earlier imagery are necessarily lost in this process. Thus a dynamic tension remains. Yet the Spirit helps us in interpretation (cf. 1 Cor

2:11–13; 2 Cor 3:14–18). Indeed, even when we have conceptually merely images of the future world, for example, experientially we can participate in a foretaste of that world through the Spirit (1 Cor 2:9–10).

Recontextualization for a New Context in Scripture

Recontextualization—applying principles or images in different ways for new contexts—was practiced already within Scripture. For example, NT writers recontextualized OT images for new settings. Thus Revelation updates OT images of heavenly cavalry (with chariots; 2 Kgs 6:17; Isa 66:15; cf. 2 Kgs 2:11; Zech 6:1–8) to the cavalry of Revelation's day (mounted riders; Rev 19:14). Perhaps today's imagery would be closer to fighter jets.

Likewise, Revelation adapts oracles against literal Babylon (e.g., Isa 21:9; 47:7–9; Jer 51:6–14) to apply them to Rome (Rev 18:2–8). This transference was logical because for Jewish people Rome constituted the Babylon-type empire of its day—what Jewish interpreters of the day construed as Babylon's ultimate successor among Daniel's four kingdoms (Dan 2:37–45; 7:3–14).[52] Some Jewish thinkers depicted Rome as a new Babylon,[53] since it had destroyed the temple and enslaved God's people like Babylon of old; people also *regularly* referred to Rome as a city on seven hills or mountains (Rev 17:9),[54] saw it as the city that ruled the kings of the earth (17:18),[55] the city that traded in the merchandise listed in Rev 18:12–13,[56] and so forth. Because Revelation's beast, however, blends all four of Daniel's beasts (Dan 7:3–14; Rev 13:1–7), it seems clear that John did not expect Rome to exhaust the image's significance. The spirit of evil empire outlived Rome—though it is ultimately as doomed as were Babylon and Rome (cf. 2 Thess 2:8).

Similarly, Paul applies the figure of Eve to some women in 1 Tim 2:13–14 but to the Corinthian church in 2 Cor 11:3. In 1 Tim 5:14, women ideally rule the domestic sphere, as in Greek ideals appropriate in Ephesus; in various OT passages, however, they sometimes work outside the home (Gen 29:9; Prov 31:16, 24; Song 1:6).[57]

To reduce misunderstanding as much as possible, the ideal should be to resolve linguistic issues linguistically—by translation—and contextual problems by supplying contextual knowledge.[58] We thus recontextualize by taking our hearers into the world of the text and helping them to hear it better.[59] To my thinking, the ideal resource would be a good translation with plentiful notes that supply elements of ancient culture that inform the passages yet remain otherwise foreign to modern readers.[60]

Conclusion

If we take seriously in Acts the Spirit's role of bridging cultural and ethnic divides (as argued in chapter 3), we need to heed Scripture's Spirit-inspired but concretely enculturated message and the dynamics of cross-cultural communication exemplified by Scripture itself. God contextualized his message, and we must also contextualize our interpretation for new settings, while remaining faithful to the original message. We can perform this task more adequately with input from other cultures.

CHAPTER 5

Needing Other Cultures' Input

In seeking to distinguish the permanent *message* of Scripture from its concrete cultural *applications* to its original audience, many Christians are often tempted to resort merely to our own assumptions, which are often culturally informed.[1] Western churches and denominations often even divide today over which issues are cultural and which are transcultural, although all texts, whatever transcultural points they communicate, are communicated in culturally and linguistically specific ways.

Contextualization Is Inevitable

Contextualization is necessary, and we practice it regularly. Principles applied one way in biblical cultures may be expressed in different ways in different contexts. How many of us follow biblical building codes? Deuteronomy 22:8 requires a parapet or rim around the roof lest we incur bloodguilt. Israelites could perform various activities on their flat roofs and thus were required to have protection against someone falling off and getting hurt or dying.[2] Most of us today spend little time on our roofs, but the principle of caring for our neighbors' safety and following safety protocols remains whether or not we build a parapet there.

Relating Scripture to target cultures, including our own, should also enable us to hear its message all the more graphically—hence not only its message of comfort, but sometimes also its offense. Thus, for example, so long as we do not understand the status expectations that influential members of the Corinthian church faced from their peers, we can dismiss their spiritual immaturity easily. When we understand their situation better and find analogous situations in our own settings today, however, we cannot so easily evade the text's challenges to our own prejudices and behavior.

But while contextualization is inevitable, it is possible to contextualize in ways that are inconsistent with the spirit of the original message—indeed, often to exchange contextualization for syncretism. Counterreading of texts by reading them in the wrong context creates a new problem. Reading Scripture in the way that they had learned, Paul's rivals in Galatia mixed their own culture up with the gospel. When they went so far as to impose this mixture on believers in another culture, Paul resisted their approach as heretical.

The history of modern missions includes abundant cases of cross-cultural mishaps. For example, nineteenth-century Western missionaries tried to impose a covering for women's breasts in one culture; by ignoring the covering's function as a status marker they provoked social unrest.[3] Elsewhere the same missionary concern with covering skin deeply wounded the spirits of some Christians using a culturally indigenous way to express their faith.[4]

Culture Shapes What We Think Is Cultural

These questions can arise in any culture. When I was teaching a course at the University of Jos in Plateau State, Nigeria, some students believed that the Bible commands women in all cultures to wear head coverings in church. Yet they laughed when I asked why none of them had greeted me with a holy kiss, commanded even more often in the Bible (Rom 16:16; 1 Cor 16:20; 2 Cor 13:12; 1 Thess 5:26; 1 Pet 5:14).[5]

Kisses did not function as a form of greeting in their culture, whereas head coverings functioned as markers of gender and modesty in their culture. As we explored the issues of sexual modesty, ostentation, and class conflict in the text, however, most students recognized that the principles in the text went far beyond head coverings. Wearing head coverings was appropriate in their setting, but would not function the same way in all settings; some students complained that some other people even used head coverings ostentatiously or to attract cross-gender attention at times.

A friend from Indonesia noted that when she first began driving in the United States, driving the way she was accustomed to drive in Jakarta, she thought that Americans were waving at her in a friendly manner. She was not yet aware that displaying the middle finger was an obscene gesture here. Displaying the middle finger was also inappropriate in ancient Greece,[6] but not necessarily for the same reasons, so both Indonesians and North Americans would intuitively misconstrue the point of such a signal in a classical text.

Some African friends have expressed surprise to learn that their cultures' traditional customs of bridewealth and family-arranged marriages are more like the Jewish marriage arrangements of Jesus's day than are expensive church weddings and wedding rings.[7] This insight proved valuable because some African Christians were living together for years while saving money for a church wedding. In this case, the problematic custom was partly imported by Western missionaries who assumed that their cultures' customs were de facto Christian.

Almost everyone today recognizes that at least some texts address local situations. Most Christians, for example, do not set aside money every Sunday to send to the church in Jerusalem (1 Cor 16:1–3). Still fewer have gone to Troas to try to find Paul's cloak and take it to him (2 Tim 4:13). But texts have cultural and often situational contexts even when the case is not so obvious. When we do not pay attention to biblical texts' original cultural setting, we intuitively read them in light of our own; we cannot read them without any setting whatsoever filling in the blanks of the text.[8] For many readers today Jesus himself becomes no more than a "Rorschach inkblot," "standing for and legitimating whatever individuals and groups choose to do 'in his name.'"[9] Such, for example, was the Aryan Jesus of the Third Reich.[10]

As Christians, we embrace all of Scripture as God's message, but we also must recognize that it is contextualized within languages and cultures. Indeed, Christians cannot question whether God's Word could be communicated in concrete contexts that invite our consideration, for we affirm the incarnation. The ultimate contextualization is the Word that became flesh as a first-century Galilean Jewish man, in a particularity that could better identify with us in our particularities than could an impossibly generic, cultureless person.

Much of the New Testament simply reinforces the basic message of the apostolic gospel and its ethical implications, contextualizing it for a variety of concrete situations. In so doing, the New Testament writers provide us with models for how to apply their teachings in often quite different concrete situations today, whether in Nigeria, Nepal, Nicaragua, or North America.

Blind Spots

Many theological interests are contextual; but one generation's theologizing or apologetics can simply become the next generation's tradition. It is often mission and encounter with new cultures that liberate theology from captivity to theologians' cultures.[11] New cultural settings raise new questions that some-times contribute to important theological insights. This happened in biblical times as well; Scripture probably first speaks of Satan by name, for example, in texts of the Persian period. Whenever the resurrection belief[12] began, it is first articulated most explicitly in the Persian period, when the surrounding culture may have been raising for Judahites new questions about personal eschatology. New situations and interaction with surrounding cultures sometimes raise new questions that open the door for fresh divine answers, answers that sometimes resemble and sometimes resist those of the surrounding culture.

We all have cultural blind spots, and too often we are ready to remove the splinter from someone else's eye before removing the log from our own (Matt 7:3). For example, most North American evangelicals are more inclined to think of syncretism in terms of, say, east Asian ancestor veneration than in terms of worshiping both God and mammon, though Jesus explicitly deemed the latter idolatry (Matt 6:24; Luke 16:13).[13] In our culture, secularism and unbridled consumerism compete with Christian values; yet monotheism is not supposed to mean one God or less.

Similarly, some Western Christians quick to criticize allusions from Chris-tians in other cultures to local pagan traditions nevertheless tell their children about tooth fairies, an Easter bunny, divinatory traditions about seasonal ac-tivity of groundhogs, or recount tales of morally positive witches and wizards. Western Christians who are confident that they can isolate such story worlds from the sphere of faith often do not grant such expressions of confidence toward mature Christians in other cultures.

This problem is normally most acute for members of a dominant culture. Members of minority cultures have to learn about a majority culture to survive, but members of a dominant culture can live their entire lives without knowing much about minority cultures. Western Christian critiques of tribalism and ethnic strife in other parts of the world ring hollow to others who observe North American churches' frequent racial segregation and ideological sepa-ration along racial and often cultural lines.

Prioritizing Texts

Most Christians function with a de facto canon within a canon, prioritizing some texts and teachings above others.[14] Martin Luther's analogy of faith her-meneutic created a canon within the canon fairly overtly,[15] but various church traditions have functional canons all the time. Messianic Jewish believers thus, for example, rightly call Gentile Christians' attention to positive texts about the law or the Jewish people that we have historically neglected. Because of traditional Confucian values, Chinese and Korean believers rightly highlight for Westerners the values of honor and respect found in Scripture.[16] In our Western individualism, it is easy for us to neglect biblical teachings about honoring parents and those in authority; indeed, it seems almost a North American duty to criticize political leaders even when we voted for them!

At the same time, those of us shaped by the Western Jesus revival of the 1970s or by some revolutionary contexts in Latin America may contribute emphases on justice and liberation even when these emphases lead to prophetic challenges to authority. The Confessing Church in Nazi Germany and anti-apartheid Christians in South Africa rightly raised such challenges to churches subservient to demonic political ideologies. Too often Christian readings domesticate the Bible in ways acceptable to our own settings, but listening to Christians from different settings helps challenge our hermeneutical blind spots and canons within the canon. This is true whether the corrections come from studying the history of interpretation (reception history) or from global voices of living churches today. Because we are the body of Christ, we must allow each member to bring needed gifts and insights.[17]

Bible Teaching and Cultural Imperialism

None of us[18] lives in precisely the cultures first addressed in Scripture, and this limits our intuitive grasp of the language of biblical texts. Even outsiders who know a culture better than other outsiders come to it with blind spots, as may be easily illustrated from history. Historically many missionaries far surmounted the prejudices of their sending culture to identify with indigenous cultures, such as many Jesuit missionaries in East Asia, William Carey in India, or much of Hudson Taylor's China Inland Mission.[19] Even in the heyday of colonialism, European evangelical missionaries to Africa were often the least ethnocentric of the Europeans.[20]

Nevertheless, Westerners traditionally conducted missions very often from a culturally insensitive and even imperialistic standpoint.[21] Missionaries often imposed their culture, most forcefully where they supposed indigenous cultures inferior (such as in much of Africa), and sometimes conquerors introduced forms of Christianity by means of the sword (such as in much of Latin America).[22]

Such ethnocentric approaches are not unlike Paul's opponents in Galatia who demanded conformity to the sending culture's norms for the converts to be fully integrated into the people of God. Clearly Scripture condemns this behavior. Some sorts of texts readily address cultural imperialism, such as texts that provide positive models for mission (e.g., Paul in Acts)[23] or condemn negative models of mission (e.g., Paul's letter to the Galatians).[24] (Postcolonial criticism addresses some of these issues, although it offers only one facet of the voices of the global church; see Appendix B.)

Listening to other Christians today means listening to the global church. Western academics have long privileged our own readings and approaches and need to be made aware of our blind spots. At the same time, hearing Scripture as itself authoritative means that we do not privilege a reading from any one extrabiblical culture, Western or not. Believers from all cultures must do our best to gather around the text and bring our varied readings to the table to learn from one another. Some traditional academic approaches continue to have much to contribute, so long as they are humble and culturally sensitive.

Hearing Today's Global Church

By reading globally, I am not implying that any reading is as good as any other. For example, someone who understands rebirth in John's Gospel in light of Hindu reincarnation reads the texts in a way far removed from their original setting. But a Western reading should *also* not be privileged over the original setting, and reading texts together with Christians from other cultures and eras can help us all surmount some of our cultural blinders.[25]

Today interpretive communities are far more diverse than they were a century ago. As Daniel Carroll Rodas and I noted in the introduction to *Global Voices*, "Many estimate that in 1900 . . . 16.7 percent of Christians lived in Africa, Asia, and Latin America. By 2010 it was 63.2 percent, and by 2025 it will be nearly 70 percent."[26] In the past half-century, evangelicals on these continents have multiplied roughly twelve times over, and already represent more than 80 percent of evangelicals in the world, far outnumbering those in the West. This is true even though Western evangelicals continue to control a majority of evangelical theological education.[27]

Meanwhile, the Christian world has also experienced other dramatic changes, some relevant to "charismatic" or "pentecostal" readings of Scripture. "Independent" churches have been growing from 1 percent of Christians in 1900 to what may be an estimated one quarter by 2050.[28] Overlapping with this group at many points, charismatics and Pentecostals by 2050 will likely constitute one-third of Christians and 11 percent of the global population.[29] Addressing the future of global Christianity, Moonjang Lee notes, "The growing churches in the non-Western world are mostly Pentecostal-Charismatic, as seen in the Pentecostal movements in Latin America, Independent Churches in Africa, and Charismatic movements in Asia." Observing that Christianity is losing its traditional Western forms, Lee warns that it will need to fully recover its early charismatic character to survive and flourish.[30]

Mainline historian Robert Bruce Mullin observes that already by the end of the twentieth century, there were "more Pentecostals worldwide" than mainline Protestants.[31] Sociologist Peter Berger contends that Pentecostalism, presumably in the broad sense, "accounts for something like 80 percent of its [evangelical Protestantism's] worldwide growth."[32] Although such claims actually include an amorphous array of groups in their figure, it remains significant that many estimate nearly half a billion charismatics worldwide; a recent article in the *International Bulletin of Missionary Research* even estimates 614 million.[33] If such estimates are even close to accurate, the charismatic branch of Christendom is now second in size in Christendom only to Roman Catholicism (with which it overlaps).

As the center of world Christianity has shifted to the Global South, the dominant Christian perspectives in the world have shifted with it.[34] This shift has important implications for the task of biblical interpretation for the church.[35] The interests of mid-twentieth-century Western biblical scholarship are no longer the issues of most of the global church. The mushrooming church in the Majority World is in desperate need of more biblical scholarship, but it must be a biblical scholarship in touch with the genuine issues confronted by the global church. The median Christian today is a young woman with limited education from the Global South, whose interests may well lie more with understanding biblical narrative than with parsing the details of *Formgeschichte*.[36]

Traditional historical-critical methods are not without value, and I emphasize them myself when addressing historical questions.[37] It is simply that they focus on historical questions rather than preaching or theological ones; they are methods designed for one sort of goal rather than for other sorts of goals.[38] Nevertheless, the hegemony of such methods, or whatever other approach constructed for a particular setting, can become coercive yet irrelevant when promulgated as "the true scholarship" in settings for which they were not designed. Whatever latest critical methodology the professor has learned (sometimes in long-finished doctoral work) is often taught to students as the best way to do scholarship, and then exported into contexts all over the world where those issues are usually irrelevant to the lives of the churches.[39] Following R. S. Sugirtharajah, postcolonial exegete Davina Lopez warns that this approach has itself served as an intellectually colonizing activity.[40]

Extreme historical criticism's undue speculation further compounds irrelevance; Hans Frei of Yale Divinity School emphasized, as Richard Hays puts it, "that the message of the Gospels is first of all to be found" in what the Gospels say about Jesus, "not in a speculative reconstruction of events or communities behind the text."[41] Another frequent challenge is the a priori exclusion of the supernatural from the older sort of historical criticism, which has often followed David Friedrich Strauss (1808–1874) in valuing the text for its psychological component while stripping it of any "unhistorical" supernaturalist elements.[42]

Keep in mind that I am not referring to simply reading Scripture in its historical context, which we *must* do if we are to be consistent in genuine cross-cultural listening, as suggested above. If we affirm hearing the global church in its contexts, we are grossly inconsistent to deny the same privilege to the voices that we deem canonical. Reactions against historical criticism's preoccupation with sources (often hypothetical) are thus no excuse to reject concern for a text's historical *context*,[43] a concern that long predated modern apologetic and critical concerns. Claiming that background is not helpful for understanding texts designed for a different historical setting is analogous to expecting English readers to appreciate Greek and Hebrew biblical manuscripts without translation.[44]

The critics remain correct, however, that many of our traditional critical methods were designed to answer questions that prevail or prevailed in particular contexts (e.g., addressed to Enlightenment skepticism). Such questions remain valuable in their appropriate contexts, but other concerns take priority for believers in other contexts. One earlier Chinese church leader, for example, warned that some Western Christians' theological acumen would benefit them little in his country "if when the need arose you could not cast out a demon."[45] One reason that scholars have pursued a distinctively pentecostal hermeneutic is the desire to escape "unbridled rationalism," which has tended toward a spiritual dead end in the church's use of Scripture.[46]

Moreover, as noted above, some non-Western readings are from cultures with values more like those directly addressed in Scripture, and these cultures sometimes therefore ask questions more like the questions that the authors of Scripture were directly answering. Thus, for example, when my wife Médine and I first studied Genesis together, I contributed insights on some passages from my literary knowledge of ancient Near Eastern sources. Médine, however, contributed more insights in the patriarchal narratives based on her intuitive grasp of pastoral cultures. Similarly, the unusual births that I found so strange in Genesis were in fact not unfamiliar in her culture.

Those raised in rural Middle Eastern cultures might be able to answer still more precisely many of my interpretive questions about Genesis (e.g., in 21:23–24, when Abraham agrees to repay Abimelech's treatment of him, might this function ironically on a larger narrative level?)[47] At this point I feel competent in answering most NT questions from my knowledge of Greco-Roman antiquity, but even my cross-cultural sensitivity often leaves me with more questions than answers for the OT. If I lack decisive information regarding the specific ancient setting, the more varied cultural interpretive options I can get on the table alongside my own, the better.

Taking into account interpretations from a wider range of backgrounds is helpful because our experience often shapes or expands our range of interpretive options. Before I became part of the Black Church, I merely wished that Scripture addressed ethnic reconciliation. Once the question became an existential one for me, however, I began considering how Jewish-Samaritan and Jewish-Gentile issues in the New Testament provided many potential concrete models for reconciliation. There were differences, of course, but also helpful analogies: if God summoned his people to surmount an ethnic and cultural barrier that he himself established in history, how much more would he summon us to surmount all others?[48] If my new experience was a sort of "bias," was my previous inexperience any less so?

Brief Excursus on Method

Welcoming a multicultural range of perspectives to the table checks biases far better than welcoming only a single perspective, but the ideal is that, once at the table, dialogue can help all of us to hear more clearly not simply ourselves or even (more helpfully) one another but the biblical text and how it speaks to our various situations.

Insofar as hearing the message of the authoritative text remains our objective, we should keep in mind the historical context of some of our approaches and the risks they carry of aborting our achievement of this objective. I introduce some of these risks here, since concerns regarding them inform subsequent portions of the book, but develop the question further in Part III (with what I believe are some supporting reasons for my approach in Parts IV and V). They remain a special danger in tandem with the potential for subjectivity and competing, autonomous readings in Spirit hermeneutics.

Some hermeneutical approaches have tried to make more room for the interpreter's horizon in interpretation than earlier methods welcomed (see further Appendix A and B). Sometimes, however, they obliterated the first horizon in doing so. The formalist claim that a text can mean something autonomous from what its author meant should have given more attention to the generative sociolinguistic setting in which the text first communicated or evoked some meaning. Unfortunately, many thinkers instead developed this autonomy even further.

Deconstructionists posited that the range of possible meanings of texts was virtually unlimited, given the range of possible contexts in which to read them.[49] This is where the new criticism ultimately led. Others challenged the significance of deconstructionist approaches; language may be imperfect without being wholly inadequate.[50] Even deconstructionists, of course, expected their own readers to understand their basic point by recognizing the historically developed and culturally conditioned function of the alphabetic symbols, words, and media of communication in which their views were encoded.[51]

Reader-response critics followed deconstructionists by observing the ways that texts are read in different settings.[52] As a descriptive tool, reader-response criticism that identifies different interpretations in different interpretive communities can be helpful, laying new questions and interpretive options on the table for consideration.[53] At the basic level, such an approach is hardly objectionable: readers who consult commentaries lay various opinions on the table, and drawing insights from a wider range of cultures merely enriches our options.[54]

But reader-response criticism has been used in other ways.[55] Many critics have located meaning in the heads of interpretive communities. Interpretation thus becomes a political act, prescribing meaning for communities; its success rests not with correspondence to implied communicators' interests, but with interpreters' social or political power. Most communication and aesthetic literary artifice thus deconstruct into propaganda to achieve the interpreter's ends; critical readers now become those who resist implied authors' persuasive strategies and instead exploit or even manipulate texts for the readers' own goals.

That language is often used politically is clear. But when reader-response criticism moves from its descriptive role to a prescriptive one, it ranks some meanings as more authoritative for a community than others, except that the new authority lies in the interpreter, the head of the interpretive community, or in the socially constructed values or politics favored by the interpreter.

The descriptive approach is valuable by bringing all voices to the table; the prescriptive approach, however, raises questions for those who seek to hear the text as God's word. Granted, people often use texts to promote their own agendas; certainly biblical texts are quite often used that way. This descriptive observation is not, however, an invitation to us to simply exploit texts more effectively than others for our supposedly better causes (since we no longer have any concrete canonical basis for preferring some causes over others). If we have the Spirit, do we really need to control politically the reading of texts in God's community, the church, where the least should be the greatest? Is it the voice of the most powerful interpreters or the divine Author's voice for which we relentlessly pursue the canonical texts?

We recognize (descriptively) the reality of social power dynamics in influencing interpretation, a reality that confronts us on both popular and academic levels. But we resist these not first of all by establishing our own following (so perpetuating abusive power dynamics) but by seeking to hear the biblical texts in ways faithful to their first contexts, ways that analogously challenge us afresh in our own contexts, and helping others to read faithfully for their own contexts as well.[56] The common basis for discussion that readers from various vantage points share is the text and (as best as we can reconstruct it) how that text would have been heard by the audience for which its author(s) constructed it with ancient vocabulary, idioms, and cultural assumptions. (On this point, see further Part III.)

Conclusion

Each culture has contributions to make as well as some blind spots; dominant cultures tend to be blinder culturally because they alone have had freedom to function without attention to other voices. Our ultimate goal should not be any single group's hegemony, but conversation, engaged in the loving and humble spirit of Christ. Given the global dissemination of movements of God's Spirit today, and especially given the biblical model of Pentecost, a true Spirit hermeneutic today must be one that considers a range of concrete contextualizations. When executed optimally, contextualizations also help us better identify with how the biblical texts confronted their first audiences.

We must listen critically, with believers from all cultures tethered to the same canon that binds us together. Yet we should also recognize that particular sorts of experiences of believers in some settings are closer to those assumed in the biblical texts than are others. On some points, Majority World churches are ready to teach Western Christians lessons that our own heritage once knew but has long forgotten.[57]

CHAPTER 6

Some Valuable Majority World Insights

In principle, many of us are willing to learn from believers in a range of cultures. But what happens when their input challenges centuries-old assumptions in our own cultures? We are not obligated to abandon our assumptions uncritically, but often believers from other cultures can help us in the areas where our assumptions reflect cultural blind spots. Some cultures understand biblical principles of hospitality, courage, sacrifice and faith much better than does most of our Western culture at this time in history.

Here I summarize two sample areas where believers in many parts of the world may help the Western church and Western seminaries challenge traditional modern Western materialistic monism: the issues of spirits and miracles. Not everything that all believers say in these contexts is compatible with biblical revelation, but much of it poses a potent challenge to the typical Western academic dismissal of these notions.

Case Study I: Spirits[1]

Missionary anthropologist Paul Hiebert notes that Christians in India addressed a cultural blind spot that he carried: his scientific training stressed a naturalistic, empirical approach; his theological training emphasized theistic explanations. But he had lacked a functional category for superhuman activity other than that of the supreme God, despite its prevalence in parts of Scripture as well as many cultures' belief in it. In recent centuries, Western thought had left no intermediate category between God and the natural world, but in his dialogue with Indian Christians he came to believe that such a sphere existed.[2]

There are dangers of seeing spirits more pervasively than Scripture warrants; it should be noted that cultures that believe in possession by a spirit are more likely to generate more cases of the phenomenon so interpreted.[3] Still, one suspects that most Western Christians probably recognize spiritual realities far less than Scripture suggests.

Global Experiences concerning Spirits

John Pilch suggests that 90 percent of the world today accepts both "ordinary reality and non-ordinary reality," the latter including God and spirits.[4] Further, anthropologist Erika Bourguignon points out that belief in spirit possession is widespread in varied cultures around the world, "as any reader of ethnographies knows."[5] Already four decades ago she could attest spirit-possession beliefs in nearly three-quarters of representative societies studied;[6] some subsequent studies speak of altered states of consciousness in some 90 percent of societies.[7] Diverse cultures offer an array of different interpretive matrixes for these experiences,[8] although their experiences often do produce some similar beliefs even in very different societies.[9]

Many early-twentieth-century Presbyterian missionaries to Korea learned in seminary that spirits were not real, but most came to believe otherwise in the context of ministry alongside local Korean believers.[10] A generation ago noted Western missiologist Stephen Neill warned that it was next to impossible to convince most Majority World Christians "that evil spirits do not exist."[11] More recently, Peruvian missiologist Samuel Escobar reports a conversation with an indigenous teacher from the Peruvian jungle. When local people noticed demons in the Western linguist's translation of Mark, the Western linguist explained that such spirits were only for the first century. While the local teacher respected the linguist, however, he insisted that their local environment matched better what they found in Mark's Gospel: "we know that there really are demons and spirits; they're around here."[12]

African scholar John S. Mbiti dismisses the ignorance of Westerners who deny spirits and witchcraft, which are local realities.[13] Africans often report encounters with spirits as genuine experiences. A Ghanaian physician trained in the West, for example, found his arm paralyzed by electricity for a few hours after touching a patient who had been to "fetish priests."[14] Power encounters have often sparked church growth; thus tens of thousands of followers of traditional religions became Christians after early-twentieth-century African figures such as Garrick Sokari Braide or William Wadé Harris contested the older spiritual powers.[15] Such power encounters are widely reported in the spread of Christianity elsewhere, such as in Haiti, India, and the Philippines.[16] In many cases such power encounters have even led to priests of traditional religions becoming Christians.[17]

Not surprisingly, such experiences influence how believers approach what they view as analogous accounts in the biblical text.[18] In one African theological journal a Tanzanian Lutheran writer notes, "the phenomenon of demon possession is a hard reality with which a good number of East African Christians struggle daily." In contrast to Westerners, East Africans thus hear "the biblical accounts . . . not as myths, but as objective accounts of actual experiences."[19]

Western Academic vs. Indigenous Interpretations

Paul Stoller, an anthropologist working among Songhay Muslims, was warned that he would face an attack of sorcery; that night he felt pressed down by a suffocating weight and heard threatening creatures on his roof. The affliction stopped only when he recalled the locally prescribed cure (reciting some Qur'anic verses). This experience changed his perspective; indigenous understandings rather than his anthropological training enabled him to cope with the local reality.[20] Publication of his experience initially stirred controversy and disdain from some peers, though it eventually led to accolades.[21]

Likewise, Solon Kimball, a noted anthropologist,[22] notes his own completely unexpected experience of encountering an apparition during his fieldwork in Ireland.[23] He learned only afterward that many local people had encountered the same figure.[24] Anthropologist Edith Turner confesses that "anthropology marveled briefly at Solon Kimball's ghost story," but then neglected its implications until other such stories began to be published.[25] Turner herself became a believer in genuine spirits in 1985 when she witnessed what she calls "spirit substance" ejected from a patient during a Zambian spirit ritual.[26] From a pro-shamanist perspective, she now rejects her former dismissal of spirits as cultural imperialism.[27] She complains that some academics "believe that trained anthropologists . . . understand aspects of a culture" better than people from that culture.[28]

Anthropologists today often try to study experiences with alleged spirits from societies' indigenous perspectives, rather than imposing a Western interpretive grid on them.[29] In contrast to theologians and parapsychologists, most anthropologists seek to study not spiritual phenomena but indigenous *beliefs* about spirits.[30] Thus one study offers as a working definition of spirit possession "*any altered state of consciousness indigenously interpreted in terms of the influence of an alien spirit.*"[31] More recent studies work harder than most of their predecessors to take into account the indigenous frame of reference;[32] while traditional Western categories, often from a medical perspective, make cross-cultural comparison easier, more contextualized and phenomenological approaches prove more epistemologically open.[33]

Yet the approaches of anthropologists, psychiatrists, psychologists, and indigenous interpreters often vary considerably from one another.[34] Even in the West, there is no unanimity regarding the meaning of possession experiences. Thus, for example, anthropologists have criticized psychologists and psychiatrists for ethnocentric understandings of altered states of consciousness, whereas others have criticized anthropologists' limited competence in psychological and psychiatric matters.[35] Although reports from a range of sources provide valuable data, interpreting the data is often a matter of worldview. In many cases, indigenous approaches prove closer to the deliverance narratives of the Gospels than do Western materialist interpretations.[36]

Witchcraft

Despite frequent abuses and exaggerations,[37] some people in many African societies do seek to practice malevolent sorcery, as is inevitable in cultures that believe in sorcery.[38] Whatever the actual degree of efficacy, practitioners themselves, and often most of the culture, believe in their efficacy.[39] Despite the stigma in many places, some confessions of murder by sorcery appear in various societies.[40] One Western lecturer, after having denied the existence of witches, was corrected by an African student who noted that he was a witch and believed that he had an effective record of killing people through witchcraft.[41] Many others believe that witchcraft in their context kills.[42] Voodoo deaths, associated with spirits, are a real phenomenon,[43] though Western observers, usually seeking psychological rather than spiritual explanations, typically associate them with terror.[44]

Western missionaries from desupernaturalized Europe, which had declared belief in witchcraft heretical because of its own earlier excesses, often taught ideas unworkable for an African context.[45] Local people often mistrusted traditional missionaries because the latter ignored sorcery.[46] Indeed, witchcraft beliefs fulfill roles within societies that if unaddressed by newer religious cultures can persist and grow.[47]

Although harmful use of spiritual power may take different forms in different contexts, not all of which actually exercise the same degree of power, improper local accusations and responses to accusations may lead Westerners to too readily dismiss *all* indigenous beliefs about witchcraft. Negative spiritual power and sometimes power encounters with its practitioners appears in a number of biblical texts (including Exod 7:10–12; Matt 24:24; Mark 13:22; Acts 8:9–13; 13:8–12; 19:11–20; 2 Thess 2:9; Rev 13:13); the early centuries of Christianity include often still more elaborate stories of power encounters.

My own views on the subject were forced to shift after an unexpected and worldview-shattering experience of power related to traditional African curses in December of 2008.[48] Cognitive dissonance between my experience and my theological understanding of personal evil's power persisted until, two or three years after the publication of *Miracles,* I was reading Job in Hebrew and realized that my worldview had previously simply blinded me to what was already clear in the biblical text.[49]

Case Study II: Miracles[50]

Many Westerners doubt the possibility of miracles, an issue of no little importance for biblical studies, where, for example, some 30 percent of our earliest Gospel involves miracles and exorcisms.[51] Likewise, Western scholars who normally condemn allegorization sometimes welcome only spiritual applications of healing narratives. Although the Gospel writers do offer spiritual applications, it is doubtful that they intended *exclusively* spiritual applications.[52] One need only consider testimonies posted in sanctuaries of Asclepius to recall that a significant point of recounting testimonies was to encourage supplicants to have faith for their own needs, naturally including physical ones.

Some Western Christians made invaluable contributions to the world's improvement during the early English Enlightenment, especially through experimental science.[53] Nevertheless, strands of the radical Enlightenment created false dichotomies that remain with the West to this day. These remain a mainly Western issue. Invited to lecture in 2015 to hundreds of theological students in Indonesia in connection with my *Miracles* book, my suspicion was quickly confirmed that defense of the reality of the supernatural was of very limited value; of much greater interest was how to distinguish divine activity from that generated by other spirits. Unfortunately for myself as a lecturer, I probably had less experience and expertise on that level than did many of my hosts.

Sympathy vs. Antipathy

Western scholars often read biblical miracle texts unsympathetically or even with embarrassment. This is unfortunate, since, as Geza Vermes points out in a different connection, "Religious writings disclose their meaning only to those who approach them in a spirit of sympathy."[54] There is of course a place for academic attempts to construct detached readings for the purpose of allowing cross-cultural comparisons; even the etic categories designed for such comparisons, however, inevitably reflect particular cultural assumptions. Emic readings based on indigenous understandings often provide clearer insight into the thinking of a culture, although less handy rubrics for comparative evaluation among cultures.

The degree of probability assigned to miracles depends on one's prior assumptions.[55] A theistic reading of evidence here will differ from a deistic or atheistic one. On atheistic premises, miracles are implausible; on theistic premises, one expects them at least on occasion. By a priori excluding the consideration of a god who can act in nature, Hume prejudges the outcome of his inquiry against miracles.[56] A neutral starting point would not presuppose the action or inaction of a deity,[57] but Hume simply presupposes divine inaction.[58]

If on other grounds one has reason to affirm theism,[59] then what we call miracles might even be expected;[60] miracles are against the *ordinary* observed course of nature, but that is their *point*.[61] We might expect such unusual acts to occur at times, especially in particular settings that involve the message that this God seeks to communicate.[62] Thus many scholars consider the religious and theological context when evaluating miracle claims,[63] a position that has a long pedigree.[64] Indeed, if one allows for a deity who acts purposefully, then, as retired Oxford professor Keith Ward puts it, "it will be unreasonable not to accept reliable testimony" for miracles.[65]

Western skepticism toward miracles was heavily shaped by an influential essay of David Hume that most philosophers today regard as circularly argued.[66] The most relevant point for the present discussion is that one of Hume's key arguments is explicitly ethnocentric, rejecting all testimony from nonwhites and non-Western cultures, which Hume dismissed as "ignorant and barbarous."[67] Hume's racism is well-documented, and it plays a significant role in his argument against miracles.[68] (His ethnocentrism included anti-Semitism, thus prejudice against ancient Jewish civilization.)[69]

Yet medical anthropology now rejects "medicocentrism," the ethnocentric view that only current Western views of sickness and healing are authentic and that disputes the many claims to cures outside Western views.[70] Medical anthropology is a burgeoning field that has generated vast scholarship.[71] It also offers promise for biblical scholars; medical anthropology, John Pilch argues, "could help the exegete to adopt a transcultural stance"[72] when addressing healing claims in the NT.

Widespread Experiences

Social scientists have noted that, despite a variety of interpretations, "people from all cultures relate stories of spontaneous, miraculous cures," based on their experiences.[73] In addition to differing in their paradigms involving paranormal phenomena, many other cultures are in general more holistic than conventional Western culture, expecting spiritual beliefs to impinge on physical needs in ways that Western culture has often found uncomfortable.[74]

Results from a recent Pew survey of Pentecostals and charismatics suggest that even in just the ten countries that Pew surveyed, some two hundred million Pentecostals and charismatics claim to have witnessed divine healing.[75] Although a large proportion of mainline Christians in the Majority World fit the broad Western definition of charismatic,[76] such beliefs and practices are not limited to Pentecostals and charismatics. In the same Pew survey, more than one-third of Christians worldwide who do *not* identify themselves as Pentecostal or charismatic claim not simply to believe in healing but to have "witnessed divine healings."[77] However we construe many of these experiences, the number is certainly too high to accommodate Hume's default claim of no reliable witnesses as a starting point for discussion—a position that in its traditional form is, despite its many vocal supporters, simply untenable today.

Western scholar of global Christianity Philip Jenkins notes that in general Christianity in the Global South is quite interested in "the immediate workings of the supernatural, through prophecy, visions, ecstatic utterances, and healing."[78] Historian Mark Noll observes that Western Christians working in the Majority World "consistently report that most Christian experience reflects a much stronger supernatural awareness than is characteristic of even charismatic and Pentecostal circles in the West."[79]

Reading Miracles with the Global Church

The above observations have some relevance for how we approach biblical narratives involving healings. Kenneth Archer, explaining the value of a Pentecostal hermeneutic, notes, "The essence of Pentecostalism is its persistent emphasis upon the supernatual within the community."[80] This approach not surprisingly resonates with the majority of the world's cultures.

Readings of Scripture in the Global South often contrast starkly with modern Western critics' readings.[81] Thus a Western writer with experience in Africa suggests that African culture offers better foundations for understanding biblical texts addressing such issues.[82] Ghanaian theologian Kwabena Asamoah-Gyadu notes that African Christians emphasize God's power to act in ways that Western theologians too often restrict only to science.[83]

Most Christians in the Majority World, less shaped by the modern Western tradition of the radical Enlightenment, find stories of miraculous phenomena far less objectionable than do their Western counterparts.[84] These other cultures offer a check on traditional Western assumptions; as Lamin Sanneh, professor of missions and history at Yale Divinity School, points out, it is here that Western culture "can encounter . . . the gospel as it is being embraced by societies that had not been shaped by the Enlightenment," and are thus closer to the milieu of earliest Christianity.[85]

Western missionaries to one region in Africa who merely left behind Gospels reportedly returned to find a flourishing church with NT-like miracles happening daily, "because there had been no missionaries to teach that such things were not to be taken literally."[86] Indigenous readings of Scripture often noticed patterns there "that the missionaries did not want [local believers] to see."[87]

Thus, for example, one anthropologist recounts the experience of a fellow anthropologist named Jacob Loewen, who was doing Bible translation among the Choco people in Panama.[88] The wife of his host, Aureliano, was dying, and medicine was unavailable. While Loewen had translated the promise of healing in Jas 5:14–15, he felt that he lacked faith to pray. Nevertheless, reading this passage, the local believers prayed with him for her healing, and she rallied slightly. By the next morning, however, she was dying again, so the local believers anointed her with oil, without inviting Loewen, and this time she rose from the bed completely well. When Aureliano declared happily that God's Spirit had chased away the fever spirits, Loewen observed that they had not invited him and his Western colleague to pray this time. Aureliano apologized but noted, "It doesn't work when you and David are in the circle. You and David don't really believe." Loewen was a devoted Christian, yet found "himself unable to transcend the secular assumptions and understandings of his particular birth society."[89]

95

Challenging Western Skepticism about Miracles

By its own honor-shame conventions, the academy as a community of interpretation can exert no less pressure for conformity on its members than the ecclesiastical dogmas it once sought to replace.[90] Although encouraging individualistic approaches in some ways, in others members fear to contradict it, such as when some academicians have confided to me in hushed tones that they actually believe in miracles or spirits. In the Western academic worldview, everything may be subjected to critique except its own starting assumptions.[91] Thus students remain indoctrinated in traditional approaches until paradigm shifts offer new approaches, generally themselves adopted by new generations of students without critical evaluation of their underlying epistemic principles. Because belief in God is, unlike some controversial topics, excluded by the epistemic and thus methodological constraints of many disciplines, it cannot be openly discussed in those disciplines.

Cross-cultural studies suggest that socialization rather than exposure to science accounts for most of the skepticism in some circles.[92] African psychologist Regina Eya warns that all claims to extranormal healing are dismissed by many Western scholars, the credible along with the spurious, because of the inappropriate application of traditional Western scientific paradigms to matters for which they were not designed.[93]

David Friedrich Strauss was the driving force behind viewing the Gospels as late and drawing on myths and legends because they included miracle stories. Yet he was so controlled by his ontohermeneutical presuppositions that when someone he *knew* was apparently cured via the ministry of German Lutheran pastor Johann Christoph Blumhardt, Strauss explained the previous condition as psychosomatic, despite contrary medical opinion.[94] That the cure was a legend that developed over generations, however, he could not assert. Rudolf Bultmann (1884–1976), on the other hand, lived a generation after Blumhardt (1805–1880), and so felt more free to dismiss the mere "legends" about him.[95] (Karl Barth, conversely, defended Blumhardt and considered him a mentor.)[96] Today extant, firsthand sources about Blumhardt overwhelmingly show that these reports were not legends.[97] Why was Bultmann so adamant?

As Justo González remarks in his commentary on Acts, the frequent denial of narratives' historicity because of their miracle reports employs a questionable epistemological criterion. Bultmann denied that modern people who use scientific inventions such as the wireless can believe in miracles,[98] yet "what Bultmann declares to be impossible is not just possible, but even frequent." Miracles are, González points out, affirmed in most Latino churches, despite the influence of the mechanistic worldview from much Western thought.[99] Cuban Lutheran bishop Ismael Laborde Figueras notes that it is hard to find Latin American Christians who do not believe in miracles.[100]

Some Asian theologians have likewise complained that the approach of Bultmann's school is irrelevant to Asian realities. The retired Methodist bishop of Malaysia, Hwa Yung, notes that Asian worldviews affirm miracles, angels, and hostile spirits.[101] It is actually the Western, mechanistic, naturalistic Enlightenment worldview that is culturally and historically idiosyncratic.[102]

Conclusion

Western interpreters have often accumulated historical insights helpful for reading Scripture, insights that, when properly evaluated and applied, should become property of the whole global church. Likewise, some cases where most Western interpreters may learn from many Majority World believers include the latter's more common experiences with spirits, miracles, poverty, injustice, and so forth. (Some of these issues are also prominent among minority-culture Christians in the Western church.) In many of these cases, global Christianity hears the Spirit in the biblical text more faithfully than do many Western exegetes.[103] The relative strengths and weaknesses of different parts of the global church will shift over time as we grow together, so long as we are all humble enough to learn from one another.

Because of our cultural blind spots, we all need one another's help to hear Scripture fully. This is work for the entire global body of Christ, each culture bringing the contributions we are currently best equipped to contribute while also learning from others. The long-term hegemony of Western interpreters often yields less humility, and thus greater blind spots, but all of us may learn from one another. This is also the best way to forestall potential future hegemonies of different kinds.

We cannot understand the message of the inspired authors apart from the social and linguistic contexts in which they communicated; the message came to us already concretely enculturated. Neither can we fully engage or communicate their message, however, without grasping how it can engage us in our various cultures today. Scripture's principles will be illustrated and reapplied in diverse ways in different cultures who hear and enculturate its message afresh.

Both aspects are consistent with Spirit-led biblical interpretation in Acts 2, where Peter applies Scripture to his hearers. Areas where believers hear the Spirit in many cultures today, such as on miracles and deliverance, are also consistent with what we see lived out in the book of Acts. Such insights and interests match well what we might expect for a Spirit-filled hermeneutic. That is because looking at Scripture through the lens of God's own heart invites us to see there God's concern for *people* and their needs, and how God can empower us to help meet those needs.

PART III

CONNECTION WITH THE DESIGNED SENSE

Global readings (Part II) show us the important role that culture plays in interpretation. If we want to fully hear someone, we must hear them in their cultural context. Yet God inspired Scripture itself in particular cultural contexts. Modern readers are increasingly alienated from the world of the Bible, in particular the seminomadic pastoral culture of the patriarchs, the poetry of Israel's prophetic books, and so forth. Today some peoples least equipped to read the Bible in terms of basic reading skills are best equipped to understand it culturally. By contrast, many who are highly literate in reading our own languages are culturally *illiterate* in understanding many events, customs, and clusters of thought in Scripture.

If we had not guessed otherwise, the incarnation would show us that history and historical particularity matter. It is important for me to address in this book issues of original meaning[1] because some interpreters, in the *name* of "Pentecostal hermeneutics," have played down original meaning's value. Others have simply taken it for granted and emphasized the Spirit's role in engaging the modern reader with the text (as I have done to some extent earlier in this book), but with the unfortunate consequence that their readers have sometimes assumed that original context is dispensable.

Observing the designed sense, or what we might call the sense projected by the ideal author or at least the ancient cultural sense, is a vital and foundational objective for interpreting Scripture. Analogously, understanding a building's design, including in the context of contemporary architectural agendas, engineering limitations, local building codes, and other relevant data, can help us reconstruct many relevant interests of the implied architect.[2]

Something's design also is ideally consistent with its planned function, suggesting in turn its greatest spheres of usefulness. A commonly cited example is that of the hammer: one can employ it as a weapon, a doorstop, or a prop, but the specific design of the handle, face, and claws fits its designed function in pounding in and removing nails. The goals for which texts were designed point us toward the uses for which they will usually be most relevant. We cannot infallibly recover an author's thought processes; we can, however, seek to recognize the "implied author's" design in the text.[3]

CHAPTER 7

The Measuring Stick

Once when I was a pastor a visitor explained that after forty days of fasting he had achieved a particular eschatological view: pretribulational Christians would escape the tribulation, while posttribulational Christians would stay behind to evangelize during it. Although I was duly impressed with his dietary sacrifice, which undoubtedly offered many other spiritual benefits, I found his eschatological approach untenable based on the context of the verses in question. Too young to be diplomatic, I retorted that even forty days of fasting would not coerce from the Holy Spirit something that contradicted the biblical text that the Spirit had already inspired.

Although the first two sections of the book highlighted readers' engagement with the biblical text, Part III warns against what I believe is a dangerous overreaction against texts' ancient sense. Some sorts of churches have emphasized only the rational elements of Christian faith to the exclusion of others. Most of us who have spent many years in Pentecostal or charismatic churches, however, have witnessed some excesses in the other direction.

The Shape of the Canonical Documents

Insofar as we believe that God has spoken to us in Scripture, we should pay careful attention to the Scripture that God gave us, not the sort of Scripture we want God to have given us. As Craig Bartholomew, a leading theological interpreter of Scripture, rightly warns, "The text as the instantiation of a communication event comes into existence at a certain historical point: in all its synchronicity, it is embedded in history, and it is crucial that this historical aspect of the text be taken seriously in interpretation."[4]

God did not send Scripture to us in some random way, but in particular languages, cultures, and genres normally already accessible to the first audiences. The message came to us already contextualized, so if we wish to hear it fully, we must hear it first in the shape in which God provided it. Had God spoken to us most directly in a multicultural language of, for example, sparrows' chirping, we would invest considerable time in deciphering their chirps. Had God spoken through radio waves, we would invest in researching radio waves. So if God has spoken in some ancient Near Eastern narrative genres, we should learn those genres. If God has spoken through genres such as letters to particular congregations, we should try to hear what God inspired his servants to say to those congregations.

Some preachers are more committed to evoking particular audience responses than to hearing God's message in the text. This approach pragmatically reduces Scripture to, at best, Bible memory verses as useful decorations, and, at worst, a respected text to which one may deceptively appeal for authority while ignoring its message. God provided the message in texts; therefore some principles useful for studying texts will be useful for studying the Bible. God gave us this message in specific, enculturated forms and literary contexts; respecting the Bible that God actually gave us (rather than how we in our human wisdom might assume that it should be given) therefore invites us to explore its message given in these forms and contexts. Preachers should not pretend a prophetic omniscience in areas where God expects us (with the Spirit's help) to study, even if we must rely on translations and background helps to assist us.

Interpretive Goals Dictate Methods

Different interpretive approaches sometimes address different goals, and some can be complementary. Scholars continue to debate the proper goals of interpretation. To some degree, the underlying semantic question regarding determining meaning is what we mean by "meaning." Since language is socially constructed, as part of culture, a term's definition or phrase's sense normally depends on its generally accepted usage. Otherwise we could not communicate.

Different scholars have different objectives in pursuing "meaning."[5] We can speak descriptively of how reading communities understand texts; this is a useful historical and social approach already mentioned earlier. Yet we can also seek to reconstruct, insofar as possible, how authors in a given past setting could have expected hearers (whether those apparently targeted by the work or hearers more generally in that setting) to have understood their work.

This goal is extremely relevant if we care about why the text is shaped in the particular, concrete way that it is—why we have different texts in different genres addressing different situations rather than simply one universal communication that automatically transcends culture and language. That is, why we have the Bible as literature, as texts, rather than having only the testimony of nature or of (in a nontextual way) the Spirit. We have those other testimonies, but God gave us the Bible in a different way, partly because texts were needed to preserve for us the testimony of God's specific acts in history that climax in Jesus's death and resurrection—the narration of the gospel (for Paul's summary of the gospel, see 1 Cor 15:1–4). I return to this subject later in this section, drawing briefly on relevance theory and how we read many kinds of texts as communications.

Some scholars accept the legitimacy of questions about how the earliest audiences would have understood literary works, but as simply one set of possible contexts among a potentially infinite array of valuable readings.[6] That is, some accept the question of the earliest audiences' understanding as legitimate yet ultimately of relatively marginal importance.[7]

But while chronological priority need not dictate theological priority, the very use of an ancient Mediterranean or Middle Eastern text, composed in Greek or Hebrew and presupposing particular cultural assumptions, invites our attention to the text in the contexts that generated both it and the signs it employs (insofar as these contexts can be reconstructed from the interplay between the text and what we know of antiquity). Understanding the text in its earliest general cultural context is fundamental in some sense for those subsequent readings for which a major objective remains hearing the text (again, as a collection of signs generated and most directly intelligible in a particular milieu).

This approach contrasts with some interpreters who (at the extreme) are not interested in the biblical texts as we received them (written in ancient languages and presupposing specific ancient contexts), who simply wish to exploit "canonical" texts to attach canonical status to their own readings or those of their interpretive community.[8] Such readers do not, apart from that conferred status, actually *need* these particular texts to communicate the different ideas they prefer to emphasize.[9]

Our goal in interpretation shapes the approach we will take to it; but for those for whom the earliest text is foundational (or even canonical), producing readings (however recontextualized) somehow analogous to those most plausible to the text's ideal audience[10] or at least to general first-century culture[11] will be vital, hence demands careful attention to the earliest contexts. Because discussion of ancient context is often linked to discussions of authorial intention, I will address that question before returning to the ancient context and designed sense.

Pentecostal Tradition and the Canon

For Christians, Scripture has epistemic primacy. This is evident both in Jesus's appeal to the Scriptures of his day (as an authority above tradition and arbiter of spiritual activity) and in subsequent, long-standing Christian tradition itself. Nearly all Christian movements and denominations enshrined their respect for Scripture's authority in their doctrinal statements, if it was not already assumed and demonstrated in their leaders' appeals to Scripture in their writings. They presumably have believed that their other doctrines came from Scripture.

This being the case, Scripture merits epistemic priority over, and is the optimal resource for verifying or falsifying the claims of, other doctrinal statements. Indeed, for Pentecostals to value Pentecostal tradition as an arbiter of Scripture's meaning is inconsistent with a basic impulse in early Pentecostal tradition itself: the rejection of church tradition.[12] An ahistorical American restorationism often shaped this needlessly extreme rejection, but it certainly should serve as a warning against enshrining *Pentecostal* tradition.[13]

Fundamental Truths

An example in a Pentecostal church context would be Scripture's epistemic priority over the Assemblies of God's Statement of Sixteen Fundamental Truths (not all of which are equally emphasized in practice today in Assemblies of God churches).[14] (I select the Assemblies because of my appreciative affinities there and because of lively, late-night conversations among Assemblies of God Bible college students from 1978 to 1982, but one could also examine the doctrinal commitments of Church of God or other denominations accordingly.) Pentecostal historians regularly point out that the doctrines highlighted reflect the historical context in which they were written—for example, the lengthy statement on the Trinity reflects the Oneness debate that divided early US Pentecostals. In its current form, the prologue itself notes that Scripture is "our all-sufficient rule for faith and practice," that the wording of the statement is not inspired, and that it is meant to meet the church's fundamental needs rather than to articulate all possible doctrines. The first truth articulated is that of Scripture's inspiration.

What would happen if careful biblical study led to rethinking one or more of these "fundamental truths"? Do we grant epistemic priority to the church's tradition or to what exegesis of Scripture reveals? And if the former, do we really believe the first of the fundamental truths? (My interest here is not, by the way, in challenging any particular doctrines on the list, the majority of which I in fact agree with; I raise the point simply to offer what in Pentecostal circles may provide a stark illustration.)[15] Of course, the diehard defender of any church's traditions will insist that Scripture, rightly interpreted, supports their traditions. But without careful study of Scripture such a claim is offered prematurely, and removes the canonical groundwork for dialogue with other traditions that interpret Scripture differently.

If we really grant Scripture epistemic priority, we ought not to fear seeing where inductive study of Scripture will lead us, especially if we engage in this process corporately and honestly. The Roman Catholic and Orthodox churches may have more right to want to nuance such claims, but for Protestants to get defensive about someone biblically probing their tradition is inconsistent with their own Protestant tradition.[16] Such malaise might require further Luthers to prophetically challenge them back to the Scriptures.

Luther's interest in Scripture reflected a wider rediscovery of earlier sources of the faith, and wider call for renewal, that already existed within the church of his day. At great cost, many Christians reemphasized Scripture, which they regarded as more divinely inspired than church tradition, as the foundation of their faith.[17] God forbid that, in the name of fresh renewal, we should undermine earlier renewals that God has already provided, most of which called the church back to Scripture or to some neglected biblical emphases.[18]

Charismatic Granola

While all interpretations are historically contingent, some are more helpful than others.[19] One continuationist scholar recounts his experience with a charismatic preacher who insisted that the Lord had shown him the meaning of a particular passage. The scholar had worked through this passage in Greek and warned that the preacher was dependent on an inaccurate translation. The preacher and his wife maintained that the Lord had revealed this truth to them, and that someone who could not see it lacked discernment from the Spirit. The scholar then replied that the Lord had told him that his own, contrary interpretation was correct. After a protracted silence, the minister conceded, "I guess that means the Bible means different things to different people."[20] For this minister, subjective personal revelation, rather than the original communication preserved in the biblical text, functioned as the locus of authority.

A biblically grounded Pentecostal preacher once complained of some theologically fringe Pentecostals as Pentecostal granola: the nuts, fruits, and flakes of the Spirit.[21] Some charismatic pastors have had to deal with members who have insisted that their revelations were true, even when such revelations contravened Scripture. Some Christians have gone so far as to justify adultery and other sins by appeal to a word from the Lord, when in fact their passions make it difficult for them to hear God clearly. That is not a new problem; prophets supporting indulgence in sin have long troubled God's people, requiring correction by faithful shepherds with solid discernment (Jer 6:14; 8:11; 23:14–18; 2 Tim 4:3; Rev 2:14, 20).

Sometimes we have to confront interpreters who, lacking understanding of historical or even literary context, produce interpretations wholly disconnected from the sense in the text. In such cases, these interpreters often justify their interpretations by appeal to an authority that they deem higher than the contextual sense: "You see only the literal meaning, but I have greater spiritual understanding."

Yet when God inspired the first authors of Scripture, many of them apostles and prophets, they were inspired to write with particular flows of context, using particular language and allusions to particular cultures and situations. Are we so sure that we have insights so "spiritual" that they should supplant what God inspired the first authors to mean? Paul warned some prophetically gifted Corinthian Christians, "If anybody supposes that they're a prophet or a 'spiritual' person, then let them recognize that the matters I'm writing to you are the Lord's own command" (1 Cor 14:37).

Like the false prophets of Jeremiah 23, some appear to be prophesying what the Lord has not spoken. Some new traditions of interpretation, such as secure promises of material wealth and ease, defy what God's Spirit inspired through a succession of tested prophets and other servants of God for centuries. My concern with Pentecostal hermeneutics at this point is not with the teaching of fellow scholars or others who emphasize the Spirit's role in embracing the text's message; my conflict is with those who supplant the text's message by interpretations that do not flow from it.

The Purpose of Canon

When we speak not simply of biblical books but of the *Bible* we are speaking of a canon—the collection of particular books that have proved themselves among God's people over time. A "canon" is literally a "measuring stick," what we can use to evaluate other claims to revelation.[22] I am not exploring here how the canon arose but addressing those who share the belief that the canon (or, with Luther, at least most of it) provides a way to measure theological beliefs.[23]

Evaluating Other Revelations

The full experience of the Spirit cannot appeal solely to spiritual experience irrelevant to biblical foundations. On the one hand, biblical narratives offer repeated models of believers willing to be changed by their experiences of divine encounters, as we have noted. On the other, we who look to Scripture for its models should recognize that it functions in a specially authoritative way.[24] Any prophecy today must be tested (1 Cor 14:29; 1 Thess 5:20–21), but the canon is largely by definition what has passed the test.

To say that the Bible functions canonically is not to deny the existence of other revelation.[25] It is in fact quite clear from biblical narratives themselves that revelation is not limited to the Bible. For example, Obadiah hid a hundred prophets (1 Kgs 18:13), who presumably prophesied the word of the Lord; yet their prophecies are nowhere reported in Scripture. God apparently speaks to angels (Ps 103:20), yet few of these instructions are recorded in Scripture. It is God's word that acts regularly in creation (Pss 147:15–18; 148:8),[26] yet few of these divine commands in nature are preserved for us. Jesus promises in John 16:13–15 that the Spirit will continue to speak and reveal the things of Jesus; the Spirit surely did not reveal all the things of Jesus in the New Testament, and the Spirit continues to enable us to know him.[27] If even just two or three prophets prophesied in the average first-century house church per week (1 Cor 14:29; though the average could have been higher, cf. 14:5, 24, 31), and we assume for the sake of argument an impossibly low average of merely one hundred house churches in the first century,[28] we might think of nearly a million prophecies—yet barely any of them ended up in the New Testament canon.

What then is the point of speaking of a canon? It is the minimal revelation that all of us can agree on as the "measuring stick" for testing other claims to revelation. As a young Christian I was jealous of an even younger Christian who was having visions. I had been one of the first people to teach her about hearing God's voice, but I had never had a real vision. Now as an immature peer I was competing with her rather than partnering with her so that both of us could grow. My friend, however, stubbornly insisted that she did not need to read the Bible; God spoke to her just as he spoke to people in those days, so why should she get her teaching secondhand from them? Inevitably, when her hearing erred, she did not have the theological means to get herself back on track. Somehow God used me, others, and her own common sense to bring correction to that specific error, but later, when a pastor rejected her prophetic gifting, she fell away from the faith completely.[29] I still mourn her tragic loss of faith; once intimate with God, she was one of the little ones who stumbled (Matt 18:6, 10, 14).

There were many prophets in Jeremiah's day, but among them Jeremiah stood virtually alone in announcing impending judgment. The other prophets were more popular in their day, but after Jerusalem fell their words settled into the dustbin of history. By contrast, Jeremiah's message, confirmed by its fulfillment, became part of Israel's canon. The Bible is not just any claim to revelation; it is what has stood the test of time. Our personal hearing of God is important, but God will not speak something now that contradicts what he has already spoken over centuries through tested apostles and prophets. God gave us the Bible, and provided the spiritual gift of teaching it so that we could evaluate our experiences and let Scripture direct what we do with them.

The Holy Spirit can speak through a poem, a song, and even a donkey if God wills. Yet we do not grant these personal words canonical status, and we also should not treat a message from a verse out of context as that verse's public, canonical meaning.[30] If Scripture can mean whatever a given interpreter thinks or feels, if some approximation related to the original communication is not important, then how is "Scripture" special in a way different from whatever else God uses to speak to us? Does not this relativistic approach, much as it appeals to our increasingly relativistic culture and therefore is often hailed as progressive, necessarily lead to an erosion of biblical teaching and to ideas that most Spirit-people have traditionally considered false?[31] If biblical texts can mean anything, there is no such thing as erroneous teaching, nullifying many debates in the New Testament (e.g., whether Gentiles must be circumcised), since many of the criticized sides in those debates reported in Scripture also claimed to build on prior Scripture.

Moreover, far from being a distinctively Spirit-led approach to Scripture, depending on random thoughts occuring as one reads Scripture can flourish in circles that allow God to speak to them *only* there; those for whom Scripture is no special authority have no reason to read it when they think they can hear God equally elsewhere. Those who recognize its special Spirit-inspiration, though, should hear the Spirit there by studying the text carefully in the form in which God gave it.

It hardly honors the Spirit to exalt our own untested experiences above the cumulative tested experience of the Spirit preserved in Scripture. As Pentecostal tradition has long observed, the Spirit will not contradict what he has already spoken over centuries through apostles and prophets, many of them directly affirmed or commissioned by Jesus during his earthly ministry.

Discernment

The Spirit gets blamed for too much of our indiscipline with study, sometimes substituting imagination for hearing God instead of submitting our imagination to God (Jer 23:16; Ezek 13:2, 17). Those who have been charismatics very long, at least in the United States, recognize that human error and spiritual counterfeits try to derive credibility by attaching themselves to genuine experience of the Spirit. This has normally been true of past revivals, as discerning writers of those times (such as Jonathan Edwards and John Wesley) noted.[32] Indeed, in Jeremiah's day, not only did most prophets prophesy falsely (Jer 23:9–31), but many of them wanted Jeremiah killed for speaking the truth (26:8, 11). Claims of inspiration must be tested. Not all claims to hear from God are correct; prayerful consideration of Scripture feeds into a hermeneutical circle in hearing God's voice. Scripture's message remains normative for us but must be interpreted and applied afresh to the present.

How do we distinguish the Spirit's message from counterfeit claims? Consider first the difference between *Jesus's* miracles and counterfeit ones. God's miracles have always been greater (Exod 7:12; 8:18–19), but Jesus warned of a proliferation of false signs in the eschatological time (Mark 13:22; cf. 2 Thess 2:9; Rev 13:13), i.e., now (Mark 13:5–8; 2 Thess 2:7; 1 John 2:18). *Jesus's* miracles were benevolent, mostly healings and deliverances from demonic oppression. They were only rarely destructive, and then usually for a specific reason. Jesus curses a fig tree as a prophetic warning (Mark 11:12–21), and allows pigs' destruction for the sake of rescuing a human (Mark 5:11–13).[33] Indeed, they sometimes appear the opposite of judgment miracles. John's Gospel may depict Jesus's benevolent signs in contrast to the judgment signs of Moses: the first sign is water turned to wine instead of blood (John 2:7–10; cf. Exod 7:20–21), and the last sign before the resurrection is the restoring of life rather than the killing of the firstborn (John 11:43–44; cf. Exod 12:29).[34]

Another partial tool for discernment is considering whom the miracle is designed to honor. In response to Jesus's signs many people glorified the true God (e.g., Mark 2:12; cf. Deut 13:2) and Jesus himself gave glory to his Father (John 8:49–50; 17:4). Those who seek credit for God's works as opposed to offering them freely are either spiritually immature or false prophets (cf. John 5:44; Acts 3:12; 8:9–10; 14:15). Unlike other ancient exorcists, Jesus needed no magical formulas or rituals (Matt 8:16; Mark 1:27). These characterize Jesus's works, though Jesus and his followers did work through material means at times (Luke 8:44; Acts 5:13; 19:12), as had God in Moses's day (Exod 4:2, 17; 7:19–20; 8:5, 16–17; 9:23; 10:13; 14:16).

Yet Satan may imitate even benevolent activity. That might be the case in Matt 12:27//Luke 11:19: "by whom do your own sons cast out demons?" Presumably the seven sons of Sceva (Acts 19:13) had been thought successful on some earlier occasions. Perhaps demons sometimes cooperated with magical system to keep people enslaved to it. Spiritual discernment is thus needed.

We must examine claims even among professing Christians. The Spirit of God *sometimes* uses people simply because the Spirit is strong among others in a place (1 Sam 19:20–24). Likewise, someone who is disobeying God may still have a remnant of anointing for a time (Judg 16:1–3; lost eventually, 16:20). That false prophets come in sheep's clothing (Matt 7:15) means that some of them look like sheep. Some may prophesy, drive out demons and perform miracles in Jesus's name—yet be lost because they do not follow him (Matt 7:21–23). Gifts are important, but Jesus did not say, "You'll know them by their gifts"; rather, he warned, "You will know them by their *fruits*" (Matt 7:16, 20), i.e., in the context, by their obeying God (7:17–19).

Still, we must exercise great caution about judging someone a false prophet (as opposed to simply some with whom we disagree on some points). Even prophecies from genuine Christian prophets must be evaluated (1 Cor 14:29).[35] Christians in this age "know in part, and prophesy in part" (1 Cor 13:9). Even John the Baptist wrongly doubted Jesus's identity because of his preconceptions and his limited revelation (Matt 11:2–3//Luke 7:18–19). Just because someone is imperfect or we think they are wrong does not give us the right to condemn them as a false prophet. John was certainly a true prophet (Matt 11:9–11//Luke 7:26–28).

Genuine "false prophets" are a more serious threat than someone mishearing God, despite the undue weight some critics fix on the general statement of Deut 18:22.[36] Even if prophecies are accurate, the prophets are false

- if they call us to follow other gods (Deut 13:1–5)
- if a spirit denies that Jesus is the Messiah (1 John 2:22)
- if a spirit denies that Jesus came in the flesh (1 John 4:2–3)
- if a spirit says, "Jesus is accursed" (1 Cor 12:3)
- or if they promote immorality

If someone rightly emphasizing love wrongly claims that the Spirit condones sexual immorality, they are false prophets (Jer 23:14; 2 Pet 2:1–2; Rev 2:14, 20; cf. Jude 8). If they turn the teaching of grace into an excuse to sin freely, they are false (Jude 4). If they exploit God's people for their own profit, they are false (2 Pet 2:1–3; cf. 1 Tim 6:5).

But we must be careful with accusations; slander and gossip are serious sins (Rom 1:29–30). Scripture repeatedly exhorts us to love and unity (e.g., Rom 12:9–10; 13:8–10; 14:15; 1 Cor 13:1–14:1; 16:14; Gal 5:6, 13–14, 22; Eph 4:2–3, 13–16; 5:2; Phil 2:2; Col 3:14). Shepherds must guard our flocks (Acts 20:28–31), but we cannot assume that every accusation is true; many rumors get circulated about true servants of God (e.g., Acts 21:21; Rom 3:8; 2 Cor 6:8), and we are not to accept accusations against elders until we have multiple independent witnesses (though we should then reprove the elders publicly; 1 Tim 5:19–20). Even when someone sins, our goal is their repentance and restoration, not their destruction (Matt 18:12–17; 1 Cor 5:5; Gal 6:1; 2 Thess 3:14–15; 1 Tim 1:13–16, 20; 2 Tim 2:25–26).

Biblical Spirit, Spirit-inspired Bible

Scripture is the one revelation that virtually all Christians agree on as the "canon," or measuring stick, for all other claims to revelation. Thus we need to do our best to properly understand it, preach it and teach it the way God gave it to us, in context. If Scripture is our measuring stick, then it does matter what God inspired it to mean. What we can be sure it means is at least what God meant when he inspired the various authors to communicate their message (the subject of chapters 8 and 9).

Respecting Scripture Requires Respecting the First-inspired Sense

Valuing spiritual revelation requires us to value most of all the divinely commissioned and inspired message of our Lord Jesus—God in the flesh—and the circle of those whose experience of him we can be sure, by providential arrangement, was unmediated and substantial. As already noted, Paul warns us: "If anyone thinks himself a prophet or spiritual, let him acknowledge that what I write is the Lord's command. If one ignores this, he himself will be ignored" (1 Cor. 14:37–38). All claims to hear God's voice must be evaluated (1 Cor 14:29; 1 Thess 5:20–21), and listening to someone else's revelatory claim can get us in trouble if we do not test it carefully (1 Kgs 13:18–22).[37] Individual spiritual experience is necessarily subjective, but it can be balanced with something objective: tested past revelation, corporately affirmed by God's people in all times and places since its books' acceptance.

The purpose of a canon is not to provide fodder (one might say, "cannon fodder") for whatever we wish to find there. Its purpose is to provide a measuring stick for other claims to revelation, an objective standard against which we may compare our own subjective experience. This is by no means, as we have pointed out already, an invitation to ignore experience; it is rather an invitation to read our experience in light of Scripture. The reverse is true, but not in the same way: we will intuitively read Scripture in light of our experience, bringing our questions to the text. Rather than imposing our answers on the text, however, we must submit to the text's guidance.

That means that it matters what the text is saying in its context. Exploiting the Bible to say only what *we* mean—to communicate merely our own opinions—is simply wrapping our own ideas in the cloak of biblical authority. Hijacking the biblical text's authority for our own agendas is a dangerous venture. The Bible spoke harshly of prophets who claimed God's authority for their own ideas.

Apart from context, including the context of the languages and cultures of which they were a part, the letters on a page are simply scratches that communicate nothing in particular.[38] When we read in context, we need to read Scripture the way God provided it, which in general means a book at a time. A passage in Mark fulfills a particular role in the larger context of Mark's full story; a passage in Esther likewise fulfills a particular role in the larger context of that book. Knowing the customs and culture to which these books regularly allude also helps us understand the original point.

When I was a new Christian, I was taking second-year Latin and was supposed to be translating Caesar for my homework.[39] Wanting to read only my Bible and not do my homework, I flipped open the Bible and stuck my finger down, hoping to find a text that said, "Forsake all and follow me." Instead, I found, "Render therefore to Caesar the things that are Caesar's, and to God the things that are God's" (Luke 20:25). God chose to answer my random approach to Scripture on the level that it merited, but this hardly means that God revealed to me a new, universal meaning for this passage. It would be unfortunate indeed if I began traveling the lecture circuit summoning all Christians to heed this passage by translating Caesar's *Gallic War*!

Nor do all appropriations of Scripture out of context prove so fortuitous. The true story is told of a woman who "explained to her therapist that God had told her to divorce her husband and marry another man (with whom she was romantically involved). She cited Paul's command in Eph 4:24 (KJV), 'Put on the new man,' as the key to her 'divine' guidance."[40]

Spontaneity Is Not Identical to Inspiration

Unfortunately, some Christians zealous for fresh experience do not find careful study exciting enough. This verdict may not apply to academic interpreters, but it seems a common enough malady among popular-level readers.

The Bible urges us to labor for wisdom (Prov 2:2–3; 4:5; 15:14; 22:17; 23:23); shortcuts are not the way to attain it. In our culture, we want everything instant; fast-food devotions fit our active lifestyle. Instant, however, is not always, and perhaps not usually, God's way. Sometimes in the Bible God did things instantly, such as many of Jesus's miracles, but usually God worked through a process. Consider the testing that Abraham and Sarah endured before Isaac's birth, the testing that David endured before being exalted king, and so forth. God could have formed the world or fulfilled his purposes in a moment rather than billions of years, but even young earth creationists (of whom I am not one) grant that he took at least several days to do it. God often works through long processes.[41]

Contemporary culture exalts tweets and sound bites. Sound bites out of context misrepresent people; such out-of-context quotations destroy reputations, damage ministries, end political careers, and so forth. On a popular level, however, most Christians use Bible verses like sound bites. Rather than reading Scripture deeply and imbibing the context, we use verses the way we have always heard others use them. Sometimes we employ them simply the way they strike us at the moment, sometimes blaming them on inspiration even if our application runs precisely counter to the text's point.[42]

The process of careful study may not sound inspiring to those who believe that the Spirit is experienced or pursued solely in a context of spontaneity, but Proverbs insists that we be diligent in seeking wisdom and knowledge. Pentecostals affirm that Luke wrote his work by the Spirit, yet Luke tells us that he did research before he wrote (Luke 1:1–4). Was the Spirit involved only in Luke's writing and not in the research that he did to provide accurate information about Jesus and some of his early followers? If so, why should it make much difference whether Luke was writing material that was historically true (as I and many other Acts scholars have argued) or was making his stories up like a novel (as some other scholars have suggested)?

Some of the earliest Pentecostals wanted to communicate in tongues on the mission field without having to endure the rigor of language learning;[43] Pentecostal missionaries quickly discovered the need to learn languages, and language school has long been a crucial step in their preparation. Those who want to "understand" biblical texts without using appropriate tools for textual understanding may miss the purposes for which such texts were designed, and so fail to receive communication fully just as some early Pentecostals failed to provide it.

God works through the process, not only through spontaneity. God sometimes did not even give a prophet a message until after an immediate confrontation (e.g., Jer 28:10–17), nor did a prophet always hear as soon as he asked (42:7). Granted, we often experience spontaneous blessings, but often we or someone else devoted considerable time in prayer or a daily life consecrated to God before we had those spontaneous experiences. As we read about God's servants in Scripture, nearly all of those about whom much is recorded experienced lengthy testing before God fulfilled his promises. Consider the particularly long wait of Abraham and Sarah; Joseph's years of slavery and prison; David's years of fleeing from Saul; and so forth. When the Spirit first empowered Jesus, he led him into the wilderness to be tested before the rest of his public mission; and even that mission led to the cross before the Father vindicated him with the resurrection.

The Spirit Gives the Gift of Teaching

Determining what the biblical writers were communicating in their original historical setting may not seem flashy like some revival phenomena, but it is foundational to a sound pentecostal hermeneutic. What did the Spirit inspire Spirit-moved prophets in the past to say to God's people then? This approach is not *distinctively* pentecostal, but then again, neither is calling Jesus Lord; yet the Spirit certainly inspires the confession that Jesus is Lord (1 Cor 12:3). The activity of the Spirit poured out at Pentecost is hardly limited to merely what non-Pentecostals traditionally rejected. Teaching is an essential spiritual gift, one that Paul ranks highest next to apostles and prophets (1 Cor 12:28; cf. Rom 12:6–7; Eph 4:11). Yet "teaching" at the very least often includes expounding the Scriptures (1 Tim 4:13; 2 Tim 3:16).

Some groups of Christians have been too arrogant about their gift of Scripture exposition to respect gifts that are often more spontaneous in more popular circles, but sometimes more popular circles have also been arrogant about their gifts and despised "mere" teaching. If we humbled ourselves, we might be able to learn and grow through each others' gifts. Today, happily, there are many biblically strong teachers in Pentecostalism; I suspect that in some places, however, the traditional tension between "mere" teachers and flashier gifts remains. We inherited the tension from tensions between academic and revivalist nineteenth-century evangelicalism, and for the sake of Christ's church it is high time we got over them. (See the discussion later in this book, especially p. 266.)

If what the Spirit led the biblical writers to proclaim is a normative guide for us, then it will not do to make the text mean whatever we want it to mean. That is not to say that we cannot get a sound idea from a text that was meant to teach a different sound idea; this happens all the time. But then there is little other than the Spirit to keep us from also getting an unsound idea from the text, and we are back to untested experience.

A Hermeneutical Circle

At times I have experienced the Lord speaking to me in dreams and found profound insights regarding his character or activity with regard to passages or themes in Scripture. I have found such "revelatory" experiences enlightening, as also at times when insights would come to me in prayer or preaching as well as in study.[44] Presumably such revelatory experience should qualify as a charismatic hermeneutic. But in each case I also evaluate the apparent insight in light of Scripture before deciding whether or not to accept it, because the tested deposit of countless generations of prophets in Scripture must trump any individual's (or even any contemporary community's) apparently revelatory insight. That is, it is more truly the way of the Spirit to honor the greater inspiration over the lesser one.

Scripture is meant to function as a measuring stick—not as just a place where, when we get a revelation, we can look up verses to support our experience. If we come to Scripture only to support our experience and not to understand it, we are justifying rather than *measuring* our experience by

Scripture. This approach sometimes leads to almost complete subjectivity, so that if one's experience is not divinely directed, one lacks a superior authority to expose and correct it. Rather than wrapping Scripture around our experience, we should be so full of the biblical message—not simply its wording but its *message* and theology—that we read our experience in light of Scripture.

But this process also inevitably involves a hermeneutical circle. Whenever we bring theological or other questions to the text, we read the text in light of the present. When pastors seek answers in Scripture for issues with which their congregations are struggling, they read the text in light of current needs (even when they do so to challenge overindulgence of felt needs). *Everyone* does this, whether the questions are prompted by their experience, their church's teaching, current ethical or social issues, or something else.

In 2008 I experienced an abrupt, extreme, and unrelenting spiritual attack for two days; it made no sense in my immediate context. On the third day I was recovering, and my wife, son David, and I went for a walk. We paused under a tree that was some three stories tall, and within moments after we stepped out from under it, the tree suddenly split at the bottom—without uprooting—and crashed where we had been standing. Because of the tree's wide structure, all three of us would have been crushed to death. The information that reached us from Congo soon after this event made clear that this was a direct and deliberate spiritual attack, from which God had protected us.

It was an experience too direct to deny, yet it violated my theology.[45] Without assuming that every detail of reality is addressed in Scripture, I did not understand biblically how a spirit could have power to do more than deceive and work in individuals. How could forces of evil actually knock down a tree? For several years I left my experience and my theology in tension, not understanding how to resolve the question. Then one day I was reading Job 1 in Hebrew for my devotions, and suddenly noticed what I had read many times previously: Satan sent a strong wind, causing a house to collapse on Job's children (Job 1:12, 19). I had already written a commentary on Revelation, where an evil figure brings fire from heaven (Rev 13:13). But somehow it had remained disconnected from my theology about the real power of evil. Experience helped trigger that recognition of what was already in the text, albeit belatedly.

Basic Principles

Spirit hermeneutics, then, may be *more* than simply traditional exegesis, as argued earlier. Yet it should also not be *less* than traditional exegesis. Granted, when believers lack understanding of literary context a true relationship with the Spirit often protects them from serious error; access to background is even more often limited, and we must trust the Spirit's help to cover lacunae in our knowledge. But the Spirit is not a shortcut to reading Scripture deeply, for the Spirit surely leads us to engage Scripture deeply if we have access to Scripture at all. And whatever else reading deeply may involve, it must include reading Scripture in the shape in which God gave it, rather than isolated verses out of context. My sense is that those who ignore context or minimize the value of background are generally those who spend little time engaging the texts as God has given them.

If we use the Spirit as an excuse to forego deeply reading the very works that we claim that the Spirit inspired, our spiritualized shortcut will short-circuit the point of having a canon as an objective external control on our more subjective claims to inspiration. I merely summarize some traditional principles here, since they are widely known, taught elsewhere, and so fundamental to the process of reading intelligently that a reader unfamiliar with them would probably not have reached this point in the book.[46]

- Read a passage in light of its immediate context
- Read a passage for its function as part of the larger book to which it belongs
- Read a passage in light of the cultural context that its language, assumptions and often allusions take for granted

The last point includes considering the way the ancient audiences would have understood the text's genre. In some circles it is popular to argue that these principles stem from modern historical critical method and that ancient readers did not follow them. Unhappily for those who so argue, this claim is not correct. As I will explain in greater detail later, reading a work in its context is not a modern invention but is the usual way of writing and reading texts;[47] it is also common sense, and the inspired book of Proverbs values common sense.[48]

The New Dynamic

The new Spirit dynamic is not a dismissal of the old, textual one; it simply submits to the Spirit's leading and affirms application by analogy, which we seek to do with the Spirit's guidance. The OT sometimes speaks of "walking" or "going" in God's commandments or ways informed by his commandments, employing a Hebrew idiom for behavior (Exod 18:20; Lev 26:3; Deut 8:6; 19:9; 26:17; 28:9; 30:16). For Paul, believers do not need to be under the law in the traditional sense because we "walk" by the Spirit and are led by the Spirit (Gal 5:14–23, esp. 16, 18, 23). Surely whatever else this guidance may involve it also informs our ethics and behavior; and if Paul is a model of following such guidance, this guidance is compatible with looking to the OT for models by means of analogy (a pattern often found in his letters; e.g., Rom 8:36; 13:8–10; 1 Cor 1:31; 9:9; 10:7).[49]

Nevertheless, as we embrace the new dynamic by the Spirit, we need to keep in mind that the more subjective our guidance, the more it is that our personal revelation needs testing, and the further we move from the objective standard by which it must be tested. Keeping Word and Spirit in balance is essential; because of our respective giftings, a teacher may emphasize one side more and a prophetically gifted person the other, but the body of Christ needs both.

In Josiah's day, the words of the Book declared God's standard, and Huldah the prophetess declared what that violated standard would mean for their time (2 Kgs 22:8–20). All prophecy must be tested, and teaching likewise is fallible, for we "know in part, and prophesy in part" (1 Cor 13:9). Keeping the right balance between sound exegesis and Spirit-guided, relevant application for our lives is important. We cannot emphasize only the latter because it has been seen as more distinctive to some of our faith communities.

Conclusion

A prominent early Pentecostal leader prophesied a revival greater than the Pentecostal revival that he had experienced; this new revival would bring together Word and Spirit.[50] Imagine what can happen when we bring together the best of charismatic experience with the best of evangelical attention to biblical exposition (and, for that matter, the best of many churches' emphases on caring for the poor, for ethnic reconciliation, and so forth).

The Spirit still speaks today; that is what Scripture leads us to expect. We can be most confident of the Spirit's voice, however, when we attend to what the Spirit has already spoken. The canon provides us the opportunity and the responsibility to submit our hearing the Spirit to what the tested prophetic tradition has heard, and thus to grow in hearing correctly.

CHAPTER 8

Do Ancient Meanings Matter?

Eager to emphasize readers' experience, some critics today play down the foundational importance of the ancient meaning. Those divided between emphasizing the modern and the ancient meanings include contemporary Pentecostal interpreters, with both sides claiming the heritage of the Spirit.

The ancient meaning, however, does matter, and, continuing a theme already broached in the previous chapter, that ancient, canonical meaning must be the anchor and arbiter for claims to interpret the text today. Moreover, continuing a theme in Part II, we must listen to voices from other cultures with sensitivity to their varied cultural contexts; how can we grant modern readers that respect yet deny it to the biblical authors? Concern for the ancient meaning is not a modern invention, and I argue that it is a concern shared by the Spirit who first inspired the text.

(Post)modern or Ancient Meanings?

Many argue for multiple meanings, although to at least some extent this argument may be a semantic one: most interpreters recognize some importance of both the ancient meaning and readers' reception, even if the nomenclature by which they describe this varies. Some, however, do seem to devalue the connection between ideal reception and ancient meaning.

Postmodern Pentecostal Hermeneutics?

A current tension in Western Pentecostal scholarship exists between those who favor a historical-critical hermeneutic and emphasize historical context, on the one hand, and those who, on the other, favor a postmodern hermeneutic and play down the importance of the original historical horizon.[1]

In reality, we should recognize the historical contingency of both the ancient and modern horizons. As William Oliverio rightly laments, Pentecostal interpreters, often divided today into one of two hermeneutical camps, have sometimes unhelpfully caricaturized the opposing camp. Those favoring a contextual hermeneutic "have accused those of the Evangelical-Pentecostal hermeneutic of problematically striving for an illusory goal of pure objectivity, followed by rejoinders from representatives of that hermeneutic accusing their critics of coming near (or falling into) an abyss of unconstrained relativism."[2]

A number of Pentecostal scholars have found valuable features in postmodern approaches;[3] others have objected to these.[4] While some aspects of postmodernity require critique, postmodernity does provide experientially informed voices a place at the table, and thus provides a valuable opportunity for those who can speak its language. By welcoming a range of cultures, it also welcomes many Christian voices of deep faith and spiritual experience from whom Western biblical scholars have much to learn.

Some trace the development of Pentecostal hermeneutics from precritical to modernist to postmodern approaches. Such a development is not surprising, although neither should we regard it as prescriptive: Albert Schweitzer, for example, naturally presented his own view as the climax of a long development of Jesus scholarship, yet many of Schweitzer's positions today appear eccentric.[5] Noting that many Pentecostal scholars today articulate themselves particularly in the approaches in which they have been trained hardly suggests that these approaches characterize Pentecostal experience per se.[6]

But while postmodern approaches may overlap with conventional Pentecostal approaches at points, they are not the same. Most Pentecostals who appreciate aspects of postmodernism readily distance themselves from extreme postmodernism's moral and theological relativism.[7] New approaches appear periodically, but when we wed ourselves to them too closely our very linkage to now cutting-edge approaches will date us eventually. Bultmann wedded his gospel to Heidegger; that may have been intended as contextualization for his generation, but it is passé now.

One could approach Pentecostal hermeneutics as a sort of postmodern potluck: all meaning is restricted to the eyes of the beholder, so we simply describe all interpretations offered by various Pentecostals and treat them all as equally normative. Like some other special interest hermeneutical approaches, we might then be taking descriptions of interpretations of a group—or even our preferred element of that group—and making them prescriptive or at least acting as if the practice of these approaches automatically legitimizes them as beneficial.[8]

In practice, few of us would go so far: most Pentecostals, for example, reject extreme practices associated with Pentecostal fringes such as snake handling and claims of believers becoming gods. Some Western interpreters have argued that Scripture's meaning is determined only by the reader's context.[9] Yet if, with respect to reader-driven approaches, we consider global Pentecostalism as a community of readers, it is helpful to note that most global Pentecostals and charismatics reject this relativistic and Scripture-relativizing approach of meaning being determined only by the readers' context.[10]

Is Any Interpretation as Good as Any Other?

We can learn from a range of cultural and even theological voices, but I believe that a true Spirit hermeneutic must go back to Scripture itself, in the form and thus the context in which God chose to inspire it. It is true that we will not always understand exactly what the original point of some texts was. But it is also true that no specific modern, "contextualized" reading is normative for all cultures.[11]

Subjective experience is not self-interpreting, and abundant historic abuses (whether by gnostics, Bogomils, Münster Anabaptists, some early Quakers, or Charles Capps's modern prosperity teaching) invite some objective criteria. The interplay between experience and Scripture involves a sort of hermeneutical circle,[12] but, as with Wesley's incorporation of reason, tradition, and experience, Scripture must remain paramount. Thus as Pentecostal theologian Cheryl Bridges Johns urges, "The written text has an objective, historical reality which cannot properly be understood outside of the bounds of reason. Yet, it is a personal subjective word that is carried along by the Spirit."[13] A Pentecostal biblical scholar, Lee Roy Martin, warns that focus on subjective feelings "rather than seeking God for God's sake" is the sort of "shallow emotionalism" that earlier Pentecostals called "'wild fire.'"[14]

If some deem an extreme postmodern approach that equalizes the value of all interpretations the most "Pentecostal" reading, they do so only by baptizing a modern academic or cultural approach, not by reflecting the dominant approach of early Pentecostalism. Early Pentecostal interpretation may have hosted a degree of polyvalence restricted by evangelical theological boundaries.[15] Nevertheless, their frequent, commendable tolerance on secondary issues[16] did not entail endorsing all interpretations as correct.

Pentecostals fought and divided over issues such as sanctification in ways that today embarrass many of us (including myself). Many of them affirmed that *everyone,* not just their groups, should embrace speaking in tongues and a new experience of the Holy Spirit. It is difficult to doubt that, on some points at least, most early Pentecostals believed that some readings were normative, and insisted that Scripture was to be decisive. Indeed, in the 1918 Assemblies of God debate over initial evidence, biblical evidence was deemed more important and nonnegotiable than experience.[17]

Joel Green, himself critical of sterile traditional approaches, rightly protests the extreme relativism of some newer approaches:

> More recently, some have migrated to forms of study for which there are no "facts," only "perspectives." Texts are sundered from the sociohistorical contexts within which they were generated, . . . and from whatever interpretive constraints might have been suggested by the texts themselves. Because these impulses continue the modern agenda of sundering the present from the past, it is arguable whether these forms of study are only *late-modern,* and not yet *postmodern* after all.[18]

Polyvalence?

What we emphasize is often shaped by what we seek to correct. Like Gordon Fee,[19] I have reacted against, and thus spent much of my hermeneutical instruction addressing, popular proof-texting, especially when it is blamed on the Holy Spirit. Those more shaped by combatting sterile academic traditions will have a different emphasis, although of course some of their emphasis also appears in Fee's and my work. It is misappropriation of texts with counterreadings, and not resistance to application, that drives our concern with potential uses of claims about polyvalence.

For those apparently unaware how far such unbridled charismatic subjectivity can go, here are just a few of the examples I have personally encountered of justifying new doctrines on this basis, from eschatological revelations incompatible with Scripture, to Word of Faith teachings, to claims that victorious Christians will achieve immortality by faith or will become Christ or part of the Trinity. (Retaining the nomenclature "Trinity" after this last-mentioned addition might remain feasible only for the severely mathematically challenged.) Proponents usually claim textual support for such views, but fairly consistently resist literary and historical context that challenges their "inspired" interpretations.

Some ancient interpreters affirmed polyvalence, especially rabbis approaching their sacred texts.[20] The widespread ancient approach of allegory could lend itself to such claims, but some approaches tended to prevail in particular schools.

How far should informed Christian interpreters press polyvalence today? Even at the level of authorial intention, texts can sometimes have different implications for different intended readers.[21] No one disputes that texts can be read in various ways, many of which may indeed genuinely arrange evidence from the text; but not all of these interpretations are necessarily helpful or necessarily consistent with larger biblical theology or Christian faith.[22]

Texts with indeterminate elements naturally lend themselves to multiple significations. "The only danger," one writer warns, "is that we will too easily accept our understandings as truly residing in and springing from the text itself, rather than deriving from our own vision."[23] Yet this observation suggests another, unstated danger insofar as we are concerned to hear the text rather than our own voice as authoritative. When our constructions of textual meaning diverge widely from its contextual sense, we may simply invest our own opinions with biblical authority.

The assumptions we bring to the text help determine the meaning that we supply to textual indeterminacies.[24] To the extent that we share the assumptions of the first ideal audience, our reading is likely to approximate the reading designed by the ideal author. Ideally, our assumptions are shaped by what we know of the canonical texts and how they are shaped in particular contexts to communicate.

Fee thus warns of the danger of simply mirroring our own views in the text; because Scripture must be heard as God's Word, good exegesis means "to hear the text first on *its* own terms, not *our* own."[25] This is a vitally important point: if Scripture is God's Word, we must hear his voice there rather than our own. God's Word may speak different things to different contexts, but if we hear merely a reflection of our context (and never a challenge to it) we hear not God's voice contextualized but a syncretistic deification of our context.

Potentially Ambiguous Nomenclature

Many who affirm the importance of modern horizons do not for that reason reject that of ancient ones. For some, Pentecostal hermeneutics emphasize the Spirit's role in multiple interpretations.[26] Insofar as we understand "meaning" or "interpretations" as applications and recontextualizations guided by the framework of the biblical text in its original context, scholars from a wide range of perspectives will agree in principle, despite differences in vocabulary.

Nevertheless, some can find the language misleading if it is not qualified. That misunderstandings are inevitable given the proliferation of divergent nomenclatures may be illustrated by actual readings of such claims.

Some of Kenneth Archer's proposals, for example, have generated controversy. Using familiar academic language, Kenneth Archer concludes, "Meaning is not something we discover then appropriate. Meaning is something that we construct."[27] In specifically *biblical* interpretation, however, our usual stated goal is to hear the message of the canonical text, so we cannot construct "meaning" (what others call application) without first discovering meaning in the text.

Speaking of readers constructing meaning in biblical texts, then, has provoked the concerns of some critics that this approach shifts the locus of authority from the designed text to its actual readers.[28] Although I would not suggest that Archer's views are identical with my own or his critics, however, he has provided us some authorial signals of his own intention; other statements in his work suggest that he is describing the process of reading here, not prescribing dismissal of the canonical sense. What he describes as "meaning" being "produced through the on-going interdependent dialectical interaction of the text and reader"[29] I would label "understanding," but again, these are primarily semantic differences. Social contexts determine the meaning that terms carry, and Archer is using some terminology familiar in literary studies.

In personal correspondence, Archer has explained that his critics misunderstood his point.[30] (I might suggest, only partly tongue-in-cheek, that his explanation thereby asserts the value of his own authorial intention in approaching his work.)[31] Archer affirms "the intentionality of the text to communicate with an appreciation for it being a social-cultural product that was written in a certain time and place by a person(s)."[32] He does reject historical-critical methodology as a way of discovering what the text means and thinks that discovering original intent does not deliver a straightforward understanding of what the text means; but he does appreciate social-cultural context and values both horizons.[33] "The world behind the text" informs but does not control the conversation about meaning.[34]

Some of our debates, then, may be especially matters of emphasis shaped by the differing contexts that we address. Without denying that other differences do exist, the lack of a standardized nomenclature for discussing these differences complicates communication.

Wrong-headed Rejection of Ancient Context

I can have sympathy for scholars who feel the tension between historical criticism and hearing the text itself. Indeed, that is partly what Bultmann's existential approach (see Appendix A) and, I believe more helpfully, modern literary-theological approaches are meant to surmount. I took a break from significant work on John's Gospel for a couple years after my dissertation on John because it had become difficult for me to read it without thinking of all the secondary literature on the various passages. Years later, I can again hear the Gospel afresh on its own terms without being distracted by modern critical questions. Such questions have their place, and some even arise naturally from reading the text, but secondary literature often builds layer upon layer of speculative interpretive glosses no less coercive for interpreters than the ecclesiastical constraints and traditions about which early modern scholars complained.

By contrast, careful research that aids us in hearing these works in their ancient contexts can make the texts and their scenes come alive to us more fully. Insofar as testimony of spiritual experience is valued, I can certainly testify concerning this rewarding experience. Understanding better the first horizon does not resolve all issues but it fills many lacunae that the text did not answer because, at the time of its writing, the answers were obvious.[35]

Speaking of a view as "wrong" may offend some postmodern sensibilities, but insofar as one's goal is receiving a communication from another—what we affirm when we speak of Scripture as God's message through concrete human agents—there are plainly unhelpful ways to do it. Some scholars do wrongly speak as if the first horizon is not important.

In some cases scholars value both horizons and simply emphasize one over the other in their writing. In many parts of the world, popular interpretation often neglects issues of background because it is rarely available to the interpreters. Nevertheless, I have found popular readers almost uniformly enthusiastic about ancient background when I have presented it and made it more available to them.[36]

Yet one Pentecostal scholar, apparently using prescriptively a description of popular Pentecostal practice,[37] suggests that a fuller understanding the Bible is not particularly desirable,[38] that "encounter" is preferable to "exegesis," that "spiritualising readers" need "little interest . . . in the surface meaning of the text" or attention "to the original intention of the author."[39]

On this view, Pentecostal hermeneutics opposes, in an adversarial manner, appreciating the text in its own right, and suggests that "Pentecostals are infinitely less interested in" what texts mean to their original audiences than in how the texts challenge us today.[40] The author goes so far as to suggest, though not with a completely straight face, that "now that progressive scholars" have mortally struck the Goliath of "grammatico-historical criticism," Pentecostal Davids should finish the job by cutting off Goliath's head.[41]

The analogy works better as a rhetorical device than an argument, since the voices of all prophets must be tested and it remains to be seen who genuinely speaks for God on the matter. Fortunately, this author lacks the position to define for others what a Pentecostal hermeneutic should look like.

Texts' Ancient Meaning

Inspiration does not make texts any less texts. Whether or not one wishes to speak of the authors' intention, one cannot easily avoid speaking of what the text meant in its originating context. It was, after all, written in ancient Greek and Hebrew. The first-century Mediterranean world was the setting in which New Testament authors' Greek vocabulary, syntax, and so forth made the most sense (and for which they were designed). How one defines "meaning" depends largely on one's goal in interpretation, but its real, originating historical level in which a writer sought to communicate content in a socially shared system of signs clearly shaped the texts as we have them.

Moreover, if we cannot take into account the biblical texts' cultural context, we are left with insoluble problems concerning slavery (e.g., Exod 21:21) and, in my opinion, some passages addressing women's subordination (esp. 1 Tim 2:11–12), and a host of other issues in the Old Testament and some in the New.[42]

As Bruce Malina rightly observes, our Scriptures were written in Middle Eastern and Mediterranean languages and settings. If they "made immediate and direct sense in that cultural form within our American social context, you might rightly suspect the New Testament writings of being twentieth-century forgeries," which they obviously are not.[43] It is when we hear most clearly what the biblical writers communicated, often forcefully, to their own generations that we can hear most clearly what these texts speak to us in our very different contexts.[44] It is easy for us to simply dismiss the relevance of the Corinthians' folly, for example, until we hear how logical their views sounded within their own culture—just as some of our practices sound logical to us until truly challenged by Paul's point.

Modern contextual readings that are most faithful to that original sense as their foundation will have the greatest common ground and ability to dialogue with other contextual readings. Without a common foundation—not only in the words of the texts but in what those linguistically and culturally specific words meant in their culturally, situationally, and authorially shaped contexts—one can make any text say virtually anything. In one SBL session that I attended early in my academic career, the presenter suggested that if one does not like what the text says, one should read the spaces between the lines to produce a counterreading. (When I shared this theory with a doctoral student from another institution, he remarked wryly, "Oh, that sounds just like what we used to just call eisegesis.")

Culture makes a difference on both ends of interpretation: understanding the ancient context and relating to the interpreter's context. Thus, for example, Abraham's negotiations with local Hittites for a burial plot for Sarah (Gen 23) fit what we find in Hittite business documents.[45] Had Abraham not known the culture, he might have thanked Ephron the Hittite for offering to give him the land free (23:11) instead of paying him for it (23:13–16). In that case, he would have expended all his favor with the Hittites and incurred enmity; the offer was a courtesy, not meant for the receiver to take advantage of. By contrast, in Paul's world, to refuse a gift or try to pay for it insulted and risked incurring the enmity of the benefactor who offered it.[46] Neither in antiquity nor in cross-cultural interactions today can one determine the appropriate response simply by supplying dictionary equivalents of words as translations; one must grasp the cultural context that informs them. Otherwise one risks sometimes understanding precisely the *opposite* of the speaker's point!

The disconnect readers often feel with the ancient meaning is one reason that many readers today seem baffled by the Bible and struggle to keep reading it. Believers need to hear and appropriate the text corporately and personally. One of the best ways to make this happen, however, is for some teachers of Scripture to explore relevant features of ancient culture and translate the message in their expositions. Most of us recognize the value of contextualizing the message for our hearers; what is so controversial about scholars using the same skills to reconstruct how contextualization was modeled for us in Scripture, which regularly contextualized the message for its first audiences?

My Pentecostal Testimony for Ancient Context

Since testimony is both a valued element in Christian epistemology and a conventional element of the Pentecostal heritage,[47] I shall offer mine. For what it is worth, to those for whom subjective revelation holds a place of special authority, a revelatory experience set my course toward understanding. As a young Christian, reacting against my preconversion intellectualism, I decided that I did not need to understand Scripture; I needed only to "get the revelation in my spirit."

One day during prayer the Spirit confronted my view; when I tried to protest, God flashed about ten texts into my mind simultaneously, proving me incontrovertibly wrong. Scripture values understanding (e.g., Prov 1:6; 2:2–3; 8:1 and passim; Rom 12:2), including understanding God's word (Deut 4:6; Ps 119:34, 73, 104, 130, 169; Matt 13:23).

Nor did I come to value historical context because of academic indoctrination. Indeed, although our education does influence each of us, my views have differed quite starkly from my esteemed and learned doctoral hermeneutics professor, Dan Via, a Bultmannian existentialist and former structuralist. Quite the contrary, my approach came by reading the Bible forty chapters a day, often through the New Testament every week, until it forced me to abandon my previous way of reading the biblical text and begin to read it according to the shape in which God actually inspired it, such as letters to concrete congregations.

To ignore that the texts invite attention to their ancient context—indeed, were written in ancient languages—is simply to show that one has not spent enough time reading them—at least, the way God inspired them, usually a book at a time. This is not to say that God does not provide insights to Scripture in other ways; it is simply to say that one way that God clearly does so is to help us understand the texts in context, and I was led to focus on this approach to make more of that context available.

I did not focus on background because my professors told me to; I gravitated toward the professors who gave me what helped me understand the background, and thus the Bible, better. I did not need so much a professor to tell me what the text said because I was reading the text enough on my own. I went into scholarship because it gave me more access to the background I now craved to help me—and help the church—understand the Bible better. I had to understand whether we should practice holy kisses, women wearing head coverings, and so forth; if I was not to dismiss these texts on subjective grounds that made modern readers' intuition rather than Scripture the canon, I had to discover why Paul wrote such instructions in his context.

My only desire, originally, was to fulfill my calling by preaching God's Word as accurately as I could. Might this call also summon the church to a paradigm shift on the popular level? The Bible is full of examples of God using servants to bring paradigm shifts, and unlike Jeremiah, I am at least not alone in inviting this one. God gave me a special passion for background, often spending ten hours a day mining collections of ancient texts, searching for any information that would illumine any biblical passage. After collecting roughly 70,000 index cards of information and finishing my doctorate, I resolved to put the information at the fingertips of ordinary preachers, such as I had been. No teaching position opened for me that summer, but within twenty-four hours of my prayer for a specified figure to live on that year, I was offered an unexpected advance of that very figure to write the background commentary I had proposed. The revised edition twenty years later is better, but God was at work in this process from the beginning.[48]

I believe that the Spirit has often helped me in my exegesis also, often facilitating my cognitive skills (which seems usual in the exegetical process), for example, by striking my attention with all sorts of potential connections as I read the background sources and still more as I wrestle with the text. Yet this also happens by guiding me in ways traditionally considered more "charismatic." Thus, for example, when several decades ago I was struggling with the point of the tabernacle material in Exodus, praying desperately, I felt that God directed me to study ancient Near Eastern temples to understand the symbolism.[49] On a different level, at times various ideas come together and something "clicks" in a special way. I do not want to elevate such insights as if they are perfect or immune to correction; again, "we know in part and prophesy in part" (1 Cor 13:9). I mention them simply to illustrate that I do expect and experience what I believe to be the Spirit's guidance even at the exegetical stage.

Premodern as Well as Modern Way of Reading

Later in this chapter I address ancient precedent for exploring authorial intention.[50] Here I turn more generally to interest in ancient context. Discovering a text's "original meaning and intention" is the goal of historical-grammatical methodology.[51] As noted further in chapter 9, some associate authorial intention with "an Enlightenment rationalistic hermeneutic"[52] or "the historical-critical method."[53] Yet interpreters clearly already used "historical-grammatical exegesis" before the dominance of modern historical criticism.[54] Reformers such as Zwingli emphasized attention to matters such as "grammar, rhetoric and historical research in explaining the biblical text."[55] Anyone who doubts the sophisticated nature of much ancient literary criticism need only survey Aristotle's *Poetics* or other ancient critical works.[56]

Greco-Roman Antiquity

Some critics have complained that reading in historical context is a modern notion irrelevant to Greco-Roman texts.[57] Even a cursory survey of Greco-Roman sources will expose the fallacy of this complaint, even if many interpreters were inconsistent in their application of the principle.[58] Thus one Roman writer complains that some older Roman laws are no longer intelligible, because the "words and customs" identified in the laws have become "obsolete, and it is in the light of those words and customs that the sense of the laws is to be understood."[59] Everyone also understood the reality of cultural differences.[60]

Granted, ancients were readier than we usually are today to cite snippets more verbally than contextually relevant to their situations;[61] consulting the original was also far more difficult for them.[62] But the first hearers of the Gospels, for example, would have heard them read whole, rather than piecemeal.[63]

For those with historical interest, the question is not anachronistic: contrary to some modern suppositions, ancient writers were not shy about debating intention, whether regarding the actions of someone on trial[64] or the purpose of legislators.[65] Certainly ancient authors were ready to challenge those who quoted them out of context by producing the context of their words.[66] Indeed, many current literary approaches resemble ancient antecedents,[67] though not all correspond as closely to their alleged ancient analogues as is sometimes supposed.[68] Contrary to what some modern writers have opined, historical interests are not a purely modern concern limited to an Enlightenment mentality; just as the Renaissance emphasized classical learning, the Enlightenment emphasis on historical context harks back to classical models.

Ancient writers, like modern ones, could assume a degree of shared knowledge on the part of their readers or hearers.[69] Writers regularly alluded to situations that they did not need to state explicitly,[70] because their ideal audiences shared this knowledge; being outside these ideal audiences, we sometimes find ourselves in the dark as to the precise referent of the allusion (e.g., Luke 13:1–4; 1 Cor 1:11; 2 Thess 2:5).[71] (Some ancient interpreters admitted that they faced the same problem with still earlier writers.)[72] Writers sometimes respond to interlocutors clearly enough that we understand the question (e.g., Sen. *Ep. Lucil.* 68.1; 74.1; 75.1; perhaps 1 Cor 7:1); at other times, however, we cannot reconstruct the question (e.g., Sen. *Ep. Lucil.* 72.1).

They could examine a writer's meaning in a text based on that writer's usage elsewhere.[73] (Jerome even noticed linguistic problems in Paul.)[74] They could also take into account an earlier writer's historical context; thus, for example, when Dionysius of Halicarnassus practices rhetorical criticism on

Thucydides, he complains that the latter employs a style not used even in his own time (Dion. Hal. *Thuc.* 29).[75]

Ancient writers might likewise note that older texts had grown less intelligible because words and customs had changed, and urged reading those texts in light of the original wording and customs (Aul. Gel. 20.1.6, on Rome's early laws). Critics sometimes debated whether particular words were available in a given past writer's period.[76] None of these interests precludes recontextualization of a message; indeed, ancient writers, no less than modern ones, approached historical information also in light of their own contemporary concerns.[77]

Reformation Interests

Nor is this way of reading texts exclusively ancient. Luther, for example, emphasized "the historical and grammatical principle" against the fourfold scholastic approach.[78] This historical and grammatical approach also characterized Calvin[79] and the Reformers more generally.[80] Even with respect to the historical-critical method, Erasmus, Luther, Calvin and Zwingli all broached matters that today are regarded as considerations of critical study.[81] Without the Renaissance's renewed interest in foundational sources and Erasmus's production of a Greek New Testament, it is questionable whether the Reformation would have happened.

Indeed, until the nineteenth century the NT and classics were often approached by scholars together.[82] Church fathers and medieval-period writers often quoted "classical authors" for explaining biblical texts. The humanist training of many Reformers highlighted this approach even further; Calvin's first published work was on Seneca.[83] In the seventeenth century, John Lightfoot began writing a NT commentary based on insights from rabbinic texts.[84] Although Enlightenment exegetes could use these tools in a reductionist manner, interest in ancient context certainly did not begin with them.

Early Pentecostals sometimes used historical background and sometimes even biblical languages—normally when needed to resolve a difficulty;[85] they "were concerned about both the 'historical-cultural' and 'grammatical' contexts of a passage." Nevertheless, although most clearly did not oppose using background, access to background was rarely available on a popular level. As popular preachers more than academicians, early Pentecostals normally did not and could not "use the academically tutored historical-grammatical exegetical method."[86]

Does their limited use of background mean that a more disciplined and consistent approach to background information would have done them harm? Or might they have deployed more background and knowledge of ancient languages had they had fuller access to these? Smith Wigglesworth read only the Bible, but this was not true of most Pentecostal Bible college teachers. Certainly my esteemed teacher, Stanley M. Horton, whose roots go back to the Azusa Street Revival,[87] brought his academic training into the service of the Assemblies of God (including regarding language and cultural background), and the movement depended heavily on him and other academicians who were able to work within its structures.

Conclusion

Debates about texts' range of "meaning" often depend on how "meaning" is defined; certainly readers may experience texts' implications for their own situations in a wide range of ways. Nevertheless, implications are connected with the message originally invested in the texts as we have them. Those messages include textual communicative lacunae because in their original linguistic and cultural context certain features of the setting could be assumed rather than needing to be explained. Our interest may be in wider principles, but we encounter these principles in inspired texts the particularities of which reflect their cultural, situational and authorial distinctives.

Interest in ancient meaning is neither a purely modernist nor historical-critical way of thinking. It is demanded by the shape of the texts themselves, a shape recognized by interpreters even in antiquity.

CHAPTER 9

Room Left for Authors?

Although we can speak of the original cultural horizon shared between a text's ideal author and audience without addressing the more controversial question of authorial intention, the current debate on this subject invites some attention to this subject as part of this discussion. Here I contend that seeking to understand the ideal author's textual design helps us better understand how to discern, and therefore how to accurately reapply, the message that shaped the text.

Those who read Scripture enough recognize that inspiration normally used, rather than obliterated, different biblical writers' distinctive vocabularies and styles, even in the books of the prophets. This observation has serious implications for hermeneutics. Scholars may argue whether it can ever mean *more* than what it originally meant to its authors (the debate often centering on definitions of "meaning," sometimes as well as what it originally meant to *whom*), but we should not expect it to mean less than that.[1] Those of us who believe that God knows the future will affirm that God surely intended implications beyond what the authors imagined, perhaps especially in prophetic literature. But since God normally inspired the authors to write in their own vocabulary and style and in the language of their culture, that is the surest place to start.

Authorial Intention Today?

Emphasis on authorial intention has both supporters and critics, noted below. Although some current theories of literary interpretation reject the priority of the author's historical intention as the "intentional fallacy," most do not rule out the validity of this historical question,[2] recognizing the author's intention as at least one level of meaning, especially for those with historical interest.[3]

Well before postmodernity, formalists studying poetry warned against limiting artistic value to a text's meaning in the original historical context. Significance, they argued, lies in the text and not in the author.[4] These are, however, primarily aesthetic considerations. Seminal challenges to authorial intention did not, despite widespread citation to this end, dismiss interest in authors or historical criticism. They merely distinguished them from the different approach of poetic studies,[5] arguing that it is more valid to ask what an author *might* have thought rather than what they did think.[6] Notably, Wimsatt and Beardsley, in their widely cited seminal work against authorial intention, applied their critique only to aesthetic, poetic texts; they viewed communication as successful only insofar as readers accurately inferred authorial intention.[7]

counter side

Listening to Communication

Advocates of paying attention to the original meaning of a passage usually appeal to the intention of the passage's author. Whenever we read texts as communications, we try to reconstruct what the author was trying to communicate.[8] If a text is encoded in a particular language and culture, we can seek to decode it to understand it before reencoding it for a different language and culture.[9] If one takes a completely reader- or hearer-oriented approach to communication, this exclusive or excessive emphasis on the reader's understanding can lead to a situation in which readers find offense or feel insulted about a remark and often cannot accept an author's explanation of what he or she really meant.[10]

As an author, I hope that you understand what I am saying, and I work to try to facilitate that understanding. I presume that readers of good will seek to understand my books; I expect even more fully that my students will seek to understand my syllabus, since there are serious consequences for misconstruing my intentions. Because I believe that God inspired the biblical authors to communicate his message, I am interested in understanding what those texts communicated in the settings in which they were framed. They are written in Hebrew, Aramaic, and Greek, not English, Spanish, or Chinese. Likewise, because I believe that God inspired the biblical authors to communicate his message, I am further interested in how I can respond to the heart of that message today, by means of analogy and in keeping with the original principles informing these models.

A conversation affords us direct communication. When we read ancient texts for meaning, we move to what relevance theory identifies as a secondary level of communication—hearing what an author was saying to a different original audience; even if the author wished for an audience as wide as possible,[11] the author would rarely envision one in a different culture and era for whom some of the text's allusions might not be intelligible.

Yet if we seek to hear the wisdom of those texts, we must be willing to grapple with those allusions, which requires presupposing, to the extent possible, the ancient context. Normally the particularities of the text invite us to consider what the author that may be inferred from the ancient text was communicating to the ancient audience. Whatever else we might suppose that a text could mean in a different context, a text's range of potential receptions will normally mean no *less* than what we can observe that it was designed to communicate in its own general social and linguistic context. If, for example, the Stoic philosopher Seneca commented on an earlier Stoic thinker such as Chrysippus, it was often because he wanted to learn from (or cite the authority of) that thinker's wisdom. Yet Seneca was normally interested in what that thinker meant historically, and was therefore ready to criticize him if he disagreed.[12]

If authors design texts to communicate, one goal of the ideal audience for which the text was designed will be for them to understand, insofar as possible, what the text's author apparently wished to communicate.[13] (How readers evaluate the communication in practice may depend on their relationship with the text and with its author.) Thus if we put ourselves in the place of the text's implied readers, this is what we shall seek to hear.

In academia, we like to simplify complex issues and complicate simple ones, but outside academia, we would normally consider listening to the author as common sense. If we believe that Paul would be the best person to explain what he wrote in his letters, we are interested in Paul's intention; that is why scholars comb Paul's other letters to help understand what he was communicating more than we explore Shakespeare or Dickens to do so.[14] Likewise, narrative critics normally read Acts in light of Luke's Gospel more than in light of Mary Shelley or Isaac Asimov.

The closest we can come to a normative foundation for other readings is what the Spirit inspired the biblical authors to say to the contexts they originally explicitly addressed—the audiences in whose languages they wrote, and whose situations they cared about and sometimes referenced. Whatever else meaning includes, it must include at least what these inspired authors sought to communicate to their audiences. Insofar as we hear texts as communications, it should matter to us what the author was trying to communicate.

As noted earlier, the Spirit usually communicated through these authors' individual styles rather than a cosmic voice—prophetically rather than the heavenly voice at Mount Sinai. Of all people, those who, with Paul, value the gift of prophecy should understand that, for most of us, the Spirit does not usually produce a prophetic trance in which we cannot remember what we say; rather, the Spirit inspires our faculties and works through them (1 Cor 14:2–3, 32; Rev 1:19).[15] We may not always recognize the full implications of what we are saying to a recipient, but we do recognize that prophecies usually come in our own style, just as those of Isaiah, Jeremiah or Ezekiel reflect their respective styles. (God even used a special title for Ezekiel, "son of man" [NRSV: "mortal"], that he did not apply to others.)[16] Certainly Paul's letters reflect his style, his reasoning with his audiences and so forth; the Spirit most often works through[17] the author rather than in spite of the author.

Authorial Intention in Premodern Exegesis

Earlier, in chapter 8, I noted the premodern interest in original meaning; here I note premodern interest specifically in authors' meaning. Some critics associate commitment to discovering authors' intention with "an Enlightenment rationalistic hermeneutic"[18] or "the historical-critical method."[19] Attention to the intention of the inspired writers, however, figured prominently in evangelical hermeneutics well before evangelicalism made peace with historical criticism.[20] Indeed, interest in authors' intention even predates the Enlightenment.

Some scholars, in fact, argue that authorial intention is the oldest hermeneutical approach, "and almost the only viewpoint available to the writers of the Bible."[21] To some extent this verdict may depend on genre: ancient hearers reveled in collected stories in mythography and used psalms and hymns for praise. Many considered inspired poetry to be from the gods rather than the poets' minds,[22] although later critics sometimes accused poets of misrepresenting the gods.[23]

Nevertheless, it is certainly true that ancient thinkers studying and commenting on earlier works frequently asked the same sorts of questions that we do today, questions involving authors' style, historical context and the like, as noted in the previous chapter. These questions often included authorial intention.[24] Obviously that was true of prose narrative, letters and the like, but it proved true also even of epic poetry such as Virgil. Poirier helpfully cites Augustine's hermeneutic as seeking to discern the authors' thoughts and thus God's will.[25] Certainly second-century fathers looked askance at gnostics reinterpreting the Bible based on their extrabiblical ideas.[26]

The Hirsch Debate

Although historically people normally have read communications with the interest of discerning the author, scholars often associate the ideal of authorial intention in twentieth-century criticism with Eric Donald Hirsch. His critics are harsh and sometimes dismissive, accusing Hirsch of turning back the clock regarding current trends.[27] Nevertheless, whenever trends change, previous trends become unfashionable, and that will include trends now current. Indeed, because there is "nothing new under the sun" (Eccl 1:9), "old" ideas regularly return to fashion, often repackaged as new ones.

Partly for that reason, but particularly because my interest in Christian reading is in hearing the inspired texts, I find most helpful approaches that provide insight into the production of the texts as we have them. Some have critiqued evangelical and Pentecostal scholars who support authorial intention as being Hirschian and thus behind the times, but authorially focused scholars have generally adopted elements of Hirsch's argument because of their interest in grounding our reading in Scripture, which came to us first as ancient texts.[28]

Hirsch traces the historical banishment of the author[29] that succeeded the more necessary banishment of early positivistic biases (with their focus on causal patterns) and postromantic fascination with feelings.[30] Ultimately, however, he believes the process climaxed in critics usurping the author's place as arbiters of meaning.[31] He grants that authors' views change over time, but he contends that the meaning the author invested in a text does not change (thus an author's occasional need to qualify views earlier expressed).[32] He also acknowledges that not all attempts to communicate prove successful.[33]

Yet the author's meaning remains a legitimate goal of interpretation, he argues; authors who did not believe this would ordinarily not attempt communication.[34] Indeed, even those who argue that authors do not control texts' meaning do not imply that the author is irrelevant to texts' meaning.[35] They recognize that texts do not exist without authors and historical contexts, although they also include the history of subsequent readings (what biblical scholars might call reception history) under the widened rubric of a text's "meaning."[36] Meanwhile, Hirsch also affirms significance beyond authorial intention, which I will note below.

Some of the debate may be semantic, differing over the choice of elements included in the label "meaning." Thus, when we speak descriptively of a text's "meaning" in this wider sense, we may wish to define the context in which the text is being read; the question for us when reading Scripture prescriptively for the church is: which level(s) of meaning is/are our ideal objective?

Pentecostals and Authorial Intention

Among Pentecostals, a minority of scholars dispute the value of seeking the author's intention. Nevertheless, seeking authorial intention remains the majority view among Pentecostal scholars, as its detractors recognize.[37] Pentecostal scholar John Wyckoff, whose dissertation addressed pneumatic hermeneutics, for example, contends that Scripture is the final authority only if the authors' "original intended meaning," as opposed to the perspectives of the readers, is determinative for all other possible *valid* 'meanings,'" in which he includes what many prefer to call "applications."[38]

Many recognize Gordon Fee's seminal role in the wider academic discussion of Pentecostal hermeneutics.[39] Fee has argued that "Exegesis by definition means that one is seeking an author's own intent in what has been written"; the meaning is in what the author intended to communicate.[40] Fee concedes that deconstruction is right to note the limits on our ability to reconstruct and on our objectivity, but he argues that these caveats do not diminish the goal of understanding the author's intention. "After all, every one of those who argue against me at this point are very intentional in their writing, and would (rightly so) take great exception to me if I were to misconstrue their words in the same way they seem willing to treat the words of the biblical writer."[41]

Some criticize Fee and others for highlighting the importance of the author's intention.[42] Fee, however, grounds his interest in authorial intention in Paul, who did not appreciate the Corinthians misunderstanding his letter (1 Cor 5:9–10).[43] Likewise, Fee notes that Paul qualifies his meaning in Phil 3:12, showing that he wants to communicate, and wants his audience to care about, his true intention.[44]

The same approach to Paul's letters could be expanded beyond the examples that Fee offers. For example, some Christians in Thessalonica may have misinterpreted Paul's insistence on the imminence of Jesus's coming (1 Thess 5:1–3). A worldwide day of judgment was foreign to Greek thought, and some apparently "contextualized" Paul's message wrongly, believing that the future day of the Lord had already come (2 Thess 2:2). Paul corrects such misunderstanding by reminding them of his teaching, thus appealing to authorial context (2 Thess 2:3–5; cf. 1 Thess 5:4–5).[45]

As noted above, we normally read in this way communications—including letters—as a matter of common sense. It is no coincidence, however, that Fee is especially a Pauline scholar and that authorial intention functions particularly clearly in letters, which typically name authors and function as direct communications to their readers or listeners. Intentions are sometimes more difficult to recognize in some other genres, especially narratives of various kinds.[46]

not letters

Implied Authors and Limits in Ascertaining Authorial Intention

Inferring an author's intended meaning is not the same as the older, romantic psychologizing approach of reconstructing the author's feelings or thoughts. Authorial intention as inferred from texts differs from the author's inaccessible "thought processes."[47] We have no infallible access to an author's mind; technically we may speak more plausibly of what the text appears designed to communicate, given our limited knowledge of the author and the author's and ideal audience's contexts.

Following Umberto Eco, some value the text's intention for limiting interpretation but distinguish this textual intention from the intention of the author.[48] But as Dale Allison suggests, "once we acknowledge 'the limits of interpretation' (Umberto Eco), it is all but impossible to define those limits without taking into account a work's original historical context," in which Allison includes coherence with what we can reconstruct of an author's intention.[49]

The method that one uses for interpretation depends on one's goal in interpretation. Hirsch argues that there is nothing self-evident in texts that requires a universal norm, unless that norm is what the author meant when composing the text.[50] Here postmodernists will demur, doubting that any universal, validating norm is necessary to begin with.

In later work, Hirsch admits that he tied meaning and normativity too tightly to the author, but he appeals to widely shared ethical considerations to support listening to the author as a person distinct from us as readers.[51] The ethical consideration merits more than dismissal as a last line of defense. For example, Gordon Fee lambasts the travesty of an interpreter who twisted Charles Dickens's *Christmas Carol,* inverting its meaning to suggest Scrooge as a positive character and Bob Cratchit as a negative one, the opposite of what Dickens intended his story to communicate.[52]

Norms are not in fact necessary for all interpretive tasks (especially descriptive ones); for those whose objective is hearing the voice of sacred documents, however, a foundation is necessary at the level of production and not merely at the level of various historical receptions. Those documents are in turn more fully understood when we take into account the formative context (shared between originating authors and audiences) that informs them, shapes their choice of potentially valuable content and presentation, and that they therefore necessarily assume.

The modern objection that the author's intention is unrecoverable, while strictly speaking true with regard to attaining sophisticated levels of certainty, raises the bar too high for historical inquiry. All historical endeavor is necessarily conditioned by probability, and scholars often make probable inferences about the *implied* author from the text's literary strategies in their originating context.[53]

While intention is not fully recoverable, however, in texts that function as instruction it does make a difference whether one construes the intention of a passage, say, as irony, or as straightforward instruction,[54] contrary interpretations that the words could receive in settings other than their first ones. Other approaches that do not focus on the author and the author's context ("unconscious constraints" on the author) often include it as at least an element of meaning.[55]

We might express in a more nuanced way this interest in approximating authorial intention, given the limitations of evidence available to us. Strictly speaking, we cannot infallibly reconstruct an author's intention; nevertheless, this limitation does not prevent us from examining the text's design and inferring from such strategies relevant aspects of the text's *implied* author's interests.[56] The approximation is imperfect but usually sufficient for communication to work.[57]   nice !

Some who object to the language of "authors" emphasize an "implied reader";[58] an implied author mostly simply projects the textual interests in the other direction. The "implied reader" can help us hear the text as addressed to its first horizon, thus making it particularly useful in hearing the designed message of the text.[59]

Conclusion

The debate today is not whether authors provide a factor in meaning, but whether they control it. The answer we give depends largely on how we define "meaning." The meaning of "meaning," as with other terms, is determined by its usage, and scholars often talk past one another by using the term in different ways. The author's influence is minimal insofar as "meaning" includes all possible readings, with the authorial proportion of influence increasing when the range of accepted uses of "meaning" is constricted.

If our interest is original meaning, however, the author's agendas are maximal to the extent that the author communicates optimally for the "original" context. For those who value the text in its current shape as authoritative, rather than simply the text as a useful mine of symbols for our agendas or traditions of interpretation, "original" meaning certainly remains a valuable goal.

Of course, we cannot perfectly reconstruct the original meaning. We have access neither to everything authors thought nor to the full original contexts that they assumed their ideal audiences shared, the information needed to fill lacunae in secondary communication. But whatever else a biblical text might mean, it usually means *at least* what it meant to the inspired author, who understood his own language, idioms, and cultural allusions better than we do. Offering historical reconstructions as responsibly as possible (given the limits of the evidence and our own horizons) is a reasonable objective that need not be discounted simply because it cannot be perfectly achieved.

Our goal, then, remains to hear the design of biblical works (a literary approach) in their ancient context (a culturally and historically sensitive approach). The latter element invites us to take into account everything we can know about that ancient context, including whatever we know about the author's thinking. Thus, for example, we can read Paul's vocabulary in light of his use of terms elsewhere, as well as in light of how that term was used in the contexts of early Christianity, Scripture, and more widely in Greek sources. This observation invites us to use both literary and historical approaches (chapter 10).

Both-And

From chapters 7–9 it follows that both literary and historical approaches provide valuable information for the study of Scripture. The majority of scholars today recognize this balance, although various writers and teachers today may provide fuller contributions in one approach or the other. Likewise, most scholars do value both ancient and modern meanings (on a broad definition of meaning) or the ancient range of meaning and subsequent contextual applications (on a more traditional definition of meaning).

What is often considered distinctive about Spirit hermeneutics is on the level of contextualization, since the Spirit already inspired texts in their ancient form. As already noted, however, the Spirit can help us in the entire process of reception, so a full-orbed Spirit hermeneutic ultimately includes both. In practice, one may emphasize the Spirit to supplement traditional teaching regarding exegetical method, but one should not emphasize only the Spirit's role in application or modern meaning as a substitute for inculcating basic exegetical skills (including literary context and, insofar as possible, ancient cultural context and language skills).

Both Literary and Historical Approaches[1]

Many think of critical scholarship until the mid-twentieth century as primarily historically oriented, followed by a shift toward interest in rhetorical (persuasive) techniques in the texts.[2] Yet even earlier approaches to Acts scholarship, for example, often attended to Luke's distinctive perspective and approach,[3] and today historical interests remain alive and well in this area of study.[4]

Although contemporary literary and historical criticism were once often at odds (primarily because the former was responding to a traditional overemphasis on the latter), most scholars now accept the value of both approaches.[5] Even apparently purely intrinsic literary approaches themselves arise in and reflect particular historical and social contexts.[6]

Need for Both Approaches

Questions from the broader historical context are inescapable if we concern ourselves with how ancient audiences, whose language and culture the text plainly presupposes, would have heard various passages. Writers such as Luke sought "to communicate with intended readers," and this purpose helped shape the text as we have it, regardless of how we utilize the text for subsequent purposes foreign to those authors.[7] The audience implied by the text is historically conditioned by the world addressed in the text.[8]

To read the text as a whole, we must read it in light of not only the intrinsic data throughout the text but also the extrinsic data that the original communication presupposes.[9] At a minimum this includes the language in which the text was written (without which, as already noted, the extant alphabetic characters become nothing more than random marks)[10] and those cultural, theological and literary assumptions that are shared between author and audience without needing to be made explicit. Often the real author and audience also shared knowledge of a more particular situation, although this specific knowledge often eludes us as secondary readers.[11]

Historical context affects matters such as how readers approach genre;[12] some modern Jesus mythers approach the Gospels as mythography, whereas I would argue that any competent ancient reader, recognizing Jesus as a recent historical figure, would recognize them as ancient biography.[13] Although these disparate conclusions do involve different preunderstandings (in this case, some want to treat any supernatural claims as mythical), they remain substantially a matter of comparative historical analysis.

Contrary to what some suggest, ancient audiences cared about genre. Ancient readers were aware of various categories of genre;[14] in fact, technical rhetorical works often defined specific genres of letters and speeches more strictly than the empirical examples allow.[15] Ancient editors divided Pindar's poems according to the kinds of hymns and songs they were, thereby arranging them into books.[16] Of various models for genre criticism in antiquity, Aristotle's prevailed longest.[17]

In contrast to those who avoid extratextual approaches for methodological reasons, some may avoid them because they recognize that they have limited expertise in such areas; and such avoidance is, at least, better than pretending expertise they lack. Martin Hengel and Anna Maria Schwemer, whose expertise in the ancient sources is self-evident, rightly warn that many NT scholars show little acquaintance with the ancient sources, and that their deficiency proves particularly conspicuous in work that sometimes collapses into "completely uninhibited ahistorical speculation."[18] Such theories tend to arise in artificial vacuums: scholars too often explain away all the historical evidence that we do have, then create arguments from the silence that remains; "a radical form of criticism" that uncritically ignores the only extant sources we have "in order to make room for its own fantastic constructions."[19]

Approaches That Draw on Larger Contexts

Insofar as modern literary theory focuses on communication (a primary purpose of texts), it indicates that "texts display not only internal reference (in relation to structures within the text itself), but also external reference (in relation to circumstances outside the text); they tacitly presuppose the entire cultural knowledge of the period."[20] As readers are drawn into a narrative, they are drawn into the narrative world that the text presupposes; this is not always the author's real world, but it cannot but be somehow informed by the author's real world.[21]

William Kurz, citing speech-act theories, notes that narratives normally occur

> in a context of communication. The writer of Luke and Acts was not merely amusing himself by doodling on papyrus or parchment but was attempting to communicate with intended readers through his written text. The key participants and factors of this act of communication are objective (extramental) realities, not figments of readers' imaginations, as some might deduce from certain forms of literary criticism. Thus the writer of Luke existed as a historical individual, whether or not we can identify him today. If there had been no writer, there would be no text.[22]

Explaining sociostylistic interpretation, Todd Klutz notes that "Like rhetorical criticism, . . . this type of stylistics assumes that the communicative force of a text's style usually has something to do with the goals of the text's producer, whose conformity to expectations of relevance normally entails that the assumed audience and situation are implied in the text itself."[23] In contrast to formalism's focus on aesthetic "properties of texts," "sociostylistics and related linguistic methods pay just as much attention to the extratextual conditions, causes, motives and effects of texts as they do to the aesthetic qualities of the texts themselves."[24]

One fruitful blending of historical and literary approaches reads "texts using many of the reading and listening conventions in vogue at the time of composition."[25] This blended approach has many implications. It might challenge, for example, some narrative critics' almost exclusive focus on first-time readers; ancient readers recognized the value of rereading a document as often as necessary to catch the main themes and subtleties.[26]

One line of literary criticism focuses on "the authorial audience,"[27] as reconstructed not only from the text but from the cultural world "in which the text was produced."[28] Other scholars, interested in addressing the needs of philologists, have developed the text-analytical approach to specific intertextuality, which allows for authorial intention in deliberate associations between texts and their pre-texts.[29] As historian Andreas Bendlin points out, "The intention of the author and the unity of the transmitted text have not lost their appeal for classical philologists. Here, intertextuality mostly in its restricted text-analytical form, is employed in analyzing the use of Greek precursors and models in Latin literature."[30]

One particularly helpful current approach, grounded in cognitive neuroscience and empirical study of how human communication functions, is relevance theory (treated also above in chapter 4).[31] This theory observes that a communicator can leave some information implicit[32] because it may be inferred from the social context that the anticipated audience shares with the communicator. Where such information cannot be inferred, the communication fails.

Such failure is especially a risk in secondary communication, where we interpret texts not addressed to us, particularly when they were not originally addressed even to our own social or linguistic contexts.[33] Because so much communication depends on inference, Gutt notes that the intended sense "is recoverable not in just any context, but *only in a context where the requirements of optimal processing are fulfilled,* that is, where there are adequate contextual effects, without unnecessary processing effort."[34]

Both Ancient and Modern Meanings[35]

A polarization between the value of an "original" meaning and modern ones may be common in some circles, but for Christian interpretation it is unhelpful

ful. Historical study need not be played off against theological interest as if they are mutually incompatible.[36]

The Usual Consensus

Today most scholars recognize the value of both approaches, wherever their own emphases may lie. Joel Green, especially known for literary and theological interpretation, differentiates between speculative historical criticism and the more valuable sort that provides historical context valuable for hearing the text.[37] As he points out, the dichotomy between history and theology or ideology is a modernist one that neglects the role of ideology in shaping historical writing (particularly in terms of selection and arrangement).[38] Indeed, he observes, hearing the text in its own historical context may help us hear it more clearly, as opposed to domesticating it, distancing from it or merely exploiting our excavations of it.[39]

Kevin L. Spawn and Archie T. Wright note that most scholars in renewal traditions support both dependence on the Spirit and "rigorous academic research."[40] North American Pentecostal scholar Lee Roy Martin likewise emphasizes that "appreciation for the affective dimension" of reading Scripture "is only one aspect of a holistic hermeneutic. The affective elements become clearer and more precise when they emerge from sound exegesis."[41] Australian Pentecostal scholar Jacqueline Grey notes that reading with sensitivity to both horizons "does not contradict the legitimacy of the historical and cultural context of the text, but (to use the terminology of Childs) *extends* it."[42]

Nor are these recognitions new. Early charismatic scholar Howard M. Ervin valued "Linguistic, literary and historical analysis" as a vital element in understanding the text.[43] Walter Hollenweger, long noted as a leading scholar on Pentecostalism, emphasizes the contribution that reading Scripture in its historical contexts can make to Pentecostal hermeneutics.[44]

Before his death, charismatic theologian Clark Pinnock, though using a broader sense of the term "meaning" than evangelicals traditionally have embraced, reminded readers that a genuinely Spirit-led reading will be consistent "with the apostolic witness," which he deems "an important check." Although meaning is not limited to its historical sense, texts "cannot mean just anything we want"; respect for the text requires us to let "it establish the range of possible meanings." Most relevantly here, he notes that "Texts of the Bible do have definite meanings in the historical situation and that meaning is the anchor of our interpretation."[45]

Need for Ancient as Well as Modern Meanings

Of all people, readers with a deep experience of the Spirit should be ready to distinguish divine revelation from human insights and contextualized practices. Although God also speaks through and adapts human insights (witness the similarities between Proverbs and Egyptian wisdom literature, for example), there is a reason that we give priority to the apostolic and prophetic message of Scripture as a whole over subsequent opinions about what it meant.

Studying Scripture first in the languages and cultures in which God gave it to us provides a crucial foundation for helping us understand its message. Revelatory insights are possible, but as emphasized in chapter 7, it is Scripture itself that gives us an objective anchor by which to test and guide our subjective experiences. Without that objective anchor, we can easily drift into "every wind of teaching" (Eph 4:14) that someone today claims gave them an adrenaline rush.

In the older formalist fashion, some might appeal to the text alone to prevent possible counterreadings that would undermine the text's message. Unfortunately, the textual delimitation of meaning alone is not always adequate, since an uninformed modern reader will supply meaning in perceived lacunae not by ancient context but by his or her own interpretive systems;[46] a clever persuader could even construct such a system for the very purpose of recruiting the text for one's agenda.

Indeed, even reading texts for merely the syntactical relation of terms without fuller social context would exclude any possibility of clearly recognizing when an author may have intended such literary devices as irony. Further, languages develop over time, so in principle the meaning of key words even in the same language could change, eliciting new interpretations inconsistent with the original (cf., e.g., how we could today read the expression "the gay 20s"). Anchoring the range of meaning within what remains consistent with the text's design in its historical context provides clearer limitations.[47]

Renewalist scholars Spawn and Wright thus have warned against "Pentecostal" methods that minimize "the historical, cultural and literary dimensions of Scripture," "[s]ince these issues related to the provenance of the biblical text result from divine initiatives" and therefore are essential to truly Spirit-attentive readings.[48] Likewise Pentecostal scholar Gordon L. Anderson notes that a sound Pentecostal hermeneutic should not be "a new exegetical method." Despite the role of the Spirit and subjectivity at other levels, "Exegesis is a method of getting at the original intended meaning of the text. To do so one must study language, culture, history, word history, etc. This is the standard method of studying texts."[49]

Some Readings Are More Helpful Than Others

Paul Ricoeur noted that because words are polysemous and sentences can have plurivocity, interpretation is debatable—but because these elements of communication appear in contexts they are "subject also to a validation of probability." The critic can thus avoid not only dogmatism but also thorough-going skepticism about meaning.[50]

Some have treated the recognition of the reader's horizon as an invitation to simply read texts from the standpoint of one's own doctrinal or theological presuppositions. Calling this Pentecostal hermeneutics would make Pentecostal tradition, rather than Scripture, the new norming norm. This rhetorical appeal might fit the postmodern propensity to equalize all truth claims, but it misrepresents the conventional hermeneutic of blending horizons. Anthony Thiselton warns, "The problem of pre-understanding, however, does not give grounds for the cynical response that the modern interpreter understands the Bible only on the basis of his own presuppositions. For there is an ongoing process of dialogue with the text in which the text itself progressively corrects and reshapes the interpreter's own questions and assumptions."[51] Thiselton's seminal study thus concludes with the vital observation: "The hermeneutical goal is that of a steady progress towards a fusion of horizons. But this is to be achieved in such a way that the particularity of each horizon is fully taken into account and respected. This means *both* respecting the rights of the text *and* allowing it to speak."[52]

Simply reading our agendas into the text makes us masters over the text rather than submitting to it.[53] (This prioritization of reader over text differs from what early Pentecostals would have recognized as a Pentecostal herme-neutic,[54] though like most readers, they sometimes did it.) Readers too readily hear in Scripture simply "divine license" for what we desire or to confirm our biases against others,[55] or, against everything we affirm about divine grace, even our theological or ethical superiority to others. Respecting the text's first horizon, in a sense, is an ethical responsibility; insofar as we receive the text as a communication, we respect "the other" that comes to us in the text by hearing it rather than simply treating it as a reflection of ourselves.[56]

Beyond the Ancient Meaning

One might say that, like Abel, whose blood cried from the ground, the ancient text "still speaks" (Heb 11:4); NT writers were not shy about presenting Scripture as "speaking"[57] (the way pagan contemporaries also spoke of the work of revered poets). Most of my academic work so far has focused on ancient meaning and background, but the purpose of this labor was to help people hear the biblical text more accurately, not to suggest that believers should approach it as a mere specimen for historical analysis.

The disconnect that readers often feel with the ancient meaning is one reason many readers seem baffled by and reticent to keep reading the Bible. Believers need to hear and appropriate the text corporately and personally. I have taken it for granted that my Christian readers will not simply teach the background by itself as if that gives spiritual life to their hearers.[58] Background helps us understand, for example, what Jesus really meant in some hard sayings, or what it means for him to be meek and kind.

If we do not, however, communicate the real meaning of those sayings or help people to relate to Jesus's kindness, we have not communicated the heart of the message. It is by seeing Jesus that we are transformed into his likeness (2 Cor 3:18).[59] For Paul, this also included people being able to witness Jesus's death and resurrection through how Paul lived (2 Cor 2:15–16; 4:10; 13:3–4; Gal 2:20–3:1).

Ancient Foundations for Newer Significance

This ancient meaning must be foundational for any other meaning or significance we find in the text, if we hear it as a communication. "There is a line of continuity," one Pentecostal scholar notes, "between the original 'meaning' of Scripture and any contemporary meaning."[60] The original sense, another Pentecostal scholar notes, can help set parameters for the range of desirable reception today.[61]

If our application reflects no correlation to the specific communications that the author offered in the social and linguistic milieu that he shared with his first audience, we no longer attend to the particulars of this text or its formation.[62] Instead, we make it a generic reflection of our own interests, one in principle little different from any other text that we might read the same way. This approach is not uncommon and is sometimes justified with hermeneutical language. But for those who respect the text as communication and are interested in anything analogous to what it first communicated, an approach more attuned to its original context will prove more helpful.[63] The first horizon cannot fully define our experience of reading,[64] but it should be foundational for the analogies we draw.[65]

Common Ground

Having said that, Spirit hermeneutics cannot stop with just the normative, ancient meaning of the text, but must also concern itself with how that meaning speaks in new settings today. Exploring examples of those readings in various settings and examining reading communities are valuable pursuits. Learning from the contemporary insights of these other readers (and sometimes from their failed experiments) is no less helpful than when we listen to the insights and failed experiments of our predecessors in church history. "Whoever has an ear," the Lord reminds us, "let them hear what the Spirit says" not only to their own church but "to the churches" (Rev 2:7, 11, 17, 29; 3:6, 13, 22). The messages to the seven churches were each contextualized for their local audiences, but all the churches could learn from them, because the Spirit can apply the message to our own situations.

Even the most ardent defenders of authorial intention usually do not disagree here, provided that the new insights are connected with the design implied by texts in their historical context. Despite some interpretations being incompatible with the original sense,[66] Hirsch contends that some differing interpretations may be compatible, insofar as they reflect the same *type* of meaning.[67] Ultimately Hirsch allows for a text's "implications" or "significance" in new settings[68]—which in fact does allow for what others call applications or "meaning" beyond, though not disconnected from, the author's intention.[69] Despite differences on the role of the author, then, both Hirsch and his more postmodern detractors allow for what we have called recontextualization.[70]

Writers do communicate more (and less) than their conscious intention.[71] But cultural and linguistic assumptions shared with the original audience determine many of the "indeterminacies," or lacunae, in their texts. We cannot fully recover authors' thoughts, but neither do words or phrases have some normative meaning apart from their literary and sociolinguistic contexts. A term's semantic range supplies potential meanings for the term, but its particular sense is narrowed by the social and literary setting of the text in which it appears. Those who object that the pursuit of authorial intention demands too much from our evidence should at least consider the shared context of the text's implied author and its implied audience.[72]

The ideal author's intention, or works' design in their original contexts, was more than merely informing their audience. Most biblical writers wanted their audiences to respond to their message by how they lived.[73] Given what we know of ancient narratives, including histories, this was as true for authors in narrative genres as in others. Indeed, it was more true of ancient Near Eastern royal narratives and Greco-Roman histories and biographies than it was for typical letters or novels.[74]

Conclusion

The works included in our canon were shaped in particular linguistic and cultural circumstances. We can thus better understand what these texts were designed to communicate, and how they can be applied analogously today, to the extent that we understand the circumstances shaping them. Nevertheless, if we stop with merely historical observations about the text, we have failed to appropriate its inspired message. Once we understand what biblical texts communicated in their first context, we must hear their challenge or comfort in our own settings as well. Only then do we truly enter the text rather than merely examining it.

PART IV

Epistemology and the Spirit

Many conventional epistemic approaches contribute valuable insights in their respective spheres; the theological sphere requires an epistemic approach appropriate to it. The infinite God is known only where he reveals himself,[1] and theological epistemology must thus begin with those places of revelation. Those sites of revelation overlap at points with other epistemic spheres—generally in science, particularly in history, and the like, inviting inquiry at those points by appropriate scientific and particularly historical methods.

But the experiential dimension of direct inspiration, illumination or revelation by the Spirit, though necessarily subject to evaluation and refinement, also points to a complementary epistemic approach not subsumed under the others (which are sometimes traditionally defined so as to exclude it). Spirit-inspired faith in the true divine Object is not fideism, as a blind faith would be; it involves a form of sight to which those who do not experience it are not privy.

Such an offensively exclusive claim is neither ideal for, nor designed for, use in apologetics or academic dialogue, since it does not depend on truth equally accessible to all parties. It nevertheless remains a biblical claim important for emic theological understanding of Christian teaching. At the same time, Christians should be wary of narrowing their epistemic boundaries too tightly; we should ensure that we are calling people to trust God's Word the *way* it invites trust, rather than according to our own preconceived interpretive grids.

153

CHAPTER 11

An Epistemology of Word and Spirit

How so?

Hermeneutics function as a special sort of epistemology.[2] Biblical hermeneutics are important especially to those who embrace an epistemology of revelation that grants Scripture an important role in that revelation. For Christians, the Spirit plays an important role in revealed theology and the theological worldview from which we interpret reality.

Whereas intrapentecostal discussions of hermeneutics often focus on what is distinctive to Pentecostalism, charismatics outside the Pentecostal movement proper tend to ask broader questions also engaged by noncharismatics: an epistemology that correctly relates Scripture and experience.[3]

Biblical epistemology differs from the epistemological approaches with which many of us in the West intuitively function. Our philosophic heritage has conditioned us to particular ways of seeking truth, some of which (such as empiricism) do correlate with aspects of reality. The Bible, however, invites us to perceive a more overarching dimension of reality, namely reality about God the creator and redeemer, who is understood in more specifically theological ways.

Just before embarking on this discussion, I should note that many of the biblical passages explored or sampled below, which sometimes employ dramatically stark language, come from contexts reinforcing believers' faith rather than contexts in which authors were seeking common ground for dialogue. They are not, then, the sort of language we normally employ in academic forums. Nevertheless, they offer demands on our personal and corporate loyalties, reminding us that Christ must ultimately be Lord of our epistemology as well as of everything else. This was something I admittedly did not always remember during my earlier academic writing. ↘ impacts?

155

Traditional Epistemic Approaches and Their Limitations

Every belief system takes for granted some philosophic premises that cannot be proven to others, premises that often cannot be proved by the belief system on its own. For example, empiricism offers the best developed method for learning details about creation itself. Nevertheless, even introductory philosophy often observes that one cannot prove empirically the assumption that truth can be learned only empirically.[4] The regularity of what we call nature, at least under given sorts of conditions, allows us to confirm observations by replication and experimentation.

We cannot, however, repeat historical events in the same way. The best available sorts of evidence that we find most useful for historiography, journalism, and interpersonal communication often fail to meet the stricter constraints of experimental science.[5] That is precisely because the activity of human beings offers less predictable regularity than is possible for larger natural entities on a less complex level.[6] In both cases, we may offer a range of predictions, but the complexity of factors involving human choices and activity differs from the range of random variation within structures with less information content. Historiography reflects a cosmologically much narrower sphere of interest than the chemistry and physics of the universe, and as such it both offers less epistemic precision and demands greater flexibility in evaluating various pieces of evidence.

While the scientific method is enormously beneficial for humanity, if all truth were limited only to what can be replicated in experiments, we would need to, as noted above, jettison not only theology but also such disciplines as historiography and journalism or anything else that deals with unique persons and unique events. We also do not normally conduct our relationships, including how we love, on purely empirical grounds, though we may understand empirical data (such as conditioning of neurological responses) that helps to explain such human connections.

Empiricism is thus useful and veridical within its sphere, but its sphere does not embrace all of reality, and empiricism does not even seek to ask, much less answer, some kinds of questions. This helps to explain why, again, an exclusively empirical epistemology cannot justify *itself* empirically.

Empiricism could examine evidence that one may present about God acting in the world, but the interpretation of that evidence (except for its potential falsification) lies beyond the competence of empiricism in the strictest sense. In fact, the process of interpretation itself involves more than simple observation and experimentation. Scientific theories use models and inferences from the best (currently available) explanation, though these should arise from accumulated empirical data and can be tested (and especially falsified) empirically.[7]

Moreover, empirical knowledge is always subject to revision based on fuller evidence (say, the limitation of a regularity to previously observed conditions when a different regularity occurs under different conditions).[8] Frameworks based solely on an accumulation of even massive empirical evidence thus offer less certainty than appears in mathematics, given the logical necessity of the underlying axioms within their logical system. Such comments are not meant to demean empirical inquiry, which is, as I continue to emphasize, valuable and even necessary within its sphere. (For an extreme example, one would be advised not to consume random substances without attention to their observed and studied effects, particularly when those effects might prove to be lethal.) It is precisely because empiricism offers so much valuable information that I employ it here as an example of epistemological limitations.

Instead, my point is that this valuable epistemic approach is not comprehensive in explaining everything, particularly what we call metaphysical questions.[9] Simply because an approach does not address a subject directly does not mean that that subject cannot be addressed by any means.

A Theocentric and Christocentric Epistemology

What would an epistemology look like with the biblical God as its starting point? By this I do not mean an epistemology of natural theology, which might seek to arrive at something like God as its conclusion.[10] Rather, what kind of epistemology would we expect if we start with the God revealed in Scripture? For example, what kind of epistemology underwrites the apostolic proclamation in Acts, where God's activity in Jesus appears as the fundamental saving message?[11]

Christ Re-presented by the Spirit in the Gospel

John 16 offers a particularly helpful depiction of this christocentric epistemology. In John 16:7, Jesus sends the Spirit to believers, so it is apparently through the believers' continuing mission (cf. 20:21–22) that the Spirit goes on in the following verses (16:8–11) to convict the world. In these verses, the Spirit continues what Jesus has already been doing in the Gospel. Like Jesus, the Spirit convicts the world of sin.[12] Like Jesus, the Spirit confronts the world with judgment (cf. 3:19; 5:22, 27, 30; 12:31). Thus in 16:7–11, the Spirit reveals Jesus to the world through believers preaching him, since Jesus sends the Spirit to believers (16:7).[13] In 16:12–15, even more clearly, the Spirit continues to reveal Jesus to his own followers; as Jesus told the disciples whatever he heard from the Father (15:15), so the Spirit reveals whatever he hears from Jesus, including what is to come (16:13).

If we wish to frame this process or experience in epistemic terminology admittedly foreign to John, we may speak of complementary objective and subjective, or in this case historical and existential, aspects. The gospel is about acts of God in genuine history verified by witnesses (and continuationists would add, continuing to be supported by witnesses concerning experiences consistent with those first ones).

When people hear the gospel, however, they are confronted not merely with one worldview among others; in John's theology, the risen Jesus is present in the message, presenting his demands by the Spirit no less plainly than he did on those who heard him in person. Thus in a similar manner Paul describes believers' response to his preaching as accepting not merely human words, but the word of God, which proves divinely efficacious among those who believe it (1 Thess 2:13).

In a sense, then, we might speak of Christian epistemology as kerygmatic epistemology: founded on historical evidence, yet confirmed by the living testimony of God's own Spirit. People become responsible for how they respond because God directly challenges their hearts in the gospel.

Historical Particularity

The historical particularity of this approach naturally will put some people off (an offense Paul finds epitomized in the cross), yet such historical particularity should be expected. Without it, we might at best suppose a deistic deity revealed in nature's laws but excluded from our own reality in historically particular settings. For both theists and deists, if a universal God were to reveal himself in the physical universe, we might reasonably expect to find his signature in the regularity of the patterns of nature, particularly in complexity that defies the reasonable probability of coincidence as an explanation.

Yet we encounter not simply a divine intelligence delighting in fashioning a regular cosmos of any sort, but a God who appears to have a special interest in humans. If a universal God were to reveal himself in humans, we might

interesting

expect humans to epitomize complexity. Humans do not in fact reside at the *geographic* center of the universe, but, so far as we have discovered, we remain the pinnacle of material complexity in terms of information content—perhaps somehow close to the center of *meaning* or *purpose* in creation.

If a universal God were to reveal himself in the particularity of human existence, we might be expected to look for that revelation in the particulars of history. There we might expect to find that revelation associated particularly with a people who (even if reluctantly at times) preserved a heritage of monotheism.

If we look at extant faiths that claim that heritage, it appears to me that the biblical prophetic tradition of God actively pursuing and challenging his people climaxes especially in the ministry of Jesus. The promised era of fulfillment that he ushers in empowers all of God's people to be the prophetic community. That church history often fails to testify to this reality, as the history of Israel often fails to honor its prophetic tradition, should not blind us to the fuller realization of those ideals in periods of revival.

Experiential and Testimonial Evidence in Kerygmatic Epistemology

Both experience and testimony, thus both personal and communal components, play a role in this epistemology. The resurrection was public evidence (Acts 17:31), appealing to witnesses (Acts 2:32; 3:15; 5:32; 10:41; 13:31; 1 Cor 15:5–8). This was not, however, the only evidence that Luke affirms; he embraces an epistemology fuller than what we often find today. Jesus did not appear to everyone in Jerusalem, but to witnesses whom God chose (Acts 10:41). Although Cornelius hears Peter's witness about Jesus rather than seeing Jesus for himself, Cornelius experiences the Holy Spirit (10:44, 46; cf. his earlier vision, 10:3–6). That is, Cornelius and his household receive confirmation through experience, after embracing the message by trusting the testimony.

Testimony and Experience in John's Gospel

interesting!

As noted above, in John's Gospel Jesus's interlocutors challenged the validity of his testimony, because he was the only one who had seen what he testified (John 8:13). Jesus responded, however, that his unique experience uniquely qualified him to testify about his claim, and that his Father testified with him (8:14, 17–18). His critics had a fleshly, worldly perspective, whereas he had a heavenly one (8:15–16, 23; cf. 3:11–13).

Those who receive testimony secondhand may nevertheless share thereby the salvific experience of the first disciples (John 20:29–31; 1 John 1:3; cf. 1 Pet 1:8, 12). John points out that Jesus after the resurrection would not reveal himself directly to the world, but to those who walked with him beforehand (John 14:21–23); this promise is initially fulfilled with Jesus's appearances to his disciples in John 20–21. On the first of these occasions, Jesus imparts the Spirit (20:22), communicating Jesus's presence to all believers (14:16–23).

The next paragraph addresses the evidence already given, the testimony of the witnesses. Thomas refuses to believe his colleagues, because he has not seen Jesus for himself (20:25). When Thomas afterward experiences Jesus directly, he offers the climactic confession of faith in John's Gospel: "My Lord and my God!" (20:28). Jesus does acknowledge this confession, with its model content, as faith, but affirms greater blessing for those who believe without having seen (20:29).

Immediately the author goes on to explain, essentially, "That's why I wrote the signs in this book—so that those of you who haven't seen may believe through my testimony" (cf. 20:30–31). This kerygmatic epistemology is clearest in John 16, already treated above. Here Jesus's own presence confronts those who hear the message, as plainly as Jesus's presence earlier confronted the world in person.

Those who have met God have access to an experience that they usually can communicate only by testimony,[14] but which outsiders cannot fully (experientially) apprehend, lacking any framework for evaluating it (1 Cor 2:14–15; 2 Cor 4:4–6; John 3:3, 8–12). Through testimony, though, some will go on to experience Jesus for themselves. This was what Andrew offered Peter, what Philip offered Nathanael and what the Samaritan woman offered her people: not mere arguments, but introducing others to Jesus himself (John 1:41–42, 46; 4:29). Arguments have their place, and Jesus offers some in the same Gospel; but Jesus also speaks in riddles (e.g., 7:28; 8:25), for it was up to the Father to draw those whose hearts were open (6:44).

Revelation and Reception

Likewise, Paul declares that his gospel came to the Thessalonians not only as words, but in the experience of power, the Holy Spirit and full assurance (1 Thess 1:5; cf. Col 2:2). The gospel proved efficacious in turning them from idols to the living God (1 Thess 1:8–10). Paul explains that his gospel did not come with insincerity (2:1–12), and, most relevant to my topic, thanks God that his hearers recognized this message as God's own speaking (2:13). Paul expected not human wisdom but the power of the Spirit to transform his hearers (1 Cor 2:4–5).[15] Paul recognized that Christ himself spoke in and through him (2 Cor 13:3; cf. 2:17; 12:19), and that Christ's cross was visible in his own suffering and message about the cross (2 Cor 2:14–16; 4:10–11; Gal 2:20; 3:1).

In the Synoptics, too, Jesus suggests a revelatory epistemology that transcends exclusive dependence on human intellect. Without revelation, earthly wisdom cannot penetrate Jesus's identity; the kingdom is given not to the wise and prudent, as if they are necessarily most meritorious, but to babes—to those who accept the message in faith (Matt 11:25–27//Luke 10:21–22; Matt 16:17). Those who receive the kingdom like children are those ready to depend on a heavenly Father (Matt 18:3).[16] Some of the early Christians, such as Paul, were very smart people; like some of the rest of us, however, Paul had to have the pride experientially knocked out of him to bring him to faith.

Jesus's movement widely recognized the Spirit as the chief agent of divine wisdom and revelation (e.g., Exod 28:3; 31:3; 35:31; Deut 34:9; Isa 11:2; Acts 6:3, 10; 1 Cor 2:13; 12:8; Eph 1:17), suggesting that kerygmatic epistemology is pneumatic epistemology. The gospel includes both a narration of God's acts and an inspired interpretation. In the gospel the Spirit reveals Jesus afresh, providing epistemic clarity and thus moral responsibility. Thus Paul expects that the full message of the Spirit can be embraced fully only by those conditioned by the Spirit (1 Cor 2:13–3:1).[17] Although Bultmann's skeptical approach toward the narrative's objective historicity gutted a central element of the gospel (1 Cor 15:1–7),[18] he was certainly right to recognize New Testament theology's role for the existential dimension in the gospel's reception.[19]

Fallen Worldviews

Belief has been difficult for Western intellectuals shaped by the legacy of Hume's skeptical epistemology. Immanuel Kant allowed room for faith and values, but in a subjective sphere distinct from objective reason; by further discounting any role for the subjective in epistemology, the Vienna Circle rejected the legitimacy of metaphysics. Many philosophers subsequently reintroduced metaphysics, but my point here is that those schooled in the modern Western intellectual tradition tend to marginalize the role of subjective experience in terms of certainty or knowledge. This tradition has certainly influenced my own thinking, for better or (often, I find) worse.

This often excessively skeptical approach, however, is no less historically contingent than the approaches it rejects, and runs counter to biblical Christian experience. "The Spirit testifies together with our spirit," Paul notes, "that we are God's children" (Rom 8:16; cf. possibly 1 John 5:6–7). The context involves the Spirit enabling us to cry out, "Abba, Father" (Rom 8:15), a subjective, relational experience and not exclusively an objective, rational recognition. "We know that he dwells in us," John declares, "by the Spirit he has given us" (1 John 3:24). That is not John's only test of faith, but it is one of them.

Romans 1 contrasts two options, the way of faith revealing God's righteousness, and the other revealing involving his wrath. In the first option, God's righteousness is revealed in the good news, embraced by faith from start to finish (1:16–17). In the second, God's righteous wrath is revealed against humanity's unrighteous suppression of truth by idolatry, which distorts the truth about God (1:18, 23), even though humanity should have known better (1:19–23).

These options also ultimately contrast faith as a perspective on reality, with minds corrupted by their resistance against divine truth. Refusal to honor God became the beginning of the sinful mind (1:20–22); neglecting the truth, humanity succumbed to foolishness. Ultimately God gave them over to failed minds because they failed to mind or acknowledge him (1:28).[20] Faith is opposed to the mind of the flesh; instead, it reveals the mind of the Spirit.

The corruption of human intellect in Rom 1:21–22, 25, 28, involves particularly human understanding about God and the principles that flow from that; the further one proceeds from directly theological and ethical matters, the less direct the influence of corruption. Paul is nevertheless clear that this corruption extends beyond the area where it starts, because no area of our life is completely independent from him (cf. Matt 5:34–35). If we demean God to the level of his creation, we eventually distort his image in and purpose for ourselves (Rom 1:23–27), and ultimately become incapable of proper moral discernment (1:28–32).[21] The greater the theological distortion, the wider the societal consequences and distortion of other truths. Theological soundness of mind is restored as the mind is renewed in Christ (12:2–3, inverting some of the language of 1:28).[22]

Faith as an Epistemic Commitment

what does that mean?

Faith, which is consistent with the mind of the Spirit, is an epistemic commitment. Evidence may be sufficient to invite belief, but rarely would thinkers today claim that evidence compels belief; belief involves a decision.[23] Even when it often produces unconscious recognition of the truth, this recognition does not compel adherence that acts as if the recognized reality is true. <u>Christian scholars sometimes guard their moral life but surrender their intellectual life to the world's skepticism.</u> If Christ is Lord of our lives, however, his realm must include our intellect.

Epistemically, Christians need be no more reticent about their starting convictions than are others.[24] Everyone has starting premises that are difficult to justify on their own terms—for example, epistemologies that are empiricist, rationalist, or existential. We may explore the options, but ultimately when we decide to follow Christ, or to the extent that we commit ourselves to follow him, this entrusting ourselves to him, and so staking the direction of our lives on him, involves an epistemic commitment. I am well aware of this issue because I have personally struggled with it for years—balancing the intellectual value of open inquiry with personal commitment of my mind to Christ.

It was not that the conclusions of my inquiry undermined my faith; more often than not they confirmed my intellectual belief in Christ, although often requiring adjustments in some other preliminary assumptions. Nor was it wrong to weigh intellectual options while pursuing more secure conclusions, nor, for heuristic purposes, to bracket some questions as I pursued evidence where it would lead. The problem was that I sometimes allowed agnostic assumptions, adopted for small-scale heuristic purposes, to bleed over into larger areas, despite their incompatibility with the Christian beliefs that I already had reason to conclude on other grounds, and thus their incompatibility with my commitment to Christ as Lord.

Most of my academic work has built on open inquiry, to some degree bracketing my faith commitment from the exploration because the approaches accepted in the sphere of inquiry were limited. While in general this limited methodology caused no problems within the sphere of the issues addressed, it promoted a mental habit of bracketing faith out of the reasoning process when (for much of each day) I was in my academic mode.

This bracketing approach, however, risked spillover into my personal faith; data was sufficient to resolve many of the intellectual questions, but no quantity of data can ever fill the vacuum of a skeptical epistemology that refuses to permit faith with less than 100 percent evidence. This is because inflexible skepticism—the way I framed the questions that needed to be answered—can always raise new objections. When such a radically untrusting epistemology moves beyond a heuristic function to become a working mental premise, it can preclude commitments. Yet no one applies this radical skepticism to ordinary life; we recognize the difference between complete evidence and *sufficient* evidence.[25] I mentioned in chapter 1 the tension that this skeptical approach needlessly created when I applied it to my wife's testimony.

As already noted, everyone works from some starting assumptions, whether methodological, cosmological or otherwise. Devoting our intellect for the service of Christ (Rom 12:2) means that we work from a grid, from assumptions attached to Christ's Lordship. This does not mean that we cannot examine questions honestly, but our academic habit of placing the bar of evidence too high for anything to surmount it is not honesty; it is practiced unbelief. Full faith comes when we are convinced enough to personally rely on the worldview entailed by the truth that Christ is Lord. That grid need not (and for me does not) require uncritical embrace of everything affirmed by some Christian tradition. It does work from Christ's Lordship and whatever that proves to entail, because this grid merits my commitment more than do other premises that wish to compete for my allegiance.

Nonbelievers and even antibelievers can contribute valuable insights about the grammar, history and even literary characteristics of Scripture. By definition, however, they do not understand Scripture in the fullest *personal* sense that Scripture invites, because such understanding includes *embracing* its truth (by virtue of which one is no longer an unbeliever), not simply explaining the grammar. The level of understanding is different, just as there is a difference between explaining the chemical properties of ink on a page and reading it, or, more analogously, between examining a map and following it.

Some Examples of Faithful Reading

Earlier chapters have addressed issues such as taking into account cultural context (chapter 8), reading narratives (chapter 1), and interpreting miracle accounts (chapter 6). Here I briefly revisit these issues in light of the present question of epistemology.

Then and Now: Culture

Works addressed to particular churches or circles of churches are not necessarily relevant only to these churches; thus Revelation invites each of the churches to hear what the Spirit says to all of them, even though the message to each church was specially tailored for that church (Rev 2:7, 11, 17, 29; 3:6, 13, 22).

But what do we do when we cannot *understand* what the Spirit was saying to a church because the language and culture are obscure to us? Most Christian readers in most cultures will apply directly to themselves passages such as "Be strong in the Lord" (Eph 6:10) or even the armor of God (6:11–17), often without giving much thought to the imagery's sources from Isaiah or Roman military apparel that this passage addressed to its ancient audience.

Readers usually become more judicious and alert when the context advises slaves to obey their holders (6:5); suddenly they recognize that they are dealing with a different culture. Similarly, modern Western readers often see no need for first-century setting when reading Paul's counsel regarding the Lord's supper in 1 Corinthians 11:17–34; the preceding passage about head coverings, however (11:2–16), they often dismiss as irrelevant to their own culture. Such readings are drastically inconsistent, as a comparison with other cultures' readings could illustrate. For example, half my university students in northern Nigeria believed that Christian women in all cultures should wear head coverings to church; they treated holy kisses, however, as a first-century custom. In my wife's culture in Central Africa, where people could employ kisses in greeting, holy kisses proved more intelligible than mandatory head coverings. What we assume as cultural often depends on what differs from the reader's own culture. This does not offer a consistent way to read Scripture.[26]

A more consistent way of reading Scripture is to recognize that even if (as Christians affirm) the message of Scripture is for every generation, its particulars do not apply equally in all circumstances. For a conspicuous example, Paul explicitly addressed the Corinthians when he wrote 1 Corinthians (1 Cor 1:2); if we take this affirmation seriously, it must shape how we read the entire letter, whether Chloe's report (1:11), food offered to idols (8:1–10:33), head coverings (11:2–16), or how the Corinthians ate the Lord's supper (11:17–34). Paul regularly brings to bear universal principles on particular situations, but because he writes to a local setting he does not have reason to pause to explain which elements are universal and which are concrete applications of those principles.

To figure out the reasons for Paul's concrete applications, we ideally need to know something about the original culture and settings that he addressed.[27] Rather than expecting everyone to digress from their other work for a few years, I believe that a primary responsibility of at least some biblical scholars should be to make this information available to ordinary readers. Once this information is available, conversion of the shared principles to readers' settings is often intuitive. By "principles," however, I do not refer to seeking to extract from texts "foundational propositional truths," the concern with "principlizing" articulated by some scholars.[28] I mean something more like recognizing how Paul contextualized God's message for his setting, and how his contextualization models for us ways to recontextualize that message for new settings.[29]

Once we can get a sense for the original setting, we can begin to use the concrete applications as case studies, as models for how we can concretely apply the same principles. Paul read earlier biblical accounts as models relevant for his own audience. Thus, for instance, stories of Israel's sins in the wilderness, though describing and written to settings different from Paul's, provided warnings for the Corinthians who were tempted by the very same sins. "These matters happened as examples for us," Paul admonished (1 Cor 10:6). They "happened to them as an example," and "were written as a warning for us" (10:11).

Reading Narrative

Although ready to apply Paul's letters directly and without much thought for their first setting, some have been more reluctant to apply *narrative*. Some use narrative only for reconstructing past salvation history. Their historical insights are usually valuable, since these accounts provide a narative structure of the Bible, with other material (such as prophecies and letters) offering samples of the message that went to given generations. Yet these narratives also contain patterns of the ways that God worked in some circumstances, and we can learn from these patterns. Scripture itself invites this approach: "All Scripture is God-inspired and beneficial for teaching, for reproof, for improvement, and for the sort of training that involves righteousness" (2 Tim 3:16).[30]

Traditionally Pentecostals, like many others,[31] approached Acts as a model.[32] Whether Acts actually teaches us that tongues-speaking should always accompany baptism in the Holy Spirit is a legitimate question on which Pentecostal scholars today themselves disagree; tongues are not narrated in every instance when people receive the Spirit in Acts. Nevertheless, tongues are repeated frequently enough to suggest that Luke intends a connection. In my view, argued in chapter 3, the clear connection is that tongues evidenced the *character* of baptism in the Holy Spirit in Luke's emphasis: power to speak for God across cultures (Acts 1:8). This does not require interpreters to suppose that tongues evidence which *individuals* receive this empowerment, but Luke's association of tongues with mission does suggest that the connection in Acts is not arbitrary. That is, Luke is *teaching* something in his narrative.

Although his position has developed somewhat,[33] Gordon Fee originally aroused reaction by arguing for greater caution in use of narrative models than he felt characterized many other Pentecostal scholars.[34] Fee is the quintessential model of a faithful Pentecostal scholar, and I esteem him as a mentor; indeed, long before I had met him I listened repeatedly to tapes of his NT course until I had taken thorough notes on and mostly mastered the material. He was one of the only role models that some of us younger Pentecostal, aspiring scholars found available. Although criticized by some fellow Pentecostals for his hesitation regarding narrative precedents, he has been a model of Spirit-filled scholarship for myself and many others.

Most scholars today, however, would not agree with his early hesitation regarding narrative. In the past few decades, biblical narrative criticism has highlighted the importance of getting theology from narrative, even more fully than the previous generation's attention to redaction criticism had.[35] (Fee's current articulation of deriving theology from narrative, nuanced after dialogue with some Pentecostal colleagues, is fairly mainstream and unobjectionable.)[36]

In addition to developments in narrative criticism, today we also know that ancient biography and historiography regularly sought to inculcate moral lessons, political agendas, and so forth. Such an observation does not mean that we should allegorize narratives, the way that some Greek philosophers allegorized old myths that they found offensive.[37] Whatever may be said for mythography, ancient writers of historiography and biography did not normally expect their readers to allegorize their narratives, but they did expect their readers to draw lessons from them. This expectation is often explicit in their writings,[38] and we are remiss if we neglect such interests. After all, "all Scripture is God-inspired and beneficial for teaching, refuting error, correction, and training for right living," so God's servants may be fully equipped to serve him (2 Tim 3:16–17). Ignoring the training value of narrative, the largest major genre in Scripture, leaves the church only partly equipped.

By grafting our lives into the biblical narrative, we become part of the extension of that narrative. Early Pentecostals often viewed Acts 28 as open-ended,[39] a conclusion that narrative critics today have usually reaffirmed.[40] So long as the mission remains to be completed, we continue to need the Spirit's power to fulfill it (Acts 1:8), and that same power is promised to us (2:39, evoking also God's promise in 1:4). Likewise, we who continue this mission remain part of the narrative of salvation history, a narrative (from our vantage point postcanonical) to which Acts points. Revelation similarly speaks of God's people from all nations, and the continuing conflict in this age by the peoples of Babylon and the New Jerusalem. We who give our allegiance to the lamb remain part of the narrative envisioned in Revelation.

Interpreting Miracles

Miracles provide an important example of where divergent epistemic approaches lead to diametrically contrary interpretations, both in biblical narratives and in modern ones. Thus, for example, the crowds were duly impressed by fire from heaven (1 Kgs 18:39), but Jezebel promised to kill Elijah, sending him into despair (19:1–3). God attested with signs his message in Iconium, but its citizens divided over the message (Acts 14:3–4).

Responses to and worldviews about miracles differ dramatically today as well. One Mozambiqan pastor reportedly raised seven people from the dead, and could not understand why the foreign interviewer seemed so interested; the pastor simply expected God to do miracles as he did in the Bible.[41]

wow!

Miracles belong to an epistemology of faith as well as to concrete material realities. Countless events that a recipient experiences as a miracle are explained quite differently by those who do not believe. Whether we accept an experience as miraculous typically depends on prior assumptions and the burden of proof. Thus, for example, if someone recovers after prayer from a usually fatal illness from which someone occasionally recovers (perhaps without prayer), those who prayed will see God's hand, but those who define a miracle only as a violation of nature (following Hume here, not the Bible) will question it. It is appropriate for us as believers to see God's hand regularly, but those who think in terms of "evidence" (the way we must argue in the academy) may reject as miraculous any actions explicable "without appeal to God." Others are skeptical no matter what explanations seem plausible.

Some skeptics carry this skepticism to remarkable lengths. Thus, for example, from a medical standpoint cataracts do not disappear immediately without surgery. A number of cases, however, report the instant disappearance of cataracts after prayer.[42] Someone committed to unbelief, however, can refuse to allow the evidence through their interpretive grid, rejecting claims that do not fit the "reality" they have constructed. They can challenge the credibility of the witnesses, videos, or even medical documentation; or they can explain the event away as a natural event working according to natural principles not yet understood (e.g., psychic power).[43] I know some of the witnesses for some of these reports, however, and one would expect psychic power, if that were the explanation, to have more consistent results (in contrast to the less known will of God as what philosophers call an intelligent, personal agent). Moreover, the common factor in a large number of reports (nearly all of those available to me) was prayer in the name of Jesus.

Likewise, resuscitations from death (or at least deep coma that appears to be death) are not easily explained psychosomatically. Yet ten such close eye-witness accounts appear in my own circle of friends and family. As I pointed out in a recent article, such an accumulation of incidents appears highly im-probable as coincidence.[44] "Unless premature burial is dangerously perva-sive, the proportion of resuscitations connected with theistic settings appears extraordinarily higher than the number of spontaneous resuscitations in the general population. At least ten people that my family knows well claim direct experience with theistic resuscitations, a figure that easily could be expanded if we include associates of those we know."[45]

If one deems such resuscitations merely rare anomalies explained by coin-cidence, the improbability of the accumulation of coincidences demonstrates that this typical nontheistic explanation is *extraordinarily* improbable. If one's starting estimate for the coincidence of one of these anomalies in one's circle were as high as one chance in ten (a very generous concession; Hume and members of his circle presumably had none in their circles)—that is, of a misdiagnosed death and instant recovery during prayer—one might thus sup-pose one chance in ten billion for ten such claims in one's circle. One cannot presuppose much higher probabilities of average resuscitations in one's circle without assuming that a radically inordinate number of people are being bur-ied prematurely. What are the odds that I was the one person in ten billion with such a coincidence, and I just happened to be one of the few persons writing an extensive book concerning miracles? Based on normal understanding of probabilities, is it not more rational to suppose that prayer sometimes has something to do with recovery?

Again, someone committed to disbelief in miracles can argue that my circle includes a disproportionate number of liars.[46] We know the witnesses too well to accept that objection as persuasive, but one would hope that even skeptics should be given pause. Why should skeptics hold so tenaciously to a worldview that is essentially a presupposition (miracles are not accepted as known in their circles) to the degree that they would dismiss other people's testimony as false, even when critical scholars who know them affirm their trustworthiness, precisely in those cases where eyewitness testimony chal-lenges their philosophic presuppositions?

As already suggested, such an inflexible epistemology that deems as liars eyewitnesses who do not simply confirm one's existing knowledge would make impossible history, journalism, and a variety of other disciplines. "Science de-mands replicable events!" they may protest. But miracles are by definition not replicable; if they were, skeptics could then dismiss them as part of nature.[47] History is also not replicable; we must use for each area of inquiry the epistemic method appropriate to it. "But we can evaluate the likelihood of kinds of events by analogy," some protest, "and there is no analogy for miracles." Such an argument against there being any analogy for a miracle is circular: it works only if one has already dismissed all other miracle claims. If that a priori approach is not closed-minded, circular reasoning, I cannot imagine what would qualify as such.

good point!

Such responses to miracle reports today should not surprise us. We often suppose that if people simply saw some incontrovertible miracle, such as someone being raised who had been dead for a few days, they would believe. Yet Scripture is more realistic about human character. John's Gospel testifies that whereas many witnesses who observed Lazarus's raising believed, some apparently responded by reporting Jesus's works to religious leaders who opposed him (John 11:45–46).

interesting

Jesus's signs did often lead to faith (e.g., 2:11; 11:42, 45, 47–48; 12:11; 13:19; 14:29; 17:21; 20:8, 30–31),[48] but in other cases they simply made observers more responsible for their unbelief (12:37; cf. 6:26, 30). Some could not believe, because God himself blinded them, handing them over (as I understand it) to their choice of unbelief (12:38–40). Some others believed secretly but were more concerned about what others thought of them than about God's demands (12:42–43). Even those who did not see directly could believe through reliable witnesses' testimony, if they were willing to do so (19:35; 20:30–31; cf. 1 Pet 1:8).

Similarly, one may think of Pharaoh's recalcitrance despite repeated plagues in Exodus. Indeed, most of the plagues against Egypt could have been explained naturally, as amplifications of plagues that were already part of Egypt's ecosystem.[49] Even Pharaoh's magicians eventually recognized God's power as greater than what they could duplicate by natural (or magical) means (Exod 8:18–19), but Pharaoh himself was too invested in a different worldview. For Pharaoh to see the God of Israel as more powerful than the gods of Egypt (Exod 12:12; Num 33:4) struck at the core of his theology and of his own identity, for he was seen as divine. Even the death of the firstborn, which transcended any natural explanation from Egypt's ecosystem, persuaded him only temporarily; after that Pharaoh pursued Israel to the sea.

How we see miracles depends on our interpretive grid, our faith. If some are naïve in believing every report they hear, others of us are too skeptical. Indeed, even buying into David Hume's definition of miracles as violations of nature prevents us from recognizing most of God's activity. Plagues that struck Egypt's ecosystem or God blowing back the sea by a strong east wind (Exod 14:21) are not violations of nature. As mere coincidence, however, they are extraordinarily improbable, especially cumulatively. Indeed, so is nature itself; nothing is more improbable as an accident than a language more complex than any originated by humans—the complexity of DNA. And we humans are most complex of all.

Some naturalistic explanations for cumulatively improbable miracles appear to believers as grasping at straws; the hypothesis of God is a much simpler and more plausible explanation. For those with faith in pure naturalism, however, any explanation that excludes God is better than any explanation that includes him, because God is a priori excluded from their explanatory scheme. That is, unbelief is a worldview, and some hold it so tenaciously, placing the bar of evidence infinitely high (or at least as high as needed to reject any proffered evidence), that they can accept no evidence. The Bible speaks of moral blindness, of inability to see truth, sometimes even among God's own people (Isa 6:10; 29:9; 42:18–19; 43:8; 56:10; Jer 5:21; Ezek 12:2).

Worldviews under Judgment

This is all to say that worldviews shape how we read miracle accounts, just as worldviews shape how we interpret reality more generally. We may start with a "hermeneutic of trust," as Richard Hays helpfully puts it,[50] or a hermeneutic of suspicion.[51] As charismatic Catholic scholar William Kurz notes, a hermeneutic of suspicion, unless used with discretion, is incompatible with reading Scripture as God's Word in the interpretive community of the church.[52] Or even as Jewish scholar Geza Vermes warned NT scholars reading early Jewish texts, "Religious writings disclose their meaning only to those who approach them in a spirit of sympathy."[53]

Suspicion has its place, as Israelite wisdom recognizes (Prov 9:16; 22:3; 27:12); indeed, Prov 14:15 warns that the naïve person will believe anything someone says, whereas wise people will consider what they are getting themselves into. Some people are untrustworthy, and human perspectives are always incomplete. Nevertheless, *God* is worthy of our trust, and at some point our resistance to true signs becomes culpable unbelief (Num 14:11, 22; Neh 9:17).[54]

We may have various reasons for explaining away the text's demands or treating them as irrelevant. Whether we call it philosophically a Humean paradigm, culturally Western skepticism, or exegetically a hermeneutic of suspicion, theologically it fits what the Bible depicts as unbelief, i.e., unbelief in the true God of Scripture. From a biblical perspective, unbelief is just as characteristic of modern atheistic paradigms as it was true of ancient polytheistic or other paradigms.

The God of the Bible is not the God of deists or the definitive non-deity of atheism; yet in the West often even Christians have committed syncretism with deism. We allow for answers to prayer so long as they do not diverge from the norms of natural expectations; otherwise they are all suspect, from reliable witnesses as well as from unreliable ones.[55] We depend on God's good gifts to us, such as resources, technology, and education, but we frequently act as if God could not help us were we stripped of such blessings. We hold to a form of godliness but deny its power (cf. 2 Tim 3:5). Some have asked whether, if (speaking purely hypothetically) God's Spirit were withdrawn from our churches, we would do anything differently than the way we now do it.

That observation is relevant not only to miracles, but to experiencing and obeying Scripture more generally. Jesus summons not only the rich ruler to surrender his possessions to care for the poor (Luke 18:22), but all his disciples (12:33; 14:33; cf. 3:11; 19:8). When the Lord poured out the Spirit, one immediate effect was that God's people shared what they had with those who needed more (Acts 2:44–45; 4:32–35); this practice later continued in sharing by churches in different regions (Rom 15:26; 2 Cor 8–9), dictated by the Spirit (Acts 11:27–30). Traveling apostles sacrificed even more dramatically (1 Cor 4:11–12; 2 Cor 11:27). A genuine pneumatic theological focus, then, should yield sacrifice rather than boasting in wealth.

Some churches dismiss such claims in Scripture as hyperbole (though the purpose of hyperbole is to invite our special attention). They then dismiss similar claims by St. Francis or John Wesley or Charles Finney as legalism, and even much tamer claims by modern contemporaries such as Ron Sider as Marxism.[56] Meanwhile we spend most of our resources on ourselves, though Scripture shows that God made parts of the global church stewards of resources so that everyone would have enough to live on. In some parts of the world Christians' children die from malnutrition and inexpensively preventable diseases like malaria while we struggle with an epidemic of obesity (in the majority of cases without a good genetic reason for it). We have adopted our culture's worldview of materialism and sometimes even a virtual social Darwinism (let those less fit to survive die off). The biblical solution to such an approach is not mere intellectual rethinking, but repentance; not conversation, but conversion.

Reading with *faith* means reading biblical narratives with *expectation*—expectation that God will speak to us in some way because the God who is active in the narrative world of the text is the real God who is also active in our world.[57] This reality is easier to believe in circles where such views are reinforced, but even in cultures where they are not, we must learn to "inhabit the text."

CHAPTER 12

Biblical Epistemology and Hermeneutics

No one need suggest that secular academia should read texts as Christians do; but Christians *as* Christians should embrace a distinctively Christian way of reading Scripture. The secular approach of reading with common historical ground rules is a helpful way of reading for that setting; it allows people from different perspectives to dialogue together about the texts.[1] The common ground rules mean that none of us can prove to everyone's satisfaction everything that any of us believes beyond that common ground. A system does not have to be perfect, however, to offer a useful function.

But we need not settle for that limitation when speaking within the community of believers; Christians may read biblical texts in a specifically Christian way. Speaking descriptively at least, interpretive communities read texts according to the rules within those communities. Secular academia has its way of reading; the church has another. Here I do not speak simply descriptively about how churches often read texts, but rather urge us to consider what the prophetic and apostolic voices in Scripture suggest about reading approaches (cf. further chapters 13–16). Indeed, Scripture indicates that God will ultimately call people to account for not believing the truth (e.g., 2 Thess 2:10), including the truth found in Scripture (Luke 16:29–31; John 5:45–47).

Scripture offers models and worldviews that we can appropriate only as we read with faith. Without ruling out valuable historical insights from other forms of research, we can learn to read Scripture at a fuller level or mode that trusts and looks for the divine purpose there. When one adopts a thoroughly believing reading, embracing God's message, one reads as a believer.

Bold Claims to the Truth

In our postmodern culture, metanarrative claims appear offensive. Such reservations have some value: we "know in part" and recognize that no moral or theological merit secures for us God's gift in Christ. Nevertheless, the apostolic message regularly presents Christ as the one way of salvation (and not only in John 14:6; Acts 4:12) and offers a compatibly offensive particularist epistemology.[2]

what does that mean?

Conflicting Views of Reality

In Scripture, spiritual experience can seem insane to those who do not share it (1 Sam 19:24; 2 Kgs 9:11; Acts 2:13; 12:15; 26:24; 1 Cor 14:23; 2 Cor 5:13).[3] Even the resurrection testimony, which transcended ordinary expectations from human experience (Acts 26:8), was initially disbelieved (Luke 24:11). Indeed, those with worldviews that rule out some sorts of divine action will often question even their *own* spiritual experience (Matt 28:17; Luke 24:37; Acts 12:9), as I can unfortunately testify.

very interesting

Paul plays at length on this idea in 1 Corinthians and especially in the first part of 2 Corinthians, in the latter work responding to suspicions concerning his apostolic ministry. Apostolic suffering resembles the cross, the epitome of weakness and foolishness to those who are perishing even though it was really the supreme sign of God's power and wisdom (1 Cor 1:18–25). True wisdom thus appears as foolishness to the world.[4] But Christ's apostles share his suffering, appearing to the world as foolish and weak (4:9–13, esp. 4:10).

In 2 Corinthians, Paul announces that Christ leads his apostles as prisoners in his triumphal procession (2 Cor 2:14); hearers of this letter in Corinth, a Roman colony, probably understood that such prisoners were executed after the procession. Paul thus speaks of his ministry in terms of dying, following Jesus's example and sharing his sufferings (1:9–10; 4:7–12, esp. 11–12; 6:9). To believers, the mortal hardship of apostolic ministry is the aroma of life; to those who are perishing, it is simply the stench of death (2:14–16). Only from the standpoint of new creation do we understand even Christ's suffering (5:16–17). That is, only believers look at the cross and see the resurrection.

Faith and Truth

Faith here is a *perspective,* a worldview that, provided it is directed toward divine truth, allows us access to that truth.[5] Everyone brings presuppositions and thus an interpretive grid to reality, based on past experiences or teaching; some are more open to adjusting their interpretive grid than are others. Skepticism, no less than faith, involves presuppositions, an interpretive grid.

We may have different names for different philosophic and religious approaches that reject a biblical message, but all of these approaches appear counter to Christian faith in Scripture. That is, whether someone disbelieved Paul's message because Roman imperialism made the cross look foolish, because they already had many deities (cf. Isa 46:6–7; Jer 10:14), or because Paul's gospel did not fit the worldview in their synagogue (1 Cor 1:22–23; 8:5–6), Paul would say that the god of this age had blinded them (2 Cor 4:3–4; cf. 3:13–14).[6]

From a Christian perspective, whether one should prefer faith or skepticism with regard to a given proposition depends on what is true. In response to Kant's separation of subjective faith from objective reason, Kierkegaard conceived of faith as a leap in the dark. This construction made sense in his philosophic context, but it is not what Paul means by faith. Biblical faith is not a Kierkegaardian leap in the dark, but a deliberate step into the light of the truth.

At the same time, although truth is often amenable to exploration from various angles, human epistemologies have their limits, as does the information to which people have access. Apart from consideration of the role of God's infinite Spirit, we always have to commit our trust with incomplete, finite knowledge because that is all that is available to us. We should be supremely grateful that we have at least enough information to justify our trust in someone infinitely wiser than we are. That is not to repudiate the importance of seeking knowledge to the best of our ability (cf. Prov 18:15; 22:17; 23:12; cf. wisdom in 2:4; 8:17); it is merely to reaffirm that fearing God is the beginning of knowledge (Prov 1:7)—the sound interpretive grid and foundation, especially for knowledge about God and God's activities.

Scripture sometimes depicts faith as a sort of sense; Heb 11:1 may describe it as proof, evidence,[7] reality or confidence. Infrared illumination and night vision goggles can allow people to see images at ranges on the electromagnetic spectrum that people could not normally see without them. Biblical faith is like another sense, a spiritual sense, that allows us to see what is genuinely present yet is hidden from those who do not believe (2 Cor 4:3–4). That truth remains concealed from them in part because their interpretive frameworks do not allow them to see it, e.g., because their worldview excludes divine activity from consideration. (For this reason Paul is concerned to correct false ideologies; cf. 2 Cor 10:5). Biblical truth, then, is perceived and embraced by trust and dependence on the God who reveals it.

Faith can certainly be naïve and misplaced if its object is not true. A religious suicide bomber or people who kill alleged child witches may believe in what they are doing, but we are convinced that their beliefs are false. Scripture emphasizes not faith in simply *anything* but faith in God and in Christ, faith warranted by the evidence of the first witnesses and the continuing witness of the Spirit. (In fact, with only a few exceptions such as 2 Thess 2:11, Paul employs the language of faith almost exclusively for faith in the truth.) When people treat biblical verses out of context like magical formulas to get what they want, their faith in biblical texts is misplaced (although in some cases God might nevertheless honor their genuine faith in Christ). By contrast, God is reliable as an object of our trust.

How often do we do that?

The Spirit of Truth and Faith

Beyond believers starting with a Christian worldview or perspective, the Spirit adds an epistemic dynamic that provides conviction. In the Gospels, especially Matthew and John, Jesus affirms that he is with his people and that his Spirit continues his presence with us (Matt 18:20; John 14:23). In practice, because we accept the truth of the affirmation's source, this should lead us also to affirm his presence. It often consequently yields an experience of being conscious of God's presence (recognized by faith, not by feeling, although the recognition may well generate or be conjoined with feelings). That does not mean that our consciousness of his presence is what makes him present; but through living faith in the reality of his presence, we can live our lives in the light of his presence.[8]

The Spirit bears witness with our spirit (Rom 8:16) and offers boldness for proclamation (Acts 4:31). One may object that this assurance is too subjective and personal to convince others, but the dynamic of the Spirit who assures us can also provide conviction to others through our presentation of Christ (1 Thess 1:5; cf. 2:13; John 16:7–11). A Spirit epistemology insists that it is not ideal merely to inherit the right worldview; we need the frame of mind given by the Spirit (Rom 8:5–7; 1 Cor 2:9–16).

Early Pentecostals applied this approach to some spiritual gifts the way their radical evangelical precursors applied it to healing and faith for provision on the mission field. Although sometimes their insistence became excessive (a common trait among most young movements excited about distinctives), they tried to confirm in their experience the worldview they found in Scripture. It was a faith in Scripture usually not based so much on debates about the precise *nice!*

meaning of biblical passages as on the reality of the biblical worldview. The Spirit both empowers and responds to such faith or desperate prayers (Luke 11:13) for what is biblically normal to become our own normal experience.

Unbelief as a Worldview

eased!

The vast majority of scholars today recognize that all interpreters bring presuppositions to the table, whether the interpreters recognize their assumptions or not. Most interpreters from renewal traditions argue that their worldview, which accepts as real biblical approaches to the supernatural, comports better with reality than the often uncritically antisupernaturalist bias that tends to pervade modern critical scholarship.[9]

Biblically, fidelity to God even in the face of potentially persuasive competing worldviews shows love for him (Deut 13:3); love demands trust and loyalty. Biblical faith is not blind, as if we lack supporting evidence for what we believe; faith is, as we have noted, sound only insofar as its object is reliable. Yet neither does biblical faith lack commitment. The semantic range of the Hebrew term translated "faith" in Scripture includes not simply assent to propositions but *fidelity,* or faithfulness.[10]

The Bible often addresses our inability to apprehend divine truth. Although theologians between and within various traditions debate the nature and extent of total depravity, Scripture is clear that human depravity affects our ability to perceive divine truth. Some depict this depravity as corruption of reason; others specify a fallenness of the will that resists divine truth. Still others, including myself, would doubt that will and reason are so easily disentangled.

Some Examples of Sin Darkening the Mind

Pharaoh's hardened heart, mentioned above, provides one example. Probably his erroneous theology—his idea that his inherited ancestral gods were far greater than the one god of his slaves—remained a factor in this hardening; thus God's plagues struck Egypt's gods (Exod 12:12; Num 33:4). God hardened Pharaoh's heart (Exod 4:21; 7:3, 13), yet Pharaoh also remained responsible for choosing a hard heart (7:14). Pharaoh was often hardened whenever God relented from pressure against him (8:15, 31–32; 9:34; 10:20).

Another factor in his initial hardness, however, was the theological belief that particular alternative explanations were equally or more plausible, despite their limited scale—his magicians could duplicate the first signs (7:11–13, 22; cf. 8:7). Eventually God made clear that polytheistic and natural explanations were inadequate, even beyond Moses announcing in advance the plagues and often the relief. Pharaoh's magicians could no longer imitate the signs (8:18–19; 9:11); Pharaoh learned that the plague did not affect any of Israel's livestock (9:6–7); and God selected each family's firstborn to strike down (12:29). Yet Pharaoh, inconsistent with coherent reason outside his inflexible worldview, still remained hostile (14:4–9).

If anyone thinks that such hardness is inconceivable, one may simply marshall in the public square some conspicuously strong evidence for God's truth and observe the responses. Pharaoh staked everything on the truth of his theology, which included his divinity. Many today likewise stake everything on God being false, not open to persuasion otherwise. Those who underestimate the stakes involved might want to reckon with Pascal's wager: if one's belief might prove false, the risk in rejecting God is higher than the risk in following him.

Another example of sin blinding the mind appears in the prophet Isaiah. Here God responds to his people's resistance by ironically commanding them to remain blind (Isa 29:9); by this point, he had prevented them from even receiving truth through prophets and seers (29:10). (As a noncessationist I would suggest that where the true prophetic voice is silenced today, we should heed the silence; sometimes it means that we have exhausted our warnings and dulled or suppressed the warning system.)

Yet Isaiah is not implying that God has not reached out to his people; instead, God has abandoned them to their own excuses. Some might refuse to recognize his message because they could not read; others, because it was sealed (29:11–12). That is, they could not hear the prophetic voice because they had already chosen not to receive it. Their mortal wisdom was not God's truth (29:14); God is the one who has perfect knowledge (29:15–16). The truly wise heed him; there is no true wisdom against him (Prov 21:30; Isa 29:14; Jer 8:9).

Blindness on a Corporate Level

"We know that we are from God," John writes, "and the entire world lies in the sphere of the evil one" (1 John 5:19). John goes on to affirm that, by contrast, Jesus has given us understanding so we could know the true one (5:20).

As already noted (on p. 162), Rom 1:18–32 describes in part how humanity began deliberately suppressing the truth about God until their worldviews became so distorted with regard to divine matters that they became incapable of recognizing truth about God. Eventually, those who have become most proficient in blindness become fools while asserting themselves to be wise (1:22).

In Paul's day, as in Pharaoh's, the distortion came through multiplying deities and reducing the divine image to images created by people. Today the distortion sometimes comes through eliminating deity altogether and attributing everything to chance (even to the extent of resorting to a practically infinite number of universes to evade belief in an intelligent creator). As distorting God's image led to distorting human sexuality in Romans 1, it leads to the same today, where many humans stripped of any transcendent dignity pursue purely animal passions. Reducing human personhood or identity to the product of pure random chance offers humanity no transcendent purpose.[11]

Three times Paul emphasizes in Rom 1:18–32 that God hands the world over to the choices it has already made. This passage depicts corporate sin, which affects those surrounded by such worldviews and the corresponding choices they make within that framework. One of the horrors of sin is its corporate effects: millions of people in today's world starve, die of treatable diseases or become refugees because of others' selfishness and greed. There is enough food available in the world to feed everyone; because of inequitable distribution, however, people starve and die of malnutrition.

Information access is likewise inequitably distributed, as are veridical paradigms. When some justify their beliefs by means of falsehood, they silence God's voice not only in themselves but also for those who trust them. Those who slaughter others in hopes of achieving paradise normally follow a falsehood of others' making. Those who live and die without hope in a world that they perceive as godless also follow falsehoods of others' making.

Paul elsewhere speaks of a spirit of lawlessness (2 Thess 2:7), so that God gives over those who took pleasure in wickedness to a deluding influence so they would believe what was false instead of true, so they would not be saved (2:10–12).[12] In other words, when people love their sin more than they love truth, God causes[13] them to become so blind that they cannot see the truth.

Degrees of Blindness

As already noted, Paul speaks generically, but does not necessarily mean that everyone is equally blinded. Like Romans 1, Ephesians 4 speaks of Gentiles being darkened in their minds by ignorance and hard hearts leading to sexual immorality (Eph 4:17–19).[14] Yet Paul acknowledges here that his own audience was converted from this darkness (4:20), suggesting that Paul does not in fact regard such corporate blindness as impenetrable.[15]

Jesus describes an open-minded scribe as "not far from the kingdom" (Mark 12:34); and Mark apparently depicts Jesus's disciples (in contrast to his enemies) as merely half-blind (8:17–18, 23–25; contrast 4:11–13). It should also go without saying that our responsibility to people who do not understand is to be kind, gentle, and patient, even toward those who not merely do not comprehend but who oppose the message (2 Tim 2:24–25). Our role is to reason gently; God is the one who can grant them the repentance that can bring them to know the truth, with a sound way of thinking (2:25–26). When those who call themselves Christians feel the need to browbeat nonbelievers (even in response to some nonbelievers browbeating them), one wonders whether these Christians remember that they have what they have only by grace (cf. Luke 15:25–32; 18:9–14; Acts 11:3, 18; 1 Tim 1:13–16). Then again, focusing on the resistant can be nonproductive (Mark 6:11; Titus 3:9–10).

Years ago I often dialogued with an agnostic friend who would raise various intellectual objections against Christianity to see if I could answer them. In each case, the answers I gave did manage to satisfy his protests, although I readily recognize that I do not have answers to all available questions. The conversation would always climax the same way, with my friend admitting, "You're right. I just don't want to give up my sin." His mind was not completely incapable of receiving truth, however, in that he could at least perceive the reasonableness of the answers to his case.

Some others, who have usually refused civil dialogue, have seemed unable to even grasp that they have presuppositions, and that a Christian vantage point is no more a bias, from a neutral, agnostic perspective, than is their own. Still others may maintain skepticism because of inherited presuppositions, yet abandon those premises when confronted with a reality that dismantles their worldview. (That is what happened to me at my conversion from atheism, though many aspects of my unbelieving worldview remained to be dismantled subsequently.)

Examples of Hostile Bias

In practice, unbelief ranges from less culpable ignorance of God's truth to apparently benign neglect to deliberate rejection, and from tolerance of it to various degrees of hostility. Overt persecution of believers is a conspicuous form of hostility,[16] but in Western academic circles it is expressed more often by dismissing or attempting to discredit genuinely reasoned arguments without needing to consider them.

Most of my readers could easily illustrate such hostile bias, so I will limit examples to this section. I initially pursued scholarship expecting an objective hearing but was quickly disillusioned by the politics of academia. (It is not my intention in this book to embrace or reject wholesale everything said by postmodernist interpreters, as if all of them would even necessarily agree with each other, but in this instance postmodernists can rightly respond, "We told you so.")

Often some critics dismiss as "uncritical" any scholar who comes to more positive conclusions about many claims in Scripture. They are quick to do so even when the more positive scholar's work displays more research, more interdisciplinary connections, and a thorough interaction with various positions. The critic, meanwhile, may normally read only "critical" sources, by which they mean those that agree with their conclusions (or what they learned from their own respected mentors). Of course, this sort of bias is not a matter of one's position, but of one's disposition; it is an uncritical fundamentalism (in the pejorative modern sense of the term) whether it occurs on the left or on the right end of the theological spectrum (and I have witnessed it on both ends).

Reviews are one place where scholars can often observe such dispositions, though often the general academic respect for objectivity helps restrain them. While many scholars across the theological spectrum do honor the honorable liberal virtue of fair-mindedness, most of us have read some reviews so unfair that it seemed unbelievable that they addressed the same book that we had already read. Some reviewers apparently write reviews to pad their resumés, without noticing even the main points of the books they are reviewing. (Sometimes, consumed with their own academic focus only, they will elaborate extensively on a point of disagreement that consumed at most a single page in the book.)

One noted, senior, mainstream scholar lamented to me, undoubtedly with some hyperbole, that he had never yet had a reviewer read his book before reviewing it.[17] Another friend, lamenting a review he had received, shared the unhappy joke about a scholar who responded to a query, "No, I haven't read that book yet, or even reviewed it."[18] Even scholars who attempt to be fair cannot escape presuppositions, but traditionally part of academic critical discipline is to evaluate fairly based on common standards of one's discipline.[19]

Still, even somewhat hostile scholars are nearly always fairer than the worst comments posted after articles or blogs on the internet, which may provide a clearer illustration of hostile bias. Whereas scholars are normally trained to try to be fair or at least to guard their own reputations by not appearing overtly biased, anonymous comments on the internet may provide a clearer indication of unrestrained human dispositions. One anonymous critic offered an inexcusably hurtful "comment" to a teenage woman who had posted herself singing: "You're ugly; go kill yourself."

For examples more related to academics, when scholars write popular-level posts, self-assured popular critics often counter in comments sections with preposterous assertions. Sometimes they will "prove" their case against the scholar by citing as authoritative another misinformed popular source, or perhaps a genuine source that the scholar, whose scholarly work the anonymous critic has never read, addressed at length elsewhere.[20]

I was not surprised that some critics on the internet refused to believe eyewitness miracle testimony; to believe that it was both accurate and represented a genuine miracle would violate their worldview. What surprised me was a comment that denied believing even that I had ever been beaten for my faith—although it is a predictable occasional outcome of some urban evangelism when a miracle does *not* happen. I take this to illustrate that part of human freedom is that, instead of critically evaluating claims to seek truth honestly, people can abuse their critical faculties to reject any claim that is inconsistent with their worldview—even when, from the veridical divine perspective, their worldview may be wrong.

Presuppositions are inevitable, and they are not always expressed in hostile bias. Scripture is repeatedly clear, however, that worldviews biased against God are damaging. Whereas one solution in the Old Testament was to eradicate societies biased against God for the purposes of judgment and of preventing the contamination of God's people,[21] the teachings of Jesus and the apostolic church (and for that matter, Israel during the exile) are quite different. God wants his people to be a light and to make a difference in the values of their societies by charity and persuasion, not by coercion.[22]

John's Epistemic Dualism

From the start, John's Gospel divides the world into those who embrace the truth and those who resist it. When God's light shines in darkness, the darkness could not "apprehend" it (John 1:5); the Greek term here carries potential nuances of both understanding and overpowering (the former perhaps being more relevant here). The world could not recognize its creator when he came among them (1:11), but those who did receive him became God's children, being born from God (1:12–13). God could be fully understood only when God became human and revealed his heart (1:18).

Misunderstanding

Nicodemus could not even see God's kingdom until he was born from above (3:3); heavenly truths remained beyond his full understanding even when aided by some earthly analogies (3:10–12). Nicodemus's condition appears characteristic of what we should expect with regard to the world even after Jesus's exaltation. The world cannot receive the Spirit of truth because it neither recognizes nor knows him (John 14:17).

Johannine epistemology divides humanity into Jesus's followers and "the world." In John's epistemology (John 3:19–21, NRSV), the judgment is "that the light has come into the world, and people loved darkness rather than light because their deeds were evil. For all who do evil hate the light and do not come to the light, so that their deeds may not be exposed. But those who do what is true come to the light, so that it may be clearly seen that their deeds have been done in God."

Jesus thus warns his interlocutors that "You cannot understand" (John 8:43), because they still belong to a hostile spiritual sphere. (Paul offers a similar idea in 1 Cor 2:14.) They cannot understand him, Jesus explains, because they cannot hear his message (John 8:43). They have a fleshly, worldly perspective, whereas he has a heavenly one (8:15–16, 23; cf. 3:11–13). Jesus speaks to them in circular riddles, leaving them in a blindness that could only be superseded by a direct experience with God (8:19, 24–25). They are not morally qualified to recognize Jesus's truth (8:45–46); they cannot hear God's words truly because they are not from God (8:47). They fail to recognize that Jesus's words cannot be understood on a mere fleshly level, but only on the level of the Spirit and divine life (6:63).[23] The only way beyond this epistemic impasse is for them to continue in Jesus's message and thus *know* Jesus and his Father (8:19, 31–32), a knowledge that constitutes eternal life (17:3).

Knowing through Encounter

Many of the Johannine narratives that emphasize witness also emphasize a personal encounter with Jesus. Thus, having met Jesus, Andrew invites his brother Simon to meet him (John 1:40–42). The shepherd who calls his sheep by name, who knows them and his sheep know him (cf. 10:3–5, 14–15, 27), then calls Simon by name (1:42) and so makes him a disciple.

By noting that Andrew "found" his brother (1:41), after "seeking" Jesus (1:38), John connects this paragraph with the next one.[24] There Jesus "found" Philip, inviting him to be a disciple (1:43). Philip then "found" Nathanael (1:45). As Jesus had invited Andrew and his friend to "come and see" (1:39), so Philip now invites Nathanael to "come and see" (1:46).[25] Although Philip's testimony about Jesus's identity prepares Nathanael for an encounter with Jesus, it is the encounter with Jesus—who knows Nathanael's heart as he knew Simon's—that convinces Nathanael (1:46–51). Likewise, Jesus reveals himself to a Samaritan woman and also something about her identity (4:17–18, 25–26), and then she invites her people to "come, see" Jesus (4:29). As a result, they declare, they (like Nathanael before them) believe him not because of testimony but because they have met him for themselves (4:42). *What about today?*

Epistemology is central in a key scene in the book and Jesus's following warnings. (John's two favorite words for "know" appear some 140 times in the book, constituting this topic as a central motif.) In John 9, one who has experienced healing cannot answer all the critics' questions; there are matters that he does not know (9:12; cf. 9:20–21). Nevertheless, he knows enough to question their skepticism: he knows his experience, that he has gone from blindness to sight (9:25). His dogmatic critics, who hold a position of intellectual social power, are more arrogant about what they know: they "know" that Jesus is a sinner (9:24) and that God has spoken to Moses (9:29a), but they dismiss Jesus's significance precisely because they do not know his place of origin (9:29b).[26]

When the healed man exercises the intellectual independence to think for himself, affirming that "we know" that this man could not have done this miracle if he were a sinner (9:30–31), they scoff at his lack of scholarly learning and exclude him from the community of God's people (9:34). John's first target audience probably experienced expulsion from or marginalization in their synagogues,[27] but any of us who have been scoffed at for our faith can identify with this man. Ultimately, however, it is not these members of the elite who can determine whether anyone belongs to God's people.

Defending this man, Jesus contends that he came to give sight to those who recognize their blindness and to blind those who think they see—those who claimed to know better than others (9:39–41). The dividing issue here is Jesus's own identity. God's true sheep recognize their shepherd and resist the self-appointed, false leaders of God's people (9:35–38). Jesus's own sheep—God's true people—know his voice and know him (10:4–5, 14–15; cf. 10:27).

Although Jesus no longer walks among us in his flesh, the Spirit continues to make Jesus present (16:7–15). As Jesus revealed to his disciples what he heard from his Father (15:15), the Spirit continues to reveal what he hears from Jesus (16:13–15). The scenario of John 9–10 thus continues to play out, with diverse responses to Jesus in every period of this age.

Although not as heavily as in the Gospel, the Johannine epistles make heavy use of the two Johannine verbs for knowledge (thirty-four times in these seven chapters, the vast majority in 1 John).[28] The epistemic claim in 1 John 4:6 sounds circular, unless it is informed by trust in the apostolic witnesses that rests on a genuine experience of the Spirit: "We are from God. Whoever knows God heeds us; whoever is not from God does not heed us. This is how we can distinguish the Spirit of truth from the spirit of error."[29]

Outside the in-group, such reasoning appears to beg the question. It is premised, however, on prior knowledge of God—experiential knowledge. John's circle of witnesses could distinguish which spirits accorded with the Jesus who came in the flesh because they had known the Jesus who came in the flesh (4:1–3).[30] Those who had the experience of the Spirit recognized the truth (3:24), and they knew that the Spirit they experienced was the genuine one because this Spirit's testimony accorded with what the authentic human witnesses reported about Jesus (4:2–3; cf. John 15:26–27). Those who experienced God were also those who loved (1 John 4:7–8), presumably in contrast to those whom John's letter elsewhere criticizes, who had abandoned the community of believers.

Johannine Dualism Uses Ideal Types

At this point it is important to add a caveat. Although Johannine epistemic dualism is most relevant to my present chapter's chief concern, it is not the only biblical perspective on the world. Elsewhere in Scripture, Egyptians oppressed God's people in Moses's day, but embraced God's people in Joseph's day. Joseph and Moses married members of families of Gentile priests. Daniel experienced divine revelation even though he was also trained in the wisdom and learning of the Chaldeans (Dan 1:4–5; 2:19). Paul was on positive terms with Asiarchs, some of whom may have also been prominent in the region's polytheistic civic religion (Acts 19:31).[31]

Likewise even Johannine dualism, like the binary contrast between the wise or foolish in Proverbs (or Stoicism), or the contrast between those in the Spirit and in the flesh in Rom 8:3–11, is something of an ideal construct.[32]

Even for John, it does not mean in practice that everyone either fully understands or fully misunderstands; John's narratives in fact present various levels of understanding and misunderstanding. For example, Jesus understands fully, the disciples understand somewhat, secret believers such as Nicodemus are searching, and the authorities are fully blind.[33] What Johannine dualism offers us, however, is a stark reminder that worldviews and backgrounds do shape much discourse and debate, more than some are willing to recognize.

How does this exploration of unbelief as a worldview—surveying some of the biblical theology of cognitive depravity—relate to the theme of Spirit hermeneutics? Most important exegetical methods can be applied by either believers or nonbelievers.[34] But whether we read the text with faith or not is closely related to the worldview that we embrace. The Holy Spirit inspires the correct framework at even the basic level of confessing Jesus as Lord (1 Cor 12:3; 1 John 4:2), as well as empowering the perspectives and approaches of divine wisdom (Acts 6:3, 10; 1 Cor 2:13; 12:8; Eph 1:17; cf. Exod 31:3; 35:31; Isa 11:2). Fuller empowerment of the Spirit to boldly stand and build on those premises also comes from the Spirit even in the face of opposition (Acts 4:8, 13, 31).

Conclusion

A Spirit epistemology, foundational for a Spirit hermeneutic, embraces God's truth. Although evidence matters, so do presuppositions; apart from the regenerating, empowering and renewing work of the Spirit, a fallen worldview becomes a lens that inevitably distorts reality. Not every society's or individual's worldview is equally corrupted, but only the omniscient God has a complete worldview, so submitting to his revelation is the wisest course. God's Spirit can help us not to bring inherited hostile biases against God's wisdom. At its best, this epistemology goes beyond believing secondhand; it rests on a genuine encounter with Christ.

CHAPTER 13

Reading the Bible as Truth

Ps 119:160 (referring to the Torah): "The sum of your word is truth, and all your just verdicts are eternal"

John 17:17 (referring to Jesus's message): "Consecrate them in the truth; your message is truth"

2 Cor 4:2 (referring to the apostolic message): ". . . not distorting God's message, but by open declaration of the truth recommending ourselves to everyone's conscience in God's sight"

2 Thess 2:10 (referring to the apostolic message): ". . . and with all the deceit of unrighteousness to those who are perishing, who did not accept the practice of loving the truth, so as to be saved"

Scripture

Such passages invite us to heed the divine message that we now find embodied most fully (textually speaking) in Scripture. One might also survey similar passages, usually referring to the gospel message, that speak of the "word of truth," passages such as 2 Cor 6:7; Col 1:5; 2 Tim 2:15; Jas 1:18 (cf. Ps 119:43).

nice!

God's Word invites more than acknowledgment and passing interest. Indeed, Scripture invites us to arrange our thoughts around and devote our entire life in light of its message:

Deut 6:6–7: "These words that I myself am commanding you today shall be on your hearts. Teach them diligently to your children. Speak about them when you are sitting at home and when you are going along a path, and when you lie down and when you get up."

Josh 1:8: "This book of the law shall not depart from your mouth, but you shall recite/meditate in it day and night; so that you may watch out to live according to all that is written in it; for then you will succeed in your path, and then you will have insight/success."

Ps 1:1–2: "How wonderful it will be for anyone . . . whose pleasure is in the law of the LORD, and who recites/meditates in his law day and night"

Trusting Scripture

Reading the biblical narrative with faith means reading it as *true*.[1] What this means is that the boundaries between the narrative world and our own world become permeable. The God of the Bible is our God; the Jesus of the Gospels is our risen Lord; the sorts of angels and demons that inhabit the New Testament exist in our world; and the Bible's verdict on human moral failure is what we see reflected around us continually. The theological message of the text remains applicable to our world, and we can expect the biblical God today to act in the surprising ways, at various times and places, that he acted in Scripture. We see ourselves and our world in the Bible.

Historically, Christians have read the Bible this way (though also usually taking for granted also some extrabiblical traditions that they wrongly assume are in the Bible). This perspective of reading the Bible as true for themselves clearly characterized early Pentecostals, who saw themselves as living in the continuation of "Bible days."[2] Many of their contemporaries made excuses for why tongues, prophecy, and other gifts did not seem to exist in their circles, at least in the West. (Some of these phenomena had appeared in revivals elsewhere.[3] Healing had already begun to make a comeback even among many evangelicals in the West,[4] though even today I as a charismatic sometimes find myself tempted to make excuses for why it does not happen here more frequently.)[5] Pentecostals, by contrast, believed that these gifts depicted as part of normal church life in the New Testament could be normal for church life today. They read Scripture with faith that it was true for them and took the initiative to ask God to let them live in the light of that reality.

When we approach the Bible simply to prove what we already believe, we are not beginning with the fear of the Lord. Loyalty to Scripture means valuing its teaching above any other doctrinal commitments that may not actually flow from that.[6] *Sola Scriptura* in the best sense means that we evaluate our other doctrinal commitments by Scripture; Scripture is not simply one doctrinal commitment meant to be harmonized somehow with the others.

The Lord is faithful to the humble even when they do not understand all the details; since none of us understand all the details, and some of what we suppose we understand may be wrong, humility indeed befits us all. There is enough that we do know to continue challenging us in how to live and honor the Lord. When, by contrast, we defend ideas that are not genuinely true just to win a doctrinal argument or support inherited beliefs, we are not seeking truth.

Affirming God's Word as truth means submitting our lives to it more than it means the sorts of issues that Christian scholars sometimes divide over. The truth of God does not rest on doctrinal distinctives or on our dating or authorship of biblical books. At the same time, neither does it come from following the culture's sometimes skeptical fashions or superstitious fascinations. As followers of Christ, we are to follow God's word and thus not be moved by the ways of the nations (Josh 23:6–7; cf. Matt 5:47; 6:7; Rom 12:2; Eph 4:14, 17; 1 Thess 4:5). Simply following received beliefs of one's church to remain acceptable there, or popular scholarly opinions to remain acceptable in the academy, or popular clichés that are known to arouse hearers' emotional responses, is not loyalty to God's word. Starting with the fear of the Lord, we must seek God's truth. Paul warns that God will judge those who never embraced love for the truth of his gospel (2 Thess 2:10, 12); more generally, this principle shows how God values loving truth and expects us to value it also.

Some argue that for Pentecostals what should matter is not a text's historical reliability but its message.[7] Whether a text's narrative demands on the reader include some historical claims depends on the text's genre,[8] but it should be noted that Pentecostals historically have nearly always taken for granted the historical reliability of the text, even beyond available historical evidence.[9] Contrary to some stereotypes of global Pentecostalism by their detractors, most Christian charismatic movements have a high view of Scripture as divinely inspired and authoritative,[10] even if to justify it many of them appeal to experience more than to inherited doctrines.[11] In this respect, most Pentecostals would agree with Calvin's argument that the Spirit's witness attests canonical Scripture.[12] Experience of the Spirit tends to give Pentecostals a high view of Scripture's authority, since they often experience what they believe (rightly or wrongly) to be the Spirit's voice in connection with reading Scripture.[13]

Because of the convoluted modern history of truth claims about the Bible, I need to expend considerable space below explaining what I am not proposing. I have less to say on what I *am* proposing because I believe that, stripped from the implications that some may be tempted to read into my words, the proposal is fairly straightforward. It is no more and no less than what is suggested by the biblical texts with which I opened this section: we rely on God's word.

Truth Is Not a Genre

Given the past century of debates in Western theology, the affirmation that we should hear the Bible as truth invites another caveat.[14] Claims of biblical authority are too often deployed uncritically against others who have not in fact rejected that authority. Reading the Bible as truth does not necessarily mean that all interpreters will understand it in the same way,[15] ideal though such unanimity—if based on truth—might be. Some who do not work in biblical studies criticize biblical scholars without recognizing the legitimate issues that biblical scholars often address.

Although I have not chosen to make these issues my academic focus, I, like other close readers of the text, have always noticed them. I read through the Gospels in the weeks after my conversion from unchurched atheism. Matthew gave me no trouble, but Jesus was crucified again in Mark, and by the time I reached the crucifixion in Luke I wondered how often this was going to happen! Having been told that the Bible was God's Word, I expected it to be dictated by God in the first person; I had not anticipated multiple perspectives on the same events by different human authors. Further, my first reading also revealed differences among the accounts that troubled me; some of these were not actually the same accounts (e.g., Matthew's wise men and Luke's shepherds), but some apparent discrepancies were more substantive. After reading the Gospels enough, however, I understood better how they were meant to be read.

After working through a synopsis of the Gospels shortly before beginning graduate work, I briefly considered making the differences among the Gospels more central to my work, until I concluded that, in view of my calling, the overall usefulness of such a focus would be limited. (Helpful patterns do appear, but proposed theological explanations for differences sometimes remain too speculative to be informative.) Many of those issues are not central to the matter of the texts' *meaning* and therefore to how Christians as believers must embrace and live the text. They are, however, real and a valid subject of interest, and as a biblical scholar I recognize and work with those issues. I thus have digressed to warn those who have never carefully examined the texts at this level of detail to avoid prematurely criticizing those who have.

Because the Bible includes books spanning a range of ancient genres, reading the Bible as true also does not require us to read it as modern history or science. Since challenges offered in the radical Enlightenment, arguments for historical reliability of our central information about Jesus and his first followers have been important. Certainly there are historical genres in the Bible that employ the literary canons of ancient forms of historiography. I have spent many years researching the latter point, and have argued at length that these sources supply us considerable accurate historical information.[16]

But ancient historians also knew how to recount their stories in engaging ways, which may help account, for example, for some differences among the Gospels and their underlying traditions. Moreover, they valued their roles as moral, political or theological interpreters, so even in these texts we must listen not only for the text's historical information but also for its *message*. This is all the more true for other kinds of texts (such as parables or psalms) where *historical* reliability cannot be a criterion of reliability at all (unless we mean reliability as "true to its cultural setting").

We should read each biblical book or collection on its own terms; to make their messages intelligible, biblical writers necessarily utilized and adapted not only the language of their contemporaries but also contemporary signals of basic genre. As believers who follow Jesus's perspective on prior Scripture and his authorization of key followers with his message, we recognize that God was speaking through these intelligible literary forms. Someone may draw the lines of genres differently than we do, but if they embrace the text's message they may heed the text more than someone who merely memorizes and defends it without embracing and obeying its teaching. What is the value of affirming Scripture's authority on history if we fail to submit to its authority for our lives?

On the basis of historical-critical epistemology, evidence is sometimes too slender to resolve given historical-critical questions. Some of these problems arise because centuries have obscured what may have once been common knowledge. Despite our own modern historical interests, we cannot force the biblical text to answer questions that it was never designed to answer. Resolving such historical questions is not a necessary precondition for trusting the text's message. It is important to recognize that God acts in history, since this is part of the theology that the text communicates to us. But we have sufficient evidence of that reality in enough cases to encourage our trust in that theology. Trusting that theology in turn clears away the most *important* concerns in most other texts without us having to resolve every question that we might conceive.

It is natural for scholars to quibble over details; our job description includes trying to resolve such questions. Yet scholars who harmonize (or hail as contradictions) details of the text that ancient hearers never would have expected to be harmonized, while resisting biblical teaching about the continuing activity of the Spirit, are not really honoring Scripture in the form in which God gave it to us. If inspiration were more about the particular words than about the meaning, then the New Testament would be wrong to quote the Greek version of the Hebrew Bible (from which it sometimes diverges)[17] and to adapt, as the writers often do, even the wording of the Greek version.[18]

Christians should not approach Scripture the way some Muslims approach the Qur'an, emphasizing memorization and recitation in the original language even if one does not understand it. Such reverence for sacred texts of one's faith is praiseworthy, but the Christian approach to reverence for Scripture must emphasize careful interpretation followed by obedience (cf. Ezra 7:10). Our focus should be understanding for the purpose of obedience and faith; the message, rather than the wording, should be the emphasis. (That is, after all, why Christians invest so much effort in translating the Bible into local languages.)

Reading the Bible as relevant for today is sometimes undertaken naïvely by ignoring differences in cultural frameworks that affect how we understand what the biblical writers articulated. To use the cultural chasm to neglect a nuanced understanding, however, puts us in the position of non-faith in the message of the text. I study material about Jesus in the Gospels for historical purposes, relevant to my academic work in early Christian history. But if we as Christians read this material for exclusively historical interest, not reading it also with reference to the risen and living Lord of the universe with whom we have a relationship, we miss a crucial dynamic. Historical scholarship requires some objective distance from the text, and those of us who work as historians must do our historical work well. But when we read as Christians, we must also read with faith, celebrating that these accounts involve the same Lord to whom we pray.

One Case Study

In some cases interpreters debate the genre of a text more than its core message. For example, although the first three chapters of Genesis belong to a larger narrative work that includes different sorts of narratives, they also reflect the genre of creation narratives, a subject of special interest in the early second millennium BCE.[19] Pagan contemporaries probably heard such narratives aetiologically, perhaps the way we would view many folktales today.

Questions of sources aside, Genesis addresses creation from two angles consecutively, focusing on different aspects of the primeval world (its creation and humanity's fall). Although Genesis expects us to read these adjacent narratives side by side and to learn from both, the narrative flavor of both accounts differs from that of the patriarchal narratives that follow in Genesis. Even some evangelical scholars find significant tensions in the details between these two narratives, which may warn us that the details in our present form of Genesis are not meant to be pressed too literally.[20] *interesting, so don't take it literally?*

Today some interpreters vigorously defend their view of the first three chapters of Genesis as "literal," insisting that this is the natural way to read them. Others, however, suggest that these interpreters are defending their own inherited hermeneutic rather than the text of Scripture. The text invites us to read it in a different way than some other parts of Scripture, a way that allows us to better hear its original message. Would ancient Israelites, accustomed to the sorts of narratives that dominated most of their tradition, have taken fully literally these introductory narratives that include a talking serpent, protagonists whose names in Hebrew are simply Man and (possibly) Life, and trees whose fruit is not of the usual edible variety but rather "knowledge of good and evil" and "life"? This is not the same sort of writing that we encounter in the Gospels, in 1 Kings, or even in Genesis's accounts of the patriarchs.

disagree?

Whether or not you agree with this conclusion, however, the question of genre need not obscure the primary points and message of the narrative, a few samples of which I may offer here. Many ancient Israelites, especially traders, scribes and civic elites, would have been exposed to the creation stories of their polytheistic neighbors, in which the world was created, for example, by deities battling other deities or (in one Egyptian account) by a deity stimulating himself sexually. By stark contrast, Genesis proclaims one God as the creator of the cosmos, the originator of fertility without his own sexual involvement, the appointing of sun and moon (elsewhere worshiped) under the only true God, and so forth.

Likewise, the opening narrative of creation declares humanity as the pinnacle of God's creation, the object of his special love, an observation fully consistent with New Testament theology as well.[21] Indeed, humans before the fall, in their ideal state, were meant to govern and steward other life forms; they held a position as high as that assigned to fertility deities in some polytheistic narratives. We may even note that God artistically and pragmatically brought about our life-filled world progressively, rather than instantly, starting from less complex organisms and climaxing in humanity. Interestingly, theists can read the scientific record in a similar way, especially if they understand the *not what McMath said*

"days" figuratively or as simply periods of time or the narrative framework of a work week. (The Hebrew term translated "day" is amorphous enough by itself to cover three different periods of time in the Genesis narrative: 1:5; 2:4.)

Whereas many readers today will enter such a world imaginatively without construing the narrative literally, most would construe differently shaped narratives such as those in 2 Kings or the Gospel of Luke very differently. In each case, though, we must hear and embrace the message of the text, even when it offends our cultural sensibilities—for example, by affirming a wise originator of the cosmos or acknowledging a divine purpose in history or challenging our vested economic interests.

When Harmonizing Details Often Misses the Point

Harmonizing and demanding precision on every detail can sometimes miss the point.[22] That is not to say that a writer is being dishonest about information; it is simply to recognize what we already noticed from relevance theory: communication uses cultural conventions, and in a given culture some expressions are simply understood, or genre conventions taken for granted, without any need for further explanation.

interesting

Matthew 8 and Luke 7 clearly speak of the same centurion, but in Matthew the centurion approaches and addresses Jesus directly whereas in Luke he does so only through intermediaries. Is this a contradiction, or merely a difference, in terms of what the writers wish to communicate? Or is it simply an ancient biographic technique that one scholar has called "spotlighting," allowing Matthew to condense the account by omitting irrelevant intermediaries (as he also does with the messengers in Mark 5:35)?[23]

Such questions are not limited to ancient sources. Take, for example, how Nabeel Qureshi explicitly articulates his literary method in his account of his coming to faith. "By its very nature, a narrative biography must take certain liberties with the story it shares." Sometimes Dr. Qureshi had to conflate conversations, displace some accounts from actual chronology to maintain topical continuity, and (as in the example from Matt 8) omit some persons present on an occasion "for the sake of clarity. All these devices are normal for narrative biographies; they are in fact normal for human mnemonics."[24] Because Dr. Qureshi also deals with questions of oral tradition and ancient genres, he is sensitive enough to how some of his dialogue partners could hear him to qualify his case. But as he points out, given the genre conventions, these minor issues are normally simply taken for granted.

Likewise, my wife and I have shared some of our experiences in a popular-level book called *Impossible Love.*[25] For this book, we could often accurately reconstruct fairly detailed scenes based on our journal entries. Nevertheless, at times the journals mentioned only that someone in a group offered advice, and so, for the sake of narration (and with the general permission of the main surviving characters), we simply named someone present as the speaker. Having cut perhaps 45 percent of the original manuscript, I left only details most relevant to the story line, having removed numerous points of explanation. We changed the names of some important characters to protect their identity, and two marginal characters because none of my sources remembered their names.

Our editor at Chosen Books, Jane Campbell, a firm inerrantist, noted this tension when people speak in nonliteral ways. "I'll hear someone saying, 'I built my house' in such-and-such a way, and think, *He didn't actually build that house.*" Were this biblical language, I could well imagine a popular-level skeptic finding here a smoking gun of testimony-discrediting contradiction, and a popular-level conservative insisting that in fact there is no reason to doubt that the speaker had built the house by himself, the carpenters and electricians merely handing him the bricks and wires.

Likewise, Jane noted, "Chosen published a narrative writer years ago, in a succession of books, who could tell a story once with Coke and another time with Pepsi. This will drive me wild in writing—'Was it Coke or was it Pepsi?'—but also set up an author for criticism that she isn't telling the truth, when—truth to tell—that author just wasn't a detail person."[26] Personally, unless I wrote it down at the time, I wouldn't know what I drank on an occasion, unless it was something special like the kunu (which included raw milk) that once made me sick in Africa, or the bissap (made from the juice of an African flower) that I find delightful. And neither I nor most readers would care; many of us simply use "Coke" and similar labels as referring to any soft drink. There is no need to harmonize—with our imaginary extreme conservative—that the narrative writer mixed Coke and Pepsi in the same glass on that occasion. (After all, it is not impossible!) Or to suggest that she must have run out of Coke and therefore added Pepsi—all speculation aside, of course.

Some twentieth-century readers in the United States tried to harmonize every detail without always taking into account the difference between ancient genres and modern ones related to them. Some circles today associate me with arguing for the historical reliability of the Gospels and Acts; and I do, with full conviction, contend that they are reliable by the standards of ancient biography and history. There is a range of variation in details (and a few cases that are unusually divergent),[27] but this is similar to what we find in some of the best cases of ancient biography.[28] Unless we artificially impose on the Gospels the standards of modern genres that did not yet exist in their day and that barely anyone expected, such variations are not problematic.

Old Testament Puzzles

The Gospels and Acts, however, are works about recent figures, written within living memory of eyewitnesses. I cannot expect colleagues in Old Testament to handle their narratives in precisely the same way that I do the Gospels. Some parts of the Old Testament follow earlier narrative models in reciting the past, sometimes employing traditions passed on orally for much longer periods of time.

While evangelical biblical scholars are generally aware of these sorts of questions, traditional lay interpreters often are not, and some passages may raise problems for them. Since some arguments are about how to interpret silence of evidence, which often involves burden of proof and the bar of evidence expected, here I want to offer some more conspicuous cases that demand of some conservative critics more charity for biblically faithful colleagues in Old Testament. For example, after killing Goliath David brought his head to Jerusalem in 1 Sam 17:54; but Jerusalem became Israelite territory only many years later (2 Sam 5:6–9). It is unlikely that it means that David dried the head and brought it to Jerusalem years later (after carrying it around in the wilderness while he fled Saul). It is also unlikely that David impaled the head outside Jerusalem shortly after Goliath's death as a warning that he was coming after the Jebusites later. One might suggest that Saul temporarily controlled Jerusalem at this time and the city was later overrun again by Jebusites, requiring David's conquest; we lack, however, clear supporting information for this idea. A likelier speculation would be that David brought the head to the house of worship that was later in Jerusalem (cf. 1 Sam 21:9); yet this solution, too, might disturb the most inflexible interpreter.

Was it in Moses's day, with the conquest of Gilead, that Jair the descendant of Manasseh captured towns there and called them Havvoth Jair (Deut 3:14; Num 32:40–41)? Or was it in the period of the judges (Judg 10:3–4)? Probably the narrator regarding Moses's day goes on to summarize work that extended beyond Moses's time, but even in this case the conquest and naming must come long after Moses if Judges recounts the leaders with any semblance of chronology (cf. "after him" in 10:3). Similarly, different sources agree that Jehu's revolt led to Ahaziah's death, but the dramatic details vary:

- When King Ahaziah of Judah saw this, he fled in the direction of Beth-haggan. Jehu pursued him, saying, "Shoot him also!" And they shot him in the chariot at the ascent to Gur, which is by Ibleam. Then he fled to Megiddo, and died there. (2 Kgs 9:27, NRSV)
- He searched for Ahaziah, who was captured while hiding in Samaria and was brought to Jehu, and put to death. They buried him, for they said, "He is the grandson of Jehoshaphat, who sought the LORD with all his heart." And the house of Ahaziah had no one able to rule the kingdom. (2 Chr 22:9, NRSV)

It is not difficult to find agreement if our concern is with the overall story, but if we hope for precision in matters of detail it appears to elude us. If one remains concerned to harmonize all details, how best should one resolve Genesis's lists of Esau's three wives?

Genesis 26:34; 28:9	Genesis 36:2–3
Judith, daughter of Beeri the Hittite	Adah, daughter of Elon the Hittite
Basemath, daughter of Elon the Hittite	Oholibamah, daughter of Anah (granddaughter of Zibeon the Hivite)
Mahalath, daughter of Ishmael, sister of Nebaioth	Basemath, Ishmael's daughter, sister of Nebaioth

Is Basemath the daughter of Elon and sister of Adah? Or is she Ishmael's daughter and sister of Mahalath? Or perhaps someone would argue that Ishmael adopted her? Some would suggest more simply that the inspired author may have correctly recorded various available traditions without trying to harmonize them or choose between them. Are we obligated to try to harmonize those traditions? Or should we allow the first recounters and scribes of this material in Genesis the same freedom their contemporaries may have taken in recording various oral traditions?

On a popular level, an *inflexible* defender of traditional approaches could dismiss the matter rhetorically the way such matters are often dismissed: by simply changing the subject after denouncing me as a liberal for admitting the existence of these differences. Denouncing me as a liberal, that is, for paying inordinately close attention to the text while reading through it devotionally in Hebrew.[29]

I raise these issues not to contend for a particular solution to them, nor to provide a comprehensive list of what interpreters sometimes call "problem passages." I raise them merely as samples to suggest that fixation on resolving details to this degree may be counter to the narratives' original purpose. Ancient Israelite hearers heard these accounts over and over, yet apparently did not find them problematic.[30] When later rabbis did try to resolve such issues, their traditions include multiple possible (as well as not a few impossible!) solutions. We may wish to grant our modern colleagues charity when they seek to grapple with such questions, just as most of us who love the book of Revelation or epistle of James grant Eusebius or Luther charity for questioning their canonicity.

What It *Really* Means to Have Faith in God's Word

To have faith in God's Word does not mean that we stand firm on our particular church's traditions or on our theoretical presuppositions about how God *should* have inspired Scripture (how we would have done it ourselves, we mean, had we been infinite) rather than on careful examination of how he chose to do so.[31] It means that we trust whatever God speaks as reliable, and, because we share the view that Scripture is God-inspired (see 2 Tim 3:16; 2 Pet 1:20–21),[32] that we stand in awe of it (Ezra 10:3; Ps 119:120, 161; cf. Isa 66:2, 5), and therefore devote our most diligent interpretive effort to honestly discerning and embracing its message (Ezra 7:10).[33]

In cases such as the examples offered above, what does it mean to have faith in God's Word? Is it only those who harmonize the passages who have faith in God's Word? Or can those who allow that many ancient writers had different interests than do modern historians also have faith in these texts? Please note that I am *not* denying that historical events stand behind historical narratives, but just allowing for different ways of writing history in different periods, some of which allow inference, varied traditions, or fleshing out a narrative, in how the story is narrated. Some may consider it more faithful to God's Word to take into account the phenomena of the inspired texts as we have them rather than to try to harmonize them in a way meant to fit modern conceptions of the way God *should* have inspired the text.

My point is to invite all of us, whether on such questions others are more "conservative" or more "liberal" than I am, to consider the demands of faith in Scripture. Having faith in God's Word does not dictate a specific historical method, apart from that we embrace what is elicited from us by the character of the texts themselves in their historical context (which ideally should include the expectations of the texts' contemporaries for the sort of historical or other genre in which the passages were composed). Embracing God's Word in faith means embracing the message it communicates. If we argue vociferously for a particular interpretive approach to the creation narratives, yet fail to respond with awe toward the genuine creator of heaven and earth, we *are not embracing the message with genuine personal faith.* If we argue for a particular historical approach to Ahaziah's death, yet fail to acknowledge that God is sovereign and judges wickedness in real history and in the present, we are rejecting the message of the text.

In these terms, hard cessationism, which offers an intellectual approach to the text (not unlike that of older liberal critics), can be an unbelieving approach, though not deliberately. In its strictest form, it fails to embrace the continuing relevance of a major aspect of the biblical message—namely, that we should expect God's continuing activity in history and in our lives. It cheapens the demand of faith because its way of believing the text raises no expectations.

Some of us—cessationist or not—may be tempted to believe that certain divine activity has ceased because it is easier for us to believe our own limited experience than to believe promises or models in God's Word that we have not experienced. That is, we sometimes prefer to leave biblical experiences of God as foreign rather than exercise faith. Particularly if the only gift we have been trained to cultivate and expect in particular circles is grappling with Scripture's grammar, we may think that we can handle this activity by purely natural skill, without any special divine help. (In many cases, seminary even trains us to think this way; our degree confers on us competence even if our course of study did not include spiritual maturation.) God does not do the same things in all times and places, but he certainly does more in a setting of faith than in a setting of unbelief! This may be especially true when pride in cessationist doctrine makes one arrogant about one's reason not to need to believe.

By contrast, the genius of the traditional pentecostal hermeneutic was to live in the biblical worldview, expecting God to act. Granted, sometimes pentecostals have embraced texts in an uncritical way. Biblical narratives often highlight dramatic miracles without the authors intending to imply that such dramatic miracles happen at all times and in all places in the same way. But we should hear in such passages the reality of a God who has acted and can act in dramatic ways, challenging our frequent reliance on purely human resources.

If we approach the Bible with sound understanding, embracing it in faith means that we walk in light of God's presence, recognizing that God may move in surprising ways. In fact, if God has granted us the light to recognize his presence in such a way, we are already living in the kind of setting where God's activity may be expected—whether by recognizing and enduring tests of our faith or by more overtly witnessing his powerful works.

Faithful Imagination

Paul's principle of "hearing with faith" the oral message about Christ (Rom 10:17; Gal 3:2) should also apply, by extension, to how we embrace all of God's words. Equipped with as much knowledge as possible about the world of Scripture, we need to enter its narrative world, suspend disbelief, cultural alienation and other forms of distancing, and expect to meet the living God there.

Entering Narrative Worlds

Because Scripture is textual and its largest genre is narrative, analogies from how we read other narratives are helpful. Without understanding or resolving debated historical questions about every detail of a text, we may enter its narrative world. Likewise, we must enter the narrative world of the Scriptures to hear there from the same God who inhabits that world, believing that ultimately that world theologically remains our world, a world in which God is active. Cultures and genres differ, but God, Christ and human nature remain the same.

Every human worldview, including any narrative about the world that we inherit in our culture as a given, is culturally shaped and thus ultimately subject to revision or reinterpretation. Some describe these frameworks as imaginative constructs, that is, incomplete interpretations of reality that structure data without accounting for all of it. Scripture, some argue, provides "an alternative imagination" that invites a new construction of reality.[34] It is, however, not pure subjectivity, but "an exercise in imagination that is grounded by the contextual realism" of experiencing the divine author who has spoken and speaks in the text.[35] Although Scripture samples rather than exhausts divine revelation, its story of redemption offers a skeletal metanarrative of true salvation history.[36] It can be related to what J. R. R. Tolkien and C. S. Lewis called a "true myth."

Literary critics emphasize that those who enjoy fantastic narratives suspend their disbelief to enter sympathetically into the novel's narrative world. We likewise often suspend our cultural judgments when we enter more verisimilar narrative worlds in historical biographies, often setting aside the dissonance created by a cultural realm that is foreign to us. We can hear biblical writers most clearly when we enter their narrative world with its assumptions, suspending disbelief and judgment and coming under the authority of the text's message.

Suspending Disbelief

We must marshall no less imaginative faith when we enter the biblical narrative world than when we enter others, although there are, of course, important differences in genres and, for Christians, in spiritual expectations. If I read science fiction or a Mayan myth or a Scandinavian folktale, I do not expect to hear there God's voice (at least not regularly and in the same way). I also do not expect such stories to narrate divinely revealed truth about the real world, except perhaps in an extended sense by evoking elements of reality. When I read nonbiblical history, I might contemplate and try to understand God's works there, but I do not ordinarily expect the historian's interpretation of events to be authoritatively, divinely inspired. As a Christian, I approach the Bible with a different, deliberate expectation. I expect to find there a guide for life (both personally and for the people of God), even though I must carefully weigh how to take into account different biblical evidence.[37]

Suspending disbelief when reading the Bible differs from suspending it with some other works, because the object of trust differs. Most believers in Christ intuitively understand the difference between different kinds of belief: children can relinquish belief in Santa Claus yet understand faith in God (or various cultural paradigms) in a different way. Engaging the imagination is valuable when we enter the biblical world, but biblical faith involves more than *simply* engaging the imagination. It also involves welcoming and embracing a worldview.

Ultimately we should embrace the worldview that the Scriptures communicate so as to view our own world in a different light (as opposed to primarily immersing ourselves in other narratives popular around us, such as those of current films, videogames, and political scripts of the left or the right). By this I do not mean uncritically embracing worldviews that some biblical texts simply take for granted as stage props based on assumptions shared by its original audience. These include such images as a three-story universe or rain falling from windows in the sky (cf., e.g., Gen 7:11; Mal 3:10; Exod 20:4).[38] That is, I am referring not to the cosmology or other cultural conventions that the biblical authors used to communicate, but to their message about God and his mission. (Again, distinguishing these elements sometimes can be complex in practice; that is my day job, focused on reconstructing the ancient contexts of the biblical passages.)

Instead I mean that we learn to envision a world alive with God's activity and presence. (Some call this a "reenchanted" world; it seems theologically more precise to simply speak of it as a world where God is active.) Because one who embraces the biblical worldview in faith recognizes that God is active and present, narratives are believable on the level of divine activity and God's employment of the human actors within the narrative world. An atheist may infer from patterns in biology and physics that nature explains itself without any need for a ghost in this machine; a Christian approaches the same scientific evidence with wonder, praising the magnificence of God's design.[39]

This is precisely the virtue of what early pentecostals and others like them brought to a church too captivated by the disenchanted worldview of modernity.[40] Instead of praying with hope that we will prove lucky, we can pray to the living God of the Bible who is not bound only by what might happen "on its own." Even in the Bible, God did not do miracles for most individuals on a regular basis. But the God of the Bible is well able to do them, and even more regularly than we might imagine—in the Bible and today—to show us his providential work in our lives over time.

One may note, however, that it is difficult for one to enter the biblical worldview, suspending disbelief, when one's mind is consumed instead by the world's narratives. A biblical worldview allows one to evaluate other narratives, but a mind saturated with popular entertainment and ideologies will continue to find Scripture a dauntingly foreign book (cf. 1 Cor 2:11–15). We must immerse our minds in the world of Scripture so that it shapes and renews our thinking toward God's perspective. Is this not part of what it means to forsake all and follow Christ?

Expectations

Expectations shape how we approach any text. In terms of genre, we read science fiction, poetry, and a journalistic report with different expectations.[41] In terms of authors, we read a letter from someone we trust differently than we read a letter from someone who is always giving excuses and undermining our trust. Sometimes we discover that our trust or suspicion has been misplaced, and our reading strategy immediately shifts. In terms of information, comprehending a summary of what follows helps us catch the main points that the summarizer wants us to catch. Knowing the context that a work was addressing also shapes how we read it.

Expectations help shape our reading of Scripture. If we expect only to put in time reading merely to fulfill a duty, we may save up information for future reference (not a bad thing in itself). But if we read Scripture genuinely expecting to regularly meet God there in some insight that we find along the way, we are far more likely to hear from him.

Wrong expectations can also distort how we hear Scripture. Expecting to hear an abusive parent's voice will falsely condition how we read God's character. So will starting with unhealthy theological assumptions extrapolated from a few misread texts.[42] Early in my Christian experience I was fearful of the devil's temptations, and by anticipating them I unwittingly simulated them to test myself.[43] Any bad idea that entered my creative imagination became a temptation for me to battle, and my pessimistic imagination did not always envision a favorable outcome. Once such an approach became habit, there remained much less for real external forces to do directly. How did this shape how I read Scripture? I felt guilty when merely reading about immoral characters, for once any sin had crossed my mind, I considered myself extraordinarily tempted. Intellectually I knew better, but eventually I had to also confront such habitual and misplaced guilt.

Likewise, as a young Christian I read Paul's binary contrast between people of the Spirit and people of the flesh in such a way that any misplaced thought made me think that I had ventured into "the flesh" and thus lost my salvation.[44] My pre-Christian immersion in Plato even led me to read some of Paul in a proto-gnostic way until I learned better. These are all examples of misplaced faith, believing a false object because of reading with false expectations.

By contrast, the central Christian message about Jesus's death and resurrection is the climactic biblical narrative, so reading in light of Jesus's cross and triumph helps us put other matters in perspective (cf. Rom 5:6–10; 8:32; 1 Cor 15:3–4). God is trustworthy, so expecting to hear from the faithful God of Scripture will condition our reading faithfully. One should not approach this expectation legalistically, frustrated if one does not have a particular experience each time or during the entire time one is reading. We are not invited to simulate a sort of spiritual intuition at every moment; God is fully capable of making his voice clear to us when we need it.[45] But one should expect that the God who speaks by his Spirit will meet us in our study of Scripture.[46]

Like biblical writers who interpreted earlier Scripture, we must interpret our lives and experience in light of Scripture; we thus must apply Scripture as well as exegete it. But we can apply it most faithfully—in a way most consistent with the texts themselves in the way that God gave them to us—when our analogies are based on the texts in their contexts. When we recognize how God worked in the past, we can live with the same sort of expectations today. That is, our experience becomes inscribed in the framework of the biblical story.[47] Expecting God to act today as he did in the Bible may be closely related to what the Bible calls "faith."

Of course, God did not always act the same way in all the events in the Bible; there are many patterns, but one pattern is that God often accomplishes his purposes in different ways so that we look to him rather than to a predictable formula. Although we may expect that God is fully consistent in his divine character, we experience him on the human level as an exciting God of surprises. But surprises or not, a life and mind immersed in Scripture will read the world in a different way than a mind shaped more by the values of the surrounding culture. Although we cannot predict how God will act, we expect God to act, we depend on God to act, and we live always in the confidence that God is at work.

Nice!

Conclusion

Reading the Bible as truth means reading it as a message from the one who is true, the one who may be trusted. Christians may disagree on some particulars of how this truth is expressed in terms of genre and cultural accommodation, but we should all learn to trust the God who speaks there. Embracing the Bible in faith means embracing its message for us today and living in the light of that embrace. When modern "faith teachers" summon their hearers to claim verses out of context, they are not truly honoring Scripture. To truly honor Scripture would require them to study the biblical text more carefully and faithfully. Such faith teachers exercise an insight that many of us neglect, however, when they call people to stand on God's word as true.

In too many parts of the church we hear much of the Bible only as a historical record without building our lives on its claims. Too often Christians also compile its commands (usually quite selectively and without regard for their cultural setting) but fear to identify with the lessons in its narratives. We have barely begun to explore Scripture's depths. But Scripture itself provides some guidelines for how we may proceed.

PART V

Intrabiblical Models for Reading Scripture

That the problem of present meaning cannot be excluded from interpretation in Christian theology is suggested partly by the attitude of the New Testament writers towards the Old Testament. (Anthony Thiselton)[1]

For some, the Old Testament is now irrelevant apart from a typological and allegorical christological reading.[2] This is not, however, the way that New Testament writers normally treated the Old Testament.[3] To be sure, they found many analogies in God's earlier workings that confirmed their view of Christ; they did not, however, dismiss everything else in Scripture.

The book thus far has been partly theoretical. First, I suggested what a reading from the vantage point of the biblical Pentecost should look like, including, for example, experiential, eschatological, and global perspectives, as well as consistency with the message that God originally inspired by his Spirit. Then I turned to underlying questions of epistemology; each epistemic approach presupposes its basis. Reading or hearing with faith is a necessary hermeneutic for those whose starting premise is Scripture.

Here, however, I turn to concrete Spirit-led models from Scripture itself.[4] How did Jesus handle Scripture? How did Paul interpret the law, and how may inductive reading of the law itself shape our reception of the law? How can we learn by analogy from biblical narratives?[5] A reading from the standpoint of Pentecost, as in Acts 2 and usually in the rest of the New Testament, is a reading that applies the biblical message to our lives today.[6]

CHAPTER 14

How Jesus Invites Us to Hear the Bible

One day Jesus told the crowds a parable about a farmer who scattered seed widely. Only a small proportion of the seed took root and yielded harvest, but that harvest far outweighed the seed initially sown. Jewish teachers used parables to illustrate points, but when their context did not make the parables self-evident, the teachers explained them. By contrast, Jesus admonished the crowds to hear, and then left them to ponder his riddle.

Luke remarks that afterward the disciples asked Jesus what the parable meant (Luke 8:9); in all three Synoptic Gospels, Jesus goes on to explain his teaching to them. The reason Jesus speaks in parables, Jesus explains, is that *aligns with what Dr Kibbe said* the precious mysteries of God's kingdom belong only to those committed enough to seek them.[7] As in Isaiah's day, the message does nothing for God's disobedient people; it falls on deaf ears, whether because it hardens hearts or increases acountability without bringing transformation (Matt 13:11–15).

This in fact was what Jesus's parable itself was about. Some failed to understand the message; others abandoned it in difficult circumstances; and still others became too distracted by matters of this age to give it its proper place (13:18–22). But the seed that more than compensated for the rest represented those who "heard the word and *understood* it" (13:23).[8] Who understood Jesus's message? At this point, it was those who stayed after the crowds left and asked Jesus what his parable meant. The true meaning belonged to disciples—to those who followed Jesus closely and listened and asked until they understood.[9]

Contrary to what some traditional academic exegesis assumes, reception matters. Moreover, contrary to what some popular postmodern interpretation assumes, the *particular* reception matters.[10] People received Jesus's message in different ways, and Jesus did not reckon all these ways of equal merit. They needed the true understanding of his message that led to discipleship—to following the kingdom's true king. This issue of reception is so important to Luke that it recurs in expanded form as Paul dialogues about the kingdom in Rome. Some people hear with closed ears, but others will hear (Acts 28:26–28).

Jesus Presupposes Context

Jesus read the Scriptures in a disciplined and sophisticated way that contrasts with the common abuse of popular Scripture verses today. Although he does not usually quote the context (at least not in the condensed version of his teaching available in the Gospels), he often does presuppose it. Yet, as we shall also note further below, attention to context did not keep Jesus from also applying Scripture to the present era, an example followed also by other NT narrative writers (and consistent with practices of many of their contemporaries).

Readers in synagogues read entire passages; those who prayed might recite entire psalms. Although scholars currently debate how widespread written literacy was in Galilee, and expositions often tied various texts together, attention to oral memory was an important part of synagogue culture and thus of public Jewish life. Sages often assumed the context of passages they cited.[11]

Although one may cite some texts simply as representatives of the larger principles they embody, the Jesus of the Gospels often presupposes the context of passages that he cites. After a heavenly voice announces that Jesus is God's son (Matt 3:17//Luke 3:22), Satan challenges or seeks to redefine the character of Jesus's sonship. "If you're God's son," he twices charges (Matt 4:3, 6; Luke 4:3, 9). The first time Satan challenges him to turn stones to bread. In response, Jesus quotes a text that not only addresses bread (Matt 4:4 and Luke 4:4, citing Deut 8:3) but also is part of a context that compares God's relationship with Israel to a father caring for his son (Deut 8:5). That is, Jesus allows his sonship to be defined by a model in *Scripture*.

Jesus responds to each of the three temptations by quoting Scripture; unwilling to even entertain disobedience to his Father's will, simply noting God's command entails his course of action. In each case, he draws from the same general context as before (Deut 6:13, 16). By contrast, Satan also quotes Scripture, but he quotes it selectively and out of context. He challenges Jesus to throw himself down because angels will protect the righteous (Ps 91:11–12). The psalm's context, however, refers to God's protection from harm that comes to the righteous, not to throwing oneself in harm's way.

Similarly, Jesus presupposes knowledge of the context on one occasion when he affirms as central loving one's neighbor as oneself (Luke 10:26–28, citing Lev

19:18). Loving everyone is a massive task, so Jesus's interlocutor wants to know who counts as a neighbor (Luke 10:29). Jesus responds by recounting the tale of the Good Samaritan (10:30–35), indicating that one's neighbor includes Samaritans. In so doing, he undoubtedly evokes the *context* of Lev 19:18. Leviticus 19:34 goes on to command Israelites to love as themselves also the foreigners residing in the land. Surely this injunction would have to include Samaritans, who even observed some of the same biblical customs that Judeans observed.[12]

Weightier Matters of the Law

Jesus honors the law (Matt 5:17–19); in fact, he implies, he honors the law at a level deeper than did the Pharisees (5:20). Nevertheless, Jesus regards some matters of the law as more central than others (Mark 12:28–31; Matt 23:23–24). This is not surprising; his contemporaries shared the same recognition.[13] I am not suggesting that Jesus regarded any of God's word as dispensable (Matt 5:17–19; Luke 16:17); neither did other Jewish sages.[14] But everyone has some hermeneutical grid through which they prioritize their reading, and Jesus's stated grid is significant. (Various circles provide various grids or centers for Scripture.[15] I believe that *God himself* and his seeking, redeeming love are central—his heart revealed through his acts in history and ultimately in Christ, most specifically in Jesus's death and resurrection.)[16]

The Torah itself included statements that summarized the heart of what God wanted most (Deut 10:12–13), and so did the prophets (Mic 6:8). Later tradition claimed that the early Jewish sage Hillel summarized the heart of the law in a manner similar to Jesus's teaching that we call the golden rule (Luke 6:31; esp. Matt 7:12).[17] First-century sages also debated which commandment was the greatest; although no consensus was achieved (the most common was apparently honor of parents), one rabbi later than Jesus came close to his view, citing love of neighbor.[18] Jesus's joint emphasis on love of God and love of neighbor (Mark 12:28–34),[19] however, became a distinctive hallmark in his movement. Others valued love, but multiple circles of Jesus's followers consistently highlighted this as the supreme commandment (Rom 13:9–10; Gal 5:14; Jas 2:8; cf. 1 Cor 13:13). This remains true even if some circles of his followers today may have forgotten this, excusing this neglect by our priorities on precise doctrine or careful observance of other commandments.[20]

When Jesus criticized the scholars of his day, it was sometimes because they had missed the forest for the trees. Pharisees were known to be meticulous in tithing;[21] Jesus declares that this is well and good, but they have neglected justice and God's love (Matt 23:23//Luke 11:42). Matthew records that Jesus's denunciation includes the warning that they had neglected these "heavier" matters of the Torah (Matt 23:23).

Although both Matthew and Luke specify justice and God's love, Matthew also mentions "mercy" or "compassion," a term that appears twice earlier in his Gospel in quotations from Hos 6:6 (Matt 9:13; 12:7). On both occasions Jesus deploys the Hosea text against the biblically knowledgeable Pharisees.[22] In the first case, the Pharisees have criticized Jesus for table fellowship with sinners; Jesus insists that reaching sinners with God's transforming power takes precedence over fears of contamination (9:11–13). In the second, Pharisees criticize Jesus for allowing his disciples to glean grain on the sabbath; Jesus responds that he has authority to define the sabbath and that his disciples' hunger matters more than Pharisaic boundaries around the Torah (12:1–8).

The Hosea text highlighted in Matthew's Gospel is not marginal but reflects the spirit of the prophets, both from Hosea's era (such as Isaiah and Amos) and later:

> For I desire steadfast love and not sacrifice, the knowledge of God rather than burnt offerings! (Hos 6:6, NRSV)

> Stop bringing meaningless offerings! Your incense is detestable to me. . . . Learn to do right; seek justice. Defend the oppressed. (Isa 1:13, 17, NIV)

> Is this the kind of fast I have chosen, only a day for people to humble themselves? Is it only for bowing one's head like a reed and for lying in sackcloth and ashes? Is that what you call a fast, a day acceptable to the LORD? Is not this the kind of fasting I have chosen: to loose the chains of injustice and untie the cords of the yoke, to set the oppressed free and break every yoke? (Isa 58:5–6, NIV)

> I loathe and reject your religious festivals. I refuse the fragrance of your sacred assemblies! Though you offer up to me your offerings and grain offerings, I won't take pleasure in them; and when you offer fattened livestock to secure peace, I won't pay any attention. Take away from me the clamor of your songs; I'm not listening to the music of your harps! Instead, let justice roll down like waters, and righteousness like a steady brook. (Amos 5:21–24)

> When I brought your ancestors out from Egypt, what I talked to them or commanded them about wasn't a burnt offering or sacrifice. No! This is

what I ordered them: Heed my voice, and I will be your God, and you will be my people. Follow in all the way that I commanded you so that it may be well for you. (Jer 7:22–23)

Jesus is not against sacrifices (Matt 5:23; Mark 1:44), but he does view the law's particulars through the lens of its heart. That is, he sees the Torah from the heart of the God who gave it. Indeed, the narrative context in which God gave the law genuinely was redemption and grace. Thus God prefaced the Ten Commandments by reminding his people that he had graciously liberated them from slavery (Exod 20:2; Deut 5:6).[23]

Likewise, after granting Moses's petition and forgiving his people for the sin of the golden calf, God graciously gave them the unmerited commandments again (Exod 33–34; Deut 9:25–10:5). In the midst of this narrative, God reveals his character to Moses, making his "goodness" pass before him (Exod 33:19). The Lord is "a compassionate and gracious God, slow to anger and great in covenant love and faithfulness to his word. He carries out his covenant love for thousands of generations,[24] forgiving evildoing, transgression, and sin." God "doesn't leave the guilty unpunished; he visits the evildoing of parents on children and grandchildren up to the third and fourth generation" (Exod 34:6–7), but his covenant love is to the thousandth generation (Deut 7:9)—so much greater is his mercy than his anger.

Jesus Applied Scripture to His Day

Jesus could translate the point of Scripture in the language of his day. Thus when he quotes the commonly recited "heart and soul and strength" of Deut 6:5, he expands this to include the "mind" (Mark 12:30). This is fully natural, since Jesus would have known that, given the biblical association of thinking or understanding with the heart in Hebrew, the Greek term translated "mind" was included in the Hebrew expression.[25] (I am assuming that in public disputes with leaders in Jerusalem, Jesus would speak Greek, even though I believe that he ordinarily spoke Aramaic in the Galilean countryside.)[26]

Jesus obviously knew that Moses and Isaiah had lived long before he spoke. He likewise knew that the contemporaries of Moses and Isaiah were dead. Nevertheless, where appropriate, he was prepared to apply to his own day their approach to their contemporaries, because God's word continued to address the human condition. "Isaiah was right to prophesy this about *you* hypocrites," he tells the Pharisees and scribes (Mark 7:5–6). "Moses wrote this because of the hardness of *your* hearts," he explains to some Pharisees (10:5).

Because leaders of Jesus's people were acting like those in Jeremiah's day who expected God's sacred temple to shield them from his judgment, Jesus also applies to them words from Jer 7:11: "*You* have made it a 'robbers' den'" (Mark 11:17). Of course, in the Gospels Jesus sometimes cites texts that directly pertain to him, but in other cases, like these, he applies principles true of God's people in earlier times to analogies in his own era.

Jesus's critics often charge him with violating the Torah; his replies make it clear that he regards himself not as violating the Torah, but as violating his critics' interpretive traditions about the Torah. In some of these cases, such as healing on the sabbath, Jesus actually violates only one line of Pharisaic tradition concerning what remained in his day a live debate among Pharisees.[27]

Jesus's responses to their criticisms reveal something of his hermeneutic. If a priest gave consecrated bread—which was set apart only for the priests—to David because he was hungry, this narrative shows that this priest valued feeding a hungry servant of God more highly than he valued the normal rule of the sanctuary (Matt 12:3–4).[28] Priests in the temple work on the sabbath, Jesus points out, and this is no violation (12:5), an argument that some other Jewish teachers in fact used to make certain other exceptions.[29] In light of Jesus's divine authorization, he has authority to make comparable exceptions (12:6–8). The context in Matthew also suggests a contrast: Jesus offers a better "rest" (11:28) than the Pharisaic interpretation of the sabbath.

Some were dedicating to the temple resources that God would rather have them use to support their aged parents (Mark 7:9–13).[30] Jesus opposed using religion as a mask to neglect our God-given obligations to our families. (We should practice stewardship well enough to be able to give as much as possible, but contributing to the church building program should not lead us to neglect feeding our children or caring for a neighbor made destitute by abandonment or other tragedy. In light of Jesus's example in John 2:1–11, the needs of friends also come before religious rituals.)[31]

Likewise, Jesus reasons that it is lawful to heal on the sabbath. Unwilling to defend themselves on the sabbath, some earlier Judeans were slaughtered by their enemies, so Jewish authorities reasonably decided that it was lawful even to fight and kill on the sabbath if one was attacked.[32] But it was also certainly lawful to save a life on the sabbath, and Jesus reasons that, because restoring is greater than harming, it is consistent also to heal on the sabbath (Mark 3:4). Although the strict wilderness Essenes disagreed, most people believed that it was appropriate even on the sabbath to rescue a person or animal that had fallen into a pit or well (Matt 12:11–12; Luke 14:5).[33] Indeed, it was acceptable to water an ox or donkey on the sabbath; how much more to release from Satan's oppression on the sabbath a member of the ancestral covenant (Luke 13:15–16)? Jesus demands what he deems consistency in interpretation, regards the law as graciously designed for the greater good of people, and thus is more interested in the spirit of the law than in making a fence around it to avoid accidental violation of its letter.

Tragically, Jesus's contemporaries failed to recognize the time of their visitation (Luke 4:18–20, 23–24, 28–29; 12:54–56; 19:44). Although they claimed to know the Word in Scripture, John's Gospel laments that they failed to recognize the full embodiment of that Word when he appeared among them (John 1:11; 5:37–40). Do we ever act like Jesus's contemporaries, missing the heart and purpose of God's commandments as we seek to protect only or primarily the letter?

As a later chapter will explore (see pp. 246–55), application to our own setting and lives is a biblical way to handle Scripture, provided we draw the right analogies. My scholarly work focuses on the exegetical tasks that help us understand what the text meant in its first contexts, but God's Spirit also helps the church understand how we can apply that original sense in appropriate settings today.

More than the Law

Whereas the law said, "You shall not kill," Jesus says, "You shall not *want* to kill" (Matt 5:21–22). Whereas the law said, "You shall not betray your spouse by being unfaithful," Jesus says, "You shall not betray your spouse by *wanting* to be unfaithful" (5:27–28) or "by abandoning your marriage covenant" (5:31–32). Jesus's interest is not just in what we do, but in who we are, not just in our behavior but also in our motivation.

In the same way, the law warned against calling God as a witness that one's promise was true and then breaking it; but Jesus points to the ultimate ideal behind the warning. "Have such integrity that you do not need to call as witness God or anything he created" (5:33–37). The law limited revenge to legal retribution in kind—an eye for an eye, for example. By contrast, Jesus goes beyond this by doing away with revenge; one should love the other person more than one's honor or even basic possessions (5:38–42). The law enjoins love of neighbor; Jesus enjoins love of enemies (5:43–47).

And lest anyone construe Jesus legalistically, attending only to what he specifically mentions, he cites God's moral perfection as a model and goal (5:48;

cf. 5:45). Intention matters at an even deeper level than the law can address. Indeed, it matters at a deeper level than most people are sometimes honest about. For example, although we should expose our good works to others for the purpose of glorifying God, we should never do it to glorify ourselves (5:16; 6:1–2, 5, 16). Only God and perhaps our own hearts will know the difference.

Jesus takes the law further than its letter to the ultimate divine desire for people behind it. Since the time that Jesus spoke these words we Christians have often understood his teaching legalistically, and have thus missed the spirit behind them—God's heart for us. Civil law cannot make people righteous; it can only limit their sin. Noting this limitation is not meant to disparage Israel's civil laws; it is simply an observation about genre, since civil law cannot address—or at least enforce its will on—the human heart. Jesus goes beyond civil law to ethics.

The best of contemporary Pharisaic ethics would have agreed with Jesus on many of these points. Pharisees, too, emphasized *kavanah,* the intention of the heart.[34] Yet Jesus warns that his hearers' righteousness must *exceed* that of the Pharisees by going to the heart (5:20). If anything should make us nervous, this should. The Pharisees shared many of Jesus's ethics in *principle;* they themselves agreed that the heart must be pure. Yet only the kingdom could transform their hearts.[35] It is not enough for us to agree with Jesus's ethics in principle; we must let his reign transform us.

But while civil laws cannot transform us, in the law God often already pointed toward the ideal. The law might prescribe right behavior, but those who delight in it, who let it dwell in their heart so as to want what God wants, will develop that same character in their hearts. The final commandment in the Ten Commandments was, "You shall not covet your neighbor's house . . . your neighbor's wife . . . or anything else that is your neighbor's" (Exod 20:17). So it was not enough just to avoid stealing from your neighbor (20:15) or committing adultery with his wife (20:14) or killing him (20:13) or bearing false witness against him (20:16) to get his property. You weren't even supposed to *want* it, because you are supposed to love your neighbor as yourself. That's what Jesus says also: he explains what God always wanted, of which Israel's civil law could be only an outline or shadow pointing to God's fuller plan.

The Kingdom Restores God's Ideal

Some Pharisees asked Jesus whether a man could divorce his wife (Mark 10:2), perhaps because they had heard about Jesus's stricter-than-the-law view on divorce (Matt 5:32//Luke 16:18). Matthew's wording reflects the language debated among Pharisaic schools in precisely Jesus's day: "Can a husband divorce his wife for any cause?" (Matt 19:3). The generally more lenient school of Hillel (more progressive or more liberal, depending on your standpoint), with whom Jesus agreed on several other issues, would in fact have answered, "Yes." They emphasized the word that I have translated "something" (i.e., anything). By contrast, the stricter Pharisaic school of Shammai construed Deut 24:1 as allowing divorce if a man found something *shameful* in his wife. The term in Deut 24:1 that I would translate "shameful" has to do with sexual exposure, so Shammaites approved divorce only for marital unfaithfulness.

Jesus recognizes what the law of Moses *says* (Mark 10:3–4), but he warns that this is less than God's ideal. "He wrote this command for you because your heart is so hard" (10:5). Jewish teachers already recognized that civil laws could not enforce God's ideal, and, considering how these laws should work, they even added rules to help ensure that no one came close to breaking them. Whether or not they agreed with Jesus, they could understand what he meant when he viewed permission to divorce (which the law technically accorded only to a husband) as a concession to human weakness.

Jesus not only regards the law of Moses as demanding less than God's ideal, but he points to a picture of what God's ideal is like. Jewish thinkers sometimes envisioned the future kingdom in light of the primeval paradise,[36] and Jesus here sees God's purpose for humanity, consummated in the kingdom's values, modeled already in creation. He appeals to God's plan for marriage from the beginning, modeled in his institution of marriage (Mark 10:6–9).

Jesus was not the only Jewish thinker to appeal to Genesis 2 for a model for marriage; we find that also in the Dead Sea Scrolls.[37] Nevertheless, his hermeneutic does not have to be unique to be valuable. The law deals with humanity as it is, but God ultimately wants humanity to be as it should be. Jesus's hermeneutic recognizes the law as God's word for Israel, but that it was a limited word. The true ideal, to which Scripture itself bears witness, is higher.

As I argued at book length elsewhere,[38] Jesus is speaking here in general terms; inspired interpreters felt free to qualify this teaching for specific situations. Thus Matthew makes explicit a probably originally implicit exception for the situation of the spouse's unfaithfulness (Matt 5:32; 19:9), and Paul also qualifies Jesus's saying for the situation of a spouse abandoning the marriage (1 Cor 7:15). Just as Jesus quotes the law in Matthew 5 and then expressly qualifies it with, "You have heard, but I say" (Matt 5:21, 27, 33, 38, 43), so Paul quotes Jesus and then qualifies his teaching for an exceptional circumstance in 1 Cor

7:10–16. The language of 7:15, in which the believer "is not bound," echoes the exact language of ancient divorce contracts for freedom to remarry.

But both Paul's exception and the Matthean one address the person whose marriage is broken by the other party; neither permits the believer to break up their marriage. That is, the hortatory point of preserving marriage is not diminished by these qualifications. The qualifications simply advance the point for which Jesus opposed divorce to begin with: to protect a spouse from betrayal of the marriage covenant (see Mark 10:11).

If we read Jesus the way that Paul did (as we should, because Paul exemplified for us that hermeneutical model), we might regard some other situations as analogous forms of betrayal—a wife being beaten by her husband or a husband being poisoned by his wife—but in each case, the marriage is being broken, ultimately irreparably,[39] by the other person. The point in all this is not to look for reasons to end a marriage, but to follow Jesus's principle of faithfulness to one's marriage. The exceptions are never excuses for a believer to break their marriage; they are only provisions for when the marriage bond is severed from the other side.

Outside the Box

Throughout the Gospels, Jesus is criticized by the religious establishment. He eats with sinners. His disciples do not fast. They pluck ears of grain on the sabbath. Jesus is not part of the religious establishment and does not seek to inculcate their favor and become part of that establishment. From the beginning, he ministers predominantly among the poor, the infirm, the socially marginalized, and others who could offer him no political support. He lived and ministered the way he died: embracing weakness and trusting his Father to vindicate him (cf. 2 Cor 13:4).

Of course, the players in our world today are different. Whereas in some periods of history the religious establishment belonged to Western power structures, that is typically not the case now. And yet in other respects I still surmise that if Jesus were doing the same sort of ministry today, he would not start by cultivating favor with our denominational leaders or scholars; certainly not with political or academic establishments either. I believe that he would start with children in the projects, with teenagers on the most impoverished Native American reservations, or the world's shantytowns.[40] He might look more like a street outreach worker in Teen Challenge than a political activist. He would start from the bottom up. That is not to criticize the rest of us—most of my time now is spent as a scholar. But it is to put our respective and needed roles in the kingdom in a larger perspective.

Jesus's Christological Interpretation[41]

Jesus's preaching about the kingdom has implications for his own identity;[42] Jesus seems to claim that the kingdom is present in him (Matt 12:28//Luke 11:20).[43] He claims to be greater than King Solomon or the temple (Matt 12:42//Luke 11:31). The earliest strands of the Jesus tradition indicate that Jesus taught that his disciples would have a role in the messianic kingdom (e.g., Matt 19:28//Luke 22:30), a promise that would naturally imply that he attributed to himself a messianic role.[44] Jesus surely recognized the frequent connection between Jewish eschatology and biblical expectations of an end-time Davidic ruler and that his growing following and invitations to follow could not but have stirred speculations.[45] Such teachings cohere well with the secure information that Jesus was executed on the charge of claiming to be Israel's rightful king.[46]

The later church or Jesus's Jewish followers could have chosen for Jesus a more militant steed, but Jesus chose a beast of burden that would convey the image of Zech 9:9,[47] which later teachers and probably Jesus's contemporaries regarded as Messianic.[48] Many scholars who observe the actions believe that Jesus was announcing that he was indeed a king, but not a warrior-king.[49] Jesus may have responded ambivalently to the title of Messiah because his mission defined the concept differently than the popular title would suggest.[50]

A central characteristic of the expected Messiah was his royal descent from David. But in Mark, Jesus begins to hint his messianic identity publicly at Mark 12:6,[51] yet quickly implies an identity greater than that of David in 12:35–37. Jesus is no mere David redivivus, no mere warrior king like David, but one far greater than David. If he is David's "lord," enthroned not simply in Jerusalem but at God's right hand, how can he be his "son"?

It seems unlikely that early Christians would have created an ambiguously worded tradition that could be used to challenge Jesus's Davidic descent, hence his messiahship.[52] Jesus's messiahship was precisely a point of debate with their Jewish contemporaries, and Jesus's wording here could be used against his movement's case on that point. Why would Mark, who clearly affirms that Jesus is Christ (Mark 1:1; 8:29; 9:41; 14:61–62) and seems to also affirm that he is son of David (Mark 10:47–48; cf. 11:10), take this risk if not following genuine tradition? That Psalm 110 became widespread in a wide range of early

Christian circles[53] probably suggests that a common authority, namely Jesus, stands behind its usage.

Indeed, in Mark's context, Jesus had just used the title "Lord" for the only true God of the Shema (Mark 12:29–30); Jewish interpreters commonly linked texts on the basis of common key words.[54] Even in the original psalm, if the psalmist spoke to a lord besides Yahweh, a lord who would be enthroned at God's right hand as his vice-regent, then this king was someone greater than an ordinary royal descendant of David. Some in the psalmist's day might have understood the image on the Near Eastern analogy of divine kings.[55]

Conclusion

Jesus knew passages in their full literary context, although he did not live in a setting where one needed to recite that context to evoke it. But Jesus did not simply exegete Scripture—he lived by its message and explained that message in fresh and relevant ways. Jesus recognized that some matters of the law were "weightier" than others—these revealed God's heart behind the laws, and therefore offered a hermeneutical key—an interpretive grid but not a canonical filter—for reapplying them.

Jesus applied Scripture to his day in ways that often violated conventional religious understanding. Whereas some approached the laws as lawyers, concerned with protecting the letter of the law as well (in principle) as the spirit, Jesus's concern was especially with the point behind the law, points more demanding and all-encompassing than the Mosaic-period concrete applications of those principles. Most distinctive, of course, is Jesus's understanding of his own identity in light of Scripture.

CHAPTER 15

Reading the Torah as the Law of Faith

Jesus and his first followers modeled a way of reading Scripture that goes beyond our modern exegetical methods. The original sense of the text, insofar as we may recover it, remains foundational, as in exegesis, but the Spirit working in God's people helps us to apply those principles in new ways in new situations. In that way, the message remains alive and fresh for each generation and new cultural setting, because its principles address many of the pressing issues that we face.

Two Ways of Reading

Reading by the Spirit and with the heart is the way Jesus and the first apostolic church read the Scriptures they had, what we call the Old Testament. Paul contrasts two ways of reading the law: the law of works and the law of faith (Rom 3:27).[1] That is, we may wrongly approach the law as a means of self-justification, or we may approach it as a witness to the way of reliance on (faith in) God's covenant grace. Thus God's own people, pursuing the law's righteousness as if it were achieved by works, failed to achieve it because they did not pursue it by faith, by trust in the God of the covenant who would graciously transform them (Rom 9:31–32).[2] As a merely external standard, the law could pronounce death; but its principles could instead be written in the heart by the Spirit (8:2). The latter way is reading with faith.

Far from annulling the law by teaching that trust in God's action in Christ makes us right with God, Paul insists that he supports the law (Rom 3:31). Then he goes on to argue his case for this principle directly from the law, which in his circles included the entire Pentateuch. In Romans 4, then, Paul argues from Abraham's example in Gen 15:6. Paul uses the context in Genesis to point out that God accounted Abraham as righteous even years before he was circumcised (Rom 4:10), so that this experience is possible without the outward sign of circumcision (4:11).

[handwritten note in margin: faith 7 law]

Paul develops his case further by drawing an analogy between Moses's era and his own: salvation and God's word came in both eras. Just as God himself redeemed Israel, bringing his people through the sea and giving them the Torah (Deut 30:12–13), so now God himself brought Jesus down and raised him from the dead (Rom 10:6–7). Just as God enjoined Israel to follow the law by keeping it in their heart and mouth (Deut 30:14), so now his message, the good news inviting faith, resides in the heart and is expressed by the mouth (Rom 10:8–10).

Deuteronomy 30:12–14[a]	Paul's application in Romans 10:6–10
Do not say, "Who will ascend to heaven?"[b] (to bring down Torah, God's gift; 30:12)	Do not say, "Who will ascend to heaven?" (to bring down Christ, God's gift; 10:6)
Do not say, "Who will descend into the deep?" (to experience redemption again, crossing the "sea"; 30:13)	Do not say, "Who will descend into the abyss?"[c] (to experience salvation again, raising Christ from the dead; 10:7)
The Word is near you (the Torah; 30:14)	The word is near you (the message of faith we now preach, 10:8)
It is in your mouth and in your heart (30:14; as Torah was to be recited continually [Deut 6:6–7])	It is in your mouth and in your heart: confess with the mouth Jesus is Lord, and believe with the heart that God raised him (10:9–10)

a. I borrow this chart from Keener, *Romans*, 126.

b. In later Jewish traditions, Moses ascended all the way to heaven to receive the Torah (*Sipre Deut.* 49.2.1).

c. The LXX uses this term at times for the depths of the sea (e.g., Job 28:14; 38:16, 30; Ps 33:7; Sir 24:29; Pr Man 3), sometimes, as here, in contrast to heaven (Ps 107:26).

Paul argues by analogy from God's salvation and word in Moses's era to God's way of saving and God's word in Paul's own era of the new covenant. In this context, Paul speaks of "faith that comes from hearing" (or from what is heard; Rom 10:17), probably equivalent to "hearing with faith" (Gal 3:2). Since most people in antiquity could receive the message about Christ only orally, Paul speaks of "hearing with faith," but in our era of wider literacy and the availability of apostolic Scripture, we might also speak, as we have spoken above, of "reading with faith" (indeed, for some people today, that will be on their tablet or iPhone so long as the power grid holds up).[3] As noted earlier, faith is the sound and appropriate response to God's reliability.

The Spirit of the Law: Continuing Principles, Adjusted Content

The principles of the law endure, but because God gave the law in a specific cultural setting and for specific circumstances in salvation history, the specifics of obedience look different in different times.

Both Different and the Same

The God of the Old Testament remains the same God in the New Testament and today, despite addressing different sorts of circumstances. Salvation has always been by grace through faith, expressed by obedience (Gen 15:6; cf. 6:8). God chose Israel not because of their righteousness (Deut 9:4–6) or their greatness, but because of his love (Deut 7:7–9; cf. Eph 2:8–10). The God of Deuteronomy longs for our obedience for our good (Deut 5:29; 30:19–20); likewise, Paul expects faith to be expressed by obedience (Rom 1:5; 16:25).[4] God writes his law in the hearts of his people by the Spirit (Rom 8:2; cf. 2 Cor 3:3); as participants in a new creation, we should live new life by God's gift of righteousness (Rom 6:4, 11).[5]

This does not mean that nothing has changed. In Scripture, covenant faithfulness is always expressed through obedience; it grows from a relationship with God initiated by God himself. Yet the specific content of obedience may change from one era to another, not only in response to changes in culture but in response to developments in God's revelation or his plan of salvation in history. In Moses's day, no one could protest, "Since Abraham did not keep the law against planting trees in worship, neither will I" (cf. Gen 21:33; Deut 16:21), or, "Since Jacob could marry sisters, so can I" (cf. Gen 29:30; Lev 18:18), or, "Since Jacob could set up a pillar for worship, so can I" (cf. Gen 28:22; 31:13; 35:14; Lev 26:1; Deut 16:22).

Likewise, the coming of Jesus the promised deliverer changed the relevance of specific content, shifting the emphasis from some outward signs of the covenant to fuller inner transformation (cf. Rom 2:29; Col 2:16–17; Heb 8:5; 10:1) by the promised eschatological Spirit (Ezek 36:27). For that matter (as some other Jewish interpreters also recognized), some stipulations of the Torah could not be observed literally once the temple was destroyed, or outside the holy land, or in non-agrarian settings. No one by Paul's day, or for that matter by Ezekiel's day, could honestly expect otherwise.

Spirit of the Law in Ancient Israel

Long before Jesus came, Scripture already illustrated the difference between following God legalistically and following him from the heart. Jewish sages widely recognized this principle, even if they did not always apply it the way that Jesus did.[6] Eli the respected high priest undoubtedly knew God's commandments better than did Hannah, but God responds to her humble heart, whereas Eli resists God's demands (1 Sam 1:9–28; 2:27–36; 3:12–18). After God gives Israel a great victory through Jonathan's courage and faith (1 Sam 14:6–12), Saul wants to kill him to honor a fast that Saul has declared (14:24, 43–45)—a fast that proves to be a bad idea anyway (14:29–34).

Whereas Saul refuses to carry out a full slaughter of the Amalekites and their animals, which God had commanded (1 Sam 15:3, 14–29), he slaughters all the priests and their animals, the antithesis of God's will (22:18–19). This is because the high priest gave bread (21:4–6) to David, a man after God's heart (13:14) whom Saul feared. The priest giving David sacred bread, incidentally, is used by Jesus to illustrate his principle of meeting hunger over always observing ritual demands, as already noted (Mark 2:26; Matt 12:3–4; cf. John 2:3–10); Jesus and his hearers naturally favor the high priest over Saul. Saul's zeal for Israel leads him to kill Gibeonites (2 Sam 21:2) despite the ancestral covenant (Josh 9:19–20), and thereby brings judgment against Israel and ultimately his own household (2 Sam 21:1, 6).

When Hezekiah and his princes realize that not enough priests will be ready to sacrifice the Passover for all the people, they reschedule the Passover (2 Chr 30:2–5). The participation of more of the people is more valuable in God's sight than the specific date; moreover, in response to Hezekiah's prayer, God overlooks that many of the people, though seeking God, have not consecrated themselves ritually beforehand (30:17–20). The narrative is clear that God favors Hezekiah and this Passover celebration (30:12, 20, 27). The people come closer to fulfilling the spirit of the law here than they have done for generations, and God is pleased, despite several breaches of ritual practice.[7]

Compare also the priest and the Levite in Jesus's story of the good Samaritan. Priests and Levites could render themselves ritually impure by touching a dead body, and the victim beside the road appears to be quite possibly dead (Luke 10:30).[8] These ministers are not heading to Jerusalem to serve but back to Jericho, where many wealthy priests lived; nevertheless, they do not risk helping someone who might be dead anyway. Instead, a despised Samaritan rescues the Jewish stranger (10:33–35).[9]

In other words, in today's language, the spirit of the law often took precedence over its details (or in some of these cases, over other attempted expressions of zeal). In Romans 7, Paul depicts a wrong approach to the law, based on the mind knowing what is right without experiencing and recognizing a new, pure identity in Christ. In contrast to the expectations of some ancient thinkers, merely knowing what was right did not produce right volition as long as the mind found itself subject to the passions rather than empowered by God's Spirit.[10]

By contrast, one could keep the spirit of the law by the Holy Spirit in one's heart (Rom 8:2).[11] The prophet Ezekiel had already promised that God would wash the hearts of his people and give them new hearts and spirits. By his Spirit in them they would fulfill his laws (Ezek 36:25–27). Paul was not the only early Christian writer to recognize this. When Jesus refers to being born of water and one's spirit being born of the Spirit, he plainly evokes Ezekiel's promise (John 3:5–6); he goes on to compare God's Spirit with wind in 3:8, an image from Ezekiel's following chapter (Ezek 37:9–14). Fulfilling God's covenant stipulations by the Spirit *looks* different than the old way of keeping commandments.

Applying Paul's Principles

Although Paul affirms that believers are not under the law in the sense of needing it for justification, he does expect believers to fulfill the moral principles of the law. Unfortunately, Christians disagree among ourselves widely on how to distinguish transcultural principles from their concrete applications, and on the degree of continuity between the law enshrined in the Pentateuch and what rules we should follow as Christians.

Despite disputes regarding details, certainly we can look for areas of continuity, for example, eternal principles (albeit expressed in concrete cultural forms), as Jesus did. We can look for God's heart in the Torah (e.g., in Exod 33:19–34:7). The Spirit was often dramatically active in ancient Israel (e.g., 1 Sam 10:5–6, 10; 19:20–24), including in prophetically inspired worship (1 Chr 25:1–3); surely in the new covenant era (Acts 2:17–18) we should expect not less but more experience of the eschatologically outpoured Spirit.

Romans 14 suggests that Paul does not require Gentile Christians to practice the kashrut, or food purity customs, that were meant to separate Israel from the nations (Deut 14:2–3). (The principles of being set apart for God and that even our eating and drinking should glorify God remain, but they are expressed differently.)

His remarks about special holy days (Rom 14:5–6; cf. Gal 4:10; Col 2:16) are more complicated. Assuming that Paul includes the sabbath,[12] how do we reconcile his theology here with other parts of Scripture? God himself models the sabbath principle for Israel in creation (Gen 2:2–3); it does not begin with Moses. Sabbath violation incurs a death penalty under the law (Exod 31:14–15; 35:2; Num 15:32–36), so it appears to be something that God takes quite seriously. God promises to welcome Gentiles into his covenant, provided they observe his sabbaths (Isa 56:6–7). Jesus used his authority to clarify the ideal character of the sabbath in some respects (e.g., Mark 2:25–28), but he did not abolish it.[13]

If Paul supports the spirit of the law, would he change one of the Ten Commandments with no explanation? Some argue that verses such as the present ones offer sufficient explanations. Others struggle with this argument. Perhaps Paul recognized that most slaves and Gentiles could not get off work; they belonged to communities that did not observe the sabbath. Perhaps Paul is being flexible about how the sabbath should be observed (for example, on which day, although Acts continues to apply the term consistently to the day of its regular observance—Acts 13:14, 27, 42, 44; 15:21; 16:13; 17:2; 18:4).[14]

Perhaps, and I think this somewhat more likely, Paul was saying that it was all right to revere special days such as the sabbath, but all right also if one revered every day. In the case of the sabbath, this would mean that we would devote not only one special day a week to God, but seek to devote all our time to him. Just as Paul's interest was in spiritual circumcision more than in the physical circumcision that had long symbolized it (Rom 2:29), physically a day of rest is likely good for us, but spiritually we can walk in God's peace every day, resting in him. One caveat should be noted here: using the continual sabbath idea as an excuse not to rest at all, as I suspect some busy Christians do, defeats the still-valid point for which God originally instituted the sabbath.

In any case, the biblical sabbath principle applied to livestock and agricultural land as well as to people (Exod 20:10; 23:11–12; Lev 25:4; Deut 5:14), probably on the principle that living things need time to rest and rejuvenate. We are created beings who must acknowledge our good limitations. It is therefore at least wise, whatever one's theology on the particulars, that humans observe a day of rest. I doubt that we should say that, because we are not under the law, our mortal bodies no longer need a day of rest. Nor should we say, because we are zealous for the sabbath, that we are so religious that we will abstain from work *seven* days a week.[15]

Most matters are less difficult to resolve than the sabbath question. To further understand Paul's approach to the law, it is valuable to digress to examine the law itself. Its principles invite interpreters to sensitively apply it in new ways when it moves beyond the settings for which its concrete forms were first designed.

Interpreting Biblical Law

> Oh, I love your law so much!
> All day long I am considering it! (Ps 119:97)

Because Jesus's and Paul's hermeneutics address especially, and today most controversially, the law, it is valuable to see how culturally sensitive exegesis invites us to interpret the law. Jesus and Paul understood the law appropriately, and their approach thus invites considerations for how we should interpret Scripture more generally. In sum, we must value its principles over culture-specific applications—although it must be admitted that in practice there is a wide range of difference among interpreters today over which are the universal principles and which are the culture-specific applications![16]

Comparing Israel's Laws with Those of Her Neighbors

If we compare Israel's law with those of Israel's neighbors, we quickly find shared legal categories as well as some differences in ethics. The shared categories show us what kinds of issues ancient Near Eastern legal collections normally addressed. Consider (or at least skim) the following chart of comparisons.

Israelite laws	Other ancient Near Eastern laws (samples from Hammurabi, Eshnunna)	Comment
Rank distinction only between slave and free	Social rank in laws, e.g., Hamm. 196–204	Israel's laws highly distinctive
Exod 21:6: boring of slave's ear	Cutting off slave's ear, cf. Hamm. 282; brand in Eshnunna 51–52; Hamm. 226	Ear or other mark to demonstrate ownership (Hamm.) or loyalty (Exodus)
Exod 21:7: debt slavery	Hamm. 117–19: debt slavery	Debt slavery
Exod 21:8; cf. Lev 25:23–28	Eshnunna 39	Redeeming "property"

Israelite laws	Other ancient Near Eastern laws (samples from Hammurabi, Eshnunna)	Comment
Exod 21:9; cf. Gen 21:10	Hamm. 170–74: slaves' children inherit *if* father accepts them	Slaves' children may get the inheritance of the slaveholder
Exod 21:10; 22:16	Returning the dowry, Hamm. 137–38	Monetary arrangements for marriage
Exod 21:12–14	Intention at issue, Hamm. 206–7	Intention matters
Exod 21:15, 17	Hamm. 195	Israel's treatment harsher
Exod 21:16; cf. Deut 24:7	Hamm. 14	Death penalty for kidnaping (i.e., slave-trading apart from war captives)
Exod 21:18–19	Hamm. 206	Compensation for injuries caused
Exod 21:20–21: punishment for killing a slave, provided the cause of death is proven (through analogy with free—21:18–19)	cf. monetary payment for killing another's slave, but death for their wife or child, Eshnunna 22–24	Laws economically valued free persons more than slaves
Exod 21:22	Hamm. 209–14 (rank-based) (cf. Eccl 6:5)	Penalties for accidentally killing a fetus, though more rank-based in Hamm.
Exod 21:23	Contrast Hamm. 210: another woman executed (qualified by class, 212, 214)	Higher penalty if wife also dies; but whereas the killer dies in the Exodus law, the killer's daughter dies in Hammurabi; the latter is also class-based
Exod 21:23–25	Hamm. 196–97 (but determined by rank—198–99, 201–4)	*Lex Talionis*, but determined by rank in Hamm.
Exod 21:26–27	Contrast Hamm. 199 (for *another's* slave)	Laws concerning slaves' injuries—but whereas Hammurabi compensates the slaveholder, Exodus compensates the slave
Exod 21:28	Hamm. 250	Limits to liability (for unanticipated goring by one's ox)

Israelite laws	Other ancient Near Eastern laws (samples from Hammurabi, Eshnunna)	Comment
Exod 21:29	Eshnunna 54—only ½ mina of silver (OT harsher); Eshnunna 58, however: death for *wall* negligence; Hamm. 251: ½ mina of silver; but Hamm. 229: capital negligence on house	Severe penalties for negligence (regarding one's bull; Eshnunna and Hammurabi inconsistent in penalties)
Exod 21:30–32	monetary payment for killing slave, death for wife or child in Eshnunna 22–24	Legal liability greater for free person (i.e., closer relation)
Exod 21:32: Owner *and* bull punished	Eshnunna 55: 15 shekels, *no* penalty for ox; Hamm. 252: ⅓ mina of silver	Penalties for negligence when slaves killed
Exod 21:33–34	Eshnunna 58; Hamm. 229, 251; cf. wall negligence above at Exod 21:29	More about negligence
Exod 21:35–36	Eshnunna 53	Ox gores another ox: same in both
Exod 22 (assumed)	Eshnunna 40; capital offense not to have sales documentation—Hamm. 7, 9–12	Property ownership
Exod 22:1–4: may kill a thief only if he breaks in at night (i.e., in potential self-defense)	Eshnunna 12–13 (thief dies if breakin is at night); harsher for state property in Hamm. 6, 8; death for all thieves in Hamm. 21–23, 25	Permissible to kill thieves—sometimes
Exod 22:5	Cf. Eshnunna 5 (negligence)	Restitution
Exod 22:7, double	Hamm. 126	Restitution twofold
Exod 22:8	Hamm. 120–26	Laws regarding deposits
Exod 22:10–11: oaths if deposit is lost	The depository must swear an oath before the god his house is burglarized: Eshnunna 37; cf. Hamm. 20, 120, 249	Oaths
Exod 22:12 (cf. 22:14–15)	Eshnunna 36–37; Hamm. 249	Losing hired or borrowed animals
Exod 22:14–15	Cf. Hamm. 249	Losing hired or borrowed animals
Exod 22:16–17	Practice of brideprice in many cultures	

Israelite laws	Other ancient Near Eastern laws (samples from Hammurabi, Eshnunna)	Comment
Exod 22:18: death for sorcery	Contrast widespread use of magic in pagan antiquity; but sorcery and murder are cap. offenses in Hamm. 1–2	
Exod 22:19	Contrast possible Canaanite ritual practice and certain Canaanite mythical example	
Exod 22:20	Contrast virtually universal ancient polytheism; sacrifice also a virtually universal practice	
Exod 22:21–24: general moral principle, not casuistic law		
Exod 23:8	Universal ancient principle condemning unjust judges (Hamm. 5)	All cultures *officially* opposed unjust judges and bribery
Lev 18: incest laws	Hamm. 154–58	Nearly all cultures have incest prohibitions, but details vary from one culture to another
Lev 25:24	Cf. Eshnunna 39; cf. Exod 21:8	But no other ANE parallels to protection of families' land and rights by Jubilee, which honors families, stability of agrarian society based on land, and prevents monopolistic accumulation of capital; cf. transcultural ethic in Lev 25:35
Num 6:3–4: Nazirite's abstention from wine	Cf. Hamm. 110: sacred women must abstain from wine, on penalty of death	Analogy
Deut 18: no divination	Contrast divination throughout ANE (e.g., Mesopotamian *baru* diviners)	Contrast
Deut. 19:15–21, false witnesses suffer the penalty they would have brought on the accused (death in capital cases)	Hamm. 1–3 (death for false witnesses in capital cases); Hamm. 4 (whatever the accuser would have suffered for other charges)	Same

Israelite laws	Other ancient Near Eastern laws (samples from Hammurabi, Eshnunna)	Comment
Deut. 21:1–9 (cf. bloodguilt in Gen 4:10; Num 35:33): if the perpetrator is not found, the locality takes responsibility	Cf. cursing a place with bloodguilt, Aqhat, 2 Sam. 1; Locality takes responsibility: Hamm. 23; for life, they pay 1 mina (Hamm. 24)	Corporate responsibility for blood shed
Deut 21:18–21: death for habitually rebellious sons	Hamm. 168–69: *Disinheriting* sons only after 2nd warning and only if the offense is extreme	Rebellious sons: Israel harsher
Deut 22:5: women wearing man's clothes or the reverse	Ancient Near Eastern transvestitism; sometimes possibly magical transvestitism (Aqhat, Hittites; cf. also 2 Sam 3:29)	
Deut 22:22: death for all adulterers	Hamm. 129: death by drowning, unless the aggrieved husband wishes to spare his wife (in which case her paramour is also spared)	Israel's law harsher
Deut 22:25	Eshnunna 26; Hamm. 130	Death sentence for raping betrothed virgins, the same
Deut 22:29; cf. Exod 22:16–17	For genuine marriage, contract with parents is essential (Eshnunna 27); cohabitation also essential to it (Eshnunna 28); but insufficient without contract (Eshnunna 27); contract also Hamm. 128	Economic character of marriage arrangements
Deut 23:15–16: do not return a slave to the slaveholder	Contrast Eshnunna 49–50: not returning a slave is theft; Hamm. 15–16, 19: the penalty for harboring an escaped slave is death	Israel's law supports the escaped slave; Hammurabi supports the slaveholder
Deut 23:17; cf. Lev 21:9 Prohibits cult prostitutes	Hamm. 181 (cf. Gen. 38:15): regulates cult prostitutes (a father may dedicate his daughter as a prostitute, but, because she cannot marry, he must nevertheless provide for her)	Israel prohibits cult prostitution

Israelite laws	Other ancient Near Eastern laws (samples from Hammurabi, Eshnunna)	Comment
Deut 24:1–4: husband must provide his wife ability to remarry if he divorces her	Divorce *more* opposed in Eshnunna 59; the *wife* may leave if the court accepts her complaint, Hamm. 142; husband has to return her dowry (Hamm. 138–40), *unless* she's at fault (Hamm. 141) (thus dowry protects her economically and gives both incentive to preserve marriage). Remarriage: cf. 2 Sam. 3:14–16; Eshnunna 29; Hamm. 134–37	Israel more lenient on divorce
Deut 24:16: children and parents are not to be executed for each other (cf. Num 26:11; 2 Kgs 14:6; Ezek 18:20)	Contrast Hamm. 210: If a man killed another's daughter, they execute *his* daughter -Hamm. 230: If a house collapses and kills the owner's son, the builder's son is executed	Familial responsibility is different: Hammurabi punishes the guilty person's family members, whereas Deuteronomy prohibits this action

Differences from the Approaches of Israel's Contemporaries

> And what other nation is so great as to have such righteous decrees and laws as this body of laws I am setting before you today? (Deut 4:8, NIV)

Despite a shared legal milieu and thus many parallels, there are some noteworthy contrasts. The Ten Commandments lack any exact parallel; usually the closest cited parallels are a much longer Egyptian list of Negative Confessions, which also include such praiseworthy denials as, "I have never eaten human dung."[17] Another major contrast was the matter of social rank. All other ancient Near Eastern and Mediterranean laws were class-based in penalties with respect to victims and perpetrators. Israel has the only known ancient Near Eastern legal collection that refuses to take class into account (with the exception of the division between slave and free, noted below).

Some laws may openly oppose contemporary customs or ideas; thus Exod 22:19 condemns human intercourse with animals, even though pagan myths depict deities sometimes turning into animals before intercourse. Sacrificing to other gods is a capital offense in Exod 22:20, but was obviously promoted by nearly all surrounding cultures. Surrounding cultures exploited various forms of divination, but in Israel it was a capital offense, and is expressly contrasted with the behavior of surrounding nations (Deut 18:9–14).

Some contrasts appear among significant formal commonalities. Canaanites, like Israelites, had thank offerings, atonement offerings, sin offerings, and so forth, but Canaanites also had sacrifices to produce rain and fertility, whereas Israel fertility came through observing God's covenant.[18] Israel had ritual purity laws about what was clean and unclean, but Hittites used such rules as magical prophylaxis against demons.[19] Most cultures had food prohibitions; Israel's are distinctive to keep them separate from the nations (cf. Lev 11:44–45; Deut 14:2–3), a separation no longer needed for believers under the new covenant, since they are consecrated and empowered for mission.

Concessions to Human Sinfulness

Recall again Mark 10:5: "Moses gave you this commandment because your hearts were hard." As noted in chapter 14, Jesus taught that God's ideal was actually higher than the requirements of the law, which often made accommodations for human sinfulness. Thus the law regulated and limited sin rather than changed hearts and all mores.

In *no* society do civil laws represent the ideal of virtue; they are simply a minimum standard to enable society to work together. Israel's laws at least limited sin, and they often, though not on every matter, did so more than surrounding cultures (e.g., by Israelites being expected to offer refuge to escaped slaves and to avoid judging by class divisions). Yet both Israel's history and ways that many Muslims in areas of *sharia* law circumvent it show that laws do not transform hearts, even if in certain periods they may improve the social conditions that affect hearts. Only Christ in the heart delivers us from sin, and even most genuinely committed Christians do not walk in the light of that reality continually.

We thus need to be careful about extrapolating ethics from law. Jesus was clear that God's morality is higher than the Law. That's why, as noted earlier, Israel's civil law said: You shall not kill or commit adultery, but Jesus said, You shall not *want* to kill or commit adultery. If we ignore the laws' *genre*, we will misunderstand God's character and intention.

When I teach hermeneutics, I usually treat laws before I treat most other genres, so that students can see how contextualized for ancient Israel's cultural context the instructions were. This divine contextualization[20] provides students a model for approaching all of Scripture, since all of it originally addressed particular cultures (obvious enough from noticing the particular languages in which it was written). To illustrate the degree to which this is the case, I ask students how many of them are against slavery. Nearly everyone raises their hands. I then ask students how many of them believe that the Bible is God's Word in at least some sense; because of the settings in which I teach, the vast majority of students raise their hands. (Some of the rest just never raise their hands regardless of *what* I ask.)

Then I turn to some concrete issues: laws that are less than God's ideal. Take, for example, indentured servants. If a slaveholder beats the slave there is punishment, analogous to that of a free person (Exod 21:18–21). But the slave is still called the slaveholder's property or (literally) "money" (Exod 21:21); that is, the slaveholder paid money for the slave. Thus the case still differs from the case of free persons. Likewise, sexual abuse of slave women was punished but not as severely as if the slave were free (cf. Lev 19:20 with Deut 22:25–26).[21] The law did not institute or ratify slavery; it in fact regulated and thus reduced abuses in a contemporary custom. But it did not abolish it. Was this God's ideal?

Most of us today regard polygyny (a husband holding multiple wives) as wrong because it is unfair to the wives. Yet the law regulated it by prohibiting sororal polygyny (such as Jacob's involuntary and uncomfortable situation) and royal polygyny (such as Solomon's); it did not abolish it.[22] Likewise the law tolerated divorce, but, as we have noted, Jesus explicitly says that this was not God's ideal. He appeals instead to the creation story for God's ideal: one husband and one wife become one flesh, i.e., constituting one new family unit.

Many also place holy war in this category.[23] If entire societies could be depraved beyond hope, God might execute corporate capital punishment through judgments. (Whether we like it or not—most of us likely don't—we cannot believe in a sovereign God and deny judgment: even all human life stands under the sentence of death.) God could execute judgment through Israel as well as through any other means. Scripture suggests that Canaan had eventually become corrupt enough for such an invasion (Gen 15:16). Yet holy war was to be limited to the land, carried out only under YHWH's orders (although Gen 14 also depicts a "just war" to liberate slaves), and devoting people and objects to deities for destruction was a culturally understood practice.

Moreover, Canaanites would (and eventually did) entice Israel to apostasy (Deut 7:4), leading to the shedding of even more innocent blood (Ps 106:34–39, esp. 37–38). Thousands of urns from Carthage containing cremated babies suggests what a Canaanite-related culture could do.[24] Canaanite towns' earlier seasonal revolts against Egypt illustrate that merely temporary subjugation would not last. Reading the Pentateuch as a whole even suggests that God had saved these Canaanites' ancestors, and thus given these Canaanites life to begin with, through Joseph's wisdom regarding famine centuries earlier (Gen 50:20). Canaanites could join Israel in allegiance to Israel's God (e.g., Josh 6:25; cf. the lesser commitment in 9:1–10:11), and their refusal to do so was so conspicuously foolish that it, like Pharaoh's hardness of heart, is explained as God's judgment (Josh 11:20). Finally, even the conquest lists in Joshua must be taken according to their genre, like other known lists of this kind from antiquity, as summary statements of victories, not genuine total annihilation. People often fled their towns in advance of approaching armies and resettled them after the armies left.

But was this ever God's ideal? Scripture explicitly declares that God does not desire the death of even the wicked (Ezek 18:23, 32). Jesus reveals an ideal higher than that in Joshua. He calls us to love our enemies (Matt 5:43–44), and he proved it by how he loved us when we were his enemies (Rom 5:8–10; cf. Luke 23:34).

Understanding and Applying God's Law Today

God originally gave these laws to an ancient Near Eastern people addressing a different legal milieu than ours today, although subsequent legal systems have retained many legal categories and approaches, such as *Lex Talionis,* issues of negligence and liability, demands for evidence, and consideration of intention.

Culture determined the legal issues to be addressed, but not necessarily the content. Capital sentences reveal some issues that the law took quite seriously. It prescribed death sentences for murder, sorcery, idolatry and blasphemy, sabbath violation, persistent drunken rebellion against parents, kidnapping (slave trading), and sex outside of marriage (adultery; premarital sex with a man other than one's future husband; homosexual intercourse; and intercourse with animals). No one would suggest that Israel's laws invite us to execute capital punishment for these offenses in the church today; this was a civil law with penalties intended as deterrents in society (Deut 13:10–11; 17:12–13; 19:18–20; 21:21). Nevertheless, they do suggest that Israel's God deemed all of these offenses serious; otherwise he presumably would have deemed execution too excessive.

But does this mean that God did not take other offenses seriously? Would it not be far better to abolish slavery than to merely regulate it? (I have suggested elsewhere that, although Paul later wrote in a culture where abolition was not a practical option, his ethics would support abolition.)[25] Remember also points where Jesus demands an ethic higher than the law, such as avoiding desiring another's spouse, breaking one's marriage, and the like.

Some principles in the law are stated quite overtly in ways that fairly easily translate beyond local culture—the Ten Commandments, for example (apodictic rather than casuistic law). The law also includes other explicit principles based on God's values, such as the following:

- Principles that uphold the value of others: Be kind to foreigners in the land for you were foreigners in Egypt (Lev 19:34; Deut 10:19); Love your neighbor as yourself (Lev 19:18)
- Ethical principles *behind* the mere limitations of sin
- Principles in which God seeks to inculcate character in his people by how they habitually treat other creatures: Don't muzzle the threshing ox (Deut 25:4), don't take a mother bird with her young (Deut 22:6), give sabbath rest to your animals (Exod 23:12; Deut 5:14)

In other cases we must work harder to understand the principles behind the rules, or to "recontextualize" the message for our own setting. For example, homeowners must have a parapet around their roof to avoid incurring blood-guilt (Deut 22:8). Why? People could entertain neighbors on their flat roofs, and someone could fall from the roof and die or be injured. This is a safety regulation, and it invites us to care for our neighbors' safety today. For many of us, this includes matters such as driving carefully, making passengers wear seatbelts, and keeping our personal and church property safe where visitors might otherwise be injured (courts today continue to regulate the contours of property liability).

One Case Study: Tithing

Tithing was already an ancient Near Eastern custom[26] and is only one facet of a much larger network of teaching about stewardship in the Torah. Israelites offered the firstborn of their flocks to the Lord, the firstfruits of their harvest, and various other sacrifices, some mandatory and some voluntary. Agrarian produce and the firstborn of the flock (e.g., Deut 14:22–23) were merely part of the system of offerings to the Lord. The tithes went to support the landless priests and Levites, and for a festival, or giant party, every third year (Deut

26:12). Although ancient Israel was an agrarian society, those traveling long distances to the sanctuary could first convert the tithe to a monetary equivalent (Deut 14:24–25).

Sometimes popular preachers warn their listeners that if they do not bring their tithes to the storehouse, they are robbing God (Mal 3:8–10).[27] They do not always mention that the storehouse was the granary where food was kept for feeding the priests and Levites who ministered in the temple. It was for supporting the work of ministry; priests and Levites also ate portions of animal sacrifices once they were sacrificed—and thus cooked—on the altar. If people must pay tithes because the law requires it, and churches or ministries do not use those tithes for the purposes designated in Scripture (supporting ministers and throwing a triennial party), are the churches or ministries robbing God?

Jesus articulates demands for stewardship more exacting than the Torah, yet without appealing to tithing. Jesus highlights the heart of biblical stewardship: we and therefore everything we have belongs to God (Luke 12:33; 14:33). He addresses tithing only in connection with the religious people of his day who tithed so scrupulously, affirming that they were right to do so, but warning that they had missed greater biblical demands such as justice and love (Matt 23:23//Luke 11:42; cf. Luke 18:12).

Is the emphasis some churches lay on the "tithe" (as opposed to more holistic biblical teaching on stewardship) more a matter of tradition than of inductive study of the Bible? (It does not appear in the New Testament except as a practice associated with Pharisees or, in Hebrews, associated with the levitical system.) Would our understanding of stewardship be more well rounded if we read the entirety of the much larger biblical witness about the subject?

Conclusion: The Old Testament God of Love

The supposed contrast between the NT God of love and the OT God of wrath owes more to Marcion than to the principles of the Torah. The civil and ritual laws in the Torah expressed divine righteousness in a limited but culturally relevant way. Ultimately, however, the Torah already revealed God's heart in many respects. The theology of Deuteronomy emphasizes God loving and choosing his people (Deut 7:6–9; 4:37; 9:5–6; 10:15; 14:2). Love for God likewise demands obedience (6:4–6; 11:1; 19:9; 30:16) and fidelity to God (avoiding false gods, 6:4–5; 13:6–10). God summons his people to circumcise their hearts (10:16; cf. Lev 26:41; Jer 4:4; 9:26), and promises to circumcise their hearts so they may love him fully (Deut 30:6).

The God of the Old Testament period did not undergo evangelical conversion just prior to the New. He had often called his people to himself for their own good (Jer 2:13; Hos 13:9). He lamented with the pain of spurned love or a forsaken parent when his people turned after other gods (Deut 32:18; Jer 3:1–2; Hos 1:2; 11:1–4), but yearned to restore them to himself (Jer 31:20; Hos 2:14–23). His heart broke when he had to punish his people (e.g., Judg 10:16; Hos 11:8–9). Indeed, recalling two cities that God overturned and burned (Deut 29:23), the Lord pleads, "How can I treat you like Admah? How can I make you like Zeboiim? [Instead] *my* heart is overturned and *my* compassions burn together" (Hos 11:8).[28]

Israel's loving God, her betrayed and wounded lover, is ultimately fully revealed in Jesus as the God of the cross, the God who would rather bear our pain than let us be estranged from him forever.

CHAPTER 16

Christological Reading or Personal Application?

It almost should go without saying that a truly *Christian* reading focuses on Christ. He, after all, is our Lord and Savior; nothing is more fundamental than that. One can rightly read the history of Israel and the failure of various human forms of government as pointing toward the ultimate kingship of Christ, the divine yet Davidic ruler whose kingdom culminates Old Testament hopes.[1] The message of the prophets points toward Christ (Acts 3:18, 24; 26:22–23, 27).

At the same time, biblical theologians who find only larger strands of theology in massive strands of Scripture may miss something that some less academically trained readers intuitively find. The Spirit who actualizes the law's principles in our lives (Rom 8:2; Gal 5:18, 22–23) certainly will apply Scripture to us personally as well. Moreover, correct understanding about God invites worship of God; the disconnect between theological reading and personal experience is misplaced.

A Forced Choice

If our approach is solely oriented to personal application, that says more about our culture in the West than something distinctively charismatic. Although Western Christians read Scripture especially for personal edification, Jesus invites us to seek first God's larger kingdom agendas (Matt 6:32–33; Luke 12:30–31). We naturally expect the Spirit to lead us to see in Scripture first God's and Christ's honor, because this fits the Spirit's interest. The Spirit came to reveal and exalt the person of Jesus Christ (John 16:14–15; 1 John 4:2–3; Rev 19:10). The disciples understood Scripture retroactively in a new way in light of Christ (John 2:17, 22).[2] Likewise, the Spirit led the church into cross-cultural, ultimately global engagement in bringing the good news about Christ (Acts 1:8; 8:29; 10:19, 45; 11:12, 15; 13:2, 4; 15:28).

Some interpreters, however, have focused on christological interpretation virtually to the exclusion of recognizing other positive and negative models for our lives in Scripture. Is the correct focus on a central, overarching theological theme a reason to exclude other applications that may also flow from careful exegesis of biblical books?

Granted that we can view even every exhortation and encouragement in light of Christ, if Christ is our life then this also has personal implications (Rom 8:10; Gal 2:20; Phil 1:21; Col 1:27; 3:3–4). The prophetic model in Scripture includes personal engagement with God (e.g., Jeremiah's struggles, Jer 15:15–18; 18:19–23; 20:7–18) and personal hearing from God. Indeed, the Spirit regularly pours out God's love for us in our hearts (see Rom 5:5–8) and reminds us that we are God's children (8:15–16). It also includes hearing from God for others. Some of us may be more gifted in one way or another, but clearly the present-tense, experiential reading of Scripture is limited to neither personal nor christological dimensions.

Ideally, a charismatic, prophetic, or continuationist hermeneutic is one that in addition to exegesis considers how we can *live* in light of the message of the text. Again, such a consideration is not unique to pentecostals; it is, however, fundamental to the identity of pentecostals.[3] I have experienced in edifying ways this personal spiritual experience of the text in Pentecostal and charismatic settings.

Too often interpreters force an artificial choice between early Christians' christological interpretation of Scripture and applying Scripture in other God-honoring ways consistent with the text's message. Although some texts were considered expressly messianic, in many other cases christological readings were simply application par excellence, applying principles about God's way of working with his people to the ultimate embodiment of his people's salvation.

Some emphasize reading Scripture through the eyes of subsequent Christian creeds. Valuable as these creeds are for addressing the issues that they had to confront, early Christian interpreters were not interested exclusively in how to explain the relationship between Jesus's divinity and humanity (essential as both of these affirmations are; see, e.g., Rom 10:9, 13; 1 Cor 12:3; and 1 John 4:2–3). They also rightly valued imitating Jesus (1 Cor 11:1), for example, his love (cf., e.g., John 13:15, 34; Eph 5:2; 1 John 2:6), sacrifice (2 Cor 8:9; Phil 2:5–8), and humility (2 Cor 10:1). Likewise, though Luther's approach was heavily christocentric, he also applied this concern to pastoral application. Indeed, without Luther's pastoral application of Paul's teaching (generalizing to legalism Paul's more specific concern about misapplying Torah), the Reformation as we know it might never have happened (although a more gradual Erasmian reform movement may have also had some advantages).[4]

Stephen's Christocentric Interpretation

Acts 7 fleshes out the kinds of interpretation that Luke presumably had in mind when he spoke of Jesus's application of the OT to himself (Luke 24:27, 44–45). Charged with speaking against the law and the temple, Stephen shows his own respect for and knowledge of the law, while also challenging his critics' theology of the temple.

Further, following the common ancient forensic strategy of returning charges against one's accusers and the occasional strategy of connecting evildoers with evildoing ancestors, Stephen charges his critics with continuing the ancestral pattern of rejecting God's deliverers. Because Scripture already promised a supreme prophet like Moses (Deut 18:15–18), Stephen can observe one way that Jesus would be like Moses: he would be a rejected deliverer (Acts 7:35–40, esp. 37). Stephen highlights the same characteristic for Joseph.

Stephen's linkage of Joseph and Moses, however, is not a mere rhetorical connection contrived for the situation. Instead, it draws on literary connections already evident in the early biblical history of God's people.[5] This makes sense as a canonical reading of Hebrew Scripture as a unity; it makes sense even from the standpoint of narrative design, since the Joseph and Moses narratives in something resembling their current form certainly appear to have belonged to the same cycle of narratives (see table on p. 240).[6]

The history that Stephen surveys in Acts 7 climaxes with Jesus, and it is appropriate for scholars to speak of Luke's ancient Christian approach as christocentric. Posing a diametric either-or between christocentric interpretation and all other applications, however, is unhelpful. The narrative also climaxes, appropriately for one returning accusers' charges, in a hostile response; this narrative evokes the familiar ancient Jewish motif of the rejected prophets.[7] Stephen teaches about the unfaithfulness of God's people as well as that, contrary to ideas of some of his contemporaries, God's supreme presence was not limited to any one earthly site.

Moreover, in the conclusion of Acts 7, Stephen himself fits the rejected deliverer paradigm; his hearers continue to "resist the Holy Spirit" who had inspired the earlier prophets (7:51–52; cf. 7:55). During his martyrdom, Stephen deliberately echoes Jesus's passion in Luke's first volume, committing himself

Joseph (Gen 37–50)	Moses (Exod 2–12)
Brothers sold him into slavery (37:27)	Family, who were slaves, rescued him from slavery (1:13–14; 2:2–9)
Midianites sold Joseph into Egypt (37:28, 36)	Midianites received Moses when he fled Egypt (2:15–22)
Joseph became "father" to Pharaoh (45:8)	Moses became son to Pharaoh's daughter (2:5–10)
In one day, Joseph was exalted from slavery, over Egypt	In one day, Moses lost his royalty in Egypt by identifying with slaves
Joseph made all Egypt Pharaoh's slaves (47:19)	Moses freed slaves; through him God judged Pharaoh's might
Joseph from Jacob's house to Egypt as a deliverer	Moses from Pharaoh's house from Egypt as a deliverer
Joseph's God delivered Egypt in famine	Moses's God struck Egypt with plagues
Joseph, exiled in Egypt, married an Egyptian (41:45, 50)	Moses, exiled from Egypt, married a Midianite (2:15, 21; cf. Num 12:1)
Asenath's father was priest of On (41:50)	Zipporah's father was priest of Midian (2:16)
Asenath bore two initial sons, the name of the first reflecting his father's sojourn in a foreign land (41:51)	Zipporah bore two initial sons, the name of the first reflecting his father's sojourn in a foreign land (2:22)
God raised him up to bring Israel to Egypt	God raised him up to bring Israel out of Egypt
Future deliverer's leadership initially rejected by his brothers (37:4, 8, 11)	Future deliverer's leadership initially rejected by his people (2:14)

to his Lord and praying for forgiveness for his persecutors (7:59–60; Luke 23:34, 46). That is, biblical leadership ideals sometimes not only foreshadow Jesus, the ultimate leader, but sometimes they also apply to those who more knowingly follow and imitate Jesus.[8]

This broader interpretive paradigm continues in Acts. Indeed, a doubly confirmed[9] vision leads to transforming centuries of the dominant approach to a significant portion of the law.[10] The book's final narrative scene, culminating in its final biblical quotation, revisits Jesus's explanation of Isaiah 6 in Luke 8:10. Quoting Isa 6:9–10, Paul, like Jesus, recognizes the hardness of God's people (Acts 28:26–27). Paul recognizes that Isaiah addressed the prophet's own generation: "The Holy Spirit rightly told your ancestors through Isaiah the prophet . . ." (28:25). Yet Luke's context makes it clear that Paul is applying that same principle to his own generation. Acts' open ending probably suggests that Luke also expects his audience to recognize their own mission as part of his narrative's trajectory.[11] This application is ecclesial and missional.

Matthew's Christocentric Reading

Few NT passages have been criticized for taking the OT out of context more than Matthew's use of Hos 11:1 ("Out of Egypt have I called my son") in Matt 2:15.[12] In context, Hosea plainly refers to God delivering Israel from Egypt (the verse's first line reads, "When Israel was just a child, I loved him"), whereas Matthew applies the text to Jesus. Yet Matthew appears to know the verse better than we assume: instead of depending on the common LXX version of Hosea here ("his children"), he offers his own more precise translation from the Hebrew ("my son").

God's Son and Israel

The apparent problem arises because we assume that Matthew was reading Hos 11:1 exclusively as an express messianic prophecy, when in fact Matthew's own context suggests that he was making instead an analogy. This is not the only place where Matthew compares Jesus with Israel: for example, as Israel was tested in the wilderness for forty years, Jesus was tested there forty days (Matt 4:1–2). Moreover, Matthew also knows Hosea's context: as God once called Israel from Egypt (Hos 11:1), he would bring about a new exodus and salvation for his people (Hos 11:10–11).[13] Jesus appears here as the harbinger, the pioneer, of this new era of salvation for his people.[14]

In the same context, Matthew applies Jer 31:15 (where Rachel weeps over Israel's exile) to the slaughter of infants in Bethlehem (Matt 2:17–18), near which Rachel was buried (Gen 35:19). Again Matthew may evoke the quoted verse's context: offering an implicit connection with Hos 11:1, which Matthew has just cited, Jer 31:20 calls Israel's God's son.[15] Further, after announcing Israel's tragedy, God promises restoration (Jer 31:16–17) and a new covenant (Jer 31:31–34; cf. Matt 26:28). Matthew thus may compare this tragedy in Jesus's childhood to one in Israel's history because he expects his first, biblically knowledgeable hearers to recognize that such tragedy formed the prelude to messianic salvation.

Isaiah's Typological Model

Matthew also seems to know the context of Isa 7:14, the verse that he quotes in Matt 1:23; the context apparently remains fresh in Matthew's mind when he quotes Isa 9:1–2 in Matt 4:15–16.[16] In the context, Isaiah was warning Judah's king, Ahaz, not to join the northern coalition of Israel and Aram against Assyria. As a sign to him that God would be with Judah ("God with us"), a child would be born. This child would signify that Israel and Aram would be crushed by Assyria while the child was still young (Isa 7:15–16). This child is undoubtedly Isaiah's own son, who portended the swift defeat of those kingdoms (8:3–4).

Yet Isaiah himself also apparently looked beyond the immediate fulfilment to an ultimate deliverance through a greater son (9:1–7; cf. 11:1–10). Isaiah's sons' names were intended as signs to Israel (8:18), but ultimately there would be a son born to the house of David who would also be called "the mighty God" (9:6–7), a phrase that Isaiah surely intends in a divine way (10:21). (Surrounded by cultures that believed in divine kings, Isaiah would hardly dare have employed such language for the future king if he did not genuinely intend divine associations.)[17] That the LXX renders the mother in 7:14 a "virgin" surely seals the connection for Matthew, but he already had reasons to view Isaiah's son from Ahaz's day as a precursor and sign of the ultimate arrival of the one whom the same verse calls "God with us."

Far from ignoring context, Matthew is comparing Jesus's ministry with Israel's history and the promises that those very literary contexts evoke. He makes after-the-fact analogies between God's working in Israel's earlier history and the new culmination of its history in Jesus. Although it may not be familiar to modern exegesis, Matthew's exegesis is hardly unsophisticated.

Matthew's attention to larger contexts continues in Matthew 12. Because Jesus is empowered by God's Spirit to cast out demons (12:28), he fulfills a prophesied mission.[18] That mission is clear to Matthew's audience because Matthew has just quoted a passage in Isaiah about God's servant endued with the Spirit (12:18). Isaiah's servant would initially be gentle rather than like a warrior (12:19–20; cf. 11:29; 21:5). That passage would be particularly noteworthy in Matthew's Gospel because Matthew has conformed its translation to fit the language of Matt 3:17, where a heavenly voice announces Jesus's mission.[19]

In the context in Isaiah, God originally gave this servant mission to Israel, but because Israel disobeyed (Isa 42:18–20), God raised up a figure within Israel to bring the people back to himself (49:5; 53:4–6, 11). The context in Isaiah further shows that the servant would bless not only his own people, but also the Gentiles (42:6; 49:6; 52:15), perhaps also announcing good news of God's reign (52:7). Because Matthew may find in Isaiah itself a connection between the mission of God's people and that of the one who would fulfill that mission on their behalf, Isaiah might even serve as a model for Matthew's connections between Jesus and Israel.

Matthew's Interpretive Interests

Matthew's use of Scripture is primarily christological; because he is writing a biography of Jesus (in the ancient sense) it comes as no surprise that his interest is particularly in Christ. Indeed, given Matthew's (and our) belief in Jesus's divine status (e.g., Matt 1:23; 18:20; 28:18–20), focus on Christ and therefore christocentric applications of Scripture would undoubtedly be paramount for him (and us) in any case.

But Matthew's approach is not *exclusively* directly about Christ. Recall his emphasis on compassion more than sacrifice (9:13; 12:7), or comments that he includes about the law's true demands (5:21–48), the obduracy of God's people (13:14–15), God's design for marriage (19:4–6), the temple's desecration (21:13), and so forth. I briefly treated some of these themes above.

Exegetes today will also recognize that Matthew's approach is considerably more sophisticated than the undisciplined sort of typology found later in the *Epistle of Barnabas,* Origen, and others.[20] Even Hebrews is more disciplined than later works; it does not, for example, actually allegorize all the details of the tabernacle the way some popular interpreters today do. (Its correspondence between heavenly and earthly sanctuaries fits the Middle Platonic ideals of Alexandrian Jewish interpretation in this period, but is also consistent with ancient Near Eastern links between the heavenly house of the deity and earthly imitations.)[21]

Even when the earliest Christian interpreters recognized that Christ epitomized a biblical model or principle, for example the righteous sufferer of the psalms, that does not mean that we cannot extrapolate additional lessons from those principles. Early Christian application to the righteous sufferer par excellence does not strip these texts of the value of their earlier, more general application. (The psalmist himself was probably thinking more generally than the christological application, and most of us would not want to say that the psalmist's applications to himself or to Israel were mistaken.)

Early Christian christocentric interpretation rightly warns us to keep our focus on Christ, as did Jesus's first followers.[22] Matthew's example, however, illustrates that their christocentric focus does not minimize the possibility of other, additional applications.[23] That is not to suggest that all exegetes today should handle these texts the way that Matthew did. It is simply to say that if we must interpret our lives and experience in light of Scripture, we will have to apply Scripture as well as exegete it. And in doing so, we should keep first the most central matters, such as God's plan that climaxes in our Lord Jesus, and how that plan invites us to respond.

Other Analogies in the Gospels

interesting

Biblical analogies are not exclusively christological. If many charismatics have sometimes overapplied analogies by transferring primarily apostolic or other individual gifts (or occasionally, in the worst cases, messianic prerogatives) to all believers, they have often simply overcompensated for the lack of adequate transferral offered by many other inattentive observers. Evangelists such as Luke and Matthew naturally had particular interest in analogies with Christ, given both their biographic subject and their (and our) faith in Christ. Nevertheless, they also recognized other analogies between more recent saving events and those of earlier Scripture.

One may note, for example, the echoes of Hannah (in 1 Sam 2) in Mary's song in Luke 1, toward the very beginning of Luke's two-volume work.[24]

1 Samuel 2:1–10	Luke 1:46–55
God exalts lowly (2:1, 4–5, 8)	God exalts lowly (1:48, 52–53)
I rejoice in your salvation (2:1)	I have rejoiced in God my savior (1:47)
No one holy like the Lord (2:2)	Holy is his name (1:49)
Proud brought down (2:3–5)	Proud brought down (1:51–53)
Humble exalted, proud brought down (2:4–5)	Humble exalted, proud brought down (1:52–53)
Celebration of God's sovereignty in such reversals (2:3, 6–9)	Celebration of God's sovereignty in such reversals (1:51–53)
Barren given children (2:5)	(Context: Elizabeth's pregnancy)
Poor vs. rich (2:7–8)	Rich empty-handed (1:53)
Hungry vs. full (2:5)	Filled the hungry (1:53)
Poor displacing nobles (*dunastōn*, 2:8)	Brought down rulers (*dunastas*, 1:52) [same term]
Raises up from death (2:6)	(Implicit Lukan subtext?)
Shift from personal deliverance to God's anointed king (2:10)	Shift from personal deliverance to Israel's deliverance

In fact, they were ready to recognize parallels among events of recent saving history, just as they did regarding the Old Testament. Not only does Luke recognize parallels among Joseph, Moses, and Jesus (as in Acts 7); he also recognizes parallels and contrasts among figures from the very beginning of his

Gospel. Thus one may note the conspicuous parallels and contrasts between Zechariah, the respected, aged priest serving in Jerusalem's temple, and Mary, a virgin in the village of Nazareth:[25]

Luke 1:12: the vision's recipient troubled	Luke 1:29: the vision's recipient troubled
1:13: do not be afraid	1:30: do not be afraid
1:13: reason for miracle	1:30: reason for miracle
1:13: child's name (John)	1:31: child's name (Jesus)
1:15: child will be great	1:32: child will be great
1:15: filled with the Holy Spirit from the womb	1:35: conceived through the Holy Spirit[a]
1:16–17: mission	1:32–33: mission
1:18: question	1:34: question
1:19–20: proof or explanation	1:35–37: proof or explanation
1:20: Zechariah muted for unbelief	1:38, 45: Mary praised for faith
1:80: child grows	2:40, 52: child grows[b]

a. For the contrasting role of the Spirit in John's and Jesus's prenatal experience, see Tatum, "Epoch," 188–89.

b. I have omitted less obvious parallels such as circumcision (Luke 1:59; implicit in 2:21) or "favor" for both Elizabeth (1:25) and Mary (1:30). Flender, *Theologian*, 29, helpfully views the contrast between Mary and Zechariah in light of a series of contrasts, often between religious insiders and others, in the Gospel (Luke 7:36–50; 10:29–37; 14:15–24; 15:24–32; 18:9–14; 20:45–21:4).

Yet Luke also follows with conspicuous parallels between Jesus in Luke's Gospel and Jesus's movement in the book of Acts, both in the Jerusalem church movement (exemplified especially but not exclusively in Peter) and in the Gentile mission (exemplified especially in Paul).[26]

Some of these parallels appear already in Mark (not surprisingly, since ancient narratives often included such echoes and parallels).[27] For example, John's coming in the wilderness prefigures Jesus's time in the wilderness (Mark 1:4, 12); his execution foreshadows that of Jesus (6:16; 9:11–13); the faithfulness of John's disciples in burying him highlights the unfaithfulness of Jesus's disciples at his passion (6:29; 14:50), fitting a Markan theme. Likewise, the summary of John's message in Matthew (Matt 3:2) prepares for both Jesus's message (4:17) and that of his followers (10:7; 28:18–20).

In Mark, Jesus's suffering prefigures that of his followers (Mark 8:34; 10:39;

13–15). Even in Mark's concise introduction, Jesus the Spirit-baptizer (1:8) becomes the model of the Spirit-baptized life: the Spirit descends on him at his baptism (1:10) and then thrusts him into the wilderness to face testing from the devil (1:12–13). Afterward Jesus begins expelling demons (1:25–26) and continues facing hardship; he expects his disciples to share both his power (6:7; 9:28–29; 11:21–25; perhaps 4:40) and, as noted, his sufferings.[28] Application does not, therefore, stop with Jesus, but follows to the lives of disciples through the example of Jesus.

Analogies and Application

Scholars use the term "meaning" in different ways; some define it in a way that includes what I mean here by "application." Some, for example, speak of respecting both the "plain meaning" and the "multiple meanings" that texts can acquire in usage[29]—what some earlier interpreters called a meaning with multiple applications.[30] Regardless of nomenclature, meaning functions differently for different contexts. Thus, for example, by "All men are created equal" the framers of the Declaration of Independence in fact meant only men, and in practice only adult, property-owning free males. Yet most readers today happily approach the valid element of the principle in light of our fuller understanding of humankind than the original authors embraced.[31]

Defining Terms

Distinctions in terminology can be helpful for practical reasons; although exegesis and contextualization overlap, for example, distinguishing them allows us to conceptualize the process more precisely.[32] Nevertheless, different labels used by different approaches sometimes overlap in meaning more than their detractors admit.[33] Words communicate meaning because they connote a range of ideas within particular linguistic and cultural frameworks; the general English meaning of "meaning" is broad enough to include a range of ideas, and arguments about which sense of the term is normative may be essentially struggles to control a definition within a particular community.

Because I have little interest in semantic arguments over definitions here, I explain here how I am using the contested but by themselves polyvalent terms, so as to define more specifically the aspects of the broader concept that I address here. I am distinguishing the senses first communicated in an ancient setting (the inspired author's sense designed for an intended audience insofar as we can discern it, and the senses received by real early audiences) from the ways we can receive these texts today.

I suggest that we receive the original communication most respectfully, and recognize its authority most fully, when our understanding for new situations (our "application") flows from our understanding of the sense it was originally designed to communicate. Relevance theory shows that a wider linguistic and social context must inform our understanding of a communication; acquiring such context requires even more work in the case of secondary communication—when, as in the case of works originally addressed to a different setting, we are reading someone else's mail (e.g., Rev 2:7a, 11a, 17a, 29a; 3:6a, 13a, 22a).

nice!

Application

Admittedly, my academic commentaries tend not to emphasize application. This is not because application is unimportant to those who read biblical texts as Scripture. It is because, first of all, the genre of academic commentaries focuses on ways of reading that are more widely embraced by the academy. It is also because, second, appropriate application is generally indigenous, and is as varied as the contexts to which the principles are meant to be applied. One cannot produce *universal* applications except in a generalized and usually obvious form.[34] Nevertheless, when I *read* Scripture personally, I do hear the Spirit applying it to my concerns (and should-be concerns), whether to my life or to the needs of the world more generally. Likewise, when we preach, sensitive pastors care about their congregations' practical reception of the message. Whether reading Scripture for personal devotion or for preaching, we are hopefully moved to pray regarding its message.[35]

good point

In Scripture we often learn of those who heard God's voice for their generation in connection with earlier Scripture; it was not simply a matter of historical interest. Deuteronomy already foretold severe judgment for God's people if they broke his covenant (Deut 27–28). In 2 Kgs 22:15–20, however, the prophetess Huldah *applies* the prophetic message accurately to her generation. Many judgments proclaimed by the prophets echoed the curses of the covenant that Israel had broken. Jeremiah expressly cites his predecessors the true prophets (Jer 26:17–19; 28:8).

The psalmist can emphasize God's kindness in the events of the exodus (e.g., Pss 74:13; 78:11–16; 105:25–45; 106:8–12; cf. Neh 9:9–15), evoking praise

(Ps 105:45). Yet the psalmist can also use the same events to highlight Israel's disobedience (78:11, 17–20, 32–37, 40–43; 95:9–11; 106:7, 13–33; cf. 78:8; Neh 9:16–18), to highlight God's mercy and powerful acts of covenant love (Ps 78:4, 23–29, 38–39, 42–55; Neh 9:19–25, 32) and the righteousness of his judgments (Ps 78:21–22, 31, 34), to challenge the sins of the psalmist's day (95:7–8; 106:6), to explain the reason for Israel's sufferings (106:40–43; cf. Neh 9:33–37), and to cry out for mercy and deliverance (Pss 74:19–23; 106:44–47; cf. Neh 9:32).

When Daniel considers the message of Jeremiah (Dan 9:2), he wants to see the relevance of Jeremiah for his own era. He is not merely interested in the causes of the past exile out of curiosity. He repents for the sin that led to exile (9:3–6), and looks for the fulfillment of God's promises, which he expects in his era. Jeremiah's seventy years become seventy sevens of years in the new, inspired application received by Daniel (Jer 29:10; Dan 9:2, 24). We may dispute which promises pertain to our own era, but since the outpoured Spirit clearly does (Acts 2:17–18), we, like Daniel, should expect that we live in an era of fulfillment.

New Testament writers often understood present experience in light of analogies with earlier figures in the Bible. For example, the conspicuously visionary (hence necessarily "charismatic") book of Revelation regularly reapplies OT images. Revelation's Old Testament allusions rarely apply OT language such that the OT passages are taken as direct prophecies of the events mentioned in Revelation. Rather, they involve events of the same *kind*. The author inhabits the text so thoroughly that he envisions for almost everything he depicts prior biblical analogies and expectations based on the *way* that God has worked.

When Revelation pervasively alludes to OT texts (though it never explicitly quotes them in the traditional way), then, it is not elaborating an exegesis of those texts. For example, the judgments associated with trumpets and bowls of God's anger evoke the plagues on Egypt in the book of Exodus, but virtually no one suggests that Revelation is simply rehearsing what happened to Egypt centuries before. Revelation is examining God's judgments on the world through the lens of God's past activity; thus the "great city" on which judgment falls is called "Sodom and *Egypt*" (Rev 11:8).

Likewise, when John hears a lament over fallen Babylon, borrowing the language of Isaiah and Jeremiah for the fall of an oppressive empire, he is not contemplating merely historical information about the Babylon that fell to Persia centuries before he wrote. He is thinking of another evil empire that was now oppressing God's people and that had destroyed the temple, and probably more generally of the spirit of evil empire that has continued in history beyond his day.[36]

Perhaps most strikingly, John's revelation sometimes even supplants the literal sense of OT promises. Thus, for example, his contemporaries who heard Ezekiel 40–48 would presumably expect a glorious new temple, with specified dimensions, when God restored his people.[37] John, however, saw no temple in the New Jerusalem—because God and the lamb would be the temple (Rev 21:22), and God would dwell among his people (21:3). Because the New Jerusalem is shaped like the holy of holies and is unimaginably more magnificent than Ezekiel's vision (Rev 21:16), no one could complain.

Ezekiel's symbolic vision had offered only a partial glimpse of glory, one expanded in the symbolism of Revelation. "In the expansive tendency of ancient Jewish and Christian end-time expectation, a *greater* fulfillment was never an abrogation of less exalted hopes. Rather, it was a yet better way to envision that which was beyond mere words and images to describe."[38] Ultimately, in human language only poetry and symbolism can attempt to evoke the glory that awaits; only the Spirit can provide a fuller taste of what that glory means (1 Cor 2:9–10).

Personal Applications Consistent with Scripture

Applying by analogy a principle on which the text draws often helps us to hear that principle more concretely. Reading about the Lord swallowing up death in Isa 25:8, a teenage Pentecostal took encouragement about God's compassion and power.[39] Another highlighted God's defense of the needy in 25:4 and applied it to her own situation in which a nonbeliever in crisis had just asked her for prayer.[40] Such readings do apply genuine elements of the passage's message about God's character.

Likewise, it seems clear that texts can convey implications beyond the original author's direct concern, where the author draws on principles that communicate in wider settings. Thus, for example, the admonition against being drunk with "wine" in Eph 5:18 originally applied to the typical ancient admixture of water and fermented grape juice; but the principle applies no less to being drunk with beer, vodka, or other substances.[41]

The Spirit Speaks through Scripture

Some scholars, appropriately focused on the larger covenant implications of Scripture, sometimes overreact against the modern Western emphasis on individualistic fulfillment by downplaying any role for personal application. A characteristic of the new covenant, however, is that all believers are to experience the Spirit's activity in our lives (e.g., Acts 2:17–18; Rom 8:4–16; 2 Cor 3:3). Surely at the least this recognition should include the Spirit bringing to our attention the implications of biblical principles for our lives as we read Scripture (see 2 Cor 3:15–18). Thus the Spirit may draw from texts wider analogies, beyond the direct communication to the first audience, that are nevertheless consistent with the text and with the larger framework of the Spirit's message in biblical theology.

Unlike continuationists, in fact, some cessationists treat personal illumination of Scripture as the Spirit's nearly *exclusive* way of speaking today.[42] Yet both continuationists and cessationists affirm the Spirit's role in illumination,[43] even if many charismatics emphasize illumination more heavily,[44] and, like others, sometimes incorrectly.[45] Church fathers also insisted on the need for divine illumination in understanding Scripture.[46] Some theologians today emphasize a continuity between original inspiration and subsequent illumination;[47] while such language is open to abuse,[48] Christians in general agree that the Spirit who acted in inspiration remains active in providing understanding.[49]

Affirming illumined application does not mean that every reading of Scripture in light of our situation stems from the Spirit's illumination. Obviously anyone can simply read their situation into the text. At the same time, issues in the text do address fundamental issues in our lives, and we do not usually need an extraordinary sort of revelation to recognize that.

By way of illustration, when a senior colleague at one institution was apparently seeking to discredit Christian faith and I was seeking to defend it, I wanted to simply withdraw from debate, but I discovered that Proverbs warns a righteous person not to give way before the wicked (Prov 25:26). I maintained my position, and by God's grace the students largely came out all right. Yet I had also prayed based on Prov 16:7 that God would give me peace even with my enemies, and the colleague and I became friends.

Sometimes guidance comes in ways that are, to varying degrees, extraordinary. At other times, including often when we read Scripture, we simply do our best to discern what God is saying or at least what is the wisest course (Prov 14:15; 22:3; 27:12), and we live with some ambiguity (cf., e.g., 1 Kgs 21:29; 2 Kgs 2:3, 5, 16; Prov 25:2; Luke 7:18–21; Acts 21:4–14; 1 Cor 13:9; 14:30–32; Rev 10:4) but trust God anyway.[50] Our trust is not in the perfection of our ability to hear God, but in his power to direct our steps (Prov 16:9; 20:24). If we do our best to hear him and obey what we sincerely believe is his will, he will lead us even in ways that we cannot recognize at the time.

Models for Personal Application in Scripture   *interesting*

Scripture indicates that believers have long appropriated many biblical models personally as well as corporately. For example, the ram in the story of Abraham offering Isaac (Gen 22:13) functions sacrificially like a "lamb" (Gen 22:7–8), probably on one level prefiguring Passover for Israelite hearers. But ancient hearers would have also learned other lessons from this passage, including a lesson about God relevant for their own lives. Gen 22:14 shows that this account was still being applied in the writer's day as a saying: "In the mountain YHWH will provide." Some Israelites probably were using this saying proverbially as a statement of their own faith in God's provision.

Paul's Jewish contemporaries often read the story of Israel's election in the Old Testament as a story of an ethnic people; Paul reads it especially as a story of God's grace to the undeserving (witness the behavior of most of Jacob's sons toward Joseph!). In Paul's view, it could be applied personally to all who, like biblical Israel when they kept the covenant, embraced God's grace without claiming to deserve it (cf. Rom 9; also 8:28–30).

Thus in Romans 4, Abraham is not simply the historical ancestor of the Jewish people; more importantly, for Paul, Abraham is the father of all who, like Abraham, have *faith,* trusting God's faithfulness. Paul *applies* Genesis here to all who *individually* become members of the covenant people.

Basic to Paul's use of historical narrative is looking for models for believers, and Jewish people already used Abraham and Sarah as moral models in addition to their function as ancestors of God's people. Of course, the reason Paul selects Abraham in particular is also salvation-historical, but this foundational role of Abraham's faith (even in God's promise in the face of deadness, Rom 4:19; cf. 4:24) grounds rather than reduces the application value in Rom 4:1–5:11. In 1 Corinthians 10 Paul uses the sinful wilderness generation as a negative example (cf. also Heb 3:7–12, 15–19; 4:6); as already noted, it was already being used that way in ancient Israel (Ps 78:5–8).

The writer of Hebrews similarly looks to earlier biblical characters for models, most extensively in Hebrews 11. For example, Joseph foresaw Israel's return to the promised land when he instructed his relatives to take his bones there when God would bring them there (Gen 50:25; Exod 13:19). The author of Hebrews is correct in seeing this as an example of faith in God's promise (Heb 11:22).

Reading Biblical Narratives for Models

Here, in the context of application, I revisit earlier comments about reading biblical narrative. Sometimes readers read positively negative models in Scripture, or read desired models into passages that do not offer them. Looking for models can be done in an undisciplined way that ignores the shape of the inspired texts; careful handling of context is always paramount. (I address some negative examples later in the book, pp. 268–73, although that is not the primary focus of this book.)

Nevertheless, reading Scripture and experience together has a long and positive legacy; it is the way the NT writers understood the OT (in light of their experience of Christ) as well as the way that many people throughout history have read Scripture. Thus, for example, in 1 Corinthians 10 Paul read Israel's sin in the wilderness as a negative example for his day, recognizing the continuity of God's character, and hence of God's judgment, for Paul's time (1 Cor 10:1–10). Paul narrates the judgments Israel experienced for its sins, and warns, "These things befell them to provide an example, and they were written down to provide a warning for us, on whom the ends of the ages have come" (10:11). Indeed, patristic writers also appealed to biblical characters as examples to follow.[51]

As noted earlier, one particularly in-house debate among Pentecostal scholars has been whether the narrative of Acts provides a normative model. In contrast to some traditional Pentecostal scholars, the careful exegete and Pentecostal scholar Gordon Fee expressed concern with deriving theology from narrative as confidently as we derive it from Paul's letters. He acknowledges the value of repeated patterns, but argues that the specific teaching of a narrative must be limited to its intention.

Fee's current way of expressing his position would likely arouse less dissent,[52] but I believe that we can learn more about narrators' intention—or at least narratives' purposeful shape—than some of his earlier discussions of the subject appeared to recognize. Ancient historians and biographers expected us to find models in their narratives, whether positive or negative ones. How we identify which ones are positive, negative, or mixed of course requires a great deal of careful thought (part of Fee's point), but the same is (as Fee would agree) no less true of Paul's letters, which themselves address concrete situations in the lives of churches. That is, even Paul's letters have a sort of narrative context.

Clearly not all models in narratives are positive, and most significant characters are round mixtures of positive and negative features, as was usual

[handwritten margin note: Keener disagrees]

in ancient biographies and histories. Nevertheless, narratives often provide internal cues concerning how to learn from them. Sometimes narratives indicate explicitly that a character is positive. For example, Matthew specifies that Joseph, Mary's husband, was righteous (Matt 1:19). While this observation does fulfill a sort of christological function—ancient biographies could praise protagonists by reporting pious ancestry or upbringing—it also offers Joseph as a positive moral model.

Custom mandated divorce if the wife or betrothed were deemed unfaithful; Joseph could have profited by divorcing Mary publicly, but even though he believes that he has been wronged, he chooses a private divorce to reduce her shame (1:19). He also embraces that shame in obedience to an angelic message (1:24), and exercises self-control, abstaining from intercourse so that this would be not merely a virgin conception but also a virgin birth (1:25). Connections with Jesus's teaching about lust, divorce (Matt 5:27–32), and compassion (9:13), as well as contrasts with Herod's sinful lack of self-control (14:3–11), reinforce this emphasis.

Sometimes narratives praise a character but also qualify that praise. John as more than a prophet (Matt 11:9) correctly understands that Jesus will baptize in the Spirit and fire (3:11), even though pouring out God's Spirit was an exclusively divine prerogative. Yet John also doubts Jesus's role, precisely because he hears about Jesus's ministry (11:2–3). Jesus is healing some sick people rather than baptizing in fire; Jesus has to reframe his ministry in language that evokes for John Isaiah's prophecies of restoration (11:5–6, evoking Isa 35:5–6; 61:1), showing that these acts do indeed portend and reveal the kingdom. John is a positive character but by virtue of his location in history he is also limited in his knowledge.

Often characters appear side by side, allowing us to learn by comparison and contrast. Greek and Roman speakers often compared figures in their speeches,[53] but the practice is much older than that. In 1 Samuel, for example, one may note the contrast between humble Hannah and proud Eli (as well as Peninnah); the contrast between Samuel and Eli's sons (1 Sam 2:12–18; 2:26–3:1; 3:13); and the contrasts between David and Saul.

Patterns for Us, Not Just Annals

Just as I have heard some popular charismatic teachers ignore literary and historical context, I have listened to some rigorous historical scholars (and, for different reasons, some biblical theologians) deny that some biblical texts, such as OT historical books, should be used for pastoral application. Such use, they contend, violates the texts' original function as annals.

Granted, the controlling thrust of such texts in their current form is often to explain the causes of exile, justifying God's anger and promising future restoration. But the same thrust warns against the sins that led to the exile, such as idolatry, sexual immorality, and the shedding of innocent blood. Even more to the present point, such sins also include neglecting or refusing to heed and implement the message of the Scriptures and the warnings of God's true prophets who stood in continuity with the earlier biblical message.

Should we search Scripture only for salvific events that are of interest to us for purely historical reasons about our heritage? That seems doubtful. We cannot deny, of course, that the narrative frame of Scripture concerns itself primarily with salvation history and God lovingly seeking to restore us to himself. God is the character about whose ways we learn consistently, and many of even the most positive human characters are weak.

Scripture focuses on David not because he walked closer to God than some of his less prominent prophetic companions, say Nathan or Gad, but because his life was a strategic step in salvation history and his line was intertwined with the promised destiny of God's people. At the same time, if we cannot learn from his actions, then Jesus made a mistake in appealing to them in Mark 2:25–26 (cf. also Heb 11:32). If we cannot learn personally from Abraham's walk of faith, we must discard John 8:39–40; Rom 4:1–25; Gal 3:6–7; Heb 11:8–19; and Jas 2:21–23.

As charismatic OT scholar Michael Brown asks, "And how do passages like Joshua 3, where the priests had to step into the river before the waters parted, or Luke 5, where Peter had to launch out into the deep before catching a miraculous amount of fish, speak to us today?"[54] Such texts function as models by inviting us to obey in faith whatever God commands. Certainly their emphasis is on God's miraculous power, but they also invite a response to that power.[55] They invite us not only to praise God's power in the past but also to trust God's power in accomplishing his purposes today.

Returning to 1 Corinthians 10, Paul does not cite the examples from the OT and say, "That is interesting history that gets us where we are today." He cites the judgment experienced by ancient Israel as a warning relevant for God's people in his own day. That is, Paul reads the Bible as if it offers patterns for God's dealings with his people. Paul expects believers to read the Bible from within its world.

An extreme cessationist could object at this point that this hermeneutic was appropriate only until the completion of the canon; yet this objection

nice!
RW

would implicitly concede that the extreme cessationist lacks any canonical evidence for their own approach, which is far more extrabiblical than the more experiential approach is. Early Pentecostals who believed that they lived in "Bible days" read the text in a sympathetic way that many purely academic approaches and hard cessationist approaches missed.

Biblical narratives offer repeated models of believers willing to be changed by their experiences of divine encounters, as we have noted in Acts 10 and other cases. This does not mean, as it did not mean for the earliest church, discarding Scripture or making one's hermeneutic so flexible that texts can mean anything (as some might wish to do). It does mean that incontrovertible experiences invite us to reread Scripture with new questions in mind, a process that sometimes requires us to set aside previous presupposed frameworks for interpretation. *nice*

Even reading the Bible carefully often summons us to do this. As a new convert I approached the Bible with rigid expectations of how it should be written, expectations that did not fit the biblical text itself. Later, after working my entire way through a synopsis of the Gospels prior to attending seminary, I had to further adjust my expectations for how the Gospels should be written in light of the way they were in fact written. Respect for the biblical text compelled me to adjust my theological expectation to fit the text, rather than the reverse. Readers who rule out the value of experience in affecting our theology are imposing a theological construct on the Bible rather than accepting the narratives as a model.

Consistency in How We Apply Scripture

We should avoid two extremes. The first extreme treats the Bible as a series of omens, in which verses or phrases out of context speak directly to our situation. Here relevance to our interests overwhelms the original message so that our interests become a compulsive interpretive grid.

The other extreme is to read the biblical text purely for historical interest. In academic biblical studies, we often read the text this way in order to provide a necessary common ground for discussion by atheists, Christians, and other readers. This approach focuses on reconstructing the historical sense, a necessary and foundational step in understanding, and is not objectionable in itself. (My academic publications generally work within this expected paradigm.) But if we as Christian readers *stop* there, the text becomes simply a museum (or a mausoleum); we are not reading the text distinctively as *Scripture,* as God's Word.

Indeed, questions of inspired functions aside, the historical sense of many or most kinds of texts goes beyond this. Ancient historians and essayists often had deliberative and epideictic interests—promoting improved behavior or praise of a subject, for example—rather than providing information solely for information's sake.[56]

With some kinds of texts, cessationism often, and historical criticism by virtue of definition, profess a merely historical interest. To be fair, virtually all Christians, including continuationists, believe not only that the cultural situation has changed, but that some matters change with developments in God's plan in history. Yet most Christian readers do value principles even from texts that belong to other eras—for example, we may learn principles in Leviticus about sin, atonement, thanksgiving, and so forth without practicing all the specified sacrifices. When a cessationist interpreter must screen out the direct relevance of even testimony from Paul's letters, however (e.g., 1 Cor 14:39), the interpreter seems to believe that Christians today live in a different era than the "last days" of Acts and the Pauline church. What is the exegetical, *biblical* basis for such an assumption? Or is it a theological imposition on the text?

Of course, even the most diehard cessationist will normally apply to himself some principles such as justification by faith. Such cessationism is selective; not all of Scripture is of merely historical interest. One may learn from Abraham's faith in Gen 15:6 because Paul does so. But should we not also learn from examples more generally because Paul models how to do this? This approach provides a more consistent hermeneutic that seeks God's living voice in all of Scripture.

Here, too, there might be wide agreement in principle, with disagreement focusing on particular genres, especially the narrative genre. Yet even in the epistles,[57] we read affirmations of spiritual gifts, exhortation to pray a prayer of faith for the sick, a prohibition to forbid speaking in tongues, and so forth. One cannot consign biblical letters to an occasional genre only where convenient. They *are* letters occasioned by circumstances, yet they contain principles relevant for today.

Granted, sometimes a change in culture or even a change in salvation-historical circumstances requires a significant change in how we apply the principle. Yet cessationism presupposes not a cultural change, but a supposed change in divine activity, activity that, for a gift such as prophecy, already existed before the New Testament and merely proliferated more fully in the New Testament era. The supposed change in salvation-historical circumstances that would support cessationism is nowhere directly attested in Scripture. Nor does early Christian history support the idea that miracles or a selective list of spiritual gifts, such as prophecy or tongues, ceased. And again, early Christians' understanding of their time as the eschatological time leaves us little room for relegating the epistles to a spiritual era different from our own.[58]

Yet when it comes to experiencing some other aspects of Scripture, such as appropriating in life Paul's emphasis on justification, affirming that we are risen with Christ, and so on, a selective cessationist may equal or even surpass a charismatic reader if the latter fails to apply a consistent continuationist hermeneutic. In other words, we all need to be more consistent in applying the continuationist approach.

interesting

Letter and Spirit

The Sinai covenant included outward writing on tablets of stone; the promised new covenant, by contrast, was to be written on the heart (Jer 31:31–34). Paul points to this contrast in 2 Cor 3:3, evoking also Ezek 36:26–27, where the Spirit would enable God's people to keep his laws.[59] (Paul's "hearts of flesh," used in a positive way in the Greek text of 2 Cor 3:3, directly evokes the hearts of flesh that replace hearts of stone in Ezek 36:26.)[60] As servants of the new covenant, Paul explains, he and his colleagues are empowered not as ministers of the letter but as ministers of the Spirit, and therefore of life (2 Cor 3:6).[61] It is the Spirit that writes the law on the heart and therefore enables the inward righteousness to which it points.

The "letter" probably refers to "the mere written details of the law"; Jewish teachers played even with matters of spelling.[62] In antiquity, legal interpreters often distinguished between what we would call the "letter" of the law and its intention.[63] Our modern way of speaking of a contrast between the letter and spirit of the law probably goes back to Paul's usage, though Paul refers to God's Spirit rather than merely the "intention" of the law.[64] Grammar is valuable because it helps us to hear and obey the message, but we must not stop there. By itself, understanding textual grammar is not the same as embracing the heart of God that the text is designed to communicate.

In fact, Paul contends elsewhere that believers have been liberated from the law insofar as it is understood as letter; instead we serve God as new persons by the Spirit (Rom 7:6). Paul is not demeaning earlier parts of Scripture, or the nature of Scripture as something written. Paul is here, as we have noted elsewhere, correcting a way of approaching Scripture that, in light of Christ, can never again be thought adequate (cf. 3:27; 8:2; 9:30–32; 10:5–10). God once used a civil law to restrain sin in Israel; it is from God (7:14; 8:4), and we still may learn from it (1 Cor 9:9; 14:21). But righteousness comes from Christ, and his Spirit inscribes the heart of the law within us, so that we fulfill the real principles that the law was ultimately meant to point toward anyway (Rom 8:2–4; 13:8–10). (When Christians do not live this way they miss Paul's point. Teachings that associate grace only with forensic justification and not also with transformation have played a tragic role in this deficiency.)

If our focus with regard to the Torah should be the Spirit's message more than mere grammar, how much more should that be true of the prophets and what we call the New Testament?[65] Again, I should clarify that I am not demeaning exegesis; for many years I have spent most of my teaching time instructing students interested in application how to do exegesis first. Exegesis is the needed foundation for genuinely analogous application, in stark contrast to eisegesis. My point is that if we teach students or members of our church communities to *stop* with exegetical observations, or to simply figure out our own applications that may run contrary to the Spirit we encounter in the gospel (such as a legalistic approach to the text), we are not hearing the Spirit who inspired the text to begin with. When we truly hear the Spirit's message in the text, we commit to it. It becomes heart work and not simply homework.

Exegesis in the usual sense focuses on the text's original horizon; reader-oriented approaches focus on the present horizons. The former without the latter is informative but requires the life-giving breath of the Spirit to transform us. Exclusive attention to a present horizon without attention to the original one can lead to overwriting the original, inspired meaning with an unrelated one.[66] If the goal is merely fusing horizons, insufficient objective distance remains to hear the text as something other than mirroring one's thoughts.[67] Gadamer warned "against a premature fusion of horizons which fails to preserve any tension between the past and the present."[68]

Yet the hearer must also be apprehended by the text; both horizons must be maintained.[69] "[I]f a text is to be *understood*," Thiselton notes, "there must occur an engagement between two sets of horizons. . . . The hearer must be able to relate his own horizons to those of the text."[70] Connecting the two horizons, without obliterating either of them, is often considered the role of hermeneutics.[71] The Spirit can guide us in exploring and researching both horizons, but the Spirit is especially helpful in bridging the gap between them, in applying the principles of the text to our lives and communities.[72] As Pentecostal scholar Russell Spittler notes, "Exegesis puts one into the vestibule of truth; the Holy Spirit opens the inner door."[73]

The Ultimate Word

Even John's Gospel's prologue sets up the epistemic contrast we earlier noted with respect to Johannine epistemology. John could have spoken of Jesus as divine Wisdom, the most common Jewish image for a preexistent divine agent, but he shifts to a related expression, the "Word," because of the comparison between Jesus and the Torah he will offer in John 1:14–18 (most explicitly in 1:17). I have argued elsewhere that John probably responds in part to an academic, text-centered, Torah-centered critique of Jesus's movement from people who claimed to know Scripture more accurately than the Jewish believers in Jesus that John especially addresses.[74] John responds by arguing that Jesus himself is the Word of God, embodying all the divine revelation of the Torah but now revealed more fully.[75]

Various allusions to Exodus 33–34 evoke the giving of the law there, elucidating both Jesus's continuity with earlier divine revelation and his superiority to it as a fuller revelation of God's heart.

Exodus 33–34[a]	John 1:14–18
The revelation of God's word, the Torah	The revelation of God's word, Jesus
God dwelt among his people in the tabernacle (33:10); Moses pleaded that God would continue to dwell with them (33:14–16)	The word "tabernacled" (literally, in 1:14) among people
Moses beheld God's glory	The disciples beheld Jesus's glory (1:14)
The glory was full of grace and truth (34:6)	The glory was full of grace and truth (1:14)
The law was given through Moses	The law was given through Moses (1:17)
No one could see all of God's glory (33:20)	No one could see all of God's glory (1:18a), but it is fully revealed in Jesus (1:18b)

a. Based on the research in Keener, *John*, 1:405–26, this chart is taken from Keener, *Background Commentary*, 250.

Moses could witness only part of God's glory, full of grace and truth, but Jesus revealed the fulness of God's heart. Although Jesus reveals his glory also in signs in this Gospel (e.g., 2:11; 11:4), the ultimate expression of his glory begins in the cross (12:23–24; cf. 7:39), his "lifting up" (3:14; 8:28; 12:32; cf. "will be lifted up and glorified" in Isa 52:13 LXX). The place where humanity's hatred for God came to its ultimate expression, when we nailed God to the cross, is the very place where his love for us found its ultimate demonstration.

John affirmed Jesus's continuity with the Torah, but mere intellectual mastery of the Torah was not enough. "You pore over the Scriptures because you expect to have eternal life in them," Jesus warns his critics. "Yet these are what testify about me, and you don't want to come to me so you may have life" (John 5:39–40). The accuser who hauls you before the Father, he continues, "is Moses, in whom you hope," since Moses wrote about Jesus (5:45–47).

Ultimately, for a Christian, christological reading and personal reading cannot be incompatible. As we learn our Lord's character from the Gospels we live our relationship with him in light of that character. For example, although Jesus privately corrected his disciples when necessary, he took up their defense against their detractors, sometimes at risk to himself (three examples in Mark 2:15–28; another in John 9:38–41). This is the heart of the same Lord who went to the cross for us. He compassionately granted healing to those rejected by society (Mark 1:41) and welcomed and transformed those viewed as moral failures by their contemporaries. He challenged the proud, unafraid of the consequences, consequences that inevitably would lead to his death. As we grow to know the Jesus of Scripture, putting ourselves in the place of his first followers, we can see why they loved him and were loyal to him. One who encounters the heart of Jesus encounters the heart of God—the way he truly is, far different from human imaginations about him.

Conclusion

The heart of the truth that God spoke in one era will be fundamentally consistent with the truth that God speaks in another. (Note the same kind of application of principles surrounding God's word as the Torah to the message about Jesus in Rom 10:6–8.) Christians all agree that Jesus is the climax of biblical revelation (Rom 10:4; Heb 1:1–2), but we do not always agree about the epistemology that got the apostolic church there. They made the application because of their experience of Christ. Then, of course, they had to deal with those they considered false prophets, bringing conflicting messages based on different experiences; but we cannot simply eliminate the problem of counterfeits by limiting epistemology to texts apart from experiences, for our canonical texts *testify* to experiences. Instead, we must learn to read the texts in tandem with the sorts of experiences the texts describe: a personal relationship with God in Jesus Christ.

A pure exegete can find many intellectual treasures in Scripture; but only a true *disciple* can experience the fulness of those treasures in his or her life.

Again, my point is never to play down exegesis; my point is that a step beyond mere academic study of the text is embracing the text with active faith to live in the sphere of its realities, a worldview about God that transforms us. The ideal exegete, then, would be like a scribe of the Torah who becomes a disciple of the kingdom, bringing forth treasures both old and new (Matt 13:52).[76]

PART VI

WHOSE CHARISMATIC INTERPRETATION?

Current discussion of Pentecostal and charismatic hermeneutics often dominates discussion about sound Spirit hermeneutics. What is it, however, that makes a hermeneutic distinctively Pentecostal or charismatic? The vast majority of Pentecostal scholars would demur from many popular Pentecostal and charismatic interpretations that have been foisted on the church, such as hard-core Word of Faith teaching.

Some have argued that the global Pentecostal community provides a safety net for interpretation, but whose interpretations in that community count? Few of us would advocate including the interpretations of movements that sociologists classify as pentecostal that nevertheless have deified founding figures in place of Jesus. Likewise, few of us would place syncretistic teaching about ghosts on a level with obvious biblical teaching supporting the continuance of spiritual gifts.

Do we then appeal to the global community of pentecostal scholarship? Yet the diversity of hermeneutical approaches among Pentecostal, charismatic and other Spirit-emphasizing scholars is almost as wide as the circles in which they were trained. What is distinctive about and usually present in these forms of Spirit hermeneutics is the embrace of experiencing the text. I continue to suggest, however, that such an embrace must be supplemented with attention to the shape of the texts. Because they are texts, often in genres recognizable to their first (and often even subsequent) audiences, God inspired them in a form that is accessible to those who know how to read texts. Thus for reading them from the standpoint of faith, we will always need not just the text or just the Spirit, but always Word and Spirit together.

CHAPTER 17

Naïve "Pentecostal" Readings vs. Biblically Sensitive Pentecostal Readings

In a sense, what I have offered above is an argument for disciplined devotional reading of Scripture. I have also suggested, however, that without a sound approach to the biblical text one may as well not be *using* the biblical text (and certainly not claiming the mantle of its authority). Sometimes Christians have sound doctrines simply because we inherited them from predecessors who studied the text in a faithful, disciplined way, but our own readings are designed merely to produce "inspiration" in the way a rousing patriotic speech or even cheerleading might do. That is never more than a faint shadow of the divine inspiration God vested in Scripture, and genuine people of the Spirit, of all people, ought to recognize that.

Too much popular charismatic teaching seems to reflect a stream-of-consciousness approach to interpretation, without careful work in the biblical text.[1] One thing reminding us of something else is not wrong—it reflects the way that our brains are wired. Through absolute trust in God's sovereignty leading us by the Spirit we can often learn from these connections. This is not, however, a disciplined hermeneutical method, and it does not give us the universal meaning of the text from which various contextual meanings or applications flow. In principle it could even resemble bibliomancy and risk divination—like ancients who divined the future or will of deities by the flight of birds or anomalies in sacrificial animals' innards.[2] Those genuinely immersing themselves in Scripture and trusting the Spirit's guidance would not normally go so far, but we do need careful attention to the biblical text to keep us on the right path.

A major part of the genius of global pentecostalism is its populist character. It has been able to raise up indigenous ministers more quickly by trusting the Spirit to empower new groups as partners in ministry (as presumably happened also in Acts 8:15–17; 10:44–47).[3] Teaching, however, is also a spiritual

265

gift (see pp. 114–15, 118). The problem is not with pentecostal emphasis on the Spirit or the pentecostal emphasis on living experientially as those who carry on the ministry portrayed in the biblical narrative. The problem is the reduced emphasis on teaching, based on a tradition that reflects US popular religion more generally.

Populist Approach

Although, as we have seen, academic hermeneutics can be limited in hearing the Spirit in the text, popular hermeneutics often carry their own perils, especially the neglect of context. Populist interpretation, including in the Wesleyan Holiness matrix from which Pentecostalism was born, often included stringing together proof-texts.[4]

The Reformation focused on recovering the message of Scripture, although not without concessions to tradition that the Reformers felt useful. It was partly a populist movement driven by nationalistic politics and information technology (the printing press), but often led by biblical scholars. The Second Great Awakening carried Protestantism's populist tradition further, however, often in ways that I would consider positive but not without some limitations. "[T]his 'democratic revolution' [in Protestantism] fostered the emergence of a populist hermeneutic." The Reformers valued biblical translations for everyday readers, but

> they did not view laity as being adequately able to understand the scriptures apart from ministerial guidance. Revivalists of the Second Great Awakening, however, stressed a Bible devoid of authoritative interpretations. . . . The maxim "no creed but the Bible" reflected not only the Protestant principle of *sola Scriptura,* but the growing emphasis on private judgment as the final court of scriptural interpretation as well. Thus, after 1800, views of biblical interpretation and democratic values were moving in the same direction— mutually reinforcing such ideas as volitional allegiance, self-reliance, and private judgment.[5]

This led to a popular emphasis on literal, "face value" interpretation.[6] In the early twentieth century, one might distinguish as the two ideal poles of evangelical diversity the highly educated, "elite east coast Old Princeton" and "the lower-class west coast Azusa Street with its roots in Methodism and the Holiness Movement."[7] We have something to learn from each.[8]

Problems with This Approach

Like charismatic experience, popular religion has its positive side, but it also has its limitations. Some parts of the church seem to take for granted that "we already know" the Bible in a cavalier sort of way that we would never treat medical expertise or legal counsel. Most of us rightly look to credentialed psychologists and counselors for the most expert counseling, but anybody who can read gives advice on the Bible. I do not believe that one needs to be a scholar or go to seminary to understand Scripture; my complaint is simply that many parts of the church neglect careful, contextual study of Scripture.

Some well-known popular Bible interpreters actually do handle Scripture well; some do have an important message, and many live with integrity. Yet some may become famous Bible teachers quoting verses out of context because they devote their career to marketing their message, not devoting an equally careful amount of time to deeply engaging Scripture.

To some, "Pentecostal hermeneutics" may sound like an oxymoron, bringing together incompatible values. The apparent incompatibility simply recycles, however, a long-standing tension between popular and academic religion, a tension that does not stem from skilled biblical writers such as Luke or Paul. In Acts itself, one of our chief examples of the Spirit-empowered life is Paul, who taught daily in the school of Tyrannus, using the culturally intelligible role of a public intellectual, while also being used by God in signs and wonders (Acts 19:9–12).[9] Likewise, he made optimum use of the best rhetorical techniques of his day in his defense speech before Felix.[10] Although not all early Pentecostal preachers were academically trained, many teachers in early Assemblies of God Bible schools had training in CMA circles.[11]

Pentecostals often employ biblical texts for "pragmatic purposes," for transforming lives today;[12] but what happens when the point for which we apply texts is not only not found in those texts, but is not taught in Scripture anywhere? And do we truly gain a well-rounded understanding of all that Scripture has to teach us if we find there only what we plan to find anyway? As scholar Olga Zaprometova laments, "in the hands of at least some ministers (preachers, teachers, and theologians are among them) the Bible means whatever they want it to mean."[13]

Many popular Pentecostal and charismatic ideas lend themselves to ready outside stereotypes of Pentecostal and charismatic theology. Naïve readings from any group, however, will lead to stereotypes; they may be more common in Global Pentecostalism than in some mainline traditions simply because teaching cannot keep up with Pentecostal evangelism.

interesting If the Spirit genuinely leads us to say something that is not related to the text, we do not have to force the text to fit; there are other spiritual gifts for communicating God's message besides teaching the text (Rom 12:6, 8; 1 Cor 12:29; 14:3). If the Spirit leads us to simply use the language of the text to make our point in merely an evocative way, it may be that the book of Revelation sometimes does the same with Old Testament prophecies (e.g., simply communicating judgment), and that Old Testament prophets sometimes did the same with the language of earlier prophets. But that is not the same as explaining the meaning of the text, and even if someone only feels led to evoke texts their ministry does not replace the gift of teaching and the responsibility for church leaders to genuinely explain the biblical texts in edifying ways (cf. 1 Tim 4:13, 16; 2 Tim 3:15–4:4).

The Wrong Kind of Experiential Reading[14]

Whereas some sectors of the church neglect personal spiritual experience, others highlight experience so much that they have to continually revise or harmonize their views as new claims of experiences come their way. Unfortunately, experiences are not always self-interpreting. For example, an experience may be genuinely cathartic without being a genuine exorcism; a hearer may learn a valuable lesson from a sermon without the sermon genuinely reflecting the point of the biblical text on which it claims to be based.

Moreover, God may genuinely bless sincere and zealous seekers without inviting us to conclude that everything that occurs in these circles is divine activity. Most revival movements in history include elements of human frailty along with the divine (note, for example, Jonathan Edwards's appraisals of the First Great Awakening).[15] God works through fallible people; there are no other kind.

Striking the right balance between the subjective and the objective is easier said than done, and not all of us will draw the line in the same place. During intense outpourings of the Spirit (such as in 1 Sam 19:20–24; Acts 10:44–46; 19:6, 11–12), God may act in unusual ways that transcend our usual limitations. Some who criticized "holy laughter" in recent renewal meetings are probably unaware that it has occurred in some earlier outpourings of the Spirit;[16] the Spirit does not *exclusively* generate weeping (as in some better-known revivals in history).[17] One fruit of the Spirit is, after all, joy (Gal 5:22), and this was the chief recorded characteristic of one of the corporate experiences of the Spirit in Acts (Acts 13:52; cf. Rom 14:17; 15:13; 1 Thess 1:6).

Frequently, however, radical subjectivity breeds mistakes that hurt people—inaccurate prophecies, too much emotional intensity for weaker human spirits, misinterpretations about spiritual authority, and so forth. There is a way forward, however: our subjective relationship with God can become anchored in objective study of God's Word.[18]

Years ago Jim Bakker preached a prosperity message on *The PTL Club*. He later confessed that he was so busy with ministry that he did not have much time to read the Bible for himself; thus he promoted what his friends taught that it said, assuming that they had read it in context. During his subsequent time in prison, he had much more time to read the Bible than he had before. To his horror, he realized that he had been teaching the exact opposite of what Jesus taught about possessions.[19] (To his credit, he afterward changed his teaching, but his revised message draws less interest on the US spiritual consumer market.) Taking for granted interpretations of Scripture because other "spiritual" people hold these views renders us immune from Scripture correcting us. These too are "traditions," even if sometimes very recent ones.[20]

Some Examples of Misapplied, Popular Pentecostal Hermeneutics

Reading the Bible differently than we would read texts comparable in genre may be commendable if we mean hearing God's voice in the Bible. But since God inspired many biblical texts in existing literary genres, we should also be reading the Bible as texts in these genres. That is, the *literary* principles through which we read the Bible are not different than the way we read analogous texts in the same literary genres. Those who treat the Bible differently often do so with a game of biblical Russian roulette: randomly seizing on verses isolated from context in a way that we would never do with other texts.[21] The genre of proverbs does provide short, succinct points, provided we hear them within the framework of the proverbial genre (i.e., as general statements of principle), but most genres do not work this way.

Some Charismatic Television Preaching

Unless those most enthusiastic today about Pentecostal hermeneutics are completely insulated from popular circles, they must be aware that on the ground, detached from scholars' safeguards[22] and attention to context, some popular charismatic interpretation is undisciplined and badly in need of correction. (My complaint here might not sound very postmodern, but I have already mentioned some sorts of popular claims circulated in the name of the Spirit.)[23]

For example, some popular interpreters link biblical identifications without regard for contexts,[24] producing such strange (and unbiblical) phrases as this: we *are* the will of God.[25] If unrestrained, this interpretive principle can produce nonsensical distortions: for instance, Jesus is God's righteousness (1 Cor 1:30) and so are we (2 Cor 5:21), so we are Jesus.[26] This method can produce devastating consequences even in adjacent texts: for instance, God is love (1 John 4:8, 16), and as he is so are we in this world (4:17), so we are love and we are God. The "transitive property of equality" (a = b, b = c, therefore a = c), valuable for Euclidean geometry, leads to erroneous conclusions when applied to decontextualized literature. Indeed, even in geometric logic, one needs to take into account that (a) may include (b) without necessarily equaling (b) precisely; and (a) and (b) may overlap without being equal.

On average, one will get better Bible exposition from traditional evangelical media preachers than from many charismatic media preachers. This is not because the former do not read their theology into the Bible—some do so regarding their eschatology, cessation of the gifts or other doctrines—but because the former usually focus on Bible exposition, whereas the latter often focus on instant cures for felt needs.

Granted, the diet of popular charismatic media differs from standard fare in most Pentecostal and charismatic pulpits; pastors must feed their flock a more consistent diet than many television ministries allow. Still, these figures achieve success only because they are followed and supported by many people—often young believers or those biblically illiterate apart from relevant proof-texts. Further granted, I know and count as friends significant exceptions who do seek to provide sound teaching.

Moreover, appealing to felt needs is one way to gain a hearing for the gospel in a crowded secular market of appeals for attention. Certainly Jesus healed and delivered as signs that drew attention to the message of the kingdom as well as demonstrated its character. This directly addressed serious needs, and Jesus usually taught with stories and memorable sayings. Yet he also posed riddles to make his audiences think, and, as we have seen, he knew Scripture in context and his message was fully in keeping with the heart of Scripture.

Breaking Generational Curses?

Nevertheless, there are charismatic circles where the focus seems to be the newest spiritual fashion to blow through. Some ride the crest of these fashionable waves, stealing their prophetic "words from each other" (Jer 23:30). To achieve "breakthroughs" in financial prosperity, popular teachings have gone from sowing seeds in faith to casting out spirits of poverty to breaking generational curses.[27] In many of these cases, the preacher exercises power to bring supernatural deliverance to the followers through a prayer or formula.

Again granted, a concept such as "generational curses" may have some biblical precedent. Children often walk in their parents' behavior (e.g., Gen 12:13; 20:2; 26:7), and walking in the ways of our ancestors can reap their blessings or judgments (e.g., Exod 20:5–6; Deut 5:9–10; 7:9). Nor do I deny that practitioners are often, probably usually, sincere, and that God often responds to a misinformed but sincere heart. But the biblically specified solution to *do we do that?* ancestral disobedience is not a prominent preacher's formulaic prayer of deliverance; it is turning from the ways of our ancestors to obey God's word. This recognition invites teaching about how to recognize inherited familial and cultural sins and how to turn from them, not consumer-sanitized and -packaged crisis experiences.[28]

Curses—especially in the sense of witchcraft in some cultures[29]—differ from ancestral judgments. Scripture is also aware of the reality of curses (e.g., Gen 27:12–13; Num 22:6, 11–12; 24:10; Prov 26:2), a reality more readily grasped in societies that practice them. Societies that practice such curses may practice them in ways different from biblical cultures, and biblical principles may still apply. Since standing against attacks from evil (Eph 6:11–13) requires faith (6:16), standing with authoritative prayer makes sense (cf. Mark 11:23). Obviously, a Christian's first response should be to turn to God in prayer, or to confront attacks in Jesus's name.[30]

Nevertheless, a sometimes-missed focus of biblical teaching regarding curses is that we should avoid deserving them (Num 23:8; 31:16; Prov 26:2), and that God can ignore curses for those who have his favor (2 Sam 16:12). Indeed, though God will normally curse those who curse us (Gen 12:3; 27:29), Jesus invites us to bless them instead (Luke 6:28; cf. Rom 12:14; 1 Pet 3:9). Forgiveness demonstrates trust that we depend on God to defend us; he then hears our prayers of dependence on him (Matt 6:14–15; cf. 1 Pet 3:7, 12). Indeed, Scripture is explicit that failure to forgive someone who is sorry plays into the devil's hands (2 Cor 2:10–11).

My interest is not this particular doctrine, but to use as an example what its unchecked spread seems to indicate. Too often we follow fads and fashions that, whether originally related to any biblical ideas or not, are developed according to popular practices and spiritual whims rather than careful biblical study. Biblically immature and not growing in the knowledge of Christ, we are blown about by every wind of teaching (Eph 4:14). True ministers of the word (apostles, prophets, evangelists, and pastor-teachers, 4:11) are supposed to protect us from that (4:11–13), and those who do the opposite are functioning as the opposite of true ministers of the word, whatever they call themselves (4:14).

Word of Faith Teachings

Popular Word of Faith teachers are known for quoting Scripture out of context; adherents sometimes insist that the Spirit supports their reading nonetheless. Consider, for example, the use of "now faith" in Heb 11:1 with regard to believing for immediate blessing.[31] Unfortunately, the Greek term that these teachers' Bible versions render as "now" (e.g., KJV, NASB, NIV, ESV, and even NRSV) is not the Greek adverb that means "now"; it is simply a conjunction with no temporal significance whatsoever.[32] Context indicates that the sort of faith articulated here is the faith that endures present suffering in hope of future reward (10:32–39; 11:8, 13–16, 26, 33–40; 12:1–3).

In context, the thief that comes to steal, kill, and destroy in John 10:10 is not specifically the devil[33] but rather anyone who exploits the sheep for one's own interests (10:1, 8, 12), most specifically exemplified in the preceding context by the Pharisees who expelled a believer from the synagogue (9:34–41). Likewise, the "cattle on a thousand hills" (Ps 50:10) means that God does not depend on his people's sacrifices (50:7–14), not that God is offering to sell some off in order to give us the cash.[34]

Ministering angels in Heb 1:14 do not refer to angels placed at our disposal and subject to our command.[35] "Sent to render service *for* "does not mean "sent to render service *at the command of*," but rather, "sent to render service *for the benefit of*." Instead, the context indicates that Christ is greater than the angels that mediated the law (1:4–8; 2:2–3), and the text presumably evokes the idea of guardian angels already known to that author's audience;[36] even our Lord Jesus did not claim to command angels, but noted that if he needed them he would ask the Father (Matt 26:53).[37]

Confessing one's faith with one's mouth may reflect a biblical principle,[38] but a key text that faith teachers regularly use for this principle applies directly only to confessing Christ as Lord (Rom 10:9–10).[39] God, not Abraham, spoke things into being in Rom 4:17.[40] Imitating God in the context of Eph 5:1 has nothing to do with creating realities by our words,[41] but with loving and forgiving as he did (4:32–5:2). Mark 11:23 is probably prophetic speaking, and thus is conditioned on God's backing. As Lamentations points out, "Who speaks and it comes to pass, unless the Lord commanded it?" (Lam 3:37).

Despite such criticisms, some of the seminal Word of Faith teachers themselves have recognized the importance of context, and that without attention to context one could make texts say virtually anything.[42] Some of them have further acknowledged that the revelation of Scripture itself takes priority over any other claims to revelation.[43] Others have been less careful.[44] Nevertheless, if even some key Word of Faith teachers acknowledge the importance of context at least in principle, how much more must we acknowledge it, insofar as we must appeal to context to challenge their approach.

Genuine Models of Faith in the Bible

To say that faith teachers have frequently taken Scripture out of context is not to pretend that the Bible does not teach about faith.[45] In fact it provides many biblical models of faith that are clear in context; faith teachers could approach their subject more helpfully and in more balanced ways if they gave greater attention to context.

An obvious example would be Abraham, a prototypical model of faith. Abram demonstrates obedient faith by obeying God's call in light of God's promise (Gen 12:1–4), as well as in the explicitly justifying faith of Gen 15:6 that Paul highlights. But it is especially exemplified when he offers up Isaac (22:1–18; Heb 11:17–19; Jas 2:21–23), which climaxes the larger Abraham narrative in Genesis. Tracing Abraham's development as a person of faith as a textual character offers encouragement that we too can mature in faith by walking with the faithful God.

Thus we recognize that Abram already has commendable faith in Gen 15:6; he trusts God's promise. Nevertheless, the context qualifies this faith; God had already promised Abram descendants and land (12:1–2). Yet in Genesis 15, Abram asks about the descendants (15:2–3). God then reiterates the promise more specifically (15:4–5), and Abram puts his trust in the one who is truly trustworthy (15:6). Immediately afterward, Abram asks how he can know that God will give him the land (15:8)—immediately after God has reiterated that promise (15:7). God then confirms that promise (15:9–21). The next scene that Genesis narrates, however, depicts Abram and Sarai using Hagar to bear Abram a son (16:1–2). This is not unbelief—God had not yet specified that Abram's son would come through Sarah directly—but neither is it the sort of faith that Abraham expresses in Genesis 22.

By contrast, in Genesis 22, Abraham must act on faith in the God who spoke to him, sacrificing even the very promise for which he had waited so many years. Justifying faith that God counts to us as righteousness, as in Gen 15:6, is fundamental. But experiencing God's faithfulness through years of testing initiates us into a deeper level of faith—a level of faith that trusts God no matter what, because we know that, whatever else might be the case, God is trustworthy.[46] We have come to know *him,* recognizing his character; and so we trust him. This is not a faith for which we can take credit as if we have worked it up by our efforts; it is a faith that flows from God's trustworthiness.

We might also consider the woman with a flow of blood (Mark 5:34). Because of her condition, she should not risk touching people in the crowd, and certainly should not touch Jesus's clothing; contact with her communicated impurity even secondhand (Lev 15:26–27). In her desperation, however, she violates purity regulations and touches Jesus's cloak (Mark 5:27–28). This is scandalous faith, and Jesus responds by publicly acknowledging her touch (5:31–34).[47] Although this acknowledgment could make him appear unclean in the sight of others, Jesus is not ashamed to be identified with us in our uncleanness and brokenness. The woman goes away healed.

Hebrews 11 is a rhetorical masterpiece.[48] It lists various heroes of the faith, including Abraham, who by faith made sacrifices in the present because they trusted God's future promise. The narration concludes in 12:2 with the ultimate hero of the faith—the founder and completer of our faith, Jesus, who endured the ultimate suffering in hope of the ultimate exaltation. As Heb 11:32 recognizes, biblical examples of faith could be multiplied.

These accounts depict faith of multiple kinds, not just the faith often celebrated by popular faith teachers. The woman with the flow of blood needed an immediate encounter with Jesus's power; Abraham and other people of faith in Hebrews 11 endured because they believed God's future promise. Scripture teaches about both kinds of faith.

Scripture's many examples of faith in God invite us to go deeper in faith as well. Against some popular faith teachers, we cannot simply claim promises to others for ourselves when their circumstances were different; God works differently with all of us, just as he worked differently with different people in the Bible. Nevertheless, just as the Spirit addressed *all* the churches through the distinctive message given to each of the seven churches in Asia Minor (Rev 2:7, 11, 17, 29; 3:6, 13, 22), we can learn from the ways God worked with others. Promises to others help us realize the range of the ways that God does work.

274

A Positive Example: Rereading 1 Corinthians 14 Experientially

What would happen if we read 1 Corinthians 14 sympathetically, as not merely a corrective for first-century Corinthian Christians but also as Paul's counter-appeal that depicted an ideal way of doing church (14:5–6, 13–19, 24–33, 39–40) to which we can also aspire? I believe that such an approach would challenge the practical cessationism of most of our churches regarding public exercise of most spiritual gifts (except that of pastor-teacher).

For its first few centuries the church met largely in homes. Although no meeting place is mandated—and I have no regrets concerning my own many years as an associate minister in an African-American Baptist megachurch—the dynamic in our traditional "services" differs starkly from the interpersonal dynamic of the NT house churches. At least in principle, smaller groups allow the participation of all members, ideally inviting them to contribute their spiritual gifts. Even typical pentecostal churches that maximize participation in worship today cannot let all members prophesy one by one (14:31); they are too large. Indeed, imagine how long a worship service would take if a *thousand* members prophesied one by one! Or imagine, more realistically, if each one brought some gift to edify others, whether a new song, a prophecy, a teaching, and so forth (14:26).

The Jerusalem church had available a large public space where, during some periods of this community's formation, they could meet together despite their growing numbers. We could thus speak of a sort of megachurch setting in Jerusalem; teaching large numbers simultaneously is not unbiblical, provided we have means to accommodate them. Nevertheless, even during this period in Jerusalem, believers also met from house to house, embracing a relational dynamic.[49] Larger meetings have distinct advantages, but if we miss the dynamic of face-to-face relationships in the church, such as what we today call small groups,[50] we are missing part of what it biblically means to be the body of Christ to each other. Churches larger than house churches need to find ways (whether cell groups or something else) to bring people into mutually edifying relationships, drawing on and cultivating the members' distinctive gifts.[51]

In 1 Corinthians 14, all members should bring their gifts to build up Christ's body. Because this is an ideal, circumstances may mitigate its full implementation. One wonders, however, why the ideal is mitigated so widely and whether we are not missing something fundamental about what it means to be the church together. Of course, such an observation should not be limited to 1 Corinthians 14. The ideal life of the earliest church depicted in Acts 2 suggests that we should be so involved in one another's lives that we sacrifice our possessions to make sure that everyone has enough.[52]

Admittedly, anyone who has pastored or mentored in a way that is sensitive to individuals recognizes that the pastoral role of shepherd includes dealing with people in their actual situations. Prophetically summoning the church to the ideal must be balanced with pastoral sensitivity. We must, however, work for both, keeping them in tension.

Conclusion

The Spirit has used populist impulses to propel the Christian movement far and wide. Nevertheless, unnecessarily undisciplined and uninformed readings have produced teachings that, when left unchecked, have produced much disillusionment and often even apostasy among many followers of Christ. Teachings on generational curses, prosperity, and, in various ways, controlling our own destinies have often proved more appealing in our consumer culture than training for personal evangelism, trusting God during hardship, or reading Scripture in context.

Experiential reading is important, but it must be genuinely consistent with the message of the text that is canonical for Christ's body. Basic principles such as literary context and sensitivity to biblical books' ancient cultural settings would go a long way toward restraining undisciplined "charismatic" interpretation. Genuine Spirit hermeneutics for the community must recognize and submit to the parameters established by the shape of the biblical text itself.

CHAPTER 18

Global Pentecostal Community as a Safety Net?

Some appeal to the Pentecostal community of interpretation to keep us on track hearing the Spirit. While there is some value in this approach, I believe that it is limited. When our views diverge from wider Christian standards, they invite greater inspection. Moreover, we explored above some common elements in Spirit hermeneutics, such as humble, experiential, eschatological, and cross-cultural readings. But Pentecostalism, including Pentecostal and charismatic scholarship, is currently too diverse to offer as much guidance on details. *What would have to change?*

Community and Interpretation

I briefly addressed the subject of communities of interpretation when discussing reader-oriented approaches in chapter 5. Communities of interpretation have become prominent in hermeneutical and theological discussion, and many who speak of Spirit hermeneutics emphasize the role of the community.[1] Christian academicians often find themselves needing to abide by different ground rules in the academy and the church, and this is understandable. For devotion and for church edification, however, exegesis occurs within the believing community.[2] Acts 15:28 does suggest the value of truly Spirit-led community understandings;[3] the community of those listening to the Spirit also is responsible to evaluate individual claims to revelation (1 Cor 14:29).

A number of writers on Pentecostal hermeneutics emphasize the matter of community; such an emphasis is not surprising, given the role of community today in theology, philosophy, and social sciences (e.g., systems theory) more generally. Naturally any community will seek to contextualize the fruits of its exegesis for its own setting, and this includes Pentecostal and charismatic circles.[4]

Christian Community

Because the theme of Christian community is so widely emphasized, I will summarize its importance only briefly here. Nevertheless, it is clearly a biblical notion; indeed, Greeks employed the Greek term ἐκκλησία, translated in English Bibles as "church," for civic assemblies, but it also evokes the assembly of God's people in the wilderness (that Hebrew term was translated into Greek even more frequently as συναγωγή, "synagogue"). Love for one another is expressed in relationships with one another (Rom 12:10; 1 Thess 4:9–10); those who withdraw from fellowship with fellow believers because they refuse to love these believers risk committing the apostasy of lovelessness (1 John 2:9–11, 19; 3:10–15, 18–19; 4:8).

Paul addressed churches in his letters and expected churches to function together even in disciplining members (1 Cor 5:4–5; 6:1–2; 2 Thess 3:14–15). Although churches were social groups that provided mutual reinforcement in the faith (see, e.g., Heb 3:13; 10:24–25), they were also more than this; the church is the many-membered body of Christ, and each member is expected to contribute for the good of the larger body (Rom 12:3–8; 1 Cor 12:7, 12–26; 14:26; Eph 4:7, 11–16). When traveling and founding churches, Paul and his colleagues initially lacked direct fellowship beyond their group, but they did have fellowship with each other. Team ministry is prominent in Acts and Paul's letters (see e.g., Acts 13:1–3; 15:39–40; 16:3; 18:5; 20:4; 27:2; Rom 16:3, 21; 2 Cor 8:23; Phil 2:22, 25; 4:3; Col 4:10–14; 1 Thess 3:2; Phlm 24).

At least sometimes we pray together (Acts 2:42; 1 Tim 2:1–2), and thus we address prayers together to *our* Father (Matt 6:9).[5] Some apply 2 Pet 1:20 to speak of community in interpretation; but others also use this passage to argue against texts meaning whatever we want (relativistic reading), and in context it may refer to the inspiration of the prophets themselves (1:20–21; cf. NET). Paul can appeal to the *global* Christian movement, even if sometimes for what most of us understand as cultural practices limited to the sphere in which Christians then moved (1 Cor 11:16; 14:33, 36).

Since the majority of people in antiquity were illiterate to one degree or another, Bible study among first-century Christians was most often a communal exercise, and a key element of believers' meetings together. Early Christians practiced corporate reading and exposition of Scripture,[6] a practice carried over from the synagogue.[7]

Dangers in Appeals to Community

Although Paul does appeal to the values of the wider community, as already noted, our appeals to community risk the danger of circularity. A set of beliefs may function coherently within a community yet confront serious challenges in dialogue with other communities.

Further, what happens when a widespread interpretation within a wider movement is a fashion that is embraced in its day yet recognized as fallacious in retrospect? In the midst of revival fervor, the Moravians, being greatly used by God, sometimes fixated on Jesus's blood in grotesque ways, such as viewing themselves as worms sucking his blood. Count Zinzendorf later recognized that they had gone too far with this approach and they returned to greater balance.[8] In the context of the Great Awakenings, most nineteenth-century US evangelicals were postmillennial, a decidedly minority position today.

Likewise, one academically trained charismatic interpreter partly supported his connection between the Toronto Blessing and Ezekiel's river by noting that "it arose from the shared experiences of the global charismatic community."[9] Although I affirm (against some critics) the value of the Toronto Blessing,[10] I would question this appeal to "the global charismatic community." Had most ordinary Spirit-filled worshipers in China and Africa, for example, even *heard* of this revival?

Most importantly, when Paul appeals to the global Christian community, it is not a single Christian communion such as Anglicans, Lutherans, or Assemblies of God coming up with interpretations suiting each such movement's own traditions to insulate them from correction by others.[11] Paul is appealing to the global *church,* Christ's body. If one argues not for the communion of self-identified Pentecostals but for all who are baptized in the Spirit, even Pentecostals today do not all agree on the definition of baptism in the Spirit. Indeed, by their most common classical definition, namely an experience that includes or climaxes with tongues, only half of classical Pentecostals themselves count.

Granted, empowerment by the Spirit grants a special dynamic in interpretation that we should seek; but how do we identify who has this gift (cf. 1 Cor 12:28; Eph 4:11; 1 Tim 4:14; 2 Tim 1:6), apart from the likely consistency of their revelation with ours, or by using Scripture as the shared measuring stick? My effort to guess which scholars were charismatic (noted later in Appendix C) often proved embarrassing, as some spiritually gifted for teaching and scholarship did not so identify; clearly the gift of teaching is not limited only to those who pray in tongues. Further, those who did self-identify as charismatic defined their experience in a range of ways. The scholars who identified as charismatic, including those who pray in tongues and are denominationally Pentecostal, also hold a range of views and use a variety of interpretive approaches.

Apostolic Authority and Communities

Further, even Paul's appeal to community may be more complicated than we at first assume. Like Jeremiah, who had to stand against the other prophets of his day (Jer 2:8, 26; 5:13, 31; 14:13–15; 15:17; 23:14–21; 26:8; 27:9, 14–18), Paul often challenged his circle of churches (1 Cor 4:21; 2 Cor 13:2), denounced false teachers (Gal 1:8–9) and sometimes had to stand against genuine but mistaken apostles (Gal 2:11–14). Toward the end of Paul's life, most Christians in the geographic sphere of his greatest ministry success had turned from him (2 Tim 1:15); had they been our community of interpretation, we would have rejected the word of the Lord.

On a local level, prophets together evaluate revelations (1 Cor 14:29). Nevertheless, Paul's apostolic or high-level prophetic authority can also supersede beliefs of local prophets (14:37). Of course, anyone can claim to have such authority, and this danger becomes an issue in 2 Corinthians, where Paul must counter rival apostles. Here, to defend his apostolic authority, Paul appeals to his sufferings and his role in founding their church by the Spirit and gospel (2 Cor 2:14–7:4); he denounces his rivals there as false apostles (11:13) and Satan's agents (11:15). Some who claim apostolic authority today appear less apt than Paul to narrate what they have sacrificed and suffered for their calling (contrast Matt 10:2, 16–20; 1 Cor 4:9–13).

Some Pentecostal denominations, like more traditional denominations, would circumvent the difficulty of defining apostolic authority by taking a cessationist position with regard to apostles and senior-level prophets. The problem with this approach is that no biblical evidence warrants this cessationism any more than for the other gifts (unless we are limiting "apostles" to its usual Lukan, but not usual Pauline, sense of the Twelve),[12] and a Pentecostal cannot make such a case without inconsistency in their hermeneutic. Still, biblical apostles' authority derives from their commission and message, not from the churches' recognition. They are known by their message and their obedience to Christ.[13]

The canon's authority was subsequently recognized by the church community, but insofar as we regard it as revelation its authority did not derive from the community. Apostles and prophets often challenged God's community, and were not always heeded in their generation. The community we must heed, then, is that of God's agents of revelation through history, with unrivaled attention to their tested revelation now available to us in Scripture. The church can be and often is an agent of revelation, but we cannot simply equate with revelation the voice of one part of the church or the voice of the church of any given generation.

Who *Is* the Pentecostal Community?

Appeal to a Pentecostal "community of interpretation" is of limited value unless we define Pentecostalism. Do those who speak of Pentecostal interpretation refer to classical Pentecostal denominations, or to global pentecostalism, a much wider category that many statisticians call renewalists?

Classical Pentecostalism is hardly small; the Assemblies of God, in particular, is now one of the world's largest Protestant denominations. Denominational Pentecostals together outnumber any of the other global Protestant communions taken by themselves.[14] Yet in the West, the majority of classical Pentecostals are *theologically* indistinguishable from other comparable non-cessationist evangelical groups apart from the initial evidence doctrine.[15]

Early critics of North American Pentecostalism sometimes derided it as the "tongues movement," but while tongues was a Pentecostal distinctive (in those days rarely discussed favorably outside that movement), it was not the heart of what Pentecostalism was about.[16] The empowerment of the Spirit was less distinctive theologically, because many others also affirmed it (before the Pentecostal revival, it was a strong Wesleyan and Keswick emphasis, for example); yet many observers would suggest that pentecostalism spread throughout the world more because of its core emphasis on the Spirit than because of its distinctive emphasis on tongues.

Recent biblical scholarship provides an analogy for distinguishing what is central from what is distinctive. In the heyday of redaction criticism, scholars highlighted Luke's or Matthew's changes to Mark to determine what was distinctive about Luke's or Matthew's theology. This approach has some value and offered more relevance for preaching than had source criticism (directed more toward historical concerns). Soon afterward, however, narrative critics began rightly pointing out that we learn Luke's theology not only from what he changes, but from what he retains. We must read Luke-Acts as a cohesive whole rather than as Lukan additions to material that Luke regards as theologically superfluous or irrelevant. It is not sufficient to focus on what is distinctive to us, any more than Matthew and Luke decided to omit whatever had already been covered by Mark. It is not just what is distinctive that defines us; if we act as if it is, we allow those outside our community to shape our identity.

Is a Pentecostal hermeneutic one that simply arrives at classical Pentecostal conclusions regarding initial evidence? Both redaction criticism and narrative criticism are sometimes employed to this end, but does this make them uniquely Pentecostal methods? And if the methods deployed to arrive at this distinctive conclusion are not uniquely Pentecostal, *is* there a *uniquely* Pentecostal hermeneutic? (I use "uniquely" here in distinction from "distinctive"; but distinctive characteristics of the pentecostal hermeneutic, such as eschatological and experiential readings, are not limited to classical Pentecostals.)

When, by contrast, we speak of more than half a billion pentecostals globally, we are including all charismatics and even many independent movements that are barely recognizable as Christian theologically, yet are counted because they are independent and experience-oriented.[17] Even in the forms that nearly all classical Pentecostals would embrace as sharing their experience of the Spirit, global pentecostalism exhibits more theological diversity than has classical Pentecostalism. It is not united regarding the initial evidence doctrine or the nomenclature of "baptism in the Spirit" for subsequent experiences. Insofar as we speak of "global Pentecostalism" as an interpretive community, or even global Pentecostal scholarship as an interpretive community, we cannot easily speak *descriptively* of a monolithic global Pentecostal theology or hermeneutic. (For discussion of this reality concerning the pentecostal scholarly community, see Appendix C below.)

Making Charismatic Distinctiveness Superfluous

As Appendix C should make obvious, the divide between charismatics and other continuationists is not really clear, insofar as we define "charismatic" as anyone who is a genuine continuationist in practice (that is, they affirm spiritual gifts for the church and practice the ones they have)[18] with the further limitation, for the purposes of the list in Appendix C, to those who are also willing to accept the title. If we were to include other explicitly continuationist scholars who affirm spiritual gifts, even though they might not call themselves charismatic, the list would make the book too long (e.g., Craig Blomberg, D. A. Carson, and my former colleague Ronald J. Sider).

When inquiring as to whether some scholars were charismatic, for compiling Appendix C, I sometimes received replies from scholars that they were not, but that they were appreciative of the valuable emphases that charismatics brought to the body of Christ. In some cases it was a matter of definition; they did not attend a charismatic fellowship or did not pray in tongues, and so did not accept the label, although some of those who accepted the label also had neither of these characteristics. (Indeed, most of my former students at Palmer Seminary will remember me as openly charismatic, yet everyone also knew that I was serving as an associate minister in a Baptist church.)

Only a very small proportion of contacts seemed to dissociate themselves from a charismatic label emphatically, and sometimes it appeared that they did so based on negative past experiences with Pentecostal or charismatic groups. (I have also had some of these negative experiences with some kinds of Pentecostals or charismatics myself, though more than enough positive experiences with other kinds of Pentecostals or charismatics to counteract them.)

During this research I suggested to Joel Carpenter, a religious history scholar at Calvin College, that the trend of the future might be most of Christendom being charismatic in the sense of practicing noncessationist (not necessarily in the sense of everyone praying in tongues). In response he observed that, "the demise of cessationist teaching, thus making 'charismatic' redundant as a special category," is happening in some parts of the West; meanwhile, most Africans never bought into cessationism to begin with.[19] No wonder John MacArthur has complained about the charismatization of the African church!

I personally do pray in tongues often during my academic work; tongues helps renew my spirit even as my mind is absorbed in the work.[20] Yet I believe that the title "pentecostal" and even the particular gift of tongues are not always the best way to determine who is genuinely practicing their spiritual gifts or experiencing blessings from the Spirit. When I taught at Palmer Seminary probably roughly a quarter of us who taught there prayed in tongues, and roughly one-third had significant accounts of healings; yet I did not observe a clearly significant correlation between those two groups. My Congolese father-in-law did not pray in tongues, yet many instant healings occurred after his simple, concise prayers.[21] I certainly pray abundantly in tongues and readily own the title charismatic, but people like my father-in-law, or spiritually gifted friends like Danny McCain (who has a flourishing ministry throughout Nigeria) or Ron Sider, seem to me no less people of the Spirit than most charismatics I know.

283

Most Christians today are abandoning cessationism, and therefore are *in principle* continuationist. At the same time, many do not actively embrace the gifts personally or seek to learn how to help their churches embrace them. That is, in *practice* many remain *functionally* cessationist. This divide unfortunately precisely characterizes many Western Pentecostals today as well—continuationists in doctrine but not in practice. There is little *theologically* distinctive about being noncessationist today; what is distinctive is actively embracing a lifestyle that expects, as God determines, the activity of God's Spirit. And that line of distinctiveness runs through Western Pentecostal churches just as it runs through others, though on average Pentecostals at least retain a corporate appreciation for, and thus often more room for, the activity of some spiritual gifts.

If we go where God is leading, however, the way of the future may be most of active Christendom becoming charismatic—in the sense of practicing noncessationist—as suggested above. If we really get past cessationism *in practice,* "charismatic" will truly become "redundant as a special category."[22] To remind us of what we already know, those of us who identify ourselves as charismatic cannot afford to boast in our giftedness, as if we gave ourselves the gifts (1 Cor 4:7), or as if we are the only members of Christ's body who are gifted (12:14–21). Nor do we need to be "special" in the sense of being different from the rest of the body of Christ; it is God's love that makes us precious to him. Christ has gifted his entire body; as more believers recognize this biblical reality—helping them to do so is our continuing contribution to Christ's body—we will recognize how each member is special and necessary for the body.

Charismatic Experience, Not Just Charismatic Doctrine

Partly because we come from a range of starting points, charismatic experience by itself does not lead everyone to the same hermeneutic (note again the diversity of names in Appendix C), though in most Catholic and mainline Protestant circles, those with this experience do tend to have higher views of Scripture and greater attentiveness to its message than, on average, do their peers. (Charismatic experience makes plausible many sorts of experiences in the biblical text that some who lack any analogous experiences are more tempted to dismiss.) The biblical purpose of charismatic experience in the narrowest sense is power for ministry; to be effective in Bible interpretation, however, it still needs to be supplemented with close attention to the biblical text.

What charismatic or other Spirit-experience does directly offer, however, *nice!* is a living encounter with the God of the text. Naturally this experience, insofar as our theology, faith and obedience welcome it to be fruitful, cultivates a love and excitement for embracing and actively obeying Scripture that we would not have if we engaged Scripture on an exclusively rational level. Nomenclature aside, all believers should welcome the Spirit's guidance in hearing and following the voice of the true God in Scripture.

Apart from noncessationism, which is widespread, what the Spirit provides is an experiential dynamic that not only welcomes us to experience the text but invades and empowers our lives to experience it. Such a dynamic is not limited to Pentecostals and charismatics, but is often more prevalent among us because we actively embrace it. Experiencing the Spirit further—whether we call the experience further baptism in the Spirit, multiple fillings of the Spirit, or simply continuing experiences with God, keeps us open to this dynamic embrace of the Spirit's power and love in our hearts. How can the presence and activity of the Third Person of the Trinity living inside us not make a difference?

Ideally, because Scripture portrays the gifts as belonging to the entire body of Christ and especially for building up the body of Christ, all Christians are charismatic (including cessationists, regarding the gifts that they do embrace and exercise).

A Pentecostal/charismatic hermeneutic is not extraordinarily distinctive today—but that is true primarily because the Pentecostal movement has already done its theological work over the past century. Tongues as initial evidence might remain an issue of debate, but nobody today can boast simply because we uphold a heritage of continuationism. Instead, if any of us want to lead the way in the Spirit today, we need to actively embrace continuationism in our lives and our churches and not just in theological principle. Of course, for that we need God's power; merely simulating old patterns of revival cannot bring back the Spirit. Yet he promised that if we recognize our dependence enough to ask him for the Spirit, he will not withhold his blessing (Luke 11:13).

Scripture Speaking Personally—and Historically

Some interpreters stress the ancient context, thus focusing on the biblical Word as it was originally shaped, whereas others stress the reception of modern readers, focusing on the need for the Spirit's guidance. Although the latter might be more distinctive to a pneumatic hermeneutic, both are necessarily at the core of a Spirit hermeneutic that acknowledges the Spirit's inspiration of the biblical authors. We need both Word and Spirit.

Here I summarize some principles that the book has addressed and note some applications that flow from these principles, and why a true Spirit hermeneutic is ultimately a Christian hermeneutic.

The Thrust of This Book → nice summary

As we observed in Part I, if we follow the model of Spirit hermeneutics offered in the New Testament as well as by the voices of many subsequent movements of the Spirit, we will read Scripture experientially, eschatologically, and missionally. We will also read Scripture with greater understanding and sympathy when we share the kind of spiritual experience that Scripture describes, and when we read with the sort of humble and broken people whom Scripture often addressed and encouraged. We may read Scripture as the eschatological people of God who resonate with and embrace the message of the text for our lives.

As we observed in Part II, the global church can help us, since we can learn from those parts of the church that are appropriating for their lives various emphases that the rest of us sometimes overlook or fail to apply. Both the Pentecost narrative and the geography of the preponderance of movements of

286

the Spirit today invite us to welcome the gifts and voice of the global church. Part III emphasized the importance of a disciplined reading that understands what biblical texts meant in their ancient contexts and thus a reading that can better empathize with those to whom these texts were first directed.

Part IV explored the contribution of the Spirit to a distinctively Christian, and thus distinctively Spirit-directed, epistemology. This is necessarily an epistemology of Word and Spirit, often functioning together in a hermeneutical circle that helps correct our misinterpretations. Such an epistemology provides a necessary foundation for any Spirit hermeneutic, which grows from a faithful relationship with God and trusting submission to what God says.

Once our epistemology invites a Spirit hermeneutic, what does such an approach look like? Part V explores how the Spirit-inspired interpreters within the canon offer models for Spirit hermeneutics. These models include, for example, Jesus's use of a hermeneutic of mercy more than sacrifice and Paul's reading of the law from the standpoint of faith in God's fulfilled promise in Christ. Such a reading will be christocentric, but, against some, it will also have implications for personal application in the sorts of situations analogous in some respects to those addressed in Scripture.

Yet not all purported Spirit readings equally reflect the mind of the Spirit. Some in fact can be fairly amiss. Part VI thus asked whose "charismatic interpretation" we will follow. It thus reinforced the importance of testing readings by their consistency with the Spirit's already-established message in Scripture.

Pentecostal Hermeneutics as a Christian Hermeneutic

The Pentecostal emphasis on the Spirit in interpretation has a long history before Pentecostals; it is thus historically a wider Christian hermeneutic. At the same time, all Christians need to be reminded of the Spirit's work in enabling us to hear and embrace God's message; by highlighting this emphasis for all believers Pentecostals and charismatics continue to offer a valuable contribution to the wider church. The noncessationist approach that Pentecostals began to proliferate particularly conspicuously a century ago invites all Christians into the biblical world, summoning us to expectancy and trust in God's present, often surprising working in his church and in our lives.

What has been most distinctive about classical Pentecostal hermeneutics has been its explicit invitation to read Scripture from the standpoint of believing and experiencing that we live in the era of spiritual gifts long neglected by the church. Today, Pentecostalism has proved so successful in its primary emphasis that this emphasis is no longer so distinctive; the global church is increasingly charismatic, and cessationism in the traditional sense[1] is on the wane.

This does not of course mean that classical Pentecostals cannot continue to have a distinctive voice in hermeneutics. Much of the church acknowledges spiritual gifts in principle yet allows them little role in practice. Here Pentecostals and charismatics can continue to play a distinctive role in renewing the rest of the church—so long as Pentecostals and charismatics give God's gifts and other experiences of the Spirit more than lipservice themselves. Being continuationist in principle does not guarantee our active embrace of the Spirit—no matter what our label. That is something we must live in daily dependence on the Holy Spirit.

Yet a movement may never be wholly defined only by elements most unique to it in any case. There are many elements of a Spirit hermeneutic that remain indispensable even if widely shared among Christ's body. These include respectful embrace of the message that the Spirit inspired biblical writers to communicate in their original setting. They also include eagerly embracing the text's implications for our lives today, recognizing that the Spirit also desires to guide us during our exegesis of biblical texts, not least in highlighting areas where the message applies to us today, and in inspiring our obedience to the message.

Ultimately a pentecostal hermeneutic—a hermeneutic from the vantage point of Pentecost—is simply a Christian hermeneutic—a hermeneutic of hearing in the text the God who is revealed in Jesus Christ. And ultimately a Christian hermeneutic is no less than a Spirit hermeneutic—an approach that humbly recognizes that it is God's voice, rather than our own, that we must hear in his Word. If not all Christians—including not all Pentecostals—currently do experience God's living voice in Scripture, we can recognize that Scripture now invites us to even greater treasures of knowledge and revelation about God.

The Spirit and Application

We can and should draw appropriate analogies, and the Holy Spirit can make more direct analogies for us, drawing our attention to promises to people in Scripture analogous to those that he also makes to God's people generally, or through which he makes analogies to our own lives individually. Some Christians who are too cautious about allowing the Spirit to speak to us forget that all Christians experience the leading of the Spirit in some ways, even if just the Spirit's witness that we are God's children (Rom 8:15–16; Gal 4:6; 1 John 3:24) or that God loves us (Rom 5:5). Being "led by the Spirit" is a fundamental characteristic of Christians (Rom 8:14; Gal 5:18).[2]

If we believe that God speaks, the idea that God would sometimes speak to us with analogies, by reminding us of his working in Scripture, seems a fairly tame suggestion. Scripture helps shape our hearing of God's voice. People often abuse hearing God's voice, just as people often abuse Scripture; "we know in part and we prophesy in part" (1 Cor 13:9). The existence of counterfeits or worn currency does not require us to abandon money, and witnessing shabby structures does not invite us to throw away our tools and quit building.

At the same time, the Holy Spirit's personal application to us does not change the original point from which such analogies may be best drawn. The original message is the foundation for all interpreters in all cultures. Personal applications are by definition not universal; they are not transferable to all people in all settings. A reading that is exclusively personal risks finding only what we want or personally need at the moment and risks missing "the full will of God" (Acts 20:27).

Moreover, we are best qualified to cite the authority of Scripture behind even our personal applications when they are most analogous to the original point. If I draw from the crowds early in Jesus's ministry the principle that fulfilling God's mission will always make me popular, I miss the point no less than Peter when he denied that Jesus would have to go to the cross. Impressed with Jesus's miracles, Galilean crowds followed Jesus, but in Jerusalem the crowds cried out for his crucifixion. If we miss the point of the text, it no longer offers an objective anchor for our subjective application and experience by the Spirit. Some err on the side of subjectivity without an anchor and others on the side of objectivity without an experience; the ideal is for both to work in tandem.

An early Pentecostal voice invites us to bring Word and Spirit together—a collaboration that I would envision as the best of evangelical exegesis of the text combined with the best of charismatic power to embrace and carry out its message. Smith Wigglesworth, one of the most prominent early Pentecostal healing evangelists, felt disappointed toward the end of his life that the Pentecostal revival had not directly ushered in the end of the age, as the earliest Pentecostals had hoped. He did not, however, relinquish hope for the future. He believed that in addition to the Pentecostal outpouring of the Spirit that brought a restoration of the gifts, there would someday come another revival emphasizing God's Word. "When these two moves of the Spirit combine," he prophesied, "we shall see the greatest move the Church of Jesus Christ has ever seen."[3] May it be so, Lord.

Some Theoretical Attempts to Bridge Understanding

Scholars have often sought to bridge the hermeneutical gaps between the ancient sense and contemporary application. Approaches to bridging the gap vary, from postmodern theological readings of the Bible as the church's book (harking back to patristic arguments)[1] to Bultmann's existential approach and so forth. Wilhelm Dilthey recognized that everyone is shaped by their contexts,[2] but he approached the possibility of understanding by presupposing some shared structures in our common humanity.[3] Dilthey was one of several influences on both Rudolf Bultmann and Hans-Georg Gadamer, although both were more deeply influenced by their associate Martin Heidegger.[4]

Hans-Georg Gadamer rightly noted that historical contexts shape all interpreters and that interpretation is impossible without such contexts. Biases in the sense of prejudgments are inevitable;[5] acknowledging them allows one to learn from and engage others who also work from biases and presuppositions. For Gadamer, all engagement with other perspectives or texts involves fusing horizons between the text's world and our own.[6] Temporal distance does exist, requiring the most competent readers to learn languages and so forth,[7] but, with Aristotle, one must relate the text to one's situation.[8]

Bultmann wanted to make New Testament theology relevant to a twentieth-century world.[9] Wedding it to a particular twentieth-century approach, however, would ultimately doom Bultmann's approach to the same fate as earlier attempts to conform Jesus to the dominant values of the interpreters' era.[10] Most scholars agree that the early Heidegger was a major influence on the thought of Rudolf Bultmann,[11] though Bultmann thought that Heidegger instead discovered a picture that accords with what Bultmann found in the NT.[12] Bultmann viewed existential interpretation not as a bias, but as a necessary perspective, like any other approach to history.[13] He insisted on beginning with grammatical, formal, and historical analysis,[14] so long as one recognized the role of preunderstanding in any interpretive work.[15]

Bultmann's philosophic assumptions, however, shaped not only how he presented his exegetical results but also the limitations on his academic theology. Although Bultmann rejects Barth's charges that the former's theology is anthropocentric rather than theocentric,[16] Bultmann argues that philosophy and theology both have humanity as their object.[17]

More problematic is his understanding of history. Although God has acted decisively in Christ,[18] Bultmann views this acting as existential and not historical.[19] Explaining theology to an antisupernatural world, Bultmann accepts rather than challenges its premise; thus no mature person can "seriously maintain" the New Testament worldview.[20] For him, whatever involves supernatural forces is "myth";[21] the historical continuum cannot be interrupted by supernatural interventions.[22]

Many scholars recognize the reuse of some "mythical" language and imagery in the New Testament, perhaps most obviously in such symbolism as Rev 12:1-4. In such cases, one might describe "demythologization" as translation from one genre to another, rather than creating a new sense unintelligible to the ideal authors' ideal contexts. Does one use modern criteria, freighted with their own cultural baggage, to determine what is "myth"?

For Bultmann, myth often demands an existential interpretation,[23] but this is not the only way to appropriate myth, especially where the original sense points in a different direction. In many cultures myths communicate aetiology, cosmology, moral lessons, and so forth. Why, for example, must the three-story universe, in terms of which virtually none of us think today, be reinterpreted in existential terms[24] rather than in spatial ones? Granted that "heaven" may be "out" rather than "up," but even from the standpoint of our geocentric experience, it remains gravitationally "up." Ancients had no reason to distinguish troposphere, ionosphere, and more distant forms of "out," but do the ranges most naturally translate into existential terms?

Likewise, for Bultmann the "future" represents an "authentic possibility of being."[25] Although Bultmann's present eschatology often correctly recites the New Testament picture,[26] in the New Testament realized eschatology anticipates rather than supplants future eschatology. Suggesting that the New Testament should be demythologized like apocalyptic and gnostic literature[27] offers an incongruous comparison. Early apocalyptic imagery had sociopolitical or mystical meanings, not "existential" ones. One might translate some gnostic texts into "existential" language,[28] but these texts postdate the New Testament and do not directly inform the earliest Christian approaches.[29] Contextually relevant, twentieth-century North Americans would likely not have written about spiritual powers the way that Paul does in Rom 8:38 or Eph 6:12, but a purely "existential" interpretation of those passages would strip them of their continuing relevance to spiritism in Brazil, Haiti, the Philippines, Nigeria, or Iceland.

If all texts translate into the same essential, existential meaning, why bother using different texts? Has not the locus of authority shifted in this case from the text (and thus its complex of symbols designed to make sense in a given historical context) to the interpreter's existential preunderstanding?[30] Bultmann has borrowed premises from a nontheistic worldview; Jaspers and other existentialists thus question whether Bultmann has gone far enough.[31] His content criticism has rendered his position unfalsifiable,[32] just as he averred that faith itself cannot be verified or falsified by history.[33] Bultmann's fideism cannot eliminate the offense of the cross.

Many other approaches to contextualization exist, but what these samples illustrate is the academic guild's recognition of the gap between comprehending grammar and embracing the message.

Postcolonial Approaches

Postcolonial readings of the Bible[1] highlight the presence of the empire,[2] which is relevant to various biblical texts.[3] Many scholars, for example, see the imperial cult as part of the regular experience of the seven churches of Asia Minor in Revelation.[4] Some of the NT declarations of "peace" may also challenge the hollow Augustan Pax Romana.[5]

Varied Approaches

Postcolonial approaches vary, but their examination of social power dynamics can be fruitful.[6] Although some early postcolonial studies did not value studying texts in their ancient context, such neglect is not inherent in postcolonial approaches per se;[7] certainly social power was regularly an issue in ancient contexts, as both sociological and social-historical approaches often highlight. Neither need postcolonial approaches oppose biblical liberationist readings, although again early studies were sometimes used in this way.[8]

At the same time, some scholars have warned uncritical users of the postcolonial label to keep in mind that not all empires are the same;[9] one cannot impose grids from one empire onto another without sensitivity to the differences.[10] Further, NT scholars' use of "imperial studies" often needs to acquaint itself better with the diversity even in the Roman imperial cult, with its range of local and generational variation.[11] A wider concern from a traditional textual perspective, however, may be simply the danger of reading all texts through the same grid, a frequent danger in ideological criticism (though also in ideologically informed readings not self-critical enough to *recognize* their ideologies).[12]

Particular postcolonial approaches vary among interpreters, often depending on their differing sociopolitical locations;[13] thus, for example, some Jewish feminists have complained about many Majority World postcolonialists' appropriation of Western anti-Semitism in treating ancient Jews as religious colonizers.[14] Indeed, in some scholars' hands, postcolonialism has become another opportunity for an educated elite to speak in the name of an underclass, and sometimes profit in their academic status by so speaking, without relinquishing personal privilege or helping the oppressed.[15]

Post-postcolonial Readings?

At the same time, part of the genius of postcolonial approaches is that they embrace readings from diverse social locations. Although the seminal works remain highly influential, as students continue to develop their own approaches for a range of contexts, one might even come to speak of emerging postcolonialisms, and to evaluate each on its own terms. Just as postcolonial approaches rightly challenge the hegemony of traditional Western cultural assumptions, their very diversity should welcome voices that diverge from the views of some leading postcolonial thinkers.[16] That is, Majority World biblical scholars should continue to feel free to forge their own ways based on their own convictions and communities of interpretation, not beholden to anyone else's consensus, including that of groups within the academy.[17]

Not everything done in the name of global readings truly involves cross-cultural listening. Some interpreters have created almost uniform interpretive grids through which they then filter all texts, often forcing awkward texts to serve incompatible political agendas just as earlier colonial readings often did (whether by forced readings or counterreadings). Like colonial readings, they can serve as assertions of power within their limited framework.

The Importance of Avoiding New Ethnocentrisms

Listening to other voices is crucial; making any particular set of voices normative, however, may bring us back to the sort of ethnocentric approach with which we began.[18] Proponents can end up imposing their group's ideology uniformly on texts and calling this ideological lens a method.[19] One danger, regardless of how commendable one's ideology might be, is that one simply rearticulates the same ideology in multiple ways, rather than being challenged by new insights from the text that stand outside one's range of vision.

Popular readers have often made a study Bible's notes the norm. Some readers today make patristic interpreters the norm through which we must read Scripture.[20] Some feminist or liberationist interpreters make their hermeneutical grids the norm for responsible interpretation, sometimes challenging other liberationist readings as deficient in a particular version of liberationism.[21] A minority of scholars today count as the norm Majority World voices, despite the diversity of such voices and most Westerners' access only to (and perhaps sometimes interest only in) the voices of a published, sometimes Western-educated minority within the Majority World rather than voices from the grassroots.[22] In many cases academicians listen only to fellow academicians, and often to those of the same basic theological persuasions, whatever their cultures.

This is not yet a problem, but is a warning for the future. Whenever new voices are made the transcultural norm, we weaken our case against Eurocentric interpreters continuing to assume, as they often have, that their own traditional perspective is the norm. If any group constitutes the new dominant norm for all, we have returned to the exaltation of our own group, whether in the form of ethnocentrism, nationalism, racism, sexism, or the like.

It should nevertheless be pointed out that most contemporary voices—say, African theology, Asian theology, or Latino/a theology—do not seek to make their own voice the transcultural norm, but only to have a place at the table. Western readings have been so long privileged that Western readers who really want to hear other voices now have an obligation to wear hearing aids or to provide non-Western voices with superior sound systems. Providing safe space and a better hearing for non-dominant voices is needed to transcend the blinders of the dominant culture.

The Global Charismatic Scholarly Community

In chapter 18 we addressed the question, who is the pentecostal community? If we narrow the views of charismatic-type renewal movements to scholars among them, the diversity of views will still be almost as great, outside of their affirmation of experiencing the Spirit, as the denominations and movements they represent. This is particularly true when we survey scholars worldwide, but it seems true even if we narrow the search further to scholars working within the Anglophone West. This appendix should incidentally lay to rest the ill-informed claim that charismatics have contributed nothing to biblical or theological scholarship.[1]

In this appendix I will list some of the charismatic scholars known in the Anglophone West. Due to space and time constraints I can name just a few, so I apologize in advance to those whom I have omitted from either ignorance or absent-mindedness. Because this list is only a sampling, and because those who teach in or have retired from distinctly Pentecostal or charismatically inclined institutions are simply too many as well as too obvious to need to be listed, I am omitting all but a handful of the latter.[2] This limitation is unfortunately somewhat arbitrary, since some of these schools, including Regent University, Oral Roberts University, and Pentecostal denominational schools,[3] have widely published faculty that I have not had occasion to cite elsewhere in the book, such as, for example, psychology and counseling faculty at Regent University (including, among others, Benjamin Keyes, Jennifer Ripley, James Sells, and Mark Yarhouse).

Also I am excluding a larger number of younger scholars who have not published as widely or do not yet have full-time teaching positions (though I include some who have had such positions and retired or diversified their ministries).[4] (I do include some younger scholars if their positions are at elite institutions.) These are samples only; although I asked an embarrassingly large number of colleagues whether they considered themselves charismatic, I did not by any means take a wide survey. I have undoubtedly omitted many charismatics, probably including some old friends, simply by virtue of forgetting that they were charismatic or never having known (since, apart from discussions of pneumatology, this is not usually the first subject that scholars discuss together). New Testament is disproportionately represented simply because I know more colleagues in that discipline.

Not all of those who have responded define "charismatic" in the same way. For example, my rough guess is that perhaps only half have prayed in tongues (the classical Pentecostal paradigm, though it has also been estimated that only half of denominational Pentecostals pray in tongues). Some define it as simply being deeply shaped spiritually during an earlier sojourn in charismatic circles; some others attend charismatic or Pentecostal services. Some define it as openly praying for the sick or for deliverance. Some define it as being involved in spiritual renewal in their denomination, with appreciation for spiritual gifts and worship.[5] Some scholars who pray in tongues asked not to be on the list, because the experience was so intimate for them that they confided in me but did not wish to make it known publicly. The names represent a range of denominations, including Catholic, Methodist, Anglican, Baptist, Lutheran, Presbyterian, Mennonite, (especially) Pentecostal, and so forth.[6]

In most cases I note their teaching positions to illustrate the range of institutions represented. A side benefit of the list is that it reminds us that being charismatic does not guarantee theological outcomes or hermeneutical approaches—for example, it could go without saying that Wayne Grudem would differ on many points from N. T. Wright; similarly, Christopher Stanley and Richard Hays represent quite different approaches to Paul's use of Scripture. Some scholars might consider some others too liberal or too conservative.[7] This might suggest the elusiveness of a *distinctively* charismatic hermeneutic, unless it is simply the same as a continuationist hermeneutic. (I believe that it is; some press that continuationism further than others, but this is not the only element that determines hermeneutical outcomes.)

Black Church studies:
Valerie Cooper (Duke Divinity School)
Felicia Howell Laboy (Louisville Presbyterian Theological Seminary)
Yolanda Pierce (Princeton Theological Seminary)

in evangelism, missiology, or global Christianity:
Afe Adogame (Edinburgh)
(the late) Kwame Bediako (Akrofi-Christaller Institute)
Peter Bellini (United Theological Seminary)
David Daniels (McCormick Theological Seminary)
Lyle Dorsett (Wheaton, Beeson)
Robert Gallagher (Wheaton College)
Sarita Gallagher (George Fox University)
Michael Green (Wycliffe Hall, Oxford)
Jehu Hanciles (Emory University)
Dale Irvin (New York Theological Seminary)
(the late) Ogbu Kalu (McCormick Theological Seminary)
Charles Kraft (Fuller Theological Seminary)
Peter Kuzmic (Gordon-Conwell)
Wonsuk and Julie Ma (Oxford Center for Mission Studies; Wonsuk is
    director)
Philip Meadows (Nazarene Theological College)
Lalsangkima Pachuau (Asbury Theological Seminary)
Angel Santiago-Vendrell (Asbury Theological Seminary)
Scott Sunquist (Fuller Theological Seminary)
Timothy Tennent (Asbury Theological Seminary)
Al Tizon (North Park Theological Seminary)
Robert Tuttle, Jr. (Asbury Theological Seminary, emeritus)
Randy Woodley (George Fox Theological Seminary)

in New Testament (where I have the most knowledge of my colleagues):
Efrain Agosto (New York Theological Seminary)
Norbert Baumert (St. Georgen)
Holly Beers (Westmont College)
Ben Blackwell (Houston Baptist University)
Lisa Bowens (Princeton Theological Seminary)
Douglas Campbell (Duke)
Daniel Darko (Gordon College)
Peter Davids (editor of Word Biblical Commentary)
James D. G. Dunn (Durham)
Paul Eddy (Bethel University)
Janet Meyer Everts (Hope College)
Gordon Fee (Gordon-Conwell, Regent College; editor of the NICNT
    series)

Crispin Fletcher-Louis
(the late) J. Massyngberde Ford (University of Notre Dame)
Eric Greaux (Winston-Salem State University)
Gene L. Green (Wheaton College)
Joel Green (Fuller Theological Seminary)
Richard Hays (Duke)
Mary Healy (Sacred Heart Major Seminary)
William Heth (Taylor University)
Jamal-Dominique Hopkins (Crichton College)
Jeff Hubing (Northern Seminary)
David Instone-Brewer (Tyndale House, Cambridge)
Luke Timothy Johnson (Candler, at Emory)
Israel Kamudzandu (Saint Paul School of Theology)
Craig Keener (Asbury Theological Seminary)
William Kurz (Marquette University)
Kenneth Litwak (Azusa Pacific University)
Fred Long (Asbury Theological Seminary)
Francis Martin (Dominican House of Studies)
Scot McKnight (Northern Seminary)
George Montague (St. Mary's University)
Stephen Noll (Trinity School for Ministry)
John C. Poirier
Mark Allan Powell (Trinity Lutheran Seminary)
Emerson Powery (Messiah College)
Siegfried Schatzmann (Southwestern Baptist Theological Seminary)
Russell Spittler (Fuller Theological Seminary)
Christopher Stanley (St. Bonaventure University)
Sam Storms (vice-president, Evangelical Theological Society)
Max Turner (London School of Theology)
Graham Twelftree (London School of Theology)
Robert W. Wall (Seattle Pacific University and Seminary)
Steve Walton (St. Mary's University)
David Watson (United Theological Seminary)
Rikk Watts (Regent College)
Cynthia Westfall (McMaster Divinity College)
Peter Williamson (Sacred Heart Major Seminary)
Mark Wilson (Asia Minor Research Center)
Ben Witherington (Asbury Theological Seminary)
N. T. Wright (University of St. Andrews)

in Old Testament/Hebrew Bible:
Harold Bennett (Morehouse College)
Mark Boda (McMaster Divinity College)
Michael Brown (Fire School of Ministry)
Jamie Coles (Seattle Pacific University)
Robert E. Cooley (Gordon-Conwell)
John Goldingay (Fuller Theological Seminary)
Gary Greig (United Theological Seminary)
Mark Hillmer (Luther Seminary)
Rebecca Idestrom (Tyndale Seminary)
Sandra Richter (Wheaton College)
Kevin Spawn (Regent University)
Beth Stovell (Ambrose College)
Wilhelm Wessels (University of South Africa)

practical theology (communication, homiletics, leadership studies, liturgical studies, reconciliation studies, spiritual formation, etc.):
Christena Cleveland (Duke Divinity School)
Richard Foster (Friends University)
Reg Johnson (Asbury Theological Seminary)
Michael Knowles (McMaster Divinity College)
(the late) George A. Maloney
Luke Powery (Duke Divinity School)
Abraham A. Ruelas (Patten University)
Siang-Yang Tan (Fuller Theological Seminary)
William Turner Jr. (Duke Divinity School)
(the late) Dallas Willard

in religious or church history:
Estralda Alexander (William Seymour College)
Linda Ambrose (Laurentian University)
Allan H. Anderson (University of Birmingham, UK)
Chris Armstrong (Wheaton College)
James Bradley (Fuller Theological Seminary)
Stanley M. Burgess (Missouri State University)
Meesaeng Choi (Asbury Theological Seminary)
David William Faupel (Wesley Theological Seminary)
Peter Hocken
Scott Kisker (United Theological Seminary)

Alan Kreider (Anabaptist Mennonite Biblical Seminary)
Timothy Larsen (Wheaton College)
Michael McClymond (Saint Louis University; University of
    Birmingham, UK)
Gerald McDermott (Roanoke College)
A. G. Miller (Oberlin College)
Luther Oconor (United Theological Seminary)
Daniel Ramírez (University of Michigan)
Mel Robeck (Fuller Theological Seminary)
Lester Ruth (Duke Divinity School)
Joy Schroeder (Trinity Lutheran Seminary)

in sociology of religion:
Margaret Poloma (University of Akron)
Michael Wilkinson (Trinity Western University)

in ethics, theology, and philosophy:
William Abraham (Perkins School of Theology)
Adetekunbo Adelekan (Palmer Theological Seminary)
Paul Alexander (Palmer Theological Seminary)
William Atkinson (London School of Theology)
Garth Kasimu Baker-Fletcher (Claremont School of Theology)
Karen Baker-Fletcher (Southern Methodist University)
Teresa Berger (Yale Divinity School)
Gregory Boyd (formerly Bethel University)
Daniel Castello (Seattle Pacific University and Seminary)
Paul Copan (Palm Beach Atlantic University)
(the late) Ralph Del Colle (Marquette)
(the late) Donald Gelpi (Jesuit School of Theology, Berkeley)
Douglas Groothuis (Denver Seminary)
Wayne Grudem (Phoenix Seminary)
Mareque Steele Ireland (Fuller Theological Seminary)
Veli-Matti Kärkkäinen (Fuller Theological Seminary)
William Kay (Chester University; Glyndwr University)
Daniel Keating (Sacred Heart Major Seminary)
Robert A. Larmer (University of New Brunswick)
Loida Martell-Otero (Palmer Theological Seminary)
Ralph Martin (Sacred Heart Major Seminary)
Kilian McDonnell (Saint John's School of Theology and Seminary)

J. P. Moreland (Talbot Seminary)
Heribert Mühlen (University of Paderborn)
Cherith Fee Nordling (Northern Seminary)
Edward O'Connor (University of Notre Dame)
Andrew Sung Park (United Theological Seminary)
(the late) Clark Pinnock (McMaster Divinity College)
Jon Ruthven (United Theological Seminary)
Steve Seamands (Asbury Theological Seminary)
(the late) Thomas Allan Smail (St. John's College)
James K. A. Smith (Calvin College)
Howard Snyder (Manchester Wesley Research Centre at Nazarene
    Theological College, Manchester)
Robert Stamps (Asbury Theological Seminary)
Steve Studebaker (McMaster Divinity College)
Bernie Van De Walle (Ambrose University)
Eldin Villafañe (Gordon-Conwell Theological Seminary)
Miroslav Volf (Yale Divinity School)
Wolfgang Vondey (Regent University)
Frederick Ware (Howard Divinity School)
Nimi Wariboko (Andover Newton)
Eric Lewis Williams (Harvard University)
Amos Yong (Fuller Theological Seminary)

This is not including present or former leaders of institutions, such as Robert Cooley (former president of Gordon-Conwell Seminary), Robert Herron (provost of Oklahoma Wesleyan University), and others, who are mentioned above, such as New York Theological Seminary's president, Dale Irvin, and Asbury Seminary's president, Timothy Tennent.

Many leading theologians and religion scholars in the Majority World are Pentecostal or charismatic (besides several that I have listed above), including, for just some African examples, Bishop Dapo Asaju (Crowther Graduate Theological Seminary, Nigeria), Kwabena Asamoah-Gyadu (Trinity Theological Seminary, Ghana), Deji Ayegboyin (University of Ibadan, Nigeria); or for Asian examples, Simon Chan (Trinity Theological College in Singapore) and retired professor and Methodist bishop Hwa Yung of Malaysia.

The list of charismatic thinkers would grow still longer if we include charismatic or continuationist academically informed and often academically trained popular writers such as R. T. Kendall, the late Walter Martin, Eric Metaxas, John Piper, and Frank Viola. Further, among leaders of the church, one may include the current archbishop of Canterbury, Justin Welby, and, according to some, Pope Francis (who is at least very supportive of the Catholic charismatic movement and its evangelistic commitment). For several decades now the official preacher of the papal household has been an Italian Capuchin priest, Father Raniero Cantalamessa, who speaks openly about his charismatic experience. Whereas John MacArthur, our beloved but cessationist brother in Christ, might lament all of this as the proliferation of dangerous leaven, I thank God for how, through the witness of the Pentecostal and charismatic and now Third Wave movements, acceptance of spiritual gifts has become fairly mainstream.

This list is meant to address two issues. The first is to combat the nonsensical claim that charismatics and Pentecostals as such contribute nothing to biblical or theological scholarship. The second is to illustrate the diversity of charismatic and Pentecostal perspectives and hermeneutical approaches, and thus to question the extent to which it is possible to speak of any monolithic "charismatic" or "pentecostal" hermeneutic, apart from dependence on the Spirit's empowerment.

Notes

Notes to the Introduction

1. For reasons explained later in the main text, I follow the convention of some recent works in using a lowercase "p" for global pentecostal experience that includes but is not limited to Pentecostal denominations.

2. Boda, "Word and Spirit," 25, rightly laments that most Christian theological approaches to hermeneutics focus on the NT. This work will be no exception, though that is because of my academic expertise, not out of theological disrespect for or devotional neglect of the OT.

3. Focused on context, background and genre, it is available free on the internet in English, Spanish, French and some other languages at http://www.craigkeener.com/free -resources/. I produced it free with special concern for providing it in places where readers had less access to published resources.

4. In addition to some explicitly charismatic works addressed elsewhere in this book, relevant, valuable and influential contributions by some of my fellow evangelical scholars include, among many others, Thiselton, *Horizons;* Osborne, *Spiral;* Klein, Blomberg, and Hubbard, *Introduction*[2]; Brown, *Scripture as Communication;* Bartholomew, *Hermeneutics;* many others, from various traditions and approaches, could be named. I explain the social-historical and rhetorical approach used in my Acts commentary (albeit as only one approach, not the necessary form for all approaches) in Keener, *Acts,* 1:16–26.

5. Green, *Seized,* 2–5, notes that reading the Bible like any other book can be helpful, but argues that this is not reading the Bible as Scripture, as God's Word. For one discussion of "confessional biblical hermeneutics," see Spawn, "Principle," 46–47, citing the work of Craig Bartholomew and others.

6. I chose the title "Spirit hermeneutics" early in the process, while seeking to draft the book inductively from biblical data before engaging modern Pentecostal readings. It was only late in the process, then, that I discovered that, fortuitously and independently, charismatic theologian Clark Pinnock had coined the same phrase; see helpfully here Pinnock, "Work of Spirit" (originally published as Pinnock, "Interpretation," in 2009), 233–34, 237–39.

7. For description, see today esp. Grey, *Crowd* (drawing on a range of popular settings; see 197–204); for the value of such description in bringing Pentecostalism's voice to the table,

see Grey, *Crowd*, 5, comparing feminist and liberationist hermeneutics. For one detailed treatment of the earliest decades of Pentecostal interpretation, see Archer, *Hermeneutic*, 89–127; for their hermeneutical context, see 47–88; for the Pentecostal community's story as a hermeneutical filter, see 128–71. Archer, *Hermeneutic*, 211, supports using this story as foundational for Pentecostal hermeneutics today, but even sympathetic observers (both outside and inside the movement) may question why the early Pentecostal story, rather than stories from more recent renewal movements, should be given such weight.

8. The definition is elusive because the boundaries are fluid, though there is a core spiritual identity (so also Archer, "Hermeneutics and Society," here 320–22). The Society of Pentecostal Studies itself is "a diverse hermeneutical community" (332–35). "Pentecostal interpretation is a contextualized theological hermeneutical activity," listening to the Spirit (331). Others also stress the need for contextual interpretation within a cultural community (as opposed to simply a general "pentecostal hermeneutic"); see here Estrada, "Hermeneutic."

9. Cf. Spawn and Wright, "Introduction," xvii, on hermeneutics in the renewal tradition (e.g., global Catholic and Protestant charismatics) but without "a specific scholarly method"; idem, "Emergence," 21–22; Thomas, "Spirit Is Saying," 115 (on the wide range of Pentecostal approaches to hermeneutics); Bauckham, "Review of Waddell"; Waddell, "Hearing," 190–91, following K. Archer, on "multiple strategies . . . without doing violence to the text"; Grey, *Crowd*, 4, on "Pentecostal" readings conformed "to fit whatever category of the wider academy each scholar considers most appropriate, whether that be postmodern, evangelical or otherwise." Others point out that, despite much theoretical discussion of "pneumatic interpretation," little has been done to describe it (Davies, "Read as Pentecostal," 261). Still, even those who expressly acknowledge Pentecostal diversity (e.g., Archer, *Hermeneutic*, 181–92) sometimes state, "Pentecostals believe" (252, 254). This problem is not limited to Pentecostals; cf. the lack of a single, distinctive Baptist identity in Kidd and Hankins, *Baptists*, 248.

10. E.g., criticizing Archer's work, see Spawn and Wright, "Emergence," 14–15; Poirier, "Critique" (brought to my attention by John Wyckoff); cf. Oliverio, *Hermeneutics*, 193, 231.

11. Also a key point in Poirier, "Critique," esp. 1, 3.

12. Many estimate roughly one hundred million; see Johnson and Ross, *Atlas*, 102.

13. Many observers today estimate at least half a billion in the Pentecostal and charismatic families of believers, comprising nearly 30 percent of global church membership and nearly 40 percent of regular church attenders; see, e.g., Johnson, Barrett, and Crossing, "Christianity 2010," 36; cf. Sanneh, *Disciples*, 275. These figures use wider definitions of charismatics than many charismatics would embrace (see Anderson, *Pentecostalism*, 11), and more refined methods in the future may require adjustments in such figures; nevertheless, they do convey a sense of the massive size and growth of such movements.

14. Thus Ellington, "Authority," 153, notes his "frustration" in describing "Pentecostal experience," since, although common to Pentecostals, it is not unique to them; note also Waddell, "Hearing," 174–75n12 and 183, regarding theological reading, and 181, regarding Pentecostal theological connections with various movements (following Land, "Passion," 29–30).

15. For the Pentecostal movement's first decades as reflecting the heart of Pentecostal spirituality, see, e.g., Thomas, "Spirit Is Saying," 119.

16. Cf. Bultmann, "Problem of Hermeneutics," 76–77, 79: once texts have first been understood according to their purposed function, they may also be used as "sources" by which we address other questions.

17. Cf. the warning in Moore, "Canon," 29–30 against "a Spirit-less Word (rationalism)"

and "a Word-less Spirit (subjectivism)"; Pinnock, "Work of Spirit," 233, 241; for valuing both affective and cognitive dimensions, see discussion later in the main text (p. 32), with the example of biblical psalms.

18. For one very important sampling, see Martin, *Reader;* the surveys of views in Grey, *Crowd,* 36–61; Macchia, "Spirit and Text"; Ahn, "Debates"; extensively, Oliverio, *Hermeneutics;* and the bibliographies in e.g., Wyckoff, *Pneuma,* 143–50; Martin, *Reader,* 285–90; Spawn and Wright, *Spirit and Scripture,* 199–211; Archer, *Hermeneutic,* 270–88; Oliverio, *Hermeneutics,* 363–76; and (though not limited primarily to hermeneutics) Mittelstadt, *Reading,* 170–205.

19. Early Pentecostals, like many of their contemporaries, read Scripture as authoritative and read it canonically (Martin, "Introduction," 4–5). This accords with Christian interpretation in general, which, while allowing for the distinctive voices of the different authors, affirms the overarching narrative and the fundamental theological unity of the canon (Brown, *Scripture as Communication,* 229). For canonical approaches, see, e.g., Childs, *Canon;* idem, *Scripture;* Childs et al., *Bible as Scripture;* Bartholomew, *Canon;* Hahn, *Kinship;* in patristic sources, e.g., Young, "Mind of Scripture"; for studies on canonical approaches, cf. also Brett, *Criticism;* Noble, *Approach.* Some would even accept the value of Mark 16:9–20 because it is canonical (though not Markan) and because of its role in early Pentecostal tradition (Thomas and Alexander, "Signs").

20. Cf. Martin, "Spirit and Flesh," 1, as cited in Johns and Johns, "Yielding," 51: "exegesis according to the Spirit" "presupposes that the reader is in living contact with the same realities about which the author in the Sacred Text is speaking."

21. See Martin, "Introduction," 6–8.

22. Cf. here Stronstad, "Experience," here 17, 25–26, as cited in Archer, "Retrospect and Prospect," 144.

23. Cf. here also Thomas, "Women," 82: far from simply desiring to articulate their own distinctive hermeneutic, Pentecostals seek to provide a hermeneutical gift to the wider church, just as they have done with their emphasis on and insights into pneumatology.

24. Cf. Polybius on the writing of history: "So that as nothing written by mere students of books is written with experience or vividness, their works are of no practical utility to readers" (Polybius 12.25g.2).

25. Others also suggest that distinctive Pentecostal insights may contribute to some more traditionally cessationist evangelical scholarship, and that evangelical priority on Scripture should also help Pentecostals; see Cartledge, "Text-Community-Spirit," 135–42.

26. Green, *Practicing Theological Interpretation,* 101–2 (following esp. Haskell, *Objectivity,* esp. 145–73), distinguishes between neutrality of personal commitment, which on issues important to a person is often self-deception, and the scholarly ideal of objectivity, by which he means honesty, fairness, openness to other views, and realistic self-appraisal.

27. For just a few samples of some important academic works on Pentecostalism, see, e.g., Anderson, *Pentecostalism;* Blumhofer, *Faith;* Blumhofer, Spittler, and Wacker, *Currents;* Bomann, *Faith in Barrios;* Cartledge, *Tongues;* Chesnut, *Born Again in Brazil;* Dempster, Klaus, and Petersen, *Globalization;* Jacobsen, *Thinking in Spirit;* Kalu, *African Pentecostalism;* Khai, *Cross;* Poloma, *Assemblies;* Satyavrata, "Globalization"; Angela Tarango, *Jesus Way;* Wacker, *Heaven;* Yong, *Spirit Poured.*

28. Cf. early concerns for institutionalization noted in Robeck, *Mission,* 290.

29. Oliverio, *Hermeneutics,* 78–81, 255–57. See also Smith Wigglesworth in Anderson,

Ends of the Earth, 206; Aimee Semple McPherson in Blumhofer, *Sister,* 16–17, 144, 167, 176–77, 207, 211, 217–21.

30. Anderson, *Pentecostalism,* 152 (but cf. 155), and idem, *Ends of the Earth,* 212–13, suggests more than 120 million Catholic charismatics; the figure is even higher in Johnson and Ross, *Atlas,* 102.

31. It offers both a useful historical and sociological study in its own right, and, most relevantly here, is useful for critiquing interpreters' various inherited biases. Translating and recontextualizing the text's message for various audiences helps us grapple with the texts more concretely.

32. Pentecostals do not even have a synod or council of the sort recommended by Calvin (Wyckoff, *Pneuma,* 28–29), and if we did, few Pentecostal scholars or denominations would trust it enough at this point to submit ourselves to its decisions. Today most theologians, both Catholic and Protestant, affirm that the Spirit can illuminate the text for any believer (Wyckoff, *Pneuma,* 90). That believers (and communities) sometimes arrive at competing "illuminations," however, remains a problem. Bullinger and some other Reformation leaders "saw the need for a kind of Protestant magisterium" to prevent individual use of convenience as an interpretive criterion (George, "Introduction," xxviii), but of course lack of consensus has always virtually doomed such an approach from the start, unless we define theological consensus in wide, Christian terms.

33. Poirier, "Critique."

34. Cf. Grey, *Crowd,* 187: Pentecostalism's growth "is not necessarily a corollary of good hermeneutics."

35. Stormont, *Wigglesworth,* 114.

36. Classical Pentecostals shared conservative Protestants' "high view of Scripture," offering natural connections (Oliverio, *Hermeneutics,* 83); they also emerged from a holiness-evangelical matrix (as often emphasized, esp. since Synan, *Movement).*

37. I adapt the latter part of this paragraph from Keener, "Biblical Fidelity," 40.

38. Cf. Stibbe, "Thoughts," 181, 192, who argues for valuing both historical criticism and subjective embrace of the text.

39. E.g., Paul wanted his audience not only to recognize his command that they practice hospitality, but also to comply with it (Brown, *Scripture as Communication,* 98).

40. See Stein, *Guide,* 60–66.

41. Walton and Sandy, *World,* 288–89.

42. Agreeing here with the majority of biblical scholars; so Wyckoff, *Pneuma,* 56, 82–84; Thiselton, "Hermeneutics," 148–49. See also Thiselton, *Horizons,* 91–92 (following T. F. Torrance), 440.

43. Wyckoff, *Pneuma,* 84. Despite my way of framing of the perspectives reflected in the choice of citations above, I believe that Stein, Walton, and Sandy would concur.

44. On the Spirit as teacher, see Wyckoff, *Pneuma,* 80, 97–122 (esp. 117–18), 129–30; Stibbe, "Thoughts," 184; for this role of the Spirit for Calvin, cf. also Wyckoff, *Pneuma,* 27, citing Forstman, *Word and Spirit,* 75. On proposed backgrounds for the Johannine image of the Spirit as teacher, see Keener, *John,* 2:977–82.

45. Arrington, "Use," 105, as cited in Archer, "Retrospect and Prospect," 145; Archer, *Hermeneutic,* 195–96.

46. I address this question at much fuller length in Keener, *Mind,* passim. Affirming both the "through" and the "beyond," I teach, prophesy, and pray in tongues.

47. Moberly, "Hermeneutics," 161–62, notes that most pneumatic hermeneutical approaches proposed by Pentecostals are not limited to Pentecostals, appearing even in the church fathers.

48. Cf., e.g., Magrassi, *Praying the Bible;* Paintner and Wynkoop, *Lectio Divina;* Robertson, *Lectio Divina;* McEntyre, *Phrase,* x.

49. See Nyunt, "*Hesychasm.*"

50. Wyckoff, *Pneuma,* 13–18, 124. See, e.g., Chrys. *Hom. Cor.* 37 (cited in Wyckoff, *Pneuma,* 16).

51. Ramm, *Interpretation,* 98; Wyckoff, *Pneuma,* 22–24. For Luther's theological, christocentric goal in historical-grammatical interpretation, see Grant and Tracy, *History,* 94; for his emphasis on application, see Wengert, "Luther," 104, 106. Unlike Luther, some of his seventeenth-century successors viewed Scripture only with critical intellect and not with the heart (Grant and Tracy, *History,* 97).

52. Luther WA 5:108, as quoted in Bartholomew, *Hermeneutics,* 198; Luther insisted that he had learned to abandon his own wisdom and depend on the Spirit to hear Scripture (WA 4:519.3–4, as quoted in Bartholomew, *Hermeneutics,* 199). Luther notes Paul's appeal to his audience's experience in Gal 3:5 (*First Lectures on Galatians,* on 3:5, in Bray, *Galatians, Ephesians,* 93).

53. George, "Introduction," xxv.

54. Wyckoff, *Pneuma,* 27, citing Calvin, *Corinthians,* 117; Calvin, *Catholic Epistles,* 389; Osborne, *Spiral,* 340, citing *Inst.* 1:93–95; George, "Introduction," xxix; see esp. now Adhinarta, *Doctrine,* 38 (addressing subsequent confessions on 39–43).

55. Oliverio, *Hermeneutics,* 85, following Grenz, *Renewing,* 69, 71.

56. Wyckoff, *Pneuma,* 43.

57. Wyckoff, *Pneuma,* 43–45. Wyckoff also cites influences in this respect such as Aquinas (18–20) and Francis Turretin (29–30).

58. Kidd and Hankins, *Baptists,* 122. Wayland was Brown's president from 1827 to 1855. One of his students founded Baylor University and another was president of the University of Michigan for nearly four decades (122–23).

59. Lightfoot, *Acts,* 51.

60. King, *Only Believe,* 207, citing Chambers, *Help,* 146 (also Chambers, *Chambers,* 152; idem, *Psychology,* 200), and distinguishing his approach from that of Karl Barth. Arguing that Scripture "is not of itself the word of God, but only becomes the word of God to the reader" through the Spirit (Ellington, "Authority," 156–57) sounds neoorthodox, but is not always intended this way (cf. the disclaimer in Davies, "Read as Pentecostal," 257, although it also sounds neoorthodox).

61. King, *Only Believe,* 207–8, citing Tozer, *Pursuit,* 68.

62. Cf. the importance of the Spirit in interpretation in Klein, Blomberg, and Hubbard, *Introduction,* 425–26. Even from a purely secular standpoint, pervasive modern appeals to Scripture require attention to method; cf. the observations of Collins, *Babel,* 133.

63. E.g., Newlands, "Ovid"; Tsouna, "Introduction," viii. Scholars can also draw contemporary insights from other older texts; see, e.g., Espinoza, "*Pia Desideria*" on a 1675 work of Phillip Spener. Scholars of Stoicism often want students to appreciate Stoicism, and try to answer some of the objections against it (Rorty, "Faces," 243; cf. also Irwin, "Stoic Inhumanity," 238). Others cite the value of ancient Stoic insights for cognitive psychology (see Sorabji, *Emotion,* 1–4, 225–26; cf. Rorty, "Faces," 260–62).

64. Bruce, "Interpretation," 566, as cited favorably in Wyckoff, *Pneuma,* 3. See at length Marshall, *Beyond Bible,* including 79: "Scripture needs interpretation and fresh application, both in our doctrine and in our practice."

65. Ramm, *Interpretation,* 60–63. Ramm also protests the liberal rejection of prophecy as carrying emphasis on the original meaning too far (68). But Ramm warns against devotional reading that uses Scripture passages as personal divination (111–12). Still, it should not escape notice that ancient Jews, Christians and pagans did open sacred texts randomly and take the message as relevant for them at that moment; see Van der Horst, "Bibliomancy," 165–67.

66. Osborne, *Spiral,* 340, going on to cite Spurgeon and Calvin. Cf. also Green, *Seized,* 94–100, emphasizing that Scripture engagement "must be Spirit-imbued"; McQuilkin, *Understanding,* 85–88, citing as requirements for understanding Scripture regeneration, prayer, humility, and (on 86–87) genuine faith in it, which involves commitment, and (on 87) dependence on the Spirit. Cf. also Wong, "Mind"; Cartledge, "Theology."

67. Bauer and Traina, *Inductive Bible Study,* 36–37, citing John 7:16–17; 1 Cor 2:14. Scripture contains various genres, but some of them are meant to be read in hortatory fashion (Poster, "Affections," 23) and most were meant to be followed or emphasize points to be followed.

68. Mulholland, *Shaped,* 19–21, 134. By this way of reading "we have ears to hear and do not hear" (23); Mulholland recommends instead viewing ourselves as the object shaped by the text (57), and, following Wesley, invites the text to evaluate us (130). His relational approach may echo Martin Buber's "I-Thou" (for whom the ultimate "Thou" is God; Buber, *I and Thou*).

69. Harrington, *Interpreting,* 126, as cited in Wyckoff, *Pneuma,* 67.

70. Thiselton, "New Hermeneutic," 80, citing Ebeling, *Word and Faith,* 318–19; Fuchs, *Hermeneutik,* 92; idem, *Studies,* 35, 191–206. For rhetorical criticism, see, e.g., Kwon, *1 Corinthians 1–4,* 3–4.

71. For Luther's emphasis on "*the organic, theological unity of the Bible,*" see Ramm, *Interpretation,* 56 (emphasis his), though Luther sometimes downgraded biblical works lacking this focus (Fuller, "Analogy," 210n13).

72. Blackman, "Exegesis," 26, insists that criticism is not sufficient; we must seek to understand a text, and then be able to relate it, first "to Christ and the central Biblical doctrine of salvation" and "to the situation of today."

73. Wyckoff, *Pneuma,* 46–48.

74. Wyckoff, *Pneuma,* 56, citing Henry, *God Who Speaks,* 256, 258. See also Wyckoff, *Pneuma,* 131.

75. Wyckoff, *Pneuma,* 57, 75, 136, citing these authors and others; see also Bloesch, "Christological Hermeneutic," 99–102.

76. Green, *Practicing Theological Interpretation,* 1.

77. See, e.g., Green and Turner, *Horizons;* Treier, *Interpretation.*

78. For most years since that ordination in 1990 (See, e.g., Johnston, "Ordination"; White, "Calling"; Usry and Keener, *Religion,* 125–29), I have served as an associate minister in African-American Baptist churches. Due to the demographics of our location, the logistics of this association became more difficult after we relocated to teach at Asbury Seminary, although my commitments and long-term plans remain the same. Partly because of where my son joined the worship team (but also because we genuinely like the church), we attend a Vineyard church here.

79. Keener, *Questions;* revised in idem, *Gift;* also idem, "Gifts for Today"; idem, "Luke's Pneumatology"; idem, "Power." Additionally, works addressing charismatic-interest topics

from a more general scholarly perspective, read more widely beyond charismatic circles, include Keener, *Miracles;* idem, *Spirit;* idem, "Acts 2:1–21"; idem, "Gifts"; idem, "Holy Spirit"; idem, "Miracle Reports in Gospels and Today"; idem, "Miracle Reports: Perspectives"; idem, "Miracles"; idem, "Miracles: Dictionary"; idem, "Pentecost"; idem, "Pneumatology"; idem, "Possession"; idem, "Raised"; idem, "Review of *Strange Fire*"; idem, "Spirit"; idem, "Spirit Perspectives"; idem, "Tongues"; idem, "Warfare."

80. Frank Collier, "Holy Spirit book not best source," *Salisbury Post* (Oct. 6, 1996).

81. *Historical Jesus.*

82. An "apologetic" is technically a defense of something.

83. One version is Keener, *Bible in Context* (more often distributed in French, and a Spanish version in Latin America); I also contributed to McCain and Keener, *Understanding and Applying.*

84. For the idea that the Bible is for the believing community, see the church fathers on the Bible as the *church's* book (esp. Tert. *Praescriptione* 5, 40, cited e.g., in Nichols, *Shape,* 170); see today Hauerwas, *Unleashing,* 9, as cited in Ellington, "Authority," 161. See also Rom 15:4; 1 Cor 10:11; one might distinguish the questions of "to whom" (the original contexts) and "for whom" (the continuing people of God) Scripture was written.

85. The earliest Pentecostals drew especially from the radical Holiness evangelicals rather than the more rationalistic tradition that ultimately developed particularly in the direction of fundamentalism (Waddell, "Hearing," 181), though during the modernist-fundamentalist controversy they readily identified with fundamentalists more than antisupernatal modernists.

86. That includes Pentecostal traditions. I am absolutely convinced, for example, that the old dispensational eschatological approach I was taught in a particular Pentecostal setting is exegetically untenable (I may have made too much of that difference when I was in that setting, but I have always found the approach very simple to deconstruct exegetically).

87. See, e.g., Alexander and Yong, *Daughters;* Wacker, *Heaven,* 158–65 (though contrast opposing tendencies in 165–76); Yong, *Spirit Poured,* 190–94; McGee, *Miracles,* 135 (though on 136–37 noting the decline in subsequent Pentecostalism); Powers, "Daughters"; idem, "Recovering"; Alexander, "Conscience," 59. In various parts of the world, see, e.g., Ma, "Women," 136–42; Espinosa, "Healing in Borderlands," 140; Kalu, *African Pentecostalism,* 161–62; Pothen, "Missions," 191–92, 255.

Notes to Chapter 1

1. For praxis in pentecostal hermeneutics, see Johns and Johns, "Yielding," 42–46 (defining praxis more specifically than I do here).

2. See, e.g., Waddell, "Hearing," 182, 186, citing here also Steinmetz, "Superiority" (also published in 65–77 in McKim, *Guide*); cf. today also Bartholomew and Thomas, *Manifesto.* For Luther's theological interpretation, see, e.g., Ramm, *Interpretation,* 55–57.

3. The Third Wave, heavily influenced by the biblical theology of George Ladd, has helpfully shifted this emphasis; see, e.g., Stibbe, "Thoughts," 188: "One of the distinctive things about charismatic interpretation and exposition is its emphasis on both the 'now' and the 'not yet' of the kingdom of God."

4. As is regularly noted, e.g., Anderson, *Pentecostalism,* 33–34; McGee, *Miracles,* 61–76; idem, "Hermeneutics," 102; idem, "Strategy," 52–53; Goff, "Theology of Parham," 64–65; Ja-

cobsen, *Thinking in Spirit,* 25, 49–50, 74, 76, 97; Robeck, *Mission,* 41–42, 236–37, 243, 252; see especially McGee, "Shortcut"; idem, "Logic"; Anderson, "Signs," 195–99.

5. See, e.g., Wacker, *Heaven,* 47–51; McGee, *People of Spirit,* 77–78; idem, "Strategies," 204; Hudson, "Strange Words," 61–63; Anderson, "Points," 167; Ma, "Eschatology," 100.

6. See, e.g., Lee, "Future," 105; Mullin, *History,* 211; Berger, "Faces," 425; Tomkins, *History,* 220; Sweeney, *Story,* 153; Barrett, "Renewal," 388; Barrett, Johnson, and Crossing, "Missiometrics 2006," 28; Barrett, Johnson, and Crossing, "Missiometrics 2007," 32; Sanneh, *Disciples,* 275; Noll, *Shape,* 22, 32, 34; Johnson and Ross, *Atlas,* 102; Hanciles, *Beyond Christendom,* 121; Satyavrata, "Globalization," 3. But for more nuance, see esp. Anderson, *Pentecostalism,* 11.

7. Sometimes it has persisted or resurfaced, however; see helpfully McGee, *Miracles,* 102; esp. Miller, *Tongues Revisited.*

8. Keener, *Acts,* 1:823–31, esp. 823–24; idem, "Tongues."

9. See the many sources cited in Keener, *Acts,* 1:148–65; among evangelicals, see the seminal work Marshall, *Historian and Theologian;* also idem, "Luke as Theologian"; among Pentecostals, cf. Stronstad, *Charismatic Theology.* For the compatibility of theological and political readings, see, e.g., Elliot, *Arrogance,* 23.

10. Polyb. 1.1.1; Dion. Hal. *Ant. rom.* 1.2.1; Livy 1, *pref.* 10; Val. Max. 2.pref.; Tac. *Agr.* 1; *Ann.* 3.65; Lucian *Hist.* 59; cf. Diod. Sic. 37.4.1; Hdn 3.13.3; Max. Tyre 22.5; for moralizing asides, see, e.g., Polyb. 1.35.1–10; Diod. Sic. 31.10.2; Dion. Hal. *Ant. rom.* 7.65.2; Vell. Paterc. 2.75.2; Dio Cass. 1.5.4; Arrian *Alex.* 4.10.8; Corn. Nep. 16 (Pelopidas), 3.1; Tac. *Ann.* 16.15.

11. For the importance of the cohesive biblical narrative for contemporary narrative theology, see, e.g., Stroup, *Promise;* Hauerwas and Jones, *Narrative;* Loughlin, *Story;* Bartholomew, *Hermeneutics,* 58–84. The emphasis on narrative does not guarantee that all scholars read that narrative in the same way or find all of the same key "phases" in the story. Nevertheless, narrative was already the most common genre in the Bible, and it provides the structure that gives context to most other pieces of the canon. On salvation history, see earlier Cullmann, *Salvation.*

12. See Klein, Blomberg, and Hubbard, *Introduction,* 350–51.

13. Dunn, *Baptism.*

14. Personal correspondence, July 26 and 27, 2015. "Excelling" is my own gloss on his humbler comments.

15. Dunn, *Unity.* See, e.g., Pinnock, "Foreword," vii: "Ironically, at this point at least, there is greater diversity in the New Testament than even Jimmy Dunn is prepared to grant."

16. E.g., for sharing possessions in Acts 2, Evans, *Wycliffe,* 155, 226; Wesley in Jennings, *Good News,* 25, 97–117 (esp. 111–16); early Moravians (Williams, *Radical Reformation,* 429; cf. 229–33); Hutterites (McGee, "Possessions," 167–68; Williams, *Radical Reformation,* 232, 426–29); and, less literally, many other Anabaptists (cf. Finger, *Meals,* 21–22); more recently, the communitarian Jesus Family in China (Anderson, *Pentecostalism,* 135; Zhaoming, "Chinese Denominations," 452–64; Yamamori and Chan, *Witnesses,* 54–62); some elements in the North American Jesus Movement of the 1960s–70s (Jackson, *Quest,* 32; Di Sabatino, "Frisbee," 395–96; Eskridge, *Family,* 88 [cf. 78–79]).

17. For the diversity of revivals, see, e.g., Shaw, *Awakening,* 203–6.

18. Certainly it helps reduce pressure for bias, whether theological (e.g., wanting to defend denominational doctrine) or cultural (e.g., offense at theocratic values). For example, I am free to explore what Jesus said about divorce or what Paul said about homosexual behavior whatever my personal predispositions and pastoral concerns regarding those issues, which I may then address and adjust after the exegesis.

19. See, e.g., Green, *Practicing Theological Interpretation,* 13–20, on reducing hermeneutical distance (cf. Green, *Seized,* 4); Fraser and Kilgore, *Friends,* 32–36, on finding ourselves and our world in the Bible, rather than highlighting cultural distance to the degree that this becomes impossible. In particular, the Eastern Orthodox churches, already emphasizing the value of the Spirit's enlightenment, have not been afflicted by the problems of hermeneutical distance that Bultmann and his successors sought to overcome (Vassiliadis, "Ermeneutike").

20. E.g., Archer, *Hermeneutic,* 167; Oliverio, *Hermeneutics,* 80. The earliest populist Pentecostals, in fact, probably paid too little attention to the original context (cf. the description of their interpretation in Byrd, "Theory," here 204–5, as cited in Archer, "Retrospect and Prospect," 134; idem, *Hermeneutic,* 167); the problem often remains today (see observations in Grey, *Crowd,* 119). Although such an approach largely ignored the first horizon rather than fusing horizons, most early Pentecostals lacked access to fuller information. Academic biblical study today usually ignores the current horizon, often without even passing the torch to those whose focus is preaching or contextualization; each approach, then, can learn from the other's strength.

21. Note the valuing of each in its sphere in Green, *Seized,* 1–2. Cf. Green, *Practicing Theological Interpretation,* 73, on how the theological lenses through which Christians read the Torah differ from those of, say, Pharisees or Essenes.

22. Green, *Practicing Theological Interpretation,* 107, citing Wesley, *Works,* 5:3; see also Mulholland, *Shaped,* 171, citing Wesley, *Works,* 14:252–53.

23. In contrast to more skeptical readings, some can approach the *letter* of the text as God's word, venerating the grammar. Nevertheless, if the grammarian fails to embrace the text's message, he or she may miss the forest for the trees, a myopic approach about which Jesus warned (Matt 23:23//Luke 11:42).

24. See, e.g., Oliverio, *Hermeneutics,* 51; Moore, "Approach," 12; Archer, "Retrospect and Prospect," 133; cf. Clarke, "Wine Skins," 180. Recent hermeneutical emphasis on readers has highlighted this subjective, experiential dimension of interpretation (Wyckoff, *Pneuma,* 87).

25. Menzies, "Methodology," 12–13 (as cited in Stronstad, "Trends"; Archer, "Retrospect and Prospect," 143), suggests that experience, while not itself the source of theology, should be able to verify biblical teachings in believers' lives. If "verification" sounds too modernist (and hence too culturally and historically specific; cf. the concern in Archer, "Retrospect and Prospect," 147), walking in the reality of one's condition, at least, is a biblical concept (Rom 6:11; 1 Cor 6:11). One may compare Wesley's role for experience, subordinate to Scripture, in what subsequent interpreters have called the Wesleyan Quadrilateral (also valuing Spirit-guided reason and tradition; for how some Pentecostal hermeneutics drew on this, see Oliverio, *Hermeneutics,* 127–28). Wesley deemed experience the strongest evidence for Christian faith apart from Scripture, and by this he meant that he *experienced* what Scripture described.

26. This is pointed out by my friend Darrell Bock, who belongs to moderate cessationist circles, but in practice we share very similar hermeneutical approaches. Darrell articulates the importance of moving from experience to the text and vice-versa (personal discussion, Nov. 19, 2015).

27. In this sense, preunderstanding simply recognizes that the interpreter begins with a hypothesis, but that this hypothesis remains open to falsification and adjustment (Hirsch, *Validity,* 260).

28. Nearly all scholars today recognize that no interpreter comes without presuppositions; see, e.g., Dilthey, *Pattern,* 81; Bultmann, "Exegesis"; Thiselton, "New Hermeneutic," 86; Klein,

Blomberg, and Hubbard, *Introduction,* 7; Fiorenza, "Hermeneutics," 361 (using this to argue for using liberative assumptions, 378–81); Green, *Seized,* 24–25; Bauer and Traina, *Inductive Bible Study,* 34–36; Spawn and Wright, "Cultivating," 191–92; Archer, *Hermeneutic,* 223.

29. Osborne, *Spiral,* 412.

30. Thiselton, *Horizons,* 11; cf. also 12, 15.

31. Thiselton, *Horizons,* 436.

32. Thiselton, *Horizons,* 436–37. Stanley, *Diffusion,* 222, also cites this passage and marks it as a major step forward in evangelical hermeneutics.

33. Cf. Ervin, "Hermeneutics," 33, as cited in Fogarty, "Hermeneutic"; Abraham, *Revelation,* 101, 108–11 (as cited in Spawn, "Principle," 51); also charismatic experiences in Spawn, "Principle," 62, 71; Thomas, "Spirit Is Saying," 121; cf. Boda, "Walking," 169; Lewis, "Epistemology."

34. Wesley allowed experience a role in interpretation (later articulated in the "Wesleyan Quadrilateral"), although subordinate to Scripture itself.

35. E.g., Keener, *Paul;* idem, "Perspective"; Keener, "Learning"; Belleville, *Leaders;* Pierce, Groothuis, and Fee, *Discovering.* Contrary views may be found in, e.g., Piper and Grudem, *Recovering;* Köstenberger, Schreiner, and Baldwin, *Women.*

36. On earlier restorationists' influence on early Pentecostal identity, see, e.g., Archer, *Hermeneutic,* 150–56; briefly, Blumhofer, *Popular History,* 16–18. Early Pentecostals viewed their revival as continuing or even completing the restoration of the church begun in the Reformation (Oliverio, *Hermeneutics,* 76).

37. Cf., e.g., the emphasis on original context in Bartholomew, *Hermeneutics,* 195–97. Many restorationists had an ahistorical approach (lacking sufficient appreciation for history or historical context as venues for divine activity), but the initial impetus of restorationism was in a sense the opposite. Christians who do not accept that "the Church" is always progressing toward greater truth (for various views, see Toon, *Development*) must regularly call Christians back to foundation documents. The idea that the church progresses toward truth, rather than must be periodically called back to it, may fit the late-nineteenth-century ethos of postmillennialism among Protestants and social evolution among some others. At the same time, restorationists' emphasis on actively calling the church back to truth may also fit the dominant Arminianism of much popular nineteenth-century evangelicalism.

38. The exception might be churches that regard tradition also as directed by the Spirit (see discussion in Toon, *Development*), but most do not put multivocal tradition on the same level as Scripture itself.

39. On using Psalms today, see, e.g., Longman, "Honest"; combined with reception history, see, e.g., Waltke, Houston, and Moore, *Psalms.*

40. In personal conversation in 2013, an old acquaintance of Heidi Baker complained to me that Dr. Baker saw God working even in the smallest details, matters that were not miracles by usual definitions. I suspect that God has honored this attitude, because God is often doing much more visible works through Heidi and her husband Rolland now (cf. Brown, Mory, Williams, and McClymond, "Effects"; Brown, *Testing Prayer,* 194–233).

41. As noted in Keener, *Mind of the Spirit,* 188: "Fleshly critical evaluation stands outside dependence on Christ and suspends belief, working from other, often unacknowledged, worldviews; Spirit-filled evaluation starts with the premise of faith and critically evaluates what is not in accordance with God's trustworthy revelation." My atheistic background simplified

evaluating theistic evidence critically, but recognizing the conflict between this scholarly approach and my new, personal, living faith in Christ took some time.

42. For biblical knowledge of God in terms of relationship and engagement with God, see Johns and Johns, "Yielding," 35–40 (esp. 35–37); Ellington, "Authority," 160 (citing Pinnock, "Spirit in Hermeneutics," here 5); in Johannine epistemology, Keener, "Knowledge" (esp. 30–43); idem, *John,* 1:233–47.

43. As noted in Keener, *Miracles,* 2:623–29, see, e.g., Hall, "Attendance," 106, 108; Wong et al., "Factors"; Ellison et al., "Involvement"; Heuch, Jacobsen, and Fraser, "Study" (among Seventh-Day Adventists, not surprisingly); Comstock and Patridge, "Attendance"; Matthews and Clark, *Faith Factor,* 158–61; Koenig, *Medicine,* 129–45; Lutgendorf et al., "Participation"; Musick, House, and Williams, "Attendance and Mortality"; Bagiella, Hong, and Sloan, "Attendance as Predictor"; Strawbridge et al., "Attendance"; Strawbridge et al., "Strength"; Cour, Avlund, and Schultz-Larsen, "Religion"; Hill et al., "Attendance and Mortality"; Helm et al., "Activity"; Krause, "Support"; Van Ness, Kasl, and Jones, "Religion"; Yeager et al., "Involvement"; Ironson et al., "Spirituality" (regarding AIDS); Eng et al., "Ties"; Oman et al., "Attendance"; Sears and Wallace, "Spirituality"; but cf. the more ambiguous results among Israelis in Kraut et al., "Association"; and negative results in Wrensch et al., "Factors" (though the sample size was fewer than 600 patients in one county). High attendance's association is indirect through lower levels of Interleukin-6 (Thoresen, "Health," 8). On will to live and "mature" religion, see Hedgespeth, "Power." Most conspicuously, note Adventists in Matthews and Clark, *Faith Factor,* 22; Koenig, *Medicine,* 109, 124–25.

44. Cf. anecdotal examples of coping with terminal illness in Lesslie, *Angels,* 45–46, 222–23.

45. Other Pentecostal and charismatic scholars have also noted many of the same features. See, for example, Martin, "Introduction," 5–9 (citing also Ellington, "Locating"; Green, *Theology,* 182–83), emphasizing the presence of the Spirit, canonical reading, entering the biblical narrative, revelatory experience, theological approach to narrative, christological focus, congregational community (esp. in Christian preaching), and eschatological reading.

46. Although Stibbe, "Thoughts," is from 1998, I discovered and read it only after I had structured and written nearly all of this book; that is to say, where our observations overlap they are mutually reinforcing. Our applications differ, however; although his suggestion that the Toronto Blessing might be like a fourth wave in Ezek 47 is stated as a tentative analogy (182), I believe his language goes beyond normal analogy (193).

47. Stibbe, "Thoughts," 182–84.

48. Stibbe, "Thoughts," 184–85. Stibbe draws a different kind of analogy than what I emphasize later, however, emphasizing the *pesher* approach (184–85); but Stibbe also now recognizes the vulnerability of such an approach (185).

49. Stibbe, "Thoughts," 185–87. Following J. Rodman Williams (*Theology,* 2:241–42), Stibbe (Stibbe, "Thoughts," 186) appropriately notes the value of sharing the biblical authors' experience of God, but he also appeals to an interpretation of "the global charismatic community" that is open to question exegetically (186).

50. Stibbe, "Thoughts," 187–88.

51. Stibbe, "Thoughts," 188–89.

52. Stibbe, "Thoughts," 189–91, rightly emphasizing that the biblical message engages the whole person and following Jonathan Edwards (*Affections*) and McQueen, *Joel and Spirit,* 111–12.

53. Stibbe, "Thoughts," 191–92.

54. Green, *Practicing Theological Interpretation,* 2, explains that theological interpretation, Latino/a exegesis, and other perspectival approaches are interests, not methods.

55. Note the range of definitions in Wyckoff, *Pneuma,* 5, 65–68; cf., e.g., Archer, *Hermeneutic,* 192, insisting on the importance of "what the text means today." For Vanhoozer, *Meaning,* 264–65, the "fuller meaning" stemming from divine authorship functions fully only at the canonical level, supervening on rather than contradicting the human authors' intention.

56. In at least some cultural settings, inductive study of the biblical text functions as a more effective tool for evangelism and discipleship; see Trousdale, *Movements.*

57. This is true even if one takes most superscriptions as authentic, which I am not inclined to do. By contrast, we can of course take into account general settings, such as ancient Near Eastern literary forms or the Hebrew language.

58. For the evocative use of the language of psalms, see Brueggemann, *Praying,* 28, as cited in Ellington, "Authority," 167; for their emotive quality, see Martin, "Psalm 63," esp. 265, 268. When I pray using psalms, my prayers quickly turn to analogous issues in my life or the world today, e.g., for the persecuted church. Some hermeneutical approaches seek to elucidate affective evocation; see, e.g., D'Sa, "Dhvani"; Soares Prabhu, "Reading." Much ancient poetry was for purely aesthetic purposes (Quint. *Inst.* 10.1.28), but the psalms were for *worship.*

59. Also in Scripture; see, e.g., John 4:23–24; Eph 5:18–20; Phil 3:3; cf. 1 Kgs 3:15; 1 Chr 25:1–2; 1 Cor 14:15; Col 3:16.

60. For the importance of both affective and cognitive dimensions of appropriating the text see Johns and Johns, "Yielding," 34–35, 40–41; Thomas, "Spirit Is Saying," 121–22. Many today follow the Stoic aversion to pathos, but Paul in Acts 20:31 did not (for Paul and pathos, see Kraftchick, "Πάθη," esp. 61–63; Sumney, "Rationalities"; Anderson, *Rhetorical Theory,* 181–82; Martin, "Voice of Emotion," 181–202; Keener, *Acts,* 3:3050–52). On the affective dimension, see also Martin, "Psalm 63," 265–69, on 266 citing earlier models in e.g., Edwards, *Affections;* Wesley in, e.g., Collins, "Topography." See further Baker, "Pentecostal Bible Reading," who notes (on 98–100) Barthes, *Pleasure,* esp. 14, but finds more relevant the model of Clapper, *Wesley,* esp. 85, 154–56.

61. Mulholland, *Shaped,* 22.

62. Cf. Beck, "Anonymity"; idem, *Paradigm* (e.g., 144).

63. For one charismatic scholar's countering of cessationist approaches on John 14, see Brown, *Authentic Fire,* 188–90.

64. For the Spirit's teaching role, see, e.g., Boda, "Word and Spirit," 41; Keener, *John,* 2:977–82; Wyckoff, *Pneuma,* passim. Nevertheless, the Johannine anointing does not invite a wholly individualistic interpretation that rejects the gift of teachers in Christ's body (see 1 John 1:2; 2:19; 4:6; cf. Rom 12:7; 1 Cor 12:28–29; Eph 4:11; 2 Tim 1:11), a point also emphasized by Calvin against "enthusiasts" (Wyckoff, *Pneuma,* 28–29).

65. See my concern in *John,* xxviii–xxix. Although I am not a deconstructionist, Moore, "Cadaver," 270, is right that biblical scholars tend to "dissect" texts like cadavers rather than feeding on them. For one discussion of the Johannine images of eating and drinking, see Webster, *Ingesting Jesus,* 53–64.

66. See esp. Goulder, *Type and History;* more carefully, Talbert, *Patterns;* Tannehill, *Luke;* idem, *Acts;* also Keener, *Acts,* 1:550–73; Edwards, "Parallels."

67. See Keener, *Acts,* 1:645, 651–53, and views cited there.

68. See Keener, *Acts,* 1:708; 4:3758–62; cf. also Dunn, *Acts,* 278; Rosner, "Progress," 232–33; Cayzer, "Ending"; Marguerat, "Enigma of Closing," 304; Moles, "Time," 117.

69. Perhaps partly because of our experience with erratic and erroneous charismatic revelatory claims, some of us older charismatics are particularly keen to emphasize objective boundaries.

70. See, e.g., Thomas, "Women," 85; Pinnock, "Work of Spirit," 236.

71. Baker, "Pentecostal Bible Reading," 95, compares, probably half-facetiously, the frequent critical approach to the passionless experience of many schizophrenic patients, for whom a brain anomaly causes *anhedonia.* For a helpful Christian approach to emotion, see Elliott, *Feelings.*

Notes to Chapter 2

1. Earlier biblical echoes include the Isaianic mission recalled in Acts 1:8 (see Pao, *Isaianic Exodus,* esp. 85, 92); the ministry transition from Elijah to Elisha (2 Kgs 2:9–15 in Acts 1:8–11; see Keener, *Acts,* 1:713–19, esp. 713, 715, 719); the echoes of theophanies in 2:2–4 (see discussion in Keener, *Acts,* 1:801–3); the table of nations and scattering at Babel, from Gen 10–11, in Acts 2:5–13 (see discussion in Keener, *Acts,* 1:841–44); and, in 2:17–39, explicit references to Joel, the Davidic line, and Psalms 16 and 110 (on Luke's use of David allusions, see further Strauss, *Messiah).*

2. On the promise being for all peoples and not limited to the eleven apostles, see discussion in Keener, *Acts,* 1:696, 987.

3. On Pentecost in Acts 2 producing a new way of reading (without rejecting traditional Jewish approaches), see also Martin, "Introduction," 2.

4. Dilthey emphasized shared humanity as an element of preunderstanding that enables readers to identify with historical persons (Dilthey, *Pattern,* 66–67, 70; cf. Rickman, *Dilthey,* 141–42; idem, "Introduction," 39–41). Here I speak of a further element of shared common ground in Scripture, because we as believers recognize the same divine Person both in Scripture and in prayer; for sharing an element of the divine mind in terms of insight (but not common identity), see, e.g., my *Mind of the Spirit,* 205–6. Jonathan Edwards went further; see McClymond and McDermott, *Theology of Edwards,* 422–23; Hastings, *Edwards and Life of God.*

5. To the pure the Lord reveals his purity, but he renders to each according to their heart (cf. Ps 18:25–26); whoever wants to do God's will will find it (John 7:17), and whoever does what is true finds the light (John 3:20–21). On a popular level, I address knowing God's heart and voice in Keener, *Gift,* 17–50.

6. For the custom evoked here, see Gordon, *Near East,* 229–30; Friedman, "Israel's Response," 202; Yamauchi, "Adultery," 20; Harrison and Yamauchi, "Clothing," 326; cf. Tacitus *Germania* 19.

7. Keener, *John,* 1:207–14, 358–63.

8. See Keener, "Knowledge"; idem, "Pneumatology."

9. Keener, *John,* 2:1035–43, esp. 1038. I revisit the relevance of John 16 in chapter 11 of the present book: "An Epistemology of Word and Spirit."

10. See also McKay, "Veil"; Wyckoff, *Pneuma,* 76.

11. Cf. Nebeker, "Spirit." Through transformational reading and meditation the Spirit thus

conforms us to Christ's image, to our originally intended image in Adam—to the purpose we were designed for.

12. McKay, "Veil," 74.

13. McKay, "Veil," 77. Cf. a similar tension described (but more fully resolved) by Moore, "Fire of God," 117–18; also Spittler, "Enterprise," 76, recognizing the legitimacy of historical-critical methodology for historical methods but its inadequacy for faith and the life of the community.

14. E.g., narratives about Rahab and Gibeonites, or the utter insanity of the Canaanites warring against Israel's God instead of fleeing (Josh 11:20, which implies that they might have survived otherwise). See further e.g., Paul Copan, *Is God a Moral Monster? Making Sense of the Old Testament God* (Grand Rapids: Baker, 2011); Hubbard, *Joshua,* 42–48; Dallaire, "Joshua," 841–45; Colesan, "Joshua," 13–17; my own thoughts at http://www.craigkeener.com/slaughtering-the-canaanites-part-i-limiting-factors/; http://www.craigkeener.com/slaughtering-the-canaanites-part-ii-switching-sides/; http://www.craigkeener.com/slaughtering-the-canaanites-part-iii-gods-ideal/; cf. also http://www.craigkeener.com/slaughtering-the-benjamites-i-benjamins-depravity-judges-191-2028/; http://www.craigkeener.com/slaughtering-the-benjamites-ii-merciless-anarchy-judges-2029-2125/.

15. I treat the historical context in Keener, *Marries Another;* briefly, idem, "Adultery"; idem, "Remarriage."

16. For missional reading of Scripture, see, e.g., Wright, *Mission.*

17. With Miller, *Empowered for Mission,* 62, 69; Hernando, "Function," 247–48.

18. For the Spirit and mission in Acts, see, e.g., Hull, *Spirit in Acts;* Marshall, "Significance of Pentecost"; Stronstad, *Charismatic Theology;* Shelton, *Mighty in Deed;* Penney, *Missionary Emphasis;* Hur, *Reading,* 275; Haya-Prats, *Believers,* 97–108, 192; Bovon, *Theologian,* 198–238; Meagher, "Pentecost Spirit"; Klaus, "Mission," 574–75; cf. Bruce, "Holy Spirit in Acts"; Russell, "Anointing"; Wyckoff, "Baptism," 448–49; Robinson and Wall, *Called,* 122; Keener, "Power."

19. With, e.g., Green, "Repetition," 292.

20. With, e.g., Johnson, *Acts,* 30; Stronstad, *Charismatic Theology,* 20–21.

21. Granted, this is Luke's distinctive emphasis, but it is not unique to him (Matt 10:20; Mark 13:10–11; John 15:26–27; 20:21–22; Rom 15:19; 1 Cor 12:7; 1 Thess 1:5–6; 1 Pet 1:12; Rev 19:10).

22. Palmer, *Hermeneutics,* 87–88, as cited in Thiselton, "Hermeneutics," 161.

23. I say "sometimes" because various biblical works directly address anyone from fallen Israel (e.g., Amos) to sharers in ministry (e.g., Titus). Cf. Green, *Practicing Theological Interpretation,* 42, for God's people as a shared context.

24. For interest in the spiritual experience behind the text, see Fee, *Listening,* 11 (we should seek empathy with the authors' spirituality); this sort of background certainly should be, though in a different way, no less valuable than "cultural background." See, e.g., the identification with Isaiah's experience in Isa 6 narrated in Grey, *Crowd,* 68–69, a pneumatic application that I would affirm. Various popular Pentecostal readings in Grey, *Crowd,* 69–76, helpfully evoke various genuine elements of the Isaiah passage, although most do not embrace the full context; cf. helpfully 176–79.

25. See Keener, *Acts,* 3:3083–84.

26. Indeed, Hannah was not even praying for revival, but simply for a son and thus vindication; but God is near the humble (1 Sam 1:10–11). In Luke-Acts, outpourings of the Spirit often followed prayer (Acts 1:14; 4:31; see the principle in Luke 11:13).

27. See here McKay, "Veil," 64–68. McKay's PhD was from Cambridge. Cf. also Moore, "Fire of God," 114–17.

28. Although concrete ancient sources are best, contemporary Middle Eastern culture normally remains closer to ancient Middle Eastern culture than is Western culture (Bailey, *Peasant Eyes,* xv). Some common elements also dominate much of Mediterranean culture (Gilmore, "Shame," 3, 16), though significant variation must not be overlooked (Eickelman, *Middle East,* 154). Nevertheless, subsequent movements, not least monotheistic religions, have reshaped local cultures (see Stanley Brandes in Brandes, "Reflections," 126, on Mediterranean culture; Eickelman, *Middle East,* 9–10, 97, on the Middle East).

29. Cf. McKay, "Veil," 66–67, on "shared experience"; cf. Pinnock, "Work of Spirit," 246, on being unable to understand Scripture's words adequately without understanding "the realities that are behind them"; Ellington, "Authority," 162, on Scripture being "*re-experienced* in the same setting in which it was originally formed, that is, in the community of faith." On Dilthey, see discussion on p. 290 in the present book; cf. p. 45, 316n4. For readings from a traditional Middle Eastern perspective, see, e.g., Kenneth Bailey, *Poet;* idem, *Peasant Eyes.*

30. McKay, "Veil," 68. Cf., for example, how witnessing miracles changed much of the worldview of Walter Wink, a member of the Jesus Seminar (Wink, "Write," esp. 4–6).

31. McKay, "Veil," 69, citing 1 Cor 13:9; 14:32.

32. E.g., in fall 1978 I gave a prophecy to a divorcée for whom my words meant more than I could have imagined (she informed me only afterward of her status); see Keener and Keener, *Impossible Love,* 24–25.

33. On humility before God in reading, see, e.g., Mulholland, *Shaped,* 59; for this insistence in early Pentecostalism, see Oliverio, *Hermeneutics,* 91 (D. W. Kerr's "poor in spirit").

34. With e.g., Archer, *Hermeneutic,* 23–29, following George Marsden and others; Grey, *Crowd,* 26.

35. Cf., e.g., the early Methodist who reportedly hurled her cousin's cards into the fire, provoking him to heed God's call (Wigger, *Saint,* 44).

36. Note the case for many healings today, e.g., Währisch-Oblau, "Healthy," 97; Chevreau, *Turnings,* 16–17; MacNutt, *Healing,* 26–27; Bomann, *Faith in Barrios;* idem, "Salve." For revivals especially flourishing in times of social upheaval, see Shaw, *Awakening,* 25–28.

37. See, e.g., Noll, *History,* 167; Wolffe, *Expansion,* 58–61.

38. See, e.g., Noll, *History,* 174–75; Wolffe, *Expansion,* 71–78.

39. Shaw, *Awakening,* 22.

40. Shaw, *Awakening,* 22–23. On Pandita Ramabai and her ministry, see, e.g., Burgess, "Pandita Ramabai"; Arles, "Study"; idem, "Appraisal"; Frykenberg, *Christianity in India,* 382–410.

41. See Shaw, *Awakening,* 33, 39.

42. As John Wesley noted, God's Spirit produces diligence and thrift, which leads to wealth, but in time this upward mobility can produce generations dependent on prior generations' blessings. If God has blessed some of us with upward mobility that our forebears in revival lacked, we must use it wisely (1 Tim 6:17–19); we dare not risk losing the special connection with the poor and broken. We may serve and empower them, but we are also blessed by them; they have something that we too need. Cf. Sanders, *Margins.*

43. Noll, *History,* 288.

44. Shaw, *Awakening,* 163–65.

45. In light of the global pentecostal population, Waddell, "Hearing," 187, affirms Pente-

costal readings as "from the bottom or from the margins," as with liberation theology, citing helpfully Johns, *Pentecostal Formation.*

46. The chart here follows my class notes, but cf. helpfully Danker, *New Age,* 24.

47. For the risk to Joseph of Arimathea's life, see Keener, *John,* 2:1160–61.

48. Joseph of Arimathea may have been (Matt 27:57; John 19:38) or become a disciple, but it is unlikely that he followed Jesus during the majority of his ministry in Galilee.

49. See, e.g., Wyckoff, *Pneuma,* 18, though contrasting the approach of Aquinas (19–20). The particular expression reflects Anselm.

50. Wyckoff, *Pneuma,* 22–23; Wengert, "Luther," 110. So also the Westminster Confession, as noted in Wyckoff, *Pneuma,* 31.

51. Edwards, "Revolution," 53, quoting one of Luther's final writings.

52. Wyckoff, *Pneuma,* 47. For God's Word coming to humans as "the subjective reality of revelation," Wyckoff, *Pneuma,* 48, cites Barth, *Church Dogmatics,* 1.2.1–25, 203–40, 717.

53. See esp. Part III.

54. Pentecostals read Scripture not exclusively for information, "but to meet God in the text"—see Davies, "Read as Pentecostal," 251–52 (also cited in Anderson, *Ends of Earth,* 122); Waddell, "Hearing," 184; Thomas, "Spirit Is Saying," 122; Archer, *Hermeneutic,* 251; Grey, *Crowd,* 3, 10, 15–21, 161; Martin, "Psalm 63," 280–81, citing a range of sources, including early Pentecostal figures and Green, *Theology,* 289.

55. Oliverio, *Hermeneutics,* 97, on D. W. Kerr.

56. The same devotional desire appears in other non-Pentecostal but Spirit-led writers such as R. A. Torrey and A. W. Tozer; see also Mickelsen, *Interpreting the Bible,* 365–66; Mulholland, *Shaped,* 21, 95; Green, *Practicing Theological Interpretation,* 5.

57. Mulholland, *Shaped,* 123; cf. Wesley on reading to discover God's will, 127.

58. See the complaint of Chan, *Grassroots Asian Theology,* 22–27. This observation is not meant to diminish the value of the academic voices; the grassroots may be influenced by popular Western or other ideologies that are unhelpful. It is simply a reminder that we must use our gifts as servants, not lording it over God's flock.

59. Cf. discussion of the latter rain motif in Archer, *Hermeneutic,* 136–50. For the shift from Latter Rain to more dispensational approaches, see, e.g., Oliverio, *Hermeneutics,* 114; Myer Pearlman more helpfully pointed toward the biblical metanarrative of redemption (Oliverio, *Hermeneutics,* 122–23, 129).

60. For their traditional self-understanding as eschatological, see, e.g., Anderson, *Ends of the Earth,* 61; Menzies, *Anointed,* 57; Blumhofer, *Sister,* 209; Waddell, "Hearing," 179–80, 187; Martin, "Psalm 63," 284; for the connection between their "missionary enthusiasm" and their "sense of eschatological destiny," see Anderson, *Ends of the Earth,* 62. Eschatological urgency unfortunately also reduced early missionary preparation, however (84). Some, such as Aimee Semple McPherson, viewed women preachers as "a legitimate part of the end-times church" (Blumhofer, *Sister,* 195); cf. Acts 2:17–18.

61. In recent centuries, see, e.g., Luther and early Puritans in Kyle, *Last Days,* 55, 61–62, 65; Gritsch, "Reformer," 35; early Baptists in Hayden, "Walk," 8; Edwards in "God's Wonderful Working," 15; Booth in Green, "Booth's Theology," 28; the Jesus movement in Eskridge, *Family,* 85–87; cf. Joseph Smale in Robeck, *Mission,* 83.

62. Although Eph 4:11–13 is always the ideal, the importance of revealing God's wisdom in the church "now" (3:10) may suggest that God plans for this ideal to be exemplified at least

once in this age, perhaps in circumstances such as those in which God's ideal people are depicted in Rev 12:10–11, 17.

63. See Keener, *Mind,* chap. 5. Cf. Mulholland, *Shaped,* 135.

64. See Keener, *Mind,* chap. 6. On 1 Cor 2:10–16, see also, briefly, Wyckoff, *Pneuma,* 142; Ervin, "Hermeneutics," as cited in Spawn and Wright, "Emergence," 6; esp. Pinnock, "Work of Spirit," 240. For reading Scripture from new "perceptual frameworks," cf. also Mulholland, *Shaped,* 33.

65. For this image for eschatological tribulation, cf. 1QHa XI, 3–18; *1 En.* 62:4; *b. Sanh.* 98b; *Šabb.* 118a; see origins for eschatological travail, for the Messiah and/or the community, in Isa 26:17–19; 66:7–8; Mic 5:2–4. The traumatic image of "birth pangs" develops judgment language (Ps 48:6; Isa 13:8; 21:3; 26:17; 42:14; Jer 4:31; 6:24; 13:21; 22:23; 30:6; 31:8; 48:41; 49:22, 24; 50:43; Hos 13:13; also Glasson, *Advent,* 175; cf. further 1QHa XI, 8, 12; XIII, 30–31; 4Q429 1 IV, 3). See also Keener, "Charismatic Reading."

66. In this section I am adapting Keener, *Acts,* 1:877–80.

67. Cf. Joel 4:1 LXX (ET 3:1). With, e.g., Ridderbos, "Speeches of Peter," 13; Horton, *Spirit,* 146. Greco-Roman audiences would also be familiar with the practice of adapting quotations to clarify their intention (Stanley, *Language of Scripture,* 291; cf. 335, 337, 342–44).

68. Also 11Q13 II, 4; *1 En.* 27:3–4 (*after* the final judgment); cf. 4Q509 II, 19; *2 Bar.* 76:5; *Test. Zeb.* 8:2; 9:5. Jewish interpreters of this era would also so understand Deut 4:30; 31:29; cf. others' restoration in Jer 48:47; 49:39. The "last days" or "last generation" is a natural feature of the pesharim (e.g., 1QpHab I, 2; II, 5–6).

69. Also 1Q22 I, 7–8; 4QpNah 3–4 III, 3; 4Q162 II, 1 in its context; 4Q163 23 II, 3–11; 4Q176 12 + 13 I, 9; 4QMMT C.21–22; *Test. Dan* 5:4; *Test. Zeb.* 9:5; *Test. Iss.* 6:1; cf. *Sib. Or.* 5.74; *Apoc. Elij.* 1:13.

70. See *Test. Iss.* 6:1; also 1Q22 I, 7–8; 4QpNah 3–4 III, 3; 4Q162 II, 2–7; 4Q390 1 7–9; *1 En.* 91:7; *3 En.* 48A:5–6; *4 Ezra* 14:16–18; *Sib. Or.* 5.74; *Test. Naph.* 4:1; *Test. Dan* 5:4; *Test. Zeb.* 9:5; *Sipre Deut.* 318.1.10; *b. Sanh.* 97a; *Pesiq. Rab Kah.* 5:9. Cf. perhaps 4Q501, line 3.

71. Wilson, *Pastoral Epistles,* 16, thinks that 1 Timothy employs "last days" in the Lukan manner.

72. As in the Qumran scrolls (e.g., 4Q162 I–II, esp. II, 1–10; 4Q163 23 II, 10–11). The Qumran scrolls used their pesher interpretation (in psalms, etc.) to apply much of Scripture to the special situation of the last days, a special era of fulfillment (e.g., 4Q162 I–II; 4Q176 12 + 13 I, 7–9; 4QpNah 3–4 IV, 3; see also *1 En.* 108:1); Peter does the same, believing the time of fulfillment has come (Acts 3:18–26). God would expose the wickedness of Israel's compromising leaders in the end time (4QpNah 3–4 III, 3). For "charismatic exegesis" in Qumran texts, see Wright, "Jewish Interpretation," 75–91.

73. Cf. similarly Paul's expectation of prophecy until Christ's return in 1 Cor 13:8–13, which I discuss briefly in Keener, *Corinthians,* 109–10.

74. That is, in modern theological terms, Luke cannot be a cessationist regarding this prophetic gift of the Spirit. For this passage and the expectation of continuing signs, see also Menzies, "Paradigm."

75. It is more likely that the idea of prophecy's cessation derived from reading into the NT the observed experience of Christians in some subsequent eras, where prophecy was either rare or demonstrably errant. Even this observation must be balanced, however, by the frequency of prophetic phenomena in many other eras of Christian history, including its current frequency in charismatic circles and especially in some regions of the world.

76. See, e.g., Shogren, "Prophecy."

77. See, e.g., Cook, *Interpretation,* 77–79.

78. John Orme Mills, as cited in Land, *Pentecostal Spirituality,* 62, and in Robinson, *Divine Healing,* 39.

79. See the influential works Faupel, *Everlasting Gospel;* Althouse, *Spirit.*

80. See Dayton, *Roots,* 145, 149–52 (distinguishing various contributing threads); King, *Disfellowshiped,* 59–60. Dayton is probably correct that dispensational influences were strongest in the parts of the movement most directly impacted by rising fundamentalism (see *Roots,* 146).

81. Dayton, *Roots,* 145.

82. See again Althouse, *Spirit.* Most organizers of the Assemblies of God at Hot Springs, Arkansas, for example, had Scofield Reference Bibles; for this work's influence on the early Assemblies of God, see, e.g., Oss, "Hermeneutics of Dispensationalism," 2, as cited in Campos, "Tensions," 149n14. For a temporary controversy about the book, see McGee, *People of Spirit,* 192–93.

83. R. A. Torrey learned this from the example of George Müller (so King, *Moving Mountains,* 28). On the nature of faith, see also Moreland and Issler, *Faith.*

84. I speak here of "hard" cessationists in a sort of idealized sense. In practice, most cessationists, at least among my friends that I know well, rule out only regular supernatural giftings, not special divine activity. I view this stance as inconsistent biblically and philosophically, but those who hold it are not all "hard" cessationists. Still, even ruling out continuing prophetic messages suggests a radical break with the practice of the entire biblical tradition, without biblical forewarnings of such. Such a break would simplify addressing the frailty of persons who claim such messages and absolve us of the need for discernment, but that is not the biblical approach to such problems.

85. Our language of "testaments" is really a misnomer, since most of the material in both sections is narrative not directly part of the covenants per se. For one survey of approaches to the relationship between the "testaments," see Baker, *Testaments,* 34–176.

86. Admittedly, the instrumental-music cessationists do produce many of the best acapella singers. And if the power grid ever goes down, no one will be better prepared than the old order Amish.

87. See Noll, *Rise,* 190; less dramatically, see Mullin, *History,* 182–83; Sweeney, *Story,* 64; cf. other early Methodist figures in Bebbington, *Dominance,* 51; Wolffe, *Expansion,* 57–62, 70; Kidd, *Awakening,* 322; cf. also Baptists (eighty times over in 72 years, in Kidd and Hankins, *Baptists,* 77). Such figures characterize other periods of revival as well (see the sources cited in Keener, *Acts,* 1:998nn64–66), such as the Korean revival of 1907 (Lee, "Korean Pentecost," 81).

88. Keep in mind that Asbury was not a politically driven or financially endowed bishop; he rode thousands of miles a year to serve all the churches, for very small pay, for the Lord Christ.

89. From Francis Asbury's valedictory address of 1813, reproduced in *Christian History* 114 (2015): 39 ("The patriarch broods over his family's future"). Rejecting "the Catholic doctrine of the historic episcopacy," Asbury sought to return to the New Testament's "true primitive order," "an apostolic order of poverty and itinerancy" (Cracknell and White, *Methodism,* 48).

Notes to Chapter 3

1. Adapted from Keener, *Acts*, 1:842–44.

2. E.g., Moule, *Messengers*, 23; Bruce, *Commentary*, 64; Dominy, "Spirit, Church, and Mission"; Smith, "Hope after Babel?"; Spencer, *Acts*, 32–33; Chéreau, "Babel à la Pentecôte"; Venter, *Reconciliation*, 155; Turner, "Experience," 32; Kim, "Mission," 40; Nasrallah, "Cities," 557; Asamoah-Gyadu, "Hearing"; Wackenheim, "Babel"; cf. B. H. Carroll (1916) in Barr, Leonard, Parsons, and Weaver, *Acts*, 120.

3. Cyril Jer. *Cat. Lect.* 17.16–17 (Martin, *Acts*, 24); Arator *Acts* 1 (Martin, *Acts*, 26); Bede *Comm. Acts* 2.4 (trans. L. Martin, *Bede*, 29; also Martin, *Acts*, 23); see other patristic sources in Marguerat, *Actes*, 81n45. Early Pentecostals also read their experience as a reversal of Babel (Anderson, *Pentecostalism*, 44).

4. See, e.g., Keener, "Tongues," 181–82. González, *Acts*, 39, emphasizes here a "second Babel" with a new scattering, underlining appreciation for cultural diversity as opposed to a demand for uniformity (e.g., by causing everyone to understand Aramaic). Cf. more fully Wagenaar, "Kumba." Similarly, Macchia, "Babel," envisions a partial reversal but a partial analogy: "a promise/fulfilment relationship between these events, in which only the folly and threat of Babel is reversed at Pentecost but not God's providential will and purposes" (51).

5. For this connection in the church's theology (whether or not Luke noticed it), see, e.g., Cloete and Smit, "Name Called Babel." Arrington, *Acts*, 20, treats the allusion as a strong but uncertain possibility.

6. Various scholars, including Polhill, *Acts*, 105; cf. Barrett, *Acts*, 112.

7. Compare unity of mind in Acts 1:14; 2:46 with "one tongue and voice" in the LXX of Gen 11:1; "every nation under heaven" in Acts 2:5 with "all the earth" in Gen 11:1, 8; the elaboration of Mesopotamian peoples not emphasized elsewhere in Luke-Acts in Acts 2:9 with Gen 11:2, 9; perhaps the honoring of Jesus's name (Acts 2:21, 38) with those honoring their own in Gen 11:4 (a deliberate contrast with 12:2). Luke's verb in 2:6 for the crowd's response in 2:6 likely alludes to language in the common Greek version of the Babel narrative (Gen 11:7, 9; Wis 10:5; cf. also the frequent use of the terms in Philo *Conf.* 1, 9, 43, 84, 109, 152, 158, and 183–98; esp. 168, 182, 189, 191; Josephus *Ant.* 1.117). Here it is the audience rather than the language that is confused, but in view of other allusions, this is likely an additional example (perhaps inverting the identity of those confused, to highlight reversal).

8. Also Goulder, *Type and History*, 158; Scott, "Horizon," 530.

9. For later Jewish comments on the Babel narrative, see, e.g., Jos. *Ant.* 1.116–18; *L.A.B.* 7; *Sib. Or.* 3.98–107; 8.4–5; 11.9–13; *y. Meg.* 1:9, §1.

10. Inowlocki, "Rewriting," finds such a rewriting, for a Gentile audience, in Josephus (who here, as elsewhere, opposes tyranny and prefigures God's judgment on Jerusalem).

11. 1QM X, 14.

12. See, e.g., Safrai, "Synagogue," 927 (doubting any fixed sequence in the early period); Perrot, "Lecture de la Bible" (some principles of later lectionaries used even if the cycle was not yet in use).

13. See Charnov, "Shavuot"; cf., cautiously, Moule, *Messengers*, 23.

14. Cf. the end of Babel's curse in the day of judgment (*Jub.* 10:22), but we should probably not read much into this.

15. Adapted from Keener, *Acts*, 1:823–30; see also more fully, Keener, "Evidence"; also Keener, *Questions*, 69; idem, *Gift*, 180; idem, "Tongues," 177–78, 180–81, 183–84; cf. Wrede,

Secret, 232; Lenski, *Acts,* 62–63; Wikenhauser, *Apostelgeschichte,* 38; Fitzmyer, *Acts,* 239; York, *Missions,* 80, 185–86; and esp. Ladd, *Young Church,* 56; Dupont, *Salvation,* 52, 59; Stendahl, *Paul,* 118–19; Kilgallen, *Commentary,* 16; Kim, "Mission," 37–40.

16. Only at Pentecost do others present understand the languages; the speakers may experience tongues as affective worship, as in Paul.

17. Barrett, *Acts,* 2:lxxxiv.

18. Bruce, *Commentary,* 56.

19. Cf. Spencer, *Acts,* 32–33.

20. For the diversity of revivals, see, e.g., Shaw, *Awakening, 203–6.*

21. For its earlier occurrence, see, e.g., Anderson, *Pentecostalism,* 24–25, 36–37; Hinson, "History of Glossolalia," 57–66.

22. Robeck, "Seymour," 81–89; McGee, "Hermeneutics," 108–10; idem, *Miracles,* 135 (Abrams); Wacker, *Heaven,* 41; Opp, *Lord for Body,* 152 (on Bosworth); Williams, "Acts," 219 (on Seymour); Alexander, *Fire,* 130–31 (Seymour); cf. Robeck, *Mission,* 178; Jacobsen, *Thinking in Spirit,* 10; Kalu, *African Pentecostalism,* 20 (on Abrams). Seymour may have played down the role of tongues rather than denied their inclusion in Spirit baptism (Jacobsen, *Thinking in Spirit,* 78; Tarr, *Foolishness,* 379–80); in keeping with his Holiness background, he connected tongues more closely to ethics (see Brathwaite, "Tongues").

23. In the early period, note esp. Pandita Ramabai (Burgess, "Evidence," 33–34; McGee, "Hermeneutics," 107–8; Hudson, "Strange Words," 67; Burgess, "Pandita Ramabai," 195) as well as Minnie Abrams, mentioned above. Many Pentecostal movements in Europe and Latin America are less insistent on tongues than are many other traditional Pentecostals (Spittler, "Glossolalia," 339).

24. Blumhofer, *Sister,* 208–14. In fact, many Pentecostal leaders and scholars have emphasized from the beginning that the focus should not be tongues but empowerment (Wyckoff, "Baptism," 450, and sources he cites; Robeck, *Mission,* 163 [on Seymour]; Jacobsen, *Thinking in Spirit,* 75–80 [esp. on Seymour], 190–91, 287, 289, 354).

25. See McGee, "Hermeneutics," 107–10; Jacobsen, *Thinking in Spirit,* 293, 314–15, 395n4. Doctrinal freedom on issues secondary to the gospel characterized early Pentecostalism (see Lederle, *Treasures,* 29–31, esp. 29; see also Hollenweger, *Pentecostals,* 32, 331–36).

26. See, e.g., Jacobsen, *Thinking in Spirit,* 62, 84, 95–98, 288–90; Johns, "New Directions"; Horton, *Spirit,* 157, 216–19, 259–60. This view was pioneered by Charles Parham (Jacobsen, *Thinking in Spirit,* 19, 48–49) and provided a definite social marker distinguishing Pentecostals from their Holiness kin (288; cf. this function of the early restorationist rhetoric, Nienkirchen, "Visions"), though preoccupation with such "evidence" may reflect modernist epistemological assumptions (Smith, *Thinking,* 124n1). Some estimate that perhaps 35 percent of Pentecostals have prayed in tongues (Lederle, "Evidence," 136, though the more recent and extensive figures in *Landscape Survey,* 55, are closer to 50 percent), statistics probably comparable to first-generation Pentecostals as well (Wacker, *Heaven,* 41). To at least some degree, Edward Irving in the nineteenth century apparently associated tongues with baptism in the Spirit; see Dorries, "Irving and Spirit Baptism"; Strachan, *Theology of Irving;* cf. Synan, *Voices,* 85–87.

27. Lederle, "Evidence," 131ff.

28. In 1918, D. W. Kerr's insistence on tongues as the initial evidence won out against F. F. Bosworth's more open view that it was an evidence but not the only one, leading to Bosworth's departure for the CMA (Oliverio, *Hermeneutics,* 101n68); today's climate might have been more inclusive on this point.

29. Menzies, "Tongues," on D. W. Kerr; this left room for some early Pentecostal leaders such as J. Roswall Flower, whose tongues experience followed his Spirit baptism experience by weeks or even months (185–86n30; cf. also E. N. Bell's flexibility in 184–85n29).

30. Severus of Antioch, in *Cat. Act.* 10.44 (Martin, *Acts,* 140), doubted that miracles and such evidences remained necessary in his own day, but he contended that in apostolic times, "those who received holy baptism both spoke with tongues and prophesied in order to prove that they had received the Holy Spirit." Cf. Aug. *Retract.* 1.13.7 (PL 32:604–5, cited in Kelsey, *Healing,* 185); McDonnell and Montague, *Initiation,* 314 (cited in McGee, "Miracles and Mission").

31. E.g., Menzies, *Empowered,* 254–55. From this he further infers that those who receive the gift of the Spirit "should *expect* to manifest tongues" (255).

32. Dunn, *Jesus and Spirit,* 189. The opposite could be argued in 8:17 (see Keener, *Acts,* 2:1520–27). But either argument is ultimately from silence.

33. Dunn, *Jesus and Spirit,* 189–90. Cf. Catholic scholar Haya-Prats, *Believers,* 120: "Luke presents glossolalia as the typical manifestation of the Spirit."

34. The logical distinction between premise *a* necessarily leading to conclusion *b* and the reverse (*b* leading to conclusion *a*) would not have been lost on ancient thinkers (e.g., Hermog. *Issues* 51.16–22; 52.1–4; Porph. *Ar. Cat.* 90.12–91.12; cf. another sort of distinction in Epict. *Diatr.* 1.8.14).

35. Dunn, *Jesus and Spirit,* 190–91; cf. similarly Turner, *Power,* 446–47 (who is also skeptical that early Jewish sources expected *any* particular "initial evidence," 448–49); Talbert, *Acts,* 33, 99; Twelftree, *People,* 98–99 (any ecstatic or supernatural manifestations). Cf. Nigerian Baptist scholar Caleb Olapido, who notes that when Yoruba Christians are filled with the Spirit, "ecstatic utterances are common" (*Development,* 108, 112–13, in Barr, Leonard, Parsons, and Weaver, *Acts,* 133).

36. Of course, prophetic empowerment should presumably lead at least to prophetic witness, and cross-cultural empowerment should lead to participation in cross-cultural witness. Luke does often report prophetic evidences of this empowerment at the time of the experience, but not in every case. Views thus vary depending on what we make of the incidents where Luke does not report any charismatic phenomena at the moment of reception. Each side, in a sense, argues what to make of certain cases of silence. It is possible that charismatic phenomena at the point of experience represent for Luke an *ideal* pattern; but Luke does not impose his ideal patterns strictly (compare, e.g., Acts 2:38 with 10:44–48).

37. See Keener, "Tongues."

38. E.g., Anderson, *Pentecostalism,* 33–34; McGee, *Miracles,* 61–76; and some sources in the following note on early Pentecostal views of xenoglossia.

39. See McGee, "Hermeneutics," 102; idem, "Strategy," 52–53; Goff, "Theology of Parham," 64–65; Jacobsen, *Thinking in Spirit,* 25, 49–50, 74, 76, 97; Robeck, *Mission,* 41–42, 236–37, 243, 252; see esp. McGee, "Shortcut"; idem, "Logic"; Anderson, "Signs," 195–99. Before Pentecostalism, some evangelical missions advocates, such as A. B. Simpson, the early Christian and Missionary Alliance, and three members of the famous "Cambridge Seven," sought missionary tongues, apparently in most cases without success (McGee, "Radical Strategy," 77–78, 80–83).

40. See esp. Parmentier, "Zungenreden"; Talbert, *Corinthians,* 90 (citing Iren. *Her.* 5.6.1; Chrys. *Hom. 1 Cor.* 29, on 12:1–11; though noting that this is less common than the glossolalia interpretation, Iren. *Her.* 5.6.1; Tert. *Marc.* 5.8).

41. For some of the exceptions, see Keener, *Acts,* 1:829; May, *Witnesses.*

42. E.g., Wacker, *Heaven*, 47–51; McGee, *People of Spirit*, 77–78; Hudson, "Strange Words," 61–63; Anderson, "Points," 167; Ma, "Eschatology," 100 (noting Goff, *Fields*, 16). Noted leader G. B. Cashwell apparently left the movement in part because xenolalia failed in mission (Alexander, *Fire*, 141). Note especially the shift in the Indian mission context, after which Garr emphasized that the point was not tongues themselves but how they symbolized baptism in the Spirit (McGee, "Calcutta Revival," 138–39). The xenolalia interpretation "was already waning by 1906," shortly after the movement's beginning (McGee, "Strategies," 204).

43. Anderson, *Pentecostalism*, 190.

44. Some others have recognized the connection, however, notably including Miller, *Tongues Revisited*. McGee, *Miracles*, 102, notes that this emphasis did continue. Certainly Global mission has remained a central issue in Pentecostal theology (with Ma, "Studies," 62–63); this emphasis has undoubtedly spurred Pentecostalism's massive growth over the course of the twentieth century.

45. Cf. at greater length Keener, *Questions*, 66–76, esp. 69; and esp. idem, *Gift*, 177–85, esp. 180; and idem, "Tongues."

46. Chrys. *Hom. 1 Cor.* 35.1 (Bray, *Corinthians*, 138); on the Corinthians exalting it as the first gift, see also Theodoret *Comm. 1 Cor.* 251. Theodoret (*Comm. 1 Cor.* 240) believes that these gifts were common in former days and reproves the Corinthians for abusing the gifts by showing off instead of edifying the church.

47. Bede *Comm. Acts* 2.3A (Martin, *Acts*, 22). Cf. Leo the Great *Sermons* 75.2 (Martin, *Acts*, 23): in Acts 2:4, "the particular voices of each distinct people become familiar in the mouth of the church." Origen *Comm. Rom.* on Rom 1:14 (CER 1:128, 130; Bray, *Romans*, 28) concludes that Paul was indebted to all peoples because he had received their languages (1 Cor 14:18). Cf. Wesley on tongues at Pentecost as a foretaste of peoples of all languages worshiping God (Wesley, *Notes*, 396, cited in McGee, *Miracles*, 61). Much more recently, see, e.g., Packer, *Acts*, 27: "The gift of tongues (*glossolalia*) was symbolic of the world-wide work they were to do (1:8)."

48. See more fully Keener, "Tongues."

49. E.g., Bediako, "African Culture," 120 (for translation in the vernacular); González, *Months*, 18; Solivan, *Spirit*, 112–18; Míguez Bonino, "Acts 2," 163–64; cf. Keener, "Acts 2:1–21," 526–27; idem, "Diversity"; Marguerat, *Actes*, 81; at length, cf. Harms, *Paradigms*. This application was also important in the early-twentieth-century Azusa Street Revival's application of Acts (e.g., Robeck, *Mission*, 88, 137–38; testimony in Horton, *Corinthians*, 66n29; cf. Synan, *Movement*, 80, 109–11, 165–69, 172, 178–79, 182–83, 221; Synan, "Seymour," 778–81; idem, "Legacies," 148–49; Lovett, "Holiness-Pentecostalism," 83; Daniels, "Differences"; Jacobsen, *Thinking in Spirit*, 63, 260–62). Ethnic and class reconciliation is a natural application of the passage (e.g., Yong, *Spirit Poured*, 94, 169–73; Park, *Healing*, 130–32; Keener, "Acts 2:1–21," 526–27; Williams, "Acts," 219–20 [noting also failures]), and was so applied at Azusa Street (Yong, *Spirit Poured*, 183) and in early Indian Pentecostalism, although the ethnic or caste status quo often quickly reasserted itself (Yong, *Spirit Poured*, 56–57); for ethnic reconciliation in a different revival in India in 1921, see Hickson, *Heal*, 62, 64, 66. In South Africa, see LaPoorta, "Unity," cited in Tarr, *Foolishness*, 379–80.

50. For William Seymour's multicultural vision, see *The Apostolic Faith* 1 (1, 1906): 1, cited in Waddell, "Hearing," 20; cf. Seymour on speaking "all the languages of the world" in Robeck, *Mission*, 162. Bartleman, *Azusa Street*, 54, famously noted that "The 'color line' was washed away in the blood"; but for the violent response from Jim Crow segregationists that motivated some changes, cf. Bosworth, "Beating."

51. Cf. 2 Macc 4:10, 13, 15; 6:9; 11:24; see Keener, *Acts,* 2:1253–59. For archaeological evidence for Diaspora Jews settling in Jerusalem, see Safrai, "Relations," 193–94.

52. Fitzmyer, *Acts,* 350; see esp. Mussies, "Greek," 1051–52, and the sources cited there. In these remaining paragraphs of this section I adapt Keener, *Acts,* 2:1287.

53. Cf. some Greek names among "the rich and well-educated" (Williams, "Names," 109), but one's class would not provide all seven with Greek names unless they really were Hellenists, which fits the point of the story (Acts 6:9).

54. Leon, *Jews of Rome,* 107–8; also Lung-Kwong, *Purpose,* 102–3.

55. *Let. Aris.* 47–50. Cohen, "Names of Translators," views Persian names as a mark of the transition from a Persian to a Hellenistic framework, but the document's Alexandrian provenance suggests Alexandrian expectation (at least in an early period) that Palestinian Jews had varied names.

56. See *y. Giṭ.* 1:1, §3.

57. With Hill, *Hellenists,* 47.

58. E.g., Klausner, *Jesus to Paul,* 289; Bruce, *Commentary,* 129; Dunn, *Acts,* 83.

59. Cf. Dunn, *Acts,* 84; Simon, *Stephen and Hellenists,* 7. Leaders in Jesus's movement can give more "ownership" of the movement (i.e., more participation in its leadership) to leaders of its culturally marginalized minorities when they too are led by God's Spirit; cf. González, *Acts,* 92–93.

60. With Larsson, "Hellenisten und Urgemeinde," this was more linguistic than due to a less law-faithful theology.

61. Cf. Hengel, *Jesus and Paul,* 26.

62. Cf. Pinnock, "Work of Spirit," 244: "The best safeguard" for Spirit hermeneutics "is the authority of the charismatic community." We should note, however, that some individual charismatic communities, pervaded by erroneous teachings and practices (e.g., extreme Word of Faith teachings), need more external input from others listening to God.

Notes to Chapter 4

1. Others have also noted that, given the makeup of global pentecostalism and the proportion of charismatics in the global church, a "pentecostal" reading should be a global reading (see, e.g., Waddell, "Hearing," 188).

2. For the Spirit and teaching, often concerning the right interpretation of Scripture, see, e.g., cf. Acts 20:28; Rom 7:6; 1 Cor 2:13; 12:8; 2 Cor 3:6, 15–18; Gal 3:2–5; 5:18, 22–23; Eph 3:5.

3. These next three chapters draw on my presentation to the interdisciplinary colloquium for biblical studies and intercultural studies PhD students, Asbury Theological Seminary, Oct. 10, 2014. It is published as Keener, "Scripture and Context," and I have condensed and adapted here with the permission of the editor, Robert Danielson, March 4, 2015. It includes material condensed from my *Miracles,* especially in the case-studies chapter. See also insights, including with regard to contextualizing the language of the Spirit, in Harrison, *Overwhelmed,* 194–96.

4. Wright, *Victory,* 359, citing his teacher, G. B. Caird.

5. Médine Moussounga Keener, Wilmore, KY, Sept. 19, 2012.

6. Ancient Mediterranean peoples also readily recognized that different peoples had different customs; see, e.g., Cornelius Nepos *Generals* pref. 5; Plutarch *Themistocles* 27.2–3; Sextus Empiricus *Eth.* passim.

7. This approach is more helpful than viewing texts not directly addressed to one as "dead language" (cf. the view noted in Patte, *Structural Exegesis*, 5). Besides relevance theory, some other approaches, more directly associated with cross-cultural communication, seek to translate larger cultural concepts. Although more recent and still less widely known in biblical studies than relevance theory, see very insightfully Zhang, "Ethics of Transreading"; Zhang works with biblical as well as other literary texts in various cultures.

8. Brown, *Scripture as Communication,* 27, notes that insofar as "texts are culturally located communicative acts, tied to a particular place and time (although with potential for speaking beyond that particularity), then questions of their authors and origins will be relevant for interpretation." For "A Communication Model of Hermeneutics," see Brown, *Scripture as Communication,* 29–56.

9. Some non-Pentecostals also expect Pentecostals to be particularly sympathetic to the dynamics of inspiration; see, e.g., Dunn, "Role," 155.

10. For Scripture being what unites all Christians, see Sunquist, *Century,* 181, commenting on Bartholomew I Ecumenical Patriarch of Constantinople, to the Synod of Bishops of the Catholic Church, "The Day Will Come When Our Two Churches Will Fully Converge" (Oct. 18, 2008).

11. See, e.g., Dunn, "Reconstructions," 296. The ancient Mediterranean world was a "high context" culture that presumed "a broadly shared, generally well-understood knowledge of the context of anything referred to in conversation or in writing" (Malina and Pilch, *Letters,* 5).

12. With, e.g., Vanhoozer, *Meaning,* 242; cf. 249 for Vanhoozer's application of the concepts of agency and emergence to how authorial intention brings meaning to linguistic signs. Cf. Hirsch, *Validity,* 23: "What has been denied here is that linguistic signs can somehow speak their own meaning—a mystical idea that has never been persuasively defended"; certainly they lack communicative value to one unfamiliar with the language (134).

13. Aune, *Dictionary of Rhetoric,* 317–18.

14. Brown, *Scripture as Communication,* 75–76.

15. See, e.g., Sperber and Wilson, *Relevance;* idem, "Précis"; Wilson and Sperber, "Representation"; in biblical studies, see, e.g., Jobes, "Relevance Theory"; Brown, *Scripture as Communication;* Green, "Relevance Theory." See further discussion in ch. 10.

16. Looking back on September 1911, that year included the following events: the Russian empire claimed Wrangel Island (Sept. 2); 200,000 Germans protested their government's militarization (Sept. 3); Mount Etna erupted, leaving an estimated 20,000 Italians homeless (Sept. 11); Boston's Cy Young achieved his final win (his 511th), setting a long-term record (Sept. 20); three hundred died when the French battleship *Liberté* exploded (Sept. 25); Italy fought Turkey and invaded Libya (Sept. 29); and seventy-eight died because a dam ruptured in Pennsylvania (Sept. 30; the actual death toll was likely much higher). Probably most dramatically, missions released news of the flooding of China's Yangtze River, a disaster that may have led to as many as 300,000 deaths.

17. Walton, *Thought,* 19, cites examples of "Kent State" (intelligible in the 1980s), the "Berlin Wall," or the "Iron Curtain."

18. This is the purpose for my Keener, *Background Commentary.*

19. See, e.g., Sider, *Cry Justice;* idem, *Fed;* in Wesley's teaching, see Jennings, *Good News.*

20. Some nineteenth-century abolitionist writers already highlighted these themes; see, e.g., Sunderlund, *Testimony;* idem, *Manual.*

21. I give more detail on this section of John in Keener, *John,* 1:584–628; more briefly, cf. Keener, "Invitations," here 195–202; most briefly, idem, "Reconciliation," 124–25.

22. E.g., *m. Abot* 1:5; *Ketub.* 7:6; *t. Shab.* 1:14; *b. Ber.* 43b, bar.; *Erub.* 53b; cf. Sir 9:9; 42:12; *T. Reub.* 6:1–2; *y. Abod. Zar.* 2:3, §1; *Sot.* 1:1, §7; among earlier Gentiles, cf. Euripides *Electra* 343–44; frg. 927; Theophrastus *Char.* 28.3; Livy 34.2.9; 34.4.1.

23. See, e.g., Justinian *Inst.* 2.10.6; Josephus *Ant.* 4.219; *m. Yeb.* 15:1, 8–10; 16:7; *Ketub.* 1:6–9; *t. Yeb.* 14:10; *Sipra Vayyiqra Dibura Dehobah* pq. 7.45.1.1. For qualifications of this general practice, see Ilan, *Women,* 163–66; Maccini, *Testimony,* 63–97.

24. For arguments against this, see Keener, *John,* 1:606–8.

25. Cf., e.g., Gen 24:11; Pizzuto-Pomaco, "Shame," 50; Eickelman, *Middle East,* 163.

26. E.g., Sus 7 (Dan 13:7 LXX); *Joseph and Asenath* 3:2/3; *Life of Aesop* 6; Virgil *Georg.* 3.331–34; Columella *Trees* 12.1; Plutarch *Them.* 30.1; Longus 1.8, 25; 2.4; Aulus Gellius 17.2.10; Suetonius *Aug.* 78.1; *Vesp.* 21; Pliny *Ep.* 1.3.1; 7.4.4; 9.36.5. For the heat, see, e.g., Aeschylus *Seven Ag. Thebes* 430–31; Sophocles *Antig.* 416; Apollonius Rhodius 2.739; 4.1312–13.

27. See, e.g., Menander *Dyskolos* 200; Arrian *Alex.* 2.3.4; Llewellyn-Jones, *Tortoise,* 88; cf. Cicero *Pro Caelio* 15.36; probably *Lam. Rab.* 1:1, §19.

28. Cf. consideration in Brant, "Husband Hunting," 211–16.

29. See *m. Nid.* 4:2; *t. Nid.* 5:1–2; cf. *m. Toh.* 5:8.

30. See Bruce, *History,* 37–38; cf. MacDonald, *Theology of Samaritans,* 15. The possible exception in Josephus *Ant.* 18.85–87 is apparently an eschatological prophet, who might be regarded as the prophet like Moses.

31. For the conflicts over these holy sites, see, e.g., Josephus *Ant.* 11.310, 346–47; 12.10, 259; 13.74; 18.10; *War* 1.62–63; 2.237.

32. For the fluid boundaries "between linguistic and cultural translation," see Thiselton, *Horizons,* 131.

33. For the return of the "implied author" in interpretation, see Brown, *Scripture as Communication,* 69–72; Osborne, *Spiral,* 393–95; more extensively, Vanhoozer, *Meaning,* 201–80. That biblical texts assume cultural information often obscure to modern readers is not a new insight; see, e.g., Ramm, *Interpretation,* 5–6, 98–99, 133–35, 150–57.

34. See, e.g., Gutt, *Relevance Theory,* 33; note above. As one critic suggests, "Every text, even the most elementary, implies information that it takes for granted and doesn't explain. Knowing such information is *the* decisive skill of reading" (Hirsch, *Literacy,* 112). This point is widely accepted by NT critics considering intertextuality with the OT.

35. Providing background on a popular level was why I offered the first "background commentary" in 1993 (see now *Background Commentary*); much will be available on an even more popular level in the *NIV Cultural Backgrounds Study Bible* (Grand Rapids: Zondervan, 2016).

36. For some earlier Western evangelical discussions of contextualization and hermeneutics see, e.g., the essays in Carson, *Interpretation;* Blomberg, "Globalization"; for some more recent contextual approaches, see, e.g., Jayakumar, *Mission Reader;* Satyavrata, *Witness.* For contextualization within the NT itself, see esp. thoroughly Flemming, *Contextualization.*

37. Some of these examples reflect a response paper I presented to the Institute of Biblical Research, Orlando, Nov. 1998. Exegesis is a cross-cultural act (deSilva, *Global Readings,* x).

38. See more fully my Keener, "Worship."

39. Nelson, "Temple," 147; Scott, "Pattern," 314; Badawy, *Architecture,* 176–77. In the Levant, see Gray, "Ugarit," 146–47; Dever, "Stratifications," 43.

40. Nelson, "Temple," 148–49; Badawy, *Architecture,* 177.

41. E.g., Kitchen, "Background," 8–11; Nelson, "Temple," 148–49; Meyers, *Exodus,* 220.

42. Haran, "Image," 202, 206.

43. See, e.g., Murray, *Splendor,* 183–84; Cassuto, *Exodus,* 322–23; Gurney, *Hittites,* 149–50; Meyers, *Exodus,* 221.

44. Also contrast the adjoining shrines for tutelary deities in many Egyptian temples (Badawy, *Architecture,* 180).

45. See Keener, "Tabernacle," 838; idem, "Worship," 130–31.

46. See, e.g., G. B. Caird, "The Exegetical Method of the Epistle to the Hebrews," *Canadian Journal of Theology* 5 (1, 1959): 44–51; cf. J. R. Sharp, "Philonism and the Eschatology of Hebrews: Another Look," *East Asia Journal of Theology* 2 (2, 1984): 289–98. Revelation is of course much more comparable to apocalyptic sources, and Hebrews to hellenistic Judaism (cf., e.g., Charles Carlston, "The Vocabulary of Perfection in Philo and Hebrews," 133–60 in *Unity and Diversity in New Testament Theology: Essays in Honor of George E. Ladd* [ed. Robert A. Guelich; Grand Rapids: Eerdmans, 1978]), but the author of Hebrews writes on a less sophisticated hellenistic level than does Philo.

47. For brief discussion, see, e.g., Keener, *Corinthians,* 80–81. Adapting to local customs could be viewed positively (Cornelius Nepos 7.11.2–6), because it was widely understood that customs varied in different lands (e.g., Apollonius Rhodius 2.1017). Aristocratic ideology regularly opposed, however, any pandering to the masses, which they viewed as demagoguery (e.g., Aristophanes *Acharnians* 371–73; *Frogs* 419; Aristotle *Pol.* 4.4.4–7, 1292a; Diodorus Siculus 10.7.3; Dionysius of Halicarnassus 7.8.1; 7.45.4; 7.56.2; Livy 6.11.7; Appian *R.H.* 2.9; 3.7.1). Philosophers and moralists who appealed to the masses thus risked alienating those of higher status (Aristotle *Rhet.* 2.20.5, 1393b; Liefeld, "Preacher," 39, 59, 162), which Paul probably did in Corinth (cf. Martin, *Slavery,* 92–116).

48. Adapting to one's audience was good rhetoric (Quintilian *Inst.* 3.7.24; for examples, see Suetonius *Rhet.* 6; Eunapius *Lives* 495–96).

49. See more fully my Keener, "Asiarchs."

50. See discussion in Keener, *Acts,* 3:3113–43, esp. 3141–43.

51. Cf. Charillus 2 in Plut. *Saying of Spartans, Mor.* 232C; Valerius Maximus 5.3.10–12; *m. Ketub.* 7:6; cf. in traditional Middle Eastern culture, Delaney, "Seeds," 42; Eickelman, *Middle East,* 165. See more fully Keener, *Paul,* 19–69; MacMullen, "Women in Public," 217–18; and esp. Keener, "Head Coverings."

52. Cf., e.g., Josephus *Ant.* 11.276; *2 Bar.* 39:4–7; *Sipre Deut.* 317.4.2; 320.2.3; *Tg. Neof.* 1 on Gen 15:12. Note also the probable interpretation of Daniel's Kittim in the latest Qumran texts as Romans; see Dupont-Sommer, *Writings,* 349; Vermes, "Elements." Earlier Greeks and Romans envisioned four eastern empires—though replacing Babylon with Assyria—before adding Rome; see Velleius Paterculus *Compendium* 1.6.6 (though some view this as a gloss); Mendels, "Empires"; cf. *Sib. Or.* 8.6–11.

53. E.g., *Sib. Or.* 5.143, 159–61; probably 1 Pet 5:13 (with Papias *frg.* 21.2); *4 Ezra* and *2 Bar.* passim. See discussion in, e.g., Gaster, *Scriptures,* 318; Kelly, *Peter,* 218; Kraybill, *Cult and Commerce,* 149–50.

54. See, e.g., *Sib. Or.* 2.18; 11.113–16; Dionysius of Halicarnassus *Ant. rom.* 4.13.2–3; Varro *Latin Language* 5.7.41; Ovid *Tristia* 1.5.69–70; Pliny *N.H.* 3.5.66; Silius Italicus 10.586; 12.608; Statius *Silvae* 2.3.21; 4.1.6–7; Symmachus *Ep.* 1.12.3. For the annual festival celebrating Rome's founding on these hills, see Suetonius *Dom.* 4.5.

55. E.g., Diodorus Siculus 1.4.3; Dionysius of Halicarnassus *Ant. rom.* 1.9.1; Cicero *Phil.* 4.6.15.

56. See, e.g., Bauckham, *Climax*, 352–66; esp. Pliny *N.H.* 37.78.204.

57. I elaborate these questions further in Keener, *Paul.*

58. Gutt, *Relevance Theory*, 73. Recontextualizing is usually more easily accomplished in contextual preaching than in translations that can quickly grow out of date (e.g., the colloquial *Cotton Patch Version*, helpful as it appears to have been for its setting).

59. With Hays, *First Corinthians*, 173, criticizing forced "relevance."

60. This is what we have endeavored to produce in the new *NIV Cultural Backgrounds Study Bible* (Grand Rapids: Zondervan, 2016). Because the cultural information itself is debatable, and interpretations of passages often dictate which ancient background is most relevant, tools such as this will remain works in progress and always secondary to a passage's immediate literary context. Nevertheless, our increasing cumulative resources for understanding ancient customs and ideas allows greater precision on many such matters today than has been possible since antiquity itself.

Notes to Chapter 5

1. Of course, most scholars are much more nuanced in their hermeneutic; see, e.g., Webb, *Slaves.*

2. E.g., Craigie, *Deuteronomy*, 289.

3. Carson, "Colonialism," 148–49; Lalitha, "Feminism," 82. For missionaries' insistence on local women covering their breasts, see also, e.g., Putney, *Missionaries*, 41.

4. Mayers, *Christianity Confronts Culture*, 204 (cf. 207).

5. The kiss was a form of greeting widely practiced in ancient Mediterranean culture (e.g., Homer *Od.* 21.224–27; Euripides *Androm.* 416; Virgil *Georg.* 2.523; Ovid *Metam.* 2.430–31; Artemidorus *Oneir.* 2.2; 1 Esd 4:47; *t. Hag.* 2:1); see in more detail Keener, "Kiss." For head coverings, see comment in the earlier note.

6. Diog. Laert. 6.2.34–35.

7. See, e.g., Keener, *Matthew*, 89–94; idem, "Marriage," on betrothal, dowry, and other customs.

8. See also, e.g., Brown, *Scripture as Communication*, 205.

9. Malina, *Anthropology*, 153.

10. See, e.g., discussion in Head, "Nazi Quest"; see selected documents in Solberg, *Church Undone.*

11. Cf. Bonk, "Missions." An increasing number of theologians today do write in the context of the new global church, e.g., Tennent, *Theology*; Yong with Anderson, *Renewing.*

12. On resurrection in the OT, see esp. Raharimanantsoa, *Mort*; for debates about Persian influence on this belief, see, e.g., Yamauchi, *Persia*, 303, 452–61.

13. Worshiping anyone other than God is prohibited; leading figures in Scripture did, however, employ many conventional expressions of honoring the deceased, at least at the time of their decease (Gen 23:2–20; Mark 14:8; John 19:38–40; Acts 8:2; 9:39).

14. Davies, "Read as Pentecostal," 257–58, rightly warns Pentecostals, who gravitate toward texts they find most spiritually meaningful personally, against this danger.

15. Fuller, "Analogy," 210, n. 13; cf. Ramm, *Interpretation*, 55–56; Grant and Tracy, *History*,

93. See, e.g., his preface to the first edition of the German NT (Mittelstadt, *Reading*, 1–2n3). Mark Allan Powell explains that, for Luther, Scripture's center was law (a way of reading that invited fear of God) and gospel (a way of reading that invited love of God; Powell, "Answers"; for Luther's hermeneutic and its place for the law rightly understood, cf. also Hafemann, "Yaein," 119; Barclay, *Gift*, 103, 340). For Reformation-period disputes over *which* texts remained binding, see Wengert, "Luther," 93.

16. With very few exceptions, Confucius's teachings resemble those of wise sages (such as Proverbs' Egyptian and Middle Eastern dialogue partners) more than those of a religious system antithetical to Christianity. In fact, traditional Confucian values, in contrast to, say, Western materialism, overlap with traditional biblical values at numerous points. See, e.g., studies by Yeo, *Musing*; Yeo, "*Xin*"; Ten Elshof, *Confucius*.

17. The Spirit (Acts 15:28) can also use "debate and deliberation" (cf. 15:6–7) to achieve outcomes (Boda, "Word and Spirit," 41). Qumran interpreters from the Second Temple period also believed that the Spirit worked in their process of interpretation; see Wright, "Jewish Interpretation," 91.

18. Not even rural Middle Eastern followers of Jesus today, although for many parts of the canon they may come closest.

19. See on the Jesuits, e.g., Spence, *Palace*; Neill, *History of Missions*, 162–65, 183–94; Tucker, *Jerusalem*, 59–66. On William Carey, see, e.g., *Christian History* 36 (1992); on Hudson Taylor, see, e.g., *Christian History* 52 (1996).

20. Isichei, *History*, 75. Missionaries who did not come from state churches that were aligned with colonial authorities also faced frequent opposition from these authorities, as did indigenous Christian movements like that of Prophet Braide in West Africa; cf., e.g., Sanneh, *West African Christianity*, 36, 167; Turaki, "Legacy"; Isichei, *History*, 233; Noll, *History*, 341. In different periods, church teaching was used for both colonialism and anticolonialism in different periods; cf., e.g., Stuart, *Missionaries*, 193–94; Sunquist, *Century*, 18–23.

21. See, e.g., accounts in Heaney, "Conversion to Coloniality," 73; Hawk and Twiss, "Indian," 47–54; Cuéllar and Woodley, "Mission," 63–69.

22. For instances of missions' linkage with colonial conquest, see, e.g., Dussel, *History*, 41–44, 59; Koschorke, Ludwig, and Delgado, *History*, 277–89; Irvin and Sunquist, *History*, 11–21; Deiros, "Cross."

23. See, e.g., Keener, "Asia and Europe," which suggests that Acts 16 depicts the reversal of Greek and Roman colonialism as an Asian faith moves into Europe.

24. See, e.g., Niang, *Faith*; deSilva, *Global Readings*.

25. See particularly helpfully Yeo, "Cultural Hermeneutics," 809: although all interpretations are welcome, some are more plausible, and these can be achieved best "through an ever-enlarging process of cross-cultural (global) interpretation."

26. Keener and Carroll, "Introduction," 1.

27. Keener and Carroll, "Introduction," 1. These statistics are from Mandryk, *Operation World*, 3, 5; Hanciles, *Beyond Christendom*, 121 (noting also that by 2050 "only about one-fifth of the world's Christians will be white"); see further Johnson and Ross, *Atlas*; Barrett, *World Christian Encyclopedia*; and the regular updates in *IBMR*.

28. Johnstone, *Future*, 113.

29. Johnstone, *Future*, 125. That Pentecostalism is already so culturally diverse also highlights the continuing need to encourage Pentecostal scholarship from a range of cultures (with Mittelstadt, *Reading*, 169).

30. Lee, "Future," 105. Cf. also Ma, "Shift," esp. 68–69, on how missiologists a century ago were utterly unprepared for a century of African and Pentecostal growth.

31. Mullin, *History*, 211; cf. similarly Noll, *Shape*, 32.

32. Berger, "Faces," 425. Cf. Tomkins, *History*, 220: "the fastest-growing form of Christianity ever." For massive church growth associated with miracles already by 1981, see De Wet, "Signs"; since then, e.g., Yung, "Integrity," 173–75; Moreland, *Triangle*, 166–67.

33. Johnson, Barrett, and Crossing, "Christianity 2010," 36; see further Johnson and Ross, *Atlas*, 102; more cautiously, Anderson, *Pentecostalism*, 11. Even if we count just one-third of this figure, the numbers are remarkable.

34. Laing, "Face," 165.

35. Cf., e.g., Nadar, "Feminism," from a South African Indian womanist perspective, noting that scholars must recognize the Spirit's role, engage widespread charismatic ideas, and seek to nurture true transformation.

36. Indeed, ethnocentric assumptions are embedded not only in some historical-critical interests but also in some of their approaches. Thus for example some suggest that the late dating of laws in the traditional Documentary Hypothesis reflects ethnocentric Hegelian assumptions rather than the actual development and dating of laws in ancient Near Eastern cultures; see, e.g., discussions in Harrison, *Introduction*, 21; Livingston, *Pentateuch*, 227, 229–30; cf. Whybray, *Making*, 46–47; Levinson, "Introduction," 10–11; cf. the philosophic underpinnings of W. de Wette's earlier nineteenth-century approach in Bartholomew, *Hermeneutics*, 214–15.

37. E.g., Keener, *Historical Jesus*; idem, "Assumptions." For Pentecostal and evangelical dialogue through historical-critical methodology, see also Cheung, "Study."

38. So also Martin, "Hearing," 212, very helpfully. As Bartholomew, *Hermeneutics*, 237, suggests, citing R. Alter and F. Kermode, historical criticism used extant biblical literature merely as ruins in which to excavate a more valuable real history behind them, a reconstruction generally eloquently informed by the interpreters' creative ingenuity.

39. For postcolonial criticism of the contexts in which traditional historical-critical methods originated, note observations by Segovia, *Decolonizing*, 119–32, as cited in Agosto, "Foreword," xiv. Many Western scholars today also challenge the objectivity of the historical-critical paradigm; see, e.g., the summary in Horrell and Adams, "Introduction," 42; Stanley, "Introduction," 3.

40. Lopez, "Visualizing," 76, citing Sugirtharajah, "Catching," 176–85; see also the concern in Heaney, "Conversion," 68–69, 77. Today many voices challenge dominant paradigms' pretensions to objectivity; see, e.g., Smith, "Tolerance"; Stanley, "Introduction," 3; Lee, "Nationalism," 223; Merrick, "Tracing."

41. Hays, *Reading Backwards*, xvi. Skeptical, speculative historical criticism and reconstruction tend to be antitextual; see Green, *Practicing Theological Interpretation*, 70. My historical Jesus work (Keener, *Historical Jesus*) drew heavily on Gospels research, but a survey of historical Jesus scholarship will reveal how much of it takes place without apparent cognizance of much published research on the Gospels.

42. See Frei, *Eclipse*, 239, 241–42; cf. 274.

43. A confusion unfortunately seriously reflected in Davies, "Read as Pentecostal," 252n10. Confusion might even be reflected in Hays's criticism of "modernist" interest in "a single clear and explicit 'original sense'" (Hays, *Reading Backwards*, 30), although I do agree with Hays's main point in his understanding of parable. The difference is clear in Green, *Practicing Theological Interpretation*, 45; Archer, *Hermeneutic*, 69 (in discussing Robert Traina's method), 221,

although at least some confusion may appear in 191. See helpfully the distinction between what Bartholomew calls "*thick* and *thin* notions of objectivity" (Bartholomew, *Hermeneutics,* 415). Archer's concern appears to be not with using cultural context to clarify the understanding of the text, but with focusing on the never fully recoverable and hypothetically reconstructed world behind the text (see Archer, *Hermeneutic,* 207).

44. Or, alternatively, to treating an arbitrarily selected English version, or all English versions (including conspicuously distorted ones such as Watchtower's version), as no less authoritative than the original text.

45. Watchman Nee in Kinnear, *Tide,* 152. Even some who do not share belief in spirits themselves argue that exorcism might constitute the most culturally sensitive therapy for those for whom possession is the most culturally intelligible explanation for their condition; see, e.g., Martínez-Taboas, "Seizures"; Hexham, "Exorcism"; Singleton, "Spirits," 478; Heinze, "Introduction," 14.

46. Thomas, "Women," 81, noting also (82) the need for academic reflection on the role of the Spirit in interpretation and paradigm shifts in hermeneutics. Cf. Cross, "Proposal," as cited in Cartledge, "Text-Community-Spirit," 132.

47. In Gen 26:29, Abimelech urges Isaac to swear not to harm them, just as they did not "touch" him but sent him away in peace; after making the covenant, they leave Isaac "in peace" (26:31). Their not "touching" him presumably refers to their not touching his wife sexually or harming either of them (26:11; the same verb appears in the other endangered matriarch accounts at 20:6, with a sexual sense, and in 12:17, quite differently for God striking the abusers with a plague). Their sending him away was not entirely friendly, however (26:16; cf. 26:20–21).

48. See, e.g., my discussion in Keener, "Reconciliation"; idem, "Invitations." One critic complained that I drew a general principle rather than a concrete application, but apparently did not read the entire article, which certainly gave concrete examples of both, as well as emphasizing justice alongside reconciliation. Finding a shared principle is relevant for making sure that one's application is truly analogous.

49. For Derrida, engaged in challenging conventional Western philosophy and ontotheology, there is nothing outside language, which is itself arbitrary (cf., e.g., Derrida, *Speech;* idem, *Writing;* Derrida and Stocker, *Derrida*). I concur that language is indeed socially constructed; nevertheless, it seeks to communicate referentially. For some biblical scholars' approach to deconstruction, see Crossan, "Metamodel"; also *Semeia*'s theme issue on "Derrida and Biblical Studies" (*Semeia* 23 [1982]); most helpfully, Moore, *Poststructuralism.*

50. See, e.g., Grunlan and Mayers, *Cultural Anthropology,* 75, 95, citing Chomsky, *Structures;* cf. Hirsch, *Validity,* 18–19; Spawn and Wright, "Cultivating," 193, following Vanhoozer, *Meaning,* 299–303. This observation is not intended to endorse structuralism, which deconstruction rightly criticized. Because of psychological research into how real readers experience texts, linguists have rejected structuralism and its immediate sequels (Malina, "Reading Theory Perspective," 13–14); for structuralism's antihistorical character, see the criticism in Kee, *Miracle,* 290–91; cf. Sanders, *Jesus and Judaism,* 128. For language's limits and texts deconstructing to some degree, see Dio Chrys. *Or.* 52.7 and examples in widely read ancient sources in Keener, *John,* 1:38–39, 901n19, and the rhetorical technique in Dio Chrys. *Or.* 11.

51. Derrida himself could acknowledge that language "works" for ordinary communication (Vanhoozer, *Meaning,* 211–12, though Vanhoozer also sees the irony of deconstructionist communication [266n21]; Smith, "Inc/arnation," 112–19 [as cited in Oliverio, *Hermeneutics,* 218–19]).

52. Hirsch, *Validity*, 10, complains that positing the text's autonomy from its author leaves the text meaning whatever it means to a given reader.

53. For examples of various readings from different social locations, see, e.g., Barreto, "Affects What I See"; Keener and Carroll, *Global Voices; Patte, Global Bible Commentary*. For the value of expanding the range of dialogue partners, see also Gross, *Preach,* 113; Brown, *Scripture as Communication*, 89–90; Klein, Blomberg, and Hubbard, *Introduction*, 148; Lines, "Readings"; even in group Bible study, in Fraser and Kilgore, *Friends,* 73.

54. See very helpfully Choi, "Hermeneutics," 114–17, on the hospitality and dialogue involved in multicultural hermeneutics.

55. Stanley Fish, for example, apparently values relativism; in the wake of Sept. 11, 2001, he opined that no universal standard of morality exists by which to evaluate either American democratic ideals or Al-Qaida's ideals (Fish, "Condemnation," as cited in Collins, *Babel,* 149–51). If texts could simply be read in any manner, however, repressive governments would not have to ban books (Davies, *Matthew,* 15).

56. Cf. Matt 23:8 (when we make disciples, it must be for Jesus, not for ourselves); 2 Cor 4:5.

57. On supernatural reports in Western church history, see Keener, *Miracles,* 1:359–425; 2:785–86, 875.

Notes to Chapter 6

1. Here I am selectively adapting various material from Keener, *Miracles,* 788–856, passim, with permission from Baker Academic.

2. Hiebert, "Excluded Middle," 43. This omission of the preternatural that he notes is traced more fully in Daston, "Marvelous Facts," 100–113.

3. Kemp, "Ravished," 75.

4. Pilch, *Visions,* 17.

5. Bourguignon, "Spirit Possession Belief," 18; cf. also idem, "Introduction," 17–19; Firth, "Foreword," ix; Lewis, *Ecstatic Religion,* 100–26; Chandra shekar, "Possession Syndrome," 80; Morsy, "Possession," 189; Boddy, "Spirit Possession," 409.

6. Bourguignon, "Spirit Possession Belief," 19–21; idem, "Appendix."

7. Ward, "Possession," 126; Pilch, *Dictionary,* 81–82.

8. See, e.g., Lewis, *Ecstatic Religion,* 44; cf. also Maquet, "Shaman," 3; Peters, *Healing in Nepal,* 11–16, 46–47, 50.

9. McClenon and Nooney, "Anomalous Experiences," 47.

10. Kim, "Reenchanted," 270–73.

11. Neill, "Demons," 161.

12. Escobar, *Tides,* 86.

13. Mbiti, *Religions,* 253–56.

14. Mensah, "Basis," 176.

15. Koschorke, Ludwig, and Delgado, *History,* 223–24; Hanciles, "Conversion," 170. Harris's ministry, though influenced by Methodism, ultimately also influenced African Pentecostalism (Ouédraogo, "Pentecostalism," 163).

16. E.g., Johnson, "Growing Church," 55–56; Pothen, "Missions," 305–8; Ma, "Encounter," 136; see more fully idem, *Spirit.*

17. E.g., De Wet, "Signs," 84–85; Koch, *Zulus,* 136–37, 143–44, 144–45, 147–48, 150, 153; Pothen, "Missions," 189; Park, "Spirituality," 52–53; Khai, "Pentecostalism," 269; Knapstad, "Power," 83–85; Tandi Randa, personal correspondence (May 26, 2012; May 13, 2014). Some converts have, however, retained significant values from their previous practice (Merz, "Witch," 203, 213).

18. For the prominence of spiritual power in African exegesis, see, e.g., LeMarquand, "Readings," 496–97.

19. Mchami, "Possession," 17; while conceding that East African interpretation could use more exegesis.

20. Stoller, "Eye," 110; as cited in Turner, "Advances," 41.

21. Turner, "Advances," 42.

22. Graduate Research Professor in anthropology at the University of Florida, visiting professor at the University of Chicago and University of California at Berkeley; and past president of the American Ethnological Society and of the Society for Applied Anthropology.

23. Kimball, "Learning," 188–92.

24. Kimball, "Learning," 189–90.

25. Turner, "Advances," 37. For other claims of apparitions, see McClenon, *Events,* xiii, 70, 72.

26. Turner, *Hands,* xxii; idem, *Experiencing Ritual,* 149, 159; idem, *Healers,* 1–23.

27. Idem, "Reality of Spirits" (from a pro-shamanist perspective).

28. Turner, *Experiencing Ritual,* 4.

29. Tippett, "Possession," 143–44. For a brief historical overview of anthropological approaches to spirit possession, see Prince, "Foreword," xi; Crapanzaro, "Introduction," 5–7; more thoroughly for recent studies, Boddy, "Spirit Possession," 410–14.

30. Bourguignon, *Possession,* 14. Some scholars warn of the impropriety of applying some Western diagnostic categories cross-culturally, since some behaviors considered disordered by therapists in one society may be norms in others (Hoffman and Kurzenberger, "Miraculous," 84–85).

31. Crapanzaro, "Introduction," 7 (emphasis his; cited also by others, e.g., Davies, *Healer,* 23); for those including any state indigenously interpreted as possession, cf. Bourguignon, *Possession,* 7; Lewis, "Spirits and Sex War," 627.

32. Thus Keller, *Hammer,* 39–40, notes that earlier anthropologists tended to explain possession in psychosocial terms, not commenting on possessing agents, but more recent research "does take seriously the agency of possessing ancestors, deities, and spirits."

33. See Boddy, "Spirit Possession," 408, 410–14, 427.

34. E.g, Wendl, "Slavery," 120, criticizes psychoanalytic (Crapanzaro), sociological (Lewis), and feminist approaches for imposing grids instead of analyzing indigenous functions for possession experience.

35. Ward, "Introduction," 9. Idem, "Cross-Cultural Study," 17, notes that psychologists' focus on "objective, quantifiable data" must be complemented by anthropologists' "incorporation of subjective experiential data." For a wide range of modern scientific (esp. psychiatric) classifications, see Chandra shekar, "Possession Syndrome," 82–83.

36. Cf. discussion of the Gospel accounts in Twelftree, *Exorcist;* idem, *Name.*

37. For some tragic examples, see Keener, *Miracles,* 804–6.

38. Shorter, *Witch Doctor,* 99; Wyk, "Witchcraft," 1202; Mensah, "Basis," 171; further evidence in Keener, *Miracles,* 806–8. Witchcraft is flourishing in Africa (Harries, "Worldview," 492; Hill, "Witchcraft," 323–25; Bähre, "Witchcraft," 300, 329; Wyk, "Witchcraft," 1203–4). For

the belief that negative shamanism is used to harm or kill, see reports in McNaughton, *Blacksmiths,* 69; Scherberger, "Shaman," 57–59; Azenabor, "Witchcraft," 30–31. For the sacrifice by witchcraft of relatives to achieve success, see Binsbergen, "Witchcraft," 243.

39. Obeyesekere, "Sorcery," 3, noting homicidal intention but (21) doubting much effectiveness. For poisoning as well as occult means (sometimes reported by self-acknowledged sorcerers) with intent to kill, see Reynolds, *Magic,* 41–44; Kapolyo, *Condition,* 77.

40. See, e.g., Shoko, *Religion,* 46; Mayrargue, "Expansion," 286; Hoare, "Approach," 127–28; Knapstad, "Power," 84, 89.

41. Hair, "Witches," 140.

42. See, e.g., Numbere, *Vision,* 136; Grindal, "Heart," 66; Turner, "Actuality," 5; West, *Sorcery,* 3–5, 9–10, 88.

43. For suffering and death caused by curses, see, e.g., Prince, "Yoruba Psychiatry," 91; Dawson, "Urbanization," 328–29; Mbiti, *Religions,* 258; cf. Remus, *Healer,* 110; Welbourn, "Healing," 364; voodoo and taboo deaths in Benson, *Healing,* 40–41; esp. Knapstad, "Power," 84, 89. Widespread beliefs in curses' efficacy appear in rural Africa (e.g., Lienhardt, "Death"; Azevedo, Prater, and Lantum, "Biomedicine"), in sixteenth- and seventeenth-century Netherlands (see Waardt, "Witchcraft"), and in some parts of the West more recently (e.g., Sebald, "Witchcraft"). No one disputes witchcraft-associated killings by physical means (e.g., BBC reports on Tanzanian witchcraft killings of albinos, from Jan. 13, 2015; Feb. 17–18, 2015; March 6, 2015).

44. See, e.g., Cannon, "Voodoo Death"; Frank, *Persuasion,* 39–42.

45. Lagerwerf, *Witchcraft,* 14–15. Conventional Western medicine cannot treat witchcraft affliction because it isolates it from its traditional social framework (16–17).

46. Lagerwerf, *Witchcraft,* 18.

47. Some African Pentecostal churches have appeared culturally relevant by addressing witchcraft (Maxwell, "Witches," 334); Hayes ("Responses," 346–47, 352) views positively the approach of Zionists like Bishop Nyasha, who simply baptizes, exorcises, and reintegrates those who confess to witchcraft. Most African Catholics, Anglicans, and Presbyterian pastors condemn witchcraft, though their parishioners do not always hear them this way (Ross, "Preaching," 12–13).

48. Recounted in *Miracles,* 854–56.

49. Addressed again, at greater length, on p. 116.

50. Here I am selectively adapting various material from Keener, *Miracles,* 209–41 passim, with permission from Baker also for Keener, "Scripture and Context."

51. See, e.g., Robinson, "Challenge," 321; Placher, *Mark,* 76.

52. Cf. Everts, "Exorcist," 360; Judge, *First Christians,* 416–23 (esp. 416). The tradition of accepting only nonphysical applications of biblical miracles narratives was already established in eighteenth-century cessationist Protestantism (see Kidd, "Healing," 166).

53. See, e.g., Frankenberry, *Faith,* ix, 34–38, 47–66, 385–86, 105, 256; Brooke, "Science," 9; idem, *Science,* 118; Wykstra, "Problem," 156; Force, "Dominion," 89, 91; idem, "Breakdown," 146; Osler, "Revolution," 95; Koestler, "Kepler"; Burtt, *Foundations,* passim.

54. Vermes, *Jesus and Judaism,* 63.

55. Ward, "Miracles and Testimony," 137–38. In this paragraph and the next one I follow my *Miracles,* 139–40, reusing its wording especially in the next paragraph.

56. Houston, *Miracles,* 133–34; Smart, *Philosophers,* 32; Twelftree, *Miracle Worker,* 41. For the influence of deism on Hume, see esp. Burns, *Debate,* 70–95 and passim.

57. Houston, *Miracles,* 148, 160; Swinburne, "Introduction," 14.

58. Houston, *Miracles*, 162; cf. likewise Sider, "Methodology," 27; Ward, "Believing," 742; Evans, *Narrative*, 156; McInerny, *Miracles*, 135–38; Breggen, "Seeds." Houston notes that if one presupposes atheism methodologically so that one's conclusions must be atheistic, no argument could satisfy the position's demands (Houston, *Miracles*, 168). Backhaus, "Falsehood," 307, argues that Hume recognized "[t]he atheist's belief" as involving faith no less than "the theist's."

59. Some would argue that one might start with a premise of theism if other grounds warranted (cf. Evans, "Naturalism," esp. 205). Some seek to establish theism before invoking God as a causal factor (Young, "Epistemology"; cf. writers cited in Tennant, *Miracle*, 63–64), or note that miracles are comprehensible as such only on theistic premises (Taylor, *Hume*, 46–51); provided that one brackets this explanation as one explanatory hypothesis, however, the questions may be approached in tandem (cf. Weintraub, "Credibility," 373, though lamenting the absence of a sufficiently coherent theistic theory). As McGrew, "Argument," 639–40, notes, "not knowing that there is a God" differs from "knowing that there is not a God" (quotation from 640).

60. See Swinburne, "Evidence," 204–6 (regarding the hypothesis of Jesus's resurrection); idem, "Introduction," 14–15; idem, "Historical Evidence," 151; Polkinghorne, *Science and Providence*, 58; Taylor, *Hume*, 51; Hambourger, "Belief," 601; Evans, *Narrative*, 155; Ward, "Miracles and Testimony," 144; Purtill, "Proofs," 43; Otte, "Treatment," 155–57; Langtry, "Probability," 70; Kelly, "Miracle," 50; cf. John Henry Newman (in Brown, *Miracles*, 137–38); Mozley, *Lectures*, 74–92; Akhtar, "Miracles" (noting the necessity of miracles in traditional Christian belief); Keene, "Possibility of Miracles," 214 (because of God's concern for humanity). Smart, *Philosophy of Religion*, 113, contends that miracles are accepted because of the authority behind them, rather than the reverse, though this dichotomy reflects modern Western assumptions. One may contrast here Hume, who denied the credibility of miracle stories recounted in religious contexts, because he deemed the latter irrational (e.g., Hume, *Miracles*, 36, 50).

61. Cf. Swinburne, "Evidence," 201–2 (regarding Jesus's resurrection); cf. this answer against Hume historically in Ellin, "Again," 209; cf. also the kingdom "sign" (significance) value of miracles in Polkinghorne, *Science and Providence*, 51. Biblical miracle stories often focus on what is naturally impossible (cf. Wire, "Story," 36–37).

62. See, e.g., Evans, *Narrative*, 159, noting that "the amount of evidence" needed to surmount appropriate epistemological caution would presumably vary "depending on the intrinsic plausibility and apparent religious significance of the miracle." On a genuinely *divine* miracle's significance (i.e., expression of the purpose of a consistent and benevolent deity), see also Polkinghorne, *Science and Providence*, 45, 51; Smart, *Philosophers*, 43, 46.

63. Many argue that miracle claims are more probable if they fit a larger theological scheme (Tonquédec, *Miracles*, 52; Ward, "Miracles and Testimony," 142; Jantzen, "Miracles," 356; Licona and Van der Watt, "Historians and Miracles," 4–5; for the theological context of gospel miracles in the larger gospel story, see, e.g., Helm, "Miraculous," 86–88; as part of the larger divine reality, McKenzie, "Signs," 17); they should have religious significance (Nicolls, "Laws"; Jensen, "Logic," 148; Beckwith, *Argument*, 11–12; Licona and Van der Watt, "Historians and Miracles," 1–2; cf. Fitzgerald, "Miracles," 60–61; Phillips, "Miracles," 38–39). Fern, "Critique," 351–54, insists that miracles to be meaningful must be not only inexplicable but also showing purposefulness. On purpose in miracles, see, e.g., Burhenn, "Miracles," 488.

64. Miracles' religious purpose dominated much discussion until the reaction against the Enlightenment (so McNamara, "Nature," suggesting that balance is now returning to the discussion); in the seventeenth century, note Joseph Glanvill (Burns, *Debate*, 49–50), Robert

Boyle (Burns, *Debate*, 55–56), and the majority of orthodox apologists (e.g., Burns, *Debate*, 114–15). Hume resists this position, thereby oversimplifying his argument (see Burns, *Debate*, 169–70, 178; but cf. Hume's mention of "a particular volition of the Deity" in *Miracles*, 32).

65. Ward, "Miracles and Testimony," 144–45 (quote from 145). A logical possibility, miracles become a *real* possibility if theism is true (Sider, "Historian," 312).

66. See, e.g., critiques of Swinburne, *Miracle*; Houston, *Miracles*; Johnson, *Hume*; Earman, *Failure*.

67. Hume, *Miracles*, 37 (cf. 37–40).

68. See Ten, "Racism"; Taliaferro and Hendrickson, "Racism"; Keener, "Case."

69. Cf. Hume, *Miracles*, 55; more clearly, idem, *History of Religion*, 50–51; comment in Johnson, *Hume*, 80; Kugel, *Bible*, 34.

70. See Pilch, "Sickness," 183; idem, "Disease," 135; cf. Barnes, "Introduction," 6–7; Crawford, "Healing," 31–32.

71. See Barnes, "Introduction," 3, and note the bibliography in Barnes and Talamantez, *Teaching Religion and Healing*, 353–78 just on religious traditions and healing (also Barnes, "World Religions," 346–52).

72. Pilch, *Healing*, 35 (cf. also 14).

73. McClenon, *Events*, 131 and sources cited there.

74. See, e.g., Welbourn, "Exorcism," 595 (African allowance of both medical and spiritual treatment); Oduyoye, "Value," 116; Jules-Rosette, "Healers," 128; González, *Tribe*, 94; Droogers, "Normalization"; Shishima, "Wholistic Nature"; Pobee, "Health," 59–60; Allen, "Whole Person Healing," 130–31 (resisting Western acculturation that suppresses traditional African interests); Bührmann, "Religion and Healing"; Dube, "Search," 135; Omenyo, "Healing," 235–38; Oblau, "Healing"; Ma, "Encounter," 130 (regarding Korea); Maggay, "Issues," 34.

75. "Spirit and Power" (2006 Pew Forum Survey 2006).

76. Noll, *Shape*, 34 (claiming "almost all" but admitting "some hyperbole").

77. "Spirit and Power."

78. Jenkins, *Next Christendom*, 107, who also complains that Westerners too often contest the legitimacy of such perspectives (on 121 offering the specific example of John Spong's ethnocentric complaints about African Anglican bishops' "superstitious" and "Pentecostal" "extremism").

79. Noll, *Shape*, 34.

80. Archer, "Retrospect and Prospect," 131. On Pentecostalism's supernatural worldview as a valuable hermeneutical preunderstanding, see also Cheung, "Study."

81. See Van der Watt, "Hermeneutics of Relevance," esp. here 237 42, though importantly warning of the danger of ignoring original contexts (243).

82. Roschke, "Healing."

83. Asamoah-Gyadu, "Mission," 4, as cited in Anderson, *Ends of Earth*, 139. For African Pentecostal healing worldview's correspondence with traditional African conceptions, see Asamoah-Gyadu, "Influence," 154–57.

84. Jenkins, *Next Christendom*, 122–31; cf. also Mullin, *History*, 279 (cf. 281); Mchami, "Possession," 17 (on spirits); Richards, "Factors," 95–96; Evans, "Judgment," 201–2; Eddy and Boyd, *Legend*, 67–73, 82–83 (also noting, on 71–73, the shift among, and citing, "many western ethnographers" and anthropologists who have grown increasingly respectful toward other cultures' approaches to the supernatural).

85. Sanneh, *Whose Religion*, 26.

86. Gardner, "Miracles," 1929, quoting Finlay, *Columba.*

87. Noll, *Shape,* 24.

88. Wilson, "Seeing," 202–4 (citing Loewen's account from 1974); cf. Neufeldt, "Legacy," 146.

89. Wilson, "Seeing," 204.

90. See Gregory, "Secular Bias," 138; cf. Hanciles, *Beyond Christendom,* 40 (following Minogue, "Religion"); Wolfe, "Potential," 34.

91. Cf. the complaint in Miller and Yamamori, *Pentecostalism,* 158, concerning experientially deprived academicians "who live out their existence within the shelter of the academy, where everything but faculty politics operates on assumptions of rationality and empirical verifiability."

92. Studies of undergraduates show that scientific training does "not reduce the frequency of anomalous reports," in contrast to beliefs in circles of elite scientists (McClenon, *Events,* 35). Likewise, in cultures like Ghana there is no inverse proportionality between scientific knowledge and paranormal beliefs (22). The academy is an elite subculture, and cultural factors (at least sometimes related to academic politics) help shape its creeds.

93. Eya, "Healing," 51–52.

94. Ising, *Blumhardt,* 222–23.

95. Kydd, *Healing,* 42n40 (citing Bultmann, *Kerygma and Myth,* 120).

96. Barth, *Letters,* 251 (cf. 270); Kelsey, *Healing,* 236–37; Kydd, *Healing,* 34; Ising, *Blumhardt,* 420; Barth, *Dogmatics,* 4.3:165ff. (noted in Kauffman, "Introduction," 7–8). Cf. also Moltmann, "Blessing," 149.

97. See Ising, *Blumhardt,* passim. On Blumhardt, see further Macchia, *Spirituality.*

98. Cf. Bultmann, "Mythology," 4. The usual scientific method does not disprove the supernatural but brackets it from discussion as an explanation (see Ellington, "Authority," 165); thus those who reject miracles on the grounds that there is no naturalistic explanation for them have stated nothing more than their naturalistic assumptions (put well by Metaxas, *Miracles,* 4).

99. González, *Acts,* 84–85. Cf. also estimates of 28 percent of all Latino Christians in the United States as Pentecostal or (especially among Catholics) charismatic (Espinosa, "Contributions," 124); their worldview is not "over-rationalized" (Alvarez, "South," 141–42, 144).

100. Ismael Laborde Figueras (interviews, Aug. 7, 8, 2010); cf. also Martell-Otero, "Satos," 16–17, 32–33; idem, "Liberating News," 384–87.

101. Yung, *Quest,* 6. This perspective fits most non-Western cultures (Yung, "Integrity," 173); it is Western antisupernatural Christianity that is now "the real aberration" (Yung, "Reformation").

102. Yung, "Integrity," 173.

103. For biblical concerns for the poor, see, e.g., Exod 22:25; 23:6, 11; Lev 19:10; 23:22; Deut 15:11; 24:14; Ps 12:5; 35:10; 37:14; 72:12–13; 82:4; 112:9; 113:7; 140:12; Prov 14:21, 31; 17:5; 21:13; 22:9, 16, 22; 28:8, 27; 29:7; 31:9, 20; Isa 10:2; 11:4; 41:17; Jer 5:28; 22:16; Ezek 16:49; 18:12, 17; 22:29; Dan 4:27; Amos 2:6; 4:1; 5:11–12; 8:4, 6; Zech 7:10; Mark 10:21; Luke 4:18; 7:22; 14:13; 19:8; Acts 4:34; Rom 15:26; 2 Cor 9:9; Gal 2:10; Jas 2:5–6. For a collection of passages, see Sider, *Cry Justice;* idem, *Fed.*

Notes to Chapter 7

1. "Original meaning" itself encompasses a range of possible senses. By "original" meaning, do we speak of what the author intended when designing the text? At which stage of

the text's production? (This is especially an issue with texts that experienced many stages of redaction; usually literary critics today prefer to work with the final form of the text, especially when its precursors remain hypothetical or their reconstruction speculative.) Do we mean what the first real audience heard? Which hearers count as the first real audience? To keep on task for this book, I must here speak simply of this range of senses, leaving largely to others intriguing debates about greater specificity.

2. Vanhoozer, *Meaning,* 249, aptly observes, "The author's intention is the real causality that alone accounts for why a text is the way it is." The author's causal role remains true regardless of the extent to which we can recover it.

3. Inferring design in the universe may be controversial in the larger culture, but inferring design in a crime scene (as opposed to an accident scene) is not. Inferring design is important in many settings, and we recognize that authors typically design their literary texts.

4. Bartholomew, *Hermeneutics,* 410.

5. For Dilthey, for example, "meaning" is especially meaningfulness (cf. Dilthey, *Pattern,* 67, 100) and thus changes (Rickman, "Introduction," 48–49). "There is no one 'meaning of life' but only the meaning which individuals have perceived in, or attributed to their own lives . . ." (Dilthey, *Pattern,* 85). On the danger of confusing different usages of the term "meaning," see also Hirsch, *Validity,* 255; Poirier, "Critique," 5–6.

6. Cf. Wittig, "Theory," 92–94: different contexts create different meanings. Wittig here offers a helpful and positive example of this principle in the different meanings of a parable in Jesus's own setting, that of the respective Gospels that report it, and subsequent exegetical traditions. The question remains, however, for theologians to resolve which of such contexts are authoritative for us and to what degree; Jesus's own setting is harder to recover, but most Christians will accept as authoritative at least the canonical meanings. More extreme is Raschke, "Textuality," who contends that "Scripture" is not canon, but the infinite possibility of language revealed through a text. "Religion . . . is the return of the repressed. It is the Dionysian force that impinges upon the Apollonian coherence of the text" (50).

7. Some of this section comes from Keener, *Acts,* 1:16–18.

8. Aryan rereadings of biblical texts to subvert their use for the Nazi cause (see, e.g., discussion in Head, "Nazi Quest"; Poewe, *Religions,* passim; Bernal, *Athena,* 1:349; Theissen and Merz, *Guide,* 163) offer an extreme example that nearly all interpreters today would censure (not least because of the cause for which the texts were exploited).

9. This transfer of "canonical" status from the text to the interpreter, when performed by a rhetorical sleight-of-hand (rather than merely as allusive and as a recognized rhetorical device), is the "transfer" persuasion technique (not unethical in all its forms, but capable of being employed deceptively; cf. Bremback and Howell, *Persuasion,* 235; McLaughlin, *Ethics,* 76, 146–47). In this limited space one cannot enter into dialogue with the ethics of radical philosophic deconstruction or its results (especially since many of its advocates would regard the ethical claims as themselves relative and subject to deconstruction). Deconstruction does offer some useful insights (such as that no texts are fully consistent, as also noted in Dio Chrys. *Or.* 52.7; on such inconsistencies in ancient narratives, see in more detail my discussion in Keener, *John,* 38–39, 901), and the contingency of all readings.

10. Admittedly, not all critics will agree with language such as "ideal audience" (as Aune, *Dictionary of Rhetoric,* 229, notes, some prefer "authorial audience" as more concrete historically).

11. Or whatever premises we can reasonably infer that the author likely shared with the ideal or authorial audience; see the discussion of relevance theory in the main text.

12. See, e.g., Oliverio, *Hermeneutics,* 56, 76, 78, 99.

13. Although it is true that "classic texts" in general "can come to 'mean more' than was originally intended" (Pinnock, "Work of Spirit," 242) in the sense of their general usage, these resonances are not usually our goal in hearing an original communication. Reception history, like global readings, rightly challenges our biases and places a wider range of options on the table. Nevertheless, restorationism aside, most observers of Pentecostal reception history will recognize that most Pentecostals, like most other populist readers, have tried (often unsuccessfully) to read the Bible on its own without such layers of subsequent interpretation. Appeal to *original* context has admittedly often been more selective, e.g., to defend women's involvement in ministry but not in less debated passages. But where such context shed light on the text, it has often been welcomed.

14. Although the time required some theological affirmations and boundaries for self-definition, some suggest that this statement started this segment of Pentecostalism on the road to sociological institutionalization (Blumhofer, *Chapter,* 2:14–15, as cited in Oliverio, *Hermeneutics,* 87).

15. Despite noting above the historical context of the Assemblies' Trinitarian emphasis, for example, I do affirm the Trinity and its importance. If I wanted to illustrate the fallibility of earlier Assemblies of God doctrine, I would use an example much more appropriate for that purpose, namely the case of the (non-binding) position paper on "The Rapture of the Church." Its dispensational eschatology, which astonishingly belongs to a larger cessationist system, was growing quite popular at the time of the Assemblies' founding in 1914, although even some key leaders in the Assemblies have historically held views dissenting from it (for diverse views from the beginning, see Menzies and Anderson, "Eschatological Diversity"). Dispensationalism's influence in the Assemblies flourished from the 1930s to the 1980s, "peaking in the 1950s" (Oliverio, *Hermeneutics,* 113), but it does not appear in the movement's original doctrinal formulation (114); nor did it flourish in similar ways in other parts of the Pentecostal movement (116). If the reader questions whether pretribulationalism could become a casualty of genuinely inductive Bible study, one need merely investigate whether any text in *context* explicitly supports such a view, and whether some texts might in fact disallow it.

16. Luther respected the opinions of earlier Christian interpreters, but insisted that even popes and councils were subject to Scripture. General assemblies and executive presbyteries must still answer to Scripture (as leaders in the Assemblies of God would agree); so must those who claim new revelations, since God's tested revelation in Scripture functions as a measuring stick by which new revelatory claims can be evaluated. Early church fathers "insisted that the church be held accountable to Scripture," although they did not read it in isolation from their context as the church (Hall, *Reading,* 13). For a helpful balance that recognizes both the values and dangers of tradition, see also Hall, *Reading,* 190–91, following Brown, "Proclamation," 85.

17. For my understanding of tradition and Scripture (though especially referring to traditions of particular churches rather than the shared Christian tradition), see Keener, "Biblical Fidelity," 34–37.

18. E.g., the emphasis on apostolic poverty among, e.g., Franciscans or Wycliffe's followers. Those embracing as authoritative early Pentecostal tradition should also recall that early Pentecostals generally held to a view of history that included stages of truths being restored, of which one was the Reformation's restoration of Scripture's primacy.

19. With Oliverio, *Hermeneutics,* 320, who, after affirming the contextual dimension of interpretation, notes that this affirmation does not imply "that I find one hermeneutic as good as another."

20. Carson, *Showing Spirit,* 173.

21. A sermon by Cal LeMon at Evangel Temple Assembly of God, Springfield, Missouri, c. 1980–1982.

22. The early church recognized Scripture as the "supreme authority in Christian belief and practice" (Graves, *Inspiration,* 38–41).

23. On the canon, see, e.g., McDonald and Sanders, *Debate;* McDonald, *Canon;* Evans and Tov, *Exploring;* Kruger, *Question;* Porter, Evans, and McDonald, *New Testament.*

24. See here the legitimate concern of Cartledge, "Text-Community-Spirit," 141–42, regarding the danger of some charismatics de facto appropriating the community or its head as "the *norming norm,* rather than Scripture."

25. Although some theologians have objected to calling any of these extrabiblical experiences "revelations," translations of Scripture frequently apply the term to such experiences (1 Cor 14:26, 30; 2 Cor 12:1, 7; Eph 1:17; cf. Matt 11:25, 27//Luke 10:21–22; 1 Cor 2:10; Phil 3:15).

26. As in Ps 33:4, 6, these commands to nature in Ps 147 are linked with God's commands to Israel in that both are God's word (Ps 147:19; see likewise Ps 119:90–91; compare Ps 19:1–6 with Ps 19:7–11). Divine laws or decrees in nature appear also elsewhere in Egypt and the ancient Middle East (see Walton, *Thought,* 192–93).

27. For more details of this argument, see Keener, *John,* 2:1035–43; cf. 1:234–51, 807–8, 817–18; cf. 1 John 2:27; 3:6, 24; 4:13.

28. At first mostly among believers in Jerusalem, with its five thousand men (Acts 4:4)—at ten families per home this alone would be five hundred homes—but eventually widely scattered, with large numbers clustered in Antioch on the Orontes and elsewhere.

29. I tell some of the story in greater detail in Keener, *Gift,* 187–89.

30. God can speak to us even through word or concept association; cf. the Hebrew wordplays in Jer 1:11–12; Amos 8:1–2; Mic 1:10–15, but these serve a rhetorical or homiletical more than an exegetical function. Grey, *Crowd,* 104, suggests, "By using the text as a symbol independent of the historical and cultural context of the passage, Pentecostal readings can continue to invite the possibility of multiple readings of the text." But how then can we evaluate readings? If the text can symbolize something other than what it was originally inspired to mean, does it any longer function as a canon, a measuring stick for other claims to revelation? Nevertheless, many of the examples of popular interpretation that Grey offers are genuinely plausible inferences from the principles articulated in the biblical texts. That is, in practice they apply the text rather than distorting its message.

31. Some interpreters selectively appropriate postmodern critiques of objectivity while referring to the original communication to avoid wholesale subjectivity (see Hannah K. Harrington, Rebecca Patten, and Clark Pinnock as cited in Grey, *Crowd,* 46–47). Reading from within a community may challenge relativism (Archer, *Hermeneutic,* 132), though one must still show that one's community's view is better than its competitors. Rejecting the discredited modernist assumption of full objectivity does not make one a relativist or allow texts to mean just anything (Archer, *Hermeneutic,* 206–7, 213–14), though it is simpler to recognize this distinction than to define boundaries of meaning or levels of textual relevance.

32. See, e.g., Edwards, *Marks;* Webster, *Methodism and Miraculous,* 29–31.

33. Possibly this destruction was caused solely by the demons.

34. Observing the benevolent character of Jesus's miracles is not to dismiss the value of biblical judgment miracles such as the exodus plagues, but to affirm that it is not the primary form of miracle that Jesus models for us. (More often in the Bible God executed judgments without direct human agents, except prophetic warnings.)

35. Since this counsel is applied to the regular evaluation of prophecies in house churches, one would not imagine that its primary purpose is to weed out those who were complete false prophets, since even large homes rarely accommodated more than fifty people. If every person in the congregation were a false prophet and one were discerned such and expelled per week (assuming that the other false prophets were qualified to recognize this), one would run out of members before the end of the year. The point here is not identifying wolves in sheep's clothing but making sure that those who are prophesying are communicating accurately God's message.

36. Although some scholars find in the NT a less authoritative form of prophecy than in the OT, prophecies were not always fulfilled even in the OT, since most were implicitly conditional; see, e.g., Jer 18:6–10; Ezek 18:21–32; Jonah 3:10. Indeed, some of Jeremiah's prophetic details may not have come to pass precisely literally (e.g., Jer 43:10–13; 46:19, 25–26; cf. Walton, Matthews, and Chavalas, *Background Commentary,* 675, 677–78; Voth, "Jeremiah," 330–31), although their spirit did (the character of biblical prophecy may have allowed the fulfillment later, through Nebuchadnezzar's successor—see Brown, "Jeremiah," 479), and the heart of his prophetic message was thoroughly fulfilled.

37. This paragraph is from my online biblical interpretation manual.

38. Cf. comments in Vanhoozer, *Meaning;* Brown, *Scripture as Communication,* 69–72; Osborne, "Hermeneutics," 391–95; fuller discussion than I can offer here in Keener, *Acts,* 1:18–23.

39. I reproduce here my story from my online biblical interpretation manual.

40. Klein, Blomberg, and Hubbard, *Introduction,* 7.

41. I borrow this paragraph from Keener, "Biblical Fidelity," 39.

42. Cf. Thiselton, "New Hermeneutic," 79 (citing Fuchs, "Proclamation," 354; Ebeling, *Theology,* 42, 100–102): "Fuchs and Ebeling are fully aware of the role of the Holy Spirit in communicating the word of God, but they rightly see that problems of understanding and intelligibility cannot be short-circuited by a premature appeal of this kind."

43. Anderson, *Pentecostalism,* 33–34; Goff, "Theology of Parham," 64–65; Jacobsen, *Thinking in Spirit,* 25, 49–50, 74, 76, 97; Robeck, *Mission,* 41–42, 236–37, 243, 252; McGee, *Miracles,* 61–76; idem, "Hermeneutics," 102; idem, "Strategy," 52–53; see esp. McGee, "Shortcut"; idem, "Logic"; Anderson, "Signs," 195–99.

44. They have often even addressed issues that would soon arise in my writing. When I was teaching in Indonesia, as the fourth volume of my Acts commentary was going to press, I was compelled in a dream to summarize the most important insight I had gleaned from my work on Acts. That insight was the frequent connection between prayer and the coming of the Spirit, a reminder that renewed my courage to appeal to Luke 11:13 in prayer—a text that therefore appears close to the end of this book.

45. This was still true when I wrote about the experience in Keener, *Miracles,* 2:854–55.

46. Unfortunately, some who read other books from start to finish treat Scripture as a magical book from which verses can be extracted at random, applying to Scripture something more relevant to I-Ching divination. Because God is sovereign and we trust him to speak through the entire canon, however, the problem is not the random selection so much as the neglect of context.

47. For a number of ancient examples, see Keener, *Acts,* 1:20–21; and in the present book, see pp. 129–31. Those who argue that trying to understand what an author wanted to communicate is a purely modern agenda are simply mistaken.

48. Despite academic detractors, common sense has value in constructing hermeneutical approaches; see helpfully Schnabel, "Fads."

49. A perspective refreshed by God differs from one's natural perspective apart from him (see Ps 73:17).

50. Stormont, *Wigglesworth,* 114.

Notes to Chapter 8

1. See, e.g., discussion in Brubaker, "Postmodernism"; Clark, "Pentecostal Hermeneutics"; idem, "Hermeneutics." Most historians are critical realists and thus reject extreme postmodern denial of facts (e.g., about the Nazi Holocaust), despite the tendentiousness of larger narratives; see Licona, *Resurrection,* 77–89 (esp. here 79, 84, 86–89).

2. Oliverio, *Hermeneutics,* 247. Oliverio himself contends for a "hermeneutical realism" that recognizes the limitations of human knowledge but also affirms that we can nevertheless separate truths from untruths (323–24). Epistemically, neither total realism nor total unrealism is a viable option (342); we need instead "a chastened form of realism" (352).

3. E.g., Cargal, "Postmodern Age"; Archer, "Retrospect and Prospect," 147; cf. also Waddell, *Spirit in Revelation;* discussion in Herms, "Review."

4. E.g., Menzies, "Bandwagon"; Poirier and Lewis, "Hermeneutics."

5. E.g., Schweitzer, *Quest,* 358–62, on Matt 10:23; see the criticisms of Perrin, *Kingdom,* 32–33; Ladd, *Theology,* 200.

6. As Karlfried Froehlich notes (Froehlich, "Hermeneutics," 179), "reconstructions of historical developments" often tendentiously present their own position as normative. Postmodern interpretation itself reflects a particular (and undoubtedly temporary) historical context (cf., e.g., the observation in Oliverio, *Hermeneutics,* 223, about postmodernism's historically conditioned denunciation of the Enlightenment).

7. Grey, *Crowd,* 48–49, 53, 104, 130–31, notes concerns about the relativistic postmodern worldview, suggesting that while Pentecostals can use postmodern tools, they should operate from within their own distinctive worldview. Cf. the concern in Green, *Seized,* 161, that (radical) postmodernism rejects history.

8. An ideologically driven approach may filter the interpretation of all texts through the same grid, rendering itself virtually immune to dialogue or correction. Cf. the complaint of Richard Israel, offered at a Society for Pentecostal Studies meeting: "A Pentecostal ideology is no hermeneutic at all; it is the obliteration of the horizon of the text by the interpreter" (Israel, Albrecht, and McNally, "Hermeneutics," A8–9; as cited in Anderson, "Pentecostal Hermeneutics"). Anderson himself notes ("Pentecostal Hermeneutics") that Pentecostals, like all other interpreters, have biases, but genuinely critical scholars recognize their biases and seek to allow texts to change our preconceptions about the texts.

9. See the criticism of this view in, e.g., Osborne, *Spiral,* 165, 379–80.

10. See Ellington, "Authority," 155. This radical reader-response approach is also rejected by Archer, *Hermeneutic,* 236, as antirealist (following Vanhoozer).

11. For theology as contextual, see, e.g., Bonk, "Missions"; Tennent, *Theology;* Yong with Anderson, *Renewing.* Cf. also Scharen, *Fieldwork.*

12. See helpfully Waddell, "Hearing," 188, following R. D. Moore. Cf. Schleiermacher's earlier hermeneutical circle between the whole and the parts in Westphal, *Community,* 28–29.

13. Johns, "Meeting God," 24, as cited in Waddell, "Hearing," 190.

14. Martin, "Psalm 63," 284.

15. Archer, "Retrospect and Prospect," 135–36.

16. See Lederle, *Treasures,* 29–31, esp. 29; Hollenweger, *Pentecostals,* 32, 331–36. Examples of some theological tolerance beyond what became traditional Pentecostal boundaries include Maria Woodworth Etter, Carrie Judd Montgomery, F. F. Bosworth, Aimee Semple McPherson, and, on some issues, William Seymour.

17. Menzies, *Anointed,* 130.

18. Green, *Seized,* 16.

19. Oliverio, *Hermeneutics,* 171n163.

20. Edwards, "Crowns," employing *b. Men.* 29b; cf. Driver, *Scrolls,* 550. Rabbis were not alone in presenting multiple views (Starr, "Flexibility"), and orators regularly practiced defending either side of a cause (e.g., Suetonius *Rhetoricians* 1; Hermog. *Inv.* 3.5.141–43, 145; 3.7.149; Fronto *Ad M. Caes.* 5.27 [42]), as did Skeptics (Lucian *Double Indictment* 15; Hippolytus *Refutation of All Heresies* 1.20), though most philosophers criticized the morality of this practice (e.g., Fronto *Ad M. Caes.* 4.13; Maximus of Tyre *Or.* 25.6). Some presenters of multiple views, however, critiqued others they thought erroneous (e.g., Porphyry *Ar. Cat.* 59.4–14, then affirming the "correct" interpreters in 59.15–19).

21. Cf. N. Wolterstorff's illustration cited in Westphal, *Community,* 66–67. Also note the range of expected audiences beyond one's most informed "core" or "target" audience, discussed in Koester, *Symbolism,* 19–22; idem, "Spectrum"; Burridge, "People," 143.

22. See also Green, *Practicing Theological Interpretation,* 74. Ancient Christians were ready to appeal to the larger theology of the canon when the sense of specific passages was unclear; cf., e.g., Young, "Mind of Scripture."

23. Wittig, "Theory," 97–98. Because "no signifier can properly re-present the thing-in-itself," Taylor argues (Taylor, "Shades," 32), "the activity of signification is inescapably fictive"; yet such an approach can lead to hermeneutical nihilism. More helpful is simple recognition of the finiteness of our partial perspectives (Westphal, *Community,* 26; cf. 1 Cor 13:9).

24. E.g., Freudian, Marxist, or other approaches (noted in Wittig, "Theory," 90). Hirsch, *Validity,* 126, permits the use of such categories for describing what is in texts, but not for investing meaning in them (e.g., a Freudian discovering Oedipal implications foreign to Shakespeare's point).

25. Fee, *Listening,* 14.

26. Hey, "Roles."

27. Archer, *Hermeneutic,* 208.

28. Strong critiques of Archer's work include Spawn and Wright, "Emergence," 14–15; Poirier, "Critique."

29. Archer, *Hermeneutic,* 232.

30. Kenneth Archer, personal correspondence, April 11, 2015.

31. One might even argue that this disclaimer demonstrates Archer's valuing of authorial intention—when it is recoverable. Of course, the "ideal author" is the author projected by the text, so an apparently ideal author's divergence from an actual author indicates a degree of

failed communication, whether by the author's failure to qualify ambiguous nomenclature or by the critics' failure to hear from the standpoint of the text's ideal audience or a combination thereof. The lack of standardized hermeneutical nomenclature, however, makes such failure to understand other critics virtually inevitable.

32. Kenneth Archer, personal correspondence, April 11, 2015. This has been a point of particular criticism; thus, e.g., Oliverio, *Hermeneutics,* 231, complains of "his neglect of a text's origination and attendant external context."

33. Kenneth Archer, personal correspondence, April 11, 2015.

34. Archer, *Hermeneutic,* 222.

35. Like modern writers, ancient ones assumed some cultural knowledge on the parts of their audiences; see, e.g., Xenophon *Cyrop.* 7.2.15 (assuming audience knowledge of the tradition also found in Herodotus *Hist.* 1.46–48); Phaedrus 5.10.10; Philost. *Hrk.* 1.3; Maclean and Aitken, "Introduction," lxxxvii. Seneca's letters often respond to, and thus presuppose, Lucilius's questions or comments (e.g., Seneca *Ep. Lucil.* 68.1; 74.1; 75.1), just as Paul sometimes responded to others (e.g., 1 Cor 7:1).

36. I say "almost" because the one exception at times is when, whether using background or not, I challenge a cherished traditional interpretation. Even then, I have not found Pentecostals more resistant than others to reconsidering their traditions. My background commentary alone has sold more than half a million copies, suggesting that at least some have an appetite for background.

37. Others also note that popular Pentecostal readings often give little attention to historical context (e.g., Grey, *Crowd,* 108–9).

38. Davies, "Read as Pentecostal," 252. In practice, Davies probably would not go as far as these polarizing claims sound; thus, for example, he counters the danger of selecting only inspirational texts by advocating "systematic expository preaching" (258).

39. Davies, "Read as Pentecostal," 254. Davies cites the reality of our subjectivity (254), which is not really in dispute, and then simply dismisses the objections from detractors to his spiritualizing approach, including among fellow Pentecostals, as "singularly unconvincing" (254–44). His lack of solid argument is also criticized by Poirier, "Critique."

40. Davies, "Read as Pentecostal," 256.

41. Davies, "Read as Pentecostal," 255. As he goes on to speak of killing "this monstrous alien" he concedes that he speaks tongue in cheek.

42. Rather than illustrating at length I refer the reader to my treatment in Keener, *Paul,* 17–235; Usry and Keener, *Religion,* 98–109 (esp. 103–4); Keener and Usry, *Faith,* 20–41 (esp. 36–38). Other works are also (and sometimes even more) helpful, including Copan, *Monster;* Dodd, *Problem;* Webb, *Slaves.*

43. Malina, *Anthropology,* 153.

44. Keck, "Ethos," 450–51. Cf. Stendahl, *Paul,* 35: "Actually there is no greater threat to serious biblical studies than a forced demand for 'relevance.' We must have patience and faith enough to listen to and seek out the original's meaning." Two examples of thorough engagement with original context in the service of contemporary mission are Schnabel, *Mission;* and idem, *Missionary.*

45. See, e.g., Wright, *Biblical Archaeology,* 51. Some acknowledge some parallels but prefer Neo-Babylonian ones (Tucker, "Background"); others counter with Hurrian language (Rabin, "L- with Imperative") or subsequent Israelites updating the language (Reviv, "Elements"; for views, cf. Katzoff, "Purchase"). Many scholars have argued that Abraham wanted only the cave

(Gen 23:9), but since he needed the land quickly, Ephron could compel him to buy the entire field (23:11), which would transfer any responsibilities for dues on the property from Ephron to Abraham (Gordon, *Near East,* 124; idem, *Common Background,* 94; Kitchen, *Orient,* 155). The narrative function, of course, is to reinforce Israel's right to possess Canaan.

46. See Marshall, *Enmity,* 13–21; most mildly, such refusals demonstrated contempt (Pliny *Ep.* 8.6.9).

47. See, e.g., Chaván de Matviuk, "Growth"; Pedraja, "*Testimonios.*"

48. Keener, *Background Commentary.*

49. Some of the fruits appear in Keener, "Tabernacle"; idem, "Worship."

50. In "Authorial Intention in Premodern Exegesis" (see p. 136).

51. Ramm, *Interpretation,* 114–15; defending this goal, see, e.g., Stein, "Benefits" (cited favorably in Hernando, *Dictionary,* 14n4); Stein, *Guide,* 11–23.

52. Noted in Grey, *Crowd,* 42.

53. Grey, *Crowd,* 56.

54. Archer, *Hermeneutic,* 58; though elsewhere he views this as a response to historical criticism (263). Nor is taking into account authorial context foreign to ancient interpreters, as is sometimes wrongly claimed; see discussion in the present book (pp. 129–31).

55. George, "Introduction," xxvii. On the Enlightenment origins of "pure" historical criticism, as opposed to the earlier Renaissance and Reformation interest in historical context (on which see, e.g., Bartholomew, *Hermeneutics,* 195–96), see Bartholomew, *Hermeneutics,* 208–24.

56. For many relevant texts, see, e.g., Russell and Winterbottom, *Criticism;* many of these include extrinsic genre criticism and other elements.

57. Much of what appears here I have borrowed from Keener, *Acts,* 1:20–21.

58. See, e.g., Quintilian *Inst.* 10.1.22; cf. Aune, *Dictionary of Rhetoric,* 397. For literary context, see, e.g., Dionysius of Halicarnassus *Dem.* 46; Apuleius *Apol.* 82–83; Hermogenes *Method in Forceful Speaking* 13.428; for sensitivity to genres, e.g., Quintilian *Inst.* 10.1.36; Maximus of Tyre *Or.* 38.4; Menander Rhetor 1.1.333.31–334.5; Philostratus *Vit. soph.* 2.33.628.

59. Aul. Gel. 20.1.6, citing a source that he treats as reliable.

60. E.g., Corn. Nep. Pref. 5–7; Plut. *Greek Questions; Roman Questions; Themistocles* 27.2–3.

61. They knew how to reapply ancient quotations in (conspicuously) new ways (e.g., Brutus's quote of Eurip. *Med.* 332 in Appian *Bell. civ.* 4.17.130; Virgil in Sen. *Suas.* 3.5–7; 4.4–5), so writers sometimes used them for rhetorical display rather than for the authority of their original sense. Nevertheless, quotations used out of context to justify wrong behaviors could call for censure (as in Alciph. *Paras.* 20 [Thambophagus to Cypellistes], 3.56, ¶2).

62. Stanley, *Language of Scripture,* 345.

63. Dewey, "Gospel of Mark," 145.

64. For the actor's intention, see Hermog. *Issues* 49.9–14; 61.16–18; 67.6–8; 72.14–73.3; Quint. *Decl.* 274.8 (for a divine actor); 281.1–3; 289.2; 311.8; 373.12; Libanius *Topics* 2.1; also Robinson, *Law,* 16; cf. Cicero *Fin.* 3.9.32; Seneca *Controv.* 10.1.9; *y. Ber.* 2:1.

65. For legislative intention, see Aeschines *Ctes.* 33; Lysias *Or.* 31.27, §189; *Rhet. Alex.* 1, 1422b.20–25; Hermog. *Issues* 40.6–19; 60.13–14; 66.12–13; 80.4–13; 82.4–5, 13–18; 83.20; 86.4–5; 91.9–13; Quint. *Decl.* 248.9; 249.3–5, 8; 251.2–3; 252.8; 274.9; 277.2; 297.8; 308; 317.9; 329; 331.3; 350.2, 6; esp. 317.2. Thus it was frequent to pit laws against each other; e.g., Quint. *Decl.* passim (e.g., 251 intro; 274 intro; 277.5; 299 intro; 303 intro; 304 intro; 304.1; 315 intro; 366 intro; esp. 304.1; 315.8). When useful for the case, however, one will play down the importance of

the actor's (e.g., Quint. *Decl.* 302.3; 314.6) or legislator's (313.5–6) intention; laws should state qualifications (Arist. *Rhet.* 1.1.7, 1354a; Philost. *Vit. soph.* 2.33.628), or one must define them (Hermogenes *Issues* 65.1–8), citing *implicit* exceptions (Seneca *Controv.* 9.4, passim). One's goal in the case determines whether one appeals to intention or wording (Hermog. *Issues* 40.6–19).

66. See Apul. *Apol.* 82–83.

67. See Pogoloff, "Isocrates," 338–62. Kohelet rightly observed that nothing new is under the sun (Eccl 1:9).

68. E.g., cf. Aristotle's μῦθος and modern plot (Belfiore, "Plots"); cf. also his conception of imitation (Rollinson, "*Mythos* and *Mimesis*").

69. Sometimes this assumption is made explicit, e.g., Dion. Hal. *Isaeus* 14 assumes that his readers/students have read Isaeus's speeches on which he comments. Maxwell, "Audience," addresses some assumed audience knowledge, and even suggests that authors may omit some information to augment audience participation.

70. E.g., Xen. *Cyr.* 7.2.15 (alluding to the well-known Delphic oracle; cf. Hdt 1.46–48); Phaedrus 5.10.10. Cf. Anonymous, *Commentary, Prologus,* Frede 15.1–16.46 (Burns, *Romans,* 11), on Paul.

71. Elsewhere in ancient sources, e.g., Phaedrus 3.1.7; Dio Chrys. *Or.* 34.3, 10. Sometimes writers even deliberately obscured their meaning to outsiders (e.g., Nicholson, "Confidentiality"; less persuasively, Callaway, "Reflections").

72. Proclus *Poet.* Essay 6, Bk. 2, K200.9–14.

73. E.g., Sen. *Ep. Lucil.* 108.24–25, who interprets the use of *fugit* in Virg. *Georg.* 3.284 in light of Virgil's use elsewhere; so also Dion. Hal. *Demosth.* 46 (on Demosthenes's speeches); Philost. *Hrk.* 11.5 on Hom. *Od.* 18.359, using Hom. *Il.* 21.197. Cf. also Aune, *Dictionary of Rhetoric,* 210–11, on ancient Homeric critics' recognition of hapax legomena.

74. Milazzo, "Sermone."

75. Cf. other examples in Libanius *Maxim* 3.9 (on Demosthenes); Proclus *Poet.* Essay 6, Bk. 1, K145.27–K146.1; K150.12–13. Although Heraclitus often simply allegorizes, sometimes (as in Heracl. *Hom. Prob.* 79.8) he appeals to circumstances in the narrative world to explain a character's speech.

76. E.g., Galen *Grief* 24b–26. Writers also acknowledged the imprecision of trying to find equivalent words for translation in different languages (Sen. *Ep. Lucil.* 111.1–12).

77. See, e.g., Verbaal, "Cicero," on Cicero's interest in Dionysius of Syracuse's tyranny (*Tusc.* Bk. 5) because of his own concerns regarding Caesar.

78. Grant and Tracy, *History,* 94; Ramm, *Interpretation,* 55; Wyckoff, *Pneuma,* 22–24.

79. Ramm, *Interpretation,* 58–59.

80. Grant and Tracy, *History,* 92–93; Wengert, "Luther," 93. For Ernesti, a classical scholar in 1761, see Ramm, *Interpretation,* 59.

81. Wyckoff, *Pneuma,* 35, following Krentz, *Method,* 7–18; cf., e.g., Luther's and Calvin's evaluation of Paul's argument in Gal 4:21–31 in Bray, *Galatians, Ephesians,* 159–60. Indeed, pre-Christian historians had already raised many critical issues developed in modern historiography (see Keener, *Acts,* 1:122–31).

82. Kennedy, "Criticism," 126.

83. Klauck, *Context,* 1.

84. See Lightfoot, *Commentary* (a reprint edition).

85. Archer, *Hermeneutic,* 125; cf. Oliverio, *Hermeneutics,* 91.

86. Archer, *Hermeneutic,* 101–2n44. On a popular level "inductive common sense reason-

ing" was deployed in proof-texting (Archer, *Hermeneutic,* 62–63; cf. Oliverio, *Hermeneutics,* 118–19, 130).

87. He was grandson of Elmer Kirk Fisher, pastor of Azusa Street Mission's sister church, the Upper Room Mission (Olena, *Horton,* 25–40).

Notes to Chapter 9

1. Even authors can gain subsequent insight into their work, especially if they are elaborating material that originally held a larger meaning. Only after writing *Impossible Love,* which formally addresses a romance between my wife and myself, did it strike me how the obvious theme of God's love for us not only runs deeper but offers a fuller (humanly) "impossible love."

2. Brown, *Scripture as Communication,* 69–72, emphasizes that the contemporary approach is more nuanced than earlier authorial approaches.

3. Burridge argues that "the purpose of the author is essential to any concept of genre as a set of expectations or contract between the author and the reader or audience" (Burridge, *Gospels,* 125; cf. also e.g., Shuler, *Genre,* 32; Allison, *Moses,* 3; Ashton, *Understanding,* 113). The classic defense of authorial intention is Hirsch, *Validity,* though the discussion has shifted since that time; for a brief discussion of this hermeneutic, see Osborne, "Hermeneutics," esp. 390–91; Meyer, *Realism,* 35–41.

4. Eliot, "Tradition," 454–55, 459–60.

5. Wimsatt and Beardsley, *Icon,* 10, 13–14.

6. Wimsatt and Beardsley, *Icon,* 18.

7. Hays, *Echoes,* 201n90 (citing Wimsatt and Beardsley, "Intentional Fallacy," 3, 5). Talbert, *Mediterranean Milieu,* 17, cites Hays approvingly. Vanhoozer, *Meaning,* 96n167, also distinguishes Wimsatt's original and reasonable objection in other respects from some subsequent applications of the essay; see also Hirsch, *Validity,* 12. From Hirsch's perspective emphasizing authorial intention, the only texts "for which aesthetic criteria would be both intrinsic and sufficient are texts which have only aesthetic aims" (*Validity,* 155).

8. See comments on relevance theory on pp. 69, 145, 194, 247 in the present book, and further theoretical comment in Brown, *Scripture as Communication,* 35–38.

9. The decoding and reencoding analogy may separate the steps too precisely where there remains significant cultural overlap.

10. One encounters these regularly in the news, although many grievances are political contrivances from the left or the right. For some examples from the left, see Powers, *Silencing,* 78, 81.

11. See Bauckham, *Gospels for Christians,* esp. idem, "Gospels." For target audiences, however, see Burridge, "People," 143.

12. Texts may also be used as propaganda, and sometimes Seneca may have used Epicurus to this effect in his letters to Lucilius. Nevertheless, Seneca's application normally had a foundation in the historical sense.

13. Interpreters often cite communication theory, on which see further Searle, *Expression;* idem, *Speech Acts;* Littlejohn and Foss, *Encyclopedia;* idem, *Theory;* cf. Searle and Vanderveken, *Foundations.*

14. Stein, *Guide,* 11.

15. Cf. also Chrysostom *Hom. Cor.* 29.2; esp. Severian of Gabala *Pauline Commentary*

from the Greek Church (Bray, *Corinthians,* 118): unclean spirits compel pagans' prophecies and the speakers do not understand, "whereas the [true] prophet's soul is enlightened and reveals what the prophet has learned and understood." Contrast the more common ancient view that ecstatic prophecy displaced the mind, e.g., in *Sib. Or.* 12.295–96; Aune, *Prophecy,* 47; Piñero, "Mediterranean View."

16. E.g., Ezek 2:1, 3, 6, 8; 3:1, 3–4, 10, 17, 25; etc.

17. Even with prophets; cf. perhaps διὰ τῶν προφητῶν (Matt 2:23; Luke 1:70; 18:31; Acts 3:18, 21; Rom 1:2).

18. Views noted in Grey, *Crowd,* 42.

19. Grey, *Crowd,* 56.

20. Henry, *God Who Speaks,* 281, as cited in Wyckoff, *Pneuma,* 67. That intention's significance for contemporary audiences remains consistent with, though stretched beyond, the original intention (Henry, *God Who Speaks,* 281, as cited in Wyckoff, *Pneuma,* 136–37).

21. Poirier, "Critique," 2; cf. Poirier and Lewis, "Hermeneutics," 12. Indeed, before the reign of modern historical criticism, Baconian induction dominated (Archer, *Hermeneutic,* 50–51, 62; Oliverio, *Hermeneutics,* 108), an approach that should support the valuing of context (see, e.g., the valuable nineteenth-century scholarship of J. B. Lightfoot).

22. Acknowledged also by Hirsch, *Validity,* 19. See, e.g., Pindar *Nem.* 3.1–5; Callim. *Aetia* 1.1.1–38; Ovid *Fasti* 6.5–8; Dio Chrys. *Or.* 36.34–35 (later poets being less inspired than earlier ones). For the biblical prophets, see, e.g., 2 Pet 1:21; Philo *Spec. Laws* 1.65; 4.49; *Num. Rab.* 18:12; Justin *Apol.* 1.36. For discussion of inspiration and possession, see further Keener, *Acts,* 1:896–909.

23. For error despite divine inspiration, cf. Philost. *Hrk.* 25.4, 8 with *Hrk.* 24.1–2; 25.10–17; Lucian *True Story* 2.32; perhaps Hierocles *How Should One Behave toward the Gods?* (Stobaeus *Anth.* 1.3.53; criticizing Homer *Il.* 9.497); Libanius *Refutation* 1.1; 2.1.

24. Also see Poirier, "Authorial Intention"; for Aristotle, Poirier also cites De Cuypere and Willems, "Meaning."

25. Poirier, "Critique," 4, cites Augustine *Doctr. Chr.* 2.5.6; 2.13.19; 3.27.38. Whether Augustine's approaches always yielded the authors' thoughts may surely be doubted, but the goal remains interesting nonetheless.

26. Iren. *Her.* 1.8.1. For Valentinian reinterpretation of NT language apart from its historical context, see Grant, *Gnosticism,* 140.

27. For criticisms, see, e.g., Lentricchia, *After New Criticism,* 256–80; Hoy, *Critical Circle,* 11–40; I owe these references to my Duke colleague Dwight N. Peterson. Archer, *Hermeneutic,* 201, cites against Seung, *Semiotics,* 10–45, and seems to agree with the dismissal of Hirsch's approach as naïve in Lundin, *Disciplining Hermeneutics,* 21. Westphal, *Community,* 46–56, critiques Hirsch's approach as problematic.

28. For Hirsch's influence on Fee's hermeneutic, see Oliverio, *Hermeneutics,* 171.

29. Hirsch, *Validity,* 1–5. Westphal, *Community,* 57–68, speaks less alarmingly of "revoking authorial privilege." Bartholomew, *Hermeneutics,* 313, cites examples of scholars who "pronounced the author dead" (Barthes, "Death"; Foucault, "Author") and others who have "declared the return of the author!" (Burke, *Death*).

30. Hirsch, *Validity,* 3. The objective is not the author's thoughts but what he sought to communicate (Hirsch, *Validity,* 18). He treats emphasis on purely intrinsic literary criticism as a reaction against nineteenth-century positivist fixation on causal patterns (145). He affirms

Gadamer's rejection of inaccessible authorial thought processes although criticizes him for going too far (248).

31. Hirsch, *Validity,* 4–5.

32. Hirsch, *Validity,* 6–9.

33. Hirsch, *Validity,* 12; for the author's meaning as "only partially accessible" see 17; for dependence on judgments of probability, see 173–79, esp. 173–74; for contrasting intention and accomplishment, 153. We cannot reconstruct fully the cultural givens (40–44), but recognizing this limitation need not produce total skepticism (40); symbols of all cultures, including our own, are learned (43), and we can misinterpret any text (44).

34. Hirsch, *Validity,* 18.

35. Westphal, *Community,* 57 (citing R. Barthes, M. Foucault, and J. Derrida), 63 and 67 (on P. Ricoeur). Even Derrida, against common misunderstanding, did not argue that texts are completely independent of authors; see Smith, "Inc/arnation," 112–19, as cited in Oliverio, *Hermeneutics,* 218–19.

36. Westphal, *Community,* 63, quoting Ricoeur, *Hermeneutics,* 91, 201. For Ricoeur, the focus is less on the author behind the text than on the text itself and the possibilities it opens (Westphal, *Community,* 64). Of course, as the inadequacies of formalism demonstrated, we cannot read texts as autonomous entities apart from contexts, which is why the conflict over which contexts take priority has been so heated.

37. See, e.g., Archer, *Hermeneutic,* 178–79, 182, 190, 200–201.

38. John Wyckoff, personal correspondence, April 26 and May 10, 2015.

39. See, e.g., Spawn and Wright, "Emergence," 4, noting his involvement "For more than thirty years."

40. Fee, *Listening,* 9. Fee also emphasizes how biblical texts are *designed* (*Listening,* 11).

41. Fee, *Listening,* 9.

42. Archer, *Hermeneutic,* 178–79, 203 (critiquing also, e.g., Gordon Anderson). To depict Archer's own view as completely dismissing authorial input, however, is probably unfair; certainly he wants readers to understand his own authorial intention, sometimes seeking to make this clear textually (note, e.g., his third-person reference to himself in Archer, *Hermeneutic,* 249: "this author is reiterating").

43. Fee, *Listening,* 9.

44. Fee, *Listening,* 10, recognizing, however, that intentionality differs by genre.

45. Cf. Keener, *Background Commentary,* 596. Regarding the authenticity of 2 Thessalonians, see 361n12 below. See sources in Keener, *Acts,* 2533; also Porter, *Paul,* 228–36.

46. This may be one reason for Fee's caution in deriving theology from narrative, discussed elsewhere in this book (pp. 166–67, 252). Intention affects genre itself (see Walton, *Thought,* 228, following Halpern, *Historians,* 8), though implied genre normally takes for granted more widely shared cultural assumptions.

47. Hernando, *Dictionary,* 26n24.

48. Archer, *Hermeneutic,* 218. On the value of Eco's "model reader," see also Green, *Practicing Theological Interpretation,* 18–19 and idem, *Seized,* 57, following esp. Eco, *Reader.*

49. Allison, *Moses,* 3.

50. Hirsch, *Validity,* 24–26. He avers, "Validity requires a norm—a meaning that is stable and determinate no matter how broad its range of implication and application" (126). Hirsch complains that, safeguarding against nihilism, Gadamer uses the text's stable meaning as a norm, yet Gadamer then contends that meanings change (251).

51. Hirsch, *Aims,* 79, 90 (brought to my attention by Dwight Peterson).

52. Fee, *Gospel,* 40. Dickens was not evangelical, but his social commitments were strongly shaped by Christian conviction (see Colledge, *God and Dickens,* 111–36; on *A Christmas Carol,* see 52–53, 121).

53. This language, too, has invited criticism, although most recognize narrative strategies (see Aune, *Dictionary of Rhetoric,* 228). For the implied author as distinct from the actual historical author, see, e.g., Bauer, "Function," 131.

54. See, e.g., Job 12:2; 1 Cor 4:8; 2 Cor 11:8; *Sib. Or.* 3.57–59; Jos. *Apion* 1.295; *Rhet. Alex.* 21, 1434a.17–32; 35, 1441b.24–28; Cicero *Fam.* 5.2.8; *Orator* 40.137; *Phil.* 13.2.4; *Sest.* 37.80; *Sulla* 24.67; *Verr.* 2.1.6.17; 2.2.31.76; 2.5.10.25; Sil. It. 11.254–55; Dio Chrys. *Or.* 31.9–10; 47.25; Lucian *Zeus Rants;* Quint. *Decl.* 306.28; 338.26; Apul. *Apol.* 75, 100; see many ancient examples in Duke, *Irony,* 8–12; O'Day, *Revelation,* 12–18; cf. Walde, "Irony"; Braund, "Satire." Some attributed irony's invention to Socrates (Cicero *Brutus* 292; Fronto *Ad M. Caes.* 3.15.2).

55. Patte, *Structural Exegesis,* 21, 25.

56. Cf. Osborne, *Spiral,* 154–55, 161–62, 394; Bartholomew, *Hermeneutics,* 418–20; cf. also seeking to remain within the boundaries of communicative intention, in Brown, *Scripture as Communication,* 85.

57. Benson, "Ignorant," 189–91.

58. Archer, *Hermeneutic,* 230 (or, more precisely, an "implied community," 245).

59. See Osborne, *Spiral,* 162–63. Critics do often distinguish the implied reader from real readers and narratees (Fowler, "Reader," esp. 10–11).

Notes to Chapter 10

1. Most of the following appears also in Keener, *Acts,* 1:18–23.

2. See Tyson, "History to Rhetoric," 23.

3. Tyson, "History to Rhetoric," 25–30.

4. Tyson, "History to Rhetoric," 30–31. For one recent survey of "background" approaches to Acts, see Baslez, "Monde"; for collections of some relevant background, see, e.g., Evans, *Texts,* 373–78; Boring, Berger, and Colpe, *Commentary;* Green and McDonald, *World.*

5. McKnight and Malbon, "Introduction," 18; Donahue, "Redaction Criticism," 45–48; Byrskog, "History," 258–59, 283; Peterson, *Acts,* 41; Padilla, *Speeches,* 10–11.

6. See, e.g., Malina and Pilch, *Acts,* 3–5, noting esp. Prickett, *Origins of Narrative.* For their plea for taking into account the original social contexts, see also Malina and Pilch, *Letters,* 5–9.

7. See Kurz, *Reading Luke-Acts,* 173, also noting the extrinsic reality of this author and audience, regardless of our ability to reconstruct them. On the importance of the rhetor's goal in modern rhetorical criticism, see, e.g., Brock and Scott, *Criticism,* 412.

8. See Bauer and Powell, "Introduction," 8n18; more fully, Powell, "Readings."

9. With e.g., Dunn, "Reconstructions," 296 (though cf. qualifications on 309–10). For the necessity of taking into account cultural context even in translation, see, e.g., Wendland, *Cultural Factor.*

10. See, e.g., Vanhoozer, *Meaning,* 242 (noting that reference to the author's language necessarily implies reference on some level to an author's intention). Thus not only idioms but even lexemes and smaller symbolic units depend on a shared cultural history for their

meaning; even language is a facet of culture (cf. Malina, *Windows*, xi), so denying its relevance for reconstructing a communication is naïve.

11. More than anticipated by the human authors, who did not expect us as secondary readers, and far more than anticipated in the confident assumptions that informed some of an earlier generation's redaction-critical excesses.

12. Cf. Hirsch, *Validity*, 102–11. The more specific to the context are our parallels, the more relevant is the evidence in question (183–93). From the standpoint of intention, cf. Shuler, *Genre*, 32.

13. See Burridge, *Gospels*; idem, "Biography"; idem, "Gospels and Acts"; idem, "Biography: Ancient"; Keener, *Historical Jesus*, 73–94.

14. E.g., Quint. *Inst.* 10.1.36; Max. Tyre 26.4; 38.4. Admittedly perhaps often not on the practical levels noticed by modern critics; see Conte and Most, "Genre." Rhetoricians distinguished various categories for literary forms (e.g., Theon *Progymn.* 2.5–33). The library at Alexandria may have played a role in emphasizing genre for library classification (see Fuller, "Classics," 189, summarizing George Kennedy's oral contribution).

15. See, e.g., examples in Malherbe, "Theorists." Different genres of speeches invited different styles (Dion. Hal. *Demosth.* 45–46).

16. Race, "Introduction," 1.

17. Burridge, *Gospels*, 27–29.

18. Hengel and Schwemer, *Between Damascus and Antioch*, ix. For some, such ahistoricism permits their privileging of their scholarly tradition's hypothetical constructs of early Christianity over the probably better-informed (albeit no less perspectival) reconstruction of Luke.

19. Hengel and Schwemer, *Between Damascus and Antioch*, ix.

20. Klauck, *Context*, 2; cf. Osborne, "Hermeneutics," 391–95. On the importance of recognizing the texts' ancient context, see also discussions in Malina, *Anthropology*, 153–54; Malina, *Windows*, xi–xiii; cf. Spencer, "Approaches," 399.

21. I used to write mythological fiction (in my childhood), science fiction, and a comic urban romance; these sorts of works all were shaped in part by my own limitations of knowledge, language, and to some extent genre (which I sometimes subverted) and even culturally and literarily shaped dimensions of my imagination.

22. Kurz, *Reading Luke-Acts*, 173; on speech-act theory, see also, e.g., Brown, *Scripture as Communication*, 32–35. See the extensive theoretical reflection on texts as communicative acts (218–29) and authors as communicative agents (229–40) in Vanhoozer, *Meaning* (including Searle's speech act theory on 243); for implications, see 240–65.

23. Klutz, *Exorcism Stories*, 16.

24. Klutz, *Exorcism Stories*, 17, emphasizing "the sociocultural facet of stylistics . . . developed . . . by the British linguist Roger Fowler" as a form of "linguistic criticism."

25. Smith, "Understand," 48.

26. For speeches (despite the fact that speeches were designed so as to invite hearers to follow the flow of thought; Theon *Progymn.* 2.149–53), see, e.g., Quint. *Inst.* 10.1.20–21; for Homer, see Hermog. *Method in Forceful Speaking* 13.428. Johnson, *Romans*, 19–20, rightly notes that an ideal reader will catch more of the meaning, reading a work multiple times if needed.

27. Talbert, *Mediterranean Milieu*, 14–15 (citing Peter J. Rabinowitz and Hans Robert Jauss). See also Aune, *Dictionary of Rhetoric*, 229, as noted above.

28. Talbert, *Mediterranean Milieu*, 15 (distinguishing this approach from W. Iser's "im-

plied reader," who is inferred solely from the text; cf. Iser, *Implied Reader*). Cf. Lang, *Kunst*, 56–89.

29. See Bendlin, "Intertextuality," 873–74. For ancient texts deliberately evoking earlier texts, see, e.g., Menander *Aspis* 426–29, 432; Libby, "Theseus"; for intertextuality in OT works, see Hays, *Echoes*, 14.

30. Bendlin, "Intertextuality," 874.

31. For some relevant seminal works, see, e.g., Sperber and Wilson, "Précis"; idem, *Relevance*; Wilson and Sperber, "Outline"; idem, "Representation"; I owe these citations to Gutt, *Relevance Theory*, 77–79. With regard to biblical studies, see, e.g., Green, "Pragmatics"; idem, "Interpretation"; idem, "Relevance Theory"; Jobes, "Relevance Theory"; Brown, *Scripture as Communication*, 35–38; Sim, "Relevance Theoretic approach," ch. 2. For its compatibility with speech-act theory (despite the different emphases), see Brown, *Scripture as Communication*, 35n16, 46–47.

32. Communication within a shared framework always leaves some information implicit, economizing language (Gutt, *Relevance Theory*, 33).

33. See further, e.g., Gutt, *Relevance Theory*, 27; Sim, "Relevance Theoretic Approach," ch. 2.

34. Gutt, *Relevance Theory*, 28; "context" here involves the hearer's "cognitive environment" (Gutt, *Relevance Theory*, 21–22). Thus some messages cannot be communicated without background information for the speaker's original context (Gutt, *Relevance Theory*, 35, 63–68, 71–74).

35. Cf. Cartledge, "Theology," who values both evangelical hermeneutical approaches (modeled by Anthony Thiselton and N. T. Wright) and charismatic interests, through the Paraclete who both preserves and develops Jesus's message (John 14:26). Cf. also Tuppurainen, "Contribution."

36. Agreeing here with Autry, "Dimensions"; Waddell, "Hearing," 175; Green, *Practicing Theological Interpretation*, 41, 124; idem, *Seized*, 59, 126–36.

37. Green, *Practicing Theological Interpretation*, 45. For the historical particularity of biblical narrative works, see also 53–54. Cf. further Green, *Seized*, 9–10.

38. Green, *Practicing Theological Interpretation*, 50–56. Others have often offered the same recognition, e.g., Marshall, *Historian and Theologian*.

39. Green, *Practicing Theological Interpretation*, 126–27. Cf. Mulholland, *Shaped*, 74: hearing "the Bible within its cultural contexts" helps us hear its countercultural elements more decisively.

40. With Spawn and Wright, "Emergence," 7.

41. Martin, "Psalm 63," 269; for valuing both the original message and how it speaks to present readers, see, e.g., Martin, "Hearing," 215. Following Brueggemann (Brueggemann, *Message*, 3–66), Martin, "Psalm 63," 265, also favors a "postcritical" approach that draws on both the best of pietist devotion and the best of scholarly insight. Cf. also Pinnock in Spawn and Wright, "Emergence," 9.

42. Grey, *Crowd*, 156, citing Childs, *Theology*, 380, and emphasizing (Grey, *Crowd*, 156–58) our participation in the history of God's people.

43. Ervin, "Hermeneutics" (*Pneuma* version), 18, as cited in Wyckoff, *Pneuma*, 131.

44. Hollenweger, "Contribution."

45. Pinnock, "Work of Spirit," 241. Less restrictively, Grey, *Crowd*, 126–27, limits meanings to those that can be connected to the language or images of the text. Archer, *Hermeneutic*,

255–59, tests interpretations by the Spirit, the historical views of the church, cross-cultural evaluation, and evaluation by academic communities. Osborne, *Spiral*, 413, urges a "polyvalent attitude" that refines readers' understanding in dialogue with the text as opposed to the relativism of "pure polyvalence." Westphal, *Community*, 43, contends that no one really advocates complete hermeneutical relativism.

46. When a sign designates a construct "not directly perceivable in extra-linguistic reality" it "*must be supplied by the perceiver of the sign*" (Wittig, "Theory," 85). Although the signified must be *congruent* with the signs (87), it need not designate the referent intended in an original context; systems such as Freudian and Jungian psychology or Marxism "providing meaning *to* the text rather than discovering meaning *in* the text," requiring us to recognize explicitly the models being employed (90–91).

47. Cf. Hirsch, *Validity*, 123: a text may *permit* various interpretations, but its genuine implications must reflect "the type of meaning" that the author could have intended. Because the author could not envision many situations, however, we might speak instead of recontextualizing in terms of how authors might have expressed themselves in the new situations.

48. Spawn and Wright, "Emergence," 15; see also 20–21, citing favorably works by Francis Martin, George Montague, and James O'Brien; see also Spawn and Wright, "Cultivating," 193, 196–97.

49. Anderson, "Pentecostal Hermeneutics"; see in this connection also the beginning of "Pentecostal Hermeneutics Part 2."

50. Dornisch, "Symbolic Systems," 11. Cf. also Gross, *Preach*, 95–96 (commenting on Ricoeur, *Interpretation Theory*, 76–79). On probability theory in approaching meaning, see Osborne, *Spiral*, 406–8.

51. Thiselton, *Horizons*, 439.

52. Thiselton, *Horizons*, 445; cf. also xx.

53. With Mulholland, *Shaped*, 19; cf. 133–34.

54. See D. W. Kerr in Oliverio, *Hermeneutics*, 91–92, contrasting reading one's views into Scripture with humbly submitting to it.

55. With Green, *Seized*, 77.

56. Vanhoozer, *Meaning*, 461; cf. 400 (noting Hirsch's application of Kant). Cf. Hirsch, *Validity*, 244: "interpretation is the construction of *another's* meaning."

57. John 19:37; Rom 9:17; 10:11; 11:2; Gal 3:16; 1 Tim 5:18; Jas 2:23; 4:5–6.

58. See wisely Foskett, *Interpreting*, 32: "To read the Bible contextually is to take seriously that Scripture is composed, read, and interpreted in particular human situations and that the word comes to life anew in them."

59. See discussion in Keener, *Mind*, 206–15; in 1 John, see Keener, "Transformation."

60. Wyckoff, *Pneuma*, 137, terming the latter form of meaning "significance." He follows here also work by Arden C. Autry. Others also prefer "significance" for a text's contemporary implications; see, e.g., Osborne, *Hermeneutical Spiral*, 397–415; Stein, *Guide*, 38–39; Klein, Blomberg, and Hubbard, *Introduction*, 401.

61. Grey, *Crowd*, 132, 152, citing also insights from others, including David Parker and Wonsuk Ma.

62. After discovering the original purpose of the communication, exposition should "drive this meaning home to our present society with the same impact it had when it was originally written" (Mickelsen, *Interpreting the Bible*, 56), contextualizing for new settings (172).

Normally this will challenge modern hearers far more than the more common approach of simply giving them what they already think.

63. See further Vanhoozer, *Meaning*, 201–452; Brown, *Scripture as Communication*.

64. Archer, *Hermeneutic*, 207, citing the work of earlier scholars, emphasizes sufficient indeterminacy in biblical texts to permit "the possibilities of future meaning."

65. Cf. Aquinas on the literal meaning being foundational (Wyckoff, *Pneuma*, 19; Crites, "Intellect," 18). For Aquinas, Scripture was the highest authority (Levy, Krey, and Ryan, *Romans*, 42, citing *Summa Theologica* 1.1.8 ad 2).

66. Hirsch, *Validity*, 128.

67. Hirsch, *Validity*, 131–32.

68. Hirsch, *Validity*, 61–71. There is no limit to possible implications, insofar as one simply selects what to emphasize (139–40). Hirsch initially tied implications very tightly to the text's original purpose (e.g., *Validity*, 113), but recognized that some authors expected their texts to be used beyond what they expressly intended (123; cf. further comment in Vanhoozer, *Meaning*, 264). "Significance" is essentially "application"; Gadamer's conflict with Hirsch is whether this objective should be excluded from the interpretive process to prevent hermeneutical relativism (Westphal, *Community*, 111).

69. Cf. Stibbe, "Thoughts," 192, disavowing exalting "significance over meaning" or disconnecting the two.

70. Brown, *Scripture as Communication*, 105–6n21, points out that, despite the authors' differences, Ricoeur's "potential meanings" are somewhat akin to Hirsch's "implications." Cf. also Gerhart, "Notion," cited in Osborne, *Spiral*, 391–92.

71. Here I do not venture into questions of the author's subconscious mind and conscious will, as in Hirsch, *Validity*, 51–57 (esp. 51–53), but am thinking of the context the author simply takes for granted.

72. Not in Iser's sense of what a text in isolation from its formative context implies, but in the wider sense of what a text in connection with its formative context implies.

73. Cf. Fee, *Listening*, 11: biblical texts are *designed*—to help people serve and worship God.

74. See, e.g., Dion. Hal. *Ant. rom.* 1.2.1; Val. Max. 2.pref.; Lucian *Hist.* 59; Max. Tyre 22.5; Fornara, *Nature of History*, 115–16; Lang, *Kunst*, 7–13, 97–167; Marguerat, *Histoire*, 28–29; Keener, *Acts*, 1:148–65; Laistner, *Historians*, 113–14; Williams, "Germanicus."

Notes to Chapter 11

1. My use of the masculine pronoun defers to majority linguistic convention and is not intended to attribute biological gender to the transcendent deity.

2. For the relationship, see, e.g., Thiselton, "New Hermeneutic," 82; in Pentecostal literature, see, e.g., Hernando, *Dictionary*, 20.

3. Stronstad, "Trends," offers this contrast between the intrapentecostal discussion of Gordon Fee and the epistemological approach of Ervin, "Hermeneutics" (*Pneuma* version). For the Spirit's epistemic role, as articulated by Bernard Ramm, Ian T. Ramsey, and others, see the summary in Wyckoff, *Pneuma*, 60–62.

4. The self-defeating character of that assertion was one significant reason for the decline

of logical positivism in philosophy (McGrath, *Universe,* 195; Geivett and Habermas, "Introduction," 14).

5. See discussion in, e.g., Copleston, *Philosophy,* 43–44; Gorsuch, "Limits," 284–85; Gerhart and Russell, "Mathematics," 122–24; Smart, *Philosophers,* 30, 40; Barbour, *Religion and Science,* 109–10; Polkinghorne and Beale, *Questions,* 26–27, 52; Jaki, *Patterns,* 200–201; Margenau, "Laws," 62; Mott, "Science"; Salam, "Science," 97–98; Townes, "Question," 123; Granit, "Attitude," 178; Snell, "Science," 211; Szentágothai, "Existence," 215; Hart, *Delusions,* 10–11; Licona, *Resurrection,* 102; also Ian Hutchinson, as cited in Ecklund, *Science,* 107–8.

6. Technically one should also add that their past is less directly observable than that of galaxy or star formation that we may view through light that has reached us after billions of years.

7. Cf. various discussions in Polanyi, *Science,* 41; Kuhn, *Structure;* Barbour, *Myths;* Gutting, *Paradigms;* Popper, *Myth of Framework.* Cf. the example of Kepler in Koestler, "Kepler," 56.

8. Cf. physicist Sylvester James Gates Jr., director of String and Particle Theory at the University of Maryland, as cited in Ecklund, *Science,* 108: "Science is about measuring things. It is not about truth, but it is about reducing the falsity of our beliefs."

9. In practice, one who approached relationships with a purely empirical epistemology, demanding replication for every claim, would likely find his or her pool of associates shrinking quickly. But then in practice no one presses empirical questioning this far, for example by mistrusting the accumulated records of many others' experiments and thus repeating all experiments directly. David Hume sometimes pressed skepticism even further than this, finding in replication only a high degree of probability (e.g., that the sun would be observed to rise daily). But Hume's concern at that point addresses certainty, which differs from sufficient probability for practical purposes. Hume did not employ his skeptical epistemology outside his study (see Taylor, *Hume,* 24–25).

10. I am not rejecting here the value of general revelation but noting that it is not my subject.

11. For the apostolic proclamation in Acts, see, e.g., Dodd, *Preaching,* 21–23; further discussion in Keener, *Acts,* 1:499–500.

12. Cf. the same term for "convict" in John 3:20; 8:46; Jesus exposing the world's sins in 8:21, 24, 34; 9:41; esp. 15:22, 24.

13. Cf. Luther *Sermon on Jn 16;* Efferin, "Paraclete"; Tribble, "Work," 278; Hunt, "Paraclete," 94; Sanders, *John,* 350; Holwerda, *Spirit,* 52; Keener, *John,* 2:1029–30; Michaels, *Gospel of John,* 833.

14. For testimony's role also in shaping spiritual formation (cf. Matt 10:32//Luke 12:8), cf. Drury, *Saying.* For its importance in Latino/a spirituality, see, e.g., Chaván de Matviuk, "Growth" (e.g., 218–22); Pedraja, "*Testimonios.*"

15. This applies not only to unbelievers but also to believers (cf. 1 John 2:27); before elaborating the content of Ephesians, Paul had been praying that his audience would understand that content (Eph 1:17–18; cf. prayers in Phil 1:9–10; Col 1:9–10).

16. Cf. children who know the Father in 1 John 2:14; knowing and understanding God is the right matter for boasting (Jer 9:23–24; 1 Cor 1:26, 31).

17. Cf. also Mulholland, *Shaped,* 67. The gospel may be grammatically intelligible yet it remains foolishness to the person without the Spirit (1 Cor 1:18–25; 2:14–3:4; see Wyckoff, *Pneuma,* 88, citing an unpublished manuscript of Arden C. Autry).

18. He defines faith as an act of decision, but sundered from a basis of objective evidence (Bultmann, *Mythology*, 38–39; cf. Thiselton, *Horizons*, 263) or concrete revelation in history (cf. Tenney in Ladd, *Bultmann*, v).

19. See his comments on decision, *Entweder-Oder*, in Bultmann, *Word*, 31, 47; Bultmann, *Theology*, 9, though his demythologization of its eschatological value (*Word*, 35; Bultmann, *Theology*, 22–23) seems to resist Jesus's authority, since Jesus understood it eschatologically (*Word*, 38) and eschatology should not be reinterpreted (*Word*, 122). This is not to imply that M. Heidegger's existentialism fits the NT, but to point to an area of overlap valuable for highlighting and translating an element sometimes neglected by other forms of NT scholarship. Bultmann saw affinity between Heidegger and Luther (Thiselton, *Horizons*, 178–79), but claimed that the NT, rather than Heidegger, dictated his Heideggerian understanding (*Horizons*, 226, 232, 262). Theology can learn from philosophy (Bultmann, "Historicity," 96), and Heidegger's analysis can be fruitfully adapted through Kierkegaard's Christian approach (Bultmann, "Historicity," 101). Bultmann claimed that existential understanding is not a bias, but a necessary perspective (Bultmann, "Exegesis," 149). Unlike Bultmann, Heidegger publicly supported the Nazi Party, although his extramarital affairs with Jewish students contradicted Nazi policy and might call into question his commitment to its ideology.

20. Keener, *Mind*, 1–29.

21. See Keener, *Mind*, 23–29.

22. See Keener, *Mind*, 143–72, esp. 155.

23. By this I do not mean, with Bultmann (Bultmann, "Mythology," 38), that faith is an act of decision apart from objective evidence, a Kierkegaardian leap in the dark. Most believers would agree that Christ "encounters us in the word of proclamation" rather than in historical analysis (Bultmann, "Mythology," 39), but this does not mean embracing information that we believe has been falsified by historical analysis.

24. This may be easier for me to say than for some others because I once started from atheistic premises and became convinced that Christ rather than atheism was true. But I am especially grateful to Dr. Claude Black, my undergraduate philosophy professor, for bringing to my attention the matter of competing presuppositions. Everyone starts with some preunderstanding, and faith is a legitimate one (see, e.g., A. Mickelsen, *Interpreting the Bible*, 69–71).

25. Epistemic certainty is not possible in ordinary matters to the degree possible, for example, in mathematics. See the helpful distinction between certainty and knowledge in Moreland, *Triangle*, 121–26, 131–33; cf. others, e.g., Boyd, *Benefit of Doubt*, 71–72. The intellectual milieu in which we move often forces this issue on Christian scholars.

26. For head coverings, as noted earlier, cf., e.g., Keener, *Paul*, 19–69; idem, "Head Coverings"; for kisses, idem, "Kiss."

27. Valuing both the original message and how it speaks to present readers, see, e.g., Martin, "Hearing," 215; Pinnock, "Work of Spirit," 241.

28. Archer, *Hermeneutic*, 203–5 (here esp. 204; see also Vanhoozer, "Beyond," 92–94, helpfully advocating instead canonical patterns). Archer, *Hermeneutic*, 205, even deems principlizing antithetical to narrative reading, but storytellers have long communicated "morals" or "lessons" in stories, and ancient historians and biographers expressly expected their hearers and readers to draw lessons from their works (see the sources in Keener, *Acts*, 1:148–65). See the appeal to universal principles in Grey, *Crowd*, 122, 126 (citing Ricoeur), although I believe that historical context helps us hear these more concretely (cf. also Grey, *Crowd*, 132, 145), providing

its own sort of narrative framework; see also Klein, Blomberg, and Hubbard, *Introduction*, 407, 421–25; Marshall, *Beyond Bible*, 55–79.

29. Cf. the idea in Brown, *Scripture as Communication*, 264–67, that principlizing is useful, but more useful is contextualization guided by the text's purpose.

30. Also noted by Klein, Blomberg, and Hubbard, *Introduction*, 350, in demurring from Fee and Stuart's approach to narrative, including in Acts.

31. See, e.g., Jennings, *Good News*, 111–16; Williams, *Radical Reformation*, 426–29; and other sources noted above at 311n16. For applications of Luke's Pentecost narrative in various cultures, see, e.g., Chempakassery, "Jerusalem Pentecost"; Bediako, "African Culture," 120; Forrester, "Pentecost" (addressing, e.g., castes); on 2:17–21, Prema, "Paradigm"; Lloyd-Jones, *Christianity;* nonviolent direct action in Alexander, "Action."

32. For the early Pentecostal fondness for narrative, especially Acts, see also Archer, *Hermeneutic*, 182, 187–89; Mittelstadt, *Reading*, 1–2, 14, 19–45 (esp. 19–31). Mittelstadt, *Reading*, 81, cites Jerry Camery-Hoggatt (in personal correspondence) thus: "Pentecostals have been doing narrative theology for years although without the added dimension of critical self-reflection."

33. See Fee, *Gospel*, 100–104, where Fee recognizes the value of Lukan narrative for theology and is merely more cautious how to discern it. Fee and his primary dialogue partners in these pages, R. Menzies and R. Stronstad, agree with his authorial intention hermeneutic.

34. Fee, "Historical Precedent"; Fee, *Gospel*, 94–99, 108–11. Other Pentecostal scholars have pushed back on this point; see, e.g., the survey in Noel, "Fee"; responding to Anthony Thiselton, see (though largely favorably) Archer, "Horizons."

35. Redaction criticism provided a key tool used to support a Pentecostal reading of Luke-Acts (Oliverio, *Hermeneutics*, 168, 179).

36. Fee, *Gospel*, 100–104. Fee accepts that Luke-Acts, taken as a whole, communicates theology (101) and that patterns in Acts suggest repeatability (102). His questioning as to whether Luke "intends his history to be precedent for the church in some way" (103) probably falls short of what we suggest here, but he is correct to note (103) the "diversity of patterns within Acts itself," and reasonable in (104) his uncertainty based on Luke's failure to narrate tongues in every instance (though it appears in three, "probably four, and perhaps five" cases).

37. E.g., Plato *Laws* 1.636CD; 2.672BC; Cic. *Nat. d.* 2.28.70 (the Stoic); Dio Chrys. *Or.* 1.62–63; 8.33; 60.8; Max. Tyre 4.5–8; 26.5–9; Heracl. *Hom. Prob.* 6.6; 8.4–5; 22.1; 26.1, 7–8; 30.1, 4; 31.1, 11; 39.2–17; 52.4–6; 53.1; 60.1; 68.8–9; 69.8–16; Proclus *Poet.* K82.10–17; K90.8–14; K141.16–21; K153.25–29. Cf. Josephus's criticism in *Ag. Ap.* 2.255; Gentile critiques in Sen. *Ep. Lucil.* 88.5; Lucian *Zeus Rants* 40.

38. See Keener, *Acts*, 1:148–58 and sources cited there.

39. See, e.g., Mittelstadt, *Reading*, 40–43.

40. See, e.g., Marguerat, *Histoire*, 333; Marguerat, *Historian*, 152–54, 230; Rosner, "Progress," 232–33; Keener, *Acts*, 4:3758–63.

41. Chevreau, *Turnings*, 54–56, with further details.

42. Salmon, *Heals*, 68; Baker, *Enough*, 76, 171–72, 173; Brown, "Awakenings," 363 (on one eye, citing the testimony of a retired radiologist); Bill Twyman, interview, Corona, CA, Nov. 11, 2007; Chester Allan Tesoro, interview, Baguio, Philippines, Jan. 30, 2009; Gebru Woldu, interview, Wynnewood, PA, May 20, 2010; cf. the "flat and clouded" eyes restored in Robin Shields, personal correspondence, Feb. 7, 2009; cf. the claim in Ogilbee and Riess, *Pilgrimage*, 43.

43. Cf. Montefiore, *Miracles*, 23–65; cf. also "extrabiological energy" in Hirschberg and Barasch, *Recovery*, 144, although not from a specifically skeptical standpoint.

44. Keener, "Raised," 79.

45. Friends include Deborah Watson; Ayodeji Adewuya; Leo Bawa; Timothy Olonade; Thérèse Magnouha; Albert Bissoussoue; Julienne Bissoussoue; Jeanne Mabiala (three accounts); André Mamadzi; Patrice Nsouami; Elaine Panelo; beyond these, witnesses contacted through my brother or mutual friends.

46. Hume deemed miracle witnesses as deceived or deceivers (*Miracles*, 32, 34, 36–37, 52–55; cf. 38: "nothing strange" that people "lie in all ages"), "fools" (39), and subject to "knavery and credulity" (43; 52: "knavery and folly"). Note the criticisms in Cramer, "Miracles," 136–37; Breggen, "Miracle Reports," 6; idem, "Seeds."

47. Cf. further Llewellyn, "Events," 253; Keener, *Miracles*, 667.

48. Sometimes in a preliminary way (John 2:23; 3:2; 4:48–53; 7:31; 10:37–38; 14:11; 16:30–32; 20:25, 29), but this could lead to greater maturity if one persevered (contrast 8:30–31, 59). Faith could also precede signs (11:40; 14:12).

49. See esp. Fretheim, "Plagues." From various perspectives, see, e.g., Hort, "Plagues" (challenged appropriately in Sarna, *Exodus*, 70–73); Stieglitz, "Plagues"; Duncan Hoyt, "Plagues"; Zevit, "Plagues."

50. See Hays, *Conversion*, 190–201. Cf. Provan, Long and Longman, *History*, 48, as cited in Spawn, "Principle," 60; also Stuhlmacher, *Criticism*, as cited in Archer, *Hermeneutic*, 176n18. Most of these scholars do employ historical criticism, but where it is helpful for historical purposes, as opposed to embracing its earlier antisupernatural assumptions (e.g., Stuhlmacher, *Criticism*, 90, as cited in Wyckoff, *Pneuma*, 39).

51. For criticisms of the inappropriate lengths to which a hermeneutic of suspicion is sometimes carried, see, e.g., Thurén, "Sincere"; Hengel and Schwemer, *Between Damascus and Antioch*, 119; for other relevant observations, see, e.g., Horrell and Adams, "Introduction," 37; Brown, *Death*, 7–8; Carson, "Mirror-Reading," 99. Of course, one may criticize an author's perspicacity without impugning his or her motives (Whitehead, *Science*, 25, as cited in Cohen, *Law*, 31). For Pentecostalism's distance from a hermeneutic of suspicion toward the biblical text, see, e.g., Waddell, "Hearing," 191.

52. Kurz, *Reading Luke-Acts*, 173–74.

53. Vermes, *Jesus and Judaism*, 63.

54. God seems more patient with those who had not yet witnessed signs (Judg 6:13–14; Matt 11:20–24//Luke 10:13–15). Passages that speak of past apparent "cessations" (such as Judg 6:13; Ps 44:1–3; 74:9) normally go on to speak of God's renewed works or to plead for God to act again.

55. This contravenes the normal historiographic approach outside miracles; see, e.g., Dilthey, *Pattern*, 141: "Even in contemporary accounts we must first examine the point of view of the reporter, his reliability, and his relation to the event."

56. See Sider, *Christians*. Ron is a close friend and former colleague (see Keener, "Biblical Fidelity," 29). He is not a Marxist; he is driven by biblical conviction consistent with his evangelical Anabaptist heritage.

57. Cf. Mulholland, *Shaped*, 135: "We should come to the scripture expectantly, receptively, openly, eagerly waiting" to meet God there.

Notes to Chapter 12

1. Cf. Seneca *Ep. Lucil.* 108.30 (trans. Richard M. Gummere, LCL 3:249) on the complementarity of many approaches: "When Cicero's book *On the State* is opened by a philologist, a scholar, or a follower of philosophy, each man pursues his investigation in his own way."

2. Cf. the arguments in Keener and Usry, *Faith,* 108–35, especially addressing the Christ-centered transitions involved in all the varied NT images related to soteriology. I confess that I still find the implications of this claim extremely painful; my attempts to exegete honestly do not always yield the outcomes I would have wished.

3. Believers are not alone in experiencing these perceptions; see discussion of ancient philosophers and their detractors in Keener, *Acts,* 4:3537–38.

4. See Keener, *Mind,* ch. 6. Viewed without faith in the God who raised Jesus, the cross itself is simply another travesty of injustice, of the powerful silencing the weak (cf. similarly Green, *Seized,* 153–54).

5. Cf. Augustine's "Believe so as to understand" (various sources cite *Sermon* 43.7, 9; *Tract. Jn.* 29.6) and Anselm's faith seeking understanding (*Proslogion* 1, end), although they cited in support a Latin mistranslation of Isa 7:9 (in *Tract. Jn.* 29.6.2, Augustine more helpfully also cites John 7:17). Some other interpreters cite the need for spiritual rebirth for correct insight (e.g., Ervin, "Hermeneutics," as cited in Spawn and Wright, "Emergence," 6).

6. This is not to say that in practice everyone is equally alienated; Paul and other biblical writers sometimes nuance these stark contrasts (a point to which I return briefly further below). Nevertheless, the stark epistemic contrast reinforces the texts' demands.

7. Note BDAG's first definition for ἔλεγχος (proof), although BDAG translates more loosely here; and possibly BDAG's fourth definition for ὑπόστασις (title deed or guarantee).

8. I am grateful, however, that he is present whether we are conscious of his presence or not, because my ADHD-brain usually fails to remain conscious of anything for a very extended period of time except perhaps when hyper-focused on a train of thought while reading or writing.

9. Spawn and Wright, "Emergence," 5–6, 21, providing especially charismatic Lutheran examples. For a charismatic anthropologist's discussions of worldviews, see, e.g., Kraft, "Worldviews"; idem, *Worldview;* for the historical development of and a challenge to the anti-supernatural worldview, see Long and McMurry, *Collapse* (Long and McMurry are renewalist Presbyterians).

10. See BDB. We believe in or rely on God because of his faithfulness, and this reliance in turn reciprocates fidelity.

11. Some argue that God uses chance to achieve divine goals. In this case, chance could be a mechanism in which God fixed the rules at the beginning to produce some desired outcomes. If one views chance as a divine mechanism, however, one still thinks in terms of ultimate design of the rules. "Design" need not be restricted to micromanagement.

12. Many critical scholars reject the authenticity of 2 Thessalonians, but, at least in the Anglophone sphere, the majority of commentators—those who work most closely with the text—do accept its authenticity. I find implausible the idea that a pseudepigrapher would write, after the temple's destruction in 70 CE, of someone desecrating the temple by enthroning himself there (2 Thess 2:3–4). Imperial worship on the site of the temple never included the emperor's own presence, and the temple was destroyed before such worship in 70 CE took place.

13. How one understands this causation depends on one's theology, and I cannot digress so far here.

14. I accept the authenticity of Ephesians but am aware of the debate. In support of authenticity, see the arguments in various commentators, esp. Hoehner, *Ephesians*, 2–61. Not everyone will agree, but I find Hoehner's case persuasive and have nothing relevant to add to it.

15. He similarly prays for them to be even more fully enlightened (Eph 1:18), even though they are already enlightened (5:8; cf. 3:9).

16. See, e.g., Marshall, *Blood;* Hefley and Hefley, *Blood;* Shortt, *Christianophobia;* Doyle, *Killing;* N, *I Am N;* esp. Marshall and Shea, *Silenced;* Marshall, Gilbert and Shea, *Persecuted.*

17. I later did review one of his books, and I did read it first. But I can well imagine that not every reviewer did.

18. One could elaborate at length here, even from personal experience. One of my favorite reviews of one of my earliest books allows that my inaccurate view of ancient slavery is understandable, since, the reviewer notes, I am African American. (I am ordained in an African-American denomination, but he made inaccurate racial assumptions on that account.) I have read some glowing reviews of my own books that seemed to miss the point no less than some negative ones. Nevertheless, on other occasions some skillful reviewers have understood and communicated my point so clearly that I found myself wishing that I had articulated it so well.

19. The expectation of fair evaluation is not an exclusively modern concept (cf., e.g., Gen 31:37).

20. Although I have observed this often, I think of some comments appended to Candy Gunther Brown's first post in the *Huffington Post* (http://www.huffingtonpost.com/candy -gunther-brown-phd/testing-prayer-science-of-healing_b_1299915.html, posted March 2, 2012). Although I have in mind here posts by some fundamentalist internet atheists, vituperative posts by some fundamentalist internet Christians can be embarrassing as well.

21. I have oversimplified here to avoid digression. See fuller discussion with much greater nuance in, e.g., Copan, *Monster;* Copan and Flannagan, *Genocide.*

22. Many of us would allow for coercive intervention to prevent genocide, but Jesus certainly would not have approved of forcing belief. A belief accepted by compulsion is not one's true belief, at least so long as known alternatives remain intellectually viable.

23. This passage provided a notorious crux in Zwingli's argument with Luther regarding the Eucharist (combined with an unfortunate miscommunication due to Zwingli's use of a Swiss idiom with which Luther was unfamiliar), but it also fits the larger Johannine emphasis on spiritual rather than earthly evaluation (3:12, 31; 7:24; 8:15).

24. Also Andrew's "following" Jesus (1:37–38, 40) connects him with Philip, whom Jesus summons to "follow" him (1:43), like his sheep (10:4–5, 27).

25. To some extent this language may be simply Johannine idiom (cf. 11:34), but the clustering of this vocabulary in these parallel locations seems significant.

26. John's informed audience knows that Jesus's place of origin is from heaven, i.e., from God; 3:13, 31; 6:32–33, 38, 41, 46, 51; 8:23, 42. This is precisely counter to what Jesus's critics aver of him in 9:16, and to which the healed man responds in 9:33.

27. Long ago argued by Aberle, "Zweck" (1861; as cited in Ashton, *Understanding,* 108); Wrede, *Origin,* 83–84; and more recently by Martyn, *Theology;* idem, "Glimpses"; since then, widely held, e.g., Koester, "Brown and Martyn"; Dunn, "John," 302–4; Perkins, *Reading,* 249–50; Hasitschka, "Anmerkungen"; Rensberger, *Faith,* 26; Kysar, "Gospel," 918; Quast, "Community." See further discussion in Keener, *John,* 1:194–214.

28. The back-and-forth exchange between the two verbs in 1 John resembles their largely random distribution also in the Gospel (for which see Keener, *John,* 1:243–46, esp. 245).

29. The specific terminology that contrasts the Spirit of truth with a false spirit already circulated in Jewish circles; see, e.g., 1QS 4.3, 9, 21; 4Q544 i.10–14; ii.13–15; *T. Jud.* 20:1–2; Brown, *Essays,* 147–50; Duhaime, "Voies"; Tigchelaar, "Names of Spirits."

30. A majority of Johannine scholars take seriously the Fourth Gospel's claim to an eyewitness tradition (John 13:23; 19:35; 21:24–25; e.g., Kysar, *John,* 12; O'Day, "John," 500; Witherington, *Wisdom,* 15–17; Smith, *John,* 400; Ridderbos, *John,* 3; Beck, *Paradigm,* 6; Bruce, *John,* 4–5; Bauckham, *Testimony,* 33–72). I have argued that the Gospel's author is also the epistle's author, and that he was an eyewitness of Jesus's ministry (Keener, *John,* 1:81–139; idem, "Beheld," 15–17). This fits the epistolary writer's claim (1 John 1:1–3).

31. They probably sponsored some of his teaching in Ephesus; see Keener, "Asiarchs."

32. Keener, "Spirit Perspectives"; idem, *Mind,* chapter 4.

33. For the ambiguity and complexity of characters' belief in John, see, e.g., Sevrin, "Nicodemus Enigma," 369; Grant, "Ambiguity"; and now esp. Hylen, *Imperfect Believers.*

34. Osborne, *Spiral,* 341, quotes approvingly Larkin, *Culture,* 289: "Paul locates the barrier in the area of evaluation rather than cognition." Nonbelievers may understand the textual meaning without believing it.

Notes to Chapter 13

1. Mulholland, *Shaped,* 144, contends that "Spiritual reading of scripture also entails an awareness that in the Bible we have something more than simply a human literary production." Klein, Blomberg, and Hubbard, *Introduction,* 93, suggest that the most decisive line among interpreters is "the level of *attitude toward the Bible's trustworthiness.*"

2. E.g., Archer, *Hermeneutic,* 166–67. Charles Parham and others in the movement assumed that Christian experience today should match that reported in Acts (Stronstad, "Trends"), an emphasis he undoubtedly carried over from the Holiness movement. Today, cf. Green, *Practicing Theological Interpretation,* 16: Scripture addresses the church (cf. also 42), so we should see ourselves addressed in Scripture.

3. E.g., McGee, "Radical Strategy," 72 (India in the 1850s), 73 (Indonesia in the 1860s). Cf. also a Methodist missionary in Africa in the 1840s, in Yung, "Integrity," 174; McGee, "Regions Beyond," 70; idem, "Miracles," 253; idem, *Miracles,* 51, 242.

4. Emphasized in some circles in the US as early as the 1860s (Curtis, *Faith,* 64–65).

5. This is not to imply that it does not happen; for reports from the West, see, e.g., Keener, *Miracles,* 1:426–507; most of the accounts in Metaxas, *Miracles.*

6. Spittler, "Enterprise," 65.

7. Scholarship cited in Grey, *Crowd,* 44.

8. Ancient historiography and biography allowed greater flexibility in narrating details than do their modern academic namesakes, but skeptical modern approaches that dismiss from historical consideration all details not verifiable externally also run contrary to our concrete evidence concerning these genres (see Keener, "Otho"). The genre of Greco-Roman historiography does make an implicit claim about the authors' historical intention, not merely recognition that a work is narrative in format.

9. Historical reliability was not their battle, but was normally assumed (see, e.g., Mittel-

stadt, *Reading,* 44; Grey, *Crowd,* 149), sometimes even in fundamentalistic ways (see, e.g., the summary in Grey, *Crowd,* 146–48).

10. E.g., Waddell, "Hearing," 174–75, 181, 197.

11. See, e.g., Ellington, "Authority," 149–50, 162–63.

12. On Calvin here, see Grant and Tracy, *History,* 96; Adhinarta, *Doctrine,* 37–38; Oliverio, *Hermeneutics,* 85; Bartholomew, *Hermeneutics,* 492 (noting also Aquinas); Calvin, *Institutes,* 1:90, as cited in Wyckoff, *Pneuma,* 26; also the Westminster Confession, as noted in Wyckoff, *Pneuma,* 31; and esp. Adhinarta, *Doctrine,* 36. Cf., e.g., Cartledge, "Text-Community-Spirit," 133.

13. See, e.g., Oliverio, *Hermeneutics,* 92; Ellington, "Authority," 162; also the appeal to experience in respondents to the informal survey in 149–50. Ellington notes, however, that it was rapprochement with the broader evangelical community and its cultural battles that led to stricter inerrantist language (151–52, 156; see also Spittler, "Enterprise," 58–60).

14. Especially since the controversies of the 1920s, those who seek to defend God's Word in Scripture have sometimes focused on "inerrancy" as a theological boundary. Others object that this way of framing boundaries may lend too much emphasis to incidental details. Some inflexibly defined inerrantism imposes preconceptions roughshod on actual texts while neglecting inductive study of those texts; it sometimes insists on detail in a manner that focuses on the letter as opposed to the Spirit (cf. Matt 23:23; 2 Cor 3:6). Some recent evangelical writers have defined inerrancy more generously, providing a larger tent that takes into account genre and focuses more on respecting Scripture as it is given; see Blomberg, *Believe;* Walton and Sandy, *World* (also some earlier scholarly definitions, as opposed to popular understanding of the term). For the range of conventional modern evangelical positions within and beyond inerrancy, see Merrick, Garrett, and Gundry, *Views;* Thorsen and Reeves, *Bible,* esp. 115–81. Some evangelicals argue that this narrower way of framing the debate over biblical authority reflects the legacy of distinctively American divide, and thus is of less value elsewhere (Bird, "Inerrancy," 160–65). Pentecostals defined their belief more narrowly as "inerrancy," and not simply inspiration (an intrinsically Pentecostal-friendly concept), when they joined 1940s evangelicalism (Archer, *Hermeneutic,* 87).

15. Luther, for example, embraced what he saw as Paul's message in Galatians while criticizing Paul for lapses in his logic (Wengert, "Luther," 97–99). Jerome "corrected" Paul based on the Hebrew text (112) and complains about Paul (*Ep. Gal.* 3.5.12; Edwards, *Galatians,* xvii, 76).

16. Especially in Keener, *Historical Jesus;* idem, *Acts* vol. 1; idem, *Miracles,* 1:22–33; idem, "Otho"; idem, "Assumptions"; idem, "Biographies."

17. Criticized for translating directly from the Hebrew text, Jerome countered that he also accepted, as did most Christians of his era, the inspiration of the Septuagint (Pollmann and Elliott, "Galatians," 50–51).

18. Hebrews quotes and builds on the LXX even when it varies from the Hebrew text. Christians do not recite Scripture in the original language as many Muslims recite the Qur'an, because we inherit a different concept of inspiration. Granted, in apparent allusions the New Testament sometimes evokes Old Testament wording more than direct meaning, but even in these cases it often suggests analogies (e.g., judgment language could be applied in new settings that invite judgment).

19. Kitchen, *Reliability,* 423. Those who complain that a book can contain only a single genre have only to turn to Exodus, which contains laws as well as narratives, to refute their complaint. Our current division of the story between the close of Genesis and the early narra-

tives of Exodus may have more to do with pragmatic questions of space than with cohesiveness of the narrative.

20. LaSor, Hubbard, and Bush, *Survey,* 18–19 (cf. also some tensions in the patriarchal narratives in 44–45). Cf. the recent, firmly evangelical discussion also by Walton, *Thought,* 179–215; idem, *Genesis One.*

21. Interestingly, in terms of information content, humans are the cosmos's most complex physical beings that we know about.

22. E.g., Luther resisted harmonizing Galatians with its source in Deuteronomy, embracing each text on its own terms (Wengert, "Luther," 112).

23. For this and some other biographic techniques, see Licona, "Biographies"; idem, *Differences.*

24. Qureshi, *Seeking,* 19.

25. Keener and Keener, *Impossible Love.*

26. Jane Campbell, personal correspondence, Aug. 14, 2015.

27. Probably the most notable are Jesus's genealogies in Matt 1:2–16 and Luke 3:23–38; and the accounts of Judas's death in Matt 27:3–5 and Acts 1:18–19 (which I treated briefly in Keener, *Matthew,* 656–62; idem, *Acts,* 1:760–65). There are points of contact but also striking divergences. Such wide variation in overlapping material is rare in the Synoptic Gospels (I am not counting omissions of material, which are less relevant), but it is one reason that most scholars, including myself, think that Luke and Matthew shared a common source or sources besides Mark, rather than that either Luke or Matthew used the other's completed Gospel.

28. See, e.g., Keener, "Otho"; Henderson, "Life"; Hillard, Nobbs, and Winter, "Corpus."

29. As Blomberg notes (*Believe,* 120), not only myself but D. A. Carson, Darrell Bock, and Craig Blomberg have been denounced as liberal by some scholars to our right.

30. And certainly the sources contain very ancient traditions. E.g., Israel would not likely have invented its exodus generation being unable to enter the land, or their continuous rebellions against Moses. Likewise, Numbers preserves a song about Sihon, still sung, about Sihon's exploits before Israel conquered him, apparently from *before* that conquest (Num 21:27–30). I addressed some of these issues in further detail in Keener and Usry, *Faith,* 147–65.

31. That God *did* inspire Scripture does, I think, follow for Christians from respect for Christ's multiply attested view of Scripture (see, e.g., Mark 12:24; Matt 5:18//Luke 16:17; Matt 26:54, 56; Luke 24:27; John 5:45–47; 17:12), pointed out, e.g., in Wenham, *Bible*; Piper, *Glory,* 98–113. For Jesus's distinctive interpretive *approach* to Scripture, however, see pp. 211–16 in the present book.

32. Also, e.g., *1 Clem.* 45.2. The question of canon naturally arises here (especially for the NT), although prophetic inspiration is a wider category than canonicity. Here I can only refer readers to several more detailed discussions and debates, e.g., as noted earlier, McDonald and Sanders, *Debate*; McDonald, *Canon*; Evans and Tov, *Exploring*; Kruger, *Question*; Porter, Evans, and McDonald, *New Testament.*

33. Thus when Green, *Seized,* 160–73, speaks of "renewing biblical authority," he speaks of submitting our lives to its message.

34. Ellington, "Authority," 167, citing here Brueggemann, *Texts under Negotiation,* 12–13.

35. Waddell, "Hearing," 184.

36. Reinforcing the importance of history (as a biblical concept, not, as some detractors complain, a purely modern one), the narrative structure of biblical salvation history provides a partial historical context for other biblical genres (poetic prophecies, poetic prayers, letters,

and so forth) that teach us lessons by means of case studies. We learn more of God's heart partly by observing how God addressed people in their various settings. Many scholars have grappled with the relationship of history to the present. For example, Dilthey values entering the past by historical imagination, but demands hearing the past first on its own terms (Rickman, "Introduction," 44–47), although in different ages we will hear different aspects of it (48). History thus throws light on present reality (60), and is read in light of the present (Dilthey, *Pattern,* 161).

37. Like other writers, biblical authors may also sometimes write in such a way as to seek to facilitate reader identification (see, e.g., Beck, "Anonymity"; idem, *Paradigm*). Some scholars have also begun exploring the inner life of biblical characters (see Leung Lai, *'I'-Window*), which further facilitates reader empathy and identification.

38. See Walton, *Thought,* 165–78, 189; Walton and Sandy, *World.*

39. This approach to nature should characterize Christians regardless of their view of origins. A theistic evolutionist, for example, may affirm that God used evolution as a mechanism to produce outcomes such as exist, and thus praise him for designing it and, if need be, guiding it to produce such outcomes. Skeptics may complain that, in their judgment, a God should not use such an inefficient process; biblical narratives are, however, full of God working in all sorts of different ways, including with human choices, yet achieving necessary outcomes. The church's survival over the centuries (both from external threats and, perhaps more markedly, its members' human failures) also appears as a cause for wonder. Instead of a sterile, robotic pure efficiency, God designed a world of glorious beauty and limited chaos and achieves his wise purposes in ways we can discover only in retrospect and only among those who recognize his wisdom (cf. Rom 11:33–36). That is also true of the way he brought about salvation (1 Cor 1:18–25).

40. Anderson, *Ends of the Earth,* 138: "Pentecostal rituals exhibit a worldview that presupposes that worship is about encountering God, including a faith in an all-powerful God who is *there* to meet human needs." Further, "the experience of the Spirit's presence is seen as a normal part of daily life and is brought to bear upon all situations" (139).

41. Our reading experience may also readjust our understanding of a text's genre (Westphal, *Community,* 29).

42. For one approach to engaging the Bible in dialogue as a friend rather than hiding from it, see Fraser and Kilgore, *Friends.*

43. In Scripture, the devil does tempt directly in major cases (e.g., Mark 1:13; Luke 4:2; 22:3, 31; John 13:27; Acts 5:3); he also is involved in other lives, though (since Satan is not omnipresent) readers may sometimes debate how directly the action is intended (e.g., Mark 4:15; Eph 2:2; Jas 4:7; 1 Pet 5:8). But Scripture is also clear on another level that people are drawn astray by their own desires (Jas 1:14).

44. This was my own misreading; my church was Arminian, but not *that* Arminian. I now understand that this was a misreading; see Keener, "Spirit Perspectives"; idem, *Mind,* 122–27.

45. Torrey, "Supernatural Guidance," 20–21 (excerpted from Torrey, *Person and Work*), warns against "bondage" because of unclear leadings, noting that, "any leading that is not perfectly clear is not from him. . . . If it is His will, the heavenly Father will make it as day." Elsewhere I suggest that we can trust God's providence, his ordering of our steps (Prov 16:9; 20:24), and normally wisdom, as well as (and often in connection with) more intuitive forms of guidance (cf. Keener, *Mind;* the example in Torrey, "Guidance," 18–19). Of course, even the commonsense realism that informed fundamentalism allowed for some pre-rational in-

tuition (cf. Oliverio, *Hermeneutics,* 109), although this may have been understood as innate knowledge.

46. As noted earlier, people in John's Gospel often responded to signs with initial faith, but only when this faith persevered did it become mature faith; even when Bible reading does not feel like an exciting adventure, we persevere because we know that God does and will change us through it.

47. Cf. Grey, *Crowd,* 155–59, on participation in God's people and thus in God's salvation-historical story (cf. also 171–72). Scripture's story offers a metanarrative "in which the Pentecostal reader can locate themselves" (160).

Notes to Chapter 14

1. Thiselton, *Horizons,* 439. For Ricoeur, the NT is the new lens through which the OT is understood; see Ricoeur, *Essays,* 49–72, summarized in Gross, *Preach,* 59–60.

2. Bultmann, *Christianity,* 187: "The Old Testament is still [considered by the NT] the word of God, though not because it contains his word spoken to Israel in the past, but because it is directly typological and allegorical. The original meaning and context of the Old Testament sayings are entirely irrelevant. God does not speak to men through history but through Christ . . ."

3. Paul's use of "allegory" language in Gal 4:24 may reflect the more general ancient sense of the term (see the range of senses in Anderson, *Glossary,* 14–16; Witherington, *Grace,* 322–23); although it may include elements of what we call allegory (see esp. Cover, "Above"; de Boer, *Galatians,* 295–96) it also includes elements of more direct analogy (and typology) in the themes of promise, inheritance, and sonship (see Hays, *Echoes,* 116, 166; Tronier, "Spørgsmålet"; Martyn, *Galatians,* 436; Schreiner, *Galatians,* 300; Harmon, "Allegory," esp. 157; Barclay, *Gift,* 415–16; Keener, *Galatians*). Although Paul probably also polemically inverts his rivals' argument here, too few clues support the suggestion (noted in Anderson, *Rhetorical Theory,* 178–79) that he employs allegory sarcastically.

4. These could also certainly include prophetic or even Deuteronomic readings of the Torah (with Martin, "Hearing," 216), but I shall retain a primary focus on NT readings, which are closer to my expertise. Others also appeal to how Jesus, Paul, and others interpreted the law to find models for Christian readings today (e.g., Brondos, "Freedom"), including models for charismatic reading (Stibbe, "Thoughts," 193).

5. Others have also considered the value of analogies with modern charismata for informing readings of biblical texts; see the thoughtful and nuanced essay by Spawn, "Principle."

6. NT readings of the OT have become a major area of study; a few seminal examples from various approaches include: Longenecker, *Exegesis;* Hays, *Echoes;* idem, *Conversion;* idem, *Reading Backwards;* Ellis, *Old Testament;* Evans and Sanders, *Luke and Scripture;* particularly extensively, see Beale and Carson, *Commentary.* For some concise but helpful observations on NT use of the OT, see also Brown, *Scripture as Communication,* 227–28; Klein, Blomberg, and Hubbard, *Introduction,* 129–31. Intertextuality features prominently in some modern Pentecostal readings (e.g., Waddell, "Hearing," 203).

7. In John's Gospel, Jesus also explains that earthly analogies were needed for humans to relate to God's heavenly truths (John 3:12), perhaps including analogies of water (3:5) and wind (3:8).

8. Probably implicit in Mark 4:20's "accept" (signifying agreement), but explicit in Matt 13:23 ("understand," fitting 13:13–15, 19, 51; 15:10; the verb appears in the quotation in Mark 4:12 and in Jesus's invitations and reproofs in 7:14; 8:17, 21).

9. Hays, *Reading Backwards*, 28–29, rightly suggests that Mark 4:11–34 addresses (29) "the hermeneutics of hearing and understanding the word"; Jesus's parables function as (28) "paradoxical veiled communication," which only some will hear. Late in the process of writing this book I was pleased to discover that Clark Pinnock also appeals to Jesus's model in his approach to Spirit hermeneutics (Pinnock, "Work of Spirit," 234–36).

10. Some scholars advocate a hermeneutic that appreciates experience as in postmodernism, yet also recognizes limits to subjectivity; see, e.g., Fogarty, "Hermeneutic." Delineating such limits, however, can become problematic, itself becoming a subjective process, unless we recognize some controls such as texts' contextual and/or canonical meanings.

11. See, e.g., *b. Sanh.* 38b; Instone-Brewer, *Techniques*, esp. 167; Keener, *Acts*, 2:1587–88. Some writers connected even disjointed material by the use of catchwords; see Perrin, *Thomas and Tatian*, 50; Longenecker, *Rhetoric.* In polemical setting teachers did sometimes adopt critics' or opponents' approaches (see Daube, "Johanan ben Zaccai," 54; cf. Rom 10:5).

12. Because Luke makes nothing of the connection, it seems logical to infer that the exegesis presupposed in this passage likely stems from the historical Jesus himself.

13. See, e.g., *m. Abot* 2:1; 4:2; *Sipra V.D. Deho.* Par. 1.34.1.3; par. 12.65.1.3; *Ab. R. Nat.* 1, §8B; fuller discussion in Keener, *Matthew*, 551. Cf. Pinnock, "Work of Spirit," 235.

14. See, e.g., *m. Abot* 2:1; *Hor.* 1:3; *Sipra Qed.* Pq. 8.205.2.6; *Behuq.* par. 5.255.1.10; *Sipre Deut.* 48.1.3; 54.3.2; fuller discussion in Johnston, "Commandments"; Keener, *Matthew*, 178–79.

15. Powell, "Answers," notes Luther's hermeneutical grid of law and gospel, the common Reformed grid of covenant, and so forth.

16. Interpreters who rightly use Scripture to interpret Scripture often differ on *which* Scriptures to use. Popular interpreters sometimes nonsensically interpret Scripture by equating unrelated objects in diverse contexts; Jesus's hermeneutic, by contrast, offers a model for us that reflects God's heart. Speaking of an experiential hermeneutic, this is a message that I have repeatedly experienced (as Luther's experience of justification made that message central for him); but I have also had other experiences, and I believe the centrality of this one in most texts relating to salvation history arises from inductive study of Scripture.

17. See, e.g., *b. Shab.* 31a; fuller discussion in Keener, *Matthew*, 248–49.

18. *Sipra Qed.* pq. 4.200.3.7; fuller discussion in Keener, *Matthew*, 531.

19. Other Jewish teachers often linked texts based on a common key term or phrase; in this case, both texts in the Torah begin with "You shall love" (Deut 6:5; Lev 19:18).

20. The other extreme is to vacate love of its divinely intended meaning by neglecting the particular commandments that it summarizes.

21. See Sanders, *Jesus to Mishnah*, 43–48.

22. Borg argues that Jesus's mercy paradigm replaces the holiness paradigm of the Pharisees (*Conflict*, 123–43); yet the Pharisees would have agreed with the principle of mercy in theory, and particularly the School of Hillel emphasized it in legal interpretation.

23. For the phrase "the Ten Commandments" (or "the Ten Words"), see Exod 34:28; Deut 4:13; 10:4; this was clearly a key part of the Torah, "the words of the covenant" (Exod 34:28; cf. Deut 5:2; 9:9–11, 15), written by God himself (Exod 31:18; 34:1; Deut 4:13; 5:22; 10:4).

24. The parallel text in Deut 7:9 suggests that "thousands" here (and in Exod 20:6; Deut

5:10) refers to thousands of generations (cf. also 1 Chr 16:15; Ps 105:8, where this can mean "forever"), in contrast to his anger to the third and fourth generations.

25. Cf. 1 Kgs 3:9; Ps 49:3; Prov 2:2; 14:33; 16:21; 20:5; Isa 6:10; 10:7; 44:18; Dan 10:12; the association also in Greek in Matt 9:4; Luke 1:51; 9:47; Acts 8:22; LXX 1 Chr 29:18; LXX Jer 38:33; Bar 1:22.

26. See Keener, *Matthew,* 502–3; for Jesus's likely bilingualism, see further my discussion in Keener, *Acts,* 3:3190–95.

27. See *t. Shab.*16:22; for various practices, see *m. Eduy.* 2:5; *Shab.* 14:4; 22:6; *Yoma* 8:6; *t. Shab.* 12:12; Keener, *Matthew,* 356–58.

28. Keener, *Matthew,* 355–56. Cf. Jesus's own preference for his friend's honor over the consecrated purpose of waterpots in John 2:6–9; see more fully Keener, *John,* 1:509–13.

29. Keener, *Matthew,* 356; see more broadly Keener, *John,* 1:716.

30. On the custom, see Sanders, *Jesus to Mishnah,* 53–57; Baumgarten, "*Korban*"; Carmon, *Inscriptions,* 75, §167; cf. *m. Ned.* passim (e.g., 3:2).

31. See discussion in Keener, *John,* 1:509–13.

32. 1 Macc 2:41; see Keener, *John,* 1:642n74.

33. See, e.g., CD 11.13–14; *b. Shab.* 128b, bar.; Keener, *Matthew,* 358.

34. On *kavanah,* see Bonsirven, *Judaism,* 95; Montefiore and Loewe, *Anthology,* 272–94; Pawlikowski, "Pharisees."

35. Very helpfully, and even before Sanders, cf. Odeberg, *Pharisaism.* For Sanders's mature distillation of his view on Pharisaic ethics, see esp. Sanders, "Nomism."

36. See, e.g., *4 Ezra* 8:52–54; *T. Dan* 5:12; *T. Levi* 18:10–12; *m. Abot* 5:20; *Sipra Behuq.* pq. 1.261.1.6; *b. Ber.* 28b; 34b; *Tg. Neof.* 1 on Gen 3:24; cf. Isa 51:3; Ezek 36:35; Rev 22:1–3; *Ep. Barn.* 6.13.

37. Albeit with a different application, to royal polygyny; see CD 4.20–5:2; 11QT 56.18–19; Keener, *Marries Another,* 40–41; cf. Vermes, "Halakah"; Nineham, *Mark,* 265; pace Schubert, "Ehescheidung," 27; Mueller, "Temple Scroll."

38. Keener, *Marries Another;* a more popular but up-to-date form of the argument appears in Keener, "Remarriage." Note also Instone-Brewer, *Divorce.* William Heth, one of the authors of Heth and Wenham, *Divorce,* has now changed his position (see Heth, "Remarriage").

39. I do not believe that a single act of adultery or abuse necessarily renders a marriage irreparable. If the underlying character flaws that permitted these transgressions to begin with are not addressed, however, they are likely to repeat themselves. Both Roman and Jewish expectations of divorce after a wife's infidelity were strong, enshrined even in law; while the same is less true today, we should never minimize the serious breach of the marriage covenant represented by either partner's unfaithfulness.

40. My revelation-interested charismatic readers might appreciate knowing that I witnessed Jesus doing this in a dream.

41. I have adapted this section from Keener, "Expectation"; and *Historical Jesus.*

42. Beasley-Murray, "Kingdom," 27–32 (indicating Jesus's Messiahship). On Jesus's own Christology, see further Witherington, *Christology of Jesus.*

43. Hengel, "Messiah," 345.

44. Cf. Sanders, *Jesus and Judaism,* 234, 307.

45. Meyer, "Deed," 171–72.

46. Hengel, "Messiah," 347.

47. Cf. Judg 10:4; 1 Kgs 1:44; cf. discussion in Sanders, *Figure,* 254.

48. E.g., *b. Sanh.* 98a; 99a; *Gen. Rab.* 75:6; Edgar, "Messianic Interpretation," 48–49; Lachs, *Commentary*, 344.

49. E.g., Moule, *Mark*, 87; Sanders, *Figure*, 242.

50. Brown, *Death*, 473–80. On contemporary messianic expectations and Jesus's role, see Keener, *Historical Jesus*, 256–67; Keener, "Parallel Figures."

51. See, e.g., Kingsbury, *Christology*, 150.

52. So, e.g., Gundry, *Use*, 200; Witherington, *Christology of Jesus*, 190.

53. Including some allusions, see, e.g., Acts 2:34–35; 7:55; Eph 1:20; Col 3:1; Heb 1:3, 13; 8:1; 10:12; 12:2; Mark 16:19; Justin *1 Apol.* 45.

54. See, e.g., CD 7.15–20; *Mek. Nez.* 10.15–16, 26, 38; 17.17; *Pisha* 5.103. Although the Hebrew terms are different, the divine name was pronounced simply as "lord."

55. On Jesus's exalted lordship at an early stage, cf. further Hurtado, *Lord Jesus Christ*, 109–18; Marshall, *Origins*, 97–111. For various articulations of Jesus's divine identity in some sense early in Christian tradition, see Hurtado, *Lord Jesus Christ*; Bauckham, *Crucified*; Keener, *Historical Jesus*, 276–81; Hays, *Reading Backwards*.

Notes to Chapter 15

1. Scholars divide on whether to translate *nomos* here as "law" or "principle"; the English choice may be forced, but if one must choose, the context has consistently employed the term for the Torah (Rom 2:12–27; 3:19–21, 28, 31). Cf. Marinus Victorinus *Gal.* 1.2.9 (Edwards, *Galatians*, 31).

2. Most Jewish interpreters would have insisted that they belonged to the covenant because they belonged to God's covenant people, a belonging that they confirmed by keeping the covenant. Paul is more rigorous in demanding righteousness and expects it from hearts transformed by the Spirit and obedient to God's Messiah, but he undoubtedly uses some hyperbole; see discussion in Keener, *Romans*, 4–9, 122–23.

3. Because many global Pentecostals are currently more hearing than reading communities, orality remains a valued element in Pentecostal appropriation of the text (see, e.g., Ellington, "Authority," 159; Waddell, "Hearing," 199; Martin, "Hearing," 217–21, esp. 219–21). Reading literacy is increasingly available globally, but visual images are also frequently displacing texts even among Western youth.

4. Note also the recent dissertation on obedience in Romans, Myers, "Obedience."

5. See at greater length Keener, *Mind*, 31–54.

6. Cf. later rabbis' comments on the different kinds of Pharisees in *m. Sot.* 3:4; *Ab. R. Nat.* 37A; 45, §124B; *b. Sot.* 22b, bar.; *y. Sot.* 5:5, §2; Moore, *Judaism*, 2:193; Sandmel, *Judaism*, 160–61.

7. This is not to say that God ordinarily welcomed such breaches; disrespect to God's presence in the ark brought death (2 Sam 6:6–8; 1 Chr 13:9–11; 15:2, 15), and God was angry with those who appointed priests who were not Levites (1 Kgs 12:32; 13:33; 2 Chr 11:14).

8. For people who are "half-dead" appearing as if dead in ancient sources, see Eurip. *Alc.* 141–43; Apollod. 3.6.8; Callim. *Hymn* 6 (to Demeter), line 59; Corn. Nep. *Generals* 4 (Pausanias), 5.4; Livy 23.15.8; 40.4.15; Catullus 50.15; Quintus Curtius 4.8.8; Suetonius *Aug.* 6; Keener, "Invitations," 204; in the rabbis, Bailey, *Peasant Eyes*, 42; for further details on the parable, see Keener, "Invitations," 202–7.

9. Some suggest that the Samaritan's action is all the more shocking because of other Jewish parables in which the third and righteous actor is an Israelite (Jeremias, *Parables*, 203).

10. See here Keener, *Mind,* chs. 2–4, esp. ch. 3.

11. Patristic interpreters often welcomed the ethos of the law while rejecting its ceremonial aspects; see, e.g., Ambrosiaster in Pollmann and Elliott, "Galatians," 46–47. Some distinguished between commandments of universal moral import and those limited to Israel (e.g., Theodoret *Epistle to the Galatians* 2.15–16 in Edwards, *Galatians,* 29). This recognition does not require us to suppose that Paul's "works of the law" must be limited only to ceremonial law, the position of Origen, Jerome, and Erasmus opposed by Augustine, Luther, and Calvin (see Barclay, *Gift,* 103–4, 121; Wengert, "Luther," 101; Hafemann, "Yaein," 119).

12. This might not be the case in Rom 14:5–6 (as opposed to Col 2:16), if the food context suggests that he refers to fast days here, as some suggest.

13. The text sometimes cited for its abolition (John 5:18) in fact reflects the interpretation of Jesus's enemies, an interpretation probably subverted in Jesus's following discourse (see esp. 5:19, 30; further discussion in Keener, "Subordination," 40–41; idem, *John,* 1:645–46).

14. Brought to my attention by my friend Anthony Kent, whose dissertation (in process) involves this subject. There can be no thought of the day having been changed to something else, since Luke applies the term only to the time always observed by the Jewish community, namely from sundown on what we call Friday to sundown on what we call Saturday. Some Gentile Christian writers did advocate a shift to Sunday as early as the second century, though.

15. For four views of the Sabbath, see Arand et al., *Perspectives on Sabbath.*

16. For two helpful attempts to model a way through the morass, see Swartley, *Slavery;* Webb, *Slaves.*

17. For some parallels and contrasts, see, e.g., Wells, "Exodus," 227, 230; cf. Sarna, *Exodus,* 139.

18. Cf. similar terminology and sometimes concepts for Canaanite sacrifices, plus some differences, in Pfeiffer, *Ras Shamra,* 38–39, 57; Rainey, "Sacrifice,"1 198; Rainey, "Sacrifice,"2 236–37; Carpenter, "Sacrifices," 264–65; Ross, *Holiness,* 29; Averbeck, "Sacrifices," 712, 715–16, 718, 720.

19. Walton, Matthews, and Chavalas, *Background Commentary,* 25–26; Gane, "Leviticus," 287.

20. What some in antiquity, such as Clement of Alexandria (following Philo), viewed as divine condescension and accommodation of human weakness in understanding; see Mitchell, "Accommodation," 205–14; challenging its presence in 1 Cor 9:19–23, cf. Glad, "Adaptability," 26–27.

21. Though the point could be protecting the slave, since she was abused rather than guilty, it also exempts her abuser from the level of punishment meted out to one who rapes a free person.

22. We lack specific biblical prohibitions of polygyny; the "two" becoming one flesh (Mark 10:8; 1 Cor 6:16; Eph 5:31) reflects the LXX, which in turn reflects the Greek practice of monogamy. The requirement for respectable elders in 1 Tim 3:2 warns against infidelity and multiple concubinage, since polygyny did not exist in Ephesus. Narratives show that polygyny was not the ideal, and because I believe the trajectory of Scripture supports egalitarian marriage I support monogamy. But this ideal does not justify breaking up existing polygynous marriages as if they are not valid unions in God's sight.

23. Cf. LaSor, Hubbard, and Bush, *Survey,* 148; note *herem* in the Moabite Mesha inscription. See discussion in Copan, *Monster;* Copan and Flannagan, *Genocide;* and other works cited earlier.

24. See further details in Quintus Curtius 4.3.23; Albright, *Yahweh*, 152, 234–35; idem, *Biblical Period*, 17; Stager and Wolff, "Child Sacrifice"; Stager, "Eroticism"; Rundin, "Pozo Moro."

25. Keener, *Paul*, 201–7; Keener and Usry, *Faith*, 37–41.

26. E.g., tithes to rulers in 1 Sam 8:15–17; De Vaux, *Israel*, 140; Kitchen, *Orient*, 158; corporate, agrarian tithes on Canaanite villages in Heltzer, "Tithe," 124. Cf. also Greek and Roman usage (e.g., the dedication in Val. Max. 1.1. ext. 4; Tertullian *Apol.* 14.1); for a tithe of grain as tribute to Rome, see Cic. *Verr.* 2.3.5.12; 2.3.6.13–15. For a tenth of military plunder dedicated to deities, see Gen 14:20; Xen. *Anab.* 5.3.4, 9, 13; *Hell.* 4.3.21; Val. Max. 5.6.8; Plut. *Camillus* 7.4–5 (for a tenth of plunder offered to a brave warrior, Plut. *Coriol.* 10.2; for the first or choice of the plunder to gods, Xen. *Cyr.* 7.3.1; 7.5.35).

27. Admittedly, I may broach a risky subject here. Challenging major sources of ecclesiastical fundraising can be a sensitive issue, as Dr. Martin Luther discovered when challenging the extrabiblical practices of Friar Johann Tetzel.

28. Although the terms for "burn" differ, the term for "overturn" is the same. The latter term admittedly appears some ninety-four times in the Hebrew Bible (many of these with a different sense), but only twice in Deuteronomy and only twice in Hosea, and in both it appears in the context of these cities.

Notes to Chapter 16

1. Some other Jewish texts also reveal messianic readings of OT passages, though without naming Jesus as the Messiah (e.g., Shepherd, "Targums").

2. What Hays, *Reading Backwards*, 85, rightly calls "hermeneutical hindsight"; see further 93–109 (ch. 6, "Retrospective Reading," including the Evangelists' model on 93–103). Humans often can detect foreordained divine patterns and meaning only after God's actions. See further Keener, *John*, 1:528–30, including concerning the disciples' requisite dependence on the Paraclete (cf. 14:26).

3. Pentecostals normally read what we call the OT from the Christian vantage point in the new covenant; see Grey, *Crowd*, 66–67.

4. As James D. G. Dunn in particular has emphasized, the new perspective's focus on Paul's original context in writing Romans (useful for recontextualization; cf. Dunn, "Justice") does not negate the principle of justification by faith that Luther found there (Dunn, *New Perspective*, 29–30; Dunn, "Old Perspective"; also Watson, *Paul, Judaism, and the Gentiles*, 346; Theissen, "Nouvelle perspective"; Westerholm, "New Perspective," 231, 240–41). Luther recontextualized that principle for his own context, although sometimes reading the recontextualization too much into Paul's original situation (though less than some have asserted; see Chester, "Introspective Conscience").

5. Historical figures may be real, their specific connection or interdependence being recognized by spiritual insight (Auerbach, *Mimesis*, 73, as cited in Hays, *Reading Backwards*, 2) or designed by rhetorical structuring (Keener, *Acts*, 1:556–57, 570–74).

6. I draw the following chart from Keener, *Acts*, 2:1363–64. The OT promise theme is also critical (Keener, *Acts*, 1:483–86, 987; 2:2051; cf. Grey, *Crowd*, 96).

7. On this motif, see Keener, *Acts*, 2:1426–27; more recently and fully, Turner, *Prophet*.

8. The prophets foretold him beforehand, and his followers proclaim him afterward (1 Pet 1:10–12); that is, there is often significant continuity before and after.

9. On the significance of paired visions, see Keener, *Acts,* 2:1644–45, 1760.

10. Scholars often note how experience shaped Peter's reading of Scripture in Acts 10 and 15 (Thomas, "Women," 85; Pinnock, "Work of Spirit," 236); and James's interpretation of Amos and the community's Spirit-led consensus (Acts 15:28); see, e.g., Moore, "God's Word," as cited in Johns and Johns, "Yielding," 51–52; Green, *Seized,* 95–96.

11. Keener, *Acts,* 4:3758–63.

12. I have adapted the paragraphs about the christocentric readings in Matt 1–4 from my popular-level interpretation manual. Fuller detail and citation of other sources appear in my commentary (*Matthew,* loc. cit.). For Isaiah, cf. now also Witherington, *Isaiah.*

13. For the expected new exodus, see, e.g., Isa 11:11, 16; 27:13; 40:3; 52:3–4; Jer 16:14–15; Ezek 20:34–36; Hos 2:14–15; 11:5, 11; Mic 7:15; Zech 10:10; *t. Ber.* 1:10; Daube, *Exodus Pattern* (esp. 11–12); Wright, *Paul,* 139–62; possibly (depending on reconstructed elements) 4Q389 f2.2. For the emphasis in Matthew, see Davies, *Setting,* 25–93; later, *b. Ber.* 12b; *y. Ber.* 1:5; *Exod. Rab.* 1:5; 3:4; 15:11; *Deut. Rab.* 9:9; *Pesiq. Rab.* 31:10; 52:8; in medieval Jewish interpretation, see Jacobs, *Exegesis,* 39–40.

14. Keener, *Matthew,* 108. For the emphasis on God's continued love for his people, see also Hays, *Reading Backwards,* 40–41, where Hays insightfully argues that Hosea provides the hermeneutical link between the first exodus story and Jesus.

15. Jewish interpreters were familiar with connecting texts based on a common key term; for *gezerah shevah,* see, e.g., Mek. *Nez.* 10.15–16, 26, 38; 17.17; *Pisha* 5.103; b. Ber. 9a; 35a; B.K. 25b; Git. 49a; Ker. 5a; Kid. 15a; 35b; Men. 76a; Naz. 48a; Nid. 22b–23a; R.H. 3b; 34a; Sanh. 40b; 51b; 52a; Shab. 64a; Tem. 16a; Zeb. 18a; 49b–50b; Ex. Rab. 1:20; cf. CD 7.15–20.

16. Some cite Matthew's use of Isaiah here in support of a *sensus plenior* approach (Pinnock, "Work of Spirit," 242). Matthew undoubtedly did find meaning beyond what Isaiah envisioned here, but it was not really unrelated to Isaiah's contextual sense. Some others, including Brown, *Answering,* 17–32, have independently read this passage in similar ways.

17. Granted, prophetic articulation of the ultimate Davidic ruler's deity is rare, but it may appear less rare proportionately when we consider the paucity of direct texts about a future Davidic ruler distinct from David. Cf. also Jer 23:5–6, although by itself it may be explained differently (cf. Jer 33:16). On a different note, "Pentecostal readings" normally apply Isa 9:1–7 to Jesus; see Grey, *Crowd,* 77–82.

18. "Spirit" in Matt 12:28 may be Matthew's interpretation of "finger" (Luke 11:20), but it is a helpful one. It also allows Matthew to highlight the theme of the Spirit in this context, showing how Jesus's activity fulfills Isaiah's expectations for the servant's mission.

19. Keener, *Spirit,* 55–59, 98, 103–4.

20. Not all church fathers supported allegory; Basil, for example, inveighs against it (Hall, *Reading,* 86–88; but cf. his extended analogies in 89–92); cf. also Victorinus in the mid 360s (Levy, Krey and Ryan, *Romans,* 9). Gnostic sects often employed allegory (Irenaeus *Her.* 1.18; Hippolytus *Her.* 5.15; Jonas, *Religion,* 91–97), but this was natural in a Greek philosophic milieu (e.g., Iamblichus *Ep.* 3, frg. 3–4; Cancik-Lindemaier et al., "Allegoresis"; Cook, *Interpretation,* 12–13), especially in Alexandria (cf. earlier Philo, e.g., *Plant.* 36, 129 [Greek myth]; *Post.* 7; *Prob.* 80; *Som.* 1.102; Badilita, "Exégèse"; Kugel and Greer, *Interpretation,* 82–85; Wolfson, *Philo,* 1:87–163; with limits, as noted in Wolfson, *Philo,* 1:57–68; Hay, "Extremism"; Long, "Allegory"), and in time it prevailed even in the West (e.g., Libanius *Encomium* 1.10). The approach was more common in Alexandria than in Antioch, but it prevailed widely, so that Jerome, for example, even viewed it as the higher, spiritual way to read (Pollmann and Elliott, "Gala-

tians," 56). After experiencing its medieval abuses (also found in medieval Jewish thought; cf., e.g., Ginsburg, *Kabbalah*, 127–29), Luther and subsequently Calvin rejected this approach (Bartholomew, *Hermeneutics*, 197–98; Luther's *Second Lectures on Galatians* on 4:24 in Bray, *Galatians, Ephesians*, 159; Calvin *Commentary on Galatians* 4:24 in Bray, *Galatians, Ephesians*, 160), as did Bucer (George, "Introduction," xxvi) and some Jewish exegetes (e.g., Ibn Ezra in the twelfth century; see Jacobs, *Exegesis*, 13–14).

21. See Keener, "Tabernacle," 838; idem, "Worship," 130–31.

22. Discussions of Pentecostal hermeneutics also often connect pneumatic hermeneutics with christological hermeneutics, since the Spirit comes to honor Christ (John 16:13–15; see Wyckoff, *Pneuma*, 137–38; cf. Grey, *Crowd*, 66–67, 188). This remains true of Christian hermeneutics in general; see Bloesch, "Christological Hermeneutic," esp. 81, 98–101. Geerlof, "Augustine and Pentecostals," argues that Augustine's christological reading of Psalms is helpful for Pentecostal interpreters.

23. E.g., for Luke, Jesus is the servant who represents God's people (Acts 3:13; 8:32–35), a light for the nations (Luke 2:32), but so are Jesus's agents (Acts 1:8; 13:47).

24. Borrowed from Keener, *Acts*, 1:557. Although other echoes may appear also (Ps 111:9 in Luke 1:49; Ps 89:10 in Luke 1:51; perhaps God doing "great things" in Deut 10:21; 11:7; cf. 34:12), even here one allusion echoes the context of Hannah's song (1 Sam 1:11 in Luke 1:48).

25. Borrowed from Keener, *Acts*, 1:556–57.

26. See Keener, *Acts*, 1:558–62; for more extensive discussion, see esp. Talbert, *Patterns*; Tannehill, *Acts*; idem, *Luke*.

27. Cf., e.g., Plutarch's parallel lives; Trompf, *Historical Recurrence*; Keener, *Acts*, 1:569–74.

28. Keener, *Spirit*, 65–71.

29. Waddell, "Hearing," 186.

30. Cf. Gillespie, "Authority," 219: the full meaning of the text does not change, but understanding changes, since full understanding applies the text's "significance." Klein, Blomberg, and Hubbard, *Introduction*, 123, employ the same distinction. See the discussion in Osborne, *Spiral*, 366–96 (surveying views), 397–415; earlier, Hirsch, *Validity*, 8, 143.

31. Pinnock, "Work of Spirit," 242. Hirsch, *Validity*, 113, suggests that valid reapplication of a text should flow from its own intrinsic purpose. Yet framers of some documents in fact expected their "texts to have applications in situations that they knew to be beyond their explicit knowledge" (Vanhoozer, *Meaning*, 264, summarizing Hirsch's later recognition; cf. also Hirsch, *Validity*, 123). Thus, for example, while one Athenian orator warns that inserting new laws was a crime (Lysias *Or.* 30.2, §183; 30.17, §184), he also recognizes that the fines in Solon's laws had to be updated and some other matters conformed to subsequent usage (Lysias *Or.* 30.2, §183).

32. Brown, *Scripture as Communication*, 26. Stanley Porter suggests that something analogous to "dynamic equivalence" in translation theory may be a helpful approach for offering concrete application today (see Porter, "Hermeneutics," 125–27). A potential risk of dynamic equivalence in translation per se, despite its value, is that translators' choices end up in the text (Fee, *Listening*, 18).

33. Brown, *Scripture as Communication*, 105–6n21.

34. Stanley Porter ("Comment[ary]ing") has criticized this as a notable problem in "application" commentaries.

35. Stibbe, "Thoughts," 192n24, distinguishes evangelical application as obeying the text from charismatic encounter of God in the text, but both are responses to God (see Jer 22:16). His concern appears to be what he perceives as the sometimes mechanical character of the

former, an Enlightenment method devoid of dependence on God. Although not in itself a method, recognizing our dependence on God is indeed necessary (cf. Ps 119:34; Prov 1:7; 2:3; 3:5) and characterizes the new covenant approach (2 Cor 3:6, 15–18).

36. See comments in Keener, *Revelation,* 408–9, 412–14; cf. also Talbert, *Apocalypse,* 80; Beale, *Revelation,* 755; Aune, *Revelation,* 919–28; Reddish, *Revelation,* 277–78, 328; Stefanovic, *Revelation,* 513; Fee, *Revelation,* 196, 237. For examples of specifically "charismatic/prophetic" readings (esp. in terms of prophetic interests) of Revelation, see, e.g., Keener, "Charismatic Reading"; Macchia, "Spirit of Lamb"; Waddell, *Spirit in Revelation;* idem, "Adventure"; Herms, "Invoking."

37. For expectation of a new temple in early Judaism, see, e.g., *1 En.* 90:28–29; 11QTemple 29.8–10.

38. Keener, *Revelation,* 504.

39. Grey, *Crowd,* 108.

40. Grey, *Crowd,* 108. Grey, *Crowd,* 186, notes the value of the Pentecostal "approach of seeking to understand the text for its significance to the individual reader" (cf. also 161).

41. Stein, *Guide,* 19.

42. See already Luther and Calvin, though in their polemic against enthusiasm (Wyckoff, *Pneuma,* 24–25, 28); John Owen (Wyckoff, *Pneuma,* 33, noting that this is, in Owen's words, "an *internal subjective revelation,*" albeit without finding *new* truths not previously revealed). For Luther's allowance of prophecy (regarding personal issues) and other revelatory experience under some circumstances, see Föller, "Luther on Miracles," 337–42, 347–48.

43. As Gordon L. Anderson notes, Pentecostal scholars' approach to illumination by the Spirit "falls within the range of views held by other evangelicals" ("Pentecostal Hermeneutics"). In contrast to this, some Pentecostals writing on hermeneutics have borrowed liberal stereotypes of evangelical scholarship as a whole that are as unfair as some critics' misrepresentation of Pentecostal scholarship (note also this concern about caricatures in Poirier, "Critique," 2n12).

44. As noted in, e.g., Holmes, "Challenge," 274.

45. McQuilkin, *Understanding,* 38, recognizes that the Spirit illumines the mind to the biblical text in a way that is subjectively meaningful, but strongly warns against claiming perfection for one's illumined understanding.

46. Graves, *Inspiration,* 43–48.

47. See, e.g., the continuity between original inspiration and subsequent illumination suggested by Karl Barth (see Wyckoff, *Pneuma,* 47, citing esp. Mueller, *Barth,* 57); Pinnock, "Spirit in Hermeneutics," 4, as cited in Ellington, "Authority," 156; Hey, "Roles"; also Mulholland, *Shaped,* 44; Peter Stuhlmacher ("Ex Auditu," 5, as cited in Wyckoff, *Pneuma,* 62–63); and others; cf. a connection in Osborne, *Spiral,* 340. "In Spirit-hermeneutics," Pinnock opined, "I believe that the breath of God which inspired the prophets and apostles binds himself to their words and opens up the significance" (Pinnock, "Work of Spirit," 241).

48. Carl Henry expressed concern that depicting illumination as continuing inspiration risks confusing the Spirit's communicating to us biblical truths individually with the Spirit's original provision in Scripture of what were then often new truths (see Henry, *God Who Speaks,* 256–66, 275, 283–84, as cited in Wyckoff, *Pneuma,* 68, 79).

49. See further discussion in the introduction, under "The Wider Christian Hermeneutic of the Spirit" (pp. 12–14).

50. Compare also 1 Kgs 20:35–37 with Jer 35:5–14, 18–19; cf. also 1 Kgs 13:18–24. After negative guidance from the Spirit (Acts 16:6–9) and an interpreted dream (16:9–10), Paul and

his colleagues used common sense to find a "place of prayer" where they would have people to preach to (16:13). When God called Saul, God already knew that he would turn out badly (cf. 1 Sam 8:10–18), but it was not yet time for David. David is anointed king in 1 Sam 16:13, but he is enthroned only after many years of hardship.

51. See Graves, *Inspiration*, 32–37.

52. Apart from his uncertainty as to whether Luke intended to provide precedent, I find little objectionable in Fee, *Gospel*, 100–104, as noted above (pp. 138–39, 166–67).

53. See, e.g., Theon *Progymn.* 2.86–88; Hermog. *Progymn.* 8. On Syncrisis 18–20; Aphthonius *Progymn.* 10. On Syncrisis, 42–44S, 31–33R; Nicolaus *Progymn.* 9. On Syncrisis 59–62; Hermog. *Inv.* 4.14.212; Marshall, *Enmity*, 348–53; Anderson, *Glossary*, 110–11; Gärtner, "Synkrisis."

54. *Brown, Authentic Fire*, 315.

55. For how miracle stories teach, see the examples in Cotter, *Miracle Stories*.

56. Genre and subject influenced applicability, as in genres in Scripture: cosmological speculation (rarely offered in Scripture, certainly for its own sake) tended toward pure information; Pliny the Elder's encyclopedia of knowledge collected information but still with a view to some of it having practical application (for example, his compilation of purported medical treatments); ethical reflections invited application for society or individuals.

57. Traditional dispensationalism found propositional truth in the epistles rather than in narratives (Archer, *Hermeneutic*, 78), thus using a sort of canon within the canon even of the NT. Early Pentecostals, by contrast, used Acts as the controlling paradigm, along with the Gospels and only afterward the epistles (Archer, *Hermeneutic*, 124).

58. Most cessationists would accept most material in the epistles as for today, but (following E. W. Bullinger) a minority of hyperdispensationalists (a far cry from progressive dispensationalists and even traditional dispensationalists) have argued that only the material in the prison epistles (and thus not, for example, the Lord's Supper) is for the present era of the church.

59. For the possible relationship between the Jeremiah and Ezekiel passages, and their special focus on interiority, see Boda, "Word and Spirit," 35–39.

60. This is Paul's only positive use of "fleshly" (out of three uses of this specific Greek adjective); it is extremely rare in the Septuagint, and is used of hearts only in the two parallel texts in Ezekiel, 11:19 and 36:26. Paul could evoke 11:19–20 (and may well read the two Ezekiel texts together), but his mention of God's Spirit suggests also Ezek 36:27.

61. Charismatic interpreters often stress seeking the Spirit more than the letter; see, e.g., Pinnock, "Work of Spirit," 240 (from Pinnock, "Interpretation"); Ellington, "Authority," 156 (following an earlier article by Pinnock).

62. Keener, *Romans*, 86.

63. See, e.g., Quint. *Decl.* 331.3; Hermog. *Issues* 40.6–19; *Inv.* 2.2.110; Cohen, *Law*, 38–50. The "letters" could also refer to basics as opposed to deeper insights (e.g., Heraclitus *Ep.* 4).

64. And certainly Paul was not thinking in Romantic "terms of outward form and inward feeling" (noted by Wright, *Paul*, 982).

65. Cf. Luther's use of the letter/Spirit contrast to value personal application and not simply grammar, noted in Gleason, "Letter." Cf. the contrast in Mulholland, *Shaped*, 95 (cf. 135), between using Scripture "as a 'rule book' for self-transformation or winning God's favor" and Scripture as a place to meet God.

66. Note the warnings in Grey, *Crowd*, 120–21, 145, of prematurely fusing horizons, collapsing the text's horizon into "the reader's own narrative biography," and thus hearing only

the reader's assumptions while silencing any independent, prophetic voice of the text (citing Thiselton, *Horizons,* 530); see also Bauer and Traina, *Inductive Bible Study,* 373. Establishing hermeneutical distance between the horizons could undercut positive proximity (Grey, *Crowd,* 122), but historical context offers a useful boundary on interpretations (132, 152).

67. Thiselton, *Horizons,* 318–19, citing Stendahl and Luther. The goal of understanding the interpretive process is to *prevent* interpreters from simply hearing echoes of their pre-understanding in the text (Thiselton, *Horizons,* xx).

68. Thiselton, *Horizons,* 319. Hirsch, *Validity,* 254, argues that an interpreter must first appropriate "the original perspective" in order to fuse it with one's own, and contends that Gadamer fails to recognize this; he complains (255) that Gadamer should have distinguished these two different sorts of "meaning."

69. Thiselton, *Horizons,* 319. Most academic charismatic interpretation values both horizons (cf., e.g., Stibbe, "Thoughts"; although Lyons, "Fourth Wave," deems the safeguards in Stibbe's approach inadequate).

70. Thiselton, *Horizons,* 15.

71. Although employing different terminology, even older writers writing with a faith perspective usually recognized this (despite newer stereotypes about them); cf. the discussion of exegesis and exposition in Mickelsen, *Interpreting the Bible,* 56–57.

72. Cf. helpfully Martin, "Renewal," 4, as cited in Spawn and Wright, "Emergence," 8. Archer, *Hermeneutic,* 126, suggests that (at least in the views of modernist critics) early Pentecostals blurred "the boundaries of the past and present as they exegeted Scripture." Ideally Pentecostal readers can affirm the value of both horizons (e.g., Archer, *Hermeneutic,* 180; Grey, *Crowd,* 99, 120, 132, 164), as can readers in general (see Thiselton, "New Hermeneutic," 100).

73. Spittler, "Enterprise," 76, emphasizing the value of both history and piety. For both history and knowing God by the Spirit, see also Autry, "Dimensions."

74. Keener, *John,* 246–47, 363–64.

75. This word continues to be presented in the message (John 8:31, 37, 43, 51, 52, 55; 12:48; 14:23; 17:6, 14, 17, 20), because the Spirit continues to reveal the person of Jesus in that message (see my discussion of 16:7–11 on pp. 157–58). Others, including Barth and Dietrich Bonhoeffer, have emphasized the presence of Christ in proclamation; see Bartholomew, *Hermeneutics,* 526–27, citing Barth, *Doctrine,* 135–36; Bonhoeffer, *Ethics,* 259; idem, "Lectures," 126.

76. Pinnock, "Work of Spirit," 241, also notes this text in this sort of connection.

Notes to Chapter 17

1. I am thinking not of pedagogical structure—sometimes conversational style communicates more effectively in our culture than tight-knit arguments such as those found in some brilliant eighteenth-century sermons. My objection here is to hermeneutical stream-of-consciousness, one text arbitrarily reminding us of another.

2. In practice it might function more like drawing lots, however, if the interpretation was transparent; see Walton, *Thought,* 271–72. Yet for all the biblical allusions to earlier Scripture, none reflect the random approach of bibliomancy (admittedly probably more difficult with scrolls than with codices). On bibliomancy and its practice, including among ancient Christians, see Van der Horst, "Bibliomancy"; cf. Roman priests' early use of Greek Sibylline oracles to find solutions to omens (Rüpke, *Religion,* 18).

3. See Wall, "Acts," 139; Keener, *Acts,* 2:1527, 1813–14; cf. further Miller, *Empowered for Mission.*

4. Archer, *Hermeneutic,* 62–63. The historical-critical objection to proof-texting was its assumption "that the Bible was equally inspired throughout" (Archer, *Hermeneutic,* 64); my most fundamental concern is that popular users of proof-texts often do not give attention to the texts' contexts. Conservative teachers, however, did advocate inductive Bible study, reading each book of the Bible as a whole (Archer, *Hermeneutic,* 66–68), and proof-texting by academicians could presuppose proper exegetical work (Archer, *Hermeneutic,* 101n44).

5. Smidt, *Evangelicals,* 22. Some Reformers such as Tyndale may have appealed to popular readers more than others, but in England as well as elsewhere, merchants, for example, remained more literate than farm workers. Working from the Anabaptist heritage of separating church and state, Baptists in the United States heralded democracy and religious liberty as their own values (e.g., Kidd and Hankins, *Baptists,* 72–75, 179, 194).

6. For Finney's commonsense hermeneutic focused on prayer and Bible study alone, see Hardesty, *Women,* 72; so with Phoebe Palmer (73). For populist, face-value interpretation in early Pentecostalism, see Martin, "Introduction," 3; Archer, *Hermeneutic,* 102, 125–26.

7. Boda, "Word and Spirit," 44, comparing the Princeton intellectuals with the biblical scribal tradition and the Azusa Street revivalists with the biblical prophetic tradition. On Wesleyan thought as a protest against (mostly academic) Reformed Protestant orthodoxy, see Archer, *Hermeneutic,* 21–22 (following R. M. Anderson; D. Dayton).

8. The latter pole also includes Calvinist Baptists in the revival tradition, who believed that they needed only the Spirit and a call to preach (see Kidd and Hankins, *Baptists,* 42).

9. See Keener, "Teaching Ministry."

10. See Keener, "Rhetorical Techniques."

11. See, e.g., Menzies, *Anointed,* 138. For a list of prominent Assemblies leaders earlier nurtured in the CMA, see Menzies, *Anointed,* 72n37. For other connections with the CMA, see Menzies, *Anointed,* 56, 66, 70–72, 126–30; McGee, *People of Spirit,* 98–100, 109, 243; Miskov, *Life on Wings* (on Carrie Judd Montgomery).

12. Grey, *Crowd,* 91, descriptively.

13. Zaprometova, "Crisis," 187.

14. Most of this material is adapted and condensed from Keener, "Biblical Fidelity," esp. here 38.

15. In *Distinguishing Marks of a Work of the Spirit of God* (1741) and *Religious Affections* (1746) Edwards notes "bodily effects" (including swoonings) that accompanied the revival of his day but were incidental to its transformative character.

16. See, e.g., Robeck, *Mission,* 12 (the Azusa Street Revival, 1906); Anderson, *Ends of Earth,* 173 (Methodists in Chile in 1909), 200 (Chinese Presbyterians c. 1929); Shaw, *Awakening,* 187 (the Shantung revival in northern China in the 1930s; on Baptist participation, see Crawford, *Shantung Revival*). I also experienced this when, in 1975, two days after my conversion, I was first filled with the Spirit. All I knew about it at that moment was that, for the first time in my life, I experienced genuine, sublime *joy.* Spiritual joy (as opposed to celebrating sporting or family events) is one area where Western Christians have much to learn from, e.g., our brothers and sisters in Africa, Latin America, or even the earlier Celtic Christian tradition.

17. Cf. both joyous "raptures" and, among the unconverted, lamentation among early Baptists in the United States in Kidd and Hankins, *Baptists,* 87. Swooning and other involuntary motor actions were also common in revival history (e.g., Dunn, *Jesus and Spirit,* 192; Wolffe,

Expansion, 57–59; Vidler, *Revolution,* 238; Synan, *Tradition,* 12–14; Moore, "Quakerism," 338; Rosen, "Psychopathology," 235–37; Kidd and Hankins, *Baptists,* 89).

18. Keener, "Biblical Fidelity," 38.

19. See Bakker, *Wrong,* 531–44.

20. Keener, "Biblical Fidelity," 39.

21. Cf. the complaint in Green, *Seized,* 69, about using the Bible "as a book of quotations from which to draw authoritative support for one's words, as a collection of proverbs for backing up moral convictions, or perhaps as a treasure chest of discussion starters."

22. Fanciful interpretations may appear in some Pentecostal circles, but they "are not taught at Pentecostal colleges and seminaries, and they do not represent a legitimate Pentecostal hermeneutic" (Anderson, "Pentecostal Hermeneutics").

23. If I need to offer another one, I was present when one candidate for freshman class president in a Bible college claimed that the Spirit had led him to run. After that claim he won handily, but after he endured a year of dealing with unruly classmates, the Spirit did not lead him to run for sophomore president the next year.

24. E.g., Capps, *Tongue,* 17, 71.

25. Hagin, "Authority in Prayer" (a lecture cassette tape).

26. Or, Jesus is Lord and so is the Spirit (2 Cor 3:17, interpreting the language of Exod 33–34), so Jesus is the Holy Spirit; and if we are Jesus, then we are thus also the Spirit. If we have sinned, and we are Jesus, then has Jesus sinned?

27. For history and criticism of some deliverance ministries, see Collins, *Exorcism.*

28. In the Great Awakenings, crisis experiences functioned as part of the conversion narrative. These were, however, deep experiences of repentance that normally led to transformed lives, not simply repeated blessings. Walking with the Lord normally will yield many experiences with him, and charismatics are good at calling for experience in response to teaching. But the habitual pursuit of "new" solutions, in some circles, when the old ones did not effect the desired change, needs to be seriously qualified to focus more on serving God's purposes.

29. Lest one doubt that hostile spiritual power can be real, see, e.g., Exod 7:11, 22; 8:7; Num 22:6, 12; Matt 24:24; Mark 13:22; Acts 8:11; 13:6; 2 Thess 2:9; Rev 13:13. These examples represent different cultural formulations of such power; it can be expressed in various ways in various societies.

30. We have biblical precedent for commanding the exit of demons that are in people; God also often honors such acts, if directed in faith toward him, regarding less direct spiritual activity. With regard to heavenly principalities, however, our conflict requires us standing (Eph 6:11–14) and continuing in prayer (Dan 10:12–13, 20–21), not addressing them or "casting them down" as in some charismatic traditions. The Spirit may direct us to symbolic prophetic actions with wider significance (e.g., Ezek 36:1, 4, 6, 8), but this is not a magic-like formula for casting down angelic powers if done enough (cf. 2 Pet 2:10–11; Jude 8–10). Contrast Copeland, *Laws,* 104 (on 105 he addresses Satan in a "sample prayer"); Capps, *Tongue,* 126.

31. Hagin, *What Faith Is,* 3–4, 6, 12, 18, 20, 30; *New Thresholds of Faith,* 11; see also *The Word of Faith* (March 1983): 3. Even the English temporal word "now" is an adverb, not an adjective to modify a noun such as "faith." Note that the popular-level works, especially by Hagin, went through numerous editions and the date of publication is not always clear on the book itself.

32. Often consulting multiple translations would prevent this sort of problem, but in this case checking the Greek or an interlinear would be necessary.

33. Pace Copeland, *Laws,* 63.

34. For the thousand cattle indicating God's wealth, see, e.g., Hagin, *Redeemed,* 9. Although this is not the point in the context, which emphasizes that God owns everything, it is true that God's resources are unlimited. The hermeneutical problem is that in popular interpretation the application has superseded the text's primary point.

35. Pace Hagin, *Visions,* 126; *Prayer Secrets,* 20; Copeland, *Laws,* 104; Capps, *Tongue,* 57. Sending to spirits to work for one appears in some cultures in sorcery; see, e.g., Fuchs, "Techniques," 129.

36. E.g., Tob 5:22 (the informed reader will catch the irony here); Heb 1:14; Matt 18:10; *L.A.B.* 11:12; 59:4; *t. Shab.* 17:2–3; *Sipre Num.* 40.1.5; *Gen. Rab.* 44:3; 60:15; *Song Rab.* 3:6, §3; Hermas 1.5. Le Cornu, *Acts,* 654, cites in addition to some of these *L.A.B.* 15:5; *Jub.* 35:17; *b. Hag.* 16a; *Ta'an.* 11a; see also Davies and Allison, *Matthew,* 2:770–72.

37. Guardian angels protect us as in Ps 91:11, at the orders of God ("*He* will give them charge over you"), but to go around using them according to *our* pleasure or discretion is to use Ps 91:11 as Satan uses it in Matt 4:6–7.

38. Every single text cited in support of this by Capps, *Tongue,* 42, 65–69, 80ff., is used out of context.

39. For the fuller context, see, e.g., Keener, *Romans,* 125–26.

40. Pace Hagin, *What Faith Is,* 26–27. His exposition of Rom 4 also runs afoul of the textual variant, though we can at least appreciate his attempt to base his teaching about faith in Scripture, in contrast to many who ignore the theme in Scripture. He acknowledges that one cannot claim what Scripture does not promise; see *Matter of a Mate,* 1–2 (differently from Capps, *Tongue,* 20).

41. Capps, *Tongue,* 103, 114, 126; cf. his perversion of the virgin birth and incarnation as positive confession in *Tongue,* 15–16. Such excesses do not stem from, but are consistent with, Hagin's claim that believers are Christ or divine (*Authority,* 11–12; *Zoe,* 41; *Name of Jesus,* 105–6; cf. *Zoe,* 35–36, 40, 42; Copeland, *Laws,* 15). Associates who studied at Rhema assure me that he meant only that we depend on and serve Christ as his body; still, given the danger of Manifested Sons distortions (e.g., Sam Fife, *Seven Steps to Perfection,* 12; idem, *Why All Things Work for Good,* 9), it would have been helpful for him to have qualified such language explicitly.

42. Hagin, *Ministering,* 8; Hagin Jr., *Faith Worketh by Love,* 3; idem, *Itching Ears,* 14. At least sometimes Kenneth Hagin did explain context carefully, e.g., 1 John 5 in *Visions,* 73; Acts 13:28–33 in *Present Day Ministry,* 11; parts of Eph 1:17–2:1 (*Authority,* 7–11, although much of this book simply repeats the work of John A. Macmillan; see McConnell, *Different Gospel,* 69–71). He also cites approvingly Greek scholars, even if it is to support a misconstrual of Greek; e.g., *Zoe,* 9. Perhaps most importantly, Hagin toward the end of his life criticized some of the movement's current extremes (*Midas Touch,* esp. 131–204)

43. Hagin, *Ticket,* 5; *Ministering,* 11; *Visions,* 20, 33; *What Faith Is,* 27; cf. *Authority,* 21; *Led By the Spirit,* 84; Hagin Jr., *Faith Worketh by Love,* 3; discussion in Harrell, *Possible,* 234.

44. Gloria Copeland has suggested that Paul wrongly failed to take authority over his thorn in the flesh ("Thorn," 5; this article was supplied to me courtesy of Jesse K. Moon). Some Word of Faith teachers distort the nature of Scripture into simply a contract spelling out Christians' rights; see Capps, *Tongue,* 8, 14, 106, 116; Copeland, *Laws,* 40. Thus biblical "laws" work equally well for anyone (so Capps, *Tongue,* 103; Copeland, *Laws,* 20–21; cf. 32: "the Jews" use them). God is thus reduced to "a faith God" (Hagin, *Name of Jesus,* 11; Capps, *Tongue,* 103), not worthy of our faith if he causes suffering for his glory (Hagin, *Don't Blame God,* 3–4)

and to be called a liar if he does not live up to his covenant to supply needs confessed in faith (Hagin, *Prayer Secrets,* 22). See the criticism in Bishop, "Prosperity," 14.

45. Indeed, some of the contemporary faith movement's ideas emerged originally, and with much greater overall balance, in nineteenth-century biblical faith teaching such as that of Hudson Taylor and A. J. Gordon; see extensively the documentation in King, *Only Believe.*

46. This differs from the way Kenneth Hagin expresses himself in *Prayer Secrets,* 22: "The offering was about $20 short of what we had claimed . . . if it were not there, then I would have to go to every church where I had preached and tell them that Jesus was a liar and that the Bible was not so. If it did not work, I wanted to throw it away. I am just that honest." In fact, in practice he probably would have come up with another explanation and waited (cf. *Prevailing Prayer,* 75), but inadvisable wording such as this can undermine people's faith.

47. Jesus's disciples treat touching him (Mark 5:31) as the equivalent of touching his garments (5:30), as does Luke's paraphrase of Mark (Luke 8:45).

48. Keener, *Background Commentary,* 658: "It follows the frequent literary practice called historical retrospective, a summary of Jewish history to make a particular point, as in texts like Acts 7, 1 Maccabees 2:49–69 and Sirach 44–50. . . . The writer builds the chapter around a literary device called anaphora (repetition of an opening word or words), beginning each new account with the same Greek word, 'by faith.'"

49. In church ministry, I also noticed, in more than one church, that even though at least one person every week explained in our services how to know that one had eternal life, some regular attenders understood this only when I explained it to them personally.

50. Also called cell groups, discipleship groups, Bible study groups, and so forth. In the first century these were house churches; in the 1700s, John Wesley called them Methodist Societies, Class Meetings, and Band Societies, not unlike his own earlier experience at Oxford in leading the Holy Club.

51. Noncharismatic writers have also offered valuable and balanced expositions of passages about spiritual gifts; these include Carson, *Showing Spirit;* Hemphill, *Gifted;* on hearing God, Blackaby and King, *Experiencing God.* Although one may quibble with some points in these writers, we charismatics do not have unanimity among ourselves on every point.

52. I address this question more extensively in Keener, *Acts,* 1:1012–28; on a popular level, see idem, "Money." Particularly extensively and helpfully, see Blomberg, *Poverty.*

Notes to Chapter 18

1. E.g., Spawn and Wright, "Emergence," 16, cite here among others Yong, *Spirit-Word--Community;* idem, "Trialectic." See also Wyckoff, *Pneuma,* 69; Grey, *Crowd,* 129, 170.

2. Fee, *Listening,* 15. Going even further, see, e.g., Green, *Seized,* 66–79.

3. With, e.g., Thomas, "Women," 88, 91.

4. Stibbe, "Thoughts," 185, comparing the practice of liberation theologians.

5. Though cf. also early manuscripts of Luke 11:2. Because prayer must never be for show, we also go into our inner room and pray so that only God who sees our heart knows (Matt 6:6).

6. 1 Tim 4:13; Justin *1 Apol.* 67; later, *Murat. Canon* 73–80. It does not appear in Acts 2:42, 46 (even if some members were literate, most would have access to Torah scrolls only through public readings in the temple or synagogues, unless, as in the case of Acts 8:27–28, they were wealthy), but the apostles' teaching in 2:42 probably included the sort of material

now included in the Gospels, what Justin later called "memoirs of the apostles" (*1 Apol.* 66–67; *Dial.* 100–107), and reading plus sound exposition was later the next best thing to an apostle's presence (cf. "until I come" in 1 Tim 4:13).

7. Luke 4:16; Acts 13:15, 27; 15:21; 2 Cor 3:15; *CIJ* 2:332–35, §1404 (the Theodotus inscription); Philo *Embassy* 156; *Good Man Free* 81; Josephus *Ag. Ap.* 2.175; *Ant.* 16.43; *m. Ber.* 1:2; see further Oesterley, *Liturgy,* 38–40; Levine, "Synagogue," 15–17; Sanders, *Jesus to Mishnah,* 78–81; Aune, *Environment,* 202; Le Cornu, *Acts,* 692; Dunn, "Synagogue," 219; Graves, "Reading"; Cohen, "Evidence on Synagogue," 164–65, citing among Christian witnesses to the practice especially Justin *Dial.* 72.3; Ps.-Justin, *Exhortation to the Greeks* 13 (PG 6.268); Hippol. *Ref.* 9.12.8 = GCS 26.247; cf. also Justin *Dial.* 29; 55. Cf. earlier Deut 31:11; Josh 8:34–35; 2 Chr 34:30; Neh 8:3, 8, 18; 9:3; 13:1.

8. Scholars often note their fondness for blood; see, e.g., Nichols, *History of Christianity,* 85; esp. Walker, *History,* 453. For Zinzendorf's largely positive influence on hymnody, see Bailey, *Gospel in Hymns,* 334–37.

9. Stibbe, "Thoughts," 186. Contextually, I believe that Ezekiel's image applies to the restoration of the coming age (as in Rev 22:1–2), but my concern here is Stibbe's appeal to community.

10. Beverley, *Laughter,* offers a balanced evaluation; supportive works include Poloma, *Mystics;* Chevreau, *Catch the Fire.* Historically, revivals and renewals have often initially overstated expected outcomes, yet exert a long-range influence on further renewals. Admittedly, my only direct experience is not with the Toronto Airport Church, but with Randy Clark, a friend who has labored commendably to bridge gaps between healing ministry and academics (see, e.g., his DMin dissertation, Clark, "Effects").

11. E.g., in most of the US Assemblies of God's first century, pretribulationalism was the dominant eschatological view, but most scholars, including, so far as I can tell, most Pentecostal scholars, deem this view exegetically untenable. (I do concede that even a few of my own esteemed mentors, including Stanley Horton, with whom I dialogued about this matter, sincerely held this view, much to my astonishment.) Appealing to the Assemblies as a community for doctrinal assurance over against scholarship may sometimes appeal to popular traditions that influenced the Assemblies at its beginning against possibly less biased exegesis—to tradition rather than God's Word or God's Spirit. Many of today's apostolic-type movements in the US, by contrast, are openly posttribulational (e.g., Randy Clark's Global Awakening; International House of Prayer). Yet appealing to views of charismatic communities can be dangerous; some more extreme charismatic movements have, in the name of the prophetic Spirit, advocated Manifested Sons eschatology, which in its pure form (as espoused by Sam Fife) is false prophecy and which I and most other charismatics deem heretical (see Keener, *Miracles,* 2:612–13).

12. The *Didache* (11.3–6) is somewhat closer to Paul's usage, but in general the early church fathers adapt Luke's usual usage: they simply add Paul to the Twelve. Both Luke's and Paul's usages are biblical, but it helps dialogue if we specify which usage we are following. Few apostolic movements today claim that their apostles belong to the Twelve (despite some historic anomalies, such as the twelve apostles of the nineteenth-century Catholic Apostolic Church [see, e.g., Strachan, *Theology of Irving,* 14; cf. Christenson, *Message,* 47–48, 108–9], and, further from historic Christian orthodoxy, the origins of the Mormon Church).

13. For testing apostles and prophets, see, e.g., 1 Cor 14:29; 1 Thess 5:20–21; Rev 2:2; *Did.* 11.3–12.5. For one initial and mostly balanced challenge to some modern apostolic movements,

see Geivett and Pivec, *New Apostolic Reformation.* I do recognize some ministers today as fulfilling these ministries, but I believe that others are employing the label too cavalierly.

14. In the year 2000, for example, in terms of the numbers of global congregations, Pentecostals had 751,000 congregations, independent charismatic networks 413,000, Baptists 226,000, Lutherans 106,000, Anglicans 82,000, and so forth. There were nearly 200 million Pentecostals, whereas the other groups just named ranged between 75 and 100 million each (Johnstone, *Future,* 115).

15. One could add views about subsequence of baptism in the Holy Spirit, but this is shared by some Wesleyan and most Holiness groups.

16. See, e.g., Seymour in Robeck, *Mission,* 163. Even Parham focused more on a historical and apocalyptic metanarrative than on tongues (Oliverio, *Hermeneutics,* 53, following esp. Jacobsen, *Thinking in Spirit,* 28–35). Similarly, what was distinctive about Baptists differed from their focus (Kidd and Hankins, *Baptists,* 249).

17. See Anderson, *Pentecostalism,* 11.

18. Although word meanings are not primarily derived by etymology, this would be the sense of "charismatic" if we follow Paul's discussion of *charismata:* they belong to Christ's entire body.

19. Personal correspondence, July 10, 2015 (quotation); July 11, 2015. He does not define himself as "charismatic," but had previously observed (July 9) that "There's hardly anyone around Calvin College or Calvin Seminary now that would buy into the 'cessationist' idea about apostolic miracles that John Calvin taught."

20. I have also found it helpful in times of intellectual or spiritual crisis or difficulty (or during unpleasant tasks such as reading magical papyri), as well as in times of physical pain. I have experienced it benefiting my ability to do my scholarly work; but I recognize that God also grants other gifts of his grace to others doing such work.

21. This ministry began after his friend Jacques Vernaud, a Swiss Pentecostal missionary, laid hands on him.

22. To borrow Joel Carpenter's summary of my hope, cited above (personal correspondence, July 10, 2015).

Notes to the Conclusion

1. I exclude here those who define cessationism as simply that God does not do the same thing all the time, who allow a greater degree of sovereignty in his giftings and outpourings of the Spirit. That broad a definition also embraces many charismatics, including myself. I would not define such a position as cessationist, but that is how some moderate cessationists have expressed it in conversation with me.

2. Paul emphasizes the moral dimension of that in the context of these passages, but Luke emphasizes the missional dimension in his narrative illustrations of the Spirit's guidance (Acts 8:29; 10:19; 16:6–7), and John a christocentric, revelatory dimension (John 16:13–15). The psalmist needs divine leading (Ps 25:5; 43:3; 143:10). Each writer emphasizes the aspect of the Spirit's leading relevant to the context, but together they speak of a wider experience.

3. Stormont, *Wigglesworth,* 114. Stormont personally knew Wigglesworth, who himself read only the Bible (a Bible now held by Canon Andrew White).

Notes to Appendix A

1. See, e.g., Bauer and Traina, *Inductive Bible Study*, 377–78, summarizing the points of Robert Wall and others.

2. Dilthey, *Pattern*, 81: "Even when they believe that their work is not based on presuppositions they are determined by their horizon," including their generation and what it inherits from its predecessors. Nevertheless, human sciences should *strive* for objectivity. Cf. also 147–48.

3. Dilthey, *Pattern*, 102, 123; for human connectedness (something like modern psychology's systems approach), see chs. 4–6, esp. 122–23, 127, 131, 137–38, 161. Enamored with scientific objectivity, he hoped to overcome relativity by methodological rules (Westphal, *Community*, 32). By contrast, Gadamer, *Truth and Method*, 245, critiques as inadequate Dilthey's starting points in "Self-reflection and autobiography" (cf. Dilthey, *Pattern*, ch. 2, esp. 85–86). For Gadamer, the text helps us find the universal, rather than the reverse (*Truth and Method*, 305); "A common world—even if it is only an invented one—is always the presupposition of language" (367).

4. Like Dilthey, Bultmann sees the commonality between author and interpreter as a condition for the possibility of understanding (Bultmann, "Problem of Hermeneutics," 73; cf. Poland, *Criticism*, 45). Bultmann emphasizes persons' concrete existence in historical contexts ("Science and Existence," 133; Perrin, *Bultmann*, 39; for Heidegger, see Thiselton, *Horizons*, 150); every encounter is possible only through commonality, through preunderstanding (cf. Bultmann, "Problem of Hermeneutics," 85; idem, "Historicity," 98; Perrin, *Bultmann*, 80; for Heidegger, see Thiselton, *Horizons*, 166).

5. For Gadamer, prejudices are not always unfounded; against Enlightenment pretensions to objectivity, one starts with some knowledge or assumptions that may then be augmented, adjusted, or corrected; see Gadamer, *Truth and Method*, 239–40, 245–46; cf. also Gerhart, "Generic Studies," 314; cf. Osborne, *Spiral*, 388, 412, regarding Ricoeur. Despite the work's title, Gadamer is less interested in developing a detailed hermeneutical methodology than in articulating an epistemological foundation for hermeneutics.

6. Cf. Gadamer, *Truth and Method*, 404: "language has its true being only in conversation, in the exercise of understanding between people"; personal worldviews are "disclosed."

7. Gadamer, *Truth and Method*, 258ff. Even translation, however, involves conversation, understanding something not precisely identical with the original message (348).

8. Gadamer, *Truth and Method*, 289 (cf. 274 on Pietist application).

9. Cf. Perrin, *Bultmann*, 70 (though the ideas of that world were in flux, cf. Perrin, *Bultmann*, 61).

10. Manson, "Life of Jesus," 220.

11. Perrin, *Bultmann*, 15; Hasel, *New Testament Theology*, 85. Bultmann met Heidegger over ten years before the latter formally joined the Nazi party. Other influences include old liberalism (though cf. Bultmann, "Mythology," 12–13; Poland, *Criticism*, 26–27, 29), Neo-Kantianism, and his extended form of Lutheranism (Thiselton, *Horizons*, 205–26; cf. Poland, *Criticism*, 19–20).

12. Bultmann, "Mythology," 23–25; Thiselton, *Horizons*, 178–79, 226, 232, 262. Bultmann averred that theology could learn from philosophy (Bultmann, "Historicity," 96, 101), but that philosophy's insights could not actualize existence; authentic existence is an ontological possibility but not an ontic one (Bultmann, "Historicity," 95, 103; idem, "Mythology," 25–27; Perrin,

Bultmann, 30), and may be achieved only by a decision for Christ (Bultmann, "Mythology," 28). All understanding rests on a particular way of asking questions (Bultmann, "Problem of Hermeneutics," 72–73); only the question about God enables us to grasp revelation (Bultmann, "Problem of Hermeneutics," 87).

13. Bultmann, "Exegesis," 149; cf., e.g., Bultmann, *Word,* 11. Thus what Thielicke charges is a corruption of the Bible by secular philosophy (Thiselton, *Horizons,* 3), Bultmann considers a necessary part of the theological enterprise.

14. Bultmann, "Problem of Hermeneutics," 86. One cannot presuppose the results of one's exegesis beforehand (Bultmann, "Exegesis," 145; Thiselton, *Horizons,* 284), though one cannot but presuppose one's exegetical method (Bultmann, "Exegesis," 146–47), which is determined by one's goal (Bultmann, "Historicity," 92).

15. Bultmann, "Problem of Hermeneutics," 72–73, 86. Johns and Johns, "Yielding," 50, note that Bultmann was correct to emphasize preunderstanding, but Pentecostals differ from him in insisting on the text's objective authority.

16. Bultmann counters that Barth has misunderstood the point of existential analysis, in that humans exist only in encounters ("Problem of Hermeneutics," 89). Yet he redefines Jesus's God as something within humans (*Word,* 102–3), and seeks for our human nature to be "realized" (*Mythology,* 25; though cf. Paul's understanding of conformity to the new Adam). While Bultmann's theology may have become anthropology in practice, "this was never Bultmann's intention" (Thiselton, *Horizons,* 223). Just as love and kindness are not objective phenomena (Bultmann, "Science and Existence," 140), it is not possible to speak of a transcendent God as an object (cf. Perrin, *Bultmann,* 19, 50); he is thus outside the realm of scientific inquiry (Bultmann, "Science and Existence," 131).

17. Bultmann, "Historicity," 94. For examples of anthropocentric interpretation, see Bultmann, *Word,* 55, 102–3. Much of German theology in the early twentieth century was anthropocentric, to Barth's dismay; see Poewe, *Religions,* 50.

18. Bultmann, "Mythology," 32–35.

19. Bultmann, "Demythologizing," 110. He redefines God's invisibility as excluding the visibility of his acts ("Demythologizing," 122), even though the biblical sources that affirm his invisibility also affirm his acting visibly in history. To argue that God cannot cause an event in history or he would not be God (cf. Perrin, *Bultmann,* 86) redefines God's activity in a manner antithetical to traditional monotheistic belief. Denying that God's act can be considered apart from our existence, on the ground that "God is not a phenomenon within the world" (161), would seem to presuppose that God's act is identical with God, and that he cannot be both above the world and capable of working in it. Instead of balancing God's transcendence and immanence, Bultmann's God is so wholly other that he resembles the god of deism, who does not act in history.

20. Bultmann, "Mythology," 4.

21. "Demythologizing," 95.

22. E.g., Bultmann, "Exegesis," 147.

23. Bultmann, "Mythology," 9.

24. Bultmann, "Mythology," 1.

25. Bultmann, "Historicity," 96–97.

26. E.g., Bultmann, "Between Times," 250–52, 256; idem, "Mythology," 17–20, 38–39. Still, Jewish intermediate-era eschatology was not fixed ("Between Times," 248).

27. Bultmann, "Mythology," 14–15.

28. See, e.g., Jonas, *Religion*.

29. See esp. Yamauchi, *Gnosticism;* idem, "Gnosticism"; Smith, *Gnostic Origins.* The Gnostic Redeemer myth is absent even in what some wish to call proto-gnostic trajectories (Drane, "Background," 123; Bruce, "History," 49; cf. Wilson, *Gnostic Problem,* 226).

30. Thus Bultmann can regard Paul as being unintentionally inconsistent, because the resurrection cannot validly constitute a unity with the cross and yet remain an authenticating miracle (Bultmann, "Mythology," 36–37).

31. Hasel, *New Testament Theology,* 89.

32. Thiselton, *Horizons,* 274; cf. 290.

33. Cf. Ladd, *Bultmann,* 24, 26.

Notes to Appendix B

1. See Moore and Segovia, *Criticism;* Punt, "Criticism"; England, "Criticism"; for examples, see Stanley, *Colonized Apostle;* the surveys in Kahl, "Bibelinterpretation"; Küster, "Kontextualisierung"; for the Gospels and Acts, Diehl, "Rhetoric"; for newer approaches in general, e.g., Runesson, "Treasure."

2. See, e.g., Joy, "Transitions"; Moore, "Empire"; idem, "Turn"; Punt, "Empire"; Barreto, "Affects What I See."

3. This appendix adapts material from my "Scripture and Context."

4. See already Ramsay, *Letters,* 231–32, 283, 366–67, 410.

5. See arguments in Yorke, "Hearing"; Keener, *Acts,* 2:1799–1800; and most clearly on 1 Thess 5, on which see, e.g., Weima, "'Peace.'"

6. See, e.g., Rukundwa, "Theory."

7. See helpfully here Lopez, "Visualizing," 93; idem, *Apostle,* 10.

8. Lopez, *Apostle,* 10, rightly warning that when the approach is applied with hostility toward Scripture, it ends up undermining Scripture's potential for liberating and transforming people. Wheaton professor Gene Green, who supports an evangelical postcolonial approach, also warns that the approach must be constructive as well as critical. He further raises the need for genuinely evangelical interpreters to balance postcolonial criticism with evangelical "commitments to Scripture and Christ" (Green, "Response," 22). Cf. the postcolonial but Asiacentric approach in Keener, "Asia and Europe."

9. Contrast, for example, the Moghul empire; British colonialism; the Soviet empire; ISIS; Japan in 1930s–40s; traditional US exploitation in Latin America; and Chinese expansionism in Asia today. The form of French colonialism differed even from one colony to another, making some more "French" than others. For different colonialisms, see Sunquist, *Century,* 18–20.

10. See Fitzpatrick, "Carneades."

11. See Galinsky, "Cult."

12. Gundry, "Hearing," contends that Richard Horsley wrongly reads Mark's Gospel as anticolonial, but Horsley (in *JSNT* 26 [2, 2003]: 151–69) challenges Gundry's reading of Horsley's book.

13. See discussion in Samuel, *Reading,* 14–34; cf. idem, "Mission," 27–28. Cf. the warning in Moore, "Paul after Empire," 21–23.

14. See Levine, "Disease."

15. Lozano and Roth, "Problem," 187–88, following Spivak, *Critique,* 358; and Ramachandra, *Subverting,* 240–42.

16. For postcolonial theory's ability to accommodate multiple and at times even competing perspectives, see, e.g., Wills, "Response."

17. For concerns that theological reconstructions from Western-trained elites often neglect the actual grassroots beliefs of Majority World Christians, see, e.g., Chan, *Grassroots Asian Theology,* 22–27; cf. Hwa Yung, *Quest²,* xiv; Johnson and Wu, *Families,* 11.

18. Given Jesus's teachings, a hybridized evangelical postcolonialism, like any other expression of Christian faith, must start with Christ as unrivaled Lord (cf. Usry and Keener, *Religion,* 140n4); an academic approach or an ethnic loyalty dare not become so hegemonic that it replaces Christ for Christians. The Jerusalem church effectively contextualized (Acts 21:20), but nationalism and ethnocentrism limited proper unity with other (in this case, Gentile) Christians (21:21; see discussion in Keener, *Acts,* 3:3118–32).

19. While appreciating and employing the new approaches, Moore, "Manifesto," points out that they do not offer new methodologies in the sense traditionally understood during the literary turn in biblical studies.

20. I articulate this concern more fully in my "Biblical Fidelity," 34–37.

21. Interestingly, many early Christian abolitionists and feminists offered essentially liberationist readings that followed the tenor of Scripture itself, e.g., Sunderland, *Testimony* (1835); Booth, *Women* (1861).

22. See again the complaint of Chan, *Grassroots Asian Theology,* 22–27. This observation is not meant to diminish the value of the academic voices, but to consider a wider range of perspectives.

Notes to Appendix C

1. Cf., e.g., MacArthur, *Fire,* xviii, 113, and online clips. I also responded to this claim more briefly in Keener, "Review of *Strange Fire,*" 46; this was the claim that initially prompted me to respond to his critique, as well as to beginning this (not previously published) list. If MacArthur's critique focused only on certain *kinds* of charismatics, it would be true that they are not well-represented in academia, but his claims are more sweeping (see, e.g., MacArthur, *Fire,* xiii-xix, 137, noted in Keener, "Review of *Strange Fire,*" 43–45). Other responses to MacArthur, *Fire,* include Brown, *Authentic Fire;* Graves, *Strangers;* and, most graciously, Kendall, *Fire.*

2. Though some scholars at Pentecostal institutions also have affiliations elsewhere, e.g., John Christopher Thomas at Bangor University.

3. To name just a few of the institutions where I know faculty, I could list many scholars, a number of them my friends, at Alphacrucis, Evangel, Lee, North Central, Northwestern, Southeastern, Southwestern, Valley Forge and Vanguard Universities, Emmanuel College, as well as Bible colleges (such as SUM), seminaries (Westminster Theological Centre, UK) and other institutions, for example. Some of these scholars are as published as other scholars listed below and not cited elsewhere in the book (e.g., Lee's Daniela Augustine in theological ethics). Other published scholars, such as Paul King and Derek Morphew, are especially training leaders in less traditional settings, or are in research settings, such as Harold Hunter.

4. One could name so many younger scholars, including Mary Catherine Brown (PhD Asbury), Matt Croasman (PhD Yale, working at Yale), T. Michael W. Halcomb (PhD Asbury,

authoring books), Brittany Kim (PhD Wheaton, teaching at Roberts Wesleyan College), Kris Miller (PhD Durham, teaching at Lipscomb University), Jack Poirier (DHL Jewish Theological Seminary), Michael Raburn (PhD Duke, teaching at Wake Forest), David Sloan (PhD, Trinity), Joel Soza (Malone). There are large numbers of Pentecostals and charismatics working on PhDs at the time of my writing; just a few that have been mentioned to me: Joy Ames Vaughan (Asbury), Camilla Belfon (Iliff), Benjamin Dwayne Cowan (Claremont), Anna Marie Droll (Fuller), Wilmer Estrada-Carrasquillo (Asbury), Samantha Fong (Duke), Janna Gonwa (Yale), Alicia Jackson (University of Birmingham, UK), Thomas Lyons (Asbury), Caleb J. D. Maskell (Princeton University), Leila Ortiz (Lutheran Seminary of Philadelphia), Meghan Musy (McMaster Divinity College), Judith Odor (Asbury), and Ekaputra Tupamahu (Vanderbilt).

5. Clearly the line between continuationist and charismatic is hard to draw; in fact, some self-identified as charismatic but were not known as such to their colleagues, or did not self-identify as charismatic (hence are not on this list) even though their colleagues identified them as such.

6. For just a sampling of the diversity: Anglicans include Allan Anderson, Lyle Dorsett, Michael Green, Michael Knowles, and N. T. Wright; Baptists include myself, Loida Martell-Otero, Luke Powery, and William Turner; Catholics include Mary Healy and Peter Williamson (the two editors of the Catholic Commentary on Holy Scripture), Teresa Berger, Luke Timothy Johnson, and George Montague (former editor of *Catholic Biblical Quarterly*); Christian & Missionary Alliance includes Robert Gallagher and Paul King; Lutherans include Mark Hillmer, Mark Allan Powell, and Joy Schroeder; Mennonites include Alan Kreider; Presbyterians, Ogbu Kalu, and Lalsangkima Pachuau; Quakers, Richard Foster; and so forth. Outside of Pentecostals, Methodists might win the prize on my list, but only because my immediate location and the venue of my PhD work gave me access to learn of many more of them, including William Abraham, Valerie Cooper, Gene Green, Richard Hays, Israel Kamudzandu, Fred Long, Luther Oconor, Lester Ruth, Steve Seamands, Howard Snyder, Timothy Tennent, Robert Tuttle, David Watson, and Ben Witherington.

7. Even apart from charismatic elements, many of John MacArthur's followers might deem the less conservative elements as contaminating the entire sample; Pastor MacArthur belongs to a tradition that rejects Catholics and mainline Protestants and is highly suspicious of those who have fellowship with them. Nevertheless, I am guessing that most readers of this book will be interested in the wider list.

Bibliography of Sources Cited

Aberle, "Zweck." • Aberle, M. von. "Über den Zweck des Johannesevangelium." *Theologische Quartalschrift* 42 (1861): 37–94.

Abraham, *Revelation.* • Abraham, William J. *Divine Revelation and the Limits of Historical Criticism.* Oxford: Oxford University Press, 1982.

Adhinarta, *Doctrine.* • Adhinarta, Yuzo. *The Doctrine of the Holy Spirit in the Major Reformed Confessions and Catechisms of the Sixteenth and Seventeenth Centuries.* Carlisle, Cumbria, UK: Langham Monographs, 2012.

Agosto, "Foreword." • Agosto, Efraín. "Foreword." xiii–xvi in *Colonized Apostle: Paul through Postcolonial Eyes.* Edited by Christopher D. Stanley. Minneapolis: Fortress, 2011.

Ahn, "Debates." • Ahn, Yongnan Jeon. "Various Debates in the Contemporary Pentecostal Hermeneutics." *Spirit & Church* 2 (1, 2000): 19–52.

Akhtar, "Miracles." • Akhtar, Shabbir. "Miracles as Evidence for the Existence of God." *SJRS* 11 (1, 1990): 18–23.

Albright, *Biblical Period.* • Albright, William Foxwell. *The Biblical Period from Abraham to Ezra.* New York: Harper & Row, 1963.

Albright, *Yahweh.* • Albright, William Foxwell. *Yahweh and the Gods of Canaan.* Jordan Lectures, 1965. Garden City, NY: Doubleday, 1968.

Alexander, "Action." • Alexander, Paul. "Nonviolent Direct Action in Acts 2: The Holy Spirit, the Early Church, and Martin Luther King, Jr." 114–24 in *Trajectories in the Book of Acts: Essays in Honor of John Wesley Wyckoff.* Edited by Paul Alexander, Jordan Daniel May, and Robert G. Reid. Eugene, OR: Wipf & Stock, 2010.

Alexander, "Conscience." • Alexander, Kimberly Ervin. "Matters of Conscience, Matters of Unity, Matters of Orthodoxy: Trinity and Water Baptism in Early Pentecostal Theology and Practice." *JPT* 17 (1, 2008): 48–69.

Alexander, *Fire.* • Alexander, Estrelda Y. *Black Fire: One Hundred Years of African American Pentecostalism.* Downers Grove, IL: InterVarsity, 2011.

Alexander and Yong, *Daughters.* • Alexander, Estrelda, and Amos Yong, eds. *Philip's Daughters: Women in Pentecostal-Charismatic Leadership.* PrTMS 104. Eugene, OR: Pickwick, Wipf & Stock, 2009.

Allen, "Whole Person Healing." • Allen, E. Anthony. "Whole Person Healing, Spiritual Realism, and Social Disintegration: A Caribbean Case Study in Faith, Health, and Healing." *IntRevMiss* 90 (356/357, January-April 2001): 118–33.

Allison, *Moses.* • Allison, Dale C., Jr. *The New Moses: A Matthean Typology.* Minneapolis: Fortress, 1993.

Althouse, *Spirit*. • Althouse, Peter. *Spirit of the Last Days: Pentecostal Eschatology in Conversation with Jürgen Moltmann.* New York: T&T Clark International, 2003.

Alvarez, "South." • Alvarez, Miguel. "The South and the Latin America Paradigm of the Pentecostal Movement." *AJPS* 5 (1, 2002): 135–53.

Anderson, *Ends of the Earth*. • Anderson, Allan Heaton. *To the Ends of the Earth: Pentecostalism and the Transformation of World Christianity.* New York: Oxford University Press, 2013.

Anderson, *Glossary*. • Anderson, R. Dean, Jr. *Glossary of Greek Rhetorical Terms Connected to Methods of Argumentation, Figures, and Tropes from Anaximenes to Quintilian.* Leuven: Peeters, 2000.

Anderson, "Pentecostal Hermeneutics." • Anderson, Gordon L. "Pentecostal Hermeneutics." *Enrichment Journal* (April 14, 2010). At http://enrichmentjournal.ag.org/top/holyspirit _articledisplay.cfm?targetBay=1b574def-b227-4617-bfc7-a02cdb926902&ModID=2 &Process=DisplayArticle&RSS_RSSContentID=15177&RSS_OriginatingChannelID =1170&RSS_OriginatingRSSFeedID=4486&RSS_Source=.

Anderson, "Pentecostal Hermeneutics 2." • Anderson, Gordon L. "Pentecostal Hermeneutics Part 2." http://enrichmentjournal.ag.org/top/holyspirit_articledisplay.cfm?targetBay =1b574def-b227-4617-bfc7-a02cdb926902&ModID=2&Process=DisplayArticle&RSS_ RSSContentID=15178&RSS_OriginatingChannelID=1170&RSS_OriginatingRSSFeedID =4486&RSS_Source=.

Anderson, *Pentecostalism*. • Anderson, Allan. *An Introduction to Pentecostalism: Global Charismatic Christianity.* Cambridge: Cambridge University Press, 2004.

Anderson, "Points." • Anderson, Allan. "To All Points of the Compass: The Azusa Street Revival and Global Pentecostalism." *Enr* 11 (2, 2006): 164–72.

Anderson, *Rhetorical Theory*. • Anderson, R. Dean, Jr. *Ancient Rhetorical Theory and Paul.* Rev. ed. CBET 18. Leuven: Peeters, 1999.

Anderson, "Signs." • Anderson, Allan. "Signs and Blunders: Pentecostal Mission Issues at 'Home and Abroad' in the Twentieth Century." *JAM* 2 (2, 2000): 193–210.

Arand et al., *Perspectives on Sabbath*. • Arand, Charles P., et al. *Perspectives on the Sabbath: Four Views.* Nashville: B&H Academic, 2011.

Archer, *Hermeneutic*. • Archer, Kenneth J. *A Pentecostal Hermeneutic: Spirit, Scripture and Community.* Cleveland, TN: CPT Press, 2009.

Archer, "Hermeneutics and Society." • Archer, Kenneth J. "Pentecostal Hermeneutics and the Society for Pentecostal Studies: Reading and Hearing in One Spirit and One Accord." *Pneuma* 37 (3, 2015): 317–39.

Archer, "Horizons." • Archer, Kenneth J. "Horizons and Hermeneutics of Doctrine: A Review Essay." *JPT* 18 (2009): 150–56.

Archer, "Retrospect and Prospect." • Archer, Kenneth J. "Pentecostal Hermeneutics: Retrospect and Prospect." 131–48 in *Pentecostal Hermeneutics: A Reader.* Edited by Lee Roy Martin. Leiden: Brill, 2013. Reprint of Archer, Kenneth J. "Pentecostal Hermeneutics: Retrospect and Prospect." *JPT* 8 (1996): 63–81.

Arles, "Appraisal." • Arles, Nalini. "Pandita Ramabai—An Appraisal from Feminist Perspective." *BangTF* 31 (1, July 1999): 64–86.

Arles, "Study." • Arles, Nalini. "Pandita Ramabai and Amy Carmichael: A Study of Their Contributions toward Transforming the Position of Indian Women." MTh thesis, University of Aberdeen, 1985.

Arrington, *Acts*. • Arrington, French L. *The Acts of the Apostles: An Introduction and Commentary.* Peabody, MA: Hendrickson, 1988.

Arrington, "Use." • Arrington, French L. "The Use of the Bible by Pentecostals." *Pneuma* 16 (1, 1994): 101–7.

Asamoah-Gyadu, "Hearing." • Asamoah-Gyadu, Kwabena. "'Hearing in Our Own Tongues the Wonderful Works of God': Pentecost, Ecumenism and Renewal in African Christianity." *Missionalia* 35 (3, November 2007): 128–45.

Asamoah-Gyadu, "Influence." • Asamoah-Gyadu, J. Kwabena. "Pentecostalism and the Influence of Primal Realities in Africa." 139–61 in *The Many Faces of Global Pentecostalism*. Edited by Harold D. Hunter and Neil Ormerod. Cleveland, TN: CPT Press, 2013.

Asamoah-Gyadu, "Mission." • Asamoah-Gyadu, J. Kwabena. "Reversing Christian Mission: African Pentecostal Pastor Establishes 'God's Embassy' in the Ukraine." Unpublished paper, May 2004.

Ashton, *Understanding*. • Ashton, John. *Understanding the Fourth Gospel*. Oxford: Clarendon, 1991.

Auerbach, *Mimesis*. • Auerbach, Erich. *Mimesis: The Representation of Reality in Western Literature*. Princeton: Princeton University Press, 1953.

Aune, *Dictionary of Rhetoric*. • Aune, David E. *The Westminster Dictionary of New Testament and Early Christian Literature and Rhetoric*. Louisville: Westminster John Knox, 2003.

Aune, *Environment*. • Aune, David E. *The New Testament in Its Literary Environment*. LEC 8. Philadelphia: Westminster, 1987.

Aune, *Prophecy*. • Aune, David E. *Prophecy in Early Christianity and the Ancient Mediterranean World*. Grand Rapids: Eerdmans, 1983.

Aune, *Revelation*. • Aune, David E. *Revelation*. 3 vols. WBC 52, 52b, 52c. Dallas: Word, 1997.

Autry, "Dimensions." • Autry, Arden C. "Dimensions of Hermeneutics in Pentecostal Focus." *JPT* 3 (1993): 29–50.

Averbeck, "Sacrifices." • Averbeck, Richard E. "Sacrifices and Offerings." 706–33 in *Dictionary of the Old Testament: Pentateuch*. Edited by T. Desmond Alexander and David W. Baker. Downers Grove, IL: InterVarsity, 2003.

Azenabor, "Witchcraft." • Azenabor, Godwin Ehi. "The Idea of Witchcraft and the Challenge of Modern Science." 21–35 in *Studies in Witchcraft, Magic, War, and Peace in Africa*. Edited by Beatrice Nicolini. Lewiston, NY: Edwin Mellen, 2006.

Azevedo, Prater, and Lantum, "Biomedicine." • Azevedo, Mario J., Gwendolyn S. Prater, and Daniel N. Lantum. "Culture, Biomedicine, and Child Mortality in Cameroon." *SSMed* 32 (12, 1991): 1341–49.

Backhaus, "Falsehood." • Backhaus, Wilfried K. "Advantageous Falsehood: The Person Moved by Faith Strikes Back." *PhilTheol* 7 (1993): 289–310.

Badawy, *Architecture*. • Badawy, Alexander. *A History of Egyptian Architecture: The Empire (1580–1085 B.C.)*. Berkeley and Los Angeles: University of California Press, 1968.

Badilita, "Exégèse." • Badilita, Smaranda. "Philon d'Alexandrie et l'exégèse allégorique." *FoiVie* 107 (4, 2008): 63–76.

Bagiella, Hong, and Sloan, "Attendance as Predictor." • Bagiella, Emilia, Victor Hong, and Richard P. Sloan. "Religious Attendance as a Predictor of Survival in the EPESE Cohorts." *IntJEpid* 34 (2005): 443–51.

Bähre, "Witchcraft." • Bähre, Erik. "Witchcraft and the Exchange of Sex, Blood, and Money among Africans in Cape Town, South Africa." *JRelAf* 32 (3, 2002): 300–334.

Bailey, *Gospel in Hymns*. • Bailey, Albert Edward. *The Gospel in Hymns: Backgrounds and Interpretations*. New York: Scribner's, 1950.

Bailey, *Peasant Eyes*. • Bailey, Kenneth Ewing. *Through Peasant Eyes: More Lucan Parables, Their Culture and Style*. Grand Rapids: Eerdmans, 1980.

Bailey, *Poet*. • Bailey, Kenneth Ewing. *Poet and Peasant: A Literary-Cultural Approach to the Parables in Luke*. Grand Rapids: Eerdmans, 1976.

Baker, *Enough*. • Baker, Rolland, and Heidi Baker. *There Is Always Enough: The Story of Rolland and Heidi Baker's Miraculous Ministry among the Poor*. Grand Rapids: Baker, 2003.

Baker, "Pentecostal Bible Reading." • Baker, Robert O. "Pentecostal Bible Reading: Toward a Model of Reading for the Formation of the Affections." 94–108 in *Pentecostal Hermeneutics: A Reader*. Edited by Lee Roy Martin. Leiden: Brill, 2013.

Baker, Testaments. • Baker, David L. *Two Testaments, One Bible: A Study of the Theological Relationship between the Old and New Testaments.* Downers Grove, IL: InterVarsity, 1991.

Bakker, Wrong. • Bakker, Jim, with Ken Abraham. *I Was Wrong.* Nashville: Thomas Nelson, 1996.

Barbour, Myths. • Barbour, Ian G. *Myths, Models, and Paradigms: A Comparative Study in Science and Religion.* New York: Harper & Row, 1974.

Barbour, Religion and Science. • Barbour, Ian G. *Religion and Science: Historical and Contemporary Issues.* San Francisco: HarperSanFrancisco, 1997.

Barnes, "Introduction." • Barnes, Linda L. "Introduction." 3–26 in *Teaching Religion and Healing.* Edited by Linda L. Barnes and Inés Talamantez. AARTRSS. Oxford: Oxford University Press, 2006.

Barnes, "World Religions." • Barnes, Linda L. "World Religions and Healing." 341–52 in *Teaching Religion and Healing.* Edited by Linda L. Barnes and Inés Talamantez. AARTRSS. Oxford: Oxford University Press, 2006.

Barnes and Talamantez, Religion and Healing. • Barnes, Linda L., and Inés Talamantez, eds. *Teaching Religion and Healing.* AARTRSS. Oxford: Oxford University Press, 2006.

Barr, Leonard, Parsons, and Weaver, Acts. • Barr, Beth Allison, Bill J. Leonard, Mikeal C. Parsons, and C. Douglas Weaver, eds. *The Acts of the Apostles: Four Centuries of Baptist Interpretation. The Baptists' Bible.* Waco: Baylor University Press, 2009.

Barreto, "Affects What I See." • Barreto, Raimundo Cesar. "How Who I Am Affects What I See: Reading Mark with Latin American Eyes." *Review & Expositor* 107 (3, 2010): 395–410.

Barrett, Acts. • Barrett, C. K. *A Critical and Exegetical Commentary on the Acts of the Apostles.* 2 vols. Edinburgh: T&T Clark, 1994–98.

Barrett, "Renewal." • Barrett, David B. "The Worldwide Holy Spirit Renewal." 381–414 in *The Century of the Holy Spirit: One Hundred Years of Pentecostal and Charismatic Renewal, 1901–2001.* Edited by Vinson Synan. Nashville: Thomas Nelson, 2001.

Barrett, World Christian Encyclopedia. • David B. Barrett, *World Christian Encyclopedia.* 2nd ed. New York: Oxford University Press, 2001.

Barrett, Johnson, and Crossing, "Missiometrics 2006." • Barrett, David B., Todd M. Johnson, and Peter F. Crossing. "Missiometrics 2006: Goals, Resources, Doctrines of the 350 Christian World Communions." *IBMR* 30 (1, January 2006): 27–30.

Barrett, Johnson, and Crossing, "Missiometrics 2007." • Barrett, David B., Todd M. Johnson, and Peter F. Crossing. "Missiometrics 2007: Creating Your Own Analysis of Global Data." *IBMR* 31 (1, January 2007): 25–32.

Barth, Church Dogmatics. • Barth, Karl. *Church Dogmatics.* Edinburgh: T&T Clark, 1956–75.

Barth, Doctrine. • Barth, Karl. *The Doctrine of the Word of God.* Vol. 1.1 of *Church Dogmatics.* Edited by G. W. Bromiley and T. F. Torrance. Translated by G. W. Bromiley et al. Edinburgh: T&T Clark, 1956.

Barthes, "Death." • Barthes, Roland. "The Death of an Author." 167–71 in *Modern Criticism and Theory.* Edited by David Lodge. New York: Longman, 1988.

Barthes, Pleasure. • Barthes, Roland. *The Pleasure of the Text.* Trans. R. Miller. New York: Hill & Wang, 1975.

Bartholomew, Canon. • Bartholomew, Craig G. *Canon and Biblical Interpretation.* Grand Rapids: Zondervan, 2006.

Bartholomew, Hermeneutics. • Bartholomew, Craig G. *Introducing Biblical Hermeneutics: A Comprehensive Framework for Hearing God in Scripture.* Grand Rapids: Baker Academic, 2015.

Bartholomew and Thomas, Manifesto. • Bartholomew, Craig G., and Heath A. Thomas, editors. *A Manifesto for Theological Interpretation.* Grand Rapids: Baker Academic, 2016.

Bartleman, Azusa Street. • Bartleman, Frank. *Azusa Street.* Foreword by Vinson Synan. 1925. Repr., Plainfield, NJ: Logos, 1980.

Baslez, "Monde." • Baslez, Marie-Françoise. "Le monde des Actes des apôtres: Approches littéraires et études documentaires." 63–84 in *Les Actes des apôtres—Histoire, récit, théologie: XXe congrès de l'Association catholique française pour l'étude de la Bible (Angers, 2003)*. Edited by Michel Berder. LD 199. Paris: Cerf, 2005.

Bauckham, *Climax*. • Bauckham, Richard. *The Climax of Prophecy: Studies on the Book of Revelation*. Edinburgh: T&T Clark, 1993.

Bauckham, *Crucified*. • Bauckham, Richard. *God Crucified: Monotheism and Christology in the New Testament*. Grand Rapids: Eerdmans, 1998.

Bauckham, "Gospels." • Bauckham, Richard. "For Whom Were the Gospels Written?" 9–48 in *The Gospels for All Christians: Rethinking the Gospel Audiences*. Edited by Richard Bauckham. Grand Rapids: Eerdmans, 1998.

Bauckham, *Gospels for Christians*. • Bauckham, Richard, ed. *The Gospels for All Christians: Rethinking the Gospel Audiences*. Grand Rapids: Eerdmans, 1998.

Bauckham, "Review of Waddell." • Bauckham, Richard. "Review of Robby Waddell, *The Spirit of the Book of Revelation*." *JPT* 17 (1, 2008): 3–8.

Bauckham, *Testimony*. • Bauckham, Richard. *The Testimony of the Beloved Disciple: Narrative, History, and Theology in the Gospel of John*. Grand Rapids: Baker Academic, 2007.

Bauer, "Function." • Bauer, David R. "The Literary and Theological Function of the Genealogy in Matthew's Gospel." 129–59 in *Treasures New and Old: Recent Contributions to Matthean Studies*. Edited by David R. Bauer and Mark Allan Powell. SBLSymS 1. Atlanta: Scholars Press, 1996.

Bauer and Powell, "Introduction." • Bauer, David R., and Mark Allan Powell, "Introduction." 1–25 in *Treasures New and Old: Recent Contributions to Matthean Studies*. Edited by David R. Bauer and Mark Allan Powell. SBLSymS 1. Atlanta: Scholars Press, 1996.

Bauer and Traina, *Inductive Bible Study*. • David R. Bauer and Robert A. Traina, *Inductive Bible Study: A Comprehensive Guide to the Practice of Hermeneutics*. Foreword by Eugene H. Peterson. Grand Rapids: Baker Academic, 2011.

Baumgarten, "Korban." • Baumgarten, Albert I. "*Korban* and the Pharisaic *Paradosis*." *Journal of the Ancient Near Eastern Society* 16–17 (1984–1985): 5–17.

Beale, *Revelation*. • Beale, Gregory K. *The Book of Revelation: A Commentary on the Greek Text*. NIGTC. Grand Rapids: Eerdmans, 1999.

Beale and Carson, *Commentary*. • Beale, Gregory K., and D. A. Carson, eds. *Commentary on the New Testament Use of the Old Testament*. Grand Rapids: Baker Academic, 2007.

Beasley-Murray, "Kingdom." • Beasley-Murray, George R. "The Kingdom of God and Christology in the Gospels." 22–36 in *Jesus of Nazareth, Lord and Christ: Essays on the Historical Jesus and New Testament Christology*. Edited by Joel B. Green and Max Turner. Grand Rapids: Eerdmans; Carlisle, UK: Paternoster, 1994.

Bebbington, *Dominance*. • Bebbington, David W. *The Dominance of Evangelicalism: The Age of Spurgeon and Moody*. A History of Evangelicalism 3. Downers Grove, IL: InterVarsity, 2005.

Beck, "Anonymity." • Beck, David R. "The Narrative Function of Anonymity in Fourth Gospel Characterization." *Semeia* 63 (1993): 143–58.

Beck, *Paradigm*. • Beck, David R. *The Discipleship Paradigm: Readers and Anonymous Characters in the Fourth Gospel*. Leiden: Brill, 1997.

Beckwith, *Argument*. • Beckwith, Francis J. *David Hume's Argument against Miracles: A Critical Analysis*. Lanham, MD: University Press of America, 1989.

Bediako, "African Culture." • Bediako, Kwame. "Jesus in African Culture: A Ghanaian Perspective." 93–121 in *Emerging Voices in Global Christian Theology*. Edited by William A. Dyrness. Grand Rapids: Zondervan, 1994.

Belfiore, "Plots." • Belfiore, Elizabeth. "Aristotle's *muthos* and Narratological Plots." *CBull* 73 (2, 1997): 141–47.

Belleville, *Leaders*. • Belleville, Linda L. *Women Leaders and the Church: Three Crucial Questions*. Grand Rapids: Baker, 2000.

Bendlin, "Intertextuality." • Bendlin, Andreas. "Intertextuality." 6:873–75 in *BrillPauly*.

Benson, *Healing*. • Benson, Herbert, with Marg Stark. *Timeless Healing: The Power and Biology of Belief*. New York: Scribner, 1996.

Benson, "Ignorant." • Benson, Bruce Ellis. "'Now I Would Not Have You Ignorant': Derrida, Gadamer, Hirsch and Husserl on Authors' Intentions." 173–91 in *Evangelicals and Scripture: Tradition, Authority and Hermeneutics*. Edited by Vincent Bacote, Laura C. Miguélez, and Dennis L. Ockholm. Downers Grove, IL: InterVarsity, 2004.

Berger, "Faces." • Berger, Peter L. "Four Faces of Global Culture." 419–27 in *Globalization and the Challenges of a New Century: A Reader*. Edited by Patrick O'Meara, Howard D. Mehlinger, and Matthew Krain. Bloomington: Indiana University Press, 2000.

Bernal, *Athena*. • Bernal, Martin. *Black Athena: The Afroasiatic Roots of Classical Civilization*. 3 vols. London: Free Association; New Brunswick, NJ: Rutgers University Press, 1987–2006.

Beverley, *Laughter*. • Beverley, James A. *Holy Laughter and the Toronto Blessing: An Investigative Report*. Grand Rapids: Zondervan, 1995.

Binsbergen, "Witchcraft." • Binsbergen, Wim van. "Witchcraft in Modern Africa as Virtualized Boundary Conditions of the Kinship Order." 212–63 in *Witchcraft Dialogues: Anthropological and Philosophical Exchanges*. Edited by George Clement Bond and Diane M. Ciekawy. Athens: Center for International Studies, Ohio University, 2001.

Bird, "Inerrancy." • Bird, Michael F. "Inerrancy Is Not Necessary for Evangelicalism outside the USA." 145–73 in *Five Views on Biblical Inerrancy*. Edited by J. J. Merrick and Stephen M. Garrett. Grand Rapids: Zondervan, 2013.

Bishop, "Prosperity." • Bishop, Larry. "Prosperity." *Cornerstone* 10 (54, May-June 1981): 12–16.

Blackaby and King, *Experiencing God*. • Blackaby, Henry T., and Claude V. King. *Experiencing God: How to Live the Full Adventure of Knowing and Doing the Will of God*. Nashville: Broadman & Holman, 1994.

Blackman, "Exegesis." • Blackman, E. C. "The Task of Exegesis." 3–26 in *The Background of the New Testament and Its Eschatology: Essays in Honour of Charles Harold Dodd*. Edited by W. D. Davies and D. Daube. Cambridge: Cambridge University Press, 1964.

Bloesch, "Christological Hermeneutic." • Bloesch, Donald G. "A Christological Hermeneutic: Crisis and Conflict in Hermeneutics." 78–102 in *The Use of the Bible in Theology: Evangelical Options*. Edited by Robert K. Johnston. Atlanta: John Knox, 1985.

Blomberg, *Believe*. • Blomberg, Craig L. *Can We Still Believe the Bible? An Evangelical Engagement with Contemporary Questions*. Grand Rapids: Brazos, 2014.

Blomberg, "Globalization." • Blomberg, Craig L. "The Globalization of Hermeneutics." *JETS* 38 (4, December 1995): 581–93.

Blomberg, *Poverty*. • Blomberg, Craig L. *Neither Poverty nor Riches: A Biblical Theology of Material Possessions*. Grand Rapids: Eerdmans, 1999.

Blumhofer, *Chapter*. • Blumhofer, Edith L. *The Assemblies of God: A Chapter in the Story of American Pentecostalism*. 2 vols. Springfield, MO: Gospel Publishing House, 1989.

Blumhofer, *Faith*. • Blumhofer, Edith Waldvogel. *Restoring the Faith: The Assemblies of God, Pentecostalism, and American Culture*. Urbana: University of Illinois Press, 1993.

Blumhofer, *Popular History*. • Blumhofer, Edith Waldvogel. *The Assemblies of God: A Popular History*. Springfield, MO: Gospel Publishing House, 1985.

Blumhofer, *Sister*. • Blumhofer, Edith L. *Aimee Semple McPherson: Everybody's Sister*. Grand Rapids: Eerdmans, 1993.

Blumhofer, Spittler, and Wacker, *Currents*. • Blumhofer, Edith L., Russell P. Spittler, and Grant Wacker. *Pentecostal Currents in American Protestantism*. Urbana: University of Illinois Press, 1999.

Boda, "Walking." • Boda, Mark J. "Walking with the Spirit in the Word: A Response." 169–72 in *Spirit and Scripture: Exploring a Pneumatic Hermeneutic*. Edited by Kevin L. Spawn and Archie T. Wright. New York: Bloomsbury, 2012.

Boda, "Word and Spirit." • Boda, Mark J. "Word and Spirit, Scribe and Prophet in Old Testament Hermeneutics." 25–45 in *Spirit and Scripture: Exploring a Pneumatic Hermeneutic*. Edited by Kevin L. Spawn and Archie T. Wright. New York: Bloomsbury, 2012.

Boddy, "Spirit Possession." • Boddy, Janice. "Spirit Possession Revisited: Beyond Instrumentality." *ARAnth* 23 (1994): 407–34.

Bomann, *Faith in Barrios*. • Bomann, Rebecca Pierce. *Faith in the Barrios: The Pentecostal Poor in Bogotá*. Boulder, CO, and London: Lynn Rienner, 1999.

Bomann, "Salve." • Bomann, Rebecca Pierce. "The Salve of Divine Healing: Essential Rituals for Survival among Working-Class Pentecostals in Bogotá, Colombia." 187–205 in *Global Pentecostal and Charismatic Healing*. Edited by Candy Gunther Brown. Foreword by Harvey Cox. Oxford: Oxford University Press, 2011.

Bonhoeffer, *Ethics*. • Bonhoeffer, Dietrich. *Ethics*. New York: Macmillan, 1955.

Bonhoeffer, "Lectures." • Bonhoeffer, Dietrich. "Lectures on Preaching." 123–80 in *Bonhoeffer: Worldly Preaching*. Edited and translated by C. E. Fant. Nashville: Thomas Nelson, 1975.

Bonk, "Missions." • Bonk, Jonathan J. "Missions and the Liberation of Theology." *IBMR* 34 (4, October 2010): 13–94.

Bonsirven, *Judaism*. • Bonsirven, Joseph. *Palestinian Judaism in the Time of Jesus Christ*. New York: Holt, Rinehart & Winston, 1964.

Booth, *Women*. • Booth, Catherine Mumford. *Let the Women Speak: Females Teaching in Church*. Liskeard: Diggory, 2007 (originally 1861).

Borg, *Conflict*. • Borg, Marcus J. *Conflict, Holiness and Politics in the Teachings of Jesus*. Studies in the Bible and Early Christianity 5. Lewiston, NY: Edwin Mellen, 1984.

Boring, Berger, and Colpe, *Commentary*. • Boring, M. Eugene, Klaus Berger, and Carsten Colpe, eds. *Hellenistic Commentary to the New Testament*. Nashville: Abingdon, 1995.

Bosworth, "Beating." • Bosworth, F. F. "Beating in Texas Follows Ministry to Blacks: F. F. Bosworth's 1911 Letter to His Mother, Dallas, Tex., Aug. 21, 1911." *Assemblies of God Heritage* 6 (2, Summer 1986): 5, 14.

Bourguignon, "Appendix." • Bourguignon, Erika. "Appendix." 359–76 in *Religion, Altered States of Consciousness, and Social Change*. Edited by Erika Bourguignon. Columbus: Ohio State University Press, 1973.

Bourguignon, "Introduction." • Bourguignon, Erika. "Introduction: A Framework for the Comparative Study of Altered States of Consciousness." 3–35 in *Religion, Altered States of Consciousness, and Social Change*. Edited by Erika Bourguignon. Columbus: Ohio State University Press, 1973.

Bourguignon, *Possession*. • Bourguignon, Erika. *Possession*. Chandler & Sharp Series in Cross-Cultural Themes. San Francisco: Chandler & Sharp, 1976.

Bourguignon, "Spirit Possession Belief." • Bourguignon, Erika. "Spirit Possession Belief and Social Structure." 17–26 in *The Realm of the Extra-Human: Ideas and Actions*. Edited by Agehananda Bharati. The Hague: Mouton, 1976.

Bovon, *Theologian*. • Bovon, François. *Luke the Theologian: Thirty-Three Years of Research (1950–1983)*. Translated by Ken McKinney. Allison Park, PA: Pickwick, 1987.

Boyd, *Benefit of Doubt*. • Boyd, Gregory A. *Benefit of the Doubt: Breaking the Idol of Certainty*. Grand Rapids: Baker, 2013.

Brandes, "Reflections." • Brandes, Stanley. "Reflections on Honor and Shame in the Mediterranean." 121–34 in *Honor and Shame and the Unity of the Mediterranean*. Edited by David D. Gilmore. American Anthropological Association 22. Washington, DC: American Anthropological Association, 1987.

Brant, "Husband Hunting." • Brant, Jo-Ann A. "Husband Hunting: Characterization and Narrative Art in the Gospel of John." *Biblical Interpretation* 4 (2, 1996): 205–23.

Brathwaite, "Tongues." • Brathwaite, Renea. "Tongues and Ethics: William J. Seymour and the 'Bible Evidence'; A Response to Cecil M. Robeck, Jr." *Pneuma* 32 (2010): 203–22.

Braund, "Satire." • Braund, Susanna. "Satire." 13:13–16 in *BrillPauly*.

Bray, *Corinthians*. • Bray, Gerald, ed. *1–2 Corinthians*. ACCS: New Testament 7. Downers Grove, IL: InterVarsity, 1999.

Bray, *Galatians, Ephesians*. • Bray, Gerald, ed. *Galatians, Ephesians*. Reformation Commentary on Scripture, New Testament 10. Downers Grove, IL: IVP Academic, 2011.

Bray, *Romans*. • Bray, Gerald, ed. *Romans*. ACCS: New Testament 6. Downers Grove, IL: InterVarsity, 1998.

Breggen, "Miracle Reports." • Breggen, Hendrik van der. "Miracle Reports, Moral Philosophy, and Contemporary Science." PhD dissertation, University of Waterloo, 2004.

Breggen, "Seeds." • Breggen, Hendrik van der. "The Seeds of Their Own Destruction: David Hume's Fatally Flawed Arguments against Miracle Reports." *Christian Research Journal* 30 (1, 2007): 5 pages, available online.

Bremback and Howell, *Persuasion*. • Bremback, Winston L., and William S. Howell. *Persuasion: A Means of Social Influence*. 2nd ed. Englewood Cliffs, NJ: Prentice-Hall, 1976.

Brett, *Criticism*. • Brett, Mark G. *Biblical Criticism in Crisis? The Impact of the Canonical Approach on Old Testament Studies*. New York: Cambridge University Press, 1991.

Brock and Scott, *Criticism*. • Brock, Bernard L., and Robert L. Scott. *Methods of Rhetorical Criticism: A Twentieth-Century Perspective*. 2nd ed. Detroit: Wayne State University Press, 1980.

Brondos, "Freedom." • Brondos, David A. "Freedom, the 'Letter' and the 'Spirit': Interpreting Scripture with the 'Mind of Christ.'" *Trinity Seminary Review* 26 (1, 2005): 7–15.

Brooke, *Science*. • Brooke, John Hedley. *Science and Religion: Some Historical Perspectives*. Cambridge History of Science Series. New York: Cambridge University Press, 1991.

Brooke, "Science." • Brooke, John Hedley. "Science and Theology in the Enlightenment." 7–27 in *Religion and Science: History, Method, Dialogue*. Edited by W. Mark Richardson and Wesley J. Wildman. Foreword by Ian G. Barbour. New York: Routledge, 1996.

Brown, *Answering*. • Brown, Michael L. *Answering Jewish Objections to Jesus,* vol. 3, *Messianic Prophecy Objections*. Grand Rapids: Baker, 2006.

Brown, *Authentic Fire*. • Brown, Michael L. *Authentic Fire: A Response to John MacArthur's Strange Fire*. Lake Mary, FL: Excel, 2014.

Brown, "Awakenings." • Brown, Candy Gunther. "Global Awakenings: Divine Healing Networks, and Global Community in North America, Brazil, Mozambique, and Beyond." 351–69 in *Global Pentecostal and Charismatic Healing*. Edited by Candy Gunther Brown. Foreword by Harvey Cox. Oxford: Oxford University Press, 2011.

Brown, *Death*. • Brown, Raymond E. *The Death of the Messiah—From Gethsemane to Grave: A Commentary on the Passion Narratives in the Four Gospels*. 2 vols. New York: Doubleday, 1994.

Brown, *Essays*. • Brown, Raymond E. *New Testament Essays*. Garden City, NY: Doubleday, 1968.

Brown, *Healing*. • Brown, Candy Gunther, ed. *Global Pentecostal and Charismatic Healing*. Foreword by Harvey Cox. Oxford: Oxford University Press, 2011.

Brown, "Jeremiah." • Brown, Michael L. "Jeremiah." 7:23–572 in *The Expositor's Bible Commentary*. Rev. ed. Edited by Tremper Longman III and David E. Garland. Grand Rapids: Zondervan, 2010.

Brown, *Miracles*. • Brown, Colin. *Miracles and the Critical Mind*. Grand Rapids: Eerdmans, 1984.

Brown, "Proclamation." • Brown, Harold O. J. "Proclamation and Preservation: The Necessity and Temptations of Church Tradition." 69–87 in *Reclaiming the Great Tradition: Evangelicals, Catholics and Orthodox in Dialogue*. Edited by James S. Cutsinger. Downers Grove, IL: InterVarsity, 1997.

Brown, *Scripture as Communication*. • Brown, Jeannine K. *Scripture as Communication: Introducing Biblical Hermeneutics*. Grand Rapids: Baker Academic, 2007.

Brown, *Testing Prayer*. • Brown, Candy Gunther. *Testing Prayer: Science and Healing*. Cambridge, MA: Harvard University Press, 2012.

Brown, Mory, Williams, and McClymond, "Effects." • Brown, Candy Gunther, Stephen C. Mory, Rebecca Williams, and Michael J. McClymond. "Study of the Therapeutic Effects of Proximal Intercessory Prayer (STEPP) on Auditory and Visual Impairments in Rural Mozambique." *SMedJ* 103 (9, September 2010): 864–69.

Brubaker, "Postmodernism." • Brubaker, Malcolm R. "Postmodernism and Pentecostals: A Case Study of Evangelical Hermeneutics." *Evangelical Journal* 15 (1, 1997): 33–45.

Bruce, *Commentary*. • Bruce, F. F. *Commentary on the Book of the Acts: The English Text with Introduction, Exposition, and Notes*. NICNT. Grand Rapids: Eerdmans, 1977.

Bruce, *History*. • Bruce, F. F. *New Testament History*. Garden City, NY: Doubleday, 1972.

Bruce, "History." • Bruce, F. F. "The History of New Testament Study." 21–59 in *New Testament Interpretation: Essays on Principles and Methods*. Edited by I. Howard Marshall. Grand Rapids: Eerdmans, 1977.

Bruce, "Holy Spirit in Acts." • Bruce, F. F. "The Holy Spirit in the Acts of the Apostles." *Interpretation* 27 (2, 1973): 166–83.

Bruce, "Interpretation." • Bruce, F. F. "Interpretation of the Bible." 565–68 in *Evangelical Dictionary of Theology*. Edited by Walter Elwell. Grand Rapids: Baker, 1996.

Bruce, *John*. • Bruce, F. F. *The Gospel of John: Introduction, Exposition and Notes*. Grand Rapids: Eerdmans, 1983.

Brueggemann, *Message*. • Brueggemann, Walter. *The Message of the Psalms: A Theological Commentary*. Minneapolis: Augsburg, 1984.

Brueggemann, *Praying*. • Brueggemann, Walter. *Praying the Psalms*. Winona, MN: Saint Mary's Press, 1986.

Brueggemann, *Texts under Negotiation*. • Brueggemann, Walter. *Texts under Negotiation: The Bible and the Postmodern Imagination*. Minneapolis: Fortress, 1993.

Buber, *I and Thou*. • Buber, Martin. *I and Thou*. New York: Scribner, 1958.

Bührmann, "Religion and Healing." • Bührmann, M. V. "Religion and Healing: The African Experience." 25–34 in *Afro-Christian Religion and Healing in Southern Africa*. Edited by G. C. Oosthuizen, S. D. Edwards, W. H. Wessels, and I. Hexham. AfSt 8. Lewiston, NY: Edwin Mellen, 1989.

Bultmann, "Between Times." • Bultmann, Rudolf. "Man between the Times according to the New Testament." 248–66 in *Existence and Faith: Shorter Writings of Rudolf Bultmann*. Edited by Schubert Ogden. New York: Meridian, 1960.

Bultmann, *Christianity*. • Bultmann, Rudolf. *Primitive Christianity in Its Contemporary Setting*. Translated by Reginald H. Fuller. New York: Meridian, 1956.

Bultmann, "Demythologizing." • Bultmann, Rudolf. "On the Problem of Demythologizing." 95–130 in *New Testament Mythology and Other Basic Writings*. Edited by Schubert Ogden. Philadelphia: Fortress, 1984.

Bultmann, "Exegesis." • Bultmann, Rudolf. "Is Exegesis without Presuppositions Possible?" 145–53 in *The New Testament and Mythology and Other Basic Writings*. Edited by Schubert Ogden. Philadelphia: Fortress, 1984.

Bultmann, "Historicity." • Bultmann, Rudolf. "The Historicity of Man and Faith." 90–100 in *Existence and Faith: Shorter Writings of Rudolf Bultmann*. Edited by Schubert Ogden. New York: Meridian, 1960.

Bultmann, *Jesus and Word*. • Bultmann, Rudolf. *Jesus and the Word*. Translated by Louise Pettibone Smith and Erminie Huntress Lantero. New York: Scribner's, 1958.

Bultmann, *Mythology*. • Bultmann, Rudolf. *The New Testament and Mythology and Other Basic Writings*. Edited by Schubert Ogden. Philadelphia: Fortress, 1984.

Bultmann, "Mythology." • Bultmann, Rudolf. "New Testament and Mythology." 1–43 in *New Testament Mythology and Other Basic Writings*. Edited by Schubert Ogden. Philadelphia: Fortress, 1984.

Bultmann, "Problem of Hermeneutics." • Bultmann, Rudolf. "The Problem of Hermeneutics." 69–93 in *New Testament Mythology and Other Basic Writings*. Edited by Schubert Ogden. Philadelphia: Fortress, 1984.

Bultmann, "Science and Existence." • Bultmann, Rudolf. "Science and Existence." 131–44 in *New Testament Mythology and Other Basic Writings*. Edited by Schubert Ogden. Philadelphia: Fortress, 1984.

Bultmann, *Theology.* • Bultmann, Rudolf. *Theology of the New Testament*. Translated by Kendrick Grobel. 2 vols. New York: Scribner's, 1951.

Bultmann, *Word.* • Bultmann, Rudolf. *Jesus and the Word*. Translated by Louise Pettibone Smith and Erminie Huntress Lantero. New York: Scribner's, 1958.

Burgess, "Evidence." • Burgess, Stanley M. "Evidence of the Spirit: The Medieval and Modern Western Churches." 20–40 in *Initial Evidence: Historical and Biblical Perspectives on the Pentecostal Doctrine of Spirit Baptism*. Edited by Gary B. McGee. Peabody, MA: Hendrickson, 1991.

Burgess, "Pandita Ramabai." • Burgess, Ruth Vassar. "Pandita Ramabai: A Woman for All Seasons: Pandita Ramabai Saraswati Mary Dongre Medhavi (1858–1922)." *AJPS* 9 (2, 2006): 183–98.

Burhenn, "Miracles." • Burhenn, Herbert. "Attributing Miracles to Agents—Reply to George D. Chryssides." *RelS* 13 (4, 1977): 485–89.

Burke, *Death.* • Burke, Sean. *The Death and Return of the Author: Criticism and Subjectivity in Barthes, Foucault and Derrida*. 3rd ed. Edinburgh: Edinburgh University Press, 2008.

Burns, *Debate.* • Burns, Robert M. *The Great Debate on Miracles: From Joseph Glanvill to David Hume*. London: Associated University Presses; Lewisburg, PA: Bucknell University Press, 1981.

Burns, *Romans.* • Burns, J. Patout, trans. and ed., with Father Constantine Newman. *Romans Interpreted by Early Christian Commentators*. The Church's Bible. Grand Rapids: Eerdmans, 2012.

Burridge, "Biography." • Burridge, Richard A. "Biography." 371–91 in *Handbook of Classical Rhetoric in the Hellenistic Period, 330 B.C.–A.D. 400*. Edited by Stanley E. Porter. Leiden: Brill, 1997.

Burridge, "Biography, Ancient." • Burridge, Richard A. "Biography, Ancient." 167–70 in *DNTB*.

Burridge, *Gospels.* • Burridge, Richard A. *What Are the Gospels? A Comparison with Graeco-Roman Biography*. SNTSMS 70. Cambridge: Cambridge University Press, 1992.

Burridge, "Gospels and Acts." • Burridge, Richard A. "The Gospels and Acts." 507–32 in *Handbook of Classical Rhetoric in the Hellenistic Period, 330 B.C.–A.D. 400*. Edited by Stanley E. Porter. Leiden: Brill, 1997.

Burridge, "People." • Burridge, Richard A. "About People, by People, for People: Gospel Genre and Audiences." 113–46 in *The Gospels for All Christians: Rethinking the Gospel Audiences*. Edited by Richard Bauckham. Grand Rapids: Eerdmans, 1998.

Burtt, *Foundations.* • Burtt, Edwin Arthur. *The Metaphysical Foundations of Modern Science*. Repr., Garden City, NY: Doubleday, 1954.

Byrd, "Theory." • Byrd, Joseph. "Paul Ricoeur's Hermeneutical Theory and Pentecostal Proclamation." *Pneuma* 15 (2, 1993): 203–14.

Byrskog, "History." • Byrskog, Samuel. "History or Story in Acts—A Middle Way? The 'We' Passages, Historical Intertexture, and Oral History." 257–83 in *Contextualizing Acts: Lukan Narrative and Greco-Roman Discourse*. Edited by Todd Penner and Caroline Vander Stichele. SBLSymS 20. Atlanta: SBL, 2003.

Caird, "Exegetical Method." • Caird, G. B. "The Exegetical Method of the Epistle to the Hebrews." *Canadian Journal of Theology* 5 (1, 1959): 44–51.

Callaway, "Reflections." • Callaway, Philip R. "Reflections on the Language of the 'Historical' Dead Sea Scrolls." *QC* 12 (2–4, 2004): 123–26.

Calvin, *Catholic Epistles*. • Calvin, John. *Commentaries on the Catholic Epistles.* Translated by John Owen. Grand Rapids: Eerdmans, 1948.

Calvin, *Corinthians*. • Calvin, John. *Commentaries on the Epistles of Paul the Apostle to the Corinthians.* Translated by John Pringle. Grand Rapids: Eerdmans, 1948.

Calvin, *Institutes*. • Calvin, John. *Institutes of the Christian Religion.* 2 vols. Translated by John Allen. Revised by Benjamin B. Warfield. Philadelphia: Presbyterian Board of Christian Education, 1936.

Campos, "Tensions." • Campos, Oscar A. "Premillennial Tensions and Holistic Missiology: Latin American Evangelicalism." 147–69 in *A Case for Historic Premillennialism: An Alternative to "Left Behind" Eschatology.* Edited by Craig L. Blomberg and Sung Wook Chung. Grand Rapids: Baker Academic, 2009.

Cancik-Lindemaier et al., "Allegoresis." • Cancik-Lindemaier, Hildegard, et al. "Allegoresis." 1:511–16 in *BrillPauly.*

Cannon, "Voodoo Death." • Cannon, Walter B. "'Voodoo' Death." *AmAnth* 44 (1942): 169–81.

Capps, *Tongue*. • Capps, Charles. *The Tongue: A Creative Force.* Tulsa, OK: Harrison House, 1976.

Cargal, "Postmodern Age." • Cargal, Timothy B. "Beyond the Fundamentalist-Modernist Controversy: Pentecostals and Hermeneutics in a Postmodern Age." *Pneuma* 15 (2, Fall 1993): 163–87.

Carlston, "Vocabulary." • Carlston, Charles. "The Vocabulary of Perfection in Philo and Hebrews." 133–60 in *Unity and Diversity in New Testament Theology: Essays in Honor of George E. Ladd.* Edited by Robert A. Guelich. Grand Rapids: Eerdmans, 1978.

Carmon, *Inscriptions*. • Carmon, Efrat, ed. *Inscriptions Reveal: Documents from the Time of the Bible, the Mishna, and the Talmud.* Translated by R. Grafman. Jerusalem: Israel Museum, 1973.

Carpenter, "Sacrifices." • Carpenter, Eugene E. "Sacrifices and Offerings in the OT." 4:260–73 in *The International Standard Bible Encyclopedia.* 4 vols. Rev. ed. Grand Rapids: Eerdmans, 1988.

Carson, "Colonialism." • Carson, Penelope. "Christianity, Colonialism, and Hinduism in Kerala: Integration, Adaptation, or Confrontation?" 127–54 in *Christians and Missionaries in India: Cross-cultural Communication since 1500, with Special Reference to Caste, Conversion, and Colonialism.* Edited by Robert Eric Frykenberg. Grand Rapids: Eerdmans, 2003.

Carson, *Interpretation*. • Carson, D. A., ed. *Biblical Interpretation and the Church: The Problem of Contextualization.* Nashville: Thomas Nelson, 1985.

Carson, "Mirror-Reading." • Carson, D. A. "Mirror-Reading with Paul and against Paul: Galatians 2:11–14 as a Test Case." 99–112 in *Studies in the Pauline Epistles: Essays in Honor of Douglas J. Moo.* Edited by Matthew S. Harmon and Jay E. Smith. Grand Rapids: Zondervan, 2014.

Carson, *Showing Spirit*. • Carson, D. A. *Showing the Spirit: A Theological Exposition of 1 Corinthians 12–14.* Grand Rapids: Baker, 1987.

Cartledge, "Text-Community-Spirit." • Cartledge, Mark J. "Text-Community-Spirit: The Challenges Posed by Pentecostal Theological Method to Evangelical Theology." 130–42 in *Spirit and Scripture: Exploring a Pneumatic Hermeneutic.* Edited by Kevin L. Spawn and Archie T. Wright. New York: Bloomsbury, 2012.

Cartledge, "Theology." • Cartledge, Mark J. "Empirical Theology: Towards an Evangelical-Charismatic Hermeneutic." *JPT* 9 (1996): 115–26.

Cartledge, *Tongues*. • Cartledge, Mark J., ed. *Speaking in Tongues: Multi-disciplinary Perspectives.* SPCI. Waynesboro, GA, and Bletchley, Milton Keynes, UK: Paternoster, 2006.

Cassuto, *Exodus*. • Cassuto, Umberto. *A Commentary on the Book of Exodus.* Translated by Israel Abrahams. Jerusalem: Magnes, 1967.

Cayzer, "Ending." • Cayzer, J. "The Ending of Acts: Handing on the Baton." *StMkRev* 161 (1995): 23–25.

Chambers, Chambers. • Chambers, Oswald. *Oswald Chambers: His Life and Work.* London: Simpkin Marshall, 1941.

Chambers, Help. • Chambers, Oswald. *The Place of Help.* Grand Rapids: Discovery House Publishers, 1989 (orig. 1935).

Chambers, Psychology. • Chambers, Oswald. *Biblical Psychology.* Grand Rapids: Discovery House Publishers, 1995 (orig. 1962).

Chan, Grassroots Asian Theology. • Chan, Simon. *Grassroots Asian Theology: Thinking the Faith from the Ground Up.* Downers Grove, IL: IVP Academic, 2014.

Chandra shekar, "Possession Syndrome." • Chandra shekar, C. R. "Possession Syndrome in India." 79–95 in *Altered States of Consciousness and Mental Health: A Cross-Cultural Perspective.* Edited by Colleen A. Ward. CCRMS 12. Newbury Park, CA: Sage, 1989.

Charnov, "Shavuot." • Charnov, Bruce H. "Shavuot, 'Matan Torah,' and the Triennial Cycle." *Judaism* 23 (3, 1974): 332–36.

Chaván de Matviuk, "Growth." • Chaván de Matviuk, Marcela A. "Latin American Pentecostal Growth: Culture, Orality, and the Power of Testimonies." *AJPS* 5 (2, July 2002): 205–22.

Chempakassery, "Jerusalem Pentecost." • Chempakassery, Philip. "Jerusalem Pentecost: An Indian Reinterpretation and Challenges." *Jeev* 34 (200, 2004): 108–21.

Chéreau, "Babel à la Pentecôte." • Chéreau, Georgette. "De Babel à la Pentecôte: Histoire d'une bénédiction." *NRTh* 122 (1, 2000): 19–36.

Chesnut, Born Again in Brazil. • Chesnut, R. Andrew. *Born Again in Brazil: The Pentecostal Boom and the Pathogens of Poverty.* New Brunswick, NJ: Rutgers University Press, 1997.

Chester, "Introspective Conscience." • Chester, Stephen J. "Paul and the Introspective Conscience of Martin Luther: The Impact of Luther's *Anfechtungen* on His Interpretation of Paul." *Biblical Interpretation* 14 (5, 2006): 508–36.

Cheung, "Study." • Cheung, Luke. "A Preliminary Study on Pentecostal Hermeneutics." *CGST Journal* 33 (2002): 97–118.

Chevreau, Catch the Fire. • Chevreau, Guy. *Catch the Fire: The Toronto Blessing; An Experience of Renewal and Revival.* Toronto: HarperCollins, 1995.

Chevreau, Turnings. • Chevreau, Guy. *Turnings: The Kingdom of God and the Western World.* Foreword by Rolland Baker and Heidi Baker. Tonbridge, Kent, UK: Sovereign World, 2004.

Childs, Canon. • Childs, Brevard S. *The New Testament as Canon: An Introduction.* Philadelphia: Fortress, 1984.

Childs, Scripture. • Childs, Brevard S. *Introduction to the Old Testament as Scripture.* Philadelphia: Fortress, 1979.

Childs, Theology. • Childs, Brevard S. *Biblical Theology of the Old and New Testaments: Theological Reflections on the Christian Bible.* London: SCM, 1992.

Childs et al., Bible as Scripture. • Childs, Brevard. *The Bible as Christian Scripture: The Work of Brevard S. Childs.* Edited by Robert C. Kashow, Kent Harold Richards, and Christopher R. Seitz. Atlanta: Society of Biblical Literature, 2013.

Choi, "Hermeneutics." • Choi, Hunn. "Multicultural Hermeneutics and Mission." *Asbury Journal* 70 (1, 2015): 111–39.

Chomsky, Structures. • Chomsky, Noam. *Syntactic Structures.* The Hague: Mouton, 1966.

Christenson, Message. • Christenson, Larry. *A Message to the Charismatic Movement.* Minneapolis: Dimension Books, Bethany Fellowship, 1972.

Clapper, Wesley. • Clapper, Gregory S. *John Wesley on Religious Affections.* Pietist and Wesleyan Studies 1. Metuchen: Scarecrow, 1989.

Clark, "Effects." • Clark, Randy. "A Study of the Effects of Christian Prayers on Pain or Mobility Restrictions from Surgeries Involving Implanted Materials." DMin dissertation, United Theological Seminary, 2013.

Clark, "Hermeneutics." • Clark, Matthew S. "Pentecostal Hermeneutics: The Challenge of Relating to (Post-)modern Literary Theory." *Acta Patristica et Byzantina* 12 (2001): 41–67.

Clark, "Pentecostal Hermeneutics." • Clark, Matthew S. "Pentecostal Hermeneutics: The Challenge of Relating to (Post-)modern Literary Theory." *Spirit & Church* 2 (1, 2000): 67–93.

Clarke, "Wine Skins." • Clarke, Clifton R. "Old Wine and New Wine Skins: West Indian and the New West African Pentecostal Churches in Britain and the Challenge of Renewal." 169–82 in *The Many Faces of Global Pentecostalism.* Edited by Harold D. Hunter and Neil Ormerod. Cleveland, TN: CPT Press, 2013.

Cloete and Smit, "Name Called Babel." • Cloete, G. D., and D. J. Smit. "'Its Name Was Called Babel . . .'" *JTSA* 86 (1994): 81–87.

Cohen, "Evidence on Synagogue." • Cohen, Shaye J. D. "Pagan and Christian Evidence on the Ancient Synagogue." 159–81 in *The Synagogue in Late Antiquity.* Edited by Lee I. Levine. Philadelphia: American Schools of Oriental Research, 1986.

Cohen, Law. • Cohen, Boaz. *Jewish and Roman Law: A Comparative Study.* 2 vols. New York: Jewish Theological Seminary of America Press, 1966.

Cohen, "Names of Translators." • Cohen, Naomi G. "The Names of the Translators in the Letter of Aristeas: A Study in the Dynamics of Cultural Transition." *JSJ* 15 (1, 1984): 32–64.

Colesan, "Joshua." • Colesan, Joseph. "Joshua." 3:1–183 in *Cornerstone Biblical Commentary.* Carol Stream, IL: Tyndale House, 2012.

Colledge, God and Dickens. • Colledge, Gary L. *God and Charles Dickens: Recovering the Christian Voice of a Classic Author.* Grand Rapids: Brazos, 2012.

Collins, Babel. • Collins, John J. *The Bible after Babel: Historical Criticism in a Postmodern Age.* Grand Rapids: Eerdmans, 2005.

Collins, Exorcism. • Collins, James M. *Exorcism and Deliverance Ministry in the Twentieth Century: An Analysis of the Practice and Theology of Exorcism in Modern Western Christianity.* Foreword by Ian Stackhouse. Studies in Evangelical History and Thought. Colorado Springs: Paternoster, 2009.

Collins, "Topography." • Collins, Kenneth J. "John Wesley's Topography of the Heart: Dispositions, Tempers, and Affections." *Methodist History* 36 (3, 1998): 162–75.

Comstock and Partridge, "Attendance." • Comstock, George W., and Kay B. Partridge. "Church Attendance and Health." *JChrDis* 25 (1972): 665–72.

Conte and Most, "Genre." • Conte, Gian Biagio, and Glenn W. Most. "Genre." 630–31 in *OCD³.*

Cook, Interpretation. • Cook, John Granger. *The Interpretation of the New Testament in Greco-Roman Paganism.* Peabody, MA: Hendrickson, 2002; Tübingen: J. C. B. Mohr, 2000.

Copan, Monster. • Copan, Paul. *Is God a Moral Monster? Making Sense of the Old Testament God.* Grand Rapids: Baker, 2011.

Copan and Flannagan, Genocide. • Copan, Paul, and Matt Flannagan, *Did God Really Command Genocide? Coming to Terms with the Justice of God.* Grand Rapids: Baker, 2014.

Copeland, Laws. • Copeland, Kenneth. *The Laws of Prosperity.* Fort Worth, TX: Kenneth Copeland Publications, 1974.

Copeland, "Thorn." • Copeland, Gloria. "Paul's Thorn in the Flesh." *Believer's Voice of Victory* 11 (11, November 1983): 5, 8.

Copleston, Philosophy. • Copleston, Frederick. *Contemporary Philosophy: Studies of Logical Positivism and Existentialism.* Rev. ed. London: Search; Paramus, NJ: Newman, 1972.

Cotter, Miracle Stories. • Cotter, Wendy J. *The Christ of the Miracle Stories: Portrait through Encounter.* Grand Rapids: Baker Academic, 2010.

Cour, Avlund, and Schultz-Larsen, "Religion." • Cour, Peter la, Kirsten Avlund, and Kirsten Schultz-Larsen. "Religion and Survival in a Secular Region: A Twenty-Year Follow-up of 734 Danish Adults Born in 1914." *SSMed* 62 (2006): 157–64.

Cover, "Above." • Cover, Michael B. "'Now and Above; Then and Now' (Gal. 4:21–31: Platonizing and Apocalyptic Polarities in Paul's Eschatology." 220–29 in *Galatians and Christian Theology: Justification, the Gospel, and Ethics in Paul's Letter.* Edited by Mark W. Elliott et al. Grand Rapids: Baker Academic, 2014.

Cracknell and White, *Methodism*. • Cracknell, Kenneth, and Susan J. White. *An Introduction to World Methodism*. Cambridge: Cambridge University Press, 2005.

Craigie, *Deuteronomy*. • Craigie, Peter C. *The Book of Deuteronomy*. NICOT. Grand Rapids: Eerdmans, 1976.

Cramer, "Miracles." • Cramer, John A. "Miracles and David Hume." *PScChrF* 40 (3, September 1988): 129–37.

Crapanzaro, "Introduction." • Crapanzaro, Vincent. "Introduction." 1–40 in *Case Studies in Spirit Possession*. Edited by Vincent Crapanzaro and Vivian Garrison. New York: John Wiley & Sons, 1977.

Crawford, "Healing." • Crawford, Suzanne J. "Religion, Healing, and the Body." 29–45 in *Teaching Religion and Healing*. Edited by Linda L. Barnes and Inés Talamantez. AARTRSS. Oxford: Oxford University Press, 2006.

Crawford, *Shantung Revival*. • Crawford, Mary K. *The Shantung Revival*. Shanghai: China Baptist Publication Society, 1933.

Crites, "Intellect." • Crites, Garry J. "Intellect That Illuminates Christian Truth: Thomas Aquinas's *Summa Theologiae*." *Christian History* 116 (2015): 16–19.

Cross, "Proposal." • Cross, Terry L. "A Proposal to Break the Ice: What Can Pentecostal Theology Offer Evangelical Theology?" *JPT* 10 (2, 2002): 44–73.

Crossan, "Metamodel." • Crossan, John Dominic. "A Metamodel for Polyvalent Interpretation." *Semeia* 9 (1977): 105–47.

Cuéllar and Woodley, "Mission." • Cuéllar, Gregory Lee, and Randy S. Woodley. "North American Mission and Motive: Following the Markers." 61–74 in *Evangelical Postcolonial Conversations: Global Awakenings in Theology and Practice*. Edited by Kay Higuera Smith, Jayachitra Lalitha, and L. Daniel Hawk. Downers Grove, IL: IVP Academic, 2014.

Cullmann, *Salvation*. • Cullmann, Oscar. *Salvation in History*. New York: Harper & Row, 1967.

Curtis, *Faith*. • Curtis, Heather D. *Faith in the Great Physician: Suffering and Divine Healing in American Culture, 1860–1900*. Baltimore: Johns Hopkins University Press, 2007.

Dallaire, "Joshua." • Dallaire, Hélène M. "Joshua." 2:815–1042 in *The Expositor's Bible Commentary*. Rev. ed. Grand Rapids: Zondervan, 2012.

Daniels, "Differences." • Daniels, David D., III. "God Makes No Differences in Nationality: The Fashioning of a New Racial/Nonracial Identity at the Azusa Street Revival." *Enr* 11 (2, 2006): 72–76.

Danker, *New Age*. • Danker, Frederick W. *Jesus and the New Age, according to St. Luke*. St. Louis: Clayton, 1972.

Daston, "Marvelous Facts." • Daston, Lorraine. "Marvelous Facts and Miraculous Evidence in Early Modern Europe." *Critical Inquiry* 18 (Autumn 1991): 93–124.

Daube, *Exodus Pattern*. • Daube, David. *The Exodus Pattern in the Bible*. All Souls Studies 2. London: Faber & Faber, 1963.

Daube, "Johanan ben Zaccai." • Daube, David. "Three Notes Having to Do with Johanan ben Zaccai." *JTS* 11 (1, 1960): 53–62.

Davies, *Healer*. • Davies, Stevan L. *Jesus the Healer: Possession, Trance, and the Origins of Christianity*. New York: Continuum, 1995.

Davies, *Matthew*. • Davies, Margaret. *Matthew*. Readings. Sheffield, UK: JSOT Press, 1993.

Davies, "Read as Pentecostal." • Davies, Andrew. "What Does It Mean to Read the Bible as a Pentecostal?" 249–62 in *Pentecostal Hermeneutics: A Reader*. Edited by Lee Roy Martin. Leiden: Brill, 2013.

Davies, *Setting*. • Davies, W. D. *The Setting of the Sermon on the Mount*. Cambridge: Cambridge University Press, 1964.

Davies and Allison, *Matthew*. • Davies, W. D., and Dale C. Allison. *A Critical and Exegetical Commentary on the Gospel according to Saint Matthew*. 3 vols. ICC. Edinburgh: T&T Clark, 1988–97.

Dawson, "Urbanization." • Dawson, John. "Urbanization and Mental Health in a West African

Community." 305–42 in *Magic, Faith, and Healing: Studies in Primitive Psychotherapy Today.* Edited by Ari Kiev. Introduction by Jerome D. Frank. New York: Free Press, 1964.

Dayton, *Roots.* • Dayton, Donald W. *Theological Roots of Pentecostalism.* Peabody, MA: Hendrickson, 1987.

De Boer, *Galatians.* • De Boer, Martinus C. *Galatians: A Commentary.* NT Library. Louisville: Westminster John Knox, 2011.

De Cuypere and Willems, "Meaning." • De Cuypere, Ludovic, and Klaas Willems. "Meaning and Reference in Aristotle's Concept of Linguistic Signs." *Foundations of Science* 13 (2008): 307–24.

Deiros, "Cross." • Deiros, Pablo A. "Cross and Sword." *Christian History* 35 (1992): 30–31.

Delaney, "Seeds." • Delaney, Carol. "Seeds of Honor, Fields of Shame." 35–48 in *Honor and Shame and the Unity of the Mediterranean.* Edited by David D. Gilmore. AAAM 22. Washington, DC: American Anthropological Association, 1987.

Dempster, Klaus, and Petersen, *Globalization.* • Dempster, Murray W., Byron D. Klaus, and Douglas Petersen. *The Globalization of Pentecostalism: A Religion Made to Travel.* Foreword by Russell P. Spittler. Carlisle: Paternoster; Oxford: Regnum, 1999.

Derrida, *Speech.* • Derrida, Jacques. *Speech and Phenomena: And Other Essays on Husserl's Theory of Signs.* Evanston: Northwestern University Press, 1973.

Derrida, *Writing.* • Derrida, Jacques. *Writing and Difference.* Chicago: University of Chicago Press, 1978.

Derrida and Stocker, *Derrida.* • Derrida, Jacques, and Barry Stocker. *Jacques Derrida: Basic Writings.* New York: Routledge, 2007.

DeSilva, *Global Readings.* • DeSilva, David A. *Global Readings: A Sri Lankan Commentary on Paul's Letter to the Galatians.* Eugene, OR: Cascade, 2011.

De Vaux, *Israel.* • De Vaux, Roland. *Ancient Israel: Its Life and Institutions.* 2 vols. Translated by John MacHugh. New York: McGraw-Hill, 1961.

Dever, "Stratifications." • Dever, William G. "The MB IIC Stratifications in the Northwest Gate Area at Shechem." *BASOR* 216 (December 1974): 43.

De Wet, "Signs." • De Wet, Christiaan Rudolph. "Signs and Wonders in Church Growth." MA thesis, Fuller School of World Mission, December 1981.

Dewey, "Gospel of Mark." • Dewey, Joanna. "The Gospel of Mark as an Oral-Aural Event: Implications for Interpretation." 145–63 in *The New Literary Criticism and the New Testament.* Edited by Edgar V. McKnight and Elizabeth Struthers Malbon. Valley Forge, PA: Trinity Press International, 1994; Sheffield: JSOT Press, 1994.

Diehl, "Rhetoric." • Diehl, Judith A. "Anti-Imperial Rhetoric in the New Testament." *Currents in Biblical Research* 10 (1, 2011): 9–52.

Dilthey, *Pattern.* • Dilthey, Wilhelm. *Pattern and Meaning in History: Thoughts on History and Society.* Edited by H. P. Rickman. New York: Harper & Brothers, 1962; London: Allen & Unwin, 1961.

Di Sabatino, "Frisbee." • Di Sabatino, David. "Appendix 3: Lonnie Frisbee." 392–407 in *The Quest for the Radical Middle: A History of the Vineyard,* by Bill Jackson. Foreword by Todd Hunter. Cape Town: Vineyard International, 1999.

Dodd, *Preaching.* • Dodd, C. H. *The Apostolic Preaching and Its Developments.* London: Hodder & Stoughton, 1936. Repr., Grand Rapids: Baker, 1980.

Dodd, *Problem.* • Dodd, Brian. *The Problem with Paul.* Downers Grove, IL: InterVarsity, 1996.

Dominy, "Spirit, Church, and Mission." • Dominy, Bert B. "Spirit, Church, and Mission: Theological Implications of Pentecost." *SWJT* 35 (2, 1993): 34–39.

Donahue, "Redaction Criticism." • Donahue, John R. "Redaction Criticism: Has the *Hauptstrasse* Become a *Sackgasse?*" 27–57 in *The New Literary Criticism and the New Testament.* Edited by Edgar V. McKnight and Elizabeth Struthers Malbon. Valley Forge, PA: Trinity Press International; Sheffield, UK: JSOT Press, 1994.

Dornisch, "Symbolic Systems." • Dornisch, Loretta. "Symbolic Systems and the Interpretation of Scripture: An Introduction to the Work of Paul Ricoeur." *Semeia* 4 (1975): 1–26.

Dorries, "Irving and Spirit Baptism." • Dorries, David W. "Edward Irving and the 'Standing Sign' of Spirit Baptism." 41–56 in *Initial Evidence: Historical and Biblical Perspectives on the Pentecostal Doctrine of Spirit Baptism.* Edited by Gary B. McGee. Peabody, MA: Hendrickson, 1991.

Doyle, *Killing.* • Doyle, Tom, with Greg Webster. *Killing Christians: Living the Faith Where It's Not Safe to Believe.* Nashville: Thomas Nelson, 2015.

Drane, "Background." • Drane, John W. "The Religious Background." 117–25 in *New Testament Interpretation: Essays on Principles and Methods.* Edited by I. Howard Marshall. Grand Rapids: Eerdmans, 1977.

Driver, *Scrolls.* • Driver, G. R. *The Judaean Scrolls: The Problem and a Solution.* Oxford: Blackwell, 1965.

Droogers, "Normalization." • Droogers, André. "The Normalization of Religious Experience: Healing, Prophecy, Dreams, and Visions." 33–49 in *Charismatic Christianity as a Global Culture.* Edited by Karla Poewe. SCR. Columbia: University of South Carolina Press, 1994.

Drury, *Saying.* • Drury, Amanda Hontz. *Saying Is Believing: The Necessity of Testimony in Adolescent Spiritual Development.* Downers Grove, IL: InterVarsity, 2015.

D'Sa, "Dhvani." • D'Sa, Francis X. "'Dhvani' as a Method of Interpretation." *Biblebhashyam* 5 (4, 1979): 276–94.

Dube, "Search." • Dube, D. "A Search for Abundant Life: Health, Healing, and Wholeness in Zionist Churches." 109–36 in *Afro-Christian Religion and Healing in Southern Africa.* Edited by G. C. Oosthuizen, S. D. Edwards, W. H. Wessels, and I. Hexham. AfSt 8. Lewiston, NY: Edwin Mellen, 1989.

Duhaime, "Voies." • Duhaime, Jean L. "Les voies des deux esprits (1QS iv 2–14): Une analyse structurelle." *RevQ* 19 (75, 2000): 349–67.

Duke, *Irony.* • Duke, Paul D. *Irony in the Fourth Gospel.* Atlanta: John Knox, 1985.

Duncan Hoyte, "Plagues." • Duncan Hoyte, H. M. "The Plagues of Egypt: What Killed the Animals and the Firstborn?" *The Medical Journal of Australia* 158 (1993): 706–8.

Dunn, *Acts.* • Dunn, James D. G. *The Acts of the Apostles.* Narrative Commentaries. Valley Forge, PA: Trinity Press International, 1996.

Dunn, *Baptism.* • Dunn, James D. G. *Baptism in the Holy Spirit: A Re-examination of the New Testament Teaching on the Gift of the Spirit in Relation to Pentecostalism Today.* SBT, 2nd ser., 15; London: SCM, 1970.

Dunn, *Jesus and Spirit.* • Dunn, James D. G. *Jesus and the Spirit: A Study of the Religious and Charismatic Experience of Jesus and the First Christians as Reflected in the New Testament.* London: SCM, 1975.

Dunn, "John." • Dunn, James D. G. "Let John Be John: A Gospel for Its Time." 293–322 in *The Gospel and the Gospels.* Edited by Peter Stuhlmacher. Grand Rapids: Eerdmans, 1991.

Dunn, "Justice." • Dunn, James D. G. "The Justice of God: A Renewed Perspective on Justification by Faith." *JTS* 43 (1, 1992): 1–22.

Dunn, *New Perspective.* • Dunn, James D. G. *The New Perspective on Paul.* Rev. ed. Grand Rapids: Eerdmans, 2008.

Dunn, "Old Perspective." • Dunn, James D. G. "What's Right about the Old Perspective on Paul." 214–29 in *Studies in the Pauline Epistles: Essays in Honor of Douglas J. Moo.* Edited by Matthew S. Harmon and Jay E. Smith. Grand Rapids: Zondervan, 2014.

Dunn, "Reconstructions." • Dunn, James D. G. "Reconstructions of Corinthian Christianity and the Interpretation of 1 Corinthians." 295–310 in *Christianity at Corinth: The Quest for the Pauline Church.* Edited by Edward Adams and David G. Horrell. Louisville: Westminster John Knox, 2004.

Dunn, "Role." • Dunn, James D. G. "The Role of the Spirit in Biblical Hermeneutics." 154–59 in *Spirit and Scripture: Exploring a Pneumatic Hermeneutic.* Edited by Kevin L. Spawn and Archie T. Wright. New York: Bloomsbury, 2012.

Dunn, "Synagogue." • Dunn, James D. G. "Did Jesus Attend the Synagogue?" 206–22 in *Jesus and Archaeology.* Edited by James H. Charlesworth. Grand Rapids: Eerdmans, 2006.

Dunn, Unity. • Dunn, James D. G. *Unity and Diversity in the New Testament: An Inquiry into the Character of Earliest Christianity.* Louisville: Westminster John Knox, 1984.

Dupont, Salvation. • Dupont, Jacques. *The Salvation of the Gentiles: Essays on the Acts of the Apostles.* Translated by John R. Keating. New York: Paulist, 1979.

Dupont-Sommer, Writings. • Dupont-Sommer, André. *The Essene Writings from Qumran.* Translated by G. Vermes. Oxford: Blackwell, 1961. Repr., Gloucester, MA: Peter Smith, 1973.

Dussel, History. • Dussel, Enrique. *A History of the Church in Latin America: Colonialism to Liberation (1492–1979).* Translated by Alan Neely. Grand Rapids: Eerdmans, 1981.

Earman, Failure. • Earman, John. *Hume's Abject Failure: The Argument against Miracles.* Oxford: Oxford University Press, 2000.

Ebeling, Theology. • Ebeling, Gerhard. *Theology and Proclamation: A Discussion with Rudolf Bultmann.* London: Collins, 1966.

Ebeling, Word and Faith. • Ebeling, Gerhard. *Word and Faith.* Philadelphia: Fortress, 1963.

Ecklund, Science. • Ecklund, Elaine Howard. *Science vs. Religion: What Scientists Really Think.* Oxford: Oxford University Press, 2010.

Eco, Reader. • Eco, Umberto. *The Role of the Reader: Explorations in the Semiotics of Texts.* Bloomington: Indiana University Press, 1979.

Eddy and Boyd, Legend. • Eddy, Paul Rhodes, and Gregory A. Boyd. *The Jesus Legend: A Case for the Historical Reliability of the Synoptic Jesus Tradition.* Grand Rapids: Baker Academic, 2007.

Edgar, "Messianic Interpretation." • Edgar, S. L. "The New Testament and Rabbinic Messianic Interpretation." *NTS* 5 (1, 1958): 47–54.

Edwards, Affections. • Edwards, Jonathan. *Religious Affections.* Works of Jonathan Edwards. New Haven: Yale University Press, 1959.

Edwards, "Crowns." • Edwards, Laurence L. "Rabbi Akiba's Crowns: Postmodern Discourse and the Cost of Rabbinic Reading." *Judaism* 49 (4, 2000): 417–35.

Edwards, Galatians. • Edwards, Mark J., ed. *Galatians, Ephesians, Philippians.* ACCS: New Testament 8. Downers Grove, IL: InterVarsity, 1999.

Edwards, Marks. • Edwards, Jonathan. *The Distinguishing Marks of a Work of the Spirit of God.* Works of Jonathan Edwards. New Haven: Yale University Press, 1972.

Edwards, "Parallels." • Edwards, James R. "Parallels and Patterns between Luke and Acts." *BBR* 26 (2016): forthcoming.

Edwards, "Revolution." • Edwards, Mark U., Jr. "After the Revolution: The Beginning of the Reformation Was Not the End of Luther's Troubles." *Christian History* 115 (2015): 50–53.

Efferin, "Paraclete." • Efferin, Henry. "The Paraclete in John 14–16." *Stulos Theological Journal* 1 (2, 1993): 149–56.

Eickelman, Middle East. • Eickelman, Dale F. *The Middle East: An Anthropological Approach.* 2nd ed. Englewood Cliffs, NJ: Prentice Hall, 1989.

Eliot, "Tradition." • Eliot, T. S. "Tradition and the Individual Talent." 453–60 in *American Literary Criticism: 1900–1950.* Edited by Charles I. Glicksberg. New York: Hendricks, 1952.

Ellin, "Again." • Ellin, Joseph. "Again: Hume on Miracles." *HumSt* 19 (1, April 1993): 203–12.

Ellington, "Authority." • Ellington, Scott A. "Pentecostalism and the Authority of Scripture." 149–70 in *Pentecostal Hermeneutics: A Reader.* Edited by Lee Roy Martin. Leiden: Brill, 2013.

Ellington, "Locating." • Ellington, Scott A. "Locating Pentecostals at the Hermeneutical Round Table." *JPT* 22 (2, 2013): 206–25.

Elliott, *Arrogance*. • Elliott, Neil. *The Arrogance of Nations: Reading Romans in the Shadow of Empire*. Paul in Critical Contexts. Minneapolis: Fortress, 2008.

Elliott, *Feelings*. • Elliott, Matthew. *Faithful Feelings: Emotion in the New Testament*. Leicester, UK: Inter-Varsity, 2005.

Ellis, *Old Testament*. • Ellis, E. E. *The Old Testament in Early Christianity*. Grand Rapids: Baker, 1992.

Ellison et al., "Involvement." • Ellison, Christopher G., R. A. Hummer, et al. "Religious Involvement and Mortality Risk among African American Adults." *ResAg* 22 (6, 2000): 630–67.

Eng et al., "Ties." • Eng, P. M., E. B. Rimm, G. Fitzmaurice, and I. Kawachi. "Social Ties and Change in Social Ties in Relation to Subsequent Total and Cause-Specific Mortality and Coronary Heart Disease Incidence in Men." *AmJEpid* 155 (2002): 700–709.

England, "Criticism." • England, F. "Mapping Postcolonial Biblical Criticism in South Africa." *Neotestamentica* 38 (1, 2004): 88–99.

Ervin, "Hermeneutics." • Ervin, Howard M. "Hermeneutics: A Pentecostal Option." 23–35 in *Essays on Apostolic Themes: Studies in Honor of Howard M. Ervin*. Edited by Paul Elbert. Peabody, MA: Hendrickson, 1985.

Ervin, "Hermeneutics" (*Pneuma* version). • Ervin, Howard M. "Hermeneutics: A Pentecostal Option." *Pneuma* 3 (2, 1981): 11–25.

Escobar, *Tides*. • Escobar, Samuel. *Changing Tides: Latin America and World Mission Today*. AmSocMissMonS 31. Maryknoll, NY: Orbis, 2002.

Eskridge, *Family*. • Eskridge, Larry. *God's Forever Family: The Jesus People Movement in America*. Oxford: Oxford University Press, 2013.

Espinosa, "Contributions." • Espinosa, Gastón. "'The Holy Ghost Is Here on Earth?': The Latino Contributions to the Azusa Street Revival." *Enr* 11 (2, Spring 2006): 118–25.

Espinosa, "Healing in Borderlands." • Espinosa, Gastón. "Latino Pentecostal Healing in the North American Borderlands." 129–49 in *Global Pentecostal and Charismatic Healing*. Edited by Candy Gunther Brown. Foreword by Harvey Cox. Oxford: Oxford University Press, 2011.

Espinoza, "*Pia Desideria*." • Espinoza, Benjamin D. "*Pia Desideria* Reimagined for Contemporary Theological Education." *Asbury Journal* 70 (1, 2015): 140–56.

Estrada, "Hermeneutic." • Estrada, Rodolfo Galvan. "Is a Contextualized Hermeneutic the Future of Pentecostal Readings? The Implications of a Pentecostal Hermeneutic for a Chicano/Latino Community." *Pneuma* 37 (3, 2015): 341–55.

Evans, "Judgment." • Evans, C. Stephen. "Critical Historical Judgment and Biblical Faith." *FPhil* 11 (2, April 1994): 184–206.

Evans, *Narrative*. • Evans, C. Stephen. *The Historical Christ and the Jesus of Faith: The Incarnational Narrative as History*. Oxford: Clarendon, 1996.

Evans, "Naturalism." • Evans, C. Stephen. "Methodological Naturalism in Historical Biblical Scholarship." 180–205 in *Jesus and the Restoration of Israel: A Critical Assessment of N. T. Wright's* Jesus and the Victory of God. Edited by Carey C. Newman. Downers Grove, IL: InterVarsity, 1999.

Evans, *Texts*. • Evans, Craig A. *Ancient Texts for New Testament Studies: A Guide to the Background Literature*. Peabody, MA: Hendrickson, 2005.

Evans, *Wycliffe*. • Evans, G. R. *John Wycliffe: Myth and Reality*. Downers Grove, IL: IVP Academic, 2005.

Evans and Sanders, *Luke and Scripture*. • Evans, Craig A., and James A. Sanders. *Luke and Scripture: The Function of Sacred Tradition in Luke-Acts*. Minneapolis: Fortress, 1993.

Evans and Tov, *Exploring*. • Evans, Craig A., and Emmanuel Tov, eds. *Exploring the Origins of the Bible: Canon Formation in Historical, Literary, and Theological Perspective*. Grand Rapids: Baker Academic, 2008.

Everts, "Exorcist." • Everts, William W. "Jesus Christ, No Exorcist." *BSac* 81 (323, July 1924): 355–62.

Eya, "Healing." • Eya, Regina. "Healing and Exorcism: The Psychological Aspects." 44–54 in *Healing and Exorcism: The Nigerian Experience.* Proceedings, Lectures, Discussions, and Conclusions of the First Missiology Symposium on Healing and Exorcism, organized by the Spiritan International School of Theology, Attakwu, Enugu, May 18–20, 1989. Edited by Chris U. Manus, Luke N. Mbefo, and E. E. Uzukwu. Attakwu, Enugu: Spiritan International School of Theology, 1992.

Faupel, *Everlasting Gospel.* • Faupel, David William. *The Everlasting Gospel: The Significance of Eschatology in the Development of Pentecostal Thought.* JPTSup 10. Sheffield: Sheffield Academic Press, 1996.

Fee, *Gospel.* • Fee, Gordon D. *Gospel and Spirit: Issues in New Testament Hermeneutics.* Peabody, MA: Hendrickson, 1991.

Fee, "Historical Precedent." • Fee, Gordon D. "Hermeneutics and the Historical Precedent: A Major Problem in Pentecostal Hermeneutics." 118–32 in *Perspectives on the New Pentecostalism.* Edited by Russell P. Spittler. Grand Rapids: Baker, 1976.

Fee, *Listening.* • Fee, Gordon D. *Listening to the Spirit in the Text.* Grand Rapids: Eerdmans, 2000.

Fee, *Revelation.* • Fee, Gordon D. *Revelation.* New Covenant Commentary Series. Eugene, OR: Cascade, 2011.

Fee and Stuart, *Worth.* • Fee, Gordon D., and Douglas Stuart. *How to Read the Bible for All Its Worth: A Guide to Understanding the Bible.* 2nd ed. Grand Rapids: Zondervan, 1993.

Fern, "Critique." • Fern, Richard L. "Hume's Critique of Miracles: An Irrelevant Triumph." *RelS* 18 (3, 1982): 337–54.

Finger, *Meals.* • Finger, Reta Halteman. *Of Widows and Meals: Communal Meals in the Book of Acts.* Grand Rapids: Eerdmans, 2007.

Finlay, *Columba.* • Finlay, Ian. *Columba.* London: Victor Gollancz, 1979.

Fiorenza, "Hermeneutics." • Fiorenza, Elisabeth Schüssler. "Toward a Feminist Biblical Hermeneutics: Biblical Interpretation and Liberation Theology." 358–81 in *A Guide to Contemporary Hermeneutics: Major Trends in Biblical Interpretation.* Edited by Donald K. McKim. Grand Rapids: Eerdmans, 1986.

Firth, "Foreword." • Firth, Raymond. "Foreword." ix–xiv in *Spirit Mediumship and Society in Africa.* Edited by John Beattie and John Middleton. Foreword by Raymond Firth. New York: Africana Publishing Corporation, 1969.

Fish, "Condemnation." • Fish, Stanley. "Condemnation without Absolutes." *New York Times,* October 15, 2001, A19.

Fitzgerald, "Miracles." • Fitzgerald, Paul. "Miracles." *PhilFor* 17 (1, Fall 1985): 48–64.

Fitzmyer, *Acts.* • Fitzmyer, Joseph A. *The Acts of the Apostles: A New Translation with Introduction and Commentary.* AB 31. New York: Doubleday, 1998.

Fitzpatrick, "Carneades." • Fitzpatrick, Matthew P. "Carneades and the Conceit of Rome: Transhistorical Approaches to Imperialism." *Greece & Rome* 57 (1, 2010): 1–20.

Flemming, *Contextualization.* • Flemming, Dean. *Contextualization in the New Testament: Patterns for Theology and Mission.* Downers Grove, IL: InterVarsity, 2005.

Flender, *Theologian.* • Flender, Helmut. *St Luke: Theologian of Redemptive History.* Translated by Reginald H. Fuller and Ilse Fuller. London: SPCK, 1967.

Fogarty, "Hermeneutic." • Fogarty, Stephen. "Toward a Pentecostal Hermeneutic." *Pentecostal Charismatic Bible Colleges Journal* 5 (2, Aug. 2001), 11 pages, at http://webjournals.ac.edu .au/journals/PCBC/vol5-no2/toward-a-pentecostal-hermeneutic/.

Föller, "Luther on Miracles." • Föller, Oskar. "Martin Luther on Miracles, Healing, Prophecy, and Tongues." *SHE* 31 (2, October 2005): 333–51.

Force, "Dominion." • Force, James E. "Newton's God of Dominion: The Unity of Newton's Theological, Scientific, and Political Thought." 75–102 in James E. Force and Richard H. Popkin, *Essays on the Context, Nature, and Influence of Isaac Newton's Theology.* IntArHistI 129. Dordrecht: Kluwer Academic, 1990.

Fornara, *Nature of History*. • Fornara, C. W. *The Nature of History in Ancient Greece and Rome.* Berkeley: University of California Press, 1983.

Forrester, "Pentecost." • Forrester, Duncan B. "The Perennial Pentecost." *ExpT* 116 (7, 2005): 224–27.

Forstman, *Word and Spirit*. • Forstman, H. Jackson. *Word and Spirit: Calvin's Doctrine of Biblical Authority.* Stanford: Stanford University Press, 1962.

Foskett, *Interpreting*. • Foskett, Mary F. *Interpreting the Bible.* Philadelphia: Fortress, 2009.

Foucault, "Author." • Foucault, Michel. "What Is an Author?" 101–20 in *The Foucault Reader.* Edited by Paul Rabinow. New York: Pantheon, 1984.

Fowler, "Reader." • Fowler, Robert M. "Who Is 'the Reader' in Reader Response Criticism?" *Semeia* 31 (1985): 5–23.

Frank, *Persuasion*. • Frank, Jerome D. *Persuasion and Healing: A Comparative Study of Psychotherapy.* Baltimore: Johns Hopkins University Press, 1961.

Frankenberry, *Faith*. • Frankenberry, Nancy K. *The Faith of Scientists in Their Words.* Princeton: Princeton University Press, 2008.

Fraser and Kilgore, *Friends*. • Fraser, Elouise Renich, and Louis A. Kilgore. *Making Friends with the Bible.* Foreword by Dorothy Jean Weaver. Scottsdale, PA: Herald, 1994.

Frei, *Eclipse*. • Frei, Hans W. *The Eclipse of Biblical Narrative: A Study in Eighteenth- and Nineteenth-Century Hermeneutics.* New Haven: Yale University Press, 1974.

Fretheim, "Plagues." • Fretheim, Terence E. "The Plagues as Ecological Signs of Historical Disaster." *JBL* 110 (1991): 385–96.

Friedman, "Israel's Response." • Friedman, Mordechai A. "Israel's Response in Hosea 2:17b: 'You Are My Husband.'" *JBL* 99 (2, June 1980): 199–204.

Froehlich, "Hermeneutics." • Froehlich, Karlfried. "Biblical Hermeneutics on the Move." 175–91 in *A Guide to Contemporary Hermeneutics: Major Trends in Biblical Interpretation.* Edited by Donald K. McKim. Grand Rapids: Eerdmans, 1986.

Frykenberg, *Christianity in India*. • Frykenberg, Robert Eric. *Christianity in India: From Beginnings to the Present.* OHCC. New York, Oxford: Oxford University Press, 2010.

Fuchs, *Hermeneutik*. • Fuchs, Ernst. *Hermeneutik.* 4th ed. Tübingen: J. C. B. Mohr, 1970.

Fuchs, "Proclamation." • Fuchs, Ernst. "Proclamation and Speech-Event." *Theology Today* 19 (3, October 1962): 341–54.

Fuchs, *Studies*. • Fuchs, Ernst. *Studies of the Historical Jesus.* London: SCM, 1964.

Fuchs, "Techniques." • Fuchs, Stephen. "Magic Healing Techniques among the Balahis in Central India." 121–38 in *Magic, Faith, and Healing: Studies in Primitive Psychiatry Today.* Edited by Ari Kiev. Foreword by Jerome D. Frank. New York: Free Press, 1964.

Fuller, "Analogy." • Fuller, Daniel. "Biblical Theology and the Analogy of Faith." 195–213 in *Unity and Diversity in New Testament Theology: Essays in Honor of George E. Ladd.* Edited by Robert A. Guelich. Grand Rapids: Eerdmans, 1978.

Fuller, "Classics." • Fuller, Reginald H. "Classics and the Gospels: The Seminar." 173–92 in *The Relationships among the Gospels: An Interdisciplinary Dialogue.* Edited by William O. Walker Jr. San Antonio: Trinity University Press, 1978.

Gadamer, *Truth*. • Gadamer, Hans-Georg. *Truth and Method.* Translated by Garrett Barden and John Cumming. New York: Crossroad, 1988.

Galinsky, "Cult." • Galinsky, Karl. "The Cult of the Roman Emperor: Uniter or Divider?" 1–21 in *Rome and Religion: A Cross-disciplinary Dialogue on the Imperial Cult.* Edited by Jeffrey Brodd and Jonathan L. Reed. Atlanta: Society of Biblical Literature, 2011.

Gane, "Leviticus." • Gane, Roy E. "Leviticus." 284–337 in vol. 1 of *Zondervan Illustrated Bible Backgrounds Commentary: Old Testament.* Edited by John Walton. 5 vols. Grand Rapids: Zondervan, 2009.

Gardner, "Miracles." • Gardner, Rex. "Miracles of Healing in Anglo-Celtic Northumbria as

Recorded by the Venerable Bede and His Contemporaries: A Reappraisal in the Light of Twentieth-Century Experience." *BMedJ* 287 (December 24–31, 1983): 1927–33.

Gärtner, "Synkrisis." • Gärtner, Hans Armin. "Synkrisis." 14:28 in *BrillPauly*.

Gaster, *Scriptures*. • Gaster, Theodor H. *The Dead Sea Scriptures*. Garden City, NY: Doubleday, 1976.

Geerlof, "Augustine and Pentecostals." • Geerlof, Derek M. "Augustine and Pentecostals: Building a Hermeneutical Bridge between Past and Present Experience in the Psalms." *Pneuma* 37 (2, 2015): 262–80.

Geivett and Habermas, "Introduction." • Geivett, R. Douglas, and Gary R. Habermas. "Introduction." 9–26 in *In Defense of Miracles: A Comprehensive Case for God's Action in History*. Edited by R. Douglas Geivett and Gary R. Habermas. Downers Grove, IL: InterVarsity, 1997.

Geivett and Pivec, *New Apostolic Reformation*. • Geivett, R. Douglas, and Holly Pivec. *A New Apostolic Reformation: A Biblical Response to a Worldwide Movement*. Wooster, OH: Weaver Book Company, 2014.

George, "Introduction." • George, Timothy. "General Introduction." ix–xxxiv in *Galatians, Ephesians*. Edited by Gerald Bray. Reformation Commentary on Scripture, New Testament 10. Downers Grove, IL: IVP Academic, 2011.

Gerhart, "Generic Studies." • Gerhart, Mary. "Generic Studies: Their Renewed Importance in Religious and Literary Interpretation." *JAAR* 45 (3, September 1977): 309–25.

Gerhart, "Notion." • Gerhart, Mary. "Paul Ricoeur's Notion of 'Diagnostics': Its Function in Literary Interpretation." *JR* 56 (1976): 137–56.

Gerhart and Russell, "Mathematics." • Gerhart, Mary, and Allan Melvin Russell. "Mathematics, Empirical Science, and Religion." 121–29 in *Religion and Science: History, Method, Dialogue*. Edited by W. Mark Richardson and Wesley J. Wildman. Foreword by Ian G. Barbour. New York: Routledge, 1996.

Gillespie, "Authority." • Gillespie, Thomas W. "Biblical Authority and Interpretation: The Current Debate on Hermeneutics." 192–219 in *A Guide to Contemporary Hermeneutics: Major Trends in Biblical Interpretation*. Edited by Donald K. McKim. Grand Rapids: Eerdmans, 1986.

Gilmore, "Shame." • Gilmore, David D. "Introduction: The Shame of Dishonor." 2–21 in *Honor and Shame and the Unity of the Mediterranean*. Edited by David D. Gilmore. AAAM 22. Washington, DC: American Anthropological Association, 1987.

Ginsburg, *Kabbalah*. • Ginsburg, Christian D. *The Essenes: Their History and Doctrines; The Kabbalah: Its Doctrines, Development, and Literature*. London: Routledge & Kegan Paul, 1955. (The Kabbalah section is a reprint from 1863; that on the Essenes, from 1864.)

Glad, "Adaptability." • Glad, Clarence E. "Paul and Adaptability." 17–41 in *Paul in the Greco-Roman World: A Handbook*. Edited by J. Paul Sampley. Harrisburg, PA: Trinity Press International, 2003.

Glasson, *Advent*. • Glasson, T. Francis. *The Second Advent: The Origin of the New Testament Doctrine*. 3rd rev. ed. London: Epworth, 1963.

Gleason, "Letter." • Gleason, Randall C. "'Letter' and 'Spirit' in Luther's Hermeneutics." *Bibliotheca Sacra* 157 (628, 2000): 468–85.

"God's Wonderful Working." • "God's Wonderful Working." *Christian History* 23 (1989): 12–18.

Goff, *Fields*. • Goff, James R., Jr. *Fields White unto Harvest: Charles F. Parham and the Missionary Origins of Pentecostalism*. Fayetteville: University of Arkansas Press, 1988.

Goff, "Theology of Parham." • Goff, James R., Jr. "Initial Tongues in the Theology of Charles Fox Parham." 57–71 in *Initial Evidence: Historical and Biblical Perspectives on the Pentecostal Doctrine of Spirit Baptism*. Edited by Gary B. McGee. Peabody, MA: Hendrickson, 1991.

González, *Acts*. • González, Justo L. *Acts: The Gospel of the Spirit*. Maryknoll, NY: Orbis, 2001.

González, Months. • González, Justo L. *Three Months with the Spirit.* Nashville: Abingdon, 2003.

González, Tribe. • González, Justo L. *Out of Every Tribe and Nation: Christian Theology at the Ethnic Roundtable.* Nashville: Abingdon, 1992.

Gordon, Common Background. • Gordon, Cyrus H. *The Common Background of Greek and Hebrew Civilizations.* New York: W. W. Norton, 1965.

Gordon, Near East. • Gordon, Cyrus H. *The Ancient Near East.* New York: W. W. Norton, 1965.

Gorsuch, "Limits." • Gorsuch, Richard L. "On the Limits of Scientific Investigation: Miracles and Intercessory Prayer." 280–99 in *Religious and Spiritual Events.* Vol. 1 in *Miracles: God, Science, and Psychology in the Paranormal.* Edited by J. Harold Ellens. Westport, CT; London: Praeger, 2008.

Goulder, Type and History. • Goulder, Michael D. *Type and History in Acts.* London: SPCK, 1964.

Granit, "Attitude." • Granit, Ragnar. "I Have a Religious Attitude toward the Unknown." 177–78 in *Cosmos, Bios, and Theos: Scientists Reflect on Science, God, and the Origins of the Universe, Life, and* Homo Sapiens. Edited by Henry Margenau and Roy Abraham Varghese. La Salle, IL: Open Court, 1992.

Grant, "Ambiguity." • Grant, Colleen C. "Ambiguity in an Ambiguous Gospel." *Journal of Theology* 103 (1999): 1–15.

Grant, Gnosticism. • Grant, Robert M. *Gnosticism and Early Christianity.* 2nd ed. New York: Columbia University Press, 1966.

Grant and Tracy, History. • Grant, Robert M., and David Tracy. *A Short History of the Interpretation of the Bible.* 2nd rev. ed. Philadelphia: Fortress, 1984.

Graves, Inspiration. • Graves, Michael. *The Inspiration and Interpretation of Scripture: What the Early Church Can Teach Us.* Grand Rapids: Eerdmans, 2014.

Graves, "Reading." • Graves, Michael. "The Public Reading of Scripture in Early Judaism." *JETS* 50 (3, 2007): 467–87.

Graves, Strangers. • Graves, Robert W., ed. *Strangers to Fire: When Tradition Trumps Scripture.* Foreword by J. Lee Grady. Woodstock, GA: The Foundation for Pentecostal Scholarship, 2014.

Gray, "Ugarit." • Gray, J. "Ugarit." 145–67 in *Archaeology and Old Testament Study.* Edited by D. Winton Thomas. Oxford: Clarendon, 1967.

Green, "Booth's Theology." • Green, Roger J. "William Booth's Theology of Redemption." *Christian History* 26 (1990): 27–30.

Green, "Interpretation." • Green, Gene L. "Relevance Theory and Biblical Interpretation." 217–40 in *The Linguist as Pedagogue: Trends in Teaching and Linguistic Analysis of the New Testament.* Edited by Stanley E. Porter and Matthew Brook O'Donnell. NTMon. Sheffield: Sheffield Phoenix, 2009.

Green, Practicing Theological Interpretation. • Green, Joel B. *Practicing Theological Interpretation: Engaging Biblical Texts for Faith and Formation.* Grand Rapids: Baker Academic, 2011.

Green, "Pragmatics." • Green, Gene L. "Lexical Pragmatics and Biblical Interpretation." *JETS* 50 (4, 2007): 799–812.

Green, "Relevance Theory." • Green, Gene L. "Relevance Theory and Theological Interpretation: Thoughts on Metarepresentation." *Journal of Theological Interpretation* 4 (2010): 75–90.

Green, "Repetition." • Green, Joel B. "Internal Repetition in Luke-Acts: Contemporary Narratology and Lucan Historiography." 283–99 in *History, Literature, and Society in the Book of Acts.* Edited by Ben Witherington III. Cambridge: Cambridge University Press, 1996.

Green, "Response." • Green, Gene. "A Response to the Postcolonial Roundtable: Promises, Problems and Prospects." 19–28 in *Evangelical Postcolonial Conversations: Global Awak-*

enings in Theology and Practice. Edited by Kay Higuera Smith, Jayachitra Lalitha, and L. Daniel Hawk. Downers Grove, IL: IVP Academic, 2014.

Green, Seized. • Green, Joel B. *Seized by Truth: Reading the Bible as Scripture.* Nashville: Abingdon, 2007.

Green, Theology. • Green, Chris E. W. *Toward a Pentecostal Theology of the Lord's Supper: Foretasting the Kingdom.* Cleveland, TN: CPT Press, 2012.

Green and McDonald, World. • Green, Joel B., and Lee Martin McDonald, eds. *The World of the New Testament: Cultural, Social, and Historical Contexts.* Grand Rapids: Baker Academic, 2013.

Green and Turner, Horizons. • Green, Joel B., and Max Turner, eds. *Between Two Horizons: Spanning New Testament Studies and Systematic Theology.* Grand Rapids: Eerdmans, 2000.

Gregory, "Secular Bias." • Gregory, Brad S. "The Other Confessional History: On Secular Bias in the Study of Religion." *HistTh,* theme issue, 45 (4, December 2006): 132–49.

Grenz, Renewing. • Grenz, Stanley L. *Renewing the Center: Evangelical Theology in a Post-Theological Era.* 2nd ed. Grand Rapids: Baker, 2006.

Grey, Crowd. • Grey, Jacqueline. *Three's a Crowd: Pentecostalism, Hermeneutics, and the Old Testament.* Eugene, OR: Pickwick, 2011.

Grindal, "Heart." • Grindal, Bruce T. "Into the Heart of Sisala Experience: Witnessing Death Divination." *JAnthRes* 39 (1983): 60–80.

Gritsch, "Reformer." • Gritsch, Eric W. "The Unrefined Reformer." *Christian History* 39 (1993): 35–37.

Gross, Preach. • Gross, Nancy Lammers. *If You Cannot Preach Like Paul . . .* Grand Rapids: Eerdmans, 2002.

Grunlan and Mayers, Cultural Anthropology. • Grunlan, Stephen A., and Marvin K. Mayers. *Cultural Anthropology: A Christian Perspective.* Grand Rapids: Zondervan, 1979.

Gundry, "Hearing." • Gundry, Robert H. "Richard A. Horsley's Hearing the Whole Story: A Critical Review of Its Postcolonial Slant." *JSNT* 26 (2, 2003): 131–49.

Gundry, Use. • Gundry, Robert H. *The Use of the Old Testament in St. Matthew's Gospel: With Special Reference to the Messianic Hope.* NovTSup 18. Leiden: Brill, 1975.

Gurney, Hittites. • Gurney, O. R. *The Hittites.* Baltimore: Penguin, 1972.

Gutt, Relevance Theory. • Gutt, Ernst-August. *Relevance Theory: A Guide to Successful Communication in Translation.* Dallas: Summer Institute of Linguistics; New York: United Bible Societies, 1992.

Gutting, Paradigms. • Gutting, Gary, ed. *Paradigms and Revolutions: Appraisals and Applications of Thomas Kuhn's Philosophy of Science.* Notre Dame, IN: University of Notre Dame Press, 1980.

Hafemann, "Yaein." • Hafemann, Scott. "Yaein: Yes and No to Luther's Reading of Galatians 3:6–14." 117–31 in *Galatians and Christian Theology: Justification, the Gospel, and Ethics in Paul's Letter.* Edited by Mark W. Elliott et al. Grand Rapids: Baker Academic, 2014.

Hagin, Authority of the Believer. • Hagin, Kenneth E. *Authority of the Believer.* Tulsa, OK: Kenneth Hagin Ministries, 1975.

Hagin, Don't Blame God. • Hagin, Kenneth E. *Don't Blame God.* Tulsa, OK: Kenneth Hagin Ministries, 1979.

Hagin, Led By the Spirit. • Hagin, Kenneth E. *How You Can Be Led By the Spirit of God.* Tulsa, OK: Kenneth Hagin Ministries, 1978.

Hagin, Matter of a Mate. • Hagin, Kenneth E. *On the Matter of a Mate.* Tulsa, OK: Kenneth Hagin Ministries, n.d.

Hagin, Midas Touch. • Hagin, Kenneth E. *The Midas Touch: A Balanced Approach to Biblical Prosperity.* Tulsa: Faith Library Publications, 2000.

Hagin, Ministering. • Hagin, Kenneth E. *Ministering to the Oppressed.* Tulsa, OK: Kenneth Hagin Ministries, 1978.

Hagin, *Name of Jesus*. • Hagin, Kenneth E. *The Name of Jesus*. Tulsa, OK: Kenneth Hagin Ministries, 1979.

Hagin, *New Thresholds of Faith*. • Hagin, Kenneth E. *New Thresholds of Faith*. Tulsa, OK: Kenneth Hagin Ministries, 1981.

Hagin, *Prayer Secrets*. • Hagin, Kenneth E. *Prayer Secrets*. Tulsa, OK: Kenneth Hagin Ministries, n.d.

Hagin, *Present Day Ministry*. • Hagin, Kenneth E. *Present Day Ministry of Jesus Christ*. Tulsa, OK: Kenneth Hagin Ministries, n.d.

Hagin, *Prevailing Prayer*. • Hagin, Kenneth E. *Prevailing Prayer to Peace*. Tulsa, OK: Rhema Bible Church; Kenneth Hagin Ministries, n.d.

Hagin, *Redeemed*. • Hagin, Kenneth E. *Redeemed from Poverty, Sickness, Death*. Tulsa, OK: Rhema Bible Church; Kenneth Hagin Ministries, 1983.

Hagin, *Ticket*. • Hagin, Kenneth E. *How to Write Your Own Ticket with God*. Tulsa, OK: Rhema Bible Church, 1979.

Hagin, *Visions*. • Hagin, Kenneth E. *I Believe in Visions*. Old Tappan, NJ: Fleming H. Revell, 1972.

Hagin, *What Faith Is*. • Hagin, Kenneth E. *What Faith Is*. Tulsa, OK: Kenneth Hagin Ministries, 1978.

Hagin, *Zoe*. • Hagin, Kenneth E. *Zoe: The God Kind of Life*. Tulsa, OK: Kenneth Hagin Ministries, 1981.

Hagin Jr., *Faith Worketh by Love*. • Hagin, Kenneth, Jr. *Faith Worketh by Love*. Tulsa, OK: Kenneth Hagin Ministries, 1979.

Hagin Jr., *Itching Ears*. • Hagin, Kenneth, Jr. *Itching Ears*. Tulsa, OK: Rhema Bible Church, 1982.

Hahn, *Kinship*. • Hahn, Scott. *Kinship by Covenant: A Canonical Approach to the Fulfillment of God's Saving Promises*. New Haven: Yale University Press, 2009.

Hair, "Witches." • Hair, P. E. H. "Heretics, Slaves, and Witches—as Seen by Guinea Jesuits c. 1610." *JRelAf* 28 (2, 1998): 131–44.

Hall, "Attendance." • Hall, Daniel E. "Religious Attendance: More Cost-Effective Than Lipitor?" *JABFM* 19 (2, March 2006): 103–9.

Hall, *Reading*. • Hall, Christopher A. *Reading Scripture with the Church Fathers*. Downers Grove, IL: InterVarsity, 1998.

Halpern, *Historians*. • Halpern, Baruch. *The First Historians: The Hebrew Bible and History*. San Francisco: Harper & Row, 1988.

Hambourger, "Belief." • Hambourger, Robert. "Belief in Miracles and Hume's Essay." *Nous* 14 (1980): 587–604.

Hanciles, *Beyond Christendom*. • Hanciles, Jehu J. *Beyond Christendom: Globalization, African Migration, and the Transformation of the West*. Maryknoll, NY: Orbis, 2008.

Hanciles, "Conversion." • Hanciles, Jehu J. "Conversion and Social Change: A Review of the 'Unfinished Task' in West Africa." 157–80 in *Christianity Reborn: The Global Expansion of Evangelicalism in the Twentieth Century*. Edited by Donald M. Lewis. SHCM. Grand Rapids: Eerdmans, 2004.

Haran, "Image." • Haran, Menahem. "The Priestly Image of the Tabernacle." *HUCA* 36 (1965): 191–226.

Hardesty, *Women*. • Hardesty, Nancy A. *Women Called to Witness: Evangelical Feminism in the 19th Century*. Nashville: Abingdon, 1984.

Harmon, "Allegory." • Harmon, Matthew S. "Allegory, Typology, or Something Else? Revisiting Galatians 4:21–5:1." 144–58 in *Studies in the Pauline Epistles: Essays in Honor of Douglas J. Moo*. Edited by Matthew S. Harmon and Jay E. Smith. Grand Rapids: Zondervan, 2014.

Harms, *Paradigms*. • Harms, Richard B. *Paradigms from Luke-Acts for Multicultural Communities*. AUSt, series 7, Theology and Religion 216. New York, Bern: Lang, 2001.

Harrell, *Possible.* • Harrell, David Edwin, Jr. *All Things Are Possible: The Healing and Charismatic Revivals in Modern America.* Bloomington: Indiana University Press, 1975.

Harries, "Worldview." • Harries, Jim. "The Magical Worldview in the African Church: What Is Going On?" *Missiology* 28 (4, 2000): 487–502.

Harrington, *Interpreting.* • Harrington, Daniel J. *Interpreting the New Testament: A Practical Guide.* New Testament Message. Wilmington, DE: Michael Glazier, 1979.

Harrison, *Introduction.* • Harrison, Roland K. *Introduction to the Old Testament.* Grand Rapids: Eerdmans, 1969.

Harrison, *Overwhelmed.* • Harrison, Randall A. *Overwhelmed by the Spirit: A Biblical Study on Discovering the Spirit.* N.p.: Entrust Publications, 2013.

Harrison and Yamauchi, "Clothing." • Harrison, R. K., and Edwin M. Yamauchi. "Clothing." 322–36 in *Dictionary of Daily Life in Biblical and Post-Biblical Antiquity.* Edited by Edwin M. Yamauchi and Marvin R. Wilson. 3 vols. Vol. 1: A-Da. Peabody, MA: Hendrickson, 2014.

Hart, *Delusions.* • Hart, David Bentley. *Atheist Delusions: The Christian Revolution and Its Fashionable Enemies.* New Haven: Yale University Press, 2009.

Hasel, *New Testament Theology.* • Hasel, Gerhard F. *New Testament Theology: Basic Issues in the Current Debate.* Grand Rapids: Eerdmans, 1978.

Hasitschka, "Anmerkungen." • Hasitschka, Marin. "Sozialgeschichtliche Anmerkungen zum Johannesevangelium." *Protokolle zur Bibel* 1 (1, 1992): 59–67.

Haskell, *Objectivity.* • Haskell, Thomas L. *Objectivity Is Not Neutrality: Explanatory Schemes in History.* Baltimore: Johns Hopkins University Press, 1998.

Hastings, *Edwards and Life of God.* • Hastings, Ross. *Jonathan Edwards and the Life of God: Toward an Evangelical Theology of Participation.* Minneapolis: Fortress, 2015.

Hauerwas, *Unleashing.* • Hauerwas, Stanley. *Unleashing the Scripture: Freeing the Bible from Captivity to America.* Nashville: Abingdon, 1993.

Hauerwas and Jones, *Narrative.* • Hauerwas, Stanley, and L. Gregory Jones, eds. *Why Narrative? Readings in Narrative Theology.* Grand Rapids: Eerdmans, 1989.

Hawk and Twiss, "Indian." • Hawk, L. Daniel, and Richard L. Twiss. "From Good: 'The Only Good Indian Is a Dead Indian' to Better: 'Kill the Indian and Save the Man' to Best: 'Old Things Pass Away and All Things Become White!': An American Hermeneutic of Colonization." 47–60 in *Evangelical Postcolonial Conversations: Global Awakenings in Theology and Practice.* Edited by Kay Higuera Smith, Jayachitra Lalitha, and L. Daniel Hawk. Downers Grove, IL: IVP Academic, 2014.

Hay, "Extremism." • Hay, David M. "Putting Extremism in Context: The Case of Philo, *De Migratione* 89–93." *Studia Philonica Annual* 9 (1997): 126–42.

Haya-Prats, *Believers.* • Haya-Prats, Gonzalo. *Empowered Believers: The Holy Spirit in the Book of Acts.* Edited by Paul Elbert. Translated by Scott A. Ellington. Eugene, OR: Cascade, 2011.

Hayden, "Walk." • Hayden, Roger. "To Walk in All His Ways." *Christian History* 4 (2, 1985): 7–9, 35.

Hayes, "Responses." • Hayes, Stephen. "Christian Responses to Witchcraft and Sorcery." *Missionalia* 23 (3, 1995): 339–54.

Hays, *Conversion.* • Hays, Richard B. *The Conversion of the Imagination: Paul as Interpreter of Israel's Scripture.* Grand Rapids: Eerdmans, 2005.

Hays, *Echoes.* • Hays, Richard B. *Echoes of Scripture in the Letters of Paul.* New Haven: Yale University Press, 1989.

Hays, *First Corinthians.* • Hays, Richard B. *First Corinthians.* IBC. Louisville: John Knox, 1997.

Hays, *Reading Backwards.* • Hays, Richard B. *Reading Backwards: Figural Christology and the Fourfold Gospel Witness.* Waco: Baylor University Press, 2014.

Head, "Nazi Quest." • Head, Peter M. "The Nazi Quest for an Aryan Jesus." *JSHJ* 2 (1, 2004): 55–89.

Heaney, "Conversion." • Heaney, Robert S. "Conversion to Coloniality: Avoiding the Colonization of Method." *IntRevMiss* 97 (384–385, January 2008): 65–77.

Hedgespeth, "Power." • Hedgespeth, Joanne. "The Healing Power of the Will to Live." 235–48 in *Medical and Therapeutic Events.* Vol. 2 of *Miracles: God, Science, and Psychology in the Paranormal.* Edited by J. Harold Ellens. Westport, CT; London: Praeger, 2008.

Hefley and Hefley, *Blood*. • Hefley, James, and Marti Hefley. *By Their Blood: Christian Martyrs of the Twentieth Century.* 2nd ed. Grand Rapids: Baker, 1996.

Heinze, "Introduction." • Heinze, Ruth-Inge. "Introduction." 1–18 in *Proceedings of the Fourth International Conference on the Study of Shamanism and Alternate Modes of Healing, Held at the St. Sabina Center, San Rafael, California, September 5–7, 1987.* Edited by Ruth-Inge Heinze. N.p.: Independent Scholars of Asia; Madison, WI: A-R Editions, 1988.

Helm, "Miraculous." • Helm, Paul. "The Miraculous." *ScChrB* 3 (1, 1991): 83–95.

Helm et al., "Activity." • Helm, Hughes M., Judith C. Hays, Elizabeth P. Flint, Harold G. Koenig, and Dan G. Blazer. "Does Private Religious Activity Prolong Survival? A Six-Year Follow-up Study of 3,851 Older Adults." *JGBSMS* 55 (7, 2000): M400–405.

Heltzer, "Tithe." • Heltzer, M. "On Tithe Paid in Grain in Ugarit." *Israel Exploration Journal* 25 (2–3, 1975): 124–28.

Hemphill, *Gifted*. • Hemphill, Ken. *You Are Gifted: Your Spiritual Gifts and the Kingdom of God.* Nashville: B&H Publishing Group, 2009.

Henderson, "Life." • Henderson, Jordan. "Josephus's *Life* and *Jewish War* Compared to the Synoptic Gospels." *JGRCJ* 10 (2014): 113–31.

Hengel, *Jesus and Paul*. • Hengel, Martin. *Between Jesus and Paul: Studies in the History of Earliest Christianity.* Philadelphia: Fortress, 1983.

Hengel, "Messiah." • Hengel, Martin. "Jesus, the Messiah of Israel: The Debate about the 'Messianic Mission' of Jesus." 323–49 in *Authenticating the Activities of Jesus.* Edited by Bruce Chilton and Craig A. Evans. NTTS 28.2. Leiden: Brill, 1999.

Hengel and Schwemer, *Between Damascus and Antioch*. • Hengel, Martin, and Anna Maria Schwemer. *Paul between Damascus and Antioch: The Unknown Years.* Translated by John Bowden. London: SCM; Louisville: Westminster John Knox, 1997.

Henry, *God Who Speaks*. • Henry, Carl F. H. *God Who Speaks and Shows.* Vol. 4 of *God, Revelation and Authority.* Waco: Word, 1970.

Herms, "Invoking." • Herms, Ronald. "Invoking the Spirit and Narrative Intent in John's Apocalypse." 99–114 in *Spirit and Scripture: Exploring a Pneumatic Hermeneutic.* Edited by Kevin L. Spawn and Archie T. Wright. New York: Bloomsbury, 2012.

Herms, "Review." • Herms, Ronald. "Review of Robby Waddell, *The Spirit of the Book of Revelation* (JPTS 30; Blandford Forum: Deo, 2006)." *JPT* 17 (1, 2008): 9–18.

Hernando, *Dictionary*. • Hernando, James D. *Dictionary of Hermeneutics: A Concise Guide to Terms, Names, Methods, and Expressions.* Springfield, MO: Gospel Publishing House, 2005.

Hernando, "Function." • Hernando, James D. "Pneumatological Function in the Narrative of Acts: Drawing Foundational Insight for a Pentecostal Missiology." 241–76 in *Trajectories in the Book of Acts: Essays in Honor of John Wesley Wyckoff.* Edited by Paul Alexander, Jordan Daniel May, and Robert G. Reid. Eugene, OR: Wipf & Stock, 2010.

Heth, "Remarriage." • Heth, William A. "Remarriage for Adultery or Desertion." 59–83 in *Remarriage after Divorce in Today's Church.* Edited by Mark Strauss. Grand Rapids: Zondervan, 2006.

Heth and Wenham, *Divorce*. • Heth, William A., and Gordon J. Wenham. *Jesus and Divorce: The Problem with the Evangelical Consensus.* Nashville: Thomas Nelson, 1984.

Heuch, Jacobsen, and Fraser, "Study." • Heuch, Ivar, Bjarne K. Jacobsen, and Gary E. Fraser. "A Cohort Study Found That Earlier and Longer Seventh-Day Adventist Church Membership Was Associated with Reduced Male Mortality." *JClinEpid* 58 (1, 2005): 83–91.

Hexham, "Exorcism." • Hexham, Irving. "Theology, Exorcism, and the Amplification of Deviancy." *EvQ* 49 (1977): 111–16.

Hey, "Roles." • Hey, Sam. "Changing Roles of Pentecostal Hermeneutics." *Evangelical Review of Theology* 25 (3, 2001): 210–18.

Hickson, *Heal.* • Hickson, James Moore. *Heal the Sick.* 2nd ed. London: Methuen, 1924.

Hiebert, "Excluded Middle." • Hiebert, Paul G. "The Flaw of the Excluded Middle." *Missiology* 10 (1, January 1982): 35–47.

Hill, *Hellenists.* • Hill, Craig C. *Hellenists and Hebrews: Reappraising Division within the Earliest Church.* Minneapolis: Fortress, 1992.

Hill, "Witchcraft." • Hill, Harriet. "Witchcraft and the Gospel: Insights from Africa." *Missiology* 24 (3, 1996): 323–44.

Hill et al., "Attendance and Mortality." • Hill, Terrence D., Jacqueline L. Angel, Christopher G. Ellison, and Ronald J. Angel. "Religious Attendance and Mortality: An 8-Year Follow-up of Older Mexican Americans." *JGPSSS* 60 (2, 2005): S102–9.

Hillard, Nobbs, and Winter, "Corpus." • Hillard, T., A. Nobbs, and B. Winter. "Acts and the Pauline Corpus, I: Ancient Literary Parallels." 183–213 in *The Book of Acts in Its Ancient Literary Setting.* Edited by Bruce W. Winter and Andrew D. Clarke. Vol. 1 of *The Book of Acts in Its First Century Setting.* Edited by Bruce W. Winter. Grand Rapids: Eerdmans; Carlisle, UK: Paternoster, 1993.

Hinson, "History of Glossolalia." • Hinson, E. Glenn. "A Brief History of Glossolalia." 45–75 in *Glossolalia: Tongue Speaking in Biblical, Historical, and Psychological Perspective.* By Frank Stagg, E. Glenn Hinson, and Wayne E. Oates. Nashville: Abingdon, 1967.

Hirsch, *Aims.* • Hirsch, Eric Donald. *The Aims of Interpretation.* Chicago: University of Chicago Press, 1976.

Hirsch, *Literacy.* • Hirsch, Eric Donald. *Cultural Literacy.* New York: Houghton & Mifflin, 1987.

Hirsch, *Validity.* • Hirsch, Eric Donald. *Validity in Interpretation.* New Haven: Yale University Press, 1967.

Hirschberg and Barasch, *Recovery.* • Hirschberg, Caryle, and Marc Ian Barasch. *Remarkable Recovery: What Extraordinary Healings Tell Us about Getting Well and Staying Well.* New York: Riverhead, 1995.

Hoare, "Approach." • Hoare, Frank. "A Pastoral Approach to Spirit Possession and Witchcraft Manifestations among the Fijian People." *MissSt* 21 (1, 2004): 113–37.

Hoehner, *Ephesians.* • Hoehner, Harold W. *Ephesians: An Exegetical Commentary.* Grand Rapids: Baker, 2002.

Hoffman and Kurzenberger, "Miraculous." • Hoffman, Louis, and Marika Kurzenberger. "The Miraculous and Mental Illness." 65–93 in *Parapsychological Perspectives.* Vol. 3 in *Miracles: God, Science, and Psychology in the Paranormal.* Edited by J. Harold Ellens. Westport, CT; London: Praeger, 2008.

Hollenweger, "Contribution." • Hollenweger, Walter J. "The Contribution of Critical Exegesis to Pentecostal Hermeneutics." *Spirit & Church* 2 (1, 2000): 7–18.

Hollenweger, *Pentecostals.* • Hollenweger, Walter J. *The Pentecostals.* London: SCM, 1972. Repr., Peabody, MA: Hendrickson, 1988.

Holmes, "Challenge." • Holmes, Pamela. "A Never Ending Canadian Pentecostal Challenge: What to Do with the Women." 264–85 in *The Many Faces of Global Pentecostalism.* Edited by Harold D. Hunter and Neil Ormerod. Cleveland, TN: CPT Press, 2013.

Holwerda, *Spirit.* • Holwerda, David Earl. *The Holy Spirit and Eschatology in the Gospel of John: A Critique of Rudolf Bultmann's Present Eschatology.* Kampen: J. H. Kok, 1959.

Horrell and Adams, "Introduction." • Horrell, David G., and Edward Adams. "Introduction: The Scholarly Quest for Paul's Church at Corinth: A Critical Survey." 1–43 in *Christianity at Corinth: The Quest for the Pauline Church.* Edited by Edward Adams and David G. Horrell. Louisville: Westminster John Knox, 2004.

Hort, "Plagues." • Hort, Greta. "The Plagues of Egypt." Parts 1 and 2. *ZAW* 69 (1957): 84–103; 70 (1958): 48–59.

Horton, *Corinthians*. • Horton, Stanley M. *I and II Corinthians: A Logion Press Commentary.* Springfield, MO: Gospel, 1999.

Horton, *Spirit*. • Horton, Stanley M. *What the Bible Says about the Holy Spirit.* Springfield, MO: Gospel, 1976.

Houston, *Miracles*. • Houston, J. *Reported Miracles: A Critique of Hume.* Cambridge: Cambridge University Press, 1994.

Hoy, *Critical Circle*. • Hoy, David Couzens. *The Critical Circle: Literature, History, and Philosophical Hermeneutics.* Berkeley: University of California Press, 1978.

Hubbard, *Joshua*. • Hubbard, Robert L., Jr. *Joshua.* NIVAC. Grand Rapids: Zondervan, 2009.

Hudson, "Strange Words." • Hudson, Neil. "Strange Words and Their Impact on Early Pentecostals: A Historical Perspective." 52–80 in *Speaking in Tongues: Multi-disciplinary Perspectives.* Edited by Mark J. Cartledge. SPCI. Waynesboro, GA, and Bletchley, Milton Keynes, UK: Paternoster, 2006.

Hull, *Spirit in Acts*. • Hull, J. H. E. *The Holy Spirit in the Acts of the Apostles.* London: Lutterworth, 1967; Cleveland: World, 1968.

Hume, *History of Religion*. • Hume, David. *The Natural History of Religion.* Edited by H. E. Root. London: Adam & Charles Black, 1956.

Hume, *Miracles*. • Hume, David. *Of Miracles.* Introduction by Antony Flew. La Salle, IL: Open Court, 1985.

Hunt, "Paraclete." • Hunt, Dwight. "Jesus' Teaching Concerning the Paraclete in the Upper Room Discourse." Master of Theology thesis, Western Conservative Baptist Seminary, April 1981.

Hur, *Reading*. • Hur, Ju. *A Dynamic Reading of the Holy Spirit in Luke-Acts.* JSNTSup 211. Sheffield, UK: Sheffield Academic, 2001.

Hurtado, *Lord Jesus Christ*. • Hurtado, Larry W. *Lord Jesus Christ: Devotion to Jesus in Earliest Christianity.* Grand Rapids: Eerdmans, 2003.

Hylen, *Imperfect Believers*. • Hylen, Susan E. *Imperfect Believers: Ambiguous Characters in the Gospel of John.* Louisville: Westminster John Knox, 2009.

Ilan, *Women*. • Ilan, Tal. *Jewish Women in Greco-Roman Palestine.* Tübingen: Mohr, 1996.

Inowlocki, "Rewriting." • Inowlocki, Sabrina. "Josephus' Rewriting of the Babel Narrative (Gen 11:1–9)." *JSJ* 37 (2, 2006): 169–91.

Instone-Brewer, *Divorce*. • Instone-Brewer, David. *Divorce and Remarriage in the Bible: The Social and Literary Context.* Grand Rapids: Eerdmans, 2002.

Instone-Brewer, *Techniques*. • Instone-Brewer, David. *Techniques and Assumptions in Jewish Exegesis before 70 C.E.* Tübingen: J. C. B. Mohr (P. Siebeck), 1992.

Ironson et al., "Spirituality." • Ironson, G., G. F. Solomon, E. G. Balbin, et al. "Spirituality and Religiousness Are Associated with Long Survival, Healthy Behaviors, Less Distress, and Lower Cortisol in People Living with HIV/AIDS: The IWORSHIP Scale, Its Validity and Reliability." *AnnBehMed* 24 (2002): 34–48.

Irvin and Sunquist, *History*. • Irvin, Dale T., and Scott W. Sunquist. *Modern Christianity from 1454–1800.* Vol. 2 of *History of the World Christian Movement.* Maryknoll, NY: Orbis, 2012.

Irwin, "Stoic Inhumanity." • Irwin, Terence H. "Stoic Inhumanity." 219–41 in *The Emotions in Hellenistic Philosophy.* Edited by Juha Sihvola and Troels Engberg-Pedersen. TSHP 46. Dordrecht, Neth.: Kluwer Academic, 1998.

Iser, *Implied Reader*. • Iser, Wolfgang. *The Implied Reader: Patterns of Communication in Prose Fiction from Bunyan to Beckett.* Baltimore: Johns Hopkins University Press, 1974.

Isichei, *History*. • Isichei, Elizabeth. *A History of Christianity in Africa from Antiquity to the Present.* Lawrenceville, NJ: Africa World; Grand Rapids: Eerdmans, 1995.

Ising, *Blumhardt*. • Ising, Dieter. *Johann Christoph Blumhardt, Life and Work: A New Biogra-*

phy. Translated by Monty Ledford. Eugene, OR: Cascade, 2009. Translated from *Johann Christoph Blumhardt: Leben und Werk.* Göttingen: Vandenhoeck & Ruprecht, 2002.

Israel, Albrecht, and McNally, "Hermeneutics." • Israel, Richard D., Daniel E. Albrecht, and Randal G. McNally. "Pentecostals and Hermeneutics: Texts, Rituals, and Communities." Papers of the Society for Pentecostal Studies Annual Meeting. Dallas, TX, November 1990.

Jackson, *Quest.* • Jackson, Bill. *The Quest for the Radical Middle: A History of the Vineyard.* Foreword by Todd Hunter. Cape Town: Vineyard International, 1999.

Jacobs, *Exegesis.* • Jacobs, Louis. *Jewish Biblical Exegesis.* New York: Behrman House, 1973.

Jacobsen, *Thinking in Spirit.* • Jacobsen, Douglas. *Thinking in the Spirit: Theologies of the Early Pentecostal Movement.* Bloomington: Indiana University Press, 2003.

Jaki, *Patterns.* • Jaki, Stanley L. *Patterns or Principles and Other Essays.* Wilmington, DE: Intercollegiate Studies Institute, 1995.

Jantzen, "Miracles." • Jantzen, Grace. "Miracles Reconsidered." *CSR* 9 (4, 1980): 354–58.

Jayakumar, *Mission Reader.* • Jayakumar, Samuel. *Mission Reader: Historical Models for Wholistic Mission in the Indian Context.* Oxford: Oxford Centre for Mission Studies, 2002.

Jenkins, *Next Christendom.* • Jenkins, Philip. *The Next Christendom: The Coming of Global Christianity.* New York: Oxford University Press, 2002.

Jennings, *Good News.* • Jennings, Theodore W., Jr. *Good News to the Poor: John Wesley's Evangelical Economics.* Nashville: Abingdon, 1990.

Jensen, "Logic." • Jensen, Dennis. "The Logic of Miracles." *JASA* 33 (3, September 1981): 145–53.

Jeremias, *Parables.* • Jeremias, Joachim. *The Parables of Jesus.* 2nd rev. ed. New York: Scribner's, 1972.

Jobes, "Relevance Theory." • Jobes, Karen H. "Relevance Theory and the Translation of Scripture." *JETS* 50 (4, 2007): 773–97.

Johns, "Meeting God." • Johns, Cheryl Bridges. "Meeting God in the Margins, Ministry among Modernity's Refugees." 3:7–31 in *The Papers of the Henry Luce III Fellows in Theology.* 3 vols. Edited by Matthew Zyniewicz. Atlanta: Scholars Press, 1999.

Johns, "New Directions." • Johns, Donald A. "Some New Directions in the Hermeneutics of Classical Pentecostalism's Doctrine of Initial Evidence." 145–67 in *Initial Evidence: Historical and Biblical Perspectives on the Pentecostal Doctrine of Spirit Baptism.* Edited by Gary B. McGee. Peabody, MA: Hendrickson, 1991.

Johns, *Pentecostal Formation.* • Johns, Cheryl Bridges. *Pentecostal Formation: A Pedagogy among the Oppressed.* Sheffield: Sheffield Academic Press, 1993.

Johns and Johns, "Yielding." • Johns, Jackie David, and Cheryl Bridges Johns. "Yielding to the Spirit: A Pentecostal Approach to Group Bible Study." 33–56 in *Pentecostal Hermeneutics: A Reader.* Edited by Lee Roy Martin. Leiden: Brill, 2013.

Johnson, *Acts.* • Johnson, Luke Timothy. *The Acts of the Apostles.* SP 5. Collegeville, MN: Liturgical Press, 1992.

Johnson, "Growing Church." • Johnson, Harmon A. "The Growing Church in Haiti." Coral Gables, FL: West Indies Mission, 1970.

Johnson, *Hume.* • Johnson, David. *Hume, Holism, and Miracles.* CSPhilRel. Ithaca, NY: Cornell University Press, 1999.

Johnson, *Romans.* • Johnson, Luke Timothy. *Reading Romans: A Literary and Theological Commentary.* Macon, GA: Smyth & Helwys, 2001.

Johnson, Barrett, and Crossing, "Christianity 2010." • Johnson, Todd M., David B. Barrett, and Peter F. Crossing. "Christianity 2010: A View from the *New Atlas of Global Christianity.*" *IBMR* 34 (1, January 2010): 29–36.

Johnson and Ross, *Atlas.* • Johnson, Todd M., and Kenneth R. Ross, eds. *Atlas of Global Christianity, 1910–2010.* Managing editor, Sandra S. K. Lee. Edinburgh: Center for the Study of Global Christianity, 2009.

Johnson and Wu, *Families.* • Johnson, Todd M., and Cindy M. Wu. *Our Global Families:*

Christians Embracing Common Identity in a Changing World. Grand Rapids: Baker Academic, 2015.

Johnston, "Commandments." • Johnston, Robert Morris. "'The Least of the Commandments': Deuteronomy 22:6–7 in Rabbinic Judaism and Early Christianity." *AUSS* 20 (1982): 205–15.

Johnston, "Ordination." • Johnston, Flo. "Ordination Will Cross Racial Lines." *The Chicago Tribune* (August 9, 1991): section 2, 9.

Johnstone, *Future.* • Johnstone, Patrick. *The Future of the Global Church: History, Trends and Possibilities.* Downers Grove, IL: InterVarsity, 2011.

Jonas, *Religion.* • Jonas, Hans. *The Gnostic Religion: The Message of the Alien God and the Beginnings of Christianity.* 2nd rev. ed. Boston: Beacon Press, 1963.

Joy, "Transitions." • Joy, C. I. D. "Transitions and Trajectories in the Early Christian Community in the Context of Pluralism and Mission in Acts: A Postcolonial Reading." *BiBh* 32 (4, 2006): 326–41.

Judge, *First Christians.* • Judge, Edwin A. *The First Christians in the Roman World: Augustan and New Testament Essays.* Edited by James R. Harrison. WUNT 229. Tübingen: Mohr Siebeck, 2008.

Jules-Rosette, "Healers." • Jules-Rosette, Bennetta. "Faith Healers and Folk Healers: The Symbolism and Practice of Indigenous Therapy in Urban Africa." *Religion* 11 (1981): 127–49.

Kahl, "Bibelinterpretation." • Kahl, Werner. "Akademische Bibelinterpretation in Afrika, Lateinamerika und Asien angesichts der Globalisierung." *Verkündigung und Forschung* 54 (1, 2009): 45–58.

Kalu, *African Pentecostalism.* • Kalu, Ogbu. *African Pentecostalism: An Introduction.* Oxford: Oxford University Press, 2008.

Kapolyo, *Condition.* • Kapolyo, Joe M. *The Human Condition: Christian Perspectives through African Eyes.* Downers Grove, IL: InterVarsity, 2005.

Katzoff, "Purchase." • Katzoff, Louis. "Purchase of the Machpelah." *Dor le Dor* 16 (1987): 29–31.

Kauffman, "Introduction." • Kauffman, Richard A. "Introduction." 6–9 in *Essays on Spiritual Bondage and Deliverance.* Edited by Willard M. Swartley. Occasional Papers 11. Elkhart, IN: Institute of Mennonite Studies, 1988.

Keck, "Ethos." • Keck, Leander E. "On the Ethos of Early Christians." *JAAR* 42 (1974): 435–52.

Kee, *Miracle.* • Kee, Howard Clark. *Miracle in the Early Christian World: A Study in Sociohistorical Method.* New Haven: Yale University Press, 1983.

Keene, "Possibility of Miracles." • Keene, J. Calvin. "The Possibility of Miracles." *CrQ* 26 (3, July 1949): 208–14.

Keener, *Acts.* • Keener, Craig S. *Acts: An Exegetical Commentary.* 4 vols. Grand Rapids: Baker Academic, 2012–15.

Keener, "Acts 2:1–21." • Keener, Craig S. "Day of Pentecost, Years A, B, C: First Lesson—Acts 2:1–21." 524–28 in *The First Readings: The Old Testament and Acts.* Vol. 1 of *The Lectionary Commentary: Theological Exegesis for Sunday's Texts.* Edited by Roger E. Van Harn. Grand Rapids: Eerdmans; London: Continuum, 2001.

Keener, "Adultery." • Keener, Craig S. "Adultery, Divorce." 6–16 in *DNTB.*

Keener, "Asia and Europe." • Keener, Craig S. "Between Asia and Europe: Postcolonial Mission in Acts 16:8–10." *AJPS* 11 (1–2, 2008): 3–14.

Keener, "Asiarchs." • Keener, Craig S. "Paul's 'Friends' the Asiarchs (Acts 19.31)." *Journal of Greco-Roman Christianity and Judaism* 3 (2006): 134–41.

Keener, "Assumptions." • Keener, Craig S. "Assumptions in Historical Jesus Research: Using Ancient Biographies and Disciples' Traditioning as a Control." *JSHJ* 9 (1, 2011): 26–58.

Keener, *Background Commentary.* • Keener, Craig S. *The IVP Bible Background Commentary: New Testament.* 2nd rev. ed. Downers Grove, IL: InterVarsity, 2014.

Keener, "Beheld." • Keener, Craig S. "'We Beheld His Glory': John 1:14." 15–25 in *Aspects of Historicity in the Fourth Gospel.* Edited by Paul N. Anderson, Felix Just, and Tom

Thatcher. Vol. 2 of *John, Jesus and History*. SBL Early Christianity and Its Literature 2. Atlanta: SBL, 2009.

Keener, *Bible in Context*. • Keener, Craig S. *The Bible in Its Context: How to Improve Your Study of the Scriptures*. Mountlake Terrace, WA: Action International, 2013.

Keener, "Biblical Fidelity." • Keener, Craig S. "Biblical Fidelity as an Evangelical Commitment." 29–41 in *Following Jesus: Journeys in Radical Discipleship. Essays in Honor of Ronald J. Sider*. Edited by Paul Alexander and Al Tizon. Regnum Studies in Global Christianity. Oxford: Regnum, 2013.

Keener, "Biographies." • Keener, Craig S. "Reading the Gospels as Biographies of a Sage." *BurH* 47 (2011): 59–66.

Keener, "Case." • Keener, Craig S. "A Reassessment of Hume's Case against Miracles in Light of Testimony from the Majority World Today." *PRSt* 38 (3, Fall 2011): 289–310.

Keener, "Charismatic Reading." • Keener, Craig S. "One Thousand Two Hundred Sixty Days: A Charismatic-Prophetic Empowerment Reading of Time and God's People in the Book of Revelation." 235–46 in *But These Are Written . . . : Essays on Johannine Literature in Honor of Professor Benny C. Aker*. Edited by Craig S. Keener, Jeremy S. Crenshaw, and Jordan Daniel May. Eugene, OR: Pickwick, 2014.

Keener, *Corinthians*. • Keener, Craig S. *1 and 2 Corinthians*. NCamBC. Cambridge: Cambridge University Press, 2005.

Keener, "Diversity." • Keener, Craig S. "Embracing God's Passion for Diversity: A Theology of Racial and Ethnic Plurality." *Enr* 12 (3, 2007): 20–28.

Keener, "Evidence." • Keener, Craig S. "Tongues as Evidence of the Character of the Spirit's Empowerment in Acts." In *A Light to the Nations: Explorations in Ecumenism, Missions, and Pentecostalism in Honor of Gary B. McGee*. Edited by Stanley M. Burgess and Paul W. Lewis. Eugene, OR: Pickwick, forthcoming.

Keener, "Expectation." • Keener, Craig S. "Messianic Expectation." Prepared for "Expectation and Human Flourishing," Yale Center for Faith and Culture, New York City, June 22, 2015.

Keener, *Galatians*. • Keener, Craig S. *Galatians*. NCamBC. Cambridge: Cambridge University Press, forthcoming.

Keener, *Gift*. • Keener, Craig S. *Gift and Giver: The Holy Spirit for Today*. Grand Rapids: Baker, 2001.

Keener, "Gifts." • Keener, Craig S. "Gifts (Spiritual)." 155–61 in *The Westminster Theological Wordbook of the Bible*. Edited by Donald E. Gowan. Louisville: Westminster John Knox, 2003.

Keener, "Gifts for Today." • Keener, Craig S. "Are Spiritual Gifts for Today?" 135–62 in *Strangers to Fire: When Tradition Trumps Scripture*. Edited by Robert W. Graves. Foreword by J. Lee Grady. Woodstock, GA: The Foundation for Pentecostal Scholarship, 2014.

Keener, "Head Coverings." • Keener, Craig S. "Head Coverings." 442–47 in *DNTB*.

Keener, *Historical Jesus*. • Keener, Craig S. *The Historical Jesus of the Gospels*. Grand Rapids: Eerdmans, 2009.

Keener, "Holy Spirit." • Keener, Craig. "The Holy Spirit." 158–73 in *The Oxford Handbook of Evangelical Theology*. Edited by Gerald R. McDermott. New York: Oxford University Press, 2010.

Keener, "Invitations." • Keener, Craig S. "Some New Testament Invitations to Ethnic Reconciliation." *EvQ* 75 (3, 2003): 195–213.

Keener, *John*. • Keener, Craig S. *The Gospel of John: A Commentary*. 2 vols. Peabody, MA: Hendrickson; Grand Rapids: Baker Academic, 2003.

Keener, "Kiss." • Keener, Craig S. "Kiss, Kissing." 628–29 in *DNTB*.

Keener, "Knowledge." • Keener, Craig S. "Studies in the Knowledge of God in the Fourth Gospel in Light of Its Historical Context." MDiv thesis, Assemblies of God Theological Seminary, 1987.

Keener, "Learning." • Keener, Craig S. "Learning in the Assemblies: 1 Corinthians 14:34–35."

161–71 in *Discovering Biblical Equality: Complementarity without Hierarchy*. Edited by Ronald W. Pierce, Rebecca Merrill Groothuis, and Gordon D. Fee. Downers Grove, IL: InterVarsity, 2004.

Keener, "Luke's Pneumatology." • Keener, Craig S. "Luke's Pneumatology in Acts for the 21st Century." 205–22 in *Contemporary Issues in Pneumatology: Festschrift in Honor of George M. Flattery*. Edited by James E. Richardson. Springfield, MO: Global University, 2009.

Keener, "Marriage." • Keener, Craig S. "Marriage." 680–93 in *DNTB*.

Keener, *Marries Another*. • Keener, Craig S. *. . . And Marries Another: Divorce and Remarriage in the Teaching of the New Testament*. Grand Rapids: Baker Academic, 1991.

Keener, *Matthew*. • Keener, Craig S. *The Gospel of Matthew: A Socio-Rhetorical Commentary*. Grand Rapids: Eerdmans, 2009. Rev. ed. of *A Commentary on the Gospel of Matthew*. Grand Rapids: Eerdmans, 1999.

Keener, *Mind*. • Keener, Craig S. *The Mind of the Spirit: Paul's Approach to Transformed Thinking*. Grand Rapids: Baker Academic, 2016.

Keener, "Miracle Reports in Gospels and Today." • Keener, Craig S. "Miracle Reports in the Gospels and Today." Plenary address for "Special Divine Action," 2014 conference for the Ian Ramsey Centre for Science and Religion, Oxford University, Oxford, UK, July 14, 2014.

Keener, "Miracle Reports: Perspectives." • Keener, Craig S. "Miracle Reports: Perspectives, Analogies, Explanations." 53–65 in *Hermeneutik der frühchristlichen Wundererzählungen: Historiche, literarische und rezeptionsästhetische Aspekte*. Edited by Bernd Kollmann and Ruben Zimmermann. WUNT 339. Tübingen: Mohr Siebeck, 2014.

Keener, *Miracles*. • Keener, Craig S. *Miracles: The Credibility of the New Testament Accounts*. Grand Rapids: Baker Academic, 2011.

Keener, "Miracles." • Keener, Craig S. "Miracles." 2:101–7 in *The Oxford Encyclopedia of Bible and Theology*. 2 vols. Edited by Samuel E. Balentine. Oxford: Oxford University Press, 2015.

Keener, "Miracles: Dictionary." • Keener, Craig S. "Miracles." In *Dictionary of Christianity and Science*. Edited by Paul Copan et al. Grand Rapids: Zondervan, forthcoming.

Keener, "Money." • Keener, Craig S. "When Jesus Wanted All My Money: And Everything Else; How I learned He's an All-or-Nothing Lord." *Christianity Today* (May 2015): 46–50.

Keener, "Otho." • Keener, Craig S. "Otho: A Targeted Comparison of Suetonius' Biography and Tacitus' History, with Implications for the Gospels' Historical Reliability." *BBR* 21 (3, 2011): 331–55.

Keener, "Parallel Figures." • Keener, Craig S. "Jesus and Parallel Jewish and Greco-Roman Figures." 85–111 in *Christian Origins and Greco-Roman Culture: Social and Literary Contexts for the New Testament*. Edited by Stanley Porter and Andrew W. Pitts. Vol. 1 of *Early Christianity in Its Hellenistic Context*. Vol. 9 in Texts and Editions for New Testament Study. Leiden: Brill, 2013.

Keener, *Paul*. • Keener, Craig S. *Paul, Women, and Wives: Marriage and Women's Ministry in the Letters of Paul*. Peabody, MA: Hendrickson; Grand Rapids: Baker Academic, 1992.

Keener, "Pentecost." • Keener, Craig S. "Pentecost." 360–61 in *The Westminster Theological Wordbook of the Bible*. Edited by Donald E. Gowan. Louisville: Westminster John Knox, 2003.

Keener, "Perspective." • Keener, Craig S. "Women in Ministry: Another Egalitarian Perspective." 203–48 in *Two Views on Women in Ministry*. Edited by James R. Beck. Rev. ed. Grand Rapids: Zondervan, 2005.

Keener, "Pneumatology." • Keener, Craig S. "The Function of Johannine Pneumatology in the Context of Late First-Century Judaism." PhD dissertation, Duke University, 1991.

Keener, "Possession." • Keener, Craig S. "Spirit Possession as a Cross-Cultural Experience." *BBR* 20 (2010): 215–36.

Keener, "Power." • Keener, Craig S. "Power of Pentecost: Luke's Missiology in Acts 1–2." *AJPS* 12 (1, January 2009): 47–73.

Keener, *Questions*. • Keener, Craig S. *Three Crucial Questions about the Holy Spirit.* Grand Rapids: Baker, 1996.

Keener, "Raised." • Keener, Craig S. "'The Dead Are Raised' (Matthew 11:5//Luke 7:22): Resuscitation Accounts in the Gospels and Eyewitness Testimony." *BBR* 25 (1, 2015): 57–79.

Keener, "Reconciliation." • Keener, Craig S. "The Gospel and Racial Reconciliation." 117–30 in *The Gospel in Black and White: Theological Resources for Racial Reconciliation.* Edited by Dennis L. Ockholm. Downers Grove, IL: InterVarsity, 1997.

Keener, "Remarriage." • Keener, Craig S. "Remarriage for Circumstances beyond Adultery or Desertion." 103–19 in *Remarriage after Divorce in Today's Church.* Edited by Mark Strauss. Grand Rapids: Zondervan, 2006.

Keener, *Revelation*. • Keener, Craig S. *Revelation.* NIVAC. Grand Rapids: Zondervan, 2000.

Keener, "Review of *Strange Fire*." • Keener, Craig S. "A Review of MacArthur's *Strange Fire.*" 35–58 in *Strangers to Fire: When Tradition Trumps Scripture.* Edited by Robert W. Graves. Foreword by J. Lee Grady. Woodstock, GA: The Foundation for Pentecostal Scholarship, 2014.

Keener, "Rhetorical Techniques." • Keener, Craig S. "Some Rhetorical Techniques in Acts 24:2–21." 221–51 in *Paul's World.* Edited by Stanley E. Porter. PAST 4. Leiden: Brill, 2008.

Keener, *Romans*. • Keener, Craig S. *Romans.* NCCS 6. Eugene, OR: Wipf & Stock, 2009.

Keener, "Scripture and Context." • Keener, Craig S. "Scripture and Context: An Evangelical Exploration." *Asbury Journal* 70 (1, 2015): 17–62.

Keener, "Spirit." • Keener, Craig S. "Spirit, Holy Spirit, Advocate, Breath, Wind." 484–96 in *The Westminster Theological Wordbook of the Bible.* Edited by Donald E. Gowan. Louisville: Westminster John Knox, 2003.

Keener, *Spirit*. • Keener, Craig S. *The Spirit in the Gospels and Acts: Divine Purity and Power.* Peabody, MA: Hendrickson, 1997. Repr., Grand Rapids: Baker Academic, 2010.

Keener, "Spirit Perspectives." • Keener, Craig S. "'Fleshly' versus Spirit Perspectives in Romans 8:5–8." 211–29 in *Paul: Jew, Greek, and Roman.* Edited by Stanley Porter. PAST 5. Leiden: Brill, 2008.

Keener, "Subordination." • Keener, Craig S. "Is Subordination within the Trinity Really Heresy? A Study of John 5:18 in Context." *TJ* n.s. 20 (1, 1999): 39–51.

Keener, "Tabernacle." • Keener, Craig S. "Tabernacle." 837–40 in *Dictionary of Biblical Imagery.* Edited by Leland Ryken, James C. Wilhoit, and Tremper Longman III. Downers Grove, IL: InterVarsity, 1998.

Keener, "Teaching Ministry." • Keener, Craig S. "A Spirit-Filled Teaching Ministry in Acts 19:9." 46–58 in *Trajectories in the Book of Acts: Essays in Honor of John Wesley Wyckoff.* Edited by Jordan May, Paul Alexander, and Robert G. Reid. Eugene, OR: Wipf & Stock, 2010.

Keener, "Tongues." • Keener, Craig S. "Why Does Luke Use Tongues as a Sign of the Spirit's Empowerment?" *JPT* 15 (2, 2007): 177–84.

Keener, "Transformation." • Keener, Craig S. "Transformation through Divine Vision in 1 John 3:2–6." *F&M* 23 (1, 2005): 13–22.

Keener, "Warfare." • Keener, Craig S. "Paul and Spiritual Warfare." 107–23 in *Paul's Missionary Methods in His Time and Ours.* Edited by Robert Plummer and John Mark Terry. Downers Grove, IL: IVP Academic, 2012.

Keener, "Worship." • Keener, Craig S. "The Tabernacle and Contextual Worship." *Asbury Journal* 67 (1, 2012): 127–38.

Keener and Carroll, "Introduction." • Keener, Craig S., and M. Daniel Carroll R., "Introduction." 1–4 in *Global Voices: Reading the Bible in the Majority World.* Edited by Craig Keener and M. Daniel Carroll R. Peabody, MA: Hendrickson, 2013.

Keener and Carroll, *Voices*. • Keener, Craig S., and M. Daniel Carroll R., eds. *Global Voices:*

Reading the Bible in the Majority World. Foreword by Edwin M. Yamauchi. Peabody, MA: Hendrickson, 2013.

Keener and Keener, *Impossible Love.* • Keener, Craig S., and Médine Moussounga Keener. *Impossible Love: The True Story of an African Civil War, Miracles, and Love against All Odds.* Grand Rapids: Chosen Books, 2016.

Keener and Usry, *Faith.* • Keener, Craig S., and Glenn Usry. *Defending Black Faith.* Downers Grove, IL: InterVarsity, 1997.

Keller, *Hammer.* • Keller, Mary. *The Hammer and the Flute: Women, Power, and Spirit Possession.* Baltimore: Johns Hopkins University Press, 2002.

Kelly, "Miracle." • Kelly, Stewart E. "Miracle, Method, and Metaphysics: Philosophy and the Quest for the Historical Jesus." *TJ* 29 n.s. (1, 2008): 45–63.

Kelly, *Peter.* • Kelly, J. N. D. *A Commentary on the Epistles of Peter and Jude.* Thornapple Commentaries. Grand Rapids: Baker, 1981.

Kelsey, *Healing.* • Kelsey, Morton T. *Healing and Christianity in Ancient Thought and Modern Times.* New York: Harper & Row, 1973.

Kemp, "Ravished." • Kemp, Simon. "'Ravished of a Fiend': Demonology and Medieval Madness." 67–78 in *Altered States of Consciousness and Mental Health: A Cross-Cultural Perspective.* Edited by Colleen A. Ward. CCRMS 12. Newbury Park, CA: Sage, 1989.

Kendall, *Fire.* • Kendall, R. T. *Holy Fire: A Balanced Biblical Look at the Holy Spirit's Work in Our Lives.* Lake Mary, FL: Charisma House, 2014.

Kennedy, "Criticism." • Kennedy, George. "Classical and Christian Source Criticism." 125–55 in *The Relationships among the Gospels: An Interdisciplinary Dialogue.* Edited by William O. Walker Jr. San Antonio: Trinity University Press, 1978.

Khai, *Cross.* • Khai, Chin Khua. *The Cross among Pagodas: A History of the Assemblies of God in Myanmar.* Baguio City, Philippines: APTS, 2003.

Khai, "Pentecostalism." • Khai, Chin Khua. "The Assemblies of God and Pentecostalism in Myanmar." 261–80 in *Asian and Pentecostal: The Charismatic Face of Christianity in Asia.* Edited by Allan Anderson and Edmond Tang. Foreword by Cecil M. Robeck. Regnum Studies in Mission, AJPSS 3. Oxford: Regnum; Baguio City: APTS Press, 2005.

Kidd, *Awakening.* • Kidd, Thomas S. *The Great Awakening: The Roots of Evangelical Christianity in Colonial America.* New Haven: Yale University Press, 2007.

Kidd, "Healing." • Kidd, Thomas S. "The Healing of Mercy Wheeler: Illness and Miracles among Early American Evangelicals." *WMQ* 63 (1, January 2006): 149–70.

Kidd and Hankins, *Baptists.* • Kidd, Thomas S., and Barry Hankins. *Baptists in America: A History.* Oxford: Oxford University Press, 2015.

Kiev, *Magic.* • Kiev, Ari, ed. *Magic, Faith, and Healing: Studies in Primitive Psychotherapy Today.* Introduction by Jerome D. Frank. New York: Free Press, 1964.

Kilgallen, *Commentary.* • Kilgallen, John J. *A Brief Commentary on the Acts of the Apostles.* New York: Paulist, 1988.

Kim, "Mission." • Kim, Sung Hwan. "The Holy Spirit's Mission in the Book of Acts: Its Repetition and Continuation." ThM thesis, Fuller School of World Mission, 1993.

Kim, "Reenchanted." • Kim, Sean C. "Reenchanted: Divine Healing in Korean Protestantism." 267–85 in *Global Pentecostal and Charismatic Healing.* Edited by Candy Gunther Brown. Foreword by Harvey Cox. Oxford: Oxford University Press, 2011.

Kimball, "Learning." • Kimball, Solon T. "Learning a New Culture." 182–92 in *Crossing Cultural Boundaries: The Anthropological Experience.* Edited by Solon T. Kimball and James B. Watson. San Francisco: Chandler, 1972.

King, *Disfellowshiped.* • King, Gerald W. *Disfellowshiped: Pentecostal Responses to Fundamentalism in the United States, 1906–1943.* Eugene, OR: Wipf & Stock, 2011.

King, *Moving Mountains.* • King, Paul L. *Moving Mountains: Lessons in Bold Faith from Great Evangelical Leaders.* Grand Rapids: Chosen, 2004.

King, *Only Believe.* • King, Paul L. *Only Believe: Examining the Origin and Development of Classic and Contemporary Word of Faith Theologies.* Tulsa: Word & Spirit Press, 2008.

Kingsbury, *Christology.* • Kingsbury, Jack Dean. *The Christology of Mark's Gospel.* Philadelphia: Fortress, 1983.

Kinnear, *Tide.* • Kinnear, Angus. *Against the Tide: The Story of Watchman Nee.* Wheaton, IL: Tyndale House, 1978.

Kitchen, "Background." • Kitchen, Kenneth A. "Some Egyptian Background to the Old Testament." *TynBul* 5 (16, 1960): 4–18.

Kitchen, *Orient.* • Kitchen, Kenneth A. *Ancient Orient and the Old Testament.* Downers Grove, IL: InterVarsity Press, 1968.

Kitchen, *Reliability.* • Kitchen, Kenneth A. *On the Reliability of the Old Testament.* Grand Rapids: Eerdmans, 2003.

Klauck, *Context.* • Klauck, Hans-Josef. *The Religious Context of Early Christianity: A Guide to Graeco-Roman Religions.* Translated by Brian McNeil. Minneapolis: Fortress, 2003.

Klaus, "Mission." • Klaus, Byron D. "The Mission of the Church." 567–95 in *Systematic Theology: A Pentecostal Perspective.* Edited by Stanley M. Horton. Springfield, MO: Logion, 1994.

Klausner, *Jesus to Paul.* • Klausner, Joseph. *From Jesus to Paul.* Translated by W. Stinespring. Foreword by Sidney Hoenig. London: Macmillan, 1943. Repr., New York: Menorah, 1979.

Klein, Blomberg, and Hubbard, *Introduction.* • Klein, William W., Craig L. Blomberg, and Robert L. Hubbard Jr. *Introduction to Biblical Interpretation.* Dallas: Word, 1993.

Klein, Blomberg, and Hubbard, *Introduction*². • Klein, William W., Craig L. Blomberg, and Robert L. Hubbard Jr., *Introduction to Biblical Interpretation.* Rev. ed. Nashville: Nelson, 2004.

Klutz, *Exorcism Stories.* • Klutz, Todd. *The Exorcism Stories in Luke-Acts: A Sociostylistic Reading.* SNTSMS 129. Cambridge: Cambridge University Press, 2004.

Knapstad, "Power." • Knapstad, Bård Løkken. "Show Us the Power! A Study of the Influence of Miracles on the Conversion Process from Islam to Christianity in an Indonesian Context." ThM thesis, Norwegian Lutheran School of Theology, 2005.

Koch, *Zulus.* • Koch, Kurt E. *God among the Zulus.* Translated by Justin Michell and Waldemar Engelbrecht. Natal, RSA: Mission Kwa Sizabanu, 1981.

Koenig, *Medicine.* • Koenig, Harold G. *Medicine, Religion, and Health: Where Science and Spirituality Meet.* Templeton Science and Religion Series. West Conshohocken, PA: Templeton Foundation Press, 2008.

Koester, "Brown and Martyn." • Koester, Craig R. "R. E. Brown and J. L. Martyn: Johannine Studies in Retrospect." *Biblical Theology Bulletin* 21 (2, 1991): 51–55.

Koester, "Spectrum." • Koester, Craig R. "The Spectrum of Johannine Readers." 5–19 in *"What Is John?" Readers and Reading of the Fourth Gospel.* Edited by Fernando F. Segovia. SBLSymS 3. Atlanta: Scholars Press, 1996.

Koester, *Symbolism.* • Koester, Craig R. *Symbolism in the Fourth Gospel: Meaning, Mystery, Community.* Minneapolis: Fortress, 1995.

Koestler, "Kepler." • Koestler, Arthur. "Kepler and the Psychology of Discovery." 49–57 in *The Logic of Personal Knowledge: Essays Presented to Michael Polanyi on His Seventieth Birthday, 11 March 1961.* London: Routledge & Kegan Paul, 1961.

Koschorke, Ludwig, and Delgado, *History.* • Koschorke, Klaus, Frieder Ludwig, and Mariano Delgado, eds., with Roland Spliesgart. *A History of Christianity in Asia, Africa, and Latin America, 1450–1990: A Documentary Sourcebook.* Grand Rapids: Eerdmans, 2007.

Köstenberger, Schreiner, and Baldwin, *Women.* • Köstenberger, Andreas J., Thomas R. Schreiner, and H. Scott Baldwin, eds. *Women in the Church: A Fresh Analysis of 1 Timothy 2:9–15.* Grand Rapids: Baker, 1995.

Kraft, *Worldview.* • Kraft, Charles H. *Worldview for Christian Witness.* Pasadena: William Carey Library, 2008.

Kraft, "Worldviews." • Kraft, Charles. "Shifting Worldviews, Sifting Attitudes." 57–68 in *Power Encounters among Christians in the Western World*. Edited by Kevin Springer, with an introduction and afterword by John Wimber. San Francisco: Harper & Row, 1988.

Kraftchick, "Πάθη." • Kraftchick, Steven J. "Πάθη in Paul: The Emotional Logic of 'Original Argument.'" 39–68 in *Paul and Pathos*. Edited by Thomas H. Olbricht and Jerry L. Sumney. SBLSymS 16. Atlanta: SBL, 2001.

Krause, "Support." • Krause, Neal. "Church-Based Social Support and Mortality." *JGPSSS* 61 (3, 2006): S140–46.

Kraut et al., "Association." • Kraut, Allen, Samuel Melamed, et al. "Association of Self-Reported Religiosity and Mortality in Industrial Employees: The CORDIS Study." *SSMed* 58 (3, 2004): 595–602.

Kraybill, *Cult and Commerce*. • Kraybill, J. Nelson. *Imperial Cult and Commerce in John's Apocalypse*. JSNTSup 132. Sheffield, UK: Sheffield Academic, 1996.

Krentz, *Method*. • Krentz, Edgar. *The Historical-Critical Method*. Philadelphia: Fortress, 1975.

Kruger, *Question*. • Kruger, Michael J. *The Question of Canon: Challenging the Status Quo in the New Testament Debate*. Downers Grove, IL: IVP Academic, 2013.

Kugel, *Bible*. • Kugel, James L. *How to Read the Bible: A Guide to Scripture, Then and Now*. New York: Free Press, 2007.

Kugel and Greer, *Interpretation*. • Kugel, James L., and Rowan A. Greer. *Early Biblical Interpretation*. LEC 3. Philadelphia: Westminster, 1986.

Kuhn, *Structure*. • Kuhn, Thomas S. *The Structure of Scientific Revolutions*. 2nd ed. Chicago: University of Chicago Press, 1970.

Kurz, *Reading Luke-Acts*. • Kurz, William S. *Reading Luke-Acts: Dynamics of Biblical Narrative*. Louisville: Westminster John Knox, 1993.

Küster, "Kontextualisierung." • Küster, Volker. "Von der Kontextualisierung zur Glokalisierung: Interkulturelle Theologie und postkoloniale Kritik." *Theologische Literaturzeitung* 134 (3, 2009): 261–78.

Kwon, *1 Corinthians 1–4*. • Kwon, Oh-Young. *1 Corinthians 1–4: Reconstructing Its Social and Rhetorical Situation and Re-Reading It Cross-Culturally for Korean-Confucian Christians Today*. Eugene, OR: Wipf & Stock, 2010.

Kydd, *Healing*. • Kydd, Ronald A. N. *Healing through the Centuries: Models for Understanding*. Peabody, MA: Hendrickson, 1998.

Kyle, *Last Days*. • Kyle, Richard. *The Last Days Are Here Again: A History of the End Times*. Grand Rapids: Baker, 1998.

Kysar, "Gospel." • Kysar, Robert. "John, the Gospel of." 3:912–31 in *Anchor Bible Dictionary*. 6 vols. Edited by David Noel Freedman. New York: Doubleday, 1992.

Kysar, *John*. • Kysar, Robert. *John*. Augsburg Commentary on the New Testament. Minneapolis: Augsburg Publishing House, 1986.

Lachs, *Commentary*. • Lachs, Samuel Tobias. *A Rabbinic Commentary on the New Testament: The Gospels of Matthew, Mark, and Luke*. Hoboken, NJ: Ktav; New York: Anti-Defamation League of B'Nai B'Rith, 1987.

Ladd, *Bultmann*. • Ladd, George Eldon. *Rudolf Bultmann*. Chicago: InterVarsity, 1964.

Ladd, *Theology*. • Ladd, George Eldon. *A Theology of the New Testament*. Grand Rapids: Eerdmans, 1974.

Ladd, *Young Church*. • Ladd, George Eldon. *The Young Church*. Nashville: Abingdon, 1964.

Lagerwerf, *Witchcraft*. • Lagerwerf, Leny. *Witchcraft, Sorcery and Spirit Possession: Pastoral Responses in Africa*. Gweru, Zimbabwe: Mambo Press, 1987.

Laing, "Face." • Laing, Mark. "The Changing Face of Mission: Implications for the Southern Shift in Christianity." *Missiology* 34 (2, April 2006): 165–77.

Laistner, *Historians*. • Laistner, M. L. W. *The Greater Roman Historians*. Berkeley: University of California Press; London: Cambridge University Press, 1947.

Lalitha, "Feminism." • Lalitha, Jayachitra. "Postcolonial Feminism, the Bible and Native In-

Bibliography of Sources Cited

dian Women." 75–87 in *Evangelical Postcolonial Conversations: Global Awakenings in Theology and Practice.* Edited by Kay Higuera Smith, Jayachitra Lalitha, and L. Daniel Hawk. Downers Grove, IL: IVP Academic, 2014.

Land, "Passion." • Land, Steven J. "A Passion for the Kingdom: Revisioning Pentecostal Spirituality." *JPT* 1 (1992): 19–46.

Land, *Pentecostal Spirituality*. • Land, Steven J. *Pentecostal Spirituality: A Passion for the Kingdom.* Sheffield: Sheffield Academic Press, 1994.

Landscape Survey. • *U.S. Religious Landscape Survey: Religious Beliefs and Practices—Diverse and Politically Relevant.* Washington, DC: Pew Forum on Religion and Public Life, June 2008. Online: http://religions.pewforum.org/pdf/report2-religious-landscape-study-full .pdf.

Lang, *Kunst*. • Lang, Manfred. *Die Kunst des christlichen Lebens: Rezeptionsästhetische Studien zum lukanischen Paulusbild.* ABIG 29. Lepizig: Evangelische Verlagsanstalt, 2008.

Langtry, "Probability." • Langtry, Bruce. "Hume, Probability, Lotteries, and Miracles." *HumSt* 16 (1, April 1990): 67–74.

LaPoorta, "Unity." • LaPoorta, Jappie. "Unity or Division." 151–69 in *The Globalization of Pentecostalism: A Religion Made to Travel.* Edited by Murray W. Dempster, Byron D. Klaus, and Douglas Petersen. Foreword by Russell P. Spittler. Carlisle: Paternoster; Oxford: Regnum, 1999.

Larkin, *Culture*. • Larkin, William J., Jr. *Culture and Biblical Hermeneutics: Interpreting and Applying the Authoritative Word in a Relativistic Age.* Grand Rapids: Baker, 1988.

Larsson, "Hellenisten und Urgemeinde." • Larsson, Edwin. "Die Hellenisten und die Urgemeinde." *NTS* 33 (2, 1987): 205–25.

LaSor, Hubbard, and Bush, *Survey*. • LaSor, William Sanford, David Allan Hubbard, and Frederic W. Bush. *Old Testament Survey: The Message, Form, and Background of the Old Testament.* 2nd ed. Grand Rapids: Eerdmans, 1996.

Le Cornu, *Acts*. • Le Cornu, Hilary, with Joseph Shulam. *A Commentary on the Jewish Roots of Acts.* 2 vols. Jerusalem: Academon, 2003.

Lederle, "Evidence." • Lederle, Henry I. "Initial Evidence and the Charismatic Movement: An Ecumenical Appraisal." 131–41 in *Initial Evidence: Historical and Biblical Perspectives on the Pentecostal Doctrine of Spirit Baptism.* Edited by Gary B. McGee. Peabody, MA: Hendrickson, 1991.

Lederle, *Treasures*. • Lederle, Henry I. *Treasures Old and New: Interpretations of "Spirit-Baptism" in the Charismatic Renewal Movement.* Peabody, MA: Hendrickson, 1988.

Lee, "Future." • Lee, Moonjang. "Future of Global Christianity." 104–5 in *Atlas of Global Christianity, 1910–2010.* Edited by Todd M. Johnson and Kenneth R. Ross. Managing editor, Sandra S. K. Lee. Edinburgh: Center for the Study of Global Christianity, 2009.

Lee, "Korean Pentecost." • Lee, Young-Hoon. "Korean Pentecost: The Great Revival of 1907." *AJPS* 4 (1, 2001): 73–83.

Lee, "Nationalism." • Lee, Jae Won. "Paul, Nation, and Nationalism: A Korean Postcolonial Perspective." 223–35 in *The Colonized Apostle: Paul through Postcolonial Eyes.* Edited by Christopher D. Stanley. Paul in Critical Contexts (series). Minneapolis: Fortress, 2011.

LeMarquand, "Readings." • LeMarquand, Grant. "African Readings of Paul." 488–503 in *The Blackwell Companion to Paul.* Edited by Stephen Westerholm. Malden, MA, Oxford: Blackwell, 2011.

Lenski, *Acts*. • Lenski, R. C. H. *The Interpretation of the Acts of the Apostles.* Columbus, OH: Lutheran Book Concern, 1934. Repr., Minneapolis: Augsburg, 1961.

Lentricchia, *After New Criticism*. • Lentricchia, Frank. *After the New Criticism.* Chicago: University of Chicago Press, 1980.

Leon, *Jews of Rome*. • Leon, Harry J. *The Jews of Ancient Rome.* Morris Loeb Series. Philadelphia: Jewish Publication Society of America, 1960.

425

Lesslie, *Angels.* • Lesslie, Robert D. *Angels in the ER: Inspiring True Stories from an Emergency Room Doctor.* Eugene, OR: Harvest House, 2008.

Leung Lai, *'I'-Window.* • Leung Lai, Barbara M. *Through the 'I'-Window: The Inner Life of Characters in the Hebrew Bible.* Hebrew Bible Monographs 34. Sheffield: Sheffield Phoenix, 2011.

Levine, "Disease." • Levine, A.-J. "The Disease of Postcolonial New Testament Studies and the Hermeneutics of Healing." *Journal of Feminist Studies in Religion* 20 (1, 2004): 91–99.

Levine, "Synagogue." • Levine, Lee I. "The Second Temple Synagogue: The Formative Years." 7–31 in *The Synagogue in Late Antiquity.* Edited by Lee I. Levine. Philadelphia: American Schools of Oriental Research, 1986.

Levinson, "Introduction." • Levinson, Bernard M. "Introduction." 1–14 in *Theory and Method in Biblical and Cuneiform Law: Revision, Interpolation and Development.* Edited by Bernard M. Levinson. JSOTSup 181. Sheffield: Sheffield Academic Press, 1994.

Levy, Krey, and Ryan, *Romans.* • Levy, Ian Christopher, Philip D. W. Krey, and Thomas Ryan. *The Letter to the Romans.* The Bible in Medieval Tradition. Grand Rapids: Eerdmans, 2013.

Lewis, *Ecstatic Religion.* • Lewis, I. [Ioan] M. *Ecstatic Religion: An Anthropological Study of Spirit Possession and Shamanism.* Pelican Anthropology Library. Middlesex: Penguin, 1971.

Lewis, "Epistemology." • Lewis, Paul W. "Towards a Pentecostal Epistemology: The Role of Experience in Pentecostal Hermeneutics." *Spirit & Church* 2 (1, 2000): 95–125.

Lewis, "Spirits and Sex War." • Lewis, I. M. "Correspondence: Spirits and the Sex War." *Man* n.s. 2 (4, December 1967): 626–28.

Libby, "Theseus." • Libby, Brigitte B. "Forgetful Theseus and Mindful Aeneas in Catullus 64 and *Aeneid* 4." 65–88 in *Memory in Ancient Rome and Early Christianity.* Edited by Karl Galinsky. Oxford: Oxford University Press, 2016.

Licona, "Biographies." • Licona, Michael R. "Using Plutarch's Biographies to Help Resolve Differences in Parallel Gospel Accounts." Paper presented in the New Testament Backgrounds section at the Evangelical Theological Society, Baltimore, November 21, 2013.

Licona, *Differences.* • Licona, Michael R. *Why Are There Differences in the Gospels?* New York: Oxford University Press, 2016.

Licona, *Resurrection.* • Licona, Michael R. *The Resurrection of Jesus: A New Historiographical Approach.* Downers Grove, IL: InterVarsity; Nottingham, UK: Apollos, 2010.

Licona and Van der Watt, "Historians and Miracles." • Licona, Michael R., and Jan G. Van der Watt. "Historians and Miracles: The Principle of Analogy and Antecedent Probability Reconsidered." *HTS/TS* 65 (1, 2009): article 129, 6 pages. http://www.hts.org.za.

Liefeld, "Preacher." • Liefeld, Walter L. "The Wandering Preacher as a Social Figure in the Roman Empire." PhD dissertation, Columbia University, 1967.

Lienhardt, "Death." • Lienhardt, Godfrey. "The Situation of Death: An Aspect of Anuak Philosophy." *AnthrQ* 35 (2, April 1962): 74–85.

Lightfoot, *Acts.* • Lightfoot, J. B. *The Acts of the Apostles: A Newly Discovered Commentary.* Vol. 1 of The Lightfoot Legacy Set. Edited by Ben Witherington III and Todd D. Still. Downers Grove, IL: IVP Academic, 2014.

Lightfoot, *Commentary.* • Lightfoot, John. *A Commentary on the New Testament from the Talmud and Hebraica, Matthew—I Corinthians.* 4 vols. Grand Rapids: Baker, 1979.

Lines, "Readings." • Lines, Kevin P. "Exegetical and Extispicic Readings of the Bible in Turkana, Kenya, and North America." *Asbury Journal* 66 (1, 2011): 65–94.

Littlejohn and Foss, *Encyclopedia.* • Littlejohn, Stephen W., and Karen A. Foss. *Encyclopedia of Communication Theory.* Los Angeles: Sage, 2009.

Littlejohn and Foss, *Theories.* • Littlejohn, Stephen W., and Karen A. Foss. *Theories of Human Communication.* Long Grove, IL: Waveland Press, 2011.

Livingston, *Pentateuch.* • Livingston, G. Herbert. *The Pentateuch in Its Cultural Environment.* Grand Rapids: Baker, 1974.

Llewellyn, "Events." • Llewellyn, Russ. "Religious and Spiritual Miracle Events in Real-Life Experience." 241–63 in *Religious and Spiritual Events*. Vol. 1 in *Miracles: God, Science, and Psychology in the Paranormal*. Edited by J. Harold Ellens. Westport, CT: London: Praeger, 2008.

Llewellyn-Jones, *Tortoise*. • Llewellyn-Jones, Lloyd. *Aphrodite's Tortoise: The Veiled Woman of Ancient Greece*. Swansea: The Classical Press of Wales, 2003.

Lloyd-Jones, *Christianity*. • Lloyd-Jones, Martyn. *Authentic Christianity*. Studies in the Book of Acts 1. Wheaton, IL: Crossway, 2000.

Long, "Allegory." • Long, A. A. "Allegory in Philo and Etymology in Stoicism: A Plea for Drawing Distinctions." *Studia Philonica Annual* 9 (1997): 198–210.

Long and McMurry, *Collapse*. • Long, Zeb Bradford, and Douglas McMurry. *The Collapse of the Brass Heaven: Rebuilding Our Worldview to Embrace the Power of God*. Grand Rapids: Chosen, 1994.

Longenecker, *Exegesis*. • Longenecker, Richard N. *Biblical Exegesis in the Apostolic Period*. Grand Rapids: Eerdmans, 1975.

Longenecker, *Rhetoric*. • Longenecker, Bruce W. *Rhetoric at the Boundaries: The Art and Theology of the New Testament Chain-Link Transitions*. Waco, TX: Baylor University Press, 2005.

Longman, "Honest." • Longman, Tremper, III. "Getting Brutally Honest with God." *CT* April 2015: 56–59.

Lopez, *Apostle*. • Lopez, Davina C. *Apostle to the Conquered: Reimagining Paul's Mission*. Minneapolis: Fortress, 2008.

Lopez, "Visualizing." • Lopez, Davina C. "Visualizing Significant Otherness: Reimagining Paul(ine Studies) through Hybrid Lenses." 74–94 in *The Colonized Apostle: Paul through Postcolonial Eyes*. Edited by Christopher D. Stanley. Paul in Critical Contexts (series). Minneapolis: Fortress, 2011.

Loughlin, *Story*. • Loughlin, Gerard. *Telling God's Story: Bible, Church, and Narrative Theology*. Cambridge: Cambridge University Press, 1996.

Lovett, "Holiness-Pentecostalism." • Lovett, Leonard. "Black Holiness-Pentecostalism." 76–84 in *DPCM*.

Lozano and Roth, "Problem." • Lozano, Gilberto, and Federico A. Roth. "The Problem and Promise of Praxis in Postcolonial Criticism." 183–96 in *Evangelical Postcolonial Conversations: Global Awakenings in Theology and Practice*. Edited by Kay Higuera Smith, Jayachitra Lalitha, and L. Daniel Hawk. Downers Grove, IL: IVP Academic, 2014.

Lundin, *Disciplining Hermeneutics*. • Lundin, Roger. *Disciplining Hermeneutics: Interpretation in Christian Perspective*. Grand Rapids: Eerdmans, 1997.

Lung-Kwong, *Purpose*. • Lung-Kwong, Lo. *Paul's Purpose in Writing Romans: The Upbuilding of a Jewish and Gentile Christian Community in Rome*. Edited by Philip P. Chia and Yeo Khiok-khng. Jian Dao Dissertation Series 6. Bible and Literature 4. Hong Kong: Alliance Bible Seminary Press, 1998.

Lutgendorf et al., "Participation." • Lutgendorf, Susan K., Daniel Russell, Philip Ullrich, Tamara B. Harris, and Robert Wallace. "Religious Participation, Interleukin–6, and Mortality in Older Adults." *HealthPsy* 23 (5, 2004): 465–75.

Lyons, "Fourth Wave." • Lyons, John. "The Fourth Wave and the Approaching Millennium: Some Problems with Charismatic Hermeneutics." *Anvil* 15 (3, 1998): 169–80.

Ma, "Encounter." • Ma, Julie C. "'A Close Encounter with the Transcendental': Proclamation and Manifestation in Pentecostal Worship in Asian Context." 127–45 in *Asian Church and God's Mission: Studies Presented in the International Symposium on Asian Mission in Manila, January 2002*. Edited by Wonsuk Ma and Julie C. Ma. Manila: OMF Literature; West Caldwell, NJ: MWM, 2003.

Ma, "Eschatology." • Ma, Wonsuk. "Pentecostal Eschatology: What Happened When the Wave Hit the West End of the Ocean." *AJPS* 12 (1, January 2009): 95–112.

Ma, "Shift." • Ma, Wonsuk. "A Global Shift of World Christianity and Pentecostalism." 62–70 in *The Many Faces of Global Pentecostalism*. Edited by Harold D. Hunter and Neil Ormerod. Cleveland, TN: CPT Press, 2013.

Ma, *Spirit*. • Ma, Julie C. *When the Spirit Meets the Spirits: Pentecostal Ministry among the Kankana-ey Tribe in the Philippines*. SICHC 118. Frankfurt: Peter Lang, Wien, 2000.

Ma, "Studies." • Ma, Wonsuk. "Biblical Studies in the Pentecostal Tradition: Yesterday, Today, and Tomorrow." 52–69 in *The Globalization of Pentecostalism: A Religion Made to Travel*. Edited by Murray W. Dempster, Byron D. Klaus, and Douglas Petersen. Foreword by Russell P. Spittler. Carlisle, UK: Paternoster; Oxford: Regnum, 1999.

Ma, "Women." • Ma, Julie. "Asian Women and Pentecostal Ministry." 129–46 in *Asian and Pentecostal: The Charismatic Face of Christianity in Asia*. Edited by Allan Anderson and Edmond Tang. Foreword by Cecil M. Robeck. RStMiss, AJPSS 3. Oxford: Regnum; Baguio City, Philippines: APTS, 2005.

MacArthur, *Fire*. • MacArthur, John. *Strange Fire: The Danger of Offending the Holy Spirit with Counterfeit Worship*. Nashville: Thomas Nelson, 2013.

Macchia, "Babel." • Macchia, Frank D. "Babel and the Tongues of Pentecost—Reversal or Fulfilment? A Theological Perspective." 34–51 in *Speaking in Tongues: Multi-disciplinary Perspectives*. Edited by Mark J. Cartledge. SPCI. Waynesboro, GA, and Bletchley, Milton Keynes, UK: Paternoster, 2006.

Macchia, "Spirit and Text." • Macchia, Frank D. "The Spirit and the Text: Recent Trends in Pentecostal Hermeneutics." *Spirit & Church* 2 (1, 2000): 53–65.

Macchia, "Spirit of Lamb." • Macchia, Frank D. "The Spirit of the Lamb: A Reflection on the Pneumatology of Revelation." 214–20 in *But These Are Written . . . : Essays on Johannine Literature in Honor of Professor Benny C. Aker*. Edited by Craig S. Keener, Jeremy S. Crenshaw, and Jordan Daniel May. Eugene, OR: Pickwick, 2014.

Macchia, *Spirituality*. • Macchia, Frank D. *Spirituality and Social Liberation: The Message of the Blumhardts in the Light of Wuerttemberg Pietism*. Pietist and Wesleyan Studies. Metuchen, NJ: Scarecrow, 1993.

Maccini, *Testimony*. • Maccini, Robert Gordon. *Her Testimony Is True: Women as Witnesses according to John*. JSNTSup 125. Sheffield, UK: Sheffield Academic, 1996.

MacDonald, *Theology of Samaritans*. • MacDonald, John. *The Theology of the Samaritans*. Philadelphia: Westminster, 1964.

Maclean and Aitken, "Introduction." • Maclean, Jennifer K. Berenson, and Ellen Bradshaw Aitken. "Introduction." xil–xcii in *Flavius Philostratus: Heroikos*. Translated and edited by Jennifer K. Berenson Maclean and Ellen Bradshaw Aitken. SBL Writings from the Greco-Roman World, 1. Volume editor: Jackson P. Hershbell. Atlanta: Society of Biblical Literature, 2001.

MacMullen, "Women in Public." • MacMullen, Ramsay. "Women in Public in the Roman Empire." *Historia* 29 (1980): 209–18.

MacNutt, *Healing*. • MacNutt, Francis. *Healing*. Notre Dame, IN: Ave Maria, 1974.

Maggay, "Issues." • Maggay, Melba Padilla. "Early Protestant Missionary Efforts in the Philippines: Some Intercultural Issues." 29–41 in *Asian Church and God's Mission: Studies Presented in the International Symposium on Asian Mission in Manila, January 2002*. Edited by Wonsuk Ma and Julie C. Ma. Manila: OMF Literature; West Caldwell, NJ: MWM, 2003.

Magrassi, *Praying the Bible*. • Magrassi, Mariano. *Praying the Bible: An Introduction to Lectio Divina*. Collegeville, MN: Liturgical Press, 1998.

Malherbe, "Theorists." • Malherbe, Abraham J. "Ancient Epistolary Theorists." *Ohio Journal of Religious Studies* 5 (2, 1977): 3–77.

Malina, *Anthropology*. • Malina, Bruce J. *The New Testament World: Insights from Cultural Anthropology*. Atlanta: John Knox, 1981.

Malina, "Reading Theory Perspective." • Malina, Bruce J. "Reading Theory Perspective: Reading Luke-Acts." 3–23 in *The Social World of Luke-Acts: Models for Interpretation.* Edited by Jerome H. Neyrey. Peabody, MA: Hendrickson, 1991.

Malina, *Windows*. • Malina, Bruce J. *Windows on the World of Jesus: Time Travel to Ancient Judea.* Louisville: Westminster John Knox, 1993.

Malina and Pilch, *Acts*. • Malina, Bruce J., and John J. Pilch. *Social-Science Commentary on the Book of Acts.* Minneapolis: Fortress, 2008.

Malina and Pilch, *Letters*. • Malina, Bruce J., and John J. Pilch. *Social-Science Commentary on the Letters of Paul.* Minneapolis: Fortress, 2006.

Mandryk, *Operation World*. • Mandryk, Jason. *Operation World.* 7th ed. Colorado Springs: Biblica, 2010.

Manson, "Life of Jesus." • Manson, T. W. "The Life of Jesus: Some Tendencies in Present-day Research." 211–21 in *The Background of the New Testament and Its Eschatology: Essays in Honour of Charles Harold Dodd.* Edited by W. D. Davies and D. Daube. Cambridge: Cambridge University Press, 1964.

Maquet, "Shaman." • Maquet, Jacques. "Introduction: Scholar and Shaman." 1–6 in *Ecstasy and Healing in Nepal: An Ethnopsychiatric Study of Tamang Shamanism* by Larry Peters. Malibu: Undena Publications, 1981.

Margenau, "Laws." • Margenau, Henry. "The Laws of Nature Are Created by God." 57–63 in *Cosmos, Bios, and Theos: Scientists Reflect on Science, God, and the Origins of the Universe, Life, and* Homo Sapiens. Edited by Henry Margenau and Roy Abraham Varghese. La Salle, IL: Open Court, 1992.

Marguerat, *Actes*. • Marguerat, Daniel. *Les Actes des apôtres (1–12).* CNT, 2e série, 5 A. Geneva: Labor et Fides, 2007.

Marguerat, "Enigma of Closing." • Marguerat, Daniel. "The Enigma of the Silent Closing of Acts (28:16–31)." 284–304 in *Jesus and the Heritage of Israel: Luke's Narrative Claim upon Israel's Legacy.* Edited by David P. Moessner. Luke the Interpreter of Israel 1. Harrisburg, PA: Trinity Press International, 1999.

Marguerat, *Histoire*. • Marguerat, Daniel. *La première histoire du christianisme (les Actes des apôtres).* LD 180. Paris: Cerf, 1999.

Marguerat, *Historian*. • Marguerat, Daniel. *The First Christian Historian: Writing the "Acts of the Apostles."* Translated by Ken McKinney, Gregory J. Laughery, and Richard Bauckham. SNTSMS 121. Cambridge: Cambridge University Press, 2002.

Marshall, *Beyond Bible*. • Marshall, I. Howard. *Beyond the Bible: Moving from Scripture to Theology.* With essays by Kevin J. Vanhoozer and Stanley E. Porter. Grand Rapids: Baker Academic, 2004.

Marshall, *Blood*. • Marshall, Paul A. *Their Blood Cries Out: The Worldwide Tragedy of Modern Christians Who Are Dying for Their Faith.* Dallas: Word, 1997.

Marshall, *Enmity*. • Marshall, Peter. *Enmity in Corinth: Social Conventions in Paul's Relations with the Corinthians.* WUNT 2.23. Tübingen: Mohr Siebeck, 1987.

Marshall, *Historian and Theologian*. • Marshall, I. Howard. *Luke: Historian and Theologian.* Exeter, UK: Paternoster, 1970.

Marshall, "Luke as Theologian." • Marshall, I. Howard. "Luke as Theologian." 4:402–3 in *ABD.*

Marshall, *Origins*. • Marshall, I. Howard. *The Origins of New Testament Christology.* 2nd ed. Downers Grove, IL: InterVarsity, 1990.

Marshall, "Significance of Pentecost." • Marshall, I. Howard. "The Significance of Pentecost." *SJT* 30 (4, 1977): 347–69.

Marshall, Gilbert, and Shea, *Persecuted*. • Marshall, Paul, Lela Gilbert, and Nina Shea. *Persecuted: The Global Assault on Christians.* Foreword by Eric Metaxas. Afterword by Archbishop Charles J. Chaput. Nashville: Thomas Nelson, 2013.

Marshall and Shea, *Silenced*. • Marshall, Paul, and Nina Shea. *Silenced: How Apostasy and Blasphemy Codes Are Choking Freedom Worldwide.* New York: Oxford University Press, 2011.

Martell-Otero, "Liberating News." • Martell-Otero, Loida I. "Liberating News: An Emerging U.S. Hispanic/Latina Soteriology of the Crossroads." PhD dissertation, Fordham University Department of Theology, 2004.

Martell-Otero, "Satos." • Martell-Otero, Loida I. "Of Satos and Saints: Salvation from the Periphery." 7–33 in *Perspectivas*. HTIOPS 4, Summer 2001. Edited by Renata Furst-Lambert.

Martin, *Acts.* • Martin, Francis, ed., in collaboration with Evan Smith. *Acts.* ACCS: New Testament 5. Downers Grove, IL: InterVarsity, 2006.

Martin, *Bede.* • Martin, Lawrence T., ed. and trans. *Venerable Bede: Commentary on the Acts of the Apostles.* Kalamazoo, MI: Cistercian, 1989.

Martin, "Hearing." • Martin, Lee Roy. "Hearing the Voice of God: Pentecostal Hermeneutics and the Book of Judges." 205–32 in *Pentecostal Hermeneutics: A Reader.* Edited by Lee Roy Martin. Leiden: Brill, 2013.

Martin, "Introduction." • Martin, Lee Roy. "Introduction to Pentecostal Hermeneutics." 1–9 in *Pentecostal Hermeneutics: A Reader.* Edited by Lee Roy Martin. Leiden: Brill, 2013.

Martin, "Psalm 63." • Martin, Lee Roy. "Psalm 63 and Pentecostal Spirituality: An Exercise in Affective Hermeneutics." 263–84 in *Pentecostal Hermeneutics: A Reader.* Edited by Lee Roy Martin. Leiden: Brill, 2013.

Martin, *Reader.* • Martin, Lee Roy, ed. *Pentecostal Hermeneutics: A Reader.* Leiden: Brill, 2013.

Martin, "Renewal." • Martin, Francis. "The Charismatic Renewal and Biblical Hermeneutics." 1–37 in *Theological Reflections on the Charismatic Renewal.* Edited by John C. Haughey. Ann Arbor: Servant, 1978.

Martin, *Slavery.* • Martin, Dale B. *Slavery as Salvation: The Metaphor of Slavery in Pauline Christianity.* New Haven: Yale University Press, 1990.

Martin, "Spirit and Flesh." • Martin, Francis. "Spirit and Flesh in the Doing of Theology." Paper presented at the 15th annual meeting of the Society for Pentecostal Studies, 1985.

Martin, "Voice of Emotion." • Martin, Troy W. "The Voice of Emotion: Paul's Pathetic Persuasion (Gal 4:12–20)." 181–202 in *Paul and Pathos.* Edited by Thomas H. Olbricht and Jerry L. Sumney. SBLSymS 16. Atlanta: SBL, 2001.

Martínez-Taboas, "Seizures." • Martínez-Taboas, Alfonso. "Psychogenic Seizures in an Espiritismo Context: The Role of Culturally Sensitive Psychotherapy." *PsycTRPT* 42 (1, Spring 2005): 6–13.

Martyn, *Galatians.* • Martyn, J. Louis. *Galatians.* AB 33A. New Haven: Yale University Press, 1997.

Martyn, "Glimpses." • Martyn, J. Louis. "Glimpses into the History of the Johannine Community." 149–76 in *L'Évangile de Jean: Sources, rédaction, théologie.* Edited by M. De Jonge. Bibliotheca Ephemeridum Theologicarum Lovaniensium 45. Gembloux: J. Duculot; Leuven: University Press, 1977.

Martyn, *Theology.* • Martyn, J. Louis. *History and Theology in the Fourth Gospel.* Nashville: Abingdon, 1968.

Matthews and Clark, *Faith Factor.* • Matthews, Dale A., with Connie Clark. *The Faith Factor: Proof of the Healing Power of Prayer.* New York: Viking Penguin, 1998.

Maxwell, "Audience." • Maxwell, Kathy R. "The Role of the Audience in Ancient Narrative: Acts as a Case Study." *ResQ* 48 (3, 2006): 171–80.

Maxwell, "Witches." • Maxwell, David. "Witches, Prophets, and Avenging Spirits: The Second Christian Movement in North-East Zimbabwe." *JRelAf* 25 (3, 1995): 309–39.

May, *Witnesses.* • May, Jordan Daniel. *Global Witnesses to Pentecost: The Testimony of "Other Tongues."* Cleveland, TN: CPT Press, 2013.

Mayers, *Christianity Confronts Culture.* • Mayers, Marvin K. *Christianity Confronts Culture: A Strategy for Crosscultural Evangelism.* Grand Rapids: Zondervan, 1987.

Mayrargue, "Expansion." • Mayrargue, Cédric. "The Expansion of Pentecostalism in Benin: Individual Rationales and Transnational Dynamics." 274–92 in *Between Babel and Pente-*

cost: Transnational Pentecostalism in Africa and Latin America. Edited by André Corten and Ruth Marshall-Fratani. Bloomington, Indianapolis: Indiana University Press, 2001.

Mbiti, *Religions.* • Mbiti, John S. *African Religions and Philosophies.* Garden City, NY: Doubleday, 1970.

McCain and Keener, *Understanding and Applying.* • McCain, Danny, and Craig Keener. *Understanding and Applying the Scriptures.* Bukuru, Nigeria: Africa Christian Textbooks, 2003.

McClenon, *Events.* • McClenon, James. *Wondrous Events: Foundations of Religious Belief.* Philadelphia: University of Pennsylvania Press, 1994.

McClenon and Nooney, "Anomalous Experiences." • McClenon, James, and Jennifer Nooney. "Anomalous Experiences Reported by Field Anthropologists: Evaluating Theories Regarding Religion." *Anthropology of Consciousness* 13 (2, 2002): 46–60.

McClymond and McDermott, *Theology of Edwards.* • McClymond, Michael J., and Gerald R. McDermott. *The Theology of Jonathan Edwards.* New York: Oxford University Press, 2012.

McConnell, *Different Gospel.* • McConnell, D. R. *A Different Gospel: A Historical and Biblical Analysis of the Modern Faith Movement.* Peabody, MA: Hendrickson, 1988.

McDonald, *Canon.* • McDonald, Lee Martin. *The Biblical Canon: Its Origin, Transmission, and Authority.* Peabody, MA: Hendrickson, 2007.

McDonald and Sanders, *Debate.* • McDonald, Lee Martin, and James A. Sanders, eds., *The Canon Debate.* Peabody, MA: Hendrickson, 2002.

McDonnell and Montague, *Initiation.* • McDonnell, Kilian, and George T. Montague. *Christian Initiation and Baptism in the Holy Spirit: Evidence from the First Eight Centuries.* Collegeville, MN: Liturgical Press, 1991.

McEntyre, *Phrase.* • McEntyre, Marilyn Chandler. *What's in a Phrase? Pausing Where Scripture Gives You Pause.* Grand Rapids: Eerdmans, 2014.

McGee, "Calcutta Revival." • McGee, Gary B. "The Calcutta Revival of 1907 and the Reformulation of Charles F. Parham's 'Bible Evidence' Doctrine." *AJPS* 6 (1, 2003): 123–43.

McGee, "Hermeneutics." • McGee, Gary B. "Early Pentecostal Hermeneutics: Tongues as Evidence in the Book of Acts." 96–118 in *Initial Evidence: Historical and Biblical Perspectives on the Pentecostal Doctrine of Spirit Baptism.* Edited by Gary B. McGee. Peabody, MA: Hendrickson, 1991.

McGee, "Logic." • McGee, Gary B. "Taking the Logic 'a Little Further': Late Nineteenth-Century References to the Gift of Tongues in Mission-Related Literature and Their Influence on Early Pentecostalism." *AJPS* 9 (1, 2006): 99–125.

McGee, "Miracles." • McGee, Gary B. "Miracles." 252–54 in *Encyclopedia of Mission and Missionaries.* Edited by Jonathan J. Bonk. New York: Routledge, 2007.

McGee, *Miracles.* • McGee, Gary B. *Miracles, Missions, and American Pentecostalism.* AmSocMissS 45. Maryknoll, NY: Orbis, 2010.

McGee, "Miracles and Mission." • McGee, Gary B. "Miracles and Mission Revisited." *IBMR* 25 (October 2001): 146–56.

McGee, *People of Spirit.* • McGee, Gary B. *People of the Spirit: The Assemblies of God.* Springfield, MO: Gospel, 2004.

McGee, "Possessions." • McGee, Daniel B. "Sharing Possessions: A Study in Biblical Ethics." 163–78 in *With Steadfast Purpose: Essays on Acts in Honor of Henry Jackson Flanders, Jr.* Edited by Naymond H. Keathley. Waco: Baylor University Press, 1990.

McGee, "Radical Strategy." • McGee, Gary B. "The Radical Strategy in Modern Mission: The Linkage of Paranormal Phenomena with Evangelism." 69–95 in *The Holy Spirit and Mission Dynamics.* Edited by C. Douglas McConnell. Evangelical Missiological Society Series 5. Pasadena: William Carey, 1997.

McGee, "Regions Beyond." • McGee, Gary B. "To the Regions Beyond: The Global Expansion of Pentecostalism." 69–95 in *The Century of the Holy Spirit: 100 Years of Pentecostal and*

Charismatic Renewal, 1901–2001. Edited by Vinson Synan. Nashville: Thomas Nelson, 2001.

McGee, "Shortcut." • McGee, Gary B. "Shortcut to Language Preparation? Radical Evangelicals, Missions, and the Gift of Tongues." *IBMR* 25 (July 2001): 118–23.

McGee, "Strategies." • McGee, Gary B. "Strategies for Global Mission." 203–24 in *Called and Empowered: Global Mission in Pentecostal Perspective.* Edited by Murray A. Dempster, Byron D. Klaus, and Douglas Petersen. Peabody, MA: Hendrickson, 1991.

McGee, "Strategy." • McGee, Gary B. "The Radical Strategy." 47–59 in *Signs and Wonders in Ministry Today.* Edited by Benny C. Aker and Gary B. McGee. Foreword by Thomas E. Trask. Springfield, MO: Gospel, 1996.

McGrath, *Universe.* • McGrath, Alister E. *A Fine-Tuned Universe: The Quest for God in Science and Theology.* Louisville: John Knox, 2009.

McGrew, "Argument." • McGrew, Timothy. "The Argument from Miracles: A Cumulative Case for the Resurrection of Jesus of Nazareth." 593–662 in *The Blackwell Companion to Natural Theology.* Edited by J. P. Moreland and William Lane Craig. Malden, MA: Blackwell, 2009.

Mchami, "Possession." • Mchami, R. E. K. "Demon Possession and Exorcism in Mark 1:21–28." *AfThJ* 24 (1, 2001): 17–37.

McInerny, *Miracles.* • McInerny, Ralph M. *Miracles: A Catholic View.* Huntington, IN: Our Sunday Visitor Publishing Division, 1986.

McKay, "Veil." • McKay, John W. "When the Veil Is Taken Away: The Impact of Prophetic Experience on Biblical Interpretation." 57–80 in *Pentecostal Hermeneutics: A Reader.* Edited by Lee Roy Martin. Leiden: Brill, 2013.

McKenzie, "Signs." • McKenzie, John L. "Signs and Power: The New Testament Presentation of Miracles." *ChicSt* 3 (1, Spring 1964): 5–18.

McKim, *Guide.* • McKim, Donald K., ed. *A Guide to Contemporary Hermeneutics: Major Trends in Biblical Interpretation.* Grand Rapids: Eerdmans, 1986.

McKnight and Malbon, "Introduction." • McKnight, Edgar V., and Elizabeth Struthers Malbon. "Introduction." 15–26 in *The New Literary Criticism and the New Testament.* Edited by Edgar V. McKnight and Elizabeth Struthers Malbon. Valley Forge, PA: Trinity Press International; Sheffield, UK: JSOT Press, 1994.

McLaughlin, *Ethics.* • McLaughlin, Raymond W. *The Ethics of Persuasive Preaching.* Grand Rapids: Baker, 1979.

McNamara, "Nature." • McNamara, Kevin. "The Nature and Recognition of Miracles." *ITQ* 27 (1960): 294–322.

McNaughton, *Blacksmiths.* • McNaughton, Patrick R. *The Mande Blacksmiths: Knowledge, Power, and Art in West Africa.* Bloomington: Indiana University Press, 1988.

McQueen, *Joel and Spirit.* • McQueen, Larry R. *Joel and the Spirit: The Cry of a Prophetic Hermeneutic.* Cleveland, TN: CPT, 2009.

McQuilkin, *Understanding.* • McQuilkin, Robertson. *Understanding and Applying the Bible.* Rev. ed. Chicago: Moody, 2009.

Meagher, "Pentecost Spirit." • Meagher, P. M. "Pentecost Spirit: To Witness." *Vidyajyoti* 62 (4, 1998): 273–79.

Mendels, "Empires." • Mendels, Doron. "The Five Empires: A Note on a Propagandistic Topos." *American Journal of Philology* 102 (3, 1981): 330–37.

Mensah, "Basis." • Mensah, Felix Augustine. "The Spiritual Basis of Health and Illness in Africa." 171–80 in *Health Knowledge and Belief Systems in Africa.* Edited by Toyin Falola and Matthew M. Heaton. Durham, NC: Carolina Academic Press, 2008.

Menzies, *Anointed.* • Menzies, William W. *Anointed to Serve: The Story of the Assemblies of God.* Springfield, MO: Gospel, 1971.

Menzies, "Bandwagon." • Menzies, Robert P. "Jumping Off the Postmodern Bandwagon." *Pneuma* 16 (1994): 115–20.

Menzies, *Empowered.* • Menzies, Robert P. *Empowered for Witness: The Spirit in Luke-Acts.* London: T&T Clark, 2004.

Menzies, "Methodology." • Menzies, William W. "The Methodology of Pentecostal Theology: An Essay on Hermeneutics." 1–14 in *Essays on Apostolic Themes: Studies in Honor of Howard M. Ervin.* Edited by Paul Elbert. Peabody, MA: Hendrickson, 1985.

Menzies, "Paradigm." • Menzies, Robert P. "Acts 2.17–21: A Paradigm for Pentecostal Mission." *JPT* 17 (2, 2008): 200–218.

Menzies, "Revelator." • Menzies, Robert P. "Was John the Revelator Pentecostal?" 221–34 in *But These Are Written . . . : Essays on Johannine Literature in Honor of Professor Benny C. Aker.* Edited by Craig S. Keener, Jeremy S. Crenshaw, and Jordan Daniel May. Eugene, OR: Pickwick, 2014.

Menzies, "Tongues." • Menzies, Glen. "Tongues as 'The Initial Physical Sign' of Spirit Baptism in the Thought of D. W. Kerr." *Pneuma* 20 (2, Fall 1998): 175–89.

Menzies and Anderson, "Eschatological Diversity." • Menzies, Glen, and Gordon L. Anderson. "D. W. Kerr and Eschatological Diversity in the Assemblies of God." *Paraclete* (Winter 1993): 8–16.

Merrick, "Tracing." • Merrick, Teri R. "Tracing the Metanarrative of Colonialism and Its Legacy." 108–20 in *Evangelical Postcolonial Conversations: Global Awakenings in Theology and Practice.* Edited by Kay Higuera Smith, Jayachitra Lalitha, and L. Daniel Hawk. Downers Grove, IL: IVP Academic, 2014.

Merrick, Garrett, and Gundry, *Views.* • Merrick, J., Stephen M. Garrett, and Stanley N. Gundry, eds. *Five Views on Biblical Inerrancy.* Counterpoints. Grand Rapids: Zondervan, 2013.

Merz, "Witch." • Merz, Johannes. "'I Am a Witch in the Holy Spirit': Rupture and Continuity of Witchcraft Beliefs in African Christianity." *Missiology* 36 (2, April 2008): 201–17.

Metaxas, *Miracles.* • Metaxas, Eric. *Miracles: What They Are, Why They Happen, and How They Can Change Your Life.* New York: Dutton, 2014.

Meyer, "Deed." • Meyer, Ben F. "Appointed Deed, Appointed Doer: Jesus and the Scriptures." 155–76 in *Authenticating the Activities of Jesus.* Edited by Bruce Chilton and Craig A. Evans. NTTS 28.2. Leiden: Brill, 1999.

Meyer, *Realism.* • Meyer, Ben F. *Critical Realism and the New Testament.* PrTMS 17. Allison Park, PA: Pickwick, 1989.

Meyers, *Exodus.* • Meyers, Carol. *Exodus.* Cambridge: Cambridge University Press, 2005.

Michaels, *Gospel of John.* • Michaels, J. Ramsey. *The Gospel of John.* NICNT. Grand Rapids: Eerdmans, 2010.

Mickelsen, *Interpreting the Bible.* • Mickelsen, A. Berkeley. *Interpreting the Bible.* Grand Rapids: Eerdmans, 1963.

Míguez Bonino, "Acts 2." • Míguez Bonino, José. "Acts 2:1–42: A Latin American Perspective." 161–65 in *Return to Babel: Global Perspectives on the Bible.* Edited by John R. Levison and Priscilla Pope-Levison. Louisville: Westminster John Knox, 1999.

Milazzo, "Sermone." • Milazzo, Vincenza. "'Etsi imperitus sermone . . .': Girolamo e i solecismi di Paolo nei commentari alle epistole paoline." *Annali di storia dell'esegesi* 12 (2, 1995): 261–77.

Miller, *Empowered for Mission.* • Miller, Denzil R. *Empowered for Global Mission: A Missionary Look at the Book of Acts.* Foreword by John York. [Springfield, Mo.:] Life Publishers International, 2005.

Miller, *Tongues Revisited.* • Miller, Denzil R. *Missionary Tongues Revisited: More Than Evidence; Recapturing Luke's Missional Perspective on Speaking in Tongues.* Springfield, MO: PneumaLife, 2014.

Miller and Yamamori, *Pentecostalism.* • Miller, Donald E., and Tetsunao Yamamori. *Global Pentecostalism: The New Face of Christian Social Engagement.* Berkeley: University of California Press, 2007.

Minogue, "Religion." • Minogue, Kenneth. "Religion, Reason and Conflict in the Twenty-first Century." *NatInt* (Summer 2003): 127–32.

Miskov, *Life on Wings.* • Miskov, Jennifer A. *Life on Wings: The Forgotten Life and Theology of Carrie Judd Montgomery (1858–1946).* Cleveland, TN: CPT Press, 2012.

Mitchell, "Accommodation." • Mitchell, Margaret M. "Pauline Accommodation and 'Condescension' (συγκατάβασις). 1 Cor 9:19–23 and the History of Influence." 197–214 in *Paul Beyond the Judaism/Hellenism Divide.* Edited by Troels Engberg-Pedersen. Louisville: Westminster John Knox, 2001.

Mittelstadt, *Reading.* • Mittelstadt, Martin William. *Reading Luke-Acts in the Pentecostal Tradition.* Cleveland, TN: CPT Press, 2010.

Moberly, "Hermeneutics." • Moberly, R. Walter L. "Pneumatic Biblical Hermeneutics: A Response." 160–65 in *Spirit and Scripture: Exploring a Pneumatic Hermeneutic.* Edited by Kevin L. Spawn and Archie T. Wright. New York: Bloomsbury, 2012.

Moles, "Time." • Moles, John. "Time and Space Travel in Luke-Acts." 101–22 in *Engaging Early Christian History: Reading Acts in the Second Century.* Edited by Rubén R. Dupertuis and Todd Penner. Bristol, CT: Acumen, 2013.

Moltmann, "Blessing." • Moltmann, Jürgen. "The Blessing of Hope: The Theology of Hope and the Full Gospel of Life." *JPT* 13 (2, 2005): 147–61.

Montefiore, *Miracles.* • Montefiore, Hugh. *The Miracles of Jesus.* London: SPCK, 2005.

Montefiore and Loewe, *Anthology.* • Montefiore, C. G., and Herbert Loewe, eds. and trans. *A Rabbinic Anthology.* London: Macmillan, 1938. Reprinted with a new prolegomenon by Raphael Loewe. New York: Schocken, 1974.

Moore, "Approach." • Moore, Rickie D. "A Pentecostal Approach to Scripture." 11–13 in *Pentecostal Hermeneutics: A Reader.* Edited by Lee Roy Martin. Leiden: Brill, 2013.

Moore, "Cadaver." • Moore, Stephen D. "How Jesus' Risen Body Became a Cadaver." 269–82 in *The New Literary Criticism and the New Testament.* Edited by Edgar V. McKnight and Elizabeth Struthers Malbon. Valley Forge, PA: Trinity Press International, 1994; Sheffield: JSOT Press, 1994.

Moore, "Canon." • Moore, Rickie D. "Canon and Charisma in the Book of Deuteronomy." 15–31 in *Pentecostal Hermeneutics: A Reader.* Edited by Lee Roy Martin. Leiden: Brill, 2013.

Moore, "Empire." • Moore, Stephen D. "The Empire of God and the Postcolonial Era." *Reflections* 95 (1, 2008): 69–71.

Moore, "Fire of God." • Moore, Rickie D. "Deuteronomy and the Fire of God: A Critical Charismatic Interpretation." 109–30 in *Pentecostal Hermeneutics: A Reader. Pentecostal Hermeneutics: A Reader.* Edited by Lee Roy Martin. Leiden: Brill, 2013.

Moore, "God's Word." • Moore, Rick. "Approaching God's Word Biblically: A Pentecostal Perspective." Paper presented to the 19th Annual Meeting of the Society of Pentecostal Studies, Fresno, 1989.

Moore, *Judaism.* • Moore, George Foot. *Judaism in the First Centuries of the Christian Era.* 3 vols. Cambridge, MA: Harvard University Press, 1927–30. Repr., 3 vols. in 2. New York: Schocken, 1971.

Moore, "Manifesto." • Moore, Stephen D. "A Modest Manifesto for New Testament Literary Criticism: How to Interface with a Literary Studies Field That Is Post-Literary, Post-Theoretical, and Post-Methodological." *Biblical Interpretation* 15 (1, 2007): 1–25.

Moore, "Paul after Empire." • Moore, Stephen D. "Paul after Empire." 9–23 in *The Colonized Apostle: Paul through Postcolonial Eyes.* Edited by Christopher D. Stanley. Paul in Critical Contexts (series). Minneapolis: Fortress, 2011.

Moore, *Poststructuralism.* • Moore, Stephen D. *Poststructuralism and the New Testament: Derrida and Foucault at the Foot of the Cross.* Minneapolis: Fortress, 1994.

Moore, "Quakerism." • Moore, Rosemary. "Late Seventeenth-Century Quakerism and the Miraculous: A New Look at George Fox's 'Book of Miracles.'" 335–44 in *Signs, Wonders, Miracles: Representations of Divine Power in the Life of the Church. Papers Read at the*

2003 Summer Meeting and the 2004 Winter Meeting of the Ecclesiastical History Society. Edited by Kate Cooper and Jeremy Gregory. Rochester, NY: Boydell & Brewer, for the Ecclesiastical History Society, 2005.

Moore, "Turn." • Moore, Stephen D. "The 'Turn to Empire' in Biblical Studies." *Scuola Cattolica* 35 (1, 2012): 19–27.

Moore and Segovia, *Criticism*. • Moore, Stephen D., and Fernando F. Segovia. *Postcolonial Biblical Criticism: Interdisciplinary Intersections.* London: T&T Clark, 2005.

Moreland, *Triangle*. • Moreland, J. P. *Kingdom Triangle: Recover the Christian Mind, Renovate the Soul, Restore the Spirit's Power.* Grand Rapids: Zondervan, 2007.

Moreland and Issler, *Faith*. • Moreland, J. P., and Klaus Issler. *In Search of a Confident Faith: Overcoming Barriers to Trusting God.* Downers Grove, IL: InterVarsity, 2008.

Morsy, "Possession." • Morsy, Soheir A. "Spirit Possession in Egyptian Ethnomedicine: Origins, Comparison, and Historical Specificity." 189–208 in *Women's Medicine: The Zar-Bori Cult in Africa and Beyond.* Edited by I. M. Lewis, Ahmed Al-Safi, and Sayyid Hurreiz. Edinburgh: International African Institute, Edinburgh University Press, 1991.

Mott, "Science." • Mott, Nevill. "Science Will Never Give Us the Answers to All Our Questions." 64–69 in *Cosmos, Bios, and Theos: Scientists Reflect on Science, God, and the Origins of the Universe, Life, and* Homo Sapiens. Edited by Henry Margenau and Roy Abraham Varghese. La Salle, IL: Open Court, 1992.

Moule, *Mark*. • Moule, C. F. D. *The Gospel according to Mark.* Cambridge: Cambridge University Press, 1965.

Moule, *Messengers*. • Moule, C. F. D. *Christ's Messengers: Studies in the Acts of the Apostles.* New York: Association, 1957.

Mozley, *Lectures*. • Mozley, J. B. *Eight Lectures on Miracles Preached Before the University of Oxford in the Year MDCCCLXV, on the Foundation of the Late Rev. John Bampton.* 3rd ed. New York: Scribner, Welford & Co., 1872.

Mueller, *Barth*. • Mueller, David L. *Karl Barth.* Makers of the Modern Theological Mind. Waco: Word, 1972.

Mueller, "Temple Scroll." • Mueller, James R. "The Temple Scroll and the Gospel Divorce Texts." *RevQ* 10 (2, 1980): 247–56.

Mulholland, *Shaped*. • Mulholland, M. Robert, Jr., *Shaped by the Word: The Power of Scripture in Spiritual Formation.* Rev. ed. Nashville: Upper Room, 2000.

Mullin, *History*. • Mullin, Robert Bruce. *A Short World History of Christianity.* Louisville: Westminster John Knox, 2008.

Murray, *Splendor*. • Murray, Margaret A. *The Splendor That Was Egypt.* New York: Hawthorn, 1963.

Musick, House, and Williams, "Attendance and Mortality." • Musick, Marc A., James S. House, and David R. Williams. "Attendance at Religious Services and Mortality in a National Sample." *JHSocBeh* 45 (2, 2004): 198–213.

Mussies, "Greek." • Mussies, G. "Greek in Palestine and in the Diaspora." 1040–64 in *JPFC.*

Myers, "Obedience." • Myers, Jason Andrew. "Obedience across Romans: Tracing a Book Wide Theme and Illustrating Obedience with Greco-Roman Literature." PhD dissertation, Asbury Theological Seminary, 2015.

N, *I Am N*. • *I Am N: Inspiring Stories of Christians Facing Islamic Extremists.* Colorado Springs: David C. Cook, 2016.

Nadar, "Feminism." • Nadar, Sarojini. "'The Bible Says!': Feminism, Hermeneutics and Neo-Pentecostal Challenges." *Journal of Theology for Southern Africa* 134 (2009): 131–46.

Nasrallah, "Cities." • Nasrallah, Laura. "The Acts of the Apostles, Greek Cities, and Hadrian's Panhellenion." *JBL* 127 (3, 2008): 533–66.

Nebeker, "Spirit." • Nebeker, Gary L. "The Holy Spirit, Hermeneutics, and Transformation: From Present to Future Glory." *Evangelical Review of Theology* 27 (1, 2003): 47–54.

Neill, "Demons." • Neill, Stephen. "Demons, Demonology." 161–62 in *Concise Dictionary of* *the Christian World Mission.* Edited by Stephen Neill, Gerald H. Anderson, and John Goodwin. Nashville: Abingdon, 1971.

Neill, *History of Missions.* • Neill, Stephen. *A History of Christian Missions.* Harmondsworth, UK: Penguin, 1964.

Nelson, "Temple." • Nelson, Harold H. "The Egyptian Temple." 147–58 in *The Biblical Archaeologist Reader.* Edited by G. Ernest Wright and David Noel Freedman. Chicago: Quadrangle, 1961.

Neufeldt, "Legacy." • Neufeldt, Harvey G. "The Legacy of Jacob A. Loewen." *IBMR* 32 (3, July 2008): 141–48.

Newlands, "Ovid." • Newlands, Carole. "Select Ovid." *Classical World* 102 (2, 2009): 173–77.

Niang, *Faith.* • Niang, Aliou Cissé. *Faith and Freedom in Galatia and Senegal: The Apostle Paul, Colonists and Sending Gods.* BIS 97. Leiden: Brill, 2009.

Nichols, *History of Christianity.* • Nichols, James Hastings. *History of Christianity: 1650–1950; Secularization of the West.* New York: Ronald Press, 1956.

Nichols, *Shape.* • Nichols, Aidan. *The Shape of Catholic Theology: An Introduction to Its Sources, Principles, and History.* Collegeville, MN: Liturgical Press, 1991.

Nicholson, "Confidentiality." • Nicholson, John. "The Delivery and Confidentiality of Cicero's Letters." *CJ* 90 (1, 1994): 33–63.

Nicolls, "Laws." • Nicolls, William K. "Physical Laws and Physical Miracles." *ITQ* 27 (1960): 49–56.

Nienkirchen, "Visions." • Nienkirchen, Charles. "Conflicting Visions of the Past: The Prophetic Use of History in the Early American Pentecostal-Charismatic Movements." 119–33 in *Charismatic Christianity as a Global Culture.* Edited by Karla Poewe. SCR. Columbia: University of South Carolina Press, 1994.

Nineham, *Mark.* • Nineham, D. E. *Gospel of Saint Mark.* Baltimore: Penguin, 1963. Repr., Philadelphia: Westminster, 1977.

Noble, *Approach.* • Noble, Paul R. *The Canonical Approach: A Critical Reconstruction of the Hermeneutics of Brevard S. Childs.* Leiden: Brill, 1995.

Noel, "Fee." • Noel, B. T. "Gordon Fee and the Challenge to Pentecostal Hermeneutics: Thirty Years Later." *Pneuma* 26 (1, 2004): 60–80.

Noll, *History.* • Noll, Mark A. *A History of Christianity in the United States and Canada.* Grand Rapids: Eerdmans, 1992.

Noll, *Rise.* • Noll, Mark A. *The Rise of Evangelicalism: The Age of Edwards, Whitefield, and the Wesleys.* Vol. 1 in *A History of Evangelicalism: People Movements and Ideas in the English-Speaking World.* Downers Grove, IL: InterVarsity, 2003.

Noll, *Shape.* • Noll, Mark A. *The New Shape of World Christianity: How American Experience Reflects Global Faith.* Downers Grove, IL: IVP Academic, 2009.

Numbere, *Vision.* • Numbere, Nonyem E. *A Man and a Vision: A Biography of Apostle Geoffrey D. Numbere.* Diobu, Nigeria: Greater Evangelism Publications, 2008.

Nyunt, "Hesychasm." • Nyunt, Moe Moe. "*Hesychasm* Encounters *Lectio Divina*: An Intercultural Analysis of Eastern and Western Christian Contemplative Practices." *Asbury Journal* (70.1, 2015): 76–94.

Obeyesekere, "Sorcery." • Obeyesekere, Gananath. "Sorcery, Premeditated Murder, and the Canalization of Aggression in Sri Lanka." *Ethnology* 14 (1975): 1–24.

Oblau, "Healing." • Oblau, Gotthard. "Divine Healing and the Growth of Practical Christianity in China." 307–27 in *Global Pentecostal and Charismatic Healing.* Edited by Candy Gunther Brown. Foreword by Harvey Cox. Oxford: Oxford University Press, 2011.

O'Day, "John." • O'Day, Gail R. "The Gospel of John: Introduction, Commentary, and Reflections." 9:491–865 in *The New Interpreter's Bible.* 12 vols. Edited by Leander E. Keck. Nashville: Abingdon, 1995.

O'Day, *Revelation.* • O'Day, Gail R. *Revelation in the Fourth Gospel: Narrative Mode and Theological Claim.* Philadelphia: Fortress, 1986.

Odeberg, *Pharisaism.* • Odeberg, Hugo. *Pharisaism and Christianity.* Translated by J. M. Moe. St. Louis: Concordia, 1964.

Oduyoye, "Value." • Oduyoye, Mercy Amba. "The Value of African Religious Beliefs and Practices for Christian Theology." 109–16 in *African Theology en Route: Papers from the Pan-African Conference of Third World Theologians, December 17–23, 1977, Accra, Ghana.* Edited by Kofi Appiah-Kubi and Sergio Torres. Maryknoll, NY: Orbis, 1979.

Oesterley, *Liturgy.* • Oesterley, William Oscar Emil. *The Jewish Background of the Christian Liturgy.* Oxford: Clarendon, 1925.

Ogilbee and Riess, *Pilgrimage.* • Ogilbee, Mark, and Jana Riess. *American Pilgrimage: Sacred Journeys and Spiritual Destinations.* Brewster, MA: Paraclete, 2006.

Olapido, *Development.* • Olapido, Caleb Oluremi. *The Development of the Doctrine of the Holy Spirit in the African Indigenous Christian Movement.* New York: Peter Lang, 1996.

Olena, *Horton.* • Olena, Lois E., with Raymond L. Gannon. *Stanley M. Horton: Shaper of Pentecostal Theology.* Foreword by George O. Wood. Springfield, MO: Gospel Publishing House, 2009.

Oliverio, *Hermeneutics.* • Oliverio, L. William, Jr. *Theological Hermeneutics in the Classical Pentecostal Tradition: A Typological Account.* Global Pentecostal and Charismatic Studies 12. Leiden: Brill, 2012.

Oman et al., "Attendance." • Oman, Doug, John H. Kurata, et al. "Religious Attendance and Cause of Death over Thirty-one Years." *IntJPsyMed* 32 (1, 2002): 69–89.

Omenyo, "Healing." • Omenyo, Cephas N. "New Wine in an Old Bottle? Charismatic Healing in the Mainline Churches in Ghana." 231–49 in *Global Pentecostal and Charismatic Healing.* Edited by Candy Gunther Brown. Foreword by Harvey Cox. Oxford: Oxford University Press, 2011.

Opp, *Lord for Body.* • Opp, James. *The Lord for the Body: Religion, Medicine, and Protestant Faith Healing in Canada, 1880–1930.* Montreal: McGill-Queen's University Press, 2005.

Osborne, "Hermeneutics." • Osborne, Grant R. "Hermeneutics/Interpreting Paul." 388–97 in *DPL.*

Osborne, *Spiral.* • Osborne, Grant R. *The Hermeneutical Spiral: A Comprehensive Introduction to Biblical Interpretation.* Downers Grove, IL: InterVarsity, 1991.

Osler, "Revolution." • Osler, Margaret J. "That the Scientific Revolution Liberated Science from Religion." 90–98 in *Galileo Goes to Jail and Other Myths about Science and Religion.* Edited by Ronald L. Numbers. Cambridge, MA: Harvard University Press, 2009.

Oss, "Hermeneutics of Dispensationalism." • Oss, Douglas A. "The Hermeneutics of Dispensationalism within the Pentecostal Tradition." Paper at the Evangelical Theological Society, November 21, 1991.

Otte, "Treatment." • Otte, Richard. "Mackie's Treatment of Miracles." *IJPhilRel* 39 (3, 1996): 151–58.

Ouédraogo, "Pentecostalism." • Ouédraogo, Philippe. "Pentecostalism in Francophone West Africa: The Case of Burkina Faso." 162–68 in *The Many Faces of Global Pentecostalism.* Edited by Harold D. Hunter and Neil Ormerod. Cleveland, TN: CPT Press, 2013.

Packer, *Acts.* • Packer, J. W. *Acts of the Apostles.* CBC. Cambridge: Cambridge University Press, 1966.

Padilla, *Speeches.* • Padilla, Osvaldo. *The Speeches of Outsiders in Acts: Poetics, Theology, and Historiography.* SNTSMS 144. Cambridge: Cambridge University Press, 2008.

Paintner and Wynkoop, *Lectio Divina.* • Paintner, Christine Valters, and Lucy Wynkoop. *Lectio Divina: Contemplative Awakening and Awareness.* Mahwah, NJ: Paulist Press, 2008.

Palmer, *Hermeneutics.* • Palmer, Richard. *Hermeneutics: Interpretation Theory in Schleiermacher, Dilthey, Heidegger, and Gadamer.* Studies in Phenomenology and Existential Philosophy. Evanston: Northwestern University Press, 1969.

Pao, *Isaianic Exodus.* • Pao, David W. *Acts and the Isaianic New Exodus.* WUNT 2.130. Tübingen: Mohr Siebeck, 2000. Repr., Grand Rapids: Baker, 2002.

Park, *Healing*. • Park, Andrew Sung. *Racial Conflict and Healing: An Asian-American Theological Perspective.* Maryknoll, NY: Orbis, 1996.

Park, "Spirituality." • Park, Myung Soo. "Korean Pentecostal Spirituality as Manifested in the Testimonies of Members of Yoido Full Gospel Church." 43–67 in *David Yonggi Cho: A Close Look at His Theology and Ministry.* Edited by Wonsuk Ma, William W. Menzies, and Hyeon-sung Bae. AJPSS 1. Baguio City: APTS Press, Hansei University Press, 2004.

Parmentier, "Zungenreden." • Parmentier, Martin. "Das Zungenreden bei den Kirchenvätern." *Bijdr* 55 (4, 1994): 376–98.

Patte, *Global Bible Commentary*. • Patte, Daniel, ed. *Global Bible Commentary.* Nashville: Abingdon, 2004.

Patte, *Structural Exegesis*. • Patte, Daniel. *What Is Structural Exegesis?* Philadelphia: Fortress, 1976.

Pawlikowski, "Pharisees." • Pawlikowski, John T. "The Pharisees and Christianity." *BibT* 49 (1970): 47–53.

Pedraja, "*Testimonios*." • Pedraja, Luis G. "*Testimonios* and Popular Religion in Mainline North American Hispanic Protestantism." http://www.livedtheology.org/pdfs/Pedraja .pdf. Accessed February 6, 2009.

Penney, *Missionary Emphasis*. • Penney, John Michael. *The Missionary Emphasis of Lukan Pneumatology.* JPTSup 12. Sheffield, UK: Sheffield Academic, 1997.

Perkins, *Reading*. • Perkins, Pheme. *Reading the New Testament: An Introduction.* 2nd ed. New York: Paulist Press, 1988.

Perrin, *Bultmann*. • Perrin, Norman. *The Promise of Bultmann.* Philadelphia: Fortress, 1969.

Perrin, *Kingdom*. • Perrin, Norman. *The Kingdom of God in the Teaching of Jesus.* Philadelphia: Westminster, 1963.

Perrin, *Thomas and Tatian*. • Perrin, Nicholas. *Thomas and Tatian: The Relationship between the* Gospel of Thomas *and the* Diatessaron. SBL Academia Biblica 5. Atlanta: Society of Biblical Literature, 2002.

Perrot, "Lecture de la Bible." • Perrot, Charles. "La lecture de la Bible dans les synagogues au premier siècle de notre ère." *MaisD* 126 (1976): 24–41.

Peters, *Healing in Nepal*. • Peters, Larry. *Ecstasy and Healing in Nepal: An Ethnopsychiatric Study of Tamang Shamanism.* Malibu: Undena Publications, 1981.

Peterson, *Acts*. • Peterson, David. *The Acts of the Apostles.* PNTC. Grand Rapids: Eerdmans; Nottingham, UK: Apollos, 2009.

Pfeiffer, *Ras Shamra*. • Pfeiffer, Charles F. *Ras Shamra and the Bible.* Grand Rapids: Baker, 1962.

Phillips, "Miracles." • Phillips, D. Z. "Miracles and Open-Door Epistemology." *SJRS* 14 (1, 1993): 33–40.

Pierce, Groothuis, and Fee, *Discovering*. • Pierce, Ronald W., Rebecca Merrill Groothuis, and Gordon D. Fee, eds. *Discovering Biblical Equality: Complementarity without Hierarchy.* Downers Grove, IL: InterVarsity, 2004.

Pilch, *Dictionary*. • Pilch, John J. *The Cultural Dictionary of the Bible.* Collegeville, MN: Liturgical Press, 1999.

Pilch, "Disease." • Pilch, John J. "Disease." 135–40 in *The New Interpreter's Dictionary of the Bible.* 5 vols. Nashville: Abingdon, 2007.

Pilch, *Healing*. • Pilch, John J. *Healing in the New Testament: Insights from Medical and Mediterranean Anthropology.* Minneapolis: Fortress, 2000.

Pilch, "Sickness." • Pilch, John J. "Sickness and Healing in Luke-Acts." 181–209 in *The Social World of Luke-Acts: Models for Interpretation.* Edited by Jerome H. Neyrey. Peabody, MA: Hendrickson, 1991.

Pilch, *Visions*. • Pilch, John J. *Visions and Healing in the Acts of the Apostles: How the Early Believers Experienced God.* Collegeville, MN: Liturgical Press, 2004.

Piñero, "Mediterranean View." • Piñero, Antonio. "A Mediterranean View of Prophetic Inspiration: On the Concept of Inspiration in the *Liber antiquitatum biblicarum* by Pseudo-Philo." *MHR* 6 (1, 1991): 5–34.

Pinnock, "Foreword." • Pinnock, Clark H. "Foreword." vii–viii in *The Charismatic Theology of St. Luke* by Roger Stronstad. Peabody, MA: Hendrickson, 1984.

Pinnock, "Interpretation." • Pinnock, Clark H. "The Work of the Spirit in the Interpretation of Holy Scripture from the Perspective of a Charismatic Biblical Theologian." *JPT* 18 (2, 2009): 157–71.

Pinnock, "Spirit in Hermeneutics." • Pinnock, Clark H. "The Work of the Holy Spirit in Hermeneutics." *JPT* 2 (1993): 3–23.

Pinnock, "Work of Spirit." • Pinnock, Clark H. "The Work of the Spirit in the Interpretation of Holy Scripture from the Perspective of a Charismatic Biblical Theologian." 233–48 in *Pentecostal Hermeneutics: A Reader.* Edited by Lee Roy Martin. Leiden: Brill, 2013.

Piper, *Glory*. • Piper, John. *A Peculiar Glory: How the Christian Scriptures Reveal Their Complete Truthfulness.* Wheaton, IL: Crossway, 2016.

Piper and Grudem, *Recovering*. • Piper, John, and Wayne Grudem, eds. *Recovering Biblical Manhood and Womanhood: A Response to Evangelical Feminism.* Wheaton, IL: Crossway, 1991.

Pizzuto-Pomaco, "Shame." • Pizzuto-Pomaco, Julia. "From Shame to Honour: Mediterranean Women in Romans 16." PhD dissertation, University of St. Andrews, 2003.

Placher, *Mark*. • Placher, William C. *Mark.* BTCB. Louisville: Westminster John Knox, 2010.

Pobee, "Health." • Pobee, John S. "Health, Healing, and Religion: An African View." *IntRevMiss* 90 (356/357, January-April 2001): 55–64.

Poewe, *Religions*. • Poewe, Karla. *New Religions and the Nazis.* New York and London: Routledge, 2006.

Pogoloff, "Isocrates." • Pogoloff, Stephen M. "Isocrates and Contemporary Hermeneutics." 338–62 in *Persuasive Artistry: Studies in New Testament Rhetoric in Honor of George A. Kennedy.* Edited by Duane F. Watson. JSNTSup 50. Sheffield, UK: Sheffield Academic, 1991.

Poirier, "Authorial Intention." • Poirier, John C. "Authorial Intention as Old as the Hills." *Stone-Campbell Journal* 7 (2004): 59–72.

Poirier, "Critique." • Poirier, John C. "A Critique of Kenneth Archer's Hermeneutic of Scripture." Philosophy interest group paper presented at the 44th annual meeting of the Society for Pentecostal Studies, March 2015.

Poirier and Lewis, "Hermeneutics." • Poirier, John C., and B. Scott Lewis. "Pentecostal and Postmodernist Hermeneutics: A Critique of Three Conceits." *JPT* 15 (1, 2006): 3–21.

Poland, *Criticism*. • Poland, Lynn M. *Literary Criticism and Biblical Hermeneutics.* AARAS 48. Atlanta: Scholars Press, 1985.

Polanyi, *Science*. • Polanyi, Michael. *Science, Faith and Society.* Chicago: University of Chicago Press, 1964.

Polhill, *Acts*. • Polhill, John B. *Acts.* NAC 26. Nashville: Broadman, 1992.

Polkinghorne, *Science and Providence*. • Polkinghorne, John. *Science and Providence: God's Interaction with the World.* Boston: New Science Library, Shambhala, 1989.

Polkinghorne and Beale, *Questions*. • Polkinghorne, John, and Nicholas Beale. *Questions of Truth: Fifty-one Responses to Questions about God, Science, and Belief.* Louisville: Westminster John Knox, 2009.

Pollmann and Elliott, "Galatians." • Pollmann, Karla, and Mark W. Elliott. "Galatians in the Early Church: Five Case Studies." 40–61 in *Galatians and Christian Theology: Justification, the Gospel, and Ethics in Paul's Letter.* Edited by Mark W. Elliott et al. Grand Rapids: Baker Academic, 2014.

Poloma, *Assemblies*. • Poloma, Margaret M. *The Assemblies of God at the Crossroads: Charisma and Institutional Dilemmas.* Knoxville: University of Tennessee Press, 1989.

Poloma, *Mystics*. • Poloma, Margaret M. *Main Street Mystics: The Toronto Blessing and Reviving Pentecostalism.* Walnut Creek, CA: AltaMira, 2003.

Popper, *Myth of Framework*. • Popper, Karl R. *The Myth of the Framework: In Defense of Science and Rationality.* Edited by M. A. Notturno. London: Routledge, 1994.

Porter, "Comment(ary)ing on Acts." • Porter, Stanley E. Paper presented at the annual meeting of the SBL, Philadelphia, November 21, 2005.

Porter, "Hermeneutics." • Porter, Stanley E. "Hermeneutics, Biblical Interpretation, and Theology: Hunch, Holy Spirit, or Hard Work?" 97–127 in *Beyond the Bible: Moving from Scripture to Theology* by I. Howard Marshall, with essays by Kevin J. Vanhoozer and Stanley E. Porter. Grand Rapids: Baker Academic, 2004.

Porter, *Paul*. • Porter, Stanley E. *The Apostle Paul: His Life, Thought, and Letters.* Grand Rapids: Eerdmans, 2016.

Porter, Evans, and McDonald, *New Testament*. • Porter, Stanley E., Craig A. Evans, and Lee Martin McDonald, eds. *How We Got the New Testament: Text, Transmission, and Translation.* Grand Rapids: Baker Academic, 2013.

Poster, "Affections." • Poster, Carol. "The Affections of the Soul: *Pathos*, Protreptic, and Preaching in Hellenistic Thought." 23–37 in *Paul and Pathos.* Edited by Thomas H. Olbricht and Jerry L. Sumney. SBL Symposium Series 16. Atlanta: Society of Biblical Literature, 2001.

Pothen, "Missions." • Pothen, Abraham T. "Indigenous Cross-cultural Missions in India and Their Contribution to Church Growth: With Special Emphasis on Pentecostal-Charismatic Missions." PhD dissertation, Fuller Theological Seminary, 1990.

Powell, "Answers." • Powell, Mark Allan. "Old Answers to New Questions: Traditional Biblical Interpretation in Our Contemporary Context." Presentation to the biblical studies seminar, Asbury Theological Seminary, September 23, 2015.

Powell, "Readings." • Powell, Mark Allan. "Expected and Unexpected Readings of Matthew: What the Reader Knows." *ATJ* 48/2 (1993): 31–52.

Powers, "Daughters." • Powers, Janet Everts. "'Your Daughters Shall Prophesy': Pentecostal Hermeneutics and the Empowerment of Women." 313–37 in *Globalization of Pentecostalism: A Religion Made to Travel.* Edited by Murray W. Dempster, Byron D. Klaus, and Douglas Petersen. Foreword by Russell P. Spittler. Carlisle, UK: Paternoster; Oxford: Regnum, 1999.

Powers, "Recovering." • Powers, Janet Everts. "Recovering a Woman's Head with Prophetic Authority: A Pentecostal Interpretation of 1 Corinthians 11.3–16." *JPT* 10 (1, 2001): 11–37.

Powers, *Silencing*. • Powers, Kirstan. *The Silencing: How the Left Is Killing Free Speech.* Washington, DC: Regnery, 2015.

Prema, "Paradigm." • Prema, Sr. "Acts 2:17–21: A Paradigm for a Collaborative Mission." *Jeev* 34 (200, 2004): 122–36.

Prickett, *Origins of Narrative*. • Prickett, Stephen. *Origins of Narrative: The Romantic Appropriation of the Bible.* Cambridge: Cambridge University Press, 1996.

Prince, "Foreword." • Prince, Raymond. "Foreword." xi–xvi in *Case Studies in Spirit Possession.* Edited by Vincent Crapanzaro and Vivian Garrison. New York: John Wiley & Sons, 1977.

Prince, "Yoruba Psychiatry." • Prince, Raymond. "Indigenous Yoruba Psychiatry." 84–120 in *Magic, Faith, and Healing: Studies in Primitive Psychiatry Today.* Edited by Ari Kiev. Foreword by Jerome D. Frank. New York: Free Press, 1964.

Provan, Long, and Longman, *History*. • Provan, Iain, V. Philips Long, and Tremper Longman III. *A Biblical History of Israel.* Louisville: Westminster John Knox, 2003.

Punt, "Criticism." • Punt, Jeremy. "Postcolonial Biblical Criticism in South Africa: Some Mind and Road Mapping." *Neotestamentica* 37 (1, 2003): 59–85.

Punt, "Empire." • Punt, Jeremy. "Empire as Material Setting and Heuristic Grid for New Testament Interpretation: Comments on the Value of Postcolonial Criticism." *HTS/TS* 66 (1, 2010): 330, 7.

Purtill, "Proofs." • Purtill, Richard L. "Proofs of Miracles and Miracles as Proofs." *CSR* 6 (1, 1976): 39–51.

Putney, *Missionaries.* • Putney, Clifford. *Missionaries in Hawai'i: The Lives of Peter and Fanny Gulick, 1797–1883.* Amherst: University of Massachusetts, 2010.

Quast, "Community." • Quast, Kevin B. "Reexamining Johannine Community." *TJT* 5 (2, 1989): 293–95.

Qureshi, *Seeking.* • Qureshi, Nabeel. *Seeking Allah, Finding Jesus: A Devout Muslim Encounters Christianity.* Foreword by Lee Strobel. Grand Rapids: Zondervan, 2014.

Rabin, "L- with Imperative." • Rabin, C. "L- with Imperative (Gen. XXIII)." *JSS* 13 (1, 1968): 113–24.

Race, "Introduction." • Race, William H. "Introduction." 1–41 in vol. 1 of Pindar, *Odes.* Translated by William H. Race. 2 vols. LCL. Cambridge, MA: Harvard University Press, 1997.

Raharimanantsoa, *Mort.* • Raharimanantsoa, Mamy. *Mort et Espérance selon la Bible Hébraïque.* ConBOT 53. Stockholm: Almqvist & Wiksell, 2006.

Rainey, "Sacrifice"[1]. • Rainey, Anson F. "Sacrifice and Offerings." 5:194–211 in *The Zondervan Pictorial Encyclopedia of the Bible.* 5 vols. Edited by Merrill C. Tenney. Grand Rapids: Zondervan, 1975–76.

Rainey, "Sacrifice"[2]. • Rainey, Anson F. "Sacrifice and Offerings." 5:233–52 in *The Zondervan Encyclopedia of the Bible.* Rev. ed. 5 vols. Edited by Merrill C. Tenney and Moisés Silva. Grand Rapids: Zondervan, 2009.

Ramachandra, *Subverting.* • Ramachandra, Vinoth. *Subverting Global Myths: Theology and the Public Issues Shaping Our World.* Downers Grove, IL: InterVarsity, 2008.

Ramm, *Interpretation.* • Ramm, Bernard. *Protestant Biblical Interpretation: A Textbook of Hermeneutics.* 3rd rev. ed. Grand Rapids: Baker, 1970.

Ramsay, *Letters.* • Ramsay, William M. *The Letters to the Seven Churches of Asia.* London: Hodder & Stoughton, 1904. Repr., Grand Rapids: Baker, 1979.

Randa, Tandi. • Randa, Tandi. Personal correspondence, May 26, 2012; May 13, 2014.

Raschke, "Textuality." • Raschke, Carl A. "From Textuality to Scripture: The End of Theology as 'Writing.'" *Semeia* 40:39–52.

Reddish, *Revelation.* • Reddish, Mitchell G. *Revelation.* SHBC. Macon, GA: Smyth & Helwys, 2001.

Remus, *Healer.* • Remus, Harold. *Jesus as Healer.* UJT. Cambridge: Cambridge University Press, 1997.

Rensberger, *Faith.* • Rensberger, David. *Johannine Faith and Liberating Community.* Philadelphia: Westminster, 1988.

Reviv, "Elements." • Reviv, Hanoch. "Early Elements and Late Terminology in the Descriptions of the Non-Israelite Cities in the Bible." *IEJ* 27 (4, 1977): 189–96.

Reynolds, *Magic.* • Reynolds, Barrie. *Magic, Divination and Witchcraft among the Barotse of Northern Rhodesia.* Berkeley: University of California Press, 1963.

Richards, "Factors." • Richards, Wes. "An Examination of Common Factors in the Growth of Global Pentecostalism: Observed in South Korea, Nigeria, and Argentina." *JAM* 7 (1, March 2005): 85–106.

Rickman, *Dilthey.* • Rickman, Hans Peter. *Wilhelm Dilthey: Pioneer of the Human Studies.* Berkeley: University of California Press, 1979.

Rickman, "Introduction." • Rickman, Hans Peter. "General Introduction." 1–63 in *Pattern and Meaning in History: Thoughts on History and Society* by Wilhelm Dilthey. Edited by H. P. Rickman. New York: Harper & Brothers, 1962.

Ricoeur, *Essays.* • Ricoeur, Paul. *Essays on Biblical Interpretation.* Edited by Lewis S. Mudge. Philadelphia: Fortress, 1980.

Ricoeur, *Hermeneutics.* • Ricoeur, Paul. *Hermeneutics and the Human Sciences: Essays on Language, Action, and Interpretation.* Edited and translated by John B. Thompson. New York: Cambridge University Press, 1981.

Ricoeur, *Interpretation Theory.* • Ricoeur, Paul. *Interpretation Theory: Discourse and the Surplus of Meaning.* Fort Worth: Texas Christian University Press, 1976.

Ridderbos, *John.* • Ridderbos, Herman N. *The Gospel according to John: A Theological Commentary.* Translated by John Vriend. Grand Rapids: Eerdmans, 1997.

Ridderbos, *Speeches of Peter.* • Ridderbos, Herman N. *The Speeches of Peter in the Acts of the Apostles.* Tyndale New Testament Lecture, 1961. London: Tyndale, 1962.

Robeck, *Mission.* • Robeck, Cecil M., Jr. *The Azusa Street Mission and Revival: The Birth of the Global Pentecostal Movement.* Nashville: Thomas Nelson, 2006.

Robeck, "Seymour." • Robeck, Cecil M., Jr. "William J. Seymour and 'The Bible Evidence.'" 72–95 in *Initial Evidence: Historical and Biblical Perspectives on the Pentecostal Doctrine of Spirit Baptism.* Edited by Gary B. McGee. Peabody, MA: Hendrickson, 1991.

Robertson, *Lectio Divina.* • Robertson, Duncan. *Lectio Divina: The Medieval Experience of Reading.* Collegeville, MN: Liturgical Press, 2011.

Robinson, "Challenge." • Robinson, Bernard. "The Challenge of the Gospel Miracle Stories." *NBf* 60 (1979): 321–34.

Robinson, *Divine Healing.* • Robinson, James. *Divine Healing: The Years of Expansion, 1906–1930. Theological Variation in the Transatlantic World.* Eugene, OR: Pickwick, 2014.

Robinson, *Law.* • Robinson, O. F. *The Criminal Law of Ancient Rome.* London: Duckworth; Baltimore: Johns Hopkins University Press, 1995.

Robinson and Wall, *Called.* • Robinson, Anthony B., and Robert W. Wall. *Called to Be Church: The Book of Acts for a New Day.* Grand Rapids: Eerdmans, 2006.

Rollinson, "*Mythos* and *mimesis.*" • Rollinson, Philip. "*Mythos* and *mimesis* in Humanist Critical Theory." *CBull* 73 (2, 1997): 149–53.

Rorty, "Faces." • Rorty, Amélie Oksenberg. "The Two Faces of Stoicism: Rousseau and Freud." 243–70 in *The Emotions in Hellenistic Philosophy.* Edited by Juha Sihvola and Troels Engberg-Pedersen. TSHP 46. Dordrecht, Neth.: Kluwer Academic, 1998.

Roschke, "Healing." • Roschke, Ronald W. "Healing in Luke, Madagascar, and Elsewhere." *CurTM* 33 (6, December 2006): 459–71.

Rosen, "Psychopathology." • Rosen, George. "Psychopathology in the Social Process: Dance Frenzies, Demonic Possession, Revival Movements, and Similar So-called Psychic Epidemics. An Interpretation." 219–50 in *Possession and Exorcism.* Edited and with introductions by Brian P. Levack. Vol. 9 in *Articles on Witchcraft, Magic, and Demonology: A Twelve-Volume Anthology of Scholarly Articles.* New York: Garland, 1992. Reprinted from *BullHistMed* 36 (1962): 13–44.

Rosner, "Progress." • Rosner, Brian S. "The Progress of the Word." 215–34 in *Witness to the Gospel: The Theology of Acts.* Edited by I. Howard Marshall and David Peterson. Grand Rapids: Eerdmans, 1998.

Ross, *Holiness.* • Ross, Allen P. *Holiness to the Lord: A Guide to the Exposition of the Book of Leviticus.* Grand Rapids: Baker Academic, 2002.

Ross, "Preaching." • Ross, Kenneth R. "Preaching in Mainstream Christian Churches in Malawi: A Survey and Analysis." *JRelAf* 25 (1, February 1995): 3–24.

Rukundwa, "Theory." • Rukundwa, Lazare S. "Postcolonial Theory as a Hermeneutical Tool for Biblical Reading." *HTS/TS* 64 (1, 2008): 339–51.

Rundin, "Pozo Moro." • Rundin, John S. "Pozo Moro, Child Sacrifice, and the Greek Legendary Tradition." *JBL* 123 (3, 2004): 425–47.

Runesson, "Treasure." • Runesson, Anders. "Bringing Out of the Treasure What Is New and Old: Trajectories in New Testament Research Today." *Svensk Teologisk Kvartalskrift* 87 (1, 2011): 2–13.

Rüpke, *Religion.* • Rüpke, Jörg. *Religion: Antiquity and Its Legacy.* Ancients and Moderns. New York: Oxford University Press, 2013.

Russell, "Anointing." • Russell, Walt. "The Anointing with the Holy Spirit in Luke-Acts." *TJ* 7 (1, 1986): 47–63.

Russell and Winterbottom, *Criticism*. • Russell, D. A., and M. Winterbottom, *Ancient Literary Criticism: The Principal Texts in New Translations.* New York: Oxford University Press, 1972.

Safrai, "Relations." • Safrai, Shemuel. "Relations between the Diaspora and the Land of Israel." 184–215 in *JPFC*.

Safrai, "Synagogue." • Safrai, Shemuel. "The Synagogue." 908–44 in *JPFC*.

Salam, "Science." • Salam, Abdus. "Science and Religion: Reflections on Transcendence and Secularization." 93–104 in *Cosmos, Bios, and Theos: Scientists Reflect on Science, God, and the Origins of the Universe, Life, and* Homo Sapiens. Edited by Henry Margenau and Roy Abraham Varghese. La Salle, IL: Open Court, 1992.

Salmon, *Heals*. • Salmon, Elsie H. *He Heals Today, or A Healer's Case Book.* 2nd ed. Foreword by W. E. Sangster. The Drift, Evesham, Worcs.: Arthur James, 1951.

Samuel, "Mission." • Samuel, Simon. "Mission amidst Affluence and Affliction." *Doon Theological Journal* 5 (1, 2008): 21–42.

Samuel, *Reading*. • Samuel, Simon. *A Postcolonial Reading of Mark's Story of Jesus.* LNTS 340. London: T&T Clark, 2007.

Sanders, *Figure*. • Sanders, E. P. *The Historical Figure of Jesus.* New York: Penguin, 1993.

Sanders, *Jesus and Judaism*. • Sanders, E. P. *Jesus and Judaism.* Philadelphia: Fortress, 1985.

Sanders, *Jesus to Mishnah*. • Sanders, E. P. *Jewish Law from Jesus to the Mishnah: Five Studies.* London: SCM; Philadelphia: Trinity Press International, 1990.

Sanders, *John*. • Sanders, J. N. *A Commentary on the Gospel according to St. John.* Edited and completed by B. A. Mastin. Harper's New Testament Commentaries. New York: Harper & Row, 1968.

Sanders, *Margins*. • Sanders, Cheryl J. *Ministry at the Margins: The Prophetic Mission of Women, Youth and the Poor.* Downers Grove, IL: InterVarsity, 1997.

Sanders, "Nomism." • Sanders, E. P. "Covenantal Nomism Revisited." *JSQ* 16 (1, 2009): 25–55.

Sandmel, *Judaism*. • Sandmel, Samuel. *Judaism and Christian Beginnings.* New York: Oxford University Press, 1978.

Sanneh, *Disciples*. • Sanneh, Lamin. *Disciples of All Nations: Pillars of World Christianity.* New York: Oxford University Press, 2008.

Sanneh, *West African Christianity*. • Sanneh, Lamin. *West African Christianity: The Religious Impact.* Maryknoll, NY: Orbis, 1983.

Sanneh, *Whose Religion*. • Sanneh, Lamin. *Whose Religion Is Christianity? The Gospel beyond the West.* Grand Rapids: Eerdmans, 2003.

Sarna, *Exodus*. • Sarna, Nahum M. *Exploring Exodus: The Heritage of Biblical Israel.* New York: Schocken, 1986.

Satyavrata, "Globalization." • Satyavrata, Ivan. "The Globalization of Pentecostal Missions in the Twenty-First Century." JPHWMSM 4. Springfield, MO: Assemblies of God Theological Seminary, 2009.

Satyavrata, *Witness*. • Satyavrata, Ivan. *God Has Not Left Himself without a Witness.* Eugene, OR: Wipf & Stock, 2011.

Scharen, *Fieldwork*. • Scharen, Christian. *Fieldwork in Theology: Exploring the Social Context of God's Work in the World.* Grand Rapids: Baker Academic, 2015.

Scherberger, "Shaman." • Scherberger, Laura. "The Janus-Faced Shaman: The Role of Laughter in Sickness and Healing among the Makushi." *AnthHum* 30 (1, 2005): 55–69.

Schnabel, "Fads." • Schnabel, Eckhard J. "Fads and Common Sense: Reading Acts in the First Century and Reading Acts Today." *JETS* 54 (2, 2011): 251–78.

Schnabel, *Mission*. • Schnabel, Eckhard J. *Early Christian Mission.* 2 vols. Downers Grove, IL: InterVarsity; Leicester, UK: Apollos, 2004.

Schnabel, *Missionary*. • Schnabel, Eckhard J. *Paul the Missionary: Realities, Strategies and Methods.* Downers Grove, IL: InterVarsity; Leicester, UK: Apollos, 2008.

Schreiner, *Galatians*. • Schreiner, Thomas R. *Galatians.* Zondervan Exegetical Commentary on the New Testament. Grand Rapids: Zondervan, 2010.

Schubert, "Ehescheidung." • Schubert, Kurt. "Ehescheidung im Judentum zur Zeit Jesu." *TQ* 151 (1, 1971): 23–27.

Schweitzer, *Quest*. • Schweitzer, Albert. *The Quest of the Historical Jesus.* Translated by W. Montgomery. Introduction by James M. Robinson. New York: Macmillan, 1968.

Scott, "Horizon." • Scott, James M. "Luke's Geographical Horizon." 483–544 in *The Book of Acts in Its Graeco-Roman Setting.* Edited by David W. J. Gill and Conrad Gempf. Vol. 2 of *The Book of Acts in Its First Century Setting.* Edited by Bruce W. Winter. Grand Rapids: Eerdmans; Carlisle, UK: Paternoster, 1994.

Scott, "Pattern." • Scott, John Atwood. "The Pattern of the Tabernacle." PhD dissertation, University of Pennsylvania, 1965.

Searle, *Expression*. • Searle, John R. *Expression and Meaning: Studies in the Theory of Speech Acts.* New York: Cambridge, 1979.

Searle, *Speech Acts*. • Searle, John R. *Speech Acts: An Essay in the Philosophy of Language.* London: Cambridge University Press, 1969.

Searle and Vanderveken, *Foundations*. • Searle, John R., and Daniel Vanderveken. *Foundations of Illocutionary Logic.* New York: Cambridge University Press, 1984.

Sears and Wallace, "Spirituality." • Sears, Samuel F., and Robyn L. Wallace. "Spirituality, Coping, and Survival." 173–83 in *Biopsychosocial Perspectives on Transplantation.* Edited by J. R. Rodrigue. New York: Kluwer Academic/Plenum, 2001.

Sebald, "Witchcraft." • Sebald, Hans. "Franconian Witchcraft: The Demise of a Folk Magic." *AnthrQ* 53 (3, July 1980): 173–87.

Segovia, *Decolonizing*. • Segovia, Fernando F. *Decolonizing Biblical Studies: A View from the Margins.* Maryknoll, NY: Orbis, 2000.

Seung, *Semiotics*. • Seung, Hirsch T. K. *Semiotics and Thematics in Hermeneutics.* New York: Columbia University Press, 1982.

Sevrin, "Nicodemus Enigma." • Sevrin, Jean-Marie. "The Nicodemus Enigma: The Characterization and Function of an Ambiguous Actor of the Fourth Gospel." 357–69 in *Anti-Judaism and the Fourth Gospel: Papers of the Leuven Colloquium, 2000.* Edited by R. Bieringer, D. Pollefeyt, and F. Vandecasteele-Vanneuville. Assen: Royal Van Gorcum, 2001.

Sharp, "Philonism." • Sharp, J. R. "Philonism and the Eschatology of Hebrews: Another Look." *East Asia Journal of Theology* 2 (2, 1984): 289–98.

Shaw, *Awakening*. • Shaw, Mark. *Global Awakening: How Twentieth-Century Revivals Triggered a Christian Revolution.* Downers Grove, IL: IVP Academic, 2010.

Shelton, *Mighty in Deed*. • Shelton, James B. *Mighty in Word and Deed: The Role of the Holy Spirit in Luke-Acts.* Peabody, MA: Hendrickson, 1991.

Shepherd, "Targums." • Shepherd, Michael B. "Targums, the New Testament, and Biblical Theology of the Messiah." *JETS* 51 (1, 2008): 45–58.

Shishima, "Wholistic Nature." • Shishima, D. S. "The Wholistic Nature of African Traditional Medicine: The Tiv Experience." 119–26 in *Religion, Medicine and Healing.* Edited by Gbola Aderibigbe and Deji Ayegboyin. Lagos: Nigerian Association for the Study of Religions and Education, 1995.

Shogren, "Prophecy." • Shogren, Gary Steven. "Christian Prophecy and Canon in the Second Century: A Response to B. B. Warfield." *JETS* 40 (4, 1997): 609–26.

Shoko, *Religion*. • Shoko, Tabona. *Karanga Indigenous Religion in Zimbabwe: Health and Well-Being.* VitIndRel. Foreword by James L. Cox. Burlington, VT: Ashgate, 2007.

Shorter, *Witch Doctor*. • Shorter, Aylward. *Jesus and the Witch Doctor: An Approach to Healing and Wholeness.* Maryknoll, NY: Orbis, 1985.

Shortt, *Christianophobia*. • Shortt, Rupert. *Christianophobia: A Faith under Attack.* Grand Rapids: Eerdmans, 2012.

Shuler, *Genre.* • Shuler, Philip L. *A Genre for the Gospels: The Biographical Character of Matthew.* Philadelphia: Fortress, 1982.

Sider, *Christians.* • Sider, Ronald J. *Rich Christians in an Age of Hunger.* Foreword by Kenneth Kantzer. Dallas: Word, 1990.

Sider, *Cry Justice.* • Sider, Ronald J. *Cry Justice: The Bible on Hunger and Poverty.* New York: Paulist, 1980.

Sider, *Fed.* • Sider, Ronald J. *For They Shall Be Fed: Scripture Readings and Prayers for a Just World.* Dallas: Word, 1997.

Sider, "Historian." • Sider, Ronald J. "The Historian, the Miraculous, and the Post-Newtonian Man." *SJT* 25 (1972): 309–19.

Sider, "Methodology." • Sider, Ronald J. "Historical Methodology and Alleged Miracles: A Reply to Van Harvey." *FidHist* 3 (1, 1970): 22–40.

Sim, "Relevance Theoretic Approach." • Sim, Margaret Gavin. "A Relevance Theoretic Approach to the Particle ἵνα in Koine Greek." PhD dissertation, University of Edinburgh, 2006.

Simon, *Stephen and Hellenists.* • Simon, Marcel. *St Stephen and the Hellenists in the Primitive Church.* Haskell Lectures, 1956. New York: Longmans, Green, 1958.

Singleton, "Spirits." • Singleton, Michael. "Spirits and 'Spiritual Direction': The Pastoral Counseling of the Possessed." 471–78 in *Christianity in Independent Africa.* Edited by Edward Fasholé-Luke, Richard Gray, Adrian Hastings, and Godwin Tasie. Bloomington: Indiana University Press, 1978.

Smart, *Philosophers.* • Smart, Ninian. *Philosophers and Religious Truth.* 2nd ed. London: SCM, 1969.

Smart, *Philosophy of Religion.* • Smart, Ninian. *The Philosophy of Religion.* New York: Random House, 1970.

Smidt, *Evangelicals.* • Smidt, Corwin E. *American Evangelicals Today.* Lanham, MD: Rowman & Littlefield, 2013.

Smith, *Gnostic Origins.* • Smith, Carl B., II. *No Longer Jews: The Search for Gnostic Origins.* Peabody, MA: Hendrickson, 2004.

Smith, "Hope after Babel?" • Smith, David. "What Hope after Babel? Diversity and Community in Gen 11:1–9; Exod 1:1–14; Zeph 3:1–13; and Acts 2:1–13." *HBT* 18 (2, 1996): 169–91.

Smith, "Inc/arnation." • Smith, James K. A. "Limited Inc/arnation: Revisiting the Searle/Derrida Debate in Christian Context." 112–32 in *Hermeneutics at the Crossroads.* Edited by Kevin J. Vanhoozer, James K. A. Smith, and Bruce Ellis Benson. Bloomington: Indiana University Press, 2006.

Smith, *John.* • Smith, D. Moody. *John.* ANTC. Nashville: Abingdon, 1999.

Smith, *Thinking.* • Smith, James K. A. *Thinking in Tongues: Outline of a Pentecostal Philosophy.* Grand Rapids: Eerdmans, 2010.

Smith, "Tolerance." • Smith, Kathryn J. "From Evangelical Tolerance to Imperial Prejudice? Teaching Postcolonial Biblical Studies in a Westernized, Confessional Setting." *Christian Scholar's Review* 37 (4, 2008): 447–64.

Smith, "Understand." • Smith, Abraham. "'Do You Understand What You Are Reading?': A Literary Critical Reading of the Ethiopian (Kushite) Episode (Acts 8:26–40)." *JITC* 22 (1, 1994): 48–70.

Snell, "Science." • Snell, George D. "I Do Not See How Science Can Shed Light on the Origins of Design." 209–11 in *Cosmos, Bios, and Theos: Scientists Reflect on Science, God, and the Origins of the Universe, Life, and* Homo Sapiens. Edited by Henry Margenau and Roy Abraham Varghese. La Salle, IL: Open Court, 1992.

Soares Prabhu, "Reading." • Soares Prabhu, George M. "And There Was a Great Calm: A 'Dhvani' Reading of the Stilling of the Storm (Mk 4.35–41)." *BiBh* 5 (4, 1979): 295–308.

Solberg, *Church Undone.* • Solberg, Mary M., ed. *A Church Undone: Documents from the German Christian Faith Movement, 1932–1940.* Minneapolis: Fortress, 2015.

Solivan, *Spirit*. • Solivan, Samuel. *The Spirit, Pathos, and Liberation: Toward an Hispanic Pentecostal Theology.* JPTSup 14. Sheffield, UK: Sheffield Academic, 1998.

Sorabji, *Emotion*. • Sorabji, Richard. *Emotion and Peace of Mind: From Stoic Agitation to Christian Temptation.* Oxford: Oxford University Press, 2000.

Spawn, "Principle." • Spawn, Kevin L. "The Principle of Analogy and Biblical Interpretation in the Renewal Tradition." 46–72 in *Spirit and Scripture: Exploring a Pneumatic Hermeneutic.* Edited by Kevin L. Spawn and Archie T. Wright. New York: Bloomsbury, 2012.

Spawn and Wright, "Cultivating." • Spawn, Kevin L., and Archie T. Wright. "Cultivating a Pneumatic Hermeneutic." 192–98 in *Spirit and Scripture: Exploring a Pneumatic Hermeneutic.* Edited by Kevin L. Spawn and Archie T. Wright. New York: Bloomsbury, 2012.

Spawn and Wright, "Emergence." • Spawn, Kevin L., and Archie T. Wright. "The Emergence of a Pneumatic Hermeneutic in the Renewal Tradition." 3–22 in *Spirit and Scripture: Exploring a Pneumatic Hermeneutic.* Edited by Kevin L. Spawn and Archie T. Wright. New York: Bloomsbury, 2012.

Spawn and Wright, "Introduction." • Spawn, Kevin L., and Archie T. Wright. "Introduction." xvii–xviii in *Spirit and Scripture: Exploring a Pneumatic Hermeneutic.* Edited by Kevin L. Spawn and Archie T. Wright. New York: Bloomsbury, 2012.

Spawn and Wright, *Spirit and Scripture*. • Spawn, Kevin L., and Archie T. Wright, eds. *Spirit and Scripture: Exploring a Pneumatic Hermeneutic.* New York: Bloomsbury, 2012.

Spence, *Palace*. • Spence, Jonathan D. *The Memory Palace of Matteo Ricci.* New York: Viking Penguin, 1984.

Spencer, *Acts*. • Spencer, F. Scott. *Acts.* Sheffield, UK: Sheffield Academic, 1997.

Spencer, "Approaches." • Spencer, F. Scott. "Acts and Modern Literary Approaches." 381–414 in *The Book of Acts in Its Ancient Literary Setting.* Edited by Bruce W. Winter and Andrew D. Clarke. Vol. 1 of *The Book of Acts in Its First Century Setting.* Edited by Bruce W. Winter. Grand Rapids: Eerdmans; Carlisle, UK: Paternoster, 1993.

Sperber and Wilson, "Précis." • Sperber, Dan, and Deirdre Wilson. "Précis of Relevance: Communication and Cognition." *Behavioural and Brain Sciences* 10 (1987): 697–754.

Sperber and Wilson, *Relevance*. • Sperber, Dan, and Deirdre Wilson. *Relevance: Communication and Cognition.* Oxford: Blackwell, 1986.

"Spirit and Power." • "Spirit and Power: A Ten-Country Survey of Pentecostals." Pew Forum Survey (2006). http://pewforum.org/survey/pentecostal. Accessed January 4, 2009.

Spittler, "Enterprise." • Spittler, Russell P. "Scripture and the Theological Enterprise: View from a Big Canoe." 56–77 in *The Use of the Bible in Theology: Evangelical Options.* Edited by Robert K. Johnston. Atlanta: John Knox, 1985.

Spittler, "Glossolalia." • Spittler, Russell P. "Glossolalia." 335–41 in *DPCM.*

Spivak, *Critique*. • Spivak, Gayatri Chakravorty. *A Critique of Postcolonial Reason: Toward a History of the Vanishing Present.* Cambridge, MA: Harvard University Press, 1999.

Stager, "Eroticism." • Stager, Lawrence E. "Eroticism and Infanticide at Ashkelon." *BAR* 17 (4, 1991): 34–53, 72.

Stager and Wolff, "Child Sacrifice." • Stager, Lawrence E., and Samuel R. Wolff. "Child Sacrifice at Carthage—Religious Rite or Population Control; Archaeological Evidence Provides Basis for a New Analysis." *BAR* 10 (1, January 1984): 30–51.

Stanley, *Colonized Apostle*. • Stanley, Christopher D., ed. *The Colonized Apostle: Paul through Postcolonial Eyes.* Paul in Critical Contexts (series). Minneapolis: Fortress, 2011.

Stanley, *Diffusion*. • Stanley, Brian. *The Global Diffusion of Evangelicalism: The Age of Billy Graham and John Stott.* A History of Evangelicalism 5. Downers Grove, IL: InterVarsity, 2013.

Stanley, "Introduction." • Stanley, Christopher D. "Introduction." 3–7 in *The Colonized Apostle: Paul through Postcolonial Eyes.* Edited by Christopher D. Stanley. Paul in Critical Contexts (series). Minneapolis: Fortress, 2011.

Stanley, *Language of Scripture*. • Stanley, Christopher D. *Paul and the Langage of Scripture:*

Citation Technique in the Pauline Epistles and Contemporary Literature. SNTSMS 69. Cambridge: Cambridge University Press, 1992.

Starr, "Flexibility." • Starr, Raymond J. "The Flexibility of Literary Meaning and the Role of the Reader in Roman Antiquity." *Latomus* 60 (2, 2001): 433–45.

Stefanovic, *Revelation.* • Stefanovic, Ranko. *Revelation of Jesus Christ: Commentary on the Book of Revelation.* 2nd ed. Berrien Springs, MI: Andrews University Press, 2009.

Stein, "Benefits." • Stein, Robert H. "The Benefits of an Author-Oriented Approach to Hermeneutics." *JETS* 44 (3, September 2001): 451–66.

Stein, *Guide.* • Stein, Robert H. *A Basic Guide to Interpreting the Bible: Playing by the Rules.* 2nd ed. Grand Rapids: Baker Academic, 2011.

Steinmetz, "Superiority." • Steinmetz, David C. "The Superiority of Pre-Critical Exegesis." *Theology Today* 37 (1, 1980): 27–38.

Stendahl, *Paul.* • Stendahl, Krister. *Paul among Jews and Gentiles and Other Essays.* Philadelphia: Fortress, 1976.

Stibbe, "Thoughts." • Stibbe, Mark. "This Is That: Some Thoughts concerning Charismatic Hermeneutics." *Anvil: An Anglican Evangelical Journal for Theology and Mission* 15 (3, 1998): 181–93.

Stieglitz, "Plagues." • Stieglitz, Robert R. "Ancient Records and the Exodus Plagues." *BAR* 13 (6, 1987): 46–49.

Stoller, "Eye." • Stoller, Paul. "Eye, Mind, and Word in Anthropology." *L'Homme* 24 (3–4, 1984): 91–114.

Stormont, *Wigglesworth.* • Stormont, George. *Wigglesworth: A Man Who Walked with God.* Tulsa: Harrison House, 1989.

Strachan, *Theology of Irving.* • Strachan, Gordon. *The Pentecostal Theology of Edward Irving.* Peabody, MA: Hendrickson, 1973.

Strauss, *Messiah.* • Strauss, Mark L. *The Davidic Messiah in Luke-Acts: The Promise and Its Fulfillment in Lukan Christology.* JSNTSup 110. Sheffield, UK: Sheffield Academic, 1995.

Strawbridge et al., "Attendance." • Strawbridge, W. J., S. J. Shema, et al. "Religious Attendance Increases Survival by Improving and Maintaining Good Health Behaviors, Mental Health, and Social Relationships." *AnnBehMed* 23 (1, 2001): 68–74.

Strawbridge et al., "Strength." • Strawbridge, W. J., R. D. Cohen, et al. "Comparative Strength of Association between Religious Attendance and Survival." *IntJPsyMed* 30 (4, 2000): 299–308.

Stronstad, *Charismatic Theology.* • Stronstad, Roger. *The Charismatic Theology of St. Luke.* Peabody, MA: Hendrickson, 1984.

Stronstad, "Experience." • Stronstad, Roger. "Pentecostal Experience and Hermeneutics." *Paraclete* 26 (1, Winter 1992): 14–30.

Stronstad, "Trends." • Stronstad, Roger. "Trends in Pentecostal Hermeneutics." *Paraclete* 22 (Summer 1988): 1–12.

Stroup, *Promise.* • Stroup, George W. *The Promise of Narrative Theology: Recovering the Gospel in the Church.* Atlanta: John Knox, 1981.

Stuart, *Missionaries.* • Stuart, John. *British Missionaries and the End of Empire: East, Central, and Southern Africa, 1939–64.* Grand Rapids: Eerdmans, 2011.

Stuhlmacher, *Criticism.* • Stuhlmacher, Peter. *Historical Criticism and Theological Interpretation of Scripture: Toward a Hermeneutic of Consent.* Philadelphia: Fortress, 1977.

Stuhlmacher, "Ex Auditu." • Stuhlmacher, Peter. "Ex Auditu and the Theological Interpretation of Holy Scripture." *Ex auditu* 2 (1986): 1–6.

Sugirtharajah, "Catching." • Sugirtharajah, Rasiah S. "Catching the Post or How I Became an Accidental Theorist." 176–85 in *Shaping a Global Theological Mind.* Edited by Darren C. Marks. Aldershot, UK: Ashgate, 2008.

Sumney, "Rationalities." • Sumney, Jerry L. "Alternative Rationalities in Paul: Expanding Our Definition of Argument." *ResQ* 46 (1, 2004): 1–9.

Sunderland, *Manual.* • Sunderland, La Roy. *Anti Slavery Manual, Containing a Collection of Facts and Arguments on American Slavery.* New York: S. W. Benedict, 1837. Reprinted by Detroit: Negro History Press, n.d.

Sunderland, *Testimony.* • Sunderland, La Roy. *The Testimony of God against Slavery, or A Collection of Passages from the Bible Which Show the Sin of Holding Property in Man, with Notes.* Boston: Webster & Southard, 1835.

Sunquist, *Century.* • Sunquist, Scott W. *The Unexpected Cristian Century: The Reversal and Transformation of Global Christianity, 1900–2000.* Foreword by Mark A. Noll. Grand Rapids: Baker Academic, 2015.

Swartley, *Slavery.* • Swartley, Willard M. *Slavery, Sabbath, War and Women: Case Studies in Biblical Interpretation.* Scottsdale: Herald, 1983.

Sweeney, *Story.* • Sweeney, Douglas A. *The American Evangelical Story: A History of the Movement.* Grand Rapids: Baker Academic, 2005.

Swinburne, "Evidence." • Swinburne, Richard. "Evidence for the Resurrection." 191–212 in *The Resurrection: An Interdisciplinary Symposium on the Resurrection of Jesus.* Edited by Stephen T. Davis, Daniel Kendall, and Gerald O'Collins. Oxford: Oxford University Press, 1997.

Swinburne, "Historical Evidence." • Swinburne, Richard. "Historical Evidence." 133–51 in *Miracles.* Edited by Richard Swinburne. New York: Macmillan, 1989.

Swinburne, "Introduction." • Swinburne, Richard. "Introduction." 1–17 in *Miracles.* Edited by Richard Swinburne. New York: Macmillan, 1989.

Swinburne, *Miracle.* • Swinburne, Richard. *The Concept of Miracle.* NSPR. London: Macmillan, 1970.

Synan, "Legacies." • Synan, Vinson. "The Lasting Legacies of the Azusa Street Revival." *Enr* 11 (2, 2006): 142–52.

Synan, *Movement.* • Synan, Vinson. *The Holiness-Pentecostal Movement in the United States.* Grand Rapids: Eerdmans, 1971.

Synan, "Seymour." • Synan, Vinson. "Seymour, William Joseph." 778–81 in *DPCM.*

Synan, *Tradition.* • Synan, Vinson. *The Holiness-Pentecostal Tradition: Charismatic Movements in the Twentieth Century.* Grand Rapids: Eerdmans, 1997.

Synan, *Voices.* • Synan, Vinson. *Voices of Pentecost: Testimonies of Lives Touched by the Holy Spirit.* Ann Arbor: Servant, 2003.

Szentágothai, "Existence." • Szentágothai, János. "The Existence of Some Creative Impulse at the Very Beginning." 214–17 in *Cosmos, Bios, and Theos: Scientists Reflect on Science, God, and the Origins of the Universe, Life, and* Homo Sapiens. Edited by Henry Margenau and Roy Abraham Varghese. La Salle, IL: Open Court, 1992.

Talbert, *Acts.* • Talbert, Charles H. *Reading Acts: A Literary and Theological Commentary on the Acts of the Apostles.* Rev. ed. Macon, GA: Smyth & Helwys, 2005.

Talbert, *Apocalypse.* • Talbert, Charles H. *The Apocalypse: A Reading of the Revelation of John.* Louisville: Westminster John Knox, 1994.

Talbert, *Corinthians.* • Talbert, Charles H. *Reading Corinthians: A Literary and Theological Commentary on 1 and 2 Corinthians.* New York: Crossroad, 1987.

Talbert, *Mediterranean Milieu.* • Talbert, Charles H. *Reading Luke-Acts in Its Mediterranean Milieu.* NovTSup 107. Leiden: Brill, 2003.

Talbert, *Patterns.* • Talbert, Charles H. *Literary Patterns, Theological Themes, and the Genre of Luke-Acts.* SBLMS 20. Missoula, MT: Scholars Press, 1974.

Taliaferro and Hendrickson, "Racism." • Taliaferro, Charles, and Anders Hendrickson. "Hume's Racism and His Case against the Miraculous." *PhilChr* 4 (2, 2002): 427–41.

Tannehill, *Acts.* • Tannehill, Robert C. *The Acts of the Apostles.* Vol. 2 of *The Narrative Unity of Luke-Acts: A Literary Interpretation.* Minneapolis: Fortress, 1990.

Tannehill, *Luke.* • Tannehill, Robert C. *The Gospel according to Luke.* Vol. 1 of *The Narrative Unity of Luke-Acts: A Literary Interpretation.* Philadelphia: Fortress, 1986.

Tarango, *Jesus Way.* • Tarango, Angela. *American Indian Pentecostals and the Fight for the Indigenous Principle.* Chapel Hill: University of North Carolina Press, 2014.

Tarr, *Foolishness.* • Tarr, Del. *The Foolishness of God: A Linguist Looks at the Mystery of Tongues.* Foreword by Jack Hayford. Springfield, MO: Access, 2010.

Tatum, "Epoch." • Tatum, W. Barnes. "The Epoch of Israel: Luke I–II and the Theological Plan of Luke-Acts." *NTS* 13 (2, 1967): 184–95.

Taylor, *Hume.* • Taylor, A. E. *David Hume and the Miraculous.* The Leslie Stephen Lecture, Cambridge University, 1927. Cambridge: Cambridge University Press, 1927.

Taylor, "Shades." • Taylor, Mark C. "Shades of Difference." *Semeia* 40 (Fall 1987): 21–38.

Ten, "Racism." • Ten, C. L. "Hume's Racism and Miracles." *JValInq* 36 (2002): 101–7.

Ten Elshof, *Confucius.* • Ten Elshof, Gregg A. *Confucius for Christians: What an Ancient Chinese Worldview Can Teach Us about Life in Christ.* Grand Rapids: Eerdmans, 2015.

Tennant, *Miracle.* • Tennant, F. R. *Miracle and Its Philosophical Presuppositions: Three Lectures Delivered in the University of London 1924.* Cambridge: Cambridge University Press, 1925.

Tennent, *Theology.* • Tennent, Timothy C. *Theology in the Context of World Christianity: How the Global Church Is Influencing the Way We Think about and Discuss Theology.* Grand Rapids: Zondervan, 2007.

Theissen, "Nouvelle perspective." • Theissen, Gerd. "La nouvelle perspective sur Paul et ses limites. Quelques réflexions psychologiques." *ETR* 83 (4, 2008): 529–51.

Theissen and Merz, *Guide.* • Theissen, Gerd, and Annette Merz. *The Historical Jesus: A Comprehensive Guide.* Translated by John Bowden. Minneapolis: Fortress, 1998.

Thiselton, "Hermeneutics." • Thiselton, Anthony C. "Hermeneutics and Theology: The Legitimacy and Necessity of Hermeneutics." 142–74 in *A Guide to Contemporary Hermeneutics: Major Trends in Biblical Interpretation.* Edited by Donald K. McKim. Grand Rapids: Eerdmans, 1986.

Thiselton, *Horizons.* • Thiselton, Anthony C. *The Two Horizons: New Testament Hermeneutics and Philosophical Description.* Grand Rapids: Eerdmans, 1980.

Thiselton, "New Hermeneutic." • Thiselton, Anthony C. "The New Hermeneutic." 78–107 in *A Guide to Contemporary Hermeneutics: Major Trends in Biblical Interpretation.* Edited by Donald K. McKim. Grand Rapids: Eerdmans, 1986.

Thomas, "Spirit Is Saying." • Thomas, John Christopher. "'What the Spirit Is Saying to the Church'—The Testimony of a Pentecostal in New Testament Studies." 115–29 in *Spirit and Scripture: Exploring a Pneumatic Hermeneutic.* Edited by Kevin L. Spawn and Archie T. Wright. New York: Bloomsbury, 2012.

Thomas, "Women." • Thomas, John Christopher. "Women, Pentecostalism, and the Bible: An Experiment in Pentecostal Hermeneutics." 81–94 in *Pentecostal Hermeneutics: A Reader.* Reprint of "Women, Pentecostals and the Bible: An Experiment in Pentecostal Hermeneutics." *JPT* 5 (1994): 41–56. Also found in "Women in the Church: An Experiment in Pentecostal Hermeneutics." *Evangelical Review of Theology* 20 (3, 1996): 220–32.

Thomas and Alexander, "Signs." • Thomas, John Christopher, and Kimberly E. Alexander. "'And the Signs Are Following': Mark 16.9–20—A Journey into Pentecostal Hermeneutics." *JPT* 11 (2, 2003): 147–70.

Thoresen, "Health." • Thoresen, Carl E. "Spirituality, Religion, and Health: What's the Deal?" 3–10 in *Spirit, Science, and Health: How the Spiritual Mind Fuels Physical Wellness.* Edited by Thomas G. Plante and Carl E. Thoresen. Foreword by Albert Bandura. Westport, CT: Praeger, 2007.

Thorsen and Reeves, *Bible.* • Thorsen, Don, and Keith H. Reeves, *What Christians Believe about the Bible: A Concise Guide for Students.* Grand Rapids: Baker Academic, 2012.

Thurén, "Sincere." • Thurén, Lauri. "Was Paul Sincere? Questioning the Apostle's Ethos." *Scriptura* 65 (1998): 95–108.

Tigchelaar, "Names of Spirits." • Tigchelaar, Eibert J. C. "'These Are the Names of the Spirits of . . .': A Preliminary Edition of *4Qcatalogue of Spirits (4Q230)* and New Manuscript Evidence for the *Two Spirits Treatise (4Q257* and *1Q29a)." RevQ* 21 (84, 2004): 529–47.

Tippett, "Possession." • Tippett, A. R. "Spirit Possession as It Relates to Culture and Religion: A Survey of Anthropological Literature." 143–74 in *Demon Possession: A Medical, Historical, Anthropological, and Theological Symposium.* Papers presented at the University of Notre Dame, January 8–11, 1975, under the auspices of the Christian Medical Association. Edited by John Warwick Montgomery. Minneapolis: Bethany House, 1976.

Tomkins, History. • Tomkins, Stephen. *A Short History of Christianity.* Grand Rapids: Eerdmans, 2005.

Tonquédec, Miracles. • Tonquédec, Joseph de. *Miracles.* Translated by Frank M. Oppenheim. West Baden Springs, IN: West Baden College, 1955. Translated from "Miracle." 3:517–78 in *Dictionnaire Apologétique de la Foi Catholique.* Edited by A. d'Alès. Paris: Beauchesne, 1926.

Toon, Development. • Toon, Peter. *The Development of Doctrine in the Church.* Grand Rapids: Eerdmans, 1979.

Torrey, Person and Work. • Torrey, R. A. *Person and Work of the Holy Spirit.* Grand Rapids: Zondervan, 1974.

Torrey, "Supernatural Guidance." • Torrey, R. A. "Supernatural Guidance." *Paraclete* (Fall 1978): 17–21.

Townes, "Question." • Townes, Charles H. "The Question of Origin Seems Unanswered If We Explore from a Scientific View Alone." 122–24 in *Cosmos, Bios, and Theos: Scientists Reflect on Science, God, and the Origins of the Universe, Life, and* Homo Sapiens. Edited by Henry Margenau and Roy Abraham Varghese. La Salle, IL: Open Court, 1992.

Tozer, Pursuit. • Tozer, A. W. *The Pursuit of God.* Camp Hill, PA: Christian Publications, [1948, 1982,] 1993.

Treier, Interpretation. • Treier, Daniel J. *Introducing Theological Interpretation of Scripture: Recovering a Christian Practice.* Grand Rapids: Baker Academic, 2008.

Tribble, "Work." • Tribble, H. W. "The Convicting Work of the Holy Spirit, John 16:7–11." *RevExp* 32 (1935): 269–80.

Trompf, Historical Recurrence. • Trompf, G. W. *The Idea of Historical Recurrence in Western Thought.* Berkeley: University of California Press, 1979.

Tronier, "Spørgsmålet." • Tronier, Henrik. "Spørgsmålet om hermeneutisk kongruens I Pauluseksegesen. 2. del: Allegorisk og typologisk hermeneutic i eksegesen." *Dansk Teologisk Tidsskrift* 55 (3, 1992): 191–208.

Trousdale, Movements. • Trousdale, Jerry. *Miraculous Movements.* Nashville: Thomas Nelson, 2012.

Tsouna, "Introduction." • Tsouna, Voula, "Introduction." vii–viii in *Philodemus, On Property Management.* Translated with an introduction and notes by Voula Tsouna. SBL Writings from the Greco-Roman World 33. Atlanta: SBL, 2012.

Tucker, "Background." • Tucker, Gene M. "'The Legal Background of Genesis 23." *JBL* 85 (1, March 1966): 77–84.

Tucker, Jerusalem. • Tucker, Ruth. *From Jerusalem to Irian Jaya: A Biographical History of Christian Missions.* Grand Rapids: Zondervan, 1983.

Tuppurainen, "Contribution." • Tuppurainen, Riku P. "The Contribution of Socio-Rhetorical Criticism to Spirit-Sensitive Hermeneutics: A Contextual Example—Luke 11:13." *Journal of Biblical and Pneumatological Research* 4 (2012): 38–66.

Turaki, "Legacy." • Turaki, Yusufu. "The British Colonial Legacy in Northern Nigeria." PhD dissertation, Boston University, 1982.

Turner, "Actuality." • Turner, Edith. "Psychology, Metaphor, or Actuality? A Probe into Iñupiat Eskimo Healing." *AnthCons* 3 (1–2, 1992): 1–8.

Turner, "Advances." • Turner, Edith. "Advances in the Study of Spirit Experience: Drawing Together Many Threads." *AnthCons* 17 (2, 2006): 33–61.

Turner, "Experience." • Turner, Max. "Early Christian Experience and Theology of 'Tongues'—A New Testament Perspective." 1–33 in *Speaking in Tongues: Multi-disciplinary Perspectives*. Edited by Mark J. Cartledge. SPCI. Waynesboro, GA, and Bletchley, Milton Keynes, UK: Paternoster, 2006.

Turner, *Experiencing Ritual.* • Turner, Edith, with William Blodgett, Singleton Kahoma, and Fideli Benwa. *Experiencing Ritual: A New Interpretation of African Healing.* SCEthn. Philadelphia: University of Pennsylvania Press, 1992.

Turner, *Hands.* • Turner, Edith. *The Hands Feel It: Healing and Spirit Presence among a Northern Alaskan People.* DeKalb: Northern Illinois University Press, 1996.

Turner, *Healers.* • Turner, Edith. *Among the Healers: Stories of Spiritual and Ritual Healing around the World.* Religion, Health, and Healing. Westport, CT: Praeger, 2006.

Turner, *Power.* • Turner, Max. *Power from on High: The Spirit in Israel's Restoration and Witness in Luke-Acts.* Sheffield, UK: Sheffield Academic, 1996.

Turner, *Prophet.* • Turner, David L. *Israel's Last Prophet: Jesus and the Jewish Leaders in Matthew 23.* Minneapolis: Fortress, 2015.

Turner, "Reality of Spirits." • Turner, Edith. "The Reality of Spirits." *Shamanism* 10 (1, Spring/Summer 1997).

Twelftree, *Exorcist.* • Twelftree, Graham H. *Jesus the Exorcist: A Contribution to the Study of the Historical Jesus.* Peabody, MA: Hendrickson; Tübingen: J. C. B. Mohr, 1993.

Twelftree, *Miracle Worker.* • Twelftree, Graham H. *Jesus the Miracle Worker: A Historical and Theological Study.* Downers Grove, IL: InterVarsity, 1999.

Twelftree, *Name.* • Twelftree, Graham H. *In the Name of Jesus: Exorcism among Early Christians.* Grand Rapids: Baker Academic, 2007.

Twelftree, *People.* • Twelftree, Graham H. *People of the Spirit: Exploring Luke's View of the Church.* Grand Rapids: Baker Academic, 2009.

Tyson, "History to Rhetoric." • Tyson, Joseph B. "From History to Rhetoric and Back: Assessing New Trends in Acts Studies." 23–42 in *Contextualizing Acts: Lukan Narrative and Greco-Roman Discourse.* Edited by Todd Penner and Caroline Vander Stichele. SBLSymS 20. Atlanta: SBL, 2003.

Usry and Keener, *Religion.* • Usry, Glenn, and Craig S. Keener. *Black Man's Religion: Can Christianity Be Afrocentric?* Downers Grove, IL: InterVarsity, 1996.

Van der Horst, "Bibliomancy." • Van der Horst, Pieter W. "Ancient Jewish Bibliomancy." *JGRCJ* 1 (2000): 9–17.

Van der Watt, "Hermeneutics of Relevance." • Van der Watt, Jan G. "A Hermeneutics of Relevance: Reading the Bible in Dialogue in African Contexts." 237–55 in *Miracles and Imagery in Luke and John: Festschrift Ulrich Busse.* Edited by J. Verheyden, G. van Belle, and J. G. van der Watt. BETL 218. Leuven: Uitgeverij Peeters, 2008.

Vanhoozer, "Beyond." • Vanhoozer, Kevin J. "'Into the Great 'Beyond': A Theologian's Response to the Marshall Plan." 81–95 in *Beyond the Bible: Moving from Scripture to Theology* by I. Howard Marshall, with essays by Kevin J. Vanhoozer and Stanley E. Porter. Grand Rapids: Baker Academic, 2004.

Vanhoozer, *Meaning.* • Vanhoozer, Kevin J. *Is There a Meaning in This Text? The Bible, the Reader, and the Morality of Literary Knowledge.* Grand Rapids: Zondervan, 1998.

Van Ness, Kasl, and Jones, "Religion." • Van Ness, Peter H., Stanislav V. Kasl, and Beth A. Jones. "Religion, Race, and Breast Cancer Survival." *IntJPsyMed* 33 (2003): 357–76.

Vassiliadis, "Ermeneutike." • Vassiliadis, Petros. "Agiopneumatike Biblike Ermeneutike (Biblical Hermeneutics and the Holy Spirit)." *Deltion Biblikon Meleton* 14 (2, 1985): 51–60. (New Testament Abstracts)

Venter, *Reconciliation.* • Venter, Alexander. *Doing Reconciliation: Racism, Reconciliation, and Transformation in the Church and World.* Cape Town: Vineyard International, 2004.

Verbaal, "Cicero." • Verbaal, Wim. "Cicero and Dionysios the Elder, or the End of Liberty." *Classical World* 99 (2, 2006): 145–56.

Vermes, "Elements." • Vermes, Geza. "Historiographical Elements in the Qumran Writings: A Synopsis of the Textual Evidence." *JJS* 58 (1, 2007): 121–39.

Vermes, "Halakah." • Vermes, Geza. "Sectarian Matrimonial Halakah in the Damascus Rule." *JJS* 25 (1, 1974): 197–202.

Vermes, *Jesus and Judaism.* • Vermes, Geza. *Jesus and the World of Judaism.* Philadelphia: Fortress, 1984; London: SCM, 1983.

Vidler, *Revolution.* • Vidler, Alec R. *The Church in an Age of Revolution: 1789 to the Present Day.* PHC 5. London: Penguin, 1974.

Voth, "Jeremiah." • Voth, Steven. "Jeremiah." 4:228–371 in *Zondervan Illustrated Bible Backgrounds Commentary: Old Testament.* Edited by John H. Walton. 5 vols. Grand Rapids: Zondervan, 2009.

Waardt, "Witchcraft." • Waardt, Hans de. "Dutch Witchcraft in the Sixteenth and Seventeenth Centuries." *SocG* 36 (3–4, May 1989): 224–44.

Wackenheim, "Babel." • Wackenheim, Charles. "De Babel à Pentecôte." *LumVie* 58 (281, 2009): 47–56.

Wacker, *Heaven.* • Wacker, Grant. *Heaven Below: Early Pentecostals and American Culture.* Cambridge, MA: Harvard University Press, 2001.

Waddell, "Adventure." • Waddell, Robby. "Choose Your Own Adventure: Teaching, Participatory Hermeneutics, and the Book of Revelation." 178–93 in *But These Are Written . . . : Essays on Johannine Literature in Honor of Professor Benny C. Aker.* Edited by Craig S. Keener, Jeremy S. Crenshaw, and Jordan Daniel May. Eugene, OR: Pickwick, 2014.

Waddell, "Hearing." • Waddell, Robby. "Hearing What the Spirit Says to the Churches: Profile of a Pentecostal Reader of the Apocalypse." 171–203 in *Pentecostal Hermeneutics: A Reader.* Edited by Lee Roy Martin. Leiden: Brill, 2013.

Waddell, *Spirit in Revelation.* • Waddell, Robert C. *The Spirit of the Book of Revelation.* JPTSup 30. Blandford Forum, UK: Deo, 2006.

Wagenaar, "Kumba." • Wagenaar, Hinne. "Babel, Jerusalem, and Kumba: Missiological Reflections on Genesis 11:1–9 and Acts 2:1–13." *IntRevMiss* 92 (366, 2003): 406–21.

Währisch-Oblau, "Healthy." • Währisch-Oblau, Claudia. "God Can Make Us Healthy Through and Through: On Prayers for the Sick and the Interpretation of Healing Experiences in Christian Churches in China and African Immigrant Congregations in Germany." *IntRevMiss* 90 (356–57, 2001): 87–102.

Walde, "Irony." • Walde, Christine. "Irony: Rhetoric." 6:943–44 in *BrillPauly.*

Walker, *History.* • Walker, Williston. *A History of the Christian Church.* 3rd ed. Rev. Robert T. Handy. New York: Scribner's, 1970.

Wall, "Acts." • Wall, Robert W. "The Acts of the Apostles." *NIB* 10:1–368.

Waltke, Houston, and Moore, *Psalms.* • Waltke, Bruce K., James M. Houston, and Erika Moore. *The Psalms as Christian Lament: A Historical Commentary.* Grand Rapids: Eerdmans, 2014.

Walton, *Genesis One.* • Walton, John H. *The Lost World of Genesis One.* Downers Grove, IL: IVP Academic, 2009.

Walton, *Thought.* • Walton, John H. *Ancient Near Eastern Thought and the Old Testament: Introducing the Conceptual World of the Hebrew Bible.* Grand Rapids: Baker Academic, 2006.

Walton, Matthews, and Chavalas, *Background Commentary.* • Walton, John H., Victor H. Matthews, and Mark W. Chavalas. *The IVP Bible Background Commentary: Old Testament.* Downers Grove, IL: InterVarsity, 2000.

Walton and Sandy, *World.* • Walton, John H., and D. Brent Sandy. *The Lost World of Scripture: Ancient Literary Culture and Biblical Authority.* Downers Grove, IL: IVP Academic, 2013.

Ward, "Believing." • Ward, Keith. "Believing in Miracles." *Zyg* 37 (3, 2002): 741–50.

Ward, "Cross-Cultural Study." • Ward, Colleen A. "The Cross-Cultural Study of Altered States of Consciousness and Mental Health." 15–35 in *Altered States of Consciousness and Mental*

Health: A Cross-Cultural Perspective. Edited by Colleen A. Ward. CCRMS 12. Newbury Park, CA: Sage, 1989.

Ward, "Introduction." • Ward, Colleen A. "Introduction." 8–10 in *Altered States of Consciousness and Mental Health: A Cross-Cultural Perspective.* Edited by Colleen A. Ward. CCRMS 12. Newbury Park, CA: Sage, 1989.

Ward, "Miracles and Testimony." • Ward, Keith. "Miracles and Testimony." *RelS* 21 (1985): 134–45.

Ward, "Possession." • Ward, Colleen A. "Possession and Exorcism: Psychopathology and Psychotherapy in a Magico-Religious Context." 125–44 in *Altered States of Consciousness and Mental Health: A Cross-Cultural Perspective.* Edited by Colleen A. Ward. CCRMS 12. Newbury Park, CA: Sage, 1989.

Watson, *Paul, Judaism, and the Gentiles.* • Watson, Francis. *Paul, Judaism, and the Gentiles: Beyond the New Perspective.* Rev. ed. Grand Rapids: Eerdmans, 2007.

Webb, *Slaves.* • Webb, William J. *Slaves, Women, and Homosexuals: Exploring the Hermeneutics of Cultural Analysis.* Foreword by Darrell L. Bock. Downers Grove, IL: InterVarsity, 2001.

Webster, *Ingesting Jesus.* • Webster, Jane S. *Ingesting Jesus: Eating and Drinking in the Gospel of John.* SBL Academia Biblica 6. Atlanta: Society of Biblical Literature, 2003.

Webster, *Methodism and Miraculous.* • Webster, Robert. *Methodism and the Miraculous: John Wesley's Idea of the Supernatural and the Identification of Methodists in the Eighteenth Century.* Asbury Theological Seminary Series: The Study of World Christian Revitalization Movements in Pietist/Wesleyan Studies, 12. Lexington, KY: Emeth, 2013.

Weima, "Peace." • Weima, Jeffrey D. "'Peace and Security' (1 Thess 5.3): Prophetic Warning or Political Propaganda?" *NTS* 58 (2012): 331–59.

Weintraub, "Credibility." • Weintraub, Ruth. "The Credibility of Miracles." *PhilSt* 82 (1996): 359–75.

Welbourn, "Exorcism." • Welbourn, F. B. "Exorcism." *Theology* 75 (1972): 593–96.

Welbourn, "Healing." • Welbourn, F. B. "Healing as a Psychosomatic Event." 351–68 in *Afro-Christian Religion and Healing in Southern Africa.* Edited by G. C. Oosthuizen, S. D. Edwards, W. H. Wessels, and I. Hexham. AfSt 8. Lewiston, NY: Edwin Mellen, 1989.

Wells, "Exodus." • Wells, Bruce. "Exodus." 160–283 in vol. 1 of *Zondervan Illustrated Bible Backgrounds Commentary: Old Testament.* Edited by John Walton. 5 vols. Grand Rapids: Zondervan, 2009.

Wendl, "Slavery." • Wendl, Tobias. "Slavery, Spirit Possession and Ritual Consciousness: The Tchamba Cult among the Mina of Togo." 111–23 in *Spirit Possession, Modernity and Power in Africa.* Edited by Heike Behrend and Ute Luig. Madison: University of Wisconsin Press, 1999.

Wendland, *Cultural Factor.* • Wendland, Ernst R. *The Cultural Factor in Bible Translation: A Study of Communicating the Word of God in a Central African Cultural Context.* London: United Bible Societies, 1987.

Wengert, "Luther." • Wengert, Timothy. "Martin Luther on Galatians 3:6–14: Justification by Curses and Blessings." 91–116 in *Galatians and Christian Theology: Justification, the Gospel, and Ethics in Paul's Letter.* Edited by Mark W. Elliott, Scott J. Hafemann, N. T. Wright, and John Frederick. Grand Rapids: Baker Academic, 2014.

Wenham, *Bible.* • Wenham, John W. *Christ and the Bible.* Downers Grove, IL: InterVarsity, 1977.

Wesley, *Notes.* • Wesley, John. *Explanatory Notes upon the New Testament.* London: Epworth, 1966; originally 1754.

West, *Sorcery.* • West, Harry G. *Ethnographic Sorcery.* Chicago: University of Chicago Press, 2007.

Westerholm, "New Perspective." • Westerholm, Stephen. "What's Right about the New Perspective on Paul." 230–42 in *Studies in the Pauline Epistles: Essays in Honor of Douglas J. Moo.* Edited by Matthew S. Harmon and Jay E. Smith. Grand Rapids: Zondervan, 2014.

Westphal, *Community*. • Westphal, Merold. *Whose Community? Which Interpretation? Philosophical Hermeneutics for the Church.* Grand Rapids: Baker Academic, 2009.

White, "Calling." • White, Gayle. "Colorblind Calling." *The Atlanta Journal & Constitution* (November 3, 1991): M1, 4.

Whitehead, *Science*. • Whitehead, Alfred North. *Science and the Modern World.* Pelican Mentor Books 28. New York: New American Library, 1948.

Whybray, *Making*. • Whybray, R. N. *The Making of the Pentateuch: A Methodological Study.* JSOTSup 53. Sheffield, UK: JSOT Press, 1987.

Wigger, *Saint*. • Wigger, John. *American Saint: Francis Asbury and the Methodists.* Oxford: Oxford University Press, 2009.

Wikenhauser, *Apostelgeschichte*. • Wikenhauser, Alfred. *Die Apostelgeschichte.* 4th ed. RNT 5. Regensburg: Pustet, 1961.

Williams, "Acts." • Williams, Demetrius K. "The Acts of the Apostles." 213–48 in *True to Our Native Land: An African American New Testament Commentary.* Edited by Brian K. Blount, with Cain Hope Felder, Clarice J. Martin, and Emerson Powery. Minneapolis: Fortress, 2007.

Williams, "Germanicus." • Williams, Kathryn F. "Tacitus' Germanicus and the Principate." *Latomus* 68 (1, 2009): 117–30.

Williams, "Names." • Williams, Margaret H. "Palestinian Jewish Personal Names in Acts." 79–114 in *The Book of Acts in Its Palestinian Setting.* Edited by Richard Bauckham. Vol. 4 of *The Book of Acts in Its First Century Setting.* Edited by Bruce W. Winter. Grand Rapids: Eerdmans; Carlisle, UK: Paternoster, 1995.

Williams, *Radical Reformation*. • Williams, George Huntston. *The Radical Reformation.* Philadelphia: Westminster, 1962.

Williams, *Theology*. • Williams, J. Rodman. *Renewal Theology: Systematic Theology from a Charismatic Perspective.* Grand Rapids: Academie, 1988–92.

Wills, "Response." • Wills, Lawrence M. "A Response to the Roundtable Discussion 'Anti-Judaism and Postcolonial Biblical Interpretation.'" *Journal of Feminist Studies in Religion* 20 (2, 2004): 189–92.

Wilson, *Gnostic Problem*. • Wilson, R. McL. *The Gnostic Problem.* London: A. R. Mowbray, 1958.

Wilson, *Pastoral Epistles*. • Wilson, Stephen G. *Luke and the Pastoral Epistles.* London: SPCK, 1979.

Wilson, "Seeing." • Wilson, C. Roderick. "Seeing They See Not." 197–208 in *Being Changed: The Anthropology of Extraordinary Experience.* Edited by David Young and Jean-Guy Goulet. Petersborough, ON: Broadview, 1994.

Wilson and Sperber, "Outline." • Wilson, Deirdre, and Dan Sperber. "An Outline of Relevance Theory." 21–41 in *Encontro de linguistas: Actas.* Edited by H. O. Alves. UCPLA. Minho, Port.: Universidade do Minho, 1985.

Wilson and Sperber, "Representation." • Wilson, Deirdre, and Dan Sperber. "Representation and Relevance." 133–53 in *Mental Representations: The Interface between Language and Reality.* Edited by Ruth M. Kempson. Cambridge: Cambridge University Press, 1988.

Wimsatt and Beardsley, *Icon*. • Wimsatt, William K. *The Verbal Icon: Studies in the Meaning of Poetry, and Two Preliminary Essays Written in Collaboration with Monroe C. Beardsley.* London: Methuen, 1970.

Wimsatt and Beardsley, "Intentional Fallacy." • Wimsatt, W. K., and Monroe C. Beardsley. "The Intentional Fallacy." 3–18 in *The Verbal Icon: Studies in the Meaning of Poetry.* Edited by W. K. Wimsatt. Lexington: University of Kentucky, 1954.

Wink, "Write." • Wink, Walter. "Write What You See." *FourR* 7 (3, May 1994): 3–9.

Wire, "Story." • Wire, Antoinette Clark. "The Miracle Story as the Whole Story." *SEAJT* 22 (2, 1981): 29–37.

Witherington, *Christology of Jesus*. • Witherington, Ben, III. *The Christology of Jesus.* Minneapolis: Augsburg Fortress, 1990.

Witherington, *Grace*. • Witherington, Ben, III. *Grace in Galatia: A Commentary on Paul's Letter to the Galatians.* Grand Rapids: Eerdmans; Edinburgh: T&T Clark, 1998.

Witherington, *Isaiah*. • Witherington, Ben, III. *Isaiah Old and New.* Minneapolis: Fortress, forthcoming.

Witherington, *Wisdom*. • Witherington, Ben, III. *John's Wisdom: A Commentary on the Fourth Gospel.* Louisville: Westminster/John Knox, 1995.

Wittig, "Theory." • Wittig, Susan. "A Theory of Multiple Meanings." *Semeia* 9 (1977): 75–103.

Wolfe, "Potential." • Wolfe, Alan. "The Potential for Pluralism: Religious Responses to the Triumph of Theory and Method in American Academic Culture." 22–39 in *Religion, Scholarship, Higher Education: Perspectives, Models, and Future Prospects.* Edited by Andrea Sterk. Notre Dame, IN: University of Notre Dame Press, 2001.

Wolffe, *Expansion*. • Wolffe, John. *The Expansion of Evangelicalism: The Age of Wilberforce, More, Chalmers and Finney.* Downers Grove, IL: InterVarsity, 2007.

Wolfson, *Philo*. • Wolfson, Harry Austryn. *Philo: Foundations of Religious Philosophy in Judaism, Christianity, and Islam.* 2 vols. 4th rev. ed. Cambridge, MA: Harvard University Press, 1968.

Wong, "Mind." • Wong, David W. F. "The Loss of the Christian Mind in Biblical Scholarship." *Evangelical Quarterly* 64 (1, 1992): 23–36.

Wong et al., "Factors." • Wong, Y. K., W. C. Tsai, J. C. Lin, C. K. Poon, S. Y. Chao, Y. L. Hsiao, et al. "Socio-demographic Factors in the Prognosis of Oral Cancer Patients." *OrOnc* 42 (9, 2006): 893–906.

Wrede, *Origin*. • Wrede, William. *The Origin of the New Testament.* Translated by James S. Hill. London and New York: Harper & Brothers, 1909.

Wrede, *Secret*. • Wrede, William. *The Messianic Secret.* Translated by J. C. G. Greig. Cambridge, UK: James Clarke, 1971.

Wrensch et al., "Factors." • Wrensch, Margaret, Terri Chew, et al. "Risk Factors for Breast Cancer in a Population with High Incidence Rates." *BrCanRes* 5 (4, 2003): R88–102.

Wright, *Biblical Archaeology*. • Wright, G. Ernest. *Biblical Archaeology.* Philadelphia: Westminster, 1962.

Wright, "Jewish Interpretation." • Wright, Archie T. "Second Temple Period Jewish Biblical Interpretation: An Early Pneumatic Hermeneutic." 73–98 in *Spirit and Scripture: Exploring a Pneumatic Hermeneutic.* Edited by Kevin L. Spawn and Archie T. Wright. New York: Bloomsbury, 2012.

Wright, *Mission*. • Wright, Christopher J. H. *The Mission of God: Unlocking the Bible's Grand Narrative.* Downers Grove, IL: IVP Academic, 2006.

Wright, *Paul*. • Wright, N. T. *Paul and the Faithfulness of God.* 2 vols. Vol. 4 of *Christian Origins and the Question of God.* Minneapolis: Fortress, 2013.

Wright, *Victory*. • Wright, N. T. *Jesus and the Victory of God.* Vol. 2 of *Christian Origins and the Question of God.* Minneapolis: Fortress, 1996.

Wyckoff, "Baptism." • Wyckoff, John W. "The Baptism in the Holy Spirit." 423–55 in *Systematic Theology: A Pentecostal Perspective.* Edited by Stanley M. Horton. Springfield, MO: Logion, 1994.

Wyckoff, John. • Wyckoff, John, personal correspondence, April 26 and May 10, 2015.

Wyckoff, *Pneuma*. • Wyckoff, John W. *Pneuma and Logos: The Role of the Spirit in Biblical Hermeneutics.* Eugene, OR: Wipf & Stock, 2010.

Wyk, "Witchcraft." • Wyk, I. W. C. van. "African Witchcraft in Theological Perspective." *HvTSt* 60 (3, 2004): 1201–28.

Wykstra, "Problem." • Wykstra, Stephen J. "The Problem of Miracle in the Apologetic from History." *JASA* 30 (4, 1978): 154–63.

Yamamori and Chan, *Witnesses*. • Yamamori, Tetsunao, and Kim-kwong Chan. *Witnesses to*

Power: Stories of God's Quiet Work in a Changing China. Waynesboro, GA, and Carlisle, UK: Paternoster, 2000.

Yamauchi, "Adultery." • Yamauchi, Edwin M. "Adultery." 18–26 in *Dictionary of Daily Life in Biblical and Post-Biblical Antiquity.* Edited by Edwin M. Yamauchi and Marvin R. Wilson. 3 vols. Vol. 1: A-Da. Peabody, MA: Hendrickson, 2014.

Yamauchi, *Gnosticism.* • Yamauchi, Edwin M. *Pre-Christian Gnosticism: A Survey of the Proposed Evidences.* Grand Rapids: Eerdmans, 1973.

Yamauchi, "Gnosticism." • Yamauchi, Edwin M. "Gnosticism." 414–18 in *Dictionary of New Testament Background.* Edited by Craig A. Evans and Stanley E. Porter. Downers Grove, IL: InterVarsity, 2000.

Yamauchi, *Persia.* • Yamauchi, Edwin M. *Persia and the Bible.* Foreword by Donald J. Wiseman. Grand Rapids: Baker, 1990.

Yeager et al., "Involvement." • Yeager, Diane M., Dana A. Glei, Melanie Au, Hui-Sheng Lin, Richard P. Sloan, and Maxine Weinstein. "Religious Involvement and Health Outcomes among Older Persons in Taiwan." *SSMed* 63 (2006): 2228–41.

Yeo, "Cultural Hermeneutics." • Yeo, Khiok-Khng. "Cultural Hermeneutics." 1:808–9 in *The New Interpreter's Dictionary of the Bible.* 5 vols. Edited by Katharine Doob Sakenfeld. Nashville: Abingdon, 2006.

Yeo, *Musing.* • Yeo, Khiok-Khng. *Musing with Confucius and Paul: Toward a Chinese Christian Theology.* Eugene, OR: Cascade, 2008.

Yeo, "Xin." • Yeo, Khiok-Khng. "On Confucian *Xin* and Pauline *Pistis.*" *Sino-Christian Studies* 2 (2006): 25–51.

Yong, *Spirit Poured.* • Yong, Amos. *The Spirit Poured Out on All Flesh: Pentecostalism and the Possibility of Global Theology.* Grand Rapids: Baker, 2005.

Yong, *Spirit-Word-Community.* • Yong, Amos. *Spirit-Word-Community: Theological Hermeneutics in Trinitarian Perspective.* Ashgate New Critical Thinking in Religion, Theology, and Biblical Studies. Burlington, VT: Ashgate, 2002.

Yong, "Trialectic." • Yong, Amos. "The Hermeneutical Trialectic: Notes toward a Consensual Hermeneutic and Theological Method." *Heythrop Journal* 45 (2004): 22–39.

Yong with Anderson, *Renewing.* • Yong, Amos, with Jonathan A. Anderson. *Renewing Christian Theology: Systematics for a Global Christianity.* Waco: Baylor University Press, 2014.

York, *Missions.* • York, John V. *Missions in the Age of the Spirit.* Foreword by Byron D. Klaus. Springfield, MO: Logion, 2000.

Yorke, "Hearing." • Yorke, Gosnell L. "Hearing the Politics of Peace in Ephesians: A Proposal from an African Postcolonial Perspective." *JSNT* 30 (1, 2007): 113–27.

Young, "Epistemology." • Young, Robert. "Miracles and Epistemology." *RelS* 8 (2, 1972): 115–26.

Young, "Mind of Scripture." • Young, Frances. "The 'Mind' of Scripture: Theological Readings of the Bible in the Fathers." *International Journal of Systematic Theology* 7 (2, 2005): 126–41.

Yung, "Integrity." • Yung, Hwa. "The Integrity of Mission in the Light of the Gospel: Bearing the Witness of the Spirit." *MissSt* 24 (2007): 169–88.

Yung, *Quest.* • Yung, Hwa. *Mangoes or Bananas? The Quest for an Authentic Asian Christian Theology; Biblical Theology in an Asian Context.* RStMiss. Oxford: Regnum, 1997.

Yung, *Quest².* • Yung, Hwa. *Mangoes or Bananas? The Quest for an Authentic Asian Christian Theology.* 2nd ed. RStMiss. Oxford: Regnum, 2014.

Yung, "Reformation." • Yung, Hwa. "A 21st Century Reformation: Recovering the Supernatural." The Lausanne Global Conversation. http://conversation.lausanne.org/en/conversations/detail/11041, accessed October 2, 2010.

Zaprometova, "Crisis." • Zaprometova, Olga. "The Crisis of Identity or Anthropology at Risk." 183–95 in *The Many Faces of Global Pentecostalism.* Edited by Harold D. Hunter and Neil Ormerod. Cleveland, TN: CPT Press, 2013.

Zevit, "Plagues." • Zevit, Ziony. "Three Ways to Look at the Ten Plagues." *Bible Review* 6 (3, 1990): 16–23, 42, 44.

Zhang, "Ethics of Transreading." • Zhang, Huiwen (Helen). "'Translated, It Is: . . .'—An Ethics of Transreading." *Educational Theory* 64 (5, October 2014): 479–95.

Zhaoming, "Chinese Denominations." • Zhaoming, Deng. "Indigenous Chinese Pentecostal Denominations." 437–66 in *Asian and Pentecostal: The Charismatic Face of Christianity in Asia.* Edited by Allan Anderson and Edmond Tang. Foreword by Cecil M. Robeck. RStMiss, AJPSS 3. Oxford: Regnum; Baguio City, Philippines: APTS, 2005.

Index of Authors

Aberle, M. von, 362n27
Abraham, William J., 313n33
Adams, Edward, 332n39, 360n51
Adewuya, Ayodeji, 360n45
Adhinarta, Yuzo, 308n54, 364n12
Agosto, Efraín, 332n39
Ahn, Yongnan Jeon, 306n18
Aitken, Ellen Bradshaw, 346n35
Aker, Benny C., 17
Akhtar, Shabbir, 337n60
Albrecht, Daniel E., 344n8
Albright, William Foxwell, 372n24
Alexander, Estrelda Y., 310n87, 323n22
Alexander, Kimberly Ervin, 306n19, 310n87
Alexander, Paul, 325n42, 359n31
Allen, E. Anthony, 338n74
Allison, Dale C., Jr., 139, 349n3, 351n49, 380n36
Alter, Robert, 332n38
Althouse, Peter, 321n79, 321n82
Alvarez, Miguel, 339n99
Anderson, Allan Heaton, 305n13, 306n27, 306-7n29, 307n30, 310n4, 311nn4-6, 311n16, 319n54, 319n60, 322n3, 323n20, 324nn38-39, 325nn42-43, 332n33, 338n83, 343n43, 366n40, 378n16, 383n17
Anderson, Gordon L., 147, 341n15, 344n8, 351n42, 355n49, 375n43, 379n22

Anderson, Jonathan A., 330n11, 345n11
Anderson, R. Dean, Jr., 315n60, 367n3, 376n53
Anderson, Robert M., 378n7
Anselm, 319n49
Aquinas, Thomas, 308n57, 319n49, 364n12
Arand, Charles P., 371n15
Archer, Kenneth J., 94, 124, 305nn7-10, 306n18, 306n22, 307n45, 312n20, 312nn24-25, 313n28, 313n36, 315n55, 318n34, 319n54, 319n59, 332n43, 333n43, 338n80, 342n31, 344n3, 344n10, 345n15, 345nn27-31, 346nn32-34, 347n54, 348nn85-86, 349n82, 350n21, 350n27, 351n37, 351n42, 351n48, 352n58, 354-55n45, 356n64, 358n28, 359n32, 359n34, 360n50, 363n2, 364n14, 376n57, 377n72, 378n4, 378nn6-7
Arles, Nalini, 318n40
Arndt, William F., 361n7
Arrington, French L., 12, 307n45, 322n5
Asamoah-Gyadu, J. Kwabena, 95, 322n2, 338n83
Asbury, Francis, 321n89
Ashton, John, 349n3, 362n27
Auerbach, Erich, 372n5
Aune, David E., 327n13, 340n10, 347n58, 348n73, 350n15, 352n53, 353n27, 375n36, 382n7

Index of Subjects

Abduction, 156–57
Abolitionism, 327n20, 387n21. *See also* Slavery
Abraham, William, 301, 388n6
Abrams, Minnie, 62, 323nn22–23
Accommodation, divine, 204, 371n20. *See also* Contextualization
Adelekan, Adetekunbo, 301
Adogame, Afe, 298
Aesthetic function of language, 86, 134, 145, 315n58, 349n7
Affective approaches, 146, 315n58, 315n60
African-American churches, 18, 46, 85, 275, 297, 309n78, 362n18
African Christianity, 16, 79, 81, 83, 89–92, 95, 96, 195, 279, 283, 334n15, 336n47, 363n3, 378n16. *See also* Central Africa; East Africa; *and particular African nations*
African theology, 295, 335n18, 338n78, 338n83
Agency, 327n12
Agnosticism, 7, 163, 180
Agosto, Efrain, 298
Alexander, Estralda, 300
Alexander, Paul, 301
Alexandria, library at, 353n14
Allegorical reading, 49, 74, 92, 123, 167, 205, 243, 348n75, 367nn2–3, 373n20
Allison, Dale, 139

Alphacrucis University, 387n3
Already/not yet, 21, 50, 54
Altered states of consciousness, 91
Ambrose, Linda, 300
Ambrosiaster, 371n11
Amish, 321n86
Anabaptists, 6, 121, 300, 311n16, 360n56, 378n5. *See also* Mennonites
Analogies for application, 117, 118, 134, 149, 151, 203, 205, 212, 213, 249, 287, 288–89, 333n48, 342n30, 351n50, 355n62, 356n68, 356n70, 358n28; biblical examples, 220, 238, 241, 243, 244, 246, 248, 251, 258, 367n3, 367n7, 373n20, 374nn31–32, 374nn34–35, 376n56, 376n65
Analogy of faith, 80
Ancestors: curses from, 271; possession by, 335n32; veneration of, 80
Ancient Near Eastern contexts, 74, 84, 102, 127, 129, 150–51, 218, 225–30, 233, 234, 243, 315n57, 332n36, 342n26, 346n45
Anderson, Allan H., 300, 388n6
Anglicans, 30, 57, 67, 279, 297, 303, 336n47, 338n78, 383n14, 388n6
Anhedonia, 316n71
Annals, 253–54
Anselm, 48, 319n49, 361n5
Anti-Semitism, 93, 294

Index of Scripture References

Index of Ancient Sources